S0-DTD-132

MULTIDIMENSIONAL MODELS OF PERCEPTION AND COGNITION

SCIENTIFIC PSYCHOLOGY SERIES
Stephen W. Link & James T. Townsend, Editors

EDITED VOLUMES

F. Gregory Ashby Multidimensional Models of Perception and Cognition

Hans-Georg Geissler, Stephen W. Link, and James T. Townsend Cognition, Information Processing, and Psychophysics: Basic Issues

MONOGRAPHS

William R. Uttal et al. The Swimmer: An Integrated Computational Model of a Perceptual Motor System

Stephen W. Link • The Wave Theory of Difference and Similarity

MULTIDIMENSIONAL MODELS OF PERCEPTION AND COGNITION

Edited by

F. Gregory Ashby

University of California at Santa Barbara

LEA LAWRENCE ERLBAUM ASSOCIATES, PUBLISHERS

1992 Hillsdale, New Jersey Hove and London

Copyright © 1992, by Lawrence Erlbaum Associates, Inc.
All rights reserved. No part of the book may be reproduced in any form, by photostat, microform, retrieval system, or any other means, without the prior written permission of the publisher.

Lawrence Erlbaum Associates, Inc., Publishers
365 Broadway
Hillsdale, New Jersey 07642

Library of Congress Cataloging-in-Publication Data

Multidimensional models of perception and cognition / edited by F. Gregory Ashby.
p. cm.—(Scientific psychology series)
Includes bibliographical references and index.
ISBN 0-8058-0577-X
I. Ashby, F. Gregory. II. Series.
BF311.M67 1992
153.7—dc20 92-2864
CIP

Printed in the United States of America
10 9 8 7 6 5 4 3 2 1

Table of Contents

PART II: INTERACTIONS BETWEEN PERCEPTUAL DIMENSIONS

PART III: DETECTION, IDENTIFICATION, AND CATEGORIZATION

Preface

Modern psychophysical theory was born with the 1860 publication of Gustav Fechner's monumental *Elements of Psychophysics*. A cornerstone of this work was Fechner's extension of the Gaussian Theory of Error to the comparison of sensations. Thus, among his many other contributions, Fechner was the first to account for trial-by-trial variability in the sensory effects of a stimulus. According to this view, the appropriate psychological representation is probabilistic. In 1927, L. L. Thurstone (1927a, 1927b, 1927c) published a series of papers that elaborated on Fechner's ideas about probabilistic representation and extended them to the fields of test theory and attitude measurement.

Among the best known and most successful modern theories to incorporate the assumption of probabilistic stimulus representation is Signal Detection Theory (e.g., Green & Swets, 1974). Besides incorporating the assumption that the sensory effects of a stimulus are probabilistic, Signal Detection Theory elaborated on Fechner's ideas about decision processes. Specifically, Signal Detection Theory assumed that the detection process could be separated into two components: sensory and decision. The output of the sensory process was assumed to be the particular sensory value on that trial. The decision process was assumed to use the sensory value and the experimenter's instructions to select a response.

Models incorporating probabilistic representation were hugely successful and are now studied in one form or another by virtually every graduate student in Experimental Psychology (most often in the form of Signal Detection Theory or Factor Analysis). The effect of this probabilistic approach on the areas of perception and cognition has been limited however, for one very important reason. With only a few exceptions, probabilistic models have assumed unidimensional psychological representations. Therefore, they work best when the stimulus varies along one physical dimension. For example, in psychophysics, the most common application has been to experiments that ask the subject to detect a stimulus that varies over trials only in its physical intensity. Unfortunately, however, the stimuli that are most commonly used in perception and cognition experiments vary along several or many different physical dimensions.

Over the course of the last few years, researchers in several different areas have independently extended the notion of probabilistic representation to experiments in perception and cognition that involve two or more stimulus dimensions. The resulting models all assume that the perceptual effect of a given stimulus can be represented as a point in a multidimensional psychological space and that repeated presentations do not always lead to the same percept. Thus, according to this approach, the appropriate perceptual representation is a multivariate probability distribution. While many researchers assume this same perceptual representation, they apply the model to different experimental paradigms and therefore their assumptions about the decision process are often very different. Taken together, this new approach, called probabilistic multidimensional modeling, has the potential to revolutionize the study of perception and cognition in the same way that signal detection theory revolutionized the study of psychophysics.

Progress to date has been encouraging. For example, for more than 25 years the most successful mathematical model of stimulus identification has been the so-called biased choice model (Luce, 1963; Shepard, 1957). In the words of Smith:

> Luce's Biased Choice Model has never had a serious competitor as a model of identification data. Even when it has provided a poor model of such data, other models have done even less well. (1992, p. 1)

Recently, however, Ashby and Lee (1991) developed a probabilistic multidimensional model that fit the identification data of each of four subjects in two separate experiments better than the biased choice model. For one subject in the first experiment, the sum of squared errors (SSE) of the probabilistic model was more than 10 times smaller than the SSE of the biased choice model (where the two models had essentially the same number of free parameters). For one subject in the second experiment, the SSE of the probabilistic model was about four times smaller than the SSE of the biased choice model, even though the biased choice model had 35 more free parameters than the probabilistic model in this application.

Research on probabilistic multidimensional models can be found in three main areas: (1) mathematical psychology; (2) psychometrics; and (3) basic perceptual processes. The mathematical psychology group has concentrated on applications to categorization and identification. The psychometrics group has focused on understanding judgments of similarity, choice, and preference, and the (visual) perception group has focused on applications in spatial vision. Unfortunately, these three groups have little communication. They attend different meetings and read different journals. The goal of this text is to bring these different groups together and to produce a tutorial volume that surveys virtually all of the work that has been done to date on the development of models that assume probabilistic multidimensional representations of perceptual and cognitive information. Each chapter consists of an evaluative and integrative review of the important substantive and methodological issues in a particular area of perception or cognition. Besides summarizing the literature, the chapters describe the major developments in the area and they develop connections with related areas, especially those described in other chapters.

The book begins with a chapter reviewing the mathematics that the reader will need to fully understand the later chapters. This includes matrix algebra and the statistics of multivariate probability distributions. This chapter also serves to introduce the mathematical notation used throughout the text.

As noted above, probabilistic multidimensional models have proven remarkably effective in a number of different areas. Part 1, which consists of Chapters 2 through 6, surveys applications in the areas of similarity, preference, and choice and Part 3 (Chapters 10–16) surveys models of stimulus detection, identification, and categorization. In addition to their success in modeling data, probabilistic models have inspired new methods for studying how stimulus dimensions combine and interact during perceptual and cognitive processing. Part 2 (Chapter 7–9) surveys this literature.

This work has benefitted greatly from the contributions of others. Stephen Link provided valuable comments about the historical development of probabilistic representation in Experimental Psychology. William Lee and Geoffrey Boynton contributed insightful comments on earlier drafts of parts of the manuscript. Marisa Murphy provided valuable secretarial assistance and singlehandedly compiled the extensive references found at the end of the book. Art Lizza at Erlbaum patiently accommodated the many changes and alterations that were required during typesetting. Financial support was provided to me for the duration of this project by National Science Foundation Grant BNS88-19403. Other support came from the Philip Morris Research Center, both in terms of a research grant and also as sponsors of a symposium on probabilistic multidimensional models held at the Twenty-first Annual Mathematical Psychology Meetings (Northwestern University, July 26–28, 1988). Finally, my wife, Heidi Zetzer, and my son, Duncan deserve special thanks for their patience and support during the many hours of this project.

—F. Gregory Ashby

1 Multivariate Probability Distributions

F. Gregory Ashby
University of California at Santa Barbara

Many of the models discussed in this book are based on the assumption that the perceptual effect of a stimulus is random over trials, although on any single trial is has a specified fixed value. This assumption, which can be traced back to Fechner (1860, 1966), was fully exploited in signal detection theory (e.g., Green & Swets, 1974) where the focus was on unidimensional perceptual representations. The models in this book focus on multidimensional representations. Although the mathematical basis of these models is probability theory, the generalization from univariate to multivariate probability distributions involves several complications. This first chapter reviews many of the important results of multivariate probability theory upon which the later chapters depend.

We assume that most readers will have some familiarity with univariate probability theory and with the basics of matrix algebra. The first section in this chapter is a very brief survey of univariate probability theory, and those readers unfamiliar with this material might wish to supplement it with readings from an outside source, such as Parzen (1960). This chapter does not contain a review of the basics of matrix algebra, so those readers unfamiliar with basic matrix operations such as addition, multiplication, transposition, and inversion should consult any introductory matrix algebra text (often called linear algebra; e.g., Noble & Daniel, 1977).

Readers familiar with multivariate probability theory might still wish to skim this chapter. Several sections are included that contain some useful but little known results. These include techniques for generating random samples from multivariate normal distributions, for quickly performing certain numerical integrations, and for computing the predicted accuracy of the ideal observer in multidimensional categorization and identification experiments.

UNIVARIATE PROBABILITY THEORY

When there is only one stimulus dimension, many of the models in this book become equivalent to signal detection theory (e.g., Green & Swets, 1974). As an example of a signal detection application, consider a two-alternative forced-choice task in which the stimulus ensemble contains two stimuli differing only in intensity. Call the two intensities $\mathbf{A}_1$ and $\mathbf{A}_2$, and denote the perceived intensity, when a single stimulus is presented, by $\boldsymbol{X}$. The fundamental assumption of signal detection theory is that $\boldsymbol{X}$ is a random variable.

One way to characterize the subject's perceptual experience is to determine the probability that the perceived intensity falls in certain intervals. To aid these calculations, we use certain standard mathematical functions. The *cumulative probability distribution function* $F_i(x)$ gives the probability that the perceived intensity is less than or equal to a specified value x on trials when the intensity is $\mathbf{A}_i$. Formally,

$$F_i(x) = P(\boldsymbol{X} \le x|\mathbf{A}_i) \ . \tag{1}$$

The cumulative distribution function increases monotonically from 0 to 1.0 as x increases. The second standard function, known as the *probability density function,* is defined as the derivative of $F_i(x)$. Specifically,

$$f_i(x) = \frac{d\mathrm{F}_i(x)}{dx} = \lim_{\Delta x \to 0} \frac{P(x < \boldsymbol{X} \le x + \Delta x|\mathbf{A}_i)}{\Delta x} \ .$$

Whereas values of the cumulative distribution function are themselves probabilities, values of the density function are called *likelihoods,* and are not probabilities. Given the density function, probabilities can be found by integration. For example,

$$P(x_1 < \boldsymbol{X} \le x_2|\mathbf{A}_i) = \int_{x_1}^{x_2} f_i(x)\, dx = F_i(x_2) - F_i(x_1) \ , \tag{2}$$

and so probabilities are areas under the probability density function. From Equation 2 it is clear that

$$\int_{-\infty}^{\infty} f_i(x)\, dx = 1 \ .$$

To see that $f_i(x)$ is not a probability, note that even if $f_i(x) > 0$ for some value of x, if $f_i(x)$ is continuous then it is always true that

$$P(\boldsymbol{X} = x|\mathbf{A}_i) = \int_x^x f_i(y)\, dy = 0 \ .$$

Given the probability density function of a random variable X, the mean of X, denoted μ_X, is defined as the expected value of X, $E(X)$, and can be computed via

$$\mu_X = E(X) = \int_{-\infty}^{\infty} x f_X(x)\, dx\ . \tag{3}$$

The variance of X is defined as its expected squared deviation from the mean:

$$\sigma_X^2 = E(X - \mu_X)^2 = \int_{-\infty}^{\infty} (x - \mu_X)^2 f_X(x)\, dx\ . \tag{4}$$

In general, suppose $Y = h(X)$ is any function of the random variable X and that we are interested in the expected value of Y. Equation 3 indicates that this requires knowledge of the probability density function of Y, $f_Y(y)$. In many cases—for example, when h is nonlinear—finding $f_Y(y)$ is difficult. Fortunately, as the following result shows, it is possible to solve for $E(Y)$ directly in terms of the density function $f_X(x)$ of X.

Proposition 1.1. Suppose $Y = h(X)$ is any function of the random variable X. Then

$$\mu_Y = E(Y) = E[h(X)] = \int_{-\infty}^{\infty} h(x) f_X(x)\, dx\ . \tag{5}$$

Proof: An intuitive proof is given in Papoulis (1965, pp. 142–143).

One of the most common transformations occurs when h is linear, that is, when

$$Y = h(X) = \mathrm{a}X + \mathrm{b}$$

for some constants a and b. In this case, the expected value of the new random variable Y can be found from Equation 5 to be

$$\begin{aligned} E(Y) &= \int_{-\infty}^{\infty} (\mathrm{a}x + \mathrm{b}) f_X(x)\, dx \\ &= \mathrm{a} \int_{-\infty}^{\infty} x f_X(x)\, dx + \mathrm{b} \int_{-\infty}^{\infty} f_X(x)\, dx \\ &= \mathrm{a}E(X) + \mathrm{b}\ . \end{aligned} \tag{6}$$

From a similar derivation, it can be shown that the variance of Y is equal to

$$\sigma_Y^2 = \mathrm{a}^2 \sigma_X^2 \tag{7}$$

The most popular distributional assumption in signal detection theory is that the perceived intensities are normally distributed. In this case, for all $-\infty < x < \infty$,

$$f(x) = \frac{1}{\sqrt{2\pi}\sigma} exp \left[-\frac{1}{2} \left(\frac{x-\mu}{\sigma} \right)^2 \right] , \tag{8}$$

where the mean is μ and the variance is σ^2. Unfortunately, there is no closed-form expression for the cumulative normal distribution function. Examples of the normal density and distribution function are shown in Figure 1.1. The special case in which $\mu = 0$ and $\sigma^2 = 1$ is known as the **Z** distribution. Its density function is denoted by $\phi(z)$ and its cumulative distribution function by $\Phi(z)$. Although there is no closed-form expression for $\Phi(z)$, several excellent approximations exist (see, e.g., Abramowitz & Stegun, 1965, pp. 931–933). For example, for positive values of z

$$\Phi(z) = 1 - \phi(z)(a_1 t + a_2 t^2 + a_3 t^3) + \epsilon(z) , \tag{9}$$

where

$$t = \frac{1}{1 + pz}$$

and

$$p = 0.33267, \quad a_1 = 0.4361836, \quad a_2 = -0.1201676, \quad a_3 = 0.937298 .$$

The error in this approximation $\epsilon(z)$ satisfies

$$|\epsilon(z)| < 0.00001 .$$

MULTIVARIATE DISTRIBUTIONS

Introduction

Although many psychophysical stimuli have natural unidimensional sensory representations, the stimuli of perception are many-dimensional. Tones vary in frequency, intensity, and duration. Rectangles vary in length and width. Individual characters in text may vary in size, orientation, shape, and number of line segments they contain. In all of these cases a multidimensional perceptual representation is required.

Consider a stimulus constructed from two physical components (or dimensions) **A** and **B**. Let $\mathbf{A}_i\mathbf{B}_j$ denote the stimulus with component **A** at level i and component **B** at level j. For example, component $\mathbf{A}_i$ might be a sine wave grating of frequency **A** and contrast i, and $\mathbf{B}_j$ a grating of frequency **B** and contrast j. Then the stimulus $\mathbf{A}_i\mathbf{B}_j$ is constructed by superimposing two gratings: one of frequency **A** and contrast i, and another of frequency **B** and contrast j.

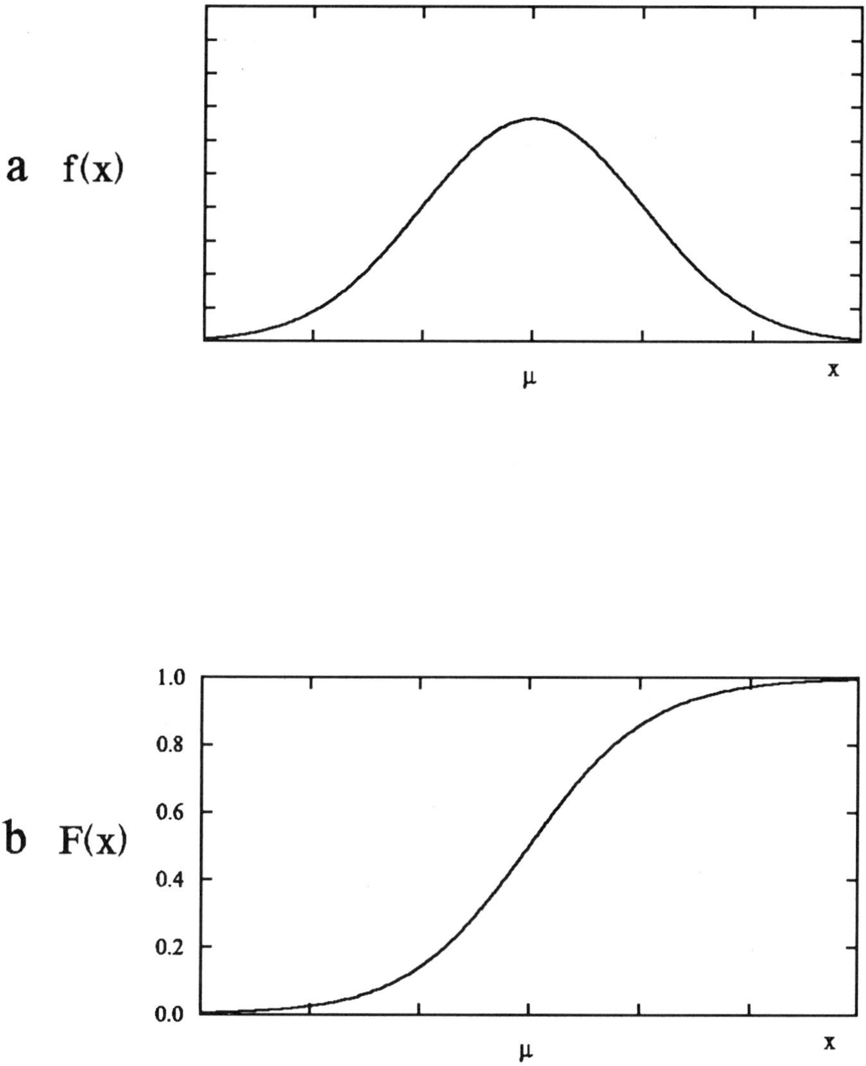

FIG. 1.1. (a) Probability density function of a normal distribution with mean μ and variance σ^2. (b) Corresponding cumulative distribution function.

Suppose that the two physical components are each associated with a separate perceptual dimension. Let X be the perceived value of component **A** and Y be the perceived value of component **B**. Most of the models discussed in this book assume that X and Y are random variables.

As in the unidimensional case, the random variables X and Y are characterized by their probability distribution. The joint probability density function of perceptual effects on trials when stimulus $\mathbf{A}_i\mathbf{B}_j$ is presented is denoted by $f_{ij}(x, y)$. The joint density can be used to compute probabilities in the multivariate case in much the same way as in the univariate case. For example,

$$P(x_1 < X \leq x_2, y_1 < Y \leq y_2) = \int_{y_1}^{y_2} \int_{x_1}^{x_2} f_{ij}(x, y)\, dx\, dy \ .$$

Given the joint density function, the marginal probability density functions are found by integrating over the irrelevant dimension. Thus,

$$g_{ij}(x) = \int_{-\infty}^{\infty} f_{ij}(x, y)\, dy$$

and

$$g_{ij}(y) = \int_{-\infty}^{\infty} f_{ij}(x, y)\, dx \ .$$

Therefore, the joint density completely determines the marginals. The converse is not true. In general, the joint density cannot be recovered from the marginals. The exception occurs in the special case when the random variables are *statistically independent.* A pair of random variables, X and Y, is statistically independent if and only if $f(x, y) = g(x)g(y)$ for all values of x and y. As Definition 1.1 indicates, perceptual effects that are statistically independent are said to satisfy perceptual independence (Ashby & Townsend, 1986).

Definition 1.1. The perceptual effects X and Y are perceived independently on trials when stimulus $\mathbf{A}_i\mathbf{B}_j$ is presented if and only if $f_{ij}(x, y) = g_{ij}(x)g_{ij}(y)$ for all values of x and y.

The Multivariate Normal Distribution

Just as normality is the most common distributional assumption in univariate Signal Detection Theory, it is also the most popular assumption in probabilistic multidimensional models. The bivariate normal probability density function is defined as

$$f(x, y) = \frac{1}{2\pi\sigma_X\sigma_Y\sqrt{1 - \rho^2}} \times exp\left\{-\frac{1}{2(1 - \rho^2)}\left[\left(\frac{x - \mu_X}{\sigma_X}\right)^2 - 2\rho\left(\frac{x - \mu_X}{\sigma_X}\right)\left(\frac{y - \mu_Y}{\sigma_Y}\right) + \left(\frac{y - \mu_Y}{\sigma_Y}\right)^2\right]\right\} \quad (10)$$

for $-\infty < x,y < \infty$. The bivariate normal distribution is characterized by five parameters: μ_X and μ_Y are the means on each dimension, σ_X^2 and σ_Y^2 are the variances on each dimension, and ρ is the correlation between X and Y. A parameter that is closely related to the correlation coefficient is the covariance, which is defined as

$$Cov = \rho\sigma_X\sigma_Y.$$

Thus, the correlation can be expressed as

$$\rho = \frac{Cov}{\sigma_X\sigma_Y},$$

and so the correlation can be interpreted as the standardized covariance.

If X and Y are jointly normally distributed, then both the X and Y marginal distributions are univariate normal. The X marginal has mean μ_X and variance σ_X^2, and the Y marginal has mean μ_Y and variance σ_Y^2. Equation 10 makes clear why the joint density is not uniquely determined by the marginals. Given the marginals, we know μ_X, μ_Y, σ_X^2, and σ_Y^2, but there is no way to determine ρ. Also note that if $\rho = 0$ in Equation 10, then the joint density is equivalent to the product of the two marginal densities. Therefore, if X and Y are normally distributed, then a zero correlation is equivalent to statistical independence. In general, however, the two concepts are not equivalent. A statistical independence always implies that the random variables are uncorrelated, but uncorrelated random variables are not necessarily statistically independent.

Equation 10 describes a three-dimension bell-shaped structure. An example is shown in Figure 1.2a. Note that the height of the bell at any point represents the likelihood that a random sample from the population will have the x and y values associated with that point. A more convenient method of presenting the same information is via the *contours of equal likelihood,* each of which is created by taking a slice parallel to the (x, y) plane (see Figure 1.2b) and looking down on the result from above. In the Figure 1.2 example, the resulting contour, depicted in Figure 1.2c, is circular. Note that all points on the same contour are associated with the same likelihood (i.e., probability density). More specifically, the contours of equal likelihood are the set of all x and y that satisfy

$$f(x,y) = k$$

for some arbitrary constant k.

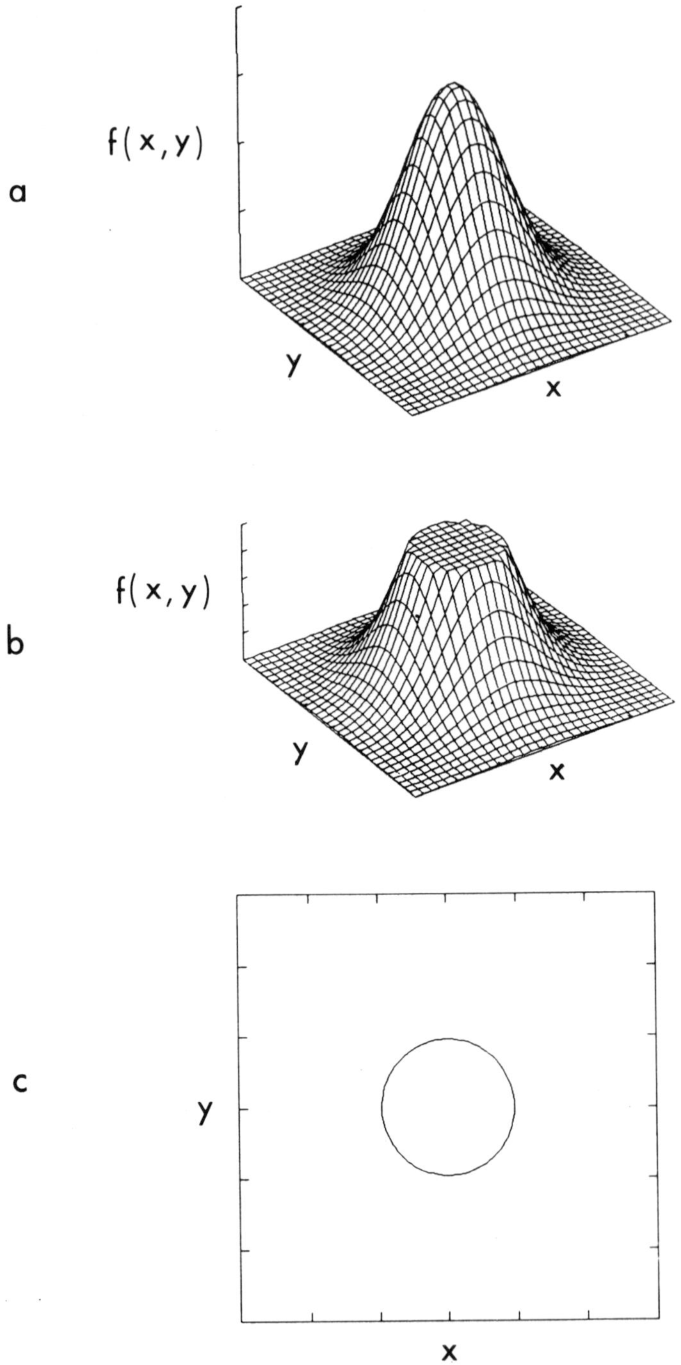

FIG. 1.2. (a) Probability density function from a bivariate normal distribution. (b) The same function with a slice taken parallel to the (*x*, *y*) plane. (c) The resulting contour of equal likelihood.

From Equation 10 it can be seen that for the bivariate normal distribution the contours of equal likelihood satisfy

$$\left(\frac{x-\mu_X}{\sigma_X}\right)^2 - 2\rho\left(\frac{x-\mu_X}{\sigma_X}\right)\left(\frac{y-\mu_Y}{\sigma_Y}\right) + \left(\frac{y-\mu_Y}{\sigma_Y}\right)^2 = \mathrm{k}\,. \quad (11)$$

This equation describes an ellipse centered at (μ_X, μ_Y). The shape of the ellipse is completely determined by the variance and covariance parameters. If $\rho = 0$ and $\sigma_X = \sigma_Y$, then, as illustrated in Figure 1.3a, the ellipse becomes a circle with a diameter that depends on the constant k. If $\rho = 0$ but $\sigma_X \neq \sigma_Y$, then the major and minor axes of the ellipse are parallel to the x and y coordinate axes. Figure 1.3b illustrates the case in which $\sigma_X > \sigma_Y$, and Figure 1.3c the case in which $\sigma_Y > \sigma_X$. Note that the larger variance is always associated with the major axis of the ellipse. Figures 1.3d and 1.3e contain examples of contours for which $\rho \neq 0$. In this case the slope of the major axis has the same sign as ρ.

Frequently, it is more convenient to describe the perceptual space with matrix notation. This is especially true when more than two dimensions are involved. With three perceptual dimensions the random vector $\mathbf{X}$ of perceptual effects is defined as

$$\mathbf{X} = \begin{bmatrix} X \\ Y \\ Z \end{bmatrix}.$$

In a similar fashion, the expected value of the random vector $\mathbf{X}$ is defined as the vector $\boldsymbol{\mu}$ whose entries are the mean perceptual effects on each dimension:

$$E\,(\mathbf{X}) = \boldsymbol{\mu} = \begin{bmatrix} \mu_X \\ \mu_Y \\ \mu_Z \end{bmatrix}.$$

The variances and covariances are specified in the *covariance matrix* $\boldsymbol{\Sigma}$, defined as

$$E[(\mathbf{X} - \boldsymbol{\mu})(\mathbf{X} - \boldsymbol{\mu})'] = \boldsymbol{\Sigma} = \begin{bmatrix} \sigma_X^2 & Cov_{XY} & Cov_{XZ} \\ Cov_{XY} & \sigma_Y^2 & Cov_{YZ} \\ Cov_{XZ} & Cov_{YZ} & \sigma_Z^2 \end{bmatrix},$$

where the prime denotes matrix transpose. Note that $\boldsymbol{\Sigma}$ is always square and symmetric. The multivariate Z distribution has mean vector

$$\boldsymbol{\mu} = \mathbf{0} = \begin{bmatrix} 0 \\ 0 \\ 0 \end{bmatrix}$$

and covariance matrix equal to the identity matrix

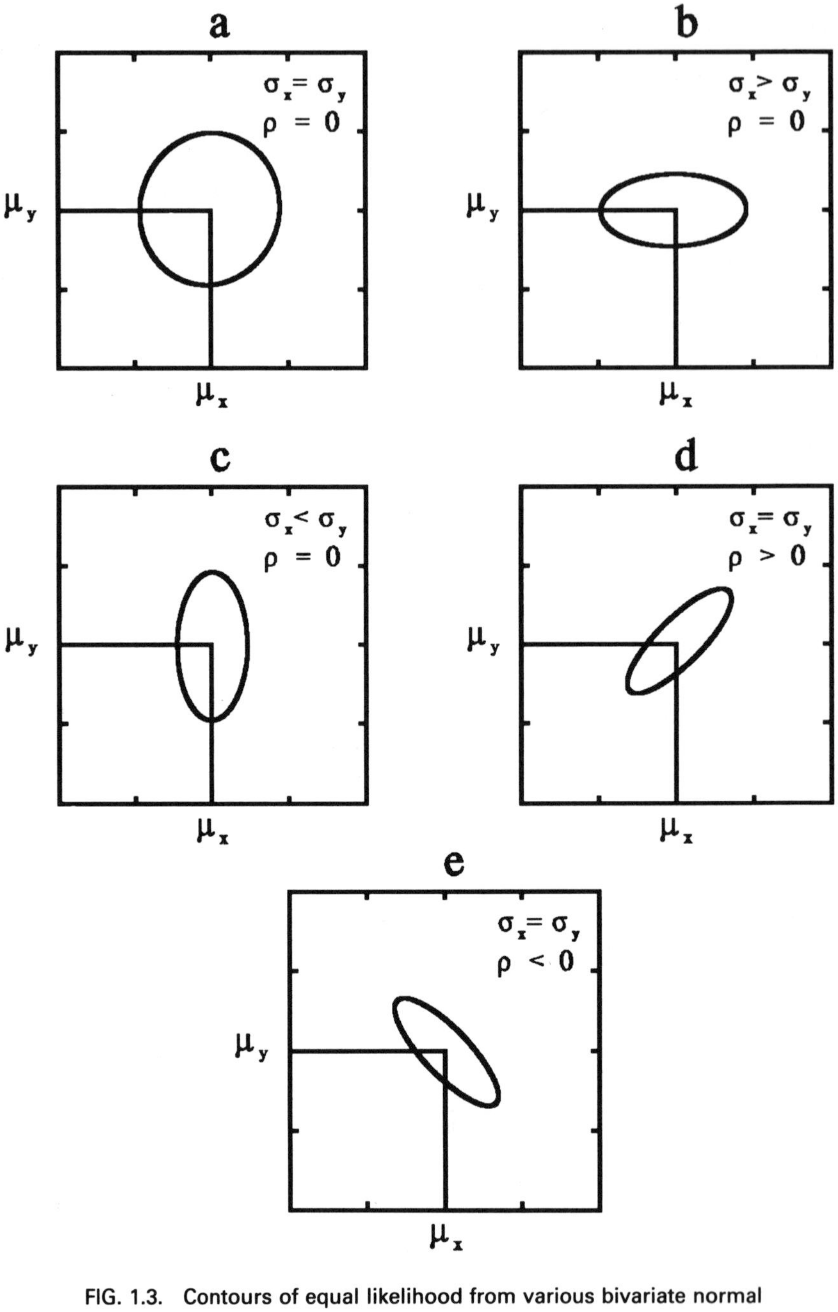

FIG. 1.3. Contours of equal likelihood from various bivariate normal distributions.

$$\boldsymbol{\Sigma} = \mathbf{I} = \begin{bmatrix} 1 & 0 & 0 \\ 0 & 1 & 0 \\ 0 & 0 & 1 \end{bmatrix} .$$

Note that each marginal is a univariate Z distribution.

The multivariate normal probability density function can be written in matrix form as

$$f(\mathbf{x}) = \frac{1}{(2\pi)^{n/2}|\boldsymbol{\Sigma}|^{1/2}} \, exp \, [-{}^{1}\!/\!_{2}(\mathbf{x} - \boldsymbol{\mu})'\boldsymbol{\Sigma}^{-1}(\mathbf{x} - \boldsymbol{\mu})] \, , \tag{12}$$

where n is the number of dimensions and $|\boldsymbol{\Sigma}|$ is the determinant of $\boldsymbol{\Sigma}$. The contours of equal likelihood are found from Equation 12 to satisfy

$$(\mathbf{x} - \boldsymbol{\mu})'\boldsymbol{\Sigma}^{-1} (\mathbf{x} - \boldsymbol{\mu}) = k \tag{13}$$

for an arbitrary constant k. Equation 11 is the special bivariate case of Equation 13.

As in the unidimensional case, one of the most useful multivariate transformations is linear. In the multivariate case, the linear transformation takes the form

$$\mathbf{Y} = \mathbf{AX} + \mathbf{b} \, ,$$

where $\mathbf{X}$ is the original n-dimensional random vector, $\mathbf{A}$ is an m $\times$ n matrix of constants, and $\mathbf{b}$ is an m $\times$ 1 vector of constants. The new random vector $\mathbf{Y}$ is m $\times$ 1. The derivation of the mean vector and covariance matrix of $\mathbf{Y}$ is similar to the univariate case:

$$\begin{aligned} \boldsymbol{\mu}_y &= E\,(\mathbf{Y}) = E\,(\mathbf{AX} + \mathbf{b}) = \mathbf{A}E\,(\mathbf{X}) + \mathbf{b} \\ &= \mathbf{A}\boldsymbol{\mu}_X + \mathbf{b} \, , \end{aligned} \tag{14}$$

$$\begin{aligned} \boldsymbol{\Sigma}_y &= E\,[(\mathbf{Y} - \boldsymbol{\mu}_Y)(\mathbf{Y} - \boldsymbol{\mu}_Y)'] \\ &= E\,[(\mathbf{AX} + \mathbf{b} - \mathbf{A}\boldsymbol{\mu}_X - \mathbf{b})(\mathbf{AX} + \mathbf{b} - \mathbf{A}\boldsymbol{\mu}_X - \mathbf{b})'] \\ &= E\,[(\mathbf{AX} - \mathbf{A}\boldsymbol{\mu}_X)(\mathbf{AX} - \mathbf{A}\boldsymbol{\mu}_X)'] \\ &= E\,[\mathbf{A}(\mathbf{X} - \boldsymbol{\mu}_X)(\mathbf{X} - \boldsymbol{\mu}_X)'\mathbf{A}'] \\ &= \mathbf{A}E\,[(\mathbf{X} - \boldsymbol{\mu}_X)(\mathbf{X} - \boldsymbol{\mu}_X)']\mathbf{A}' \\ &= \mathbf{A}\boldsymbol{\Sigma}_X\mathbf{A}' \, . \end{aligned} \tag{15}$$

Note that this last derivation used the matrix transpose property $(\mathbf{AB})' = \mathbf{B}'\mathbf{A}'$. If $\boldsymbol{\Sigma}_X$ is 1 $\times$ 1, then it can be written as σ_X^2. If $\mathbf{A}$ is the scalar a, then $a' = a$, and so Equation 15 reduces to $\boldsymbol{\Sigma}_Y = \sigma_Y^2 = a^2\sigma_X^2$, which is just Equation 7.

EIGENVECTORS AND EIGENVALUES

Introduction

When working with multivariate normal distributions, we frequently might want to select one with a certain desired property, for example, with the major axis of the equal likelihood contour oriented in a specific direction. Problems like this are easily solved by examining or manipulating the *eigenvectors* and *eigenvalues* of the distribution's covariance matrix. In addition, knowing the eigenvectors and eigenvalues of a matrix makes many computations much easier.

Definition 1.2. Consider any square matrix $\mathbf{A}$. Suppose we can find a scalar d and a vector $\mathbf{q}$ containing at least one nonzero entry such that

$$\mathbf{Aq} = d\mathbf{q} \; . \tag{16}$$

Then $\mathbf{q}$ is called an eigenvector of the matrix $\mathbf{A}$, and d is the associated eigenvalue.

If the vector $\mathbf{q}$ contains all zeros, then the equality in Equation 16 holds trivially for all values of d, and so we are specifically interested in solutions involving vectors containing at least one nonzero entry. Equation 16 implies

$$(\mathbf{A} - d\mathbf{I})\mathbf{q} = \mathbf{0} \; . \tag{17}$$

This set of homogeneous equations has a nontrivial solution only if some of the equations are linear combinations of the others. In this case the determinant of $\mathbf{A} - d\mathbf{I}$ will be zero. Therefore, the eigenvalues of $\mathbf{A}$ must satisfy the equation

$$|\mathbf{A} - d\mathbf{I}| = 0 \; . \tag{18}$$

Equation 18 is known as the *characteristic equation* of the matrix $\mathbf{A}$. If $\mathbf{A}$ is of order n × n, then Equation 18 has n solutions, $d_1, d_2, \ldots, d_n$, some of which may be zero. Once the eigenvalues are known, the eigenvectors can be found from Equation 17.

For example, the matrix

$$\mathbf{A} = \begin{bmatrix} 17 & -8 \\ -8 & 17 \end{bmatrix}$$

has characteristic equation

$$(17 - d)^2 - (-8)^2 = 0 \; ,$$

and hence $d = 9$ or 25. Substituting $d = 9$ into Equation 17 yields

$$\begin{bmatrix} 8 & -8 \\ -8 & 8 \end{bmatrix} \begin{bmatrix} q_1 \\ q_2 \end{bmatrix} = \begin{bmatrix} 0 \\ 0 \end{bmatrix} ,$$

and so $q_1 = q_2$. Clearly, there is an infinite number of solutions. However, a standard convention is to choose q_1 and q_2 so that the length of the eigenvector is 1.0, that is, so that $\mathbf{q'q} = 1$. In this case, that leads to $q_1 = q_2 = 1/\sqrt{2}$. Verifying, we see that

$$\begin{bmatrix} 17 & -8 \\ -8 & 17 \end{bmatrix} \begin{bmatrix} \frac{1}{\sqrt{2}} \\ \frac{1}{\sqrt{2}} \end{bmatrix} = 9 \begin{bmatrix} \frac{1}{\sqrt{2}} \\ \frac{1}{\sqrt{2}} \end{bmatrix} .$$

In an analogous fashion, it can be found that the second eigenvector, the one corresponding to the eigenvalue $d_2 = 25$, is

$$\underline{q}_2 = \begin{bmatrix} \frac{-1}{\sqrt{2}} \\ \frac{1}{\sqrt{2}} \end{bmatrix} .$$

Eigenvectors and eigenvalues are associated with some very convenient properties. Among the most important are the following five. Derivations can be found in any standard linear algebra text (e.g., Noble & Daniel, 1977).

Proposition 1.2. Suppose **A** is of order n × n, with eigenvalues $d_1, d_2, \ldots, d_n$. Then

$$d_1 + d_2 + \cdots + d_n = trace\ (\mathbf{A}) .$$

The trace of a matrix is defined as the sum of all elements on the main diagonal. In the previous example, *trace* (**A**) = 17 + 17 = 34 and $d_1 + d_2 = 9 + 25 = 34$.

Proposition 1.3. Suppose **A** is of order n × n, with eigenvalues $d_1, d_2, \ldots, d_n$. Then

$$d_1 d_2 \cdots d_n = |\mathbf{A}| .$$

Because computing determinants can be quite time consuming, especially for large matrices, this property can be very convenient. In our earlier example, $|\mathbf{A}| = 17^2 - (-8)^2 = 225$ and $d_1 d_2 = 9 \times 25 = 225$.

Proposition 1.4. Suppose **A** is a symmetric matrix of order n. Let **Q** be the n × n matrix whose columns are the eigenvectors of **A**, and let **D** be the n × n diagonal matrix with the corresponding eigenvalues of **A** on the diagonal (and zeros elsewhere). Then $\mathbf{Q}'\mathbf{Q} = \mathbf{I}$ (i.e., $\mathbf{Q}^{-1} = \mathbf{Q}'$) and

$$\mathbf{A} = \mathbf{QDQ}' .$$

This is the so-called diagonal representation of the matrix **A**. As we shall see, it is an extremely important result. In the earlier example,

$$\begin{bmatrix} 17 & -8 \\ -8 & 17 \end{bmatrix} = \begin{bmatrix} \frac{1}{\sqrt{2}} & \frac{-1}{\sqrt{2}} \\ \frac{1}{\sqrt{2}} & \frac{1}{\sqrt{2}} \end{bmatrix} \begin{bmatrix} 9 & 0 \\ 0 & 25 \end{bmatrix} \begin{bmatrix} \frac{1}{\sqrt{2}} & \frac{1}{\sqrt{2}} \\ \frac{-1}{\sqrt{2}} & \frac{1}{\sqrt{2}} \end{bmatrix}.$$

One useful consequence of Proposition 1.4 is the following.

Proposition 1.5. $\mathbf{A}^p = \mathbf{QD}^p\mathbf{Q}'$ for any constant p.

Proposition 1.5 is easy to verify. For example, suppose p = 2. Then

$$\begin{aligned} \mathbf{A}^2 &= (\mathbf{QDQ}')(\mathbf{QDQ}') \\ &= \mathbf{QD}(\mathbf{Q}'\mathbf{Q})\mathbf{DQ}' \\ &= \mathbf{QDIDQ}' \\ &= \mathbf{QD}^2\mathbf{Q}'. \end{aligned}$$

Because $\mathbf{D}$ is diagonal,

$$\mathbf{D}^p = \begin{bmatrix} d_1^p & 0 & \dots & 0 \\ 0 & d_2^p & \dots & 0 \\ \cdot & \cdot & & \cdot \\ \cdot & \cdot & & \cdot \\ \cdot & \cdot & & \cdot \\ 0 & 0 & \dots & d_n^p \end{bmatrix},$$

and so Proposition 1.5 can greatly simplify certain computations, particularly when p is large. Also note that if p = −1, Proposition 1.5 provides a convenient method for computing $\mathbf{A}^{-1}$.

The *rank* of a matrix is defined as its number of linearly independent rows or columns. An n × n matrix has an inverse only if its rank is n (i.e., only if it is of full rank). A square matrix with no inverse is said to be *singular*. Using standard methods to determine the rank of a matrix is often time-consuming. However, as the next result shows, if the eigenvalues are known it is trivial.

Proposition 1.6. The rank of $\mathbf{A}$ is equal to its number of nonzero eigenvalues.

Therefore, if any of the eigenvalues of $\mathbf{A}$ equal zero, then $\mathbf{A}$ is singular and has no inverse. In the numerical example, the two eigenvalues are both positive, and so $\mathbf{A}$ is of full rank. Consequently, it has an inverse. Standard methods could be used to find $\mathbf{A}^{-1}$ or Proposition 1.5 could be employed.

$$\mathbf{A}^{-1} = \mathbf{QD}^{-1}\mathbf{Q}' = \begin{bmatrix} \frac{1}{\sqrt{2}} & \frac{-1}{\sqrt{2}} \\ \frac{1}{\sqrt{2}} & \frac{1}{\sqrt{2}} \end{bmatrix} \begin{bmatrix} \frac{1}{9} & 0 \\ 0 & \frac{1}{25} \end{bmatrix} \begin{bmatrix} \frac{1}{\sqrt{2}} & \frac{1}{\sqrt{2}} \\ \frac{-1}{\sqrt{2}} & \frac{1}{\sqrt{2}} \end{bmatrix}$$

$$= \begin{bmatrix} \frac{17}{225} & \frac{8}{225} \\ \frac{8}{225} & \frac{17}{225} \end{bmatrix} .$$

In this book, the most common application of these properties will occur when **A** is a covariance matrix. In this case, Proposition 1.4 always applies because covariance matrices are symmetric. In addition, every covariance matrix is a *positive semidefinite matrix,* which means that all of its eigenvalues are nonnegative. Note that the matrix **A** from the numerical example is symmetric and all eigenvalues are positive. Therefore, **A** is a potential covariance matrix. Under this interpretation, the variance on each dimension is 17 and the covariance is -8. The correlation coefficient is therefore $\rho = -8/\sqrt{17 \times 17} = -0.47$.

Principal Components Analysis

When a random vector **X** has a multivariate normal distribution, the eigenvectors and eigenvalues of its associated covariance matrix have a special interpretation. The eigenvectors determine the axes of the ellipsoidal contours of equal likelihood, and the corresponding eigenvalues determine their length. These facts form the cornerstone of the statistical technique known as *Principal Components Analysis*. Proposition 1.7 describes the basic result that makes the technique possible.

Proposition 1.7. Consider an n-dimensional random vector **X** that has a multivariate normal distribution with mean vector $\boldsymbol{\mu}$ and covariance matrix $\boldsymbol{\Sigma}$. The ellipsoidal contours of equal likelihood (see Equation 13) are centered at $\boldsymbol{\mu}$. Suppose the n eigenvalues of $\boldsymbol{\Sigma}$ are all distinct and are ordered so that

$$d_1 > d_2 > \cdots > d_n .$$

Let $\mathbf{q}_j$ be the eigenvector corresponding to d_i. Then the major or longest axis of the Equation 13 ellipsoid lies in the direction $\mathbf{q}_1$ and the length of that axis is $2\sqrt{d_1 k}$, where k is the arbitrary Equation 13 constant. The second-longest axis lies in the direction q_2 and its length is $2\sqrt{d_2 k}$, and so on. In general, the i-th longest axis lies in the direction q_i and its length is $2\sqrt{d_i k}$.

Proof: See e.g., Morrison (1967).

To illustrate this result, suppose that the covariance matrix $\boldsymbol{\Sigma}$ is equal to the matrix **A** of our numerical example. Thus

$$\boldsymbol{\Sigma} = \begin{bmatrix} 17 & -8 \\ -8 & 17 \end{bmatrix} .$$

Suppose the distribution is centered at the origin (i.e., $\boldsymbol{\mu} = \mathbf{0}$) and that k = 1 (i.e., in Equation 13). In this case $d_1 = 25$, $d_2 = 9$,

$$\mathbf{q}_1 = \begin{bmatrix} \frac{-1}{\sqrt{2}} \\ \frac{1}{\sqrt{2}} \end{bmatrix} \quad \text{and} \quad \mathbf{q}_2 = \begin{bmatrix} \frac{1}{\sqrt{2}} \\ \frac{1}{\sqrt{2}} \end{bmatrix}.$$

Thus, the principal axis of the ellipse is coincident with the chord running from the point (0,0) to the point $(-1/\sqrt{2}, 1/\sqrt{2})$, and the length of this axis is $2\sqrt{25} = 10$. The minor axis of the ellipse is coincident with the chord connecting the points (0,0) and $(1/\sqrt{2}, 1/\sqrt{2})$. Its length is $2\sqrt{9} = 6$. The resulting contour is illustrated in Figure 1.4.

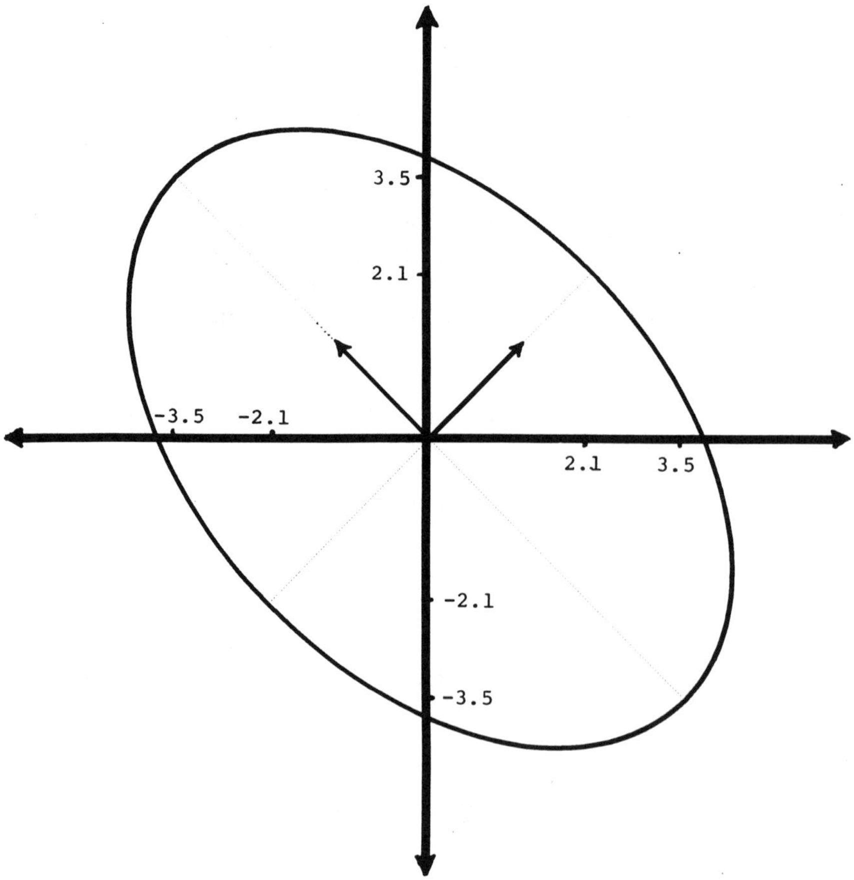

FIG. 1.4. Contour of equal likelihood from a bivariate normal distribution.

Proposition 1.7 is the cornerstone of Principal Components Analysis. Suppose a random vector **X** of order n has a multivariate normal distribution. The goal of Principal Components Analysis is to represent this set of variables in a geometric space of minimum dimensionality. Typically, some information will be lost no matter how dimensionality is reduced, but some methods will be more effective at preserving structure than others.

For example, consider the distribution represented by the Figure 1.4 contour of equal likelihood. Suppose that we rotate the x and y dimensions clockwise until they are coincident with the major and minor axes of the ellipse. Call the new dimensions x^* and y^* (i.e., x^* agrees with the major axis and y^* with the minor). Any point in the space can be represented either by the original coordinates (x, y) or by the new coordinates (x^*, y^*). Now, suppose that instead of either of these two-dimensional representations, samples from the Figure 1.4 distribution are described only by their value on the x^* dimension. In other words, instead of describing a sample by its coordinates (x^*, y^*), we use $(x^*, 0)$ or just x^*. The squared error of this one-dimensional representation is $\epsilon = (x^* - x^*)^2 + (y^* - 0)^2 = y^{*2}$. Because the variability within the distribution is greatest along the major axis and least along the minor axis, this is the most efficient method of reducing to one dimension, in the sense that the resulting mean-squared representation error is minimized (e.g., Morrison, 1967).

In fact, the resulting mean-squared error that results from eliminating $\mathbf{q}_2$ can be shown to equal d_2. Thus, the proportion of the total variance (i.e., mean-squared error) accounted for by the single $\mathbf{q}_1$ dimension is $d_1/(d_1 + d_2)$, which in our numerical example equals $25/(25 + 9) = 0.74$. Only 26% of the total variance is unaccounted for by collapsing onto one dimension.

If $\mathbf{\Sigma}$ is n $\times$ n, then the proportion of the total variance accounted for by the first eigenvector is $d_1/(d_1 + d_2 + \cdots + d_n)$. If this proportion is acceptably high, then a one-dimensional representation of the data is possible. If the first eigenvector does not account for a significant proportion of the total variance by itself, then a two-dimensional representation can be created by including the second eigenvector. The proportion of total variance accounted for by the first two eigenvectors is $(d_1 + d_2)/(d_1 + d_2 + \cdots + d_n)$. If this value is large enough, then a two-dimensional representation is possible. If not, then more dimensions are created by successively including eigenvectors until the proportion of total variance accounted for is acceptable.

RANDOM NUMBER GENERATION

Some of the analyses reported in this book entail *Monte Carlo Simulation*. In this technique, predictions of a model, usually an analytically intractable model, are investigated through computer simulation. For example, suppose a model assumes that a subject's perceptual representation of a particular stimulus has a certain multivariate probability distribution and that on each trial of the experiment of interest the subject bases his or her response on some nonlinear function of the perceptual value that occurred on that particular trial. Now suppose we are interested in the effects of perceptual dependencies on the predicted accuracy of this model. It may be impossible to obtain an analytic expression relating performance in this task to degree of perceptual dependence. If it is impossible, the following alternative research strategy can be employed.

To begin, the hypothesized multivariate probability distributions are created and many (e.g., 10,000) random samples are drawn. Each of these is subjected to the nonlinear transformation postulated by the model, and a response is then predicted. Finally, the proportion of correct responses is computed. This process can be repeated with several different values of the correlation coefficient to discover how sensitive the model is to perceptual dependence.

To conduct a simulation of this type, one must draw random samples from some specified multivariate probability distribution. On many computer systems, random number generators only give values that are uniformly distributed between 0 and 1. How can samples be obtained from other distributions? Although this problem can be difficult, its solution is often straightforward. Two cases are considered here. The first is a univariate technique, called the distribution function method. The second is a technique for generating random samples from multivariate normal distributions. For a much more thorough discussion of random number generation, see Devroye (1986).

The Distribution Function Method

Consider the problem of generating random samples from a univariate distribution with cumulative distribution function $F_X(x)$. Assume that the only random number generator available produces a value Y that is uniformly distributed over the interval (0,1). Thus,

$$F_Y(y) = P(Y \leq y) = y \qquad \text{for } 0 < y \leq 1 \ .$$

Note that y is a value between 0 and 1.0, as is $F_X(x)$ (the cumulative distribution function of the desired random variable X). Therefore, for any value of x,

$$P[Y \leq F_X(x)] = F_X(x) \ .$$

Now, if a random variable X is defined by

$$X = F_X^{-1}(Y) \ ,$$

where Y is uniformly distributed over the interval (0, 1), then

$$\begin{aligned} P(X \leq x) &= P[F_X^{-1}(Y) \leq x] \\ &= P[Y \leq F_X(x)] \\ &= F_X(x) \ . \end{aligned}$$

Thus, the random sample has the desired probability distribution. The use of this method involves the following steps: (a) write the cumulative distribution function for the desired distribution; (b) set this expression equal to Y; (c) solve for X. The resulting equation defines a transformation that converts the uniformly distributed random variable Y to a new random variable X that has the desired probability distribution.

To illustrate the technique, consider the problem of generating random samples from an exponential distribution with rate w. Thus,

$$F_X(x) = 1 - e^{-wX} \qquad \text{for } x \geq 0 \ .$$

Setting

$$Y = 1 - e^{-wX}$$

and solving for X yields

$$X = -w^{-1}\, ln\, (1 - Y)\ . \tag{19}$$

Therefore, random samples from an exponential distribution with rate w are obtained by inserting each value produced by the uniform (0, 1) random number generator into Equation 19 in place of Y and performing the specified transformation. To verify that this works, note that

$$\begin{aligned} F_X(x) = P(X \leq x) &= P[-w^{-1}\, ln\, (1 - Y) \leq x] \\ &= P[ln\, (1 - Y) \geq -wx] \\ &= P(1 - Y \geq e^{-wx}) \\ &= P(Y \leq 1 - e^{-wx}) \\ &= 1 - e^{-wx}\ , \end{aligned}$$

as required.

The Distribution Function Technique can be used only if a closed-form expression exists for the cumulative distribution function of the desired distribution. Unfortunately, the normal distribution has no closed-form expression for its cumulative distribution function, so samples that are normally distributed cannot be generated with the Distribution Function Method. However, the logistic distribution, which has a shape similar to the normal, has a closed form for its cumulative distribution function, so random samples from a logistic distribution are easily generated with the distribution function technique. In many simulations, the logistic distribution can be safely substituted for the normal. The logistic distribution function with mean μ and variance σ^2 is defined, for $-\infty < x < \infty$, as

$$F_X(x) = \left\{ 1 + exp\left[-\frac{\pi}{\sqrt{3}} \left(\frac{x - \mu}{\sigma} \right) \right] \right\}^{-1} . \tag{20}$$

Samples from this distribution can be generated from a uniform (0, 1) random number generator via the transformation

$$X = \mu - \frac{\sigma\sqrt{3}}{\pi}\left[ln\,(1 - Y) - ln\,(Y)\right].$$

Generating Normally Distributed Random Samples

As noted, the distribution function method cannot be used to generate normally distributed random numbers. However, a number of simple methods for generating normally distributed random samples from a uniform random number generator have been proposed (see, e.g., Devroye, 1986, pp. 379–390; Knuth, 1981, pp. 117–127). Among the most accurate of these is due to Box and Muller (1958). Their method involves five steps.

Step 1. Draw two independent samples, U_1 and U_2, from a population that is uniformly distributed over the interval (0, 1).

Step 2. Create two new variables, V_1 and V_2, by setting

$$V_1 = 2U_1 - 1, \qquad V_2 = 2U_2 - 1 .$$

Step 3. Create a variable S by setting

$$S = V_1^2 + V_2^2 .$$

Step 4. If $S \geq 1$, return to step 1. (The number of times steps 1 through 4 must be executed has a mean of 1.27 and a standard deviation of 0.587.)

Step 5. Create two variables,

$$Z_1 = V_1\sqrt{\frac{-2\,ln\,S}{S}}, \qquad Z_2 = V_2\sqrt{\frac{-2\,ln\,S}{S}},$$

that are independent and identically distributed random samples from a population that is normally distributed with a mean of 0 and a variance of 1.0.

Given a method for generating samples from a Z distribution, Equations 6 and 7 can be used to transform to a new normally distributed variable X that has an arbitrary mean μ and an arbitrary variance σ^2. To do this, define

$$X = \sigma Z + \mu . \tag{21}$$

From Equations 6 and 7, it is straightforward to verify that X has mean μ and variance σ^2. Note that solving this equation for Z produces

$$Z = \frac{X - \mu}{\sigma},$$

the well-known Z transformation.

Generating random samples from multivariate distributions is simple if statistical independence is desired. For example, consider the problem of generating random samples from a bivariate normal distribution with the following mean vector and covariance matrix:

$$\boldsymbol{\mu} = \begin{bmatrix} 25 \\ 40 \end{bmatrix}, \qquad \boldsymbol{\Sigma} = \begin{bmatrix} 100 & 0 \\ 0 & 144 \end{bmatrix}.$$

First, the Box and Muller (1958) algorithm is used to generate random values Z_1 and Z_2. Together Z_1 and Z_2 have a bivariate Z distribution. Next, Equation 21 is used to create two new random values X_1 and X_2:

$$X_1 = 10Z_1 + 25 ,$$
$$X_2 = 12Z_2 + 40 .$$

The pair (X_1, X_2) has the desired bivariate distribution. If a bivariate distribution with correlated variates is desired, then a generalization of Equation 21 is needed. If we define

$$X_1 = \sigma_1 Z_1 + \mu_1$$

and

$$X_2 = \sigma_2(\rho Z_1 + \sqrt{1 - \rho^2}\, Z_2) + \mu_2 ,$$

then X_1 and X_2 are normally distributed random variables with means μ_1 and μ_2, standard deviations σ_1 and σ_2, and correlation coefficient ρ.

Now suppose random samples are desired from some n-dimensional normal distribution with arbitrary mean vector $\boldsymbol{\mu}$ and arbitrary covariance matrix $\boldsymbol{\Sigma}$. Call the resulting random vector $\mathbf{X}$. To begin, generate samples from an n-dimensional Z distribution. The resulting random vector $\mathbf{Z}$ has mean vector 0 and covariance matrix $\mathbf{I}$. Linear transformations of Z distributions are normally distributed, so the next step is to find an $n \times n$ matrix $\mathbf{A}$ and a vector $\mathbf{b}$ of order n such that

$$\mathbf{X} = \mathbf{AZ} + \mathbf{b} .$$

From Equation 14, note that

$$\boldsymbol{\mu} = \mathbf{A}\, E(\mathbf{Z}) + \mathbf{b} = \mathbf{b} ;$$

and from Equation 15

$$\boldsymbol{\Sigma} = \mathbf{A}\boldsymbol{\Sigma}_Z\mathbf{A}' = \mathbf{AA}'$$

Therefore, we need to find an $n \times n$ matrix $\mathbf{A}$ such that $\mathbf{AA}' = \boldsymbol{\Sigma}$. It turns out that several such matrices $\mathbf{A}$ can be found. For example, Proposition 1.4 indicates that $\boldsymbol{\Sigma}$ can always be decomposed as

$$\begin{aligned} \boldsymbol{\Sigma} &= \mathbf{QDQ}' \\ &= \mathbf{QD}^{1/2}\mathbf{D}^{1/2}\mathbf{Q}' \\ &= (\mathbf{QD}^{1/2})(\mathbf{QD}^{1/2})' , \end{aligned}$$

where $\mathbf{Q}$ is an $n \times n$ matrix whose columns are the eigenvectors of $\boldsymbol{\Sigma}$, and $\mathbf{D}$ is a diagonal matrix whose entries on the main diagonal are the corresponding eigenvalues of $\boldsymbol{\Sigma}$. Thus, one possibility is to set $\mathbf{A} = \mathbf{QD}^{1/2}$. In this case, multivariate normal samples are generated from multivariate $\boldsymbol{Z}$ samples via the transformation

$$\mathbf{X} = \mathbf{QD}^{1/2}\mathbf{Z} + \boldsymbol{\mu} \, .$$

The only problem with this solution is that it requires knowledge of the eigenvalues and eigenvectors of $\boldsymbol{\Sigma}$. If samples from many different normal distributions are required, this extra computation may be prohibitive. Fortunately, a simpler procedure, based on a technique known as *Cholesky Factorization* (e.g., Graybill, 1976), is possible. The technique is based on the following result.

Proposition 1.8. For any covariance matrix $\boldsymbol{\Sigma}$, there exists a unique lower triangular matrix $\mathbf{A}$ such that

$$\boldsymbol{\Sigma} = \mathbf{AA}' \, .$$

Proof: See, for example, Graybill (1976, pp. 260–261).

The advantage of Cholesky Factorization is that the lower triangular matrix $\mathbf{A}$ is easy to find. To do so, first write out the equation $\boldsymbol{\Sigma} = \mathbf{AA}'$ in detail:

$$\begin{bmatrix} \sigma_1^2 & Cov_{12} & \cdots & Cov_{1n} \\ Cov_{21} & \sigma_2^2 & \cdots & Cov_{2n} \\ \cdot & \cdot & & \cdot \\ \cdot & \cdot & & \cdot \\ \cdot & \cdot & & \cdot \\ Cov_{n1} & Cov_{n2} & \cdots & \sigma_n^2 \end{bmatrix} = \begin{bmatrix} a_{11} & 0 & \cdots & 0 \\ a_{21} & a_{22} & \cdots & 0 \\ \cdot & \cdot & & \cdot \\ \cdot & \cdot & & \cdot \\ \cdot & \cdot & & \cdot \\ a_{n1} & a_{n2} & \cdots & a_{nn} \end{bmatrix} \begin{bmatrix} a_{11} & a_{21} & \cdots & a_{n1} \\ 0 & a_{22} & \cdots & a_{n2} \\ \cdot & \cdot & & \cdot \\ \cdot & \cdot & & \cdot \\ \cdot & \cdot & & \cdot \\ 0 & 0 & \cdots & a_{nn} \end{bmatrix}$$

Solving for the a_{ij} leads to:

1. $a_{11} = \sigma_1$.
2. $a_{j1} = Cov_{j1}/\sigma_1$, for j = 2, 3, . . . , n.
3. $$a_{ii} = \left[\sigma_i^2 - \sum_{k=1}^{i-1} a_{ik}^2\right]^{1/2}, \qquad \text{for } i = 2, 3, \ldots, n \, . \tag{22}$$
4. $$a_{ij} = \frac{1}{a_{ij}}\left[Cov_{ij} - \sum_{k=1}^{j-1} a_{ik}a_{jk}\right], \qquad \text{for } j < i \text{ and } i = 2, \ldots, n-1 \, .$$
5. $a_{ij} = 0$, for $j > i$ and i = 2, 3, . . . , n.

To illustrate this procedure, consider the following simple example. Suppose

$$\boldsymbol{\Sigma} = \begin{bmatrix} 9 & 12 & 6 \\ 12 & 25 & 14 \\ 6 & 14 & 24 \end{bmatrix} .$$

1. Applying formula 1 of Equation 22 leads to $a_{11} = 3$.
2. Applying 2 leads to $a_{21} = \frac{12}{3} = 4$ and $a_{31} = \frac{6}{3} = 2$.
3. Applying 3 leads to $a_{22} = (\sigma_2^2 - a_{21}^2)^{1/2} = \sqrt{9} = 3$.
4. Applying 4 leads to

$$a_{32} = \frac{Cov_{32} - a_{31}a_{21}}{a_{22}} = \frac{14 - (2)(4)}{3} = 2 .$$

5. Applying 3 leads to

$$a_{33} = (\sigma_3^2 - a_{31}^2 - a_{32}^2)^{1/2} = (24 - 2^2 - 2^2)^{1/2} = 4 .$$

6. From 5 we find that all other $a_{ij} = 0$.

Thus the lower triangular matrix **A** is found to be

$$\mathbf{A} = \begin{bmatrix} 3 & 0 & 0 \\ 4 & 3 & 0 \\ 2 & 2 & 4 \end{bmatrix} .$$

It is easily verified that $\mathbf{AA}' = \boldsymbol{\Sigma}$.

Generating random samples from a multivariate normal distribution with arbitrary mean vector $\boldsymbol{\mu}$ and covariance matrix $\boldsymbol{\Sigma}$ therefore involves the following steps. First, use the Box and Muller (1958) algorithm to generate random samples from a multivariate **Z** distribution. Second, use Equations 22 to find the lower triangular Cholesky matrix **A**. Third, transform each multivariate **Z** sample via the expression

$$\mathbf{X} = \mathbf{AZ} + \boldsymbol{\mu} .$$

The random vector **X** has the desired distribution.

Because the Cholesky matrix is lower triangular, it possesses several properties that can greatly simplify certain computations. The next result details four of these.

Proposition 1.9. If **A** is an n × n lower triangular matrix, then:

1. $\mathbf{A}^{-1}$, if it exists, is a lower triangular matrix.
2. If $\mathbf{A}^{-1}$ exists, the i-th diagonal element is $1/a_{ii}$.

3. The product of two n × n lower triangular matrices is an n × n lower triangular matrix.
4. The determinant of **A** is given by $|\mathbf{A}| = a_{11}a_{22} \cdots a_{nn}$.

Proof: The proof is left to the reader.

NUMERICAL INTEGRATION USING CHOLESKY FACTORIZATION

In addition to generating random data, one can use Cholesky Factorization to rapidly solve many numerical integration problems. For example, consider a model that assumes that a certain perceptual distribution is bivariate normal with mean vector $\boldsymbol{\mu}$ and covariance matrix $\boldsymbol{\Sigma}$. Frequently, generating predictions from such a model requires multiple integration of the bivariate normal density function. If the correlation coefficient is zero, such a multiple integral can often be easily decomposed into a product of single integrals and, in this way, quickly evaluated. However, if the correlation coefficient is nonzero, the problem is more difficult.

As a specific example, consider the integral

$$P(\mathbf{X} \in A_x) = \int \int_{A_x} \cdots \int N(\boldsymbol{\mu}, \boldsymbol{\Sigma})\, d\mathbf{x} , \tag{23}$$

where $N(\boldsymbol{\mu}, \boldsymbol{\Sigma})$ is the multivariate normal probability density function given in Equation 10 and

$$A_x = \{\mathbf{x} | h(\mathbf{x}) > 0\}$$

for some arbitrary function h. For example, if $h(\mathbf{x})$ is quadratic in $\mathbf{x}$, then A_x is the set of all points on one side of a quadratic surface.

To begin evaluating Equation 23, note that Cholesky Factorization can be used to find the lower triangular matrix **A** such that

$$\mathbf{X} = g(\mathbf{Z}) = \mathbf{AZ} + \boldsymbol{\mu} .$$

The random vector **X** has a bivariate normal distribution with mean vector $\boldsymbol{\mu}$ and covariance matrix $\boldsymbol{\Sigma}$. If **A** is nonsingular, then the function g is one-to-one and onto, so the inverse function

$$g^{-1}(\mathbf{X}) = \mathbf{A}^{-1}(\mathbf{X} - \boldsymbol{\mu})$$

exists. Now, g^{-1} maps the set A_x into the set $A_z = \{\mathbf{Z} | h[g(\mathbf{Z})] > 0\}$. To see this, note that $\mathbf{Z}^* \in A_z$ if and only if its image $\mathbf{X}^* = g(\mathbf{Z}^*) \in A_x$. Therefore,

$$P(\mathbf{X} \in A_x) = P(\mathbf{Z} \in A_z) .$$

Probabilities such as $P(\mathbf{Z} \in A_z)$ can be numerically computed quickly and accurately by using a table that contains areas under the Z distribution. The number of values needed in the table decreases with the dimensionality of the problem. With two dimensions, accurate estimates can be obtained from a list of only 25 of these values (along with linear interpolation when appropriate). Let $\Phi(z) = P(Z \leq z)$; that is, Φ is the cumulative Z distribution function. Suppose the integral in question involves n dimensions and a Z table is available that contains the m values $z_1, z_2, \ldots, z_m$. Essentially, this procedure replaces the n-dimensional continuous space with an n-dimensional discrete space containing m^n points. For each Z value, define

$$G(z_i) = \Phi\left(\frac{z_i + z_{i+1}}{2}\right) - \Phi\left(\frac{z_i + z_{i-1}}{2}\right) .$$

Note that $G(z_i)$ is the area under the Z probability density function around the point z_i [i.e., between $(z_i + z_{i+1})/2$ and $(z_{i-1} + z_i)/2$]. The $G(z_i)$ form a second table. Rather than tabling these values, we could analytically approximate them when needed by using Equation 9, but because of the extra computation involved the resulting algorithm should be significantly slower.

The $G(z_i)$ are used to approximate the probability $P(\mathbf{Z} \in A_z)$ in the following manner. First, step through all m^n points in $\mathbf{Z}$ space. The k-th point in this space, $\mathbf{Z}_k$, has coordinates

$$\mathbf{Z}_k' = (z_{k1}, z_{k2}, \cdots, z_{kn}) ,$$

where z_{kj} is equal to one of the m values in the Z table (i.e., to one of the z_i). Next, for each point $\mathbf{Z}_k$ check whether

$$h(\mathbf{A}\mathbf{Z}_k + \boldsymbol{\mu}) > 0 .$$

If not, then ignore this $\mathbf{Z}_k$ and go on to the next. If $h(\mathbf{A}\mathbf{Z}_k + \boldsymbol{\mu}) > 0$, then $\mathbf{Z}_k \in A_z$. Thus, compute the product

$$G(z_{k1})G(z_{k2}) \cdots G(z_{kn}) .$$

The sum of all such products approximates the probability $P(\mathbf{Z} \in A_z)$ and, therefore, the integral in Equation 23.

In this example, we were required to step through all m^n points in $\mathbf{Z}$ space, but, in the special case in which the region of integration is rectangular, faster methods are available. For example, consider the integral

$$P(X_1 > x_{01}, X_2 > x_{02}) = \int_{x_{02}}^{\infty} \int_{x_{01}}^{\infty} N(\boldsymbol{\mu}, \boldsymbol{\Sigma})\, dx_1\, dx_2 , \tag{24}$$

where

$$\boldsymbol{\mu} = \begin{bmatrix} \mu_1 \\ \mu_2 \end{bmatrix} \quad \text{and} \quad \boldsymbol{\Sigma} = \begin{bmatrix} \sigma_1^2 & \rho\sigma_1\sigma_2 \\ \rho\sigma_1\sigma_2 & \sigma_2^2 \end{bmatrix} .$$

Note that Equation 24 can be rewritten as

$$P(X_1 > x_{01}, X_2 > x_{02}) = P\left(\frac{X_1 - x_{01}}{\sigma_1} > 0, \frac{X_2 - x_{02}}{\sigma_2} > 0\right)$$
$$= P(W_1 > 0, W_2 > 0) ,$$

where $(W_1, W_2)'$ has a bivariate normal distribution with mean vector and covariance matrix

$$\mu_W = \begin{bmatrix} \mu_{W_1} \\ \mu_{W_2} \end{bmatrix} = \begin{bmatrix} \dfrac{\mu_1 - x_{01}}{\sigma_1} \\ \dfrac{\mu_2 - x_{02}}{\sigma_2} \end{bmatrix} \qquad \text{and} \qquad \Sigma_W = \begin{bmatrix} 1 & \rho \\ \rho & 1 \end{bmatrix} .$$

This integral can be simplified to

$$P(W_1 > 0, W_2 > 0) = \Phi(\mu_{W_1})\Phi(\mu_{W_2})$$
$$+ \int_0^{\rho} \frac{1}{2\pi\sqrt{1 - t^2}} \, exp\left[-\frac{1}{2}\left(\frac{\mu_{W_1}^2 - 2t\mu_{w_1}\mu_{w_2} + \mu_{w2}^2}{1 - t^2} \right) \right] dt . \qquad (25)$$

Equation 25 was first given by Owens (1956). The relation was independently derived by Palen and Ennis (1991), who also presented a derivation and discussed various methods for evaluating the integral numerically. A simple, but nevertheless fast alternative, uses Simpson's Rule. Sheppard (1899) showed that in the special case in which $\mu_{W1} = \mu_{W2} = 0$, the Equation 25 integral reduces to

$$P(W_1 > 0, W_2 > 0) = \frac{1}{2\pi} \, sin^{-1} \rho + \frac{1}{4} .$$

Frequently, the purpose for evaluating integrals like the one in Equation 24 is to estimate parameters and to test the goodness of fit of a particular model. If all predictions of the model involve integrals like Equation 24, then parameter estimation can be accomplished quickly via the Maximum Likelihood Procedure developed by Wickens (1992; see also chap. 9). Wickens derived the derivatives of the log-likelihood that are needed for the Newton-Raphson Algorithm, and thus his procedure should be considerably faster than a maximization routine that uses Cholesky Factorization.

DISCRIMINANT ANALYSIS

Consider a model that assumes multivariate normal perceptual representations in a simple identification experiment with stimuli $\mathbf{S}_A$ and $\mathbf{S}_B$. One problem of general interest is to compare the accuracy predictions of this model to those of the optimal responder. Specifically, given the perceptual distributions predicted by the model, what is the highest possible percentage of correct responses that can be expected? Alternatively, consider a categorization task with two overlapping categories. Suppose the exemplars in each category can be represented by a multivariate normal probability distribution. The same question can be asked. What accuracy level can be expected in this task of a subject making optimal use of the available information? In addition, one might also ask on what basis this optimal responder selects a response. These questions are the foundation of a branch of statistics known as *Discriminant Analysis* (e.g., Ashby & Gott, 1988; Fukunaga, 1972; Morrison, 1967).

As a concrete example, consider the identification experiment with stimuli $\mathbf{S}_A$ and $\mathbf{S}_B$. Suppose that on each trial stimulus $\mathbf{S}_A$ is presented with probability $P(\mathbf{S}_A)$ and stimulus $\mathbf{S}_B$ is presented with probability $P(\mathbf{S}_B)$. Call the two associated multivariate probability density functions $f_A(\mathbf{x})$ and $f_B(\mathbf{x})$ and the two identification responses $\mathbf{R}_A$ and $\mathbf{R}_B$. To maximize the probability of a correct response, the optimal responder uses the following decision rule:

$$\text{If } l(\mathbf{x}) = \frac{f_A(\mathbf{x})}{f_B(\mathbf{x})} > \frac{P(\mathbf{S}_B)}{P(\mathbf{S}_A)}\text{ , then respond } \mathbf{R}_A\text{, otherwise respond } \mathbf{R}_B\text{ .}$$

The function $l(\mathbf{x})$ is called the likelihood ratio. If the two stimuli are presented with equal probability on each trial, then $P(\mathbf{S}_B)/P(\mathbf{S}_A) = 1$, and the optimal rule is to respond $\mathbf{R}_A$ if the likelihood ratio is greater than 1.0 and $\mathbf{R}_B$ if it is less than 1.0. This rule is familiar from Signal Detection Theory.

Note that application of the likelihood ratio decision rule divides the perceptual space into two regions. In one region, $l(\mathbf{x}) > 1.0$ and response $\mathbf{R}_A$ is emitted; in the other region, $l(\mathbf{x}) < 1$ and response $\mathbf{R}_B$ is made. Points on the boundary separating these two regions satisfy $l(\mathbf{x}) = 1$. A natural question to ask is, what is the shape of this optimal decision bound? In general, there is no answer to this question. Any shape is possible. However, if the perceptual distributions are multivariate normal, then the optimal decision bound is always linear or quadratic.

To see this, suppose the perceptual space is n-dimensional. From Equation 12 the optimal decision bound satisfies

$$\begin{aligned} 1.0 = l(\mathbf{x}) &= \frac{(2\pi)^{-n/2}\,|\boldsymbol{\Sigma}_A|^{-1/2}\, exp\,[-\tfrac{1}{2}(\mathbf{x} - \boldsymbol{\mu}_A)'\,\boldsymbol{\Sigma}_A^{-1}(\mathbf{x} - \boldsymbol{\mu}_A)]}{(2\pi)^{-n/2}\,|\boldsymbol{\Sigma}_B|^{-1/2}\, exp\,[-\tfrac{1}{2}(\mathbf{x} - \boldsymbol{\mu}_B)'\,\boldsymbol{\Sigma}_B^{-1}(\mathbf{x} - \boldsymbol{\mu}_B)]} \\ &= \left(\frac{|\boldsymbol{\Sigma}_B|}{|\boldsymbol{\Sigma}_A|}\right)^{1/2} exp\,[-\tfrac{1}{2}(\mathbf{x} - \boldsymbol{\mu}_A)'\boldsymbol{\Sigma}_A^{-1}(\mathbf{x} - \boldsymbol{\mu}_A) \\ &\qquad + \tfrac{1}{2}(\mathbf{x} - \boldsymbol{\mu}_B)'\boldsymbol{\Sigma}_B^{-1}(\mathbf{x} - \boldsymbol{\mu}_B)]\ . \end{aligned}$$

Taking the natural log of both sides reduces the optimal bound to

$$0 = \tfrac{1}{2}(\mathbf{x} - \boldsymbol{\mu}_A)'\boldsymbol{\Sigma}_A^{-1}(\mathbf{x} - \boldsymbol{\mu}_A) - \tfrac{1}{2}(\mathbf{x} - \boldsymbol{\mu}_B)'\boldsymbol{\Sigma}_B^{-1}(\mathbf{x} - \boldsymbol{\mu}_B) + \tfrac{1}{2}\, ln \left(\frac{|\boldsymbol{\Sigma}_A|}{|\boldsymbol{\Sigma}_B|}\right)$$

$$= -ln\,[l(\mathbf{x})]$$

$$= h(\mathbf{x})\,. \qquad (26)$$

The optimal decision rule can therefore be written as:

If $h(\mathbf{x}) < 0$, then respond $\mathbf{R}_A$, otherwise respond $\mathbf{R}_B$.

If the stimulus presentation probabilities are unequal, this rule generalizes to:

$$\text{If } h(\mathbf{x}) < ln\,\frac{P(\mathbf{S}_A)}{P(\mathbf{S}_B)}\text{, then respond } \mathbf{R}_A\text{, otherwise respond } \mathbf{R}_B\,. \qquad (27)$$

Note that $h(\mathbf{x})$, as given by Equation 26, is quadratic in $\mathbf{x}$. Therefore, as long as the two perceptual distributions are multivariate normal, the optimal decision bound is quadratic, regardless of the values for the different variances and covariances.

If $\boldsymbol{\Sigma}_A = \boldsymbol{\Sigma}_B = \boldsymbol{\Sigma}$, then Equation 26 simplifies to

$$h(\mathbf{x}) = (\boldsymbol{\mu}_B - \boldsymbol{\mu}_A)'\boldsymbol{\Sigma}^{-1}\mathbf{x} + \tfrac{1}{2}(\boldsymbol{\mu}_A'\boldsymbol{\Sigma}^{-1}\boldsymbol{\mu}_A - \boldsymbol{\mu}_B'\boldsymbol{\Sigma}^{-1}\boldsymbol{\mu}_B)\,. \qquad (28)$$

This function is linear in $\mathbf{x}$. The statistical technique of Discriminant Analysis typically assumes a linear discriminant function; that is, in most applications the technique tries to find the linear function that best separates samples from two categories. Linear Discriminant Analysis is therefore guaranteed to be optimal only if the exemplars from the two categories have equal variances on every dimension and if the covariances between each pair of dimensions are equal.

If $\boldsymbol{\Sigma}_A = \boldsymbol{\Sigma}_B = \sigma^2\mathbf{I}$ and if the two stimuli are presented with equal probability, then the optimal bound satisfies

$$0 = h(\mathbf{x}) = (\boldsymbol{\mu}_B - \boldsymbol{\mu}_A)'\mathbf{x} + \tfrac{1}{2}(\boldsymbol{\mu}_A'\boldsymbol{\mu}_A - \boldsymbol{\mu}_B'\boldsymbol{\mu}_B)\,. \qquad (29)$$

This function, which is linear in $\mathbf{x}$, describes those points that are equidistant from the two means. All points on one side of the bound are closer to the $\mathbf{S}_A$ mean, and all points on the other side are closer to the $\mathbf{S}_B$ mean. Because of this, a subject who uses the Equation 27 decision rule along with the definition of $h(\mathbf{x})$ in Equation 29 is said to be employing *minimum distance classification*. Figure 1.5 gives two-dimensional examples of the optimal decision bound when $\boldsymbol{\Sigma}_A \neq \boldsymbol{\Sigma}_B$, $\boldsymbol{\Sigma}_A = \boldsymbol{\Sigma}_B$, and $\boldsymbol{\Sigma}_A = \boldsymbol{\Sigma}_B = \sigma^2\mathbf{I}$.

The most effective means for assessing the effectiveness of a decision rule is to compute the probability that it makes an incorrect classification. Unfortunately, although the concept is simple, the computation of error probabilities is often quite difficult. There are two main approaches. These will be illustrated for the optimal responder, but the same techniques can be used to evaluate any decision rule.

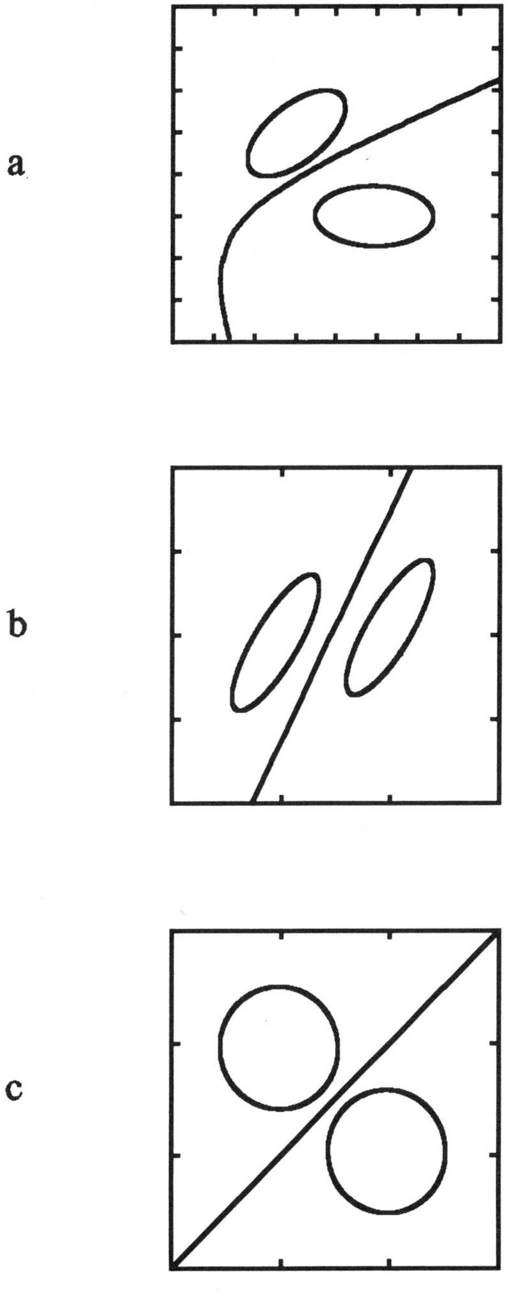

FIG. 1.5. Optimal decision bounds when (a) $\mathbf{\Sigma}_A \neq \mathbf{\Sigma}_B$, (b) $\mathbf{\Sigma}_A = \mathbf{\Sigma}_B$, and (c) when $\mathbf{\Sigma}_A = \mathbf{\Sigma}_B = \sigma^2\mathbf{I}$.

The first approach is to write an integral equation directly in terms of the category distributions $f_A(\mathbf{x})$ and $f_B(\mathbf{x})$. Let A_i denote that part of the perceptual space for which the observer responds $\mathbf{R}_i$. For example, according to Equation 27, A_A denotes the set of all $\mathbf{x}$ for which $h(\mathbf{x}) < ln\ [P(\mathbf{S}_A)/P(\mathbf{S}_B)]$. The probability of an identification error is therefore given by

$$P(\mathbf{R}_j|\mathbf{S}_i) = \int\int_{A_j} \cdots \int N(\boldsymbol{\mu}_i, \boldsymbol{\Sigma}_i)\, d\mathbf{x}\ . \tag{30}$$

Evaluating Equation 30 can be difficult, especially if any of the covariances are nonzero or if $\boldsymbol{\Sigma}_A \neq \boldsymbol{\Sigma}_B$. However, the integral always can be evaluated numerically by using Cholesky Factorization (i.e., see Equation 23).

The second method for computing error probabilities is to write an integral equation in terms of the distribution of the discriminant variable $Y = h(\mathbf{X})$. This approach has appeal because Y is univariate, no matter what the dimensionality of $\mathbf{X}$. To begin, define $X_c = ln\ [P(\mathbf{S}_A)/P(\mathbf{S}_B)]$. Next, note that

$$P(\mathbf{R}_A|\mathbf{S}_B) = P[h(\mathbf{X}) < X_c|\mathbf{S}_B] = \int_{-\infty}^{X_c} f_Y(y|\mathbf{S}_B)\, dy\ , \tag{31}$$

where $f_Y(y|\mathbf{S}_B)$ is the probability density function of the univariate decision variable $Y = h(\mathbf{X})$ on trials when stimulus $\mathbf{S}_B$ is presented. Of course, Equation 31 is useful only if $f_Y(y|\mathbf{S}_B)$ is known. However, in the case that $\boldsymbol{\Sigma}_A = \boldsymbol{\Sigma}_B$, the function $h(\mathbf{X})$ is linear (see Equation 28), and, therefore, because $\mathbf{X}$ is normally distributed, $h(\mathbf{X})$ is normally distributed—in fact, it has a univariate normal distribution, so Equation 31 is straightforward to evaluate. Only the mean and variance of $h(\mathbf{X})$ are needed.

On trials when stimulus $\mathbf{S}_i$ is presented, the mean of $h(\mathbf{X})$ can be found from Equations 14 and 28 to be

$$E\ [h(\mathbf{X})|\mathbf{S}_i] = (\boldsymbol{\mu}_B - \boldsymbol{\mu}_A)'\boldsymbol{\Sigma}^{-1}\boldsymbol{\mu}_i + \tfrac{1}{2}(\boldsymbol{\mu}_A'\boldsymbol{\Sigma}^{-1}\boldsymbol{\mu}_A - \boldsymbol{\mu}_B'\boldsymbol{\Sigma}^{-1}\boldsymbol{\mu}_B)\ ,$$

which reduces to

$$E\ [h(\mathbf{X})|\mathbf{S}_A] = -\tfrac{1}{2}(\boldsymbol{\mu}_B - \boldsymbol{\mu}_A)'\boldsymbol{\Sigma}^{-1}(\boldsymbol{\mu}_B - \boldsymbol{\mu}_A) = -\mu_h$$

and

$$E\ [h(\mathbf{X})|\mathbf{S}_B] = \tfrac{1}{2}(\boldsymbol{\mu}_B - \boldsymbol{\mu}_A)'\boldsymbol{\Sigma}^{-1}(\boldsymbol{\mu}_B - \boldsymbol{\mu}_A) = \mu_h\ .$$

The variance on $\mathbf{S}_i$ trials is found from Equation 15 to be

$$\begin{aligned} Var\ [h(\mathbf{X})|\mathbf{S}_i] &= E\ (\{h(\mathbf{X}|\mathbf{S}_i) - E\ [h(\mathbf{X})|\mathbf{S}_i]\}^2) \\ &= E\ \{[(\boldsymbol{\mu}_B - \boldsymbol{\mu}_A)'\boldsymbol{\Sigma}^{-1}(\mathbf{x} - \boldsymbol{\mu}_i)]^2\} \\ &= (\boldsymbol{\mu}_B - \boldsymbol{\mu}_A)'\boldsymbol{\Sigma}^{-1}E\ [(\mathbf{X} - \boldsymbol{\mu}_i)(\mathbf{X} - \boldsymbol{\mu}_i)'|\mathbf{S}_i]\boldsymbol{\Sigma}^{-1}(\boldsymbol{\mu}_B - \boldsymbol{\mu}_A) \\ &= (\boldsymbol{\mu}_B - \boldsymbol{\mu}_A)'\boldsymbol{\Sigma}^{-1}(\boldsymbol{\mu}_B - \boldsymbol{\mu}_A) \\ &= 2\mu_h\ . \end{aligned}$$

Therefore, using Equation 31, the probability that an ideal observer will incorrectly respond $\mathbf{R}_A$ on $\mathbf{S}_B$ trials in the special case $\boldsymbol{\Sigma}_A = \boldsymbol{\Sigma}_B$ is

$$\begin{aligned} P(\mathbf{R}_A|\mathbf{S}_B) &= P[h(\mathbf{X}) < X_c|\mathbf{S}_B] \\ &= P\left(Z < \frac{X_c - \mu_h}{\sqrt{2\mu_h}}\right) \\ &= \Phi\left(\frac{X_c - \mu_h}{\sqrt{2\mu_h}}\right), \end{aligned}$$

where $\Phi(z)$ is the standard normal cumulative distribution function evaluated at $Z = z$. Similarly,

$$\begin{aligned} P(\mathbf{R}_B|\mathbf{S}_A) &= P[h(\mathbf{X}) > X_c|\mathbf{S}_A] \\ &= P\left(Z > \frac{X_c + \mu_h}{\sqrt{2\mu_h}}\right) \\ &= 1 - \Phi\left(\frac{X_c + \mu_h}{\sqrt{2\mu_h}}\right) \end{aligned}$$

If $\boldsymbol{\Sigma}_A \neq \boldsymbol{\Sigma}_B$, then $h(\mathbf{X})$, which is described by Equation 26, is quadratic in $\mathbf{X}$. In this case, if $\mathbf{X}$ is normally distributed, then $h(\mathbf{X})$ will not be normally distributed, so there is little advantage to transforming the problem from the multivariate Equation 30 integral to the univariate Equation 31 integral. In this case, the best strategy may be to evaluate the Equation 30 integral directly by a numerical technique such as Cholesky Factorization (although see chap. 16).

PARAMETER ESTIMATION AND MODEL TESTING

Whenever the validity of a model is tested with a data set, two problems must be overcome. The first is to estimate the unknown parameters hypothesized by the model, and the second is to assess the model's ability to accurately describe the data. Each of these problems is complex, and a complete discussion is beyond the scope of this chapter. Readers wishing more information are urged to consult a standard statistics text (e.g., Bickel & Doksum, 1977; Snedecor & Cochran, 1967; see also, Wickens, 1982).

Among the most powerful estimation procedures, and one that is well suited to the kinds of models developed in this book, is Maximum Likelihood Estimation. Suppose a set of values $\mathbf{x}' = (x_1, x_2, \ldots, x_n)$ are sampled independently from a population described by the probability density function $f(x|\theta)$, where θ is the unknown parameter value that characterizes the population. Then the joint likelihood of the sample is

$$L(\mathbf{x}|\theta) = \prod_{i=1}^{n} f(x_i|\theta) .$$

The maximum likelihood estimator is that value of θ that maximizes $L(\mathbf{x}|\theta)$.

Maximum likelihood estimators have many desirable properties. First, they are always consistent. Second, if an efficient unbiased estimator exists, Maximum Likelihood Estimation will generally find it. In fact, for large sample sizes, the maximum likelihood estimate is essentially the same as the minimum variance unbiased estimate. Because of these properties, Maximum Likelihood Estimation is usually the best estimation procedure.

Much of the data modeled in this book is in the form of frequencies, specifically frequencies of various kinds of response. For example, on each trial of an identification experiment a subject is presented with one of r possible stimuli. The subject's task is to uniquely identify which of the r stimuli was presented. Data from an identification experiment are summarized in a *confusion matrix*. This is an r × r matrix with entry in row i and column j, denoted f_{ij}, equal to the frequency that response $\mathbf{R}_j$ was made to stimulus $\mathbf{S}_i$. Suppose that stimulus S_i is presented n_i times and that the true probability of responding $\mathbf{R}_j$ on $\mathbf{S}_i$ trials is $P(\mathbf{R}_j|\mathbf{S}_i)$. Then the entries in each row of the confusion matrix have a multinomial distribution. For example, the probability of observing the entries in the i-th row of the matrix is

$$\frac{n_i!}{f_{i1}!\, f_{i2}! \cdots f_{ir}!} P(\mathbf{R}_1|\mathbf{S}_i)^{f_{i1}} P(\mathbf{R}_2|\mathbf{S}_i)^{f_{i2}} \cdots P(\mathbf{R}_r|\mathbf{S}_i)^{f_{ir}} .$$

The joint likelihood associated with the whole confusion matrix is equal to the product of the likelihoods associated with each row. Therefore,

$$L = \prod_{i=1}^{r} \frac{n_i}{\prod_{j=1}^{r} f_{ij}} \prod_{j=1}^{r} P(\mathbf{R}_j|\mathbf{S}_i)^{f_{ij}}$$

Different identification models propose different forms for the $P(\mathbf{R}_j|\mathbf{S}_i)$. For example, in multidimensional signal detection models, $P(\mathbf{R}_j|\mathbf{S}_i)$ might be a multiple integral like the one expressed in Equation 23. In many such cases, the likelihood function L cannot be maximized analytically. Instead, numerical techniques are required.

Maximum likelihood estimates are also convenient when one wishes to evaluate the empirical validity of a given model. In general, evaluating the absolute goodness of fit of a model is not particularly meaningful. One can test the null hypothesis that the model is correct against the alternative that it is incorrect. Failure to reject such a null hypothesis indicates that the data are insufficient to disconfirm the model, and, as a result, one is tempted to conclude that the model conforms reasonably well to the data. No psychological model is absolutely correct, however; so whether the null hypothesis is rejected depends entirely on the sample size. Even a faulty model will be accepted if the sample size is small enough, and even the most compelling model will be rejected if the sample size is large enough. Even so, a larger sample size will be required to disconfirm a good model than to disconfirm a bad model. Thus, it is meaningful to compare the ability of two different models to account for the data. Although it would be a mistake to conclude that the winner is the correct model, one could conclude that the winner is "closer" to the correct model (at least for this data set).

One way to compare the ability of two models to account for a set of data is via a *Likelihood Ratio Test*. Consider two models M_1 and M_2. Suppose model M_1 is a special case of model M_2 in the sense that M_1 can be derived from M_2 by setting some of the free parameters in M_2 to fixed values. Now form the likelihood ratio $\lambda = L_1/L_2$, where L_i is the likelihood of the data as predicted by model i after its free parameters have been estimated via Maximum Likelihood Estimation. Note that if model M_1 is correct, $\lambda = 1$, but in every other case $\lambda < 1$. Finally, define

$$
\begin{aligned}
\chi^2 &= -2\, ln\, \lambda \\
&= -2\, ln \left(\frac{L_1}{L_2}\right) \\
&= 2[ln\, L_2 - ln\, L_1] \,.
\end{aligned}
$$

If model M_1 is correct, this statistic has an asymptotic chi-square distribution with degrees of freedom equal to the difference in the number of free parameters between the two models.

The observed value of this statistic can therefore be compared with the critical value from the appropriate chi-square distribution. If the observed value fails to exceed the critical value, then we conclude that the extra free parameters of the more general model (i.e., model M_2) lead to no real improvement in fit. The restricted model accounts for the data as well as the more general model and therefore provides a more parsimonious account of the data. If the observed value of χ^2 exceeds the critical value, we conclude that the extra complexity of the more general model captures some real psychological phenomena that is missed by the restricted model (i.e., model M_1).

One disadvantage of Likelihood Ratio Testing is that it requires models M_1 and M_2 to be nested. If neither is a special case of the other but they both happen to have the same number of free parameters, then the better model is the one with the largest likelihood L_i. If model M_1 has fewer parameters and is associated with the larger L_i, then M_1 is the better model. Difficulty arises, however, in the frequently occurring case in which the two models are not nested, they have a different number of free parameters, and the model with more parameters is associated with the larger L_i.

A goodness-of-fit statistic that controls for the number of free parameters is Akaike's (1974) Information Criterion (AIC). Suppose model M_i has v_i free parameters. Then the AIC statistic is defined as

$$AIC\ (M_i) = -2\ lnL_i + 2v_i\ .$$

Note that, with respect to AIC, a model pays a penalty for having many free parameters. In fact, the smaller the AIC, the closer a model is to the "true model," regardless of the number of free parameters. Thus, to find the best model among a given set of competitors, compute an AIC value for each model and simply choose the model associated with the smallest of these. Chapter 12 includes a thorough discussion of AIC, as well as numerous illustrations of its application.

I

SIMILARITY, PREFERENCE, AND CHOICE

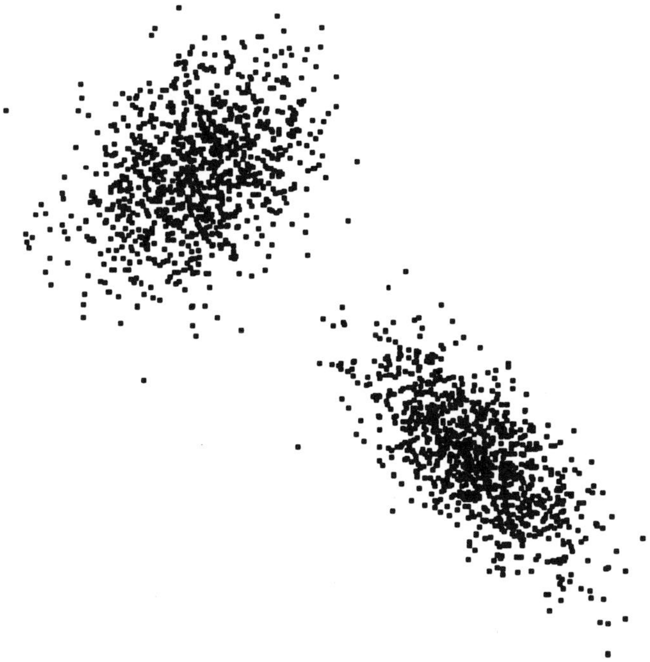

2 A Probabilistic Multidimensional Scaling Approach: Properties and Procedures

Joseph L. Zinnes
Temple University

David B. MacKay
Indiana University

Multidimensional Scaling has had a relatively long history, starting perhaps with the foundational paper by Young and Householder (1938), but, as evidenced by this book, only recently does it seem to be making contact with other areas of psychology. We like to think that this has resulted from probabilistic, multidimensional approaches gaining wider acceptance.

Our aim in this chapter is to review some of the main features of the probabilistic model that we have been working with for some time, covering some technical details, but mainly focusing on some of its properties and empirical applications. Our hope is that this introduction will make the probabilistic Multidimensional Scaling approaches more amenable and interesting to the reader, and even, perhaps, to encourage the reader to explore further their potentialities as explanatory theories.

FOUNDATIONS

This section shows how the general model has been applied to different experimental tasks involving similarity or preference judgments. In the following two sections some of the more important properties of the model are highlighted, as indicated by various simulations and empirical findings.

The General Model

As do many other authors in this volume, we assume that the perceptual aspects of each stimulus can be represented by a random vector having a multivariate normal distribution. Specifically, for stimulus $\mathbf{S}_j$, j = 1, . . . , m, we let $\mathbf{X}_j = (X_{j1}, \ldots, X_{jr})$ be the corresponding r-dimensional random vector and assume that it has an r-variate normal distribution with mean vector $\boldsymbol{\mu}_j = (\mu_{j1}, \ldots, \mu_{jr})$ and covariance matrix $\boldsymbol{\Sigma}_j$. To simplify the discussion, we treat only the case in which the components $\mathbf{X}_j = (X_{j1}, \ldots, X_{jr})$ are independently distributed, and therefore we assume that the covariance matrix $\boldsymbol{\Sigma}_j$ is just the diagonal matrix $\mathbf{D}(\sigma_{jh}^2)$, $h = 1, \ldots, r$. This does not result in any appreciable loss of generality, but we do not pursue these details here (see chap. 1).

Similarly, it will be helpful to assume that all random vectors $\mathbf{X}_1, \ldots, \mathbf{X}_m$ are independent, although this assumption also can be relaxed with little additional effort.

There are two possible interpretations of the variance parameter σ_{jh}^2, depending on the level of the analysis to be performed. For individual analyses, the variances $\sigma_{j1}^2, \ldots, \sigma_{jr}^2$ reflect the degree of unfamiliarity or uncertainty that the individual has concerning the nature of stimulus $\mathbf{S}_j$ on each of its r dimensions. For group analyses, the variances instead indicate how heterogeneous the people in the group are with respect to their perception of stimulus $\mathbf{S}_j$. In the following sections, we focus mainly on the individual and, therefore, generally refer to the variances as an uncertainty or unfamiliarity parameter.

Preferences can be incorporated into the general model by associating random vectors with individuals as well as with stimuli. Thus, for person P_i, i = m + 1, . . . , m + n, we let $\mathbf{X}_i = (\mathbf{X}_{i1}, \ldots, \mathbf{X}_{ir})$ be the associated r-dimensional random vector, and assume, as we did with the stimulus vectors, that it has an r-variate normal distribution with mean vector $\boldsymbol{\mu}_i = (\mu_{i1}, \ldots, \mu_{ir})$ and covariance matrix $\boldsymbol{\Sigma}_i = \mathbf{D}(\sigma_{ih}^2)$. The person or ideal random vector $\mathbf{X}_i$ is intended to represent the most preferred or ideal stimulus for person P_i. This aspect of the general model is, of course, precisely equivalent to the unfolding model of Coombs (1964).

These multivariate normal distribution assumptions, first given by Hefner (1958), are a direct multidimensional generalization of Thurstone's pair comparison model (1927a). Hefner's extension, while direct, was by no means obvious. Earlier attempts to generalize Thurstone's single-dimensional model (Klingberg, 1941; Richardson, 1938; Torgerson, 1951) assumed that the distances between pairs of points, not the points themselves, have a univariate normal distribution. This assumption is quite compelling because it means that interpoint distances can be treated as single-dimensional stimuli. The single-dimensional model of Thurstone can, therefore, be applied directly to judgments of pairs of interpoint distances to estimate their mean value, at least up to an additive constant. Thus, a multidimensional approach was achieved by using purely single-dimensional methods.

There are, however, some problems with this approach: The interpoint distances are only determined up to an additive constant; that is, they are only measured on an interval scale. Unlike the single-dimensional case, the effects of an additive constant in the multidimensional case are not benign. Adding a constant to a set of interpoint distances can change drastically the nature of the configuration of the points involved and, even further, their dimensionality as well. In fact, for m points, if the additive constant is sufficiently large, all the interpoint distances will tend to be equal, and the points themselves, therefore, will tend to be located at the vertices of a regular polyhedron in m − 1 dimensions. Hefner's approach, in addition to being intuitively attractive, avoids the additive constant problem. It is possible, with Hefner's assumptions, to obtain maximum likelihood (ML) estimates of all the relevant parameters—the means and variances of stimulus and ideal points—and to do this without encountering serious nonuniqueness issues.

However, a price has to be paid for the conceptual simplicity of the Hefner model, and this, no doubt, accounts for its unpopularity. The functions that make up each term of the likelihood function are, under the Hefner model, complex functions and, worst still, cannot be expressed in closed form. Despite this, it has been possible to develop reasonably simple, fast, and moderately accurate algorithms for obtaining the ML estimates for the location and variance parameters.

It will take us too far afield to cover in detail all the ML algorithms. Instead, we describe some of the main aspects of these algorithms and give references where more detailed information can be obtained.

Generally speaking, the ML algorithms that we have used have three key ingredients. First, they use simple approximations of the probability density functions that compose each term of the likelihood function. This aspect of the algorithm is essential, because the series expansions for these functions converge quite slowly for many values of the parameters to be estimated. Iterative procedures, which must of necessity be used to maximize the likelihood function, would have no hope of terminating in a reasonable period of time if, on each iteration and for each term of the likelihood function, it were necessary to evaluate a slowly converging series expansion.

Second, these ML algorithms use simple expressions for obtaining good initial estimates for the parameters to be estimated. Having good initial estimates not only speeds the rate at which the iterative process converges but it also makes it more likely that the convergence will terminate at a global maximum rather than at a local maximum. To obtain these initial parameter values, we have found that it has been sufficient to make just one simplifying assumption: the variances of the points—both the stimulus and ideal points—are assumed to be small relative to the size of most interpoint distances.

Third, the ML algorithms utilize general-purpose optimization programs (Chandler, 1969; International Mathematical and Statistical Libraries [IMSL], 1979) to control the iterative process. The value of using these programs is that they do not require a knowledge of the first or second derivatives of the function to be maximized. Given the complexity of the likelihood functions that arise when the Hefner model is used, it would not be practical to use iterative procedures, such as Steepest Descent Methods, that require analytical expressions for the derivatives.

Special Cases

Special cases of the Hefner model can be defined that are analogous to Thurstone's case 3 and case 5. However, due to the multidimensional nature of the Hefner model, it is necessary to break down the case 3 and case 5 assumptions into two subcases or conditions: an isotropic condition and an anisotropic condition. The distinction between these conditions has to do with the variance of the components of $\mathbf{X}_i$ over the r dimensions. If these variances are not correlated and do not change from dimension to dimension, the space is said to be isotropic. Otherwise, the space is anisotropic. Thus, all the directions of an isotropic space are equivalent, at least with respect to variability of the stimulus or ideal point. In contrast, anisotropic space exhibits directionality effects.

This leads us to the following definition.

Definition 2.1. Assume that the random vectors $\mathbf{X}_j = (X_{j1}, \ldots, X_{jr})$ satisfy the Hefner model; that is, they have the multivariate normal distribution $N(\boldsymbol{\mu}_j, \boldsymbol{\Sigma}_j)$. Then, for the isotropic condition,

(i) case 3i holds if and only if

$$\boldsymbol{\Sigma}_j = \mathbf{D}(\sigma^2_{j\cdot}) ;$$

(ii) case 5i holds if and only if

$$\boldsymbol{\Sigma}_j = \mathbf{D}(\sigma^2_{\cdot\cdot}) .$$

For the anisotropic condition,

(iii) case 3a holds if and only if

$$\boldsymbol{\Sigma}_j = \mathbf{D}(\sigma^2_{jh}), \qquad h = 1, \ldots, r ;$$

(iv) case 5a holds if and only if

$$\boldsymbol{\Sigma}_j = \mathbf{D}(\sigma^2_{\cdot h}), \qquad h = 1, \ldots, r .$$

Figure 2.1 illustrates these four cases graphically. As shown, the equal likelihood contours for all the points in the isotropic condition (cases 3i and 5i) are circles, whereas in the anisotropic condition (cases 3a and 5a) they are ellipses. The graphical distinction between cases 3 and 5 is equally transparent. In case 3, the sizes of the circles or ellipses differ from point to point, but in case 5 they do not.

The isotropic condition, cases 3i and 5i, is discussed in this and the following sections. The anisotropic condition is taken up in the third section.

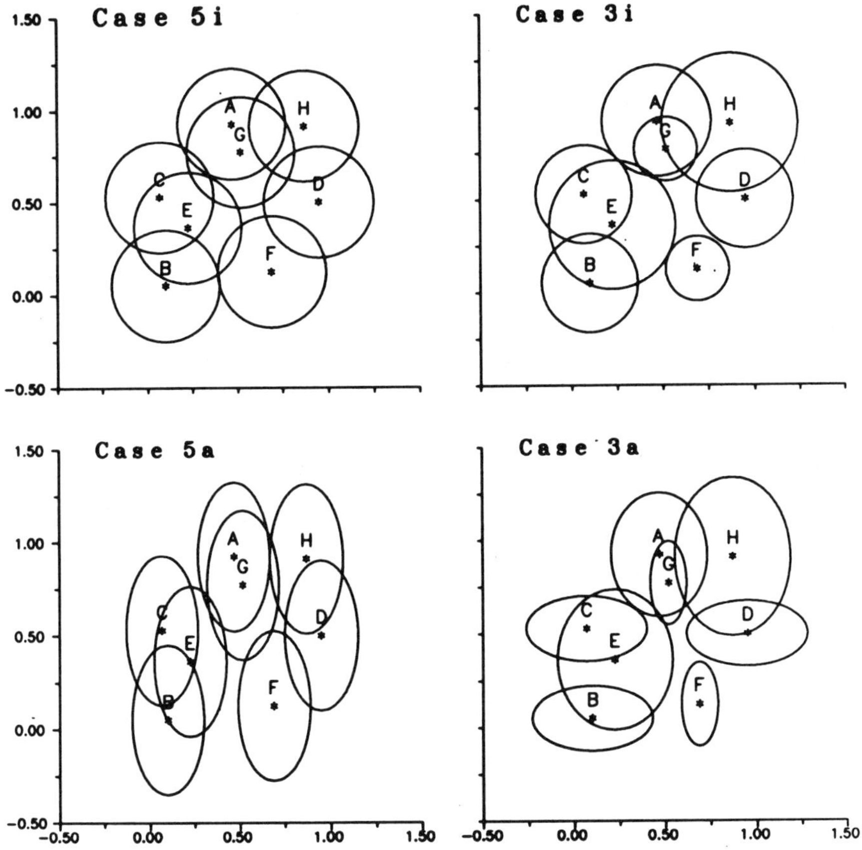

FIG. 2.1. Isotropic and anisotropic cases of the Hefner model.

Similarity

Perhaps, the simplest application of the Hefner model is in the similarity domain. Although there are a number of different similarity or dissimilarity judgments that subjects can be asked to make, depending on whether the stimuli are presented in pairs, triples, or quadruples, we consider just one of these judgments: the direct dissimilarity judgment of a pair of stimuli (MacKay & Zinnes, 1981; Zinnes & MacKay, 1983). This should suffice to illustrate some of the main issues involved in applying the Hefner model to similarity data.

The decision rule that we use for similarity judgments is the natural one. It is assumed that a subject's dissimilarity judgment of a pair of stimuli $\mathbf{S}_j$ and $\mathbf{S}_k$ directly corresponds to the Euclidean distance between these two stimuli,

$$d_{jk} = [(\mathbf{X}_j - \mathbf{X}_k)'(\mathbf{X}_j - \mathbf{X}_k)]^{1/2} , \tag{1}$$

as perceived by the subject on each trial. Since the distance $\boldsymbol{d}_{jk}$ is a random variable, its value, and thus the subjects' dissimilarity judgment, can be expected to change from trial to trial.

The observed dissimilarity judgment $\boldsymbol{d}_{jk}$ needs to be distinguished from the actual Euclidean distance δ_{jk}, defined by

$$\delta_{jk} = [(\boldsymbol{\mu}_j - \boldsymbol{\mu}_k)'(\boldsymbol{\mu}_j - \boldsymbol{\mu}_k)]^{1/2} . \tag{2}$$

Unlike $\boldsymbol{d}_{jk}$, the Euclidean distance δ_{jk} is not a random variable and therefore does not change from trial to trial. In the Hefner model, it is also important to distinguish δ_{jk} from $E(\boldsymbol{d}_{jk})$, the expected value of $\boldsymbol{d}_{jk}$. This latter distance, which can be conceptualized as the average of an infinite number of replications of the stimulus pair $\mathbf{S}_j$ and $\mathbf{S}_k$, is not, in general, equal to δ_{jk}, nor is it, in most cases, even a good estimate of δ_{jk}. This important feature of the Hefner model is discussed more fully in the second section.

In the simplest case, all stimulus pairs from a given stimulus set $\{\mathbf{S}_1, \ldots, \mathbf{S}_m\}$ are presented to the subjects, and, thus, under cases 3i or 5i, the likelihood function to be maximized equals

$$L = \prod_{k=j+1}^{m} \prod_{j=1}^{m} f(d_{jk}) , \tag{3}$$

where $f(d_{jk})$ is the probability density function (pdf) of the random variable $\boldsymbol{d}_{jk}$. The probability density function $f(d_{jk})$ is closely related to the noncentral chi-square distribution, which we define next.

Definition 2.2. Let $z_1, \ldots, z_\nu$ be independent standard normal variables, and let $\delta_1, \ldots, \delta_\nu$ be constants. Then the sum

$$\sum_{j=1}^{\nu} (z_j + \delta_j)^2$$

has the noncentral chi-square distribution $\chi'^2(\nu,\lambda)$ with ν degrees of freedom and noncentrality parameter λ equal to

$$\lambda = \sum_{j=1}^{\nu} \delta_j^2 .$$

For future reference, we note that the mean of the noncentral chi-square distribution equals

$$E(\chi'^2) = \nu + \lambda , \tag{4}$$

and the variance equals

$$Var(\chi'^2) = 2(\nu + 2\lambda) . \tag{5}$$

It can be readily seen, from the definition of the noncentral chi-square distribution and from the preceding expressions for the mean and variance, that the noncentral chi-square distribution reduces to the central or standard chi-square distribution when $\lambda = 0$. However, unlike the central chi-square distribution, the pdf of the noncentral chi-square distribution cannot be expressed in closed form. We say more on this later.

Returning to our present concern, we wish to determine the pdf of the distance $\boldsymbol{d}_{jk}$ between stimuli $\mathbf{S}_j$ and $\mathbf{S}_k$ under the case 3i assumptions. To do this, we first define the standardized variable

$$\mathbf{z}_{jkh} = \frac{\boldsymbol{d}_{jkh} - \delta_{jkh}}{\sigma_{jk\cdot}} , \tag{6}$$

where

$$\begin{aligned} \boldsymbol{d}_{jkh} &= \boldsymbol{X}_{jh} - \boldsymbol{X}_{kh} , \\ \delta_{jkh} &= \mu_{jh} - \mu_{kh} , \end{aligned} \tag{7}$$

and

$$\sigma^2_{jk\cdot} = \sigma^2_{j\cdot} + \sigma^2_{k\cdot} . \tag{8}$$

Therefore under the case 3i assumptions, z_{jkh} has the standard normal distribution $N(0,1)$. Thus, for the squared distance

$$\boldsymbol{d}^2_{jk} = \sum_{h=1}^{r} (\boldsymbol{X}_{jh} - \boldsymbol{X}_{kh})^2 ,$$

we can write

$$\boldsymbol{d}^2_{jk} = \sum_{h=1}^{r} \boldsymbol{d}^2_{jkh} ,$$

which, from Equation 6, gives

$$\boldsymbol{d}^2_{jk} = \sigma^2_{jk\cdot} \sum_{k=1}^{r} \left(z_{jkh} + \frac{\delta_{jkh}}{\sigma_{jk\cdot}} \right)^2 . \tag{9}$$

Equation 9 indicates that $\boldsymbol{d}^2_{jk}/\sigma^2_{jk\cdot}$ has the noncentral chi-square distribution $\chi'^2(\nu,\lambda_{jk})$, where $\nu = \mathrm{r}$ and

$$\lambda_{jk} = \sum_{h=1}^{r} \frac{\delta^2_{jkh}}{\sigma^2_{jk\cdot}} = \frac{\delta^2_{jk}}{\sigma^2_{jk\cdot}} . \tag{10}$$

For case 5i, the results can be simplified further, for then

$$\sigma^2_{jk\cdot} = \sigma^2_{\cdot\cdot} + \sigma^2_{\cdot\cdot} , \tag{11}$$

and since $\sigma_{\cdot\cdot}^2$ can be set equal to an arbitrary value, it is customary to set it equal to $\frac{1}{2}$, giving

$$\sigma_{jk\cdot}^2 = \frac{1}{2} + \frac{1}{2} = 1 \ . \tag{12}$$

Thus, under case 5i, $\boldsymbol{d}_{jk}^2$ has a noncentral chi-square distribution with noncentrality parameter $\lambda_{jk} = \delta_{jk\cdot\cdot}^2$.

These results can be used to obtain the pdf of $\boldsymbol{d}_{jk}$ under cases 3i and 5i. Starting with the cumulative distribution function $\boldsymbol{F}(\boldsymbol{d}_{jk})$, it follows that

$$\boldsymbol{F}(\boldsymbol{d}_{jk}) = \boldsymbol{G}\left(\frac{\boldsymbol{d}_{jk}^2}{\sigma_{jk\cdot}^2}\right) , \tag{13}$$

where $\boldsymbol{G}(\cdot)$ is the noncentral chi-square cumulative distribution function (cdf). Differentiating Equation 13 by $\boldsymbol{d}_{jk}$ and using $g(\cdot)$ for the noncentral chi-square pdf gives

$$f(\boldsymbol{d}_{jk}) = g\left(\frac{\boldsymbol{d}_{jk}^2}{\sigma_{jk\cdot}^2}\right)\left(\frac{2\boldsymbol{d}_{jk}}{\sigma_{jk\cdot}^2}\right) , \tag{14}$$

which shows that the pdf of $\boldsymbol{d}_{jk}$ can indeed be expressed in terms of the pdf of the noncentral chi-square distribution function. Thus, to evaluate $f(\boldsymbol{d}_{jk})$, it is sufficient to concentrate our attention on the function $g(\cdot)$.

As indicated earlier, the exact form of $g(\cdot)$ can be expressed only as an infinite series, whose rate of convergence depends on the values of ν and λ. When ν is large and λ is small, the series will tend to converge rapidly. However, for other values of ν and λ, the rate of convergence can be painfully slow. Fortunately, normal and central chi-square approximations have been worked out (Abdel-Aty, 1954; Patnaik, 1949; Sankaran, 1959), which, considering their simplicity, are amazingly accurate. In some applications (Zinnes & Griggs, 1974; Zinnes & Wolff, 1977), the normal distribution approximation was found to be superior, and in other applications (MacKay & Zinnes, 1986; Zinnes & MacKay, 1987) the central chi-square approximation was more useful. In still other cases (MacKay & Zinnes, 1981; Zinnes & MacKay, 1983), it turned out to be useful to piece together the normal approximation and the series expansion of the noncentral chi-square distribution. This was done by using the series expansion in the region where it converges rapidly—when $\delta_{jk}\boldsymbol{d}_{jk}/\sigma_{jk\cdot}^2 < 2.55$—and using the normal distribution approximation for the remaining regions, where it tends to be quite accurate.

Preferences

This section covers two types of preference data: binary choice data and preference ratio data. In both cases, the subject indicates which of a pair of stimuli he or she prefers. For preference ratio judgments, the subject indicates, in addition, how much he or she prefers the more preferred stimulus over the less preferred stimulus. The reason for using the preference ratio judgment is to extract more information from the subject on each trial, thus minimizing the number of replications necessary to estimate the parameters at some desired level of accuracy.

As indicated earlier, preferences can be accommodated within the Hefner model by adding to it the assumptions of the Coombs unfolding model. The preferences of subjects are then assumed to be determined by the distance between the ideal points and the stimulus points. The smaller the distance $\boldsymbol{d}_{\mathrm{ij}}$ between ideal point i and stimulus point j, the more desirable stimulus $\mathbf{S}_{\mathrm{j}}$ is to person P_{i}. The probability p_{ijk} that person P_{i} chooses $\mathbf{S}_{\mathrm{j}}$ over $\mathbf{S}_{\mathrm{k}}$ is then equal to

$$p_{\mathrm{ijk}} = P(\boldsymbol{d}_{\mathrm{ij}} \leq \boldsymbol{d}_{\mathrm{ik}}) \; , \tag{15}$$

which can also be written as

$$p_{\mathrm{ijk}} = P\left(\frac{\boldsymbol{d}_{\mathrm{ij}}^2}{\boldsymbol{d}_{\mathrm{ik}}^2} \leq 1\right) \tag{16}$$

or as

$$p_{\mathrm{ijk}} = P\left(\frac{\boldsymbol{d}_{\mathrm{ij}}^2/\sigma_{\mathrm{ij}\cdot}^2}{\boldsymbol{d}_{\mathrm{ik}}^2/\sigma_{\mathrm{ik}\cdot}^2} \leq \frac{\sigma_{\mathrm{ik}\cdot}^2}{\sigma_{\mathrm{ij}\cdot}^2}\right) . \tag{17}$$

For the case 3i model, both $\boldsymbol{d}_{\mathrm{ij}}^2/\sigma_{\mathrm{ij}\cdot}^2$ and $\boldsymbol{d}_{\mathrm{ik}}^2/\sigma_{\mathrm{ik}\cdot}^2$ have a noncentral chi-square distribution, and therefore the fraction on the left side of the inequality in Equation 17 consists of the ratio of two random variables having this distribution. This leads us to a consideration of the doubly noncentral $\boldsymbol{F}$ distribution (Johnson & Kotz, 1970, vol. 2).

> Definition 2.3. Let $\chi_1'^2(\nu_1, \lambda_1)$ and $\chi_2'^2(\nu_2, \lambda_2)$ be two independent noncentral chi-square random variables. Then the ratio
>
> $$\frac{\chi_1'^2/\nu_1}{\chi_2'^2/\nu_2}$$
>
> has the doubly noncentral $\boldsymbol{F}$ distribution $\boldsymbol{F}''(\nu_1, \nu_2, \lambda_1, \lambda_2)$ with ν_1 and ν_2 degrees of freedom and noncentrality parameters λ_1 and λ_2. If $\lambda_2 = 0$, the ratio is said to have an ordinary noncentral $\boldsymbol{F}$ distribution.

Returning to Equation 17, we see that the left side of the inequality, under certain independence conditions, is distributed as a doubly noncentral $\boldsymbol{F}$ distribution $\boldsymbol{F}''(r, r, \lambda_{\mathrm{ij}}, \lambda_{\mathrm{ik}})$, where the noncentrality parameters λ_{ij} and λ_{ik} are as defined in Equation 10. The independence condition refers to the independence of the numerator and denominator of this ratio. This could be a problem in the present case, since $\boldsymbol{d}_{\mathrm{ij}}$ and $\boldsymbol{d}_{\mathrm{ik}}$ both involve the same ideal point i. However, we can simplify matters for the present by assuming that person P_{i} selects two independent samples from his or her ideal distribution, one of which is used to determine the distance $\boldsymbol{d}_{ij}$ and the other the distance $\boldsymbol{d}_{ik}$. Under these conditions, $\boldsymbol{d}_{ij}$ and $\boldsymbol{d}_{ik}$ are independent random variables. Whether this assumption is plausible or reasonable in any given situation could very well depend on the specific details of the experimental procedure.

Making use of these results, we can write Equation 17 more simply as

$$p_{ijk} = P\left[\boldsymbol{F}''(r, r, \lambda_{ij}, \lambda_{ik}) \leq \frac{\sigma^2_{ik\cdot}}{\sigma^2_{ij\cdot}}\right], \tag{18}$$

indicating that the values of the binary choice probabilities p_{ijk} can be determined by evaluating the cdf of the doubly noncentral $\boldsymbol{F}$ distribution.

The analysis of preference ratio judgments is similar to that of binary choices. It is assumed that person P_i reports the preference ratio $\boldsymbol{R}_{ijk}$, where

$$\boldsymbol{R}_{ijk} = \frac{\boldsymbol{d}_{ik}}{\boldsymbol{d}_{ij}} \tag{19}$$

when the stimulus pair $\mathbf{S}_j$ and $\mathbf{S}_k$ is presented. To arrive at the pdf $f_{\boldsymbol{R}}(\boldsymbol{R}_{ijk})$, we start with the cumulative distribution function

$$\boldsymbol{F}_{\boldsymbol{R}}(\boldsymbol{R}_{ijk}) = \boldsymbol{H}\left(\boldsymbol{R}^2_{ijk}\,\frac{\sigma^2_{ij\cdot}}{\sigma^2_{ik\cdot}}\right), \tag{20}$$

where $\boldsymbol{H}(\cdot)$ is the cdf of $\boldsymbol{F}''(r, r, \lambda_{ij}, \lambda_{ik})$. Differentiating Equation 20 with respect to $\boldsymbol{R}_{ijk}$ gives

$$f_{\boldsymbol{R}}(\boldsymbol{R}_{ijk}) = 2\boldsymbol{R}_{ijk}\left(\frac{\sigma^2_{ij\cdot}}{\sigma^2_{ik\cdot}}\right) h\left(\frac{\boldsymbol{d}^2_{ik} / \sigma^2_{ik\cdot}}{\boldsymbol{d}^2_{ij} / \sigma^2_{ij\cdot}}\right), \tag{21}$$

where $h(.)$ is just the pdf of the doubly noncentral $\boldsymbol{F}$ distribution $\boldsymbol{F}''(\mathrm{r}, \mathrm{r}, \lambda_{ij}, \lambda_{ik})$. This shows that preference ratio data, as well as binary choice data, require working with the doubly noncentral $\boldsymbol{F}$ distribution.

The Density Function of $\boldsymbol{F}''$

The doubly noncentral $\boldsymbol{F}$ distribution $\boldsymbol{F}''(\nu_1, \nu_2, \lambda_1, \lambda_2)$ has been studied extensively (Bulgren, 1971; Chou & Arthur, 1985; Price, 1964; Tang, 1938; Tiku, 1965). As one might expect from a consideration of the noncentral chi-square pdf, the pdf of the doubly noncentral $\boldsymbol{F}''$ distribution cannot be expressed in closed form and, in fact, requires a doubly infinite series of terms, each term of which includes a number of complex functions. Obviously, to make practical use of this density function, one must use an approximation.

Two approaches have been used to approximate the pdf of the $\boldsymbol{F}''$ distribution. Both involve using one of the approximations of the noncentral chi-square distribution discussed previously. In one application (Zinnes & Griggs, 1974), the

Abdel-Aty (1954) approximation was used to convert the noncentral chi-square distribution to a normal distribution, which results in transforming the F'' ratio to a difference of two normally distributed random variables. In another application (Zinnes & MacKay, 1987), the Patnaik (1949) approximation was used to convert a noncentral chi-square distribution into a central chi-square distribution. This results in the doubly noncentral F distribution being approximated by a central F distribution.

Although these approximations of the F'' distribution would seem to be overly simplistic, nevertheless, they are reasonably accurate. Figure 2.2, for example, shows the level of accuracy that is obtained when the central F approximation is used for F''. Three different distributions are plotted in this figure, one for each of three different values of λ. The exact distributions (the solid lines) shown in this figure were determined by summing the series expansion for F''. From the discrepancy between the exact and the approximate curves (the dashed lines), it is evident that the largest absolute error occurs in the middle of the distribution, especially when the distribution is highly skewed. But, in general, it can be seen that the exact and approximate lines follow each other quite closely, even in the tails of the distribution.

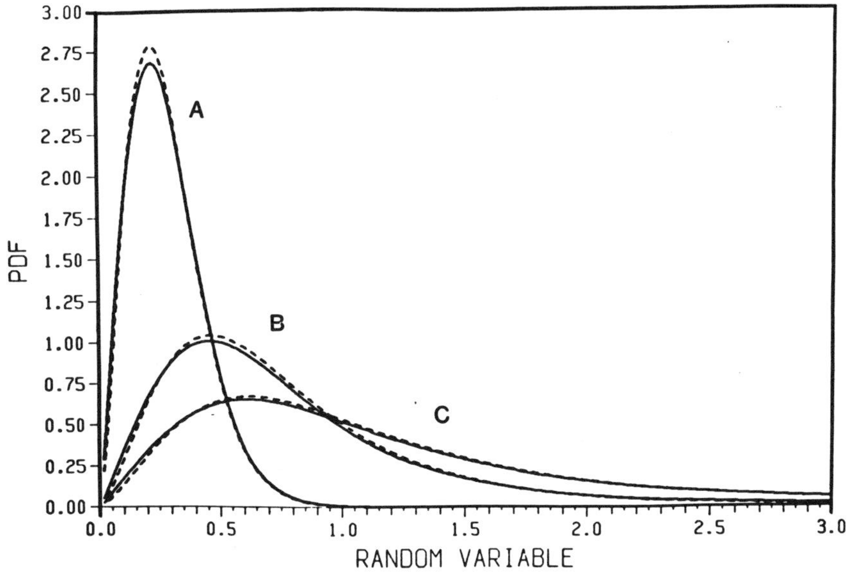

FIG. 2.2. The central F approximation of the double noncentral F distribution. Both degrees of freedom are equal to 2. The solid lines are the exact values, the dashed lines the central F approximation. For curve A, $\lambda_1 = 1, \lambda_2 = 30$; for curve B, $\lambda_1 = 1, \lambda_2 = 4$; for curve C, $\lambda_1 = 1, \lambda_2 = 1$.

PROPERTIES OF THE MODEL

The Hefner model has many interesting properties, even some counterintuitive properties, which distinguish it from other multidimensional models. In this section we cover perhaps its most controversial property, the "nonmonotonicity property."

The Nonmonotonicity Property

Most, if not all, of the multidimensional scaling models assume, either implicitly or explicitly, that the observed similarity judgment $\boldsymbol{d}_{jk}$, or, perhaps, the average dissimilarity judgment $E\ (\boldsymbol{d}_{jk})$, is monotonically related to the true distance δ_{jk} between stimuli $\mathbf{S}_j$ and $\mathbf{S}_k$. For the Hefner model, even under case 3i, this monotonicity property does not, in general, hold. The relationship between $E\ (\boldsymbol{d}_{jk})$ and δ_{jk} need not be monotonic. To show this, we consider first the condition under which monotonicity can be expected to hold. This will occur when the noncentrality parameters λ_{jk} are large. Since $\lambda_{jk} = \delta^2_{jk}/\sigma^2_{jk\cdot}$, λ_{jk} will be large when δ^2_{jk} is appreciably larger than $\sigma^2_{jk\cdot}$. Under this condition, it has been shown (Patnaik, 1949) that $E\ (\boldsymbol{d}_{jk})$ can be approximated by

$$E\ (\boldsymbol{d}_{jk}) \cong \sigma_{jk\cdot} \left(\frac{2a - (1 + b)}{2}\right)^{1/2}, \tag{22}$$

where $a = \nu + \lambda_{jk}$ and $b = \lambda_{jk}/a$. As λ_{jk} becomes indefinitely large, Equation 22 indicates that then

$$E\ (\boldsymbol{d}_{jk}) \cong \sigma_{jk\cdot}(\lambda^{1/2}_{jk})\ . \tag{23}$$

Substituting for λ_{jk} in Equation 23 and simplifying gives

$$E\ (\boldsymbol{d}_{jk}) = \delta_{jk}\ . \tag{24}$$

In other words, when $\sigma_{jk\cdot}$ is negligible relative to the size of the true distance δ_{jk}, the expected distance $E\ (\boldsymbol{d}_{jk})$ will be indistinguishable from the true distance δ_{jk}, and therefore, the Hefner model, for this case, will necessarily satisfy the monotonicity condition.

However, consider next what happens when λ_{jk} is negligibly small. This occurs when the variance $\sigma^2_{jk\cdot}$ is substantially larger than the true distance δ^2_{jk}. From Equation 4 and from the fact that $\boldsymbol{d}^2_{jk}/\sigma^2_{jk\cdot}$ has, under case 3i, a noncentral chi-square distribution, we have

$$E\ (\boldsymbol{d}^2_{jk}) = \sigma^2_{jk\cdot}(\nu + \lambda_{jk})\ ,$$

or

$$E\ (\boldsymbol{d}^2_{jk}) = \nu\sigma^2_{jk\cdot} + \delta^2_{jk}\ . \tag{25}$$

Therefore, when $\sigma^2_{jk\cdot}$ dominates δ^2_{jk},

$$E\,(\boldsymbol{d}^2_{jk}) \cong \nu\sigma^2_{jk\cdot}\ . \tag{26}$$

Equation 26 shows that when the variance $\sigma^2_{jk\cdot}$ becomes appreciably larger than the distance δ_{jk}, the expected value of $\boldsymbol{d}^2_{jk}$ will be determined almost entirely by the value of σ^2_{jk} and will tend to be almost completely insensitive to the actual distance δ_{jk}. It is clear that, under these conditions, the monotonicity condition cannot be expected to hold. In the extreme case, $E\,(\boldsymbol{d}_{jk})$ could, in fact, be indefinitely large, even when the true distance δ_{jk} is precisely equal to zero.

This property of the Hefner case 3i model may seem counterintuitive, but it actually is quite plausible. If two independent random samples are drawn from the same distribution, having a large variance, we would expect the distance or difference between these two random samples to be large most of the time. This nonmonotonicity principle also makes sense psychologically. If a person is highly uncertain about the perceptual aspects of a set of stimuli or his or her ideal stimulus, it is not unreasonable to expect that person's dissimilarity or preference judgment of the stimuli to be large and highly variable, even when, on the average, these stimuli are perceived as having identical positions on each of the relevant attributes.

Does the lack of monotonicity in the Hefner model have practical consequences? To answer this question, we consider next two simulations and the results of an empirical study. In both simulations a typical nonmetric Multidimensional Scaling algorithm (KYST, Kruskal, Young, & Seery, 1973) was applied to simulated data generated by a "subject," who follows the Hefner case 3i model. The monotonicity property, it should be noted, is an intrinsic aspect of the nonmetric approaches.

Simulation I: Hexagons

In this simulation, the data set consists of 30 replications of all the interpoint distances of a two-dimensional configuration containing 12 points. These 12 points were arranged in two hexagons, one inside the other. (See Figure 2.3a.) Two values of $\sigma_{jk\cdot}$ were used: 2.5 and 1.0. The larger value was assigned to each of the six points forming the inner hexagon, the smaller value to each of the six points forming the outer hexagon. The outer hexagon was about 2 units wide.

To summarize, the data sets were generated by obtaining random samples from a Hefner case 3i subject. These data were then analyzed by the nonmetric approach and by using the maximum likelihood approach described previously.

The recovered configurations obtained from the nonmetric and maximum likelihood approaches are shown in Figure 2.3b,c, respectively. It can be seen that the nonmetric solution interchanged the position of the two hexagons. The

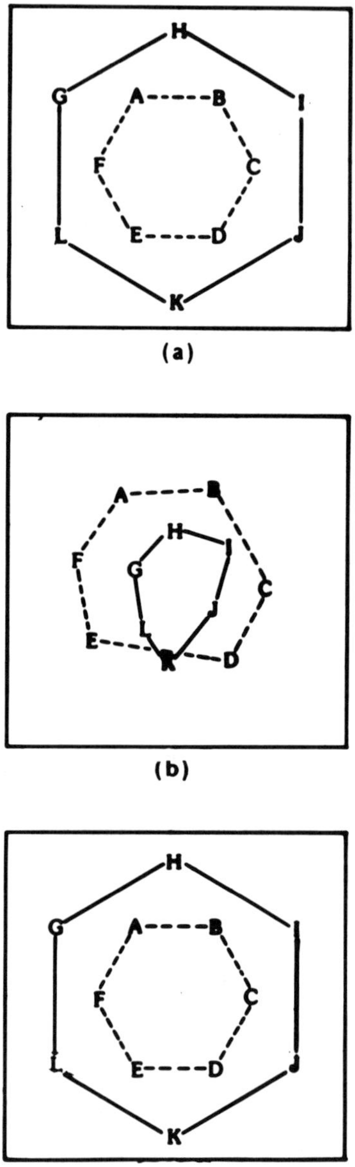

(c)

FIG. 2.3. Simulation I: (a) original configuration, (b) solution obtained using a nonmetric procedure, and (c) solution obtained using Hefner model and Maximum Likelihood Estimation.

hexagon that initially was on the outside is now contained almost entirely inside the hexagon that initially was on the inside.

This result is as expected, because as shown in the previous section, the expected value of the interpoint distances will tend to reflect, almost entirely, the uncertainty values of the stimuli when these values are large relative to the true distance. Therefore, the inner hexagon, having large variances, will tend to be "perceived" by a nonmetric approach as a large hexagon, having large interpoint distances.

The solution obtained from the maximum likelihood approach, shown in Figure 2.3c is quite accurate. There are no detectable differences between the true and recovered configurations.

Simulation II: Expected Values

In this example, unlike the previous one, the simulated data consisted of the expected values of the interpoint distances (i.e., not the true interpoint distances) rather than a finite number of independently sampled replications. This was done to simplify issues somewhat. We wish to show in this example what happens to the nonmetric solution when the uncertainty values become quite large and when the nonmetric results cannot possibly be attributed to perturbations resulting from samples having a small size.

The configuration used in this example was generated by randomly selecting 10 points along the bell-shaped curve of the normal distribution. The configuration obtained is shown in Figure 2.4a. The values of the uncertainty parameter that were assigned to each of the 10 points varied between zero and an upper bound σ_B. Seven values of σ_B, ranging from 0.15 to 9.6, were used. This effectively resulted in seven simulations, all having the same initial stimulus configuration but differing in the range of variability assigned to each point in the configuration. The relative sizes of these uncertainty values can be appreciated by comparing them to the magnitude of the configuration, which, in each of the seven simulations, was standardized to have a variance of 1 on each of the two axes.

Figure 2.4 shows the configuration recovered from each of the seven simulations by using, in each case, a nonmetric approach. Panel (a) gives the true configuration. The points in each of the panels are labeled 1 through 9 followed by A. This labeling reflects the order of magnitude of the uncertainty parameter assigned to each point. Point 1 has the lowest value, point A the highest.

From the seven nonmetric solutions shown in Figure 2.4, it is evident that the nonmetric solution degenerates considerably as the degree of variability of the points increases. When the level of σ_B is quite high, the recovered configuration bears no resemblance to the true configuration. What actually happens is that the higher numbered points, those assigned higher uncertainty values, move to the

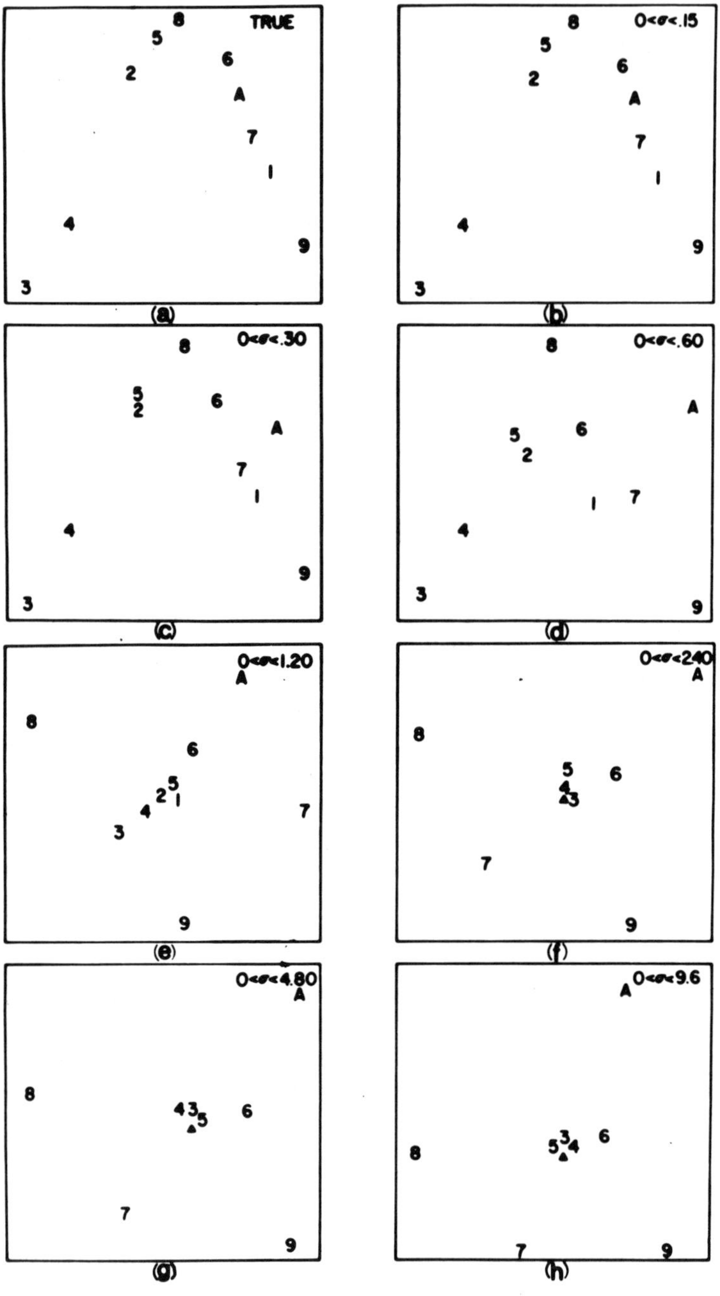

FIG. 2.4. Simulation II. The higher-numbered points have higher variances assigned to them. Point A has the highest variance. The delta symbol indicates a multiple point, consisting of points 1 and 2.

outside of the configuration as σ_B increases, and the remaining points gradually move toward the center.

These results show in a more extreme form what was evident in the previous example. When the uncertainty value of a point is large, its location in the configuration recovered by the nonmetric approach is determined almost entirely by the magnitude of its uncertainty value, not by its actual position in the true configuration. In the present example, this property generates what we call the "black hole" effect. Points having a small variance, relative to the other points, are gradually pulled into the "hole," even if they are initially quite some distance from it. Only those points with large variance succeed in not being drawn into the hole. They drift into outer space, so to speak.

Residential Locations

As a final example of the nonmonotonic property of the Hefner model, we consider an empirical study. In this experiment (MacKay and Zinnes, 1986), 20 subjects made preference judgments of 12 different apartment locations. These locations differed with respect to two variables: time (*T*) or distance from the central business district (CBD), where it was assumed the subjects worked, and the environmental quality (*E*) of the locations, as expressed by the population density of the location and by the availability of local services. Four levels of *T* (5, 10, 15, and 20 minutes) and three levels of *E* (3,000, 4,000, and 5,000 persons per square mile) were used, which, when combined factorially, resulted in 12 locations.

The specific judgment task used was a "preference ratio" judgment. Recall from the previous section that this task requires subjects to indicate not only the stimulus in each pair they prefer but also the degree of preference. A response of 2, for example, would indicate that the subject preferred one stimulus twice as much as the other. After completing the preference ratio judgments, subjects were asked to indicate what their ideal *T* and *E* values were.

The nonmonotonic solution is shown in Figure 2.5, and the maximum likelihood solution, based on the Hefner case 3i model, is shown in Figure 2.6. The 12 stimuli in these figures are labeled 0, 1 through 9, followed by A and B. The ideal points, one for each of the 20 subjects, are labeled C through V.

From Figure 2.5, it can be seen that the nonmetric solution exhibits no evidence of the factorial structure of the stimuli, which, in contrast, is clearly evident in the ML solution. It is also interesting to observe that the ideal points of the nonmetric solution are, for the most part, located far from the cluster of stimulus points. This is not consistent with the subjects' self-reported ideal *T* and *E* values. Most of the ideal values selected by the subjects were interior points, falling within the stimulus configuration, rather than at the edges of the configuration. This aspect of the data is well captured by the ML solution.

It is also interesting to compare the dimensionality test of the nonmetric and

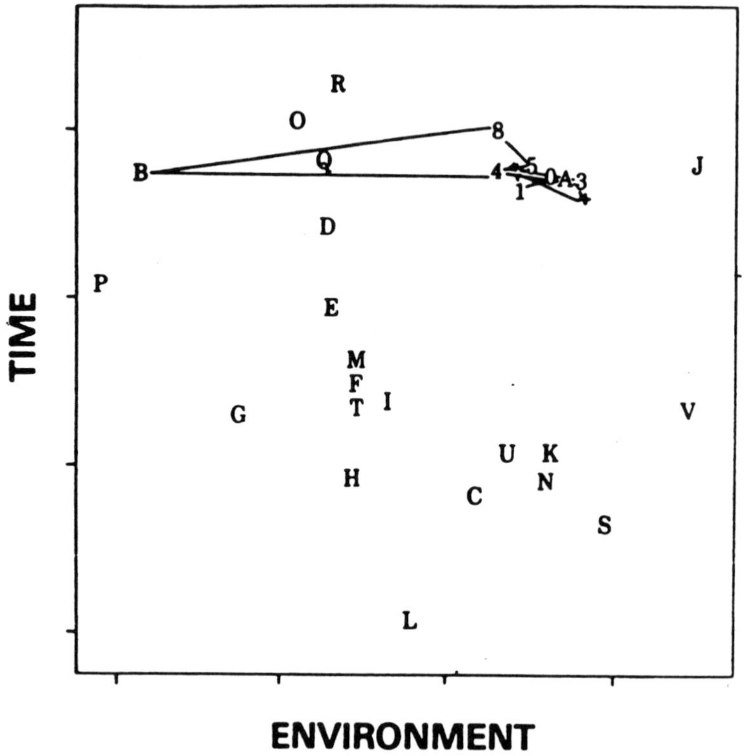

FIG. 2.5. Nonmetric solution of 12 residences and 20 ideal points. Lines connect adjacent residences. The unconnected points are the ideal points. The asterisk identifies points 2 and 7, the plus sign points 6 and 9.

the ML solutions. The likelihood ratio test for one- and two-dimensional solutions is statistically significant, while the test for two- and three-dimensional solutions is not, indicating that a two-dimensional solution is the most appropriate solution. Since there are no statistical tests for the nonmetric approach, it is customary to look at how the stress values decrease as the dimensionality of the solution increases. Stress is a measure of the degree to which the obtained solution does not account for the observed data. The stress values of the nonmetric solution decrease gradually from one to three dimensions and then less sharply from three to four dimensions. This "elbow" at three dimensions is usually taken as an indication of a three-dimensional solution. However, given the two-dimensional factorial structure of the stimuli, it is difficult not to conclude that the two-dimensional solution is, indeed, the more appropriate solution. There seems to be a tendency for nonmetric solutions to overestimate dimensionality.

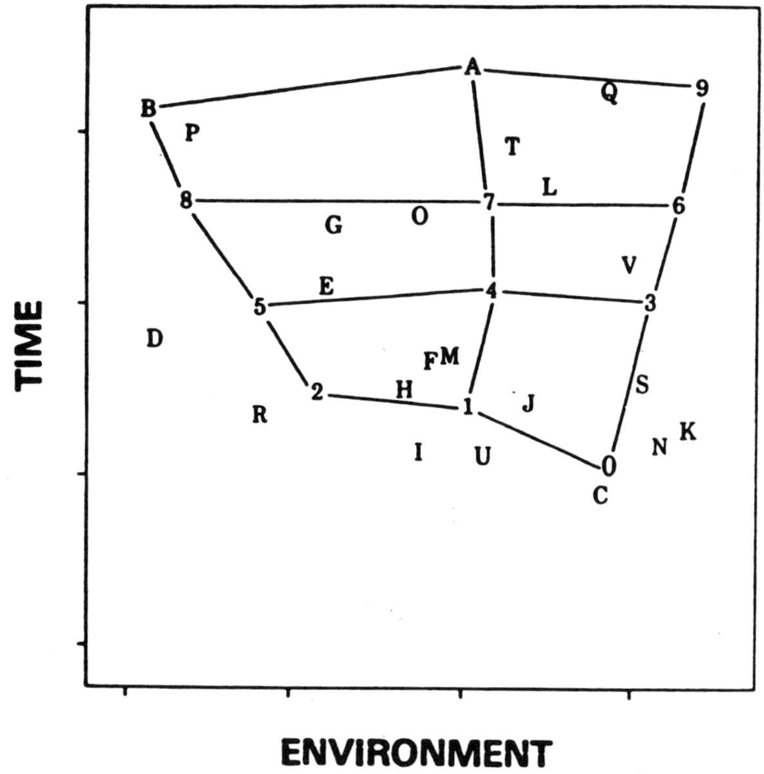

FIG. 2.6. Maximum likelihood solution using the Hefner case 3i model. Lines connect adjacent residences. The unconnected points are ideal points.

These empirical results, taken as a whole, seem to provide strong support for a Hefner-type model, even with stimuli that are relatively simple.

ANISOTROPIC CONDITION

Anisotropic spaces have fascinating properties, but, as can be surmised, they are more difficult to work with than the isotropic spaces. In anisotropic spaces, we can no longer divide d^2_{jk} by a variance expression to obtain a variable having a noncentral chi-square distribution. The best that can be done, under the anisotropic assumptions, is to rewrite Equation 9 as

$$d^2_{jk} = \sum_h \sigma^2_{jkh} \left(z_{jkh} + \frac{\delta_{jkh}}{\sigma_{jkh}} \right)^2 , \tag{27}$$

where the standardized variable z_{jkh} is now equal to

$$z_{jkh} = \frac{(x_{jh} - x_{kh}) - \delta_{jkh}}{\sigma_{jkh}} \tag{28}$$

and

$$\sigma^2_{jkh} = \sigma^2_{jh} + \sigma^2_{kh} \ . \tag{29}$$

Letting

$$\xi_{jkh} = \frac{\delta_{jkh}}{\sigma_{jkh}} \tag{30}$$

and defining the vectors

$$\mathbf{z}_{jk} = (\mathbf{z}_{jkh}) \ , \qquad \xi_{jk} = (\xi_{jkh}) \ , \tag{31}$$

we can write Equation 27 more compactly as

$$d^2_{jk} = (\mathbf{z}_{jk} + \xi_{jk})' \, \boldsymbol{\Sigma}_{jk} \, (\mathbf{z}_{jk} + \xi_{jk}) \ , \tag{32}$$

where $\boldsymbol{\Sigma}_{jk}$ is the diagonal matrix $\mathbf{D}(\sigma^2_{jkh})$. Equation 32 indicates that the squared distance d^2_{jk}, in an anisotropic space, can be expressed as a quadratic form containing normally distributed variables.

The research on quadratic forms has been reviewed by a number of writers (Johnson & Kotz, 1970; MacKay, 1989; Ruben, 1962). In the following sections, we avoid the algorithmic details of the anisotropic cases and content ourselves with describing some of the interesting properties and empirical results of cases 3a and 5a, especially how these cases differ from the isotropic cases.

Variance Properties of the Interpoint Distances

In an isotropic space, the variance of the interpoint distances exhibits what might be called a "quasi-Weber" effect. As the distance δ_{jk} between stimuli $\mathbf{S}_j$ and $\mathbf{S}_k$ increases, the variance of d_{jk} increases monotonically to an asymptotic value. In fact, the asymptote will be the sum of the variances $\sigma^2_{j\cdot}$ and $\sigma^2_{k\cdot}$ associated with $\mathbf{S}_j$ and $\mathbf{S}_k$.

In contrast, the variance of the distance d_{jk} in an anisotropic space exhibit properties that depend on the specific orientation of the contours of equal likelihood. Consider the two-dimensional example shown in Figure 2.7a. If points i and j move apart from each other in the horizontal direction, the quasi-Weber effect is observed. This is shown by the solid line in Figure 2.8.

However, if the points in the anisotropic space, shown in Figure 2.7b, move apart in this same horizontal direction, their variance first increases slightly, but then decreases and gradually approaches an asymptote at a much lower level than previously. This is shown by the dashed lines in Figure 2.8.

This radically different result between the isotropic and anisotropic cases

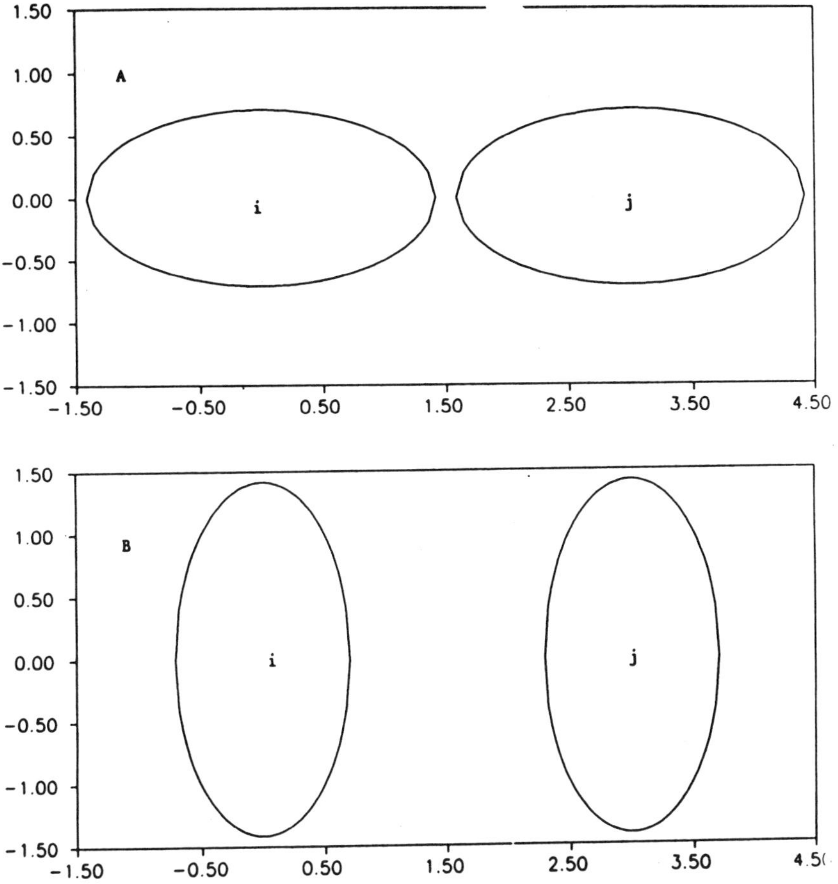

FIG. 2.7. An example of two points in an anisotropic space: (a) major axes of the equiprobability ellipses is on the line joining i and j; (b) major axes are perpendicular to a line joining i and j.

explains why it frequently happens that both cases will result in approximately the same stimulus configuration, but nevertheless have drastically different expected distances and choice probabilities. In other words, similar configurations in anisotropic spaces do not imply similar observable properties.

Properties of Choice Probabilities

Choice probabilities in an anisotropic space also exhibit nonmonotonic properties. Consider three stimulus points j, k, and m, located on the vertices of an equilateral triangle in a two-dimensional space, and an ideal point located at the centroid of this triangle (see Figure 2.9). Since ideal point i is equally far from all

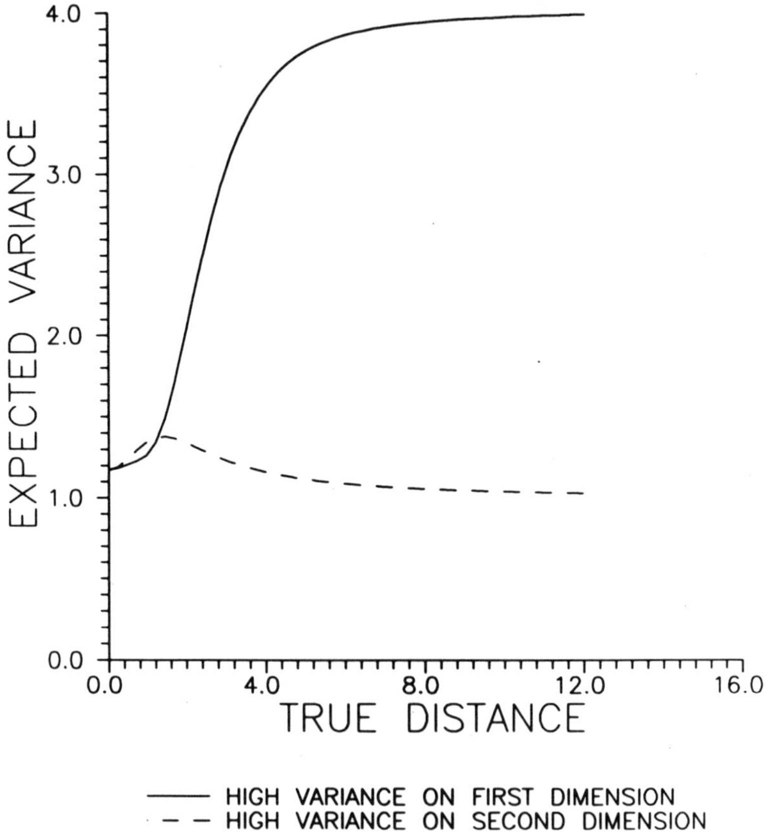

FIG. 2.8. The influence of the true distance and the variance structure on the expected variance of the distance between two points. Both the solid and dashed lines show the expected variance when the two points move apart from each other along the horizontal axis, but in the first case the points have the variance structure shown in Figure 2.7a, and in the second case the variance structure in Figure 2.7b.

three stimulus points, the choice probabilities p_j, p_k, and p_m will depend entirely on the variances associated with the three stimuli. If all three points have the same variances, and if the space is isotropic, then all three probabilities will be equal to $\frac{1}{3}$. Person P_i will be indifferent to the three stimuli. However, if the space is anisotropic, the results are quite different, even when all three points have the same variance structure. Consider the variance structure in Figure 2.9. In this example, all four points have precisely the same variance structure, which involves a large variance in the vertical direction and a smaller variance in the horizontal direction. In fact, in this example, the standard deviation on the vertical axis is 1.0 and on the horizontal axis is 0.05. Under these conditions,

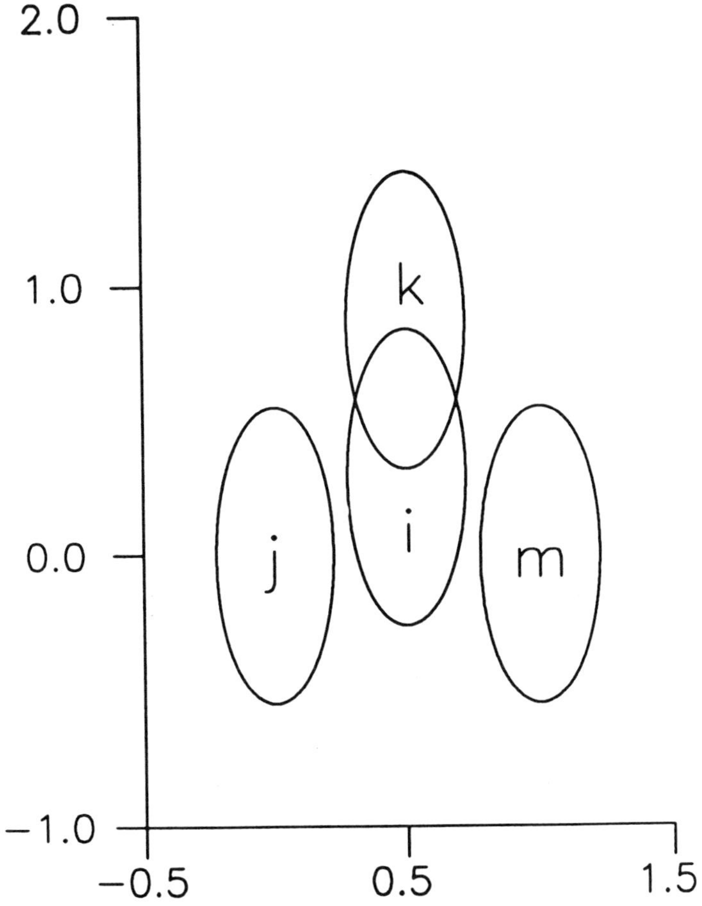

FIG. 2.9. An example of three points located at the vertices of an equilateral triangle and an ideal point located at the centroid of the triangle.

which are that of a case 5a Hefner model, the choice probability p_k is larger than both p_j and p_m, indicating that person P_i prefers $\mathbf{S}_k$ over the other two stimuli.

Consider what happens next when the variances in the vertical direction of all four points increases. One might expect the choice probability p_k to keep increasing and, therefore, person P_i to show increasing preference for stimulus $\mathbf{S}_k$ over the other two stimuli. This does not happen. As shown in Figure 2.10, p_k increases at first, but then decreases and approaches an asymptotic value of about 0.36. Thus, the choice probability p_k is not a simple monotonic function of the size of the variance in the vertical direction.

This example and the one in the previous section both illustrate some of the

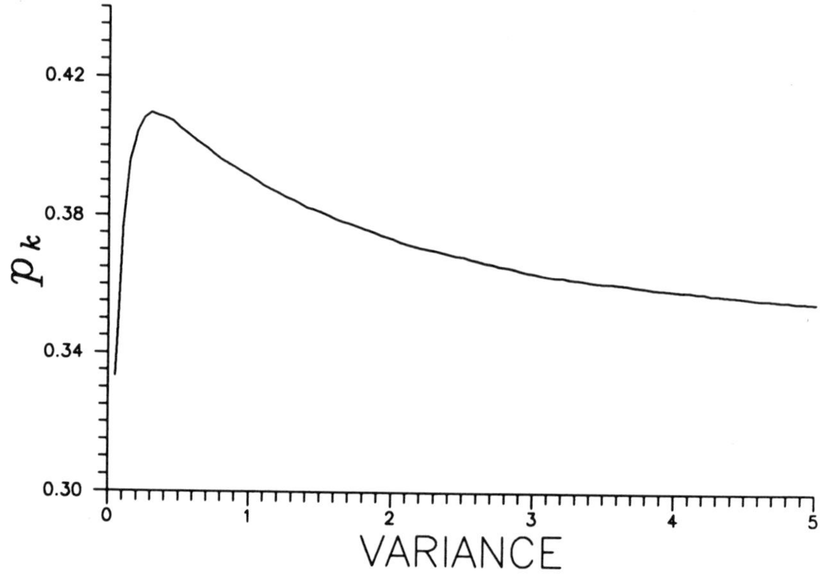

FIG. 2.10. Percent of time the ideal point i in Figure 2.9 is closest to point k, as the variance on the vertical axis increases from 0.05 to 5.0 while the variance on the horizontal axis stays fixed at 0.05.

nonintuitive properties of anisotropic spaces, which make those spaces so fascinating. To demonstrate the potential usefulness of anisotropic solutions, we consider next a simple empirical example.

An Empirical Example of an Anisotropic Space

In this experiment (MacKay & Dröge, 1990), 52 subjects judged the similarity of eight brands of toothpaste presented pairwise.

On the basis of past advertising claims, it was expected that the eight brands could be divided into three groups: (1) those brands stressing decay prevention (brands A and B), (2) those stressing breath freshening (brands C, D, E, and F), and (3) those stressing whitening (brands G and H). With this division, Likelihood Ratio Tests were carried out, in which a case 5i and a constrained case 3i solution containing three variances, one for each of the three groups, were compared. Likelihood ratio tests were also conducted for the constrained and unconstrained case 3i solution, where all stimuli have unique variances. The former test was significant but the latter was not, suggesting that the constrained case 3i solution adequately accounts for the data obtained. Similarly, results of Likelihood Ratio Tests for one, two, and three dimensions suggested that a two-dimensional solution was most appropriate.

Figure 2.11a shows the coordinates and the standard deviations of the con-

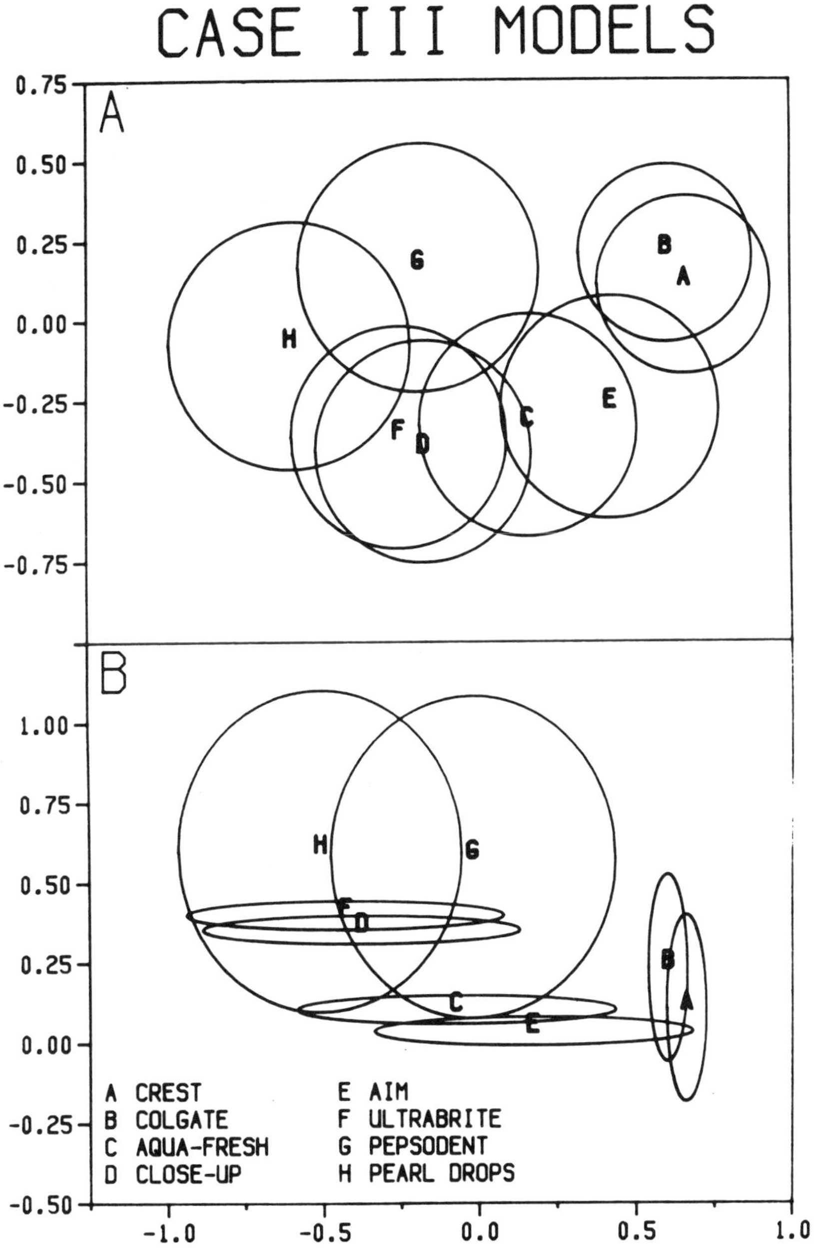

FIG. 2.11. Solution obtained for the eight toothpastes: (a) constrained case 3i solution, (b) case 3a solution.

strained case 3i solution. Generally, the results are as expected. The horizontal dimension appears to reflect decay prevention, the vertical dimension whitening and breath freshening. Also the relative sizes of variances seem plausible. Brands A and B have the smallest variance, and G and H have the largest, no doubt because brands A and B advertise heavily their decay prevention properties to college students, the subjects in this experiment. In contrast, brands G and H are positioned as a smoker's toothpaste for older consumers. Apparently, students are more concerned about decay prevention than they are about whitening and breath freshening.

However, more insight into these data can be obtained by obtaining the anisotropic solution, which is shown in Figure 2.11b. Figure 2.11a,b indicates that the isotropic and anisotropic configurations are similar, but that their variances are quite different. In Figure 2.11b, brands A and B, have small variances on dimension 1 (the decay prevention dimension) and large variances on dimension 2 (the whitening–breath freshening dimension). Just the opposite is the case for brands C, D, E, and H. These brands, which emphasize breath freshening, have a small variance on dimension 2 and a large variance on dimension 1. Brands G and H, which emphasize whitening, have nearly equal variances on both axes. Evidently, brands G and H are not well known or understood by the subjects.

The usefulness of the case 3a solution is also supported by a Likelihood Ratio Test. The comparison between a constrained case 3a and a constrained case 3i solution was statistically significant, thus providing justification for the extra variance parameters used in the case 3a solution.

These results, taken as a whole, seem to provide strong support for the appropriateness and the usefulness of the anisotropic solution. As we become more adept at working with these spaces and understanding them, it should be possible to make stronger connections with the theoretical developments in other psychological domains.

3 Probabilistic Multidimensional Models of Pairwise Choice Data

Geert De Soete
University of Ghent, Belgium

J. Douglas Carroll
Graduate School of Management
Rutgers University

INTRODUCTION

Probabilistic Models of Paired Comparisons

The inconsistency of human choice behavior led to the development of probabilistic choice models. This inconsistency is apparent in two ways. First, a subject tends to be inconsistent over replications. If a subject is repeatedly presented the same set of choice alternatives and asked to indicate which alternative he or she most prefers, he or she will not always respond in the same manner. Second, as is well known (e.g., Tversky, 1972b), a subject often experiences considerable subjective uncertainty when making such preference judgments.

When formulating choice models, this inconsistency can be taken into account in different ways. One approach consists of considering each preference judgment as an event in a probability space. Such a conception results in a probabilistic choice model that predicts the probability that a subject will select a specific object in an offered set (called a feasible set) as the most preferred alternative.

Although in principle nothing prevents us from constructing choice models that account for choices on feasible sets of more than two alternatives, most probabilistic choice models only deal with pairwise choices (i.e., choices on feasible sets consisting of only two choice objects). There are two reasons for this restriction. First, calculating choice probabilities predicted by a model for choices on feasible sets of more than two objects is usually fairly complicated because it involves the numerical evaluation of multiple integrals (see chap. 1).

Although this computational complexity is less of a problem with today's fast computers, there is a second, more fundamental, reason why researchers have mostly restricted themselves to pairwise choice models. To derive reliable estimates of the parameters in a choice model for feasible sets larger than two alternatives, one needs enormous amounts of data, such that, in practice, it might never be possible to empirically validate such a probabilistic model.

For the reasons mentioned, we concentrate in this chapter on probabilistic models for pairwise choice and resort to the time-honored Method of Paired Comparisons as a data gathering procedure (for an extensive bibliography on this method, see David, 1988, and Davidson & Farquhar, 1976). In this experimental paradigm, a subject is presented two choice objects at a time and is required to choose one. Usually, a series of such pairs are presented to each subject.

Thus, because of the inconsistency of human choice behavior we turn to a probabilistic model formulation. Due to practical and theoretical considerations, we restrict ourselves to probabilistic choice models for paired comparisons data.

Moderate Utility Models

Certainly the two most popular probabilistic choice models for paired comparisons data are Thurstone's (1927a) Law of Comparative Judgment (LCJ) Case V and the Bradley-Terry-Luce (BTL) model (Bradley & Terry, 1952; Luce, 1959). Denoting the probability of preferring object j to object k by p_{jk}, we can write Thurstone's LCJ Case V model as

$$p_{\mathrm{jk}} = \Phi(u_{\mathrm{j}} - u_{\mathrm{k}}) \ , \tag{1}$$

where Φ is the standard normal distribution function and u_{j} is the utility of object j. The BTL model is usually stated as

$$p_{\mathrm{jk}} = \frac{v_{\mathrm{j}}}{v_{\mathrm{j}} + v_{\mathrm{k}}} \ , \tag{2}$$

with v_{j} the utility of choice object j. If we define $u_{\mathrm{j}} \equiv log\ (v_{\mathrm{j}})$, Equation 2 becomes

$$p_{\mathrm{jk}} = \Psi(u_{\mathrm{j}} - u_{\mathrm{k}}) \ , \tag{3}$$

where Ψ denotes the standard logistic distribution function. As is apparent from Equations 1 and 3, Thurstone's LCJ Case V model and the BTL model are very similar. They both belong to the class of the strong utility models (cf. Luce & Suppes, 1965). A pairwise choice model is a strong utility model whenever it can be written as

$$p_{\mathrm{jk}} = F(u_{\mathrm{j}} - u_{\mathrm{k}}) \ , \tag{4}$$

where $F(\cdot)$ is a strictly increasing function with $F(x) = 1 - F(-x)$ and $0 \leq F(x) \leq 1$. A strong utility model is conceptually very simple. It states that the probability of preferring object j to object k is a strictly increasing function of the difference in utility of the two choice objects. The larger this difference, the more extreme (i.e., closer to 0 or 1) the choice probability will be. It can be shown that any set of choice probabilities obeying Equation 4 satisfies a transitivity condition that is commonly referred to as strong stochastic transitivity:

$$\text{If } p_{\mathrm{jk}} \geq \tfrac{1}{2} \text{ and } p_{\mathrm{kl}} \geq \tfrac{1}{2}, \text{ then } p_{\mathrm{jl}} \geq \max(p_{\mathrm{jk}}, p_{\mathrm{kl}}) \tag{5}$$

for all triples j, k, l. Conversely, any choice probabilities that satisfy strong stochastic transitivity can be characterized by a strong utility model.

Although a strong utility model gives a very parsimonious account of paired comparisons data, it leads to some rather counterintuitive predictions. Suppose, for instance, that the set of choice objects includes a vacation to Hawaii, a vacation to Acapulco, and a vacation to Hawaii plus \$1. Furthermore, suppose you are indifferent between a vacation to Hawaii and a vacation to Acapulco [i.e., p(Hawaii, Acapulco) = 0.5]. Most likely, when offered a choice between a vacation to Hawaii and a vacation to Hawaii plus \$1, you would prefer the vacation to Hawaii plus \$1 with absolute certainty [i.e., p(Hawaii + \$1, Hawaii) = 1]. Strong stochastic transitivity now implies that you will choose a vacation to Hawaii plus \$1 over a vacation to Acapulco with certainty [i.e., p(Hawaii + \$1, Acapulco) = 1], although you are indifferent between a trip to Hawaii and a trip to Acapulco. Although a vacation plus an extra dollar would presumably always be preferred to that *same* vacation without the extra dollar, adding an extra dollar to the Hawaii vacation is very unlikely to increase the probability of preferring the trip to Hawaii to the trip to Acapulco as predicted by strong stochastic transitivity. In fact, there is extensive empirical evidence showing that data obtained in realistic choice settings often tend to systematically violate strong stochastic transitivity (cf. Becker, DeGroot, & Marschak, 1963; Krantz, 1967; Rumelhart & Greeno, 1971; Sjöberg, 1975, 1977, 1980; Sjöberg & Capozza, 1975; Tversky & Russo, 1969; Tversky & Sattath, 1979). More precisely, it has been found that empirical choice proportions seem to be influenced not only by differences in utility between the choice objects (as predicted by a strong utility model), but also, to some extent, by the similarity or comparability of the choice alternatives. Subjects tend to be somewhat indifferent between highly dissimilar alternatives, even when these alternatives differ considerably in utility. Similar choice objects, on the other hand, tend to evoke more extreme choice proportions, even when they do not differ that much in utility. Or, put differently, a constant difference in utility will give rise to a more extreme choice proportion the more similar the choice objects are.

A family of models that can capture these empirically observed similarity effects consists of the moderate utility models. A probabilistic pairwise choice model is a moderate utility model whenever it can be written as

$$p_{\mathrm{jk}} = F\left(\frac{u_{\mathrm{j}} - u_{\mathrm{k}}}{d_{\mathrm{jk}}}\right), \tag{6}$$

where $F(\cdot)$ is a strictly increasing function, with $F(x) = 1 - F(-x)$ and $0 \leq F(x) \leq 1$, u is a utility scale, and d is a distance function that quantifies the dissimilarity (or incomparability) between the choice objects (cf. Halff, 1976). The choice probabilities defined by a moderate utility model do not necessarily satisfy Equation 5. They do, however, always satisfy a weaker transitivity condition, known as moderate stochastic transitivity:

$$\text{If } p_{jk} \geq \tfrac{1}{2} \text{ and } p_{kl} \geq \tfrac{1}{2}, \text{ then } p_{jl} \geq \min(p_{jk}, p_{kl}) \tag{7}$$

for all j, k, l. Although observed choice proportions often violate Equation 5 because of similarity effects, they usually satisfy this weaker form of stochastic transitivity. In the fictitious example discussed, moderate stochastic transitivity implies p(Hawaii + \$1, Acapulco) ≥ 0.5, which is certainly much more realistic than p(Hawaii + \$1, Acapulco) $= 1$.

Contrary to the strong utility models, the moderate utility models can account for the empirically observed similarity effects. To model paired comparisons data accurately, a pairwise choice model should be a moderate utility model. Therefore, in this chapter we only consider pairwise probabilistic choice models that belong to the class of moderate utility models.

Individual Differences

The models discussed are, in principle, models for *individual* choice behavior. Each model predicts probabilities p_{ijk} that a subject i will prefer a choice object j to another choice object k. Thus, the models explicitly allow for individual differences in preference. Stated more formally, the models belong to a class of individual differences moderate utility models

$$p_{ijk} = F\left(\frac{u_{ij} - u_{ik}}{d_{ijk}}\right), \tag{8}$$

where u_{ij} denotes the utility of object j for subject i and d_{ijk} denotes the distance (dissimilarity) between objects j and k for subject i. (The function F is defined as in Equation 6.) A model of the form of Equation 8 implies moderate stochastic transitivity at the individual subject level:

$$\text{If } p_{ijk} \geq \tfrac{1}{2} \text{ and } p_{ikl} \geq \tfrac{1}{2}, \text{ then } p_{ijl} \geq \min(p_{ijk}, p_{ikl}) \tag{9}$$

for all subjects i and objects j, k, l.

Since all the models in this chapter are moderate utility models, they parameterize not only the utility of the choice objects, but also the similarity structure among the choice objects. The models discussed in subsequent sections have distinct parameters per subject that can give rise to differences in choice probabilities among the subjects, but these models all assume that the similarity structure (be it represented spatially or by an additive tree) is common for all subjects. This common similarity representation will often, but not always, result in identical d_{ijk} across subjects. In this case, the choice model is of the form

$$p_{ijk} = F\left(\frac{u_{ij} - u_{ik}}{d_{jk}}\right). \tag{10}$$

There is no subscript i in d_{jk} because these distances are the same for all subjects.

To obtain reliable estimates of the parameters in the models discussed in the next three sections, we need within-subject replications. This is often not feasible, especially with clearly identifiable choice objects (cf. Zinnes & MacKay, 1989). Whereas with psychophysical stimuli it is often possible to have large numbers of within-subject replications, this is not possible with clearly identifiable choice objects because a subject easily recalls his or her previous responses. Therefore, in practical applications, subjects are often treated as replications of each other. In such a situation, a model of the form of Equations 8 or 10 can still be gainfully adopted to model differences among homogeneous groups of subjects. Unfortunately, in many applications one does not possess the necessary information to classify the subjects in a small number of homogeneous groups a priori. In such a case, one would like to have a procedure that, on the basis of the paired comparisons data, *simultaneously* groups the subjects into a small number of homogeneous groups *and* models the preference structures of these groups by a model of the form of Equations 8 or 10. In the fifth section, it is shown how the models discussed in the second, third, and fourth sections can be extended, using a latent class approach, to enable such an analysis.

No A Priori Known Similarity Structure

The easiest way to develop a moderate utility model is to assume that the similarity structure among the choice objects is, at least partially, known in advance. Several such models have been inspired by Restle's (1961) set-theoretic choice model. These models require an a priori feature specification of the choice objects in order to be applicable (cf., e.g., Edgell & Geisler, 1980; Marley, 1981; Strauss, 1981; Tversky, 1972b; Tversky & Sattath, 1979). Although such a specification might be possible with artificially constructed choice objects, it is usually not available in real-life applications.

In this chapter, we consider only choice models of the form of Equation 8 that do not require any a priori information about the relevant psychological dimensions or features of the choice objects. More specifically, the models discussed in the next sections use the fact that paired comparisons data are influenced not only by the utility of the choice objects but also by the similarity between the choice objects to derive from the paired comparisons data information about both the utility of the objects *and* their similarity. When external information about the psychological similarity structure of the choice objects happens to be available, this information can then be utilized to validate the choice model.

Summary

In the next sections, choice models will be discussed that take the foregoing theoretical and empirical considerations into account. The models are probabilistic because of the inconsistency of human choice behavior; they belong to the class of moderate utility models because of the empirically observed similarity effects, and, in order to be routinely applicable, they do not require a priori knowledge about the similarity structure of the choice objects. In addition, the models can deal with differences among subjects (provided that there are within-subject replications) or homogeneous groups of subjects (either known in advance or simultaneously derived as discussed in the fifth section).

THE WANDERING VECTOR MODEL

Model Formulation

The wandering vector (WV) model is a probabilistic version of the well-known vector model (Slater, 1960; Tucker, 1960) for preference data. In a vector model for choice data, both the subjects and the choice objects are represented in a joint multidimensional space. The subjects are represented by vectors emanating from the origin, and the objects are represented by points. The dimensions are assumed to correspond to attributes of the choice objects. The orthogonal projections of the object points onto a subject vector determine the utility of the choice objects for that subject. The angle between the subject vector and the dimensions indicates the relative importance of the dimensions for this subject. A vector model is compensatory in that a low value on one dimension can be compensated by a high value on another dimension. Another important property of a vector model is that it assumes a monotone preference or utility function for each dimension. This implies that, for each dimension, the utility of an object increases as its value on that dimension increases (keeping the values on the other dimensions constant).

The WV model is a probabilistic version of this vector model that was originally introduced by Carroll (1980) and subsequently generalized by De Soete and Carroll (1983). An even more general formulation of the WV model is given in De Soete and Carroll (1986) and is presented here.

In the WV model, as in the ordinary vector model, both the subjects and the choice objects are represented in an R-dimensional space. Each subject i ($i = 1, \ldots, N$) is represented by a vector emanating from the origin, with a terminus $\mathbf{V}_i$ that is an R-dimensional random variable that follows a multivariate normal distribution:

$$\mathbf{V}_i \sim N(\boldsymbol{\mu}_i, \boldsymbol{\Sigma}_i) \ . \tag{11}$$

Note that the length of the subject vector is not really important; only the direction it defines with respect to the origin is important. Therefore, the length of the mean subject vector $\boldsymbol{\mu}_i$ can be easily standardized to some arbitrary positive constant. The distributions of the end points of the N subject vectors are assumed to be independent of each other:

$$Cov\ (\mathbf{V}_i, \mathbf{V}_{i'}) = \mathbf{0}$$

for i, i′ = 1, . . . , N and i ≠ i′. Each choice object j (j = 1, . . . , M) is represented in the same multidimensional space by a fixed point $\mathbf{x}_j$.

According to the model, a subject i draws a sample $\mathbf{v}_i$ from $\mathbf{V}_i$ each time he or she is presented a pair of choice objects. Alternative j is preferred to alternative k whenever the orthogonal projection of $\mathbf{x}_j$ on the vector from the origin to $\mathbf{v}_i$ exceeds the orthogonal projection of $\mathbf{x}_i$ on that same vector, or whenever

$$\frac{\mathbf{x}_j'\mathbf{v}_i}{\|\mathbf{v}_i\|} > \frac{\mathbf{x}_k'\mathbf{v}_i}{\|\mathbf{v}_i\|}\ . \tag{12}$$

This is illustrated in Figure 3.1. In the figure the orthogonal projection of $\mathbf{x}_j$ on

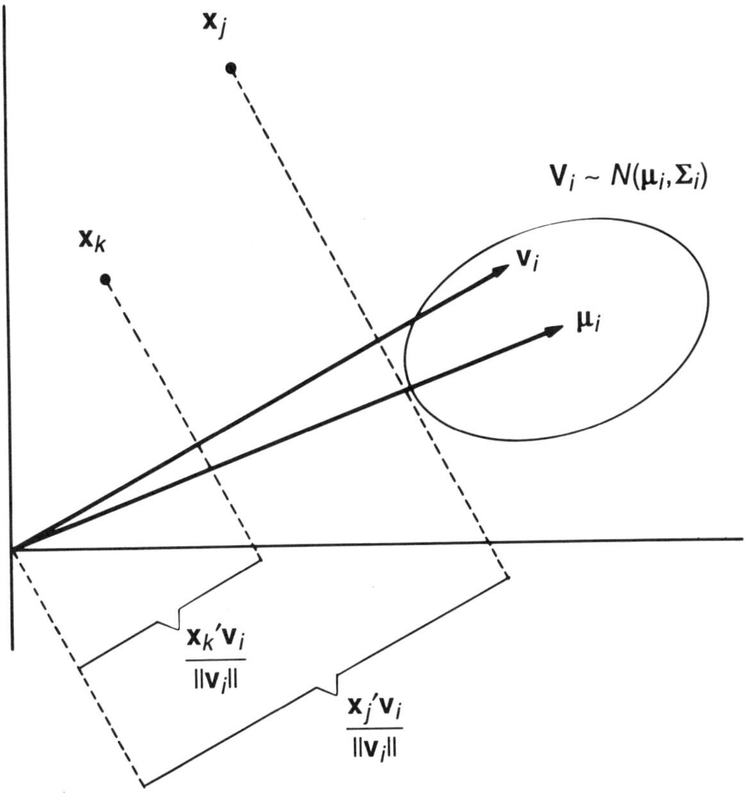

FIG. 3.1. Illustration of the WV model. The ellipse represents the distribution of the terminus of the subject vector.

the sampled vector $\mathbf{v}_i$ is larger than the orthogonal projection of $\mathbf{x}_k$ on $\mathbf{v}_i$. Therefore, the subject would on this occasion (i.e., with this realization of the random variable $\mathbf{V}_i$) prefer object j to k. Since each time the subject is presented a pair of choice objects a new $\mathbf{v}_i$ is sampled from $\mathbf{V}_i$, a subject will not necessarily respond consistently on repeated presentations of the same pair of objects. On some occasions Equation 12 will hold, and on others it will not, depending on which $\mathbf{v}_i$ was sampled. Since the end point of the subject vector "wanders" in the space from trial to trial, the model is called the wandering vector model. The covariance matrix $\boldsymbol{\Sigma}_i$ determines in which direction $\mathbf{v}_i$ is most likely to deviate from $\boldsymbol{\mu}_i$. Depending on the form of $\boldsymbol{\Sigma}_i$ (cf. infra), this information can be very useful in applications.

By multiplying both sides of Equation 12 by $\|\mathbf{v}_i\|$, one obtains that subject i prefers j to k whenever

$$\mathbf{x}_j'\mathbf{v}_i > \mathbf{x}_k'\mathbf{v}_i \ .$$

Therefore, the probability that subject i prefers object j to k is

$$\begin{aligned} p_{ijk} &= \text{Prob}\{\mathbf{x}_j'\mathbf{V}_i > \mathbf{x}_k'\mathbf{V}_i\} \\ &= \text{Prob}\{(\mathbf{x}_j - \mathbf{x}_k)'\mathbf{V}_i > 0\} \ . \end{aligned} \tag{13}$$

The distribution of $(\mathbf{x}_j - \mathbf{x}_k)'\mathbf{V}_i$ can be readily determined since $\mathbf{V}_i$ follows a multivariate normal distribution:

$$(\mathbf{x}_j - \mathbf{x}_k)'\mathbf{V}_i \sim N((\mathbf{x}_j - \mathbf{x}_k)'\boldsymbol{\mu}_i, \delta_{ijk}^2) \tag{14}$$

with

$$\delta_{ijk}^2 = (\mathbf{x}_j - \mathbf{x}_k)'\boldsymbol{\Sigma}_i(\mathbf{x}_j - \mathbf{x}_k) \ ; \tag{15}$$

that is, δ_{ijk} is the generalized distance between $\mathbf{x}_j$ and $\mathbf{x}_k$ in the metric $\boldsymbol{\Sigma}_i$. Because of Equations 14 and 15, Equation 13 becomes

$$p_{ijk} = \Phi\left(\frac{(\mathbf{x}_j - \mathbf{x}_k)'\boldsymbol{\mu}_i}{\delta_{ijk}}\right) , \tag{16}$$

which constitutes the formal definition of the WV model.

Properties

It can be easily seen that the WV model is a moderate utility model of the form in Equation 8. In the WV model, the utility of object j for subject i can be defined as

$$u_{ij} = \mathbf{x}_j'\mathbf{v}_i \ ,$$

which allows us to write Equation 16 as

$$p_{ijk} = \Phi\left(\frac{u_{ij} - u_{ik}}{\delta_{ijk}}\right) . \tag{17}$$

Since $\mathbf{\Sigma}_i$ is a covariance matrix, $\mathbf{\Sigma}_i$ is positive definite and δ_{ijk} is a metric, so that Equation 17 has the form of Equation 8.

To see that in the WV model the choice probability p_{ijk} is influenced not only by the difference in utilities $u_{ij} - u_{ik}$, but also by the generalized distance δ_{ijk} between the points $\mathbf{x}_j$ and $\mathbf{x}_k$ representing objects j and k, compare Figures 3.2 and 3.3. In these figures, the mean subject vector $\boldsymbol{\mu}_i$ is depicted along with the points representing j and k. On one side of the mean subject vector, the utility distributions $\mathbf{x}_j'\mathbf{V}_i$ and $\mathbf{x}_k'\mathbf{V}_i$ are shown, whereas on the other side the distribution of $(\mathbf{x}_j - \mathbf{x}_k)'\mathbf{V}_i$ is drawn translated such that its expectation coincides with $(\mathbf{x}_j'\boldsymbol{\mu}_i + \mathbf{x}_k'\boldsymbol{\mu}_i)/2$. The utility distribution for object j, $\mathbf{x}_j'\mathbf{V}_i$, is identical in Figures 3.2 and 3.3. The same is true for the utility distribution for object k. However, because the distance between $\mathbf{x}_j$ and $\mathbf{x}_k$ is larger in Figure 3.2 than in Figure 3.3, the variance of $(\mathbf{x}_j - \mathbf{x}_k)'\mathbf{V}_i$ is larger in Figure 3.3 than in Figure 3.2. Conse-

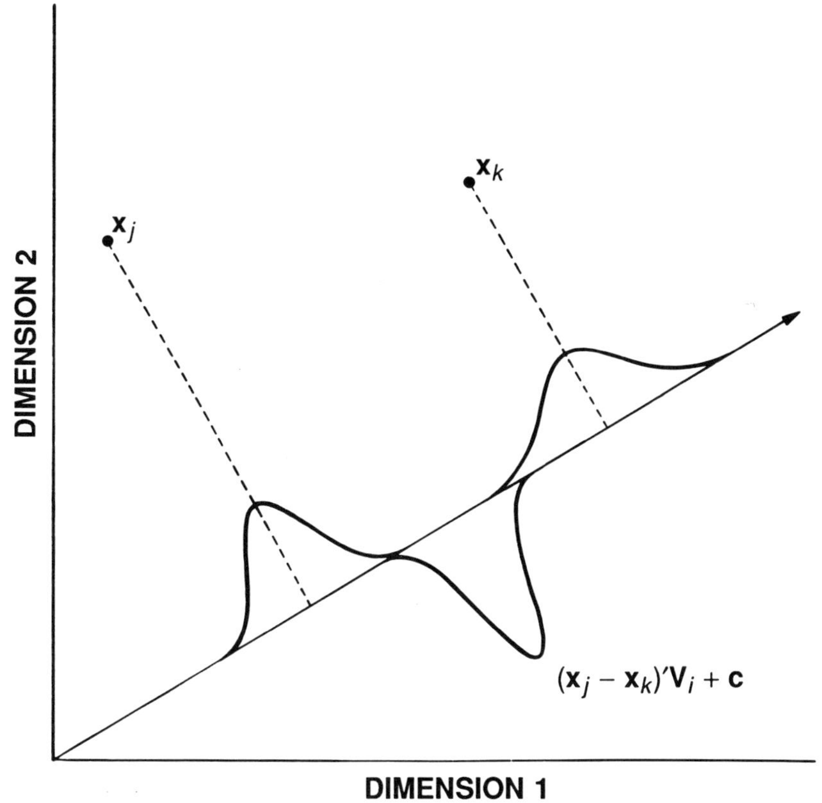

FIG. 3.2. Two choice objects and their utility distributions $\mathbf{x}_j'\mathbf{V}_i$ and $\mathbf{x}_k'\mathbf{V}_i$. The distribution of $(\mathbf{x}_j - \mathbf{x}_k)'\mathbf{V}_i$ is translated such that its expectation coincides with $(\mathbf{x}_j'\boldsymbol{\mu}_i + \mathbf{x}_k'\boldsymbol{\mu}_i)/2$.

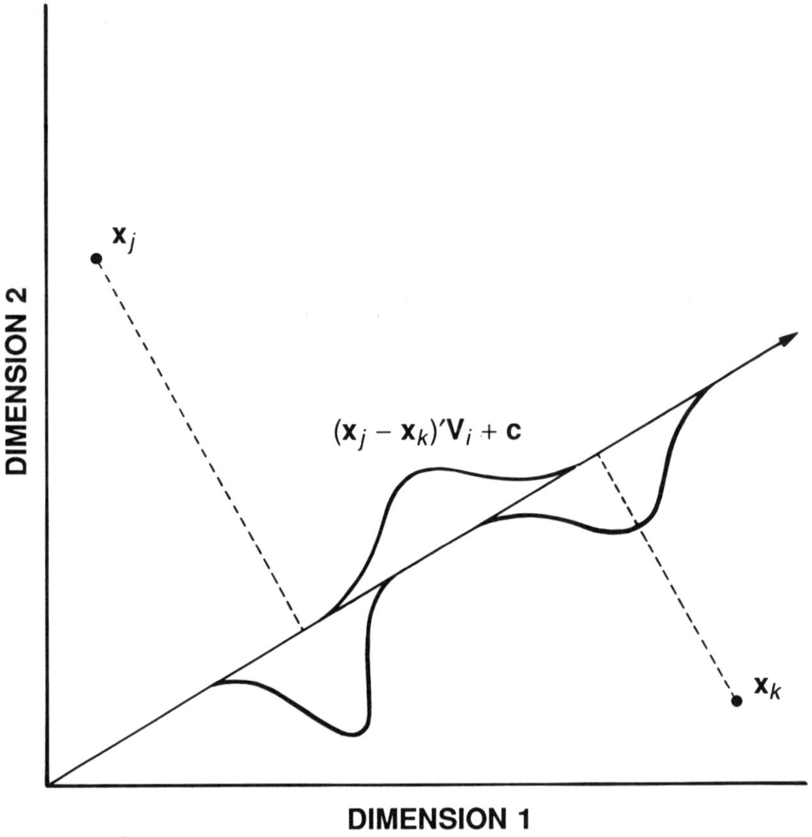

FIG. 3.3. Two objects with identical utility distributions as in Figure 3.2. But, the distribution of $(\mathbf{x}_j - \mathbf{x}_k)'\mathbf{V}_i$ has a larger variance because $\mathbf{x}_j$ and $\mathbf{x}_k$ are farther apart.

quently, p_{ijk} will be smaller for Figure 3.3 than for Figure 3.2, although the utilities of j and k are the same in the two figures.

In the single-subject case (i.e., N = 1), the WV model can be shown to be a constrained instance of a Thurstonian choice model proposed by Heiser and de Leeuw (1981) and Takane (1980) (cf. De Soete, 1983b). In Thurstone's (1927a) model of comparative judgment, the utility of each choice object j (j = 1, . . . , M) is represented by a random variable A_j. It is assumed that $\mathbf{A} = (A_1, \ldots, A_M)'$ has a multivariate normal distribution

$$\mathbf{A} \sim N(\mathbf{a},\mathbf{C}) \, . \tag{18}$$

When presented a pair of objects, the subject is assumed to choose the object with the highest momentary utility. Consequently, the probability that the subject prefers object j to object k becomes

$$p_{jk} = \Phi\left(\frac{a_j - a_k}{\gamma_{jk}}\right), \tag{19}$$

where γ_{jk} is the so-called comparatal dispersion (Gulliksen, 1958), which is equal to

$$\gamma_{jk} = \sqrt{\mathbf{e}'_{(jk)}\mathbf{C}\mathbf{e}_{(jk)}}, \tag{20}$$

with $\mathbf{e}_{(jk)}$ an M-element column vector whose l-th component is defined by $\delta^{jl} - \delta^{kl}$ (where $\delta^{\cdot\cdot}$ denotes Kronecker delta). In the model proposed by Heiser and De Leeuw (1981) and Takane (1980), the covariance matrix $\mathbf{C}$ is required to have a prescribed rank R ($R < M$). Since $\mathbf{C}$ is positive definite, it can be decomposed as

$$\mathbf{C} = \mathbf{X}\mathbf{X}', \tag{21}$$

where $\mathbf{X}$ is an $M \times R$ matrix. Denoting the j-th row of $\mathbf{X}$ by the column vector $\mathbf{x}_j$, we can write the comparatal dispersion for this constrained Thurstonian model as

$$\gamma_{jk} = \sqrt{(\mathbf{x}_j - \mathbf{x}_k)'(\mathbf{x}_j - \mathbf{x}_k)}, \tag{22}$$

which is equal to the Euclidean distance between points j and k in the column space of $\mathbf{X}$. Hence, this constrained model can be written as

$$p_{jk} = \Phi\left(\frac{a_j - a_k}{\sqrt{(\mathbf{x}_j - \mathbf{x}_k)'(\mathbf{x}_j - \mathbf{x}_k)}}\right). \tag{23}$$

If in this model the mean utilities $\mathbf{a}$ are constrained to be a linear function of $\mathbf{X}$,

$$\mathbf{a} = \mathbf{X}\boldsymbol{\nu}, \tag{24}$$

the wandering vector model with an identity covariance matrix is obtained. Note that for $N = 1$, the covariance matrix $\boldsymbol{\Sigma}$ in the WV model can always, without loss of generality, be set equal to an identity matrix (cf. De Soete & Carroll, 1986, 1990). For a more extensive discussion of the relationship between the two models, see De Soete (1983b).

In its general form, the WV model has M R parameters for the M object points $\mathbf{x}_j$ and per subject, R parameters for $\boldsymbol{\mu}_i$, and $R(R + 1)/2$ parameters for $\boldsymbol{\Sigma}_i$. This results in a total of

$$MR + N\left[R + \frac{R(R+1)}{2}\right] \tag{25}$$

model parameters. However, the WV model does not determine all these parameters uniquely. In particular, the choice probabilities defined by the WV model are invariant under a dilation of the subject vectors (i.e., replacing $\mathbf{V}_i$ by $\alpha_i\mathbf{V}_i$, where α_i is an arbitrary positive constant), a translation of the object points (i.e., adding an arbitrary constant R-component vector to all $\mathbf{x}_j$), and a nonsingular linear transformation of the object points (provided the inverse adjoint transformation is applied to the subject vectors). As a result of these indeterminacies, the degrees of freedom of the general WV model reduce to

$$MR + N\left[\frac{R(R+3)}{2} - 1\right] - R - R^2 \tag{26}$$

(see, De Soete & Carroll, 1986, 1990, for a more thorough discussion of the indeterminacies of the WV model).

Equation 16 defines the WV model in its most general form. In empirical applications, it might be interesting to impose certain restrictions on the general model, either to reduce the number of parameters that need to be estimated or to test specific hypotheses. De Soete and Carroll (1983) considered the special case where the covariance matrices $\boldsymbol{\Sigma}_i$ are constrained to be proportional to each other. That is,

$$\boldsymbol{\Sigma}_i = c_i\boldsymbol{\Sigma}\ , \tag{27}$$

with $c_i > 0$ ($i = 1, \ldots, N$). Because of what Kruskal (1978) has called the fundamental indeterminacy of bilinear models, $\boldsymbol{\Sigma}$ can, in this case, without loss of generality be set equal to the identity matrix. If we define

$$\boldsymbol{\mu}_i^* = \frac{\boldsymbol{\mu}_i}{\sqrt{c_i}}\ , \tag{28}$$

then this restricted model can be written as

$$p_{ijk} = \Phi\left(\frac{(\mathbf{x}_j - \mathbf{x}_k)'\boldsymbol{\mu}_i^*}{\delta_{jk}^*}\right), \tag{29}$$

where δ_{jk}^* denotes the Euclidean distance between $\mathbf{x}_j$ and $\mathbf{x}_k$; that is,

$$\delta_{jk}^* = \sqrt{(\mathbf{x}_j - \mathbf{x}_k)'(\mathbf{x}_j - \mathbf{x}_k)}\ . \tag{30}$$

Note that Equation 29 is of the form of Equation 10. The degrees of freedom for this restricted model are

$$(M + N)R - \frac{R(R+1)}{2} - 1\ . \tag{31}$$

De Soete and Carroll (1983) generalized Equation 29 by introducing an additional error term γ^2 to account for response variability due to an unaccounted variance associated with dimensions not present in the model:

$$p_{ijk} = \Phi\left(\frac{(\mathbf{x}_j - \mathbf{x}_k)'\boldsymbol{\mu}_i^*}{\sqrt{\delta_{jk}^{*2} + \gamma^2}}\right). \tag{32}$$

Model 32 can be shown to be a special case of the general WV model when it is assumed that, in addition to the R common dimensions, there is a unique dimension for each object (cf. De Soete & Carroll, 1986, 1990).

Parameter Estimation and Model Validation

When the model is applied to empirical data, the subject parameters $\boldsymbol{\mu}_i$, $\boldsymbol{\Sigma}_i$ (i = 1, . . . , N) and the object coordinates $\mathbf{x}_j$ (j = 1, . . . , M) must be estimated. De Soete and Carroll (1983) developed a Maximum Likelihood Estimation procedure based on a generalization of Fisher's Scoring Algorithm. Let F_{ijk} denote the number of times choice object pair (j, k) was presented to subject i, and let f_{ijk} denote the number of times (out of F_{ijk}) that subject i preferred object j to object k. Then, assuming independence across subjects and object pairs, the likelihood function is proportional to

$$L(\boldsymbol{\theta}) = \prod_{i=1}^{N} \prod_{j=2}^{M} \prod_{k=1}^{j-1} p_{ijk}^{f_{ijk}} (1 - p_{ijk})^{F_{ijk} - f_{ijk}} , \qquad (33)$$

where $\boldsymbol{\theta}$ is a column vector containing all the model parameters that need to be estimated. Fisher's scoring method amounts to iteratively improving the current estimate of $\boldsymbol{\theta}$ (starting from some initial estimate) by using the updating rule

$$\boldsymbol{\theta}^{(q+1)} = \boldsymbol{\theta}^{(q)} + \alpha^{(q)} \mathbf{I}(\boldsymbol{\theta}^{(q)})^{+} \mathbf{g}(\boldsymbol{\theta}^{(q)}) , \qquad (34)$$

where the superscript q is the iteration index, α is a step-size parameter, $\mathbf{g}(\boldsymbol{\theta}^{(q)})$ is the gradient $\nabla \; log \; L(\boldsymbol{\theta})$ evaluated at $\boldsymbol{\theta}^{(q)}$, and $\mathbf{I}(\boldsymbol{\theta}^{(q)})$ is the Fisherian information matrix

$$\mathbf{I}(\boldsymbol{\theta}) = - E \left(\frac{\partial^2 \; log \; L(\boldsymbol{\theta})}{\partial \boldsymbol{\theta} \; \partial \boldsymbol{\theta}'} \right) \qquad (35)$$

evaluated at $\boldsymbol{\theta}^{(q)}$. Because of the indeterminacies discussed in the previous section, $\mathbf{I}(\boldsymbol{\theta})$ is not of full rank and so has no regular inverse. Therefore, we use in Equation 34 its Moore-Penrose inverse $\mathbf{I}(\boldsymbol{\theta})^{+}$ (cf. Ramsay, 1978). Further details of this algorithm can be found in De Soete and Carroll (1983).

One of the main advantages of using the Maximum Likelihood Criterion for estimating the model parameters is that it enables statistical model evaluation (cf. chap. 1). When we have two models such that one model is subsumed under the other, then their goodness of fit can be compared statistically by means of a Likelihood Ratio Test. The goodness of fit of nonnested models can be compared by means of information criteria like the ones proposed by Akaike (1977), Chow (1981), and Schwarz (1978).

Examples of applications adopting this approach to parameter estimation and model evaluation can be found in Carroll, De Soete, and DeSarbo (1990), De Soete (1983b), and De Soete and Carroll (1983).

THE WANDERING IDEAL POINT MODEL

Model Formulation

As pointed out in the last section, a vector model assumes that all subjects have a monotone preference function or utility function on every dimension. Although this might be true in some situations, it certainly is not always the case. Suppose, for example, that the set of choice objects consists of job compensation plans each characterized by the amount of salary and the number of vacation days per years. It is very likely that in such a choice situation the subjects will have monotone preference function for both attributes. The more vacation, the more attractive the alternative is (assuming that the salary is constant). Conversely, given a constant number of vacation days, the higher the salary, the more preferable the object will be. For other object attributes, however, subjects tend to have a single-peaked preference function. This means that there exists an optimal value and that the farther an object is removed from that optimal value (in either direction), the less preferable it is. If, for instance, the choice objects are coffee brands varying in bitterness, most subjects will probably have a most preferred bitterness level. The farther away the bitterness of a coffee brand is from this optimal level, the smaller its utility will be.

A model that allows for single-peaked preference functions of the object dimensions is Coombs' (1964) unfolding model. In this model both the subjects and the choice objects are represented as points in a Euclidean space. The preference for an object is determined by its distance from the subject point. The closer an object is to the subject point, the more preferable it is for that subject. Because an object that coincides with the subject point would constitute an ideal object, the subject points are often called ideal points. The wandering ideal point (WIP) model was developed by De Soete, Carroll, and DeSarbo (1986) as a probabilistic version of the multidimensional unfolding model.

Just like the WV model, the WIP model attempts a joint representation of the subjects and the choice objects in a multidimensional Euclidean space of low dimensionality. Whereas in the WV model the subjects are represented by vectors emanating from the origin with termini that are multivariate normally distributed, the subjects are now represented by random points that are multivariate normally distributed. More specifically, each subject i is represented by an R-dimensional random variable $\mathbf{V}_i$:

$$\mathbf{V}_i \sim N(\boldsymbol{\mu}_i, \boldsymbol{\Sigma}_i) \; . \tag{36}$$

It is assumed that the distributions of the N subject points are independent of each other; that is,

$$Cov\,(\mathbf{V}_i, \mathbf{V}_{i'}) = \mathbf{0} \tag{37}$$

for i, $i' = 1, \ldots, N$ and $i \neq i'$. As in the WV model, the choice objects are represented as fixed points $\mathbf{x}_j$, $j = 1, \ldots, M$.

Each time a subject i is presented a pair of choice objects (j, k), he or she samples a point $\mathbf{v}_i$ from the distribution of $\mathbf{V}_i$. Following Coombs' (1964) Unfolding Theory, the subject prefers the object that is closest to the sampled point $\mathbf{v}_i$. That is, object j is preferred to k whenever the Euclidean distance between $\mathbf{v}_i$ and $\mathbf{x}_j$ is smaller than the Euclidean distance between $\mathbf{v}_i$ and $\mathbf{x}_k$, or whenever

$$(\mathbf{v}_i - \mathbf{x}_j)'(\mathbf{v}_i - \mathbf{x}_j) < (\mathbf{v}_i - \mathbf{x}_k)'(\mathbf{v}_i - \mathbf{x}_k) \; . \tag{38}$$

The WIP model is illustrated in Figure 3.4. In the figure, the realization $\mathbf{v}_i$ of $\mathbf{V}_i$ is closer to $\mathbf{x}_j$ than to $\mathbf{x}_k$. Hence, the subject will on this occasion prefer j to k. Since each time a pair of objects is presented a new $\mathbf{v}_i$ is sampled, the subject's ideal point is not fixed but "wanders" from trial to trial. That is why the model is called the wandering ideal point model. The covariance matrix $\boldsymbol{\Sigma}_i$ determines how much the sampled point $\mathbf{v}_i$ is likely to deviate from $\boldsymbol{\mu}_i$ along each dimension.

Rearranging both sides of Equation 38 shows that subject i prefers object j to k whenever

$$(\mathbf{x}_k - \mathbf{x}_j)'\mathbf{v}_i < \frac{\mathbf{x}_k'\mathbf{x}_k - \mathbf{x}_j'\mathbf{x}_j}{2} \; . \tag{39}$$

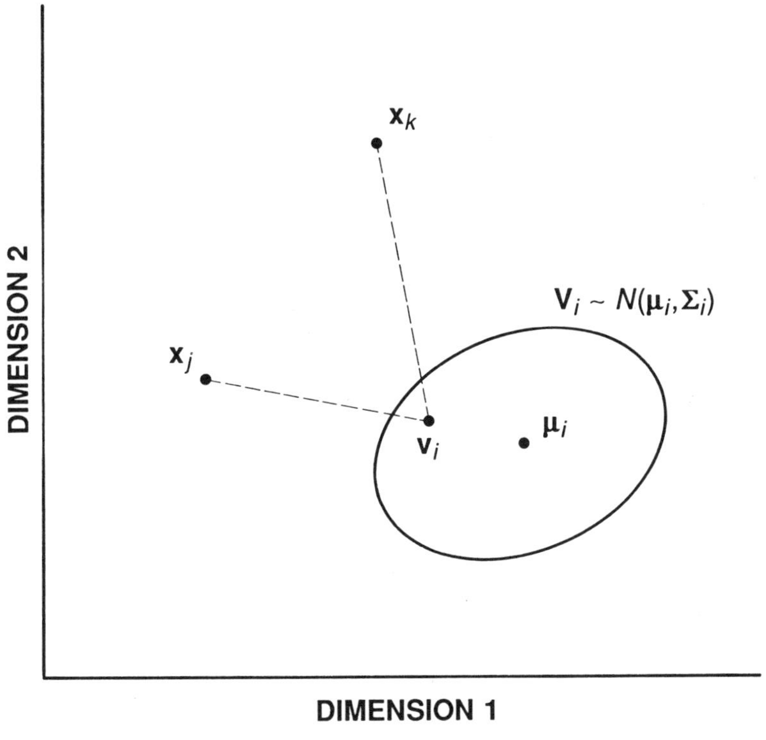

FIG. 3.4. Illustration of the WIP model. The ellipse represents the distribution of the subject point.

Hence, p_{ijk} is equal to the probability that the random variable $(\mathbf{x}_k - \mathbf{x}_j)'\mathbf{V}_i$ is smaller than $(\mathbf{x}_k'\mathbf{x}_k - \mathbf{x}_j'\mathbf{x}_j)/2$. Since the ideal points are normally distributed, the distribution of $(\mathbf{x}_k - \mathbf{x}_j)'\mathbf{V}_i$ is readily determined:

$$(\mathbf{x}_k - \mathbf{x}_j)'\mathbf{V}_i \sim N((\mathbf{x}_k - \mathbf{x}_j)'\boldsymbol{\mu}_i, \delta^2_{ijk}) , \tag{40}$$

with δ^2_{ijk} defined in Equation 15. Consequently, the probability that subject i prefers object j to k becomes

$$p_{ijk} = \Phi\left(\frac{(\mathbf{x}_k'\mathbf{x}_k - \mathbf{x}_j'\mathbf{x}_j) - 2(\mathbf{x}_k - \mathbf{x}_j)'\boldsymbol{\mu}_i}{2\delta_{ijk}}\right) , \tag{41}$$

providing the general formulation of the WIP model.

Properties

By defining the utility of choice object j for subject i as

$$u_{ij} = \mathbf{x}_j'\boldsymbol{\mu}_i - \frac{\mathbf{x}_j'\mathbf{x}_j}{2} , \tag{42}$$

we can rewrite Equation 41 as

$$p_{ijk} = \Phi\left(\frac{u_{ij} - u_{ik}}{\delta_{ijk}}\right) , \tag{43}$$

from which it follows that the WIP model is, unlike the probabilistic multidimensional unfolding models developed by Schönemann and Wang (1972; Wang, Schönemann, & Rusk, 1975) and Zinnes and Griggs (1974), a moderate utility model. The unfolding model proposed by Schönemann and Wang (1972) is based on the BTL model and is therefore a strong utility model. The probabilistic multidimensional unfolding model developed by Zinnes and Griggs (1974) has recently been shown by Bezembinder and Bossuyt (1989) to imply strong stochastic transitivity.

That in the WIP model p_{ijk} is not only influenced by the difference in utilities $u_{ij} - u_{ik}$ but also by the (generalized) distance between the two points representing objects j and k is convincingly illustrated in Figure 3.5. When the distances between $\mathbf{x}_j$ and $\boldsymbol{\mu}_i$ and between $\mathbf{x}_k$ and $\boldsymbol{\mu}_i$ (in the figure indicated by d_{ij} and d_{ik}, respectively) are kept constant, the probability that subject i prefers object j to k varies as a function of the distance between $\mathbf{x}_j$ and $\mathbf{x}_k$ (taking $R = 2$ and an identity matrix for $\boldsymbol{\Sigma}_i$). This figure shows that extreme choice probabilities are more likely to occur when the stimuli are close, while distant objects with the same difference in utility will give rise to more moderate choice probabilities.

In its general form, the WIP model has the same number of parameters as the WV model (cf. Equation 25). Again, all these parameters are not determined uniquely by the model. The choice probabilities are not affected by a translation,

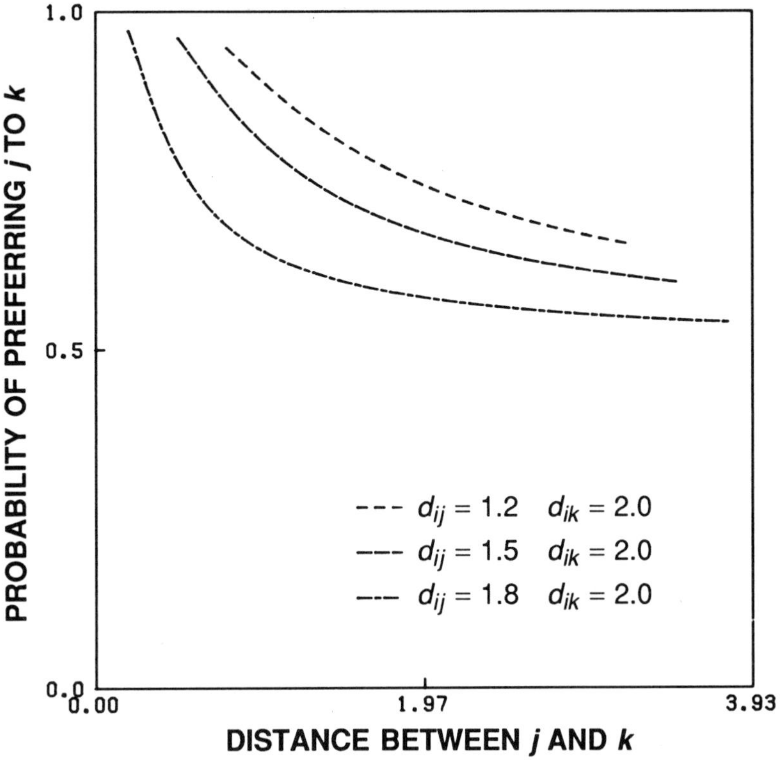

FIG. 3.5. Probability of preferring object j to k as a function of the distance between j and k keeping the distance between the object points and μ_i constant. *Note:* From "The Wandering Ideal Point Model: A Probabilistic Multidimensional Unfolding Model for Paired Comparisons Data" by D. De Soete, J. D. Carroll, and W. S. DeSarbo, 1986, *Journal of Mathematical Psychology, 30,* p. 34. Copyright 1986 by Academic Press, New York and London.

a central dilation, and an orthogonal rotation of the subject and object points. Subtracting from Equation 25 1 for the translational indeterminacy, R for the scale indeterminacy, and R(R − 1)/2 for the rotational indeterminacy yields the degrees of freedom for the general WIP model:

$$(M + N)R + (N - 1)\left[\frac{R(R + 1)}{2}\right] - 1 . \tag{44}$$

As for the WV model, it might be interesting to impose certain constraints on the general model. De Soete, Carroll, and DeSarbo (1989) discuss various restrictions that might be relevant in practical applications. The covariance matrices of the ideal point distributions can, for instance, be constrained to be diagonal or identity matrices.

Parameter Estimation and Model Validation

Maximum likelihood estimates of parameters in the WIP model can be obtained with an iterative procedure analogous to the one described in the second section. The fit of a WIP model can then be evaluated by means of a likelihood ratio test, and the fit of two WIP models can be compared by means of a similar test (when the models are nested) or by means of an information criterion such as the Aikake Information Criterion (AIC) statistic (when the models are not nested). For illustrative applications of the WIP model, the reader is referred to Carroll et al. (1990) and De Soete et al. (1986).

A PROBABILISTIC ADDITIVE TREE UNFOLDING MODEL

Introduction

Both the WV model and the WIP model rely on a spatial representation of the choice objects. This assumes that the choice objects can be thought of as objects varying along a limited number of *continuous* dimensions. Although, for certain types of stimuli the psychological similarity structure can indeed be accurately represented by a continuous spatial model, such a spatial representation is not necessarily adequate for all classes of choice objects. Pruzansky, Tversky, and Carroll (1982) provide some evidence that the similarity among "perceptual" stimuli is well represented by a spatial model, whereas the similarity structure among "conceptual" stimuli can be better accounted for by a tree model where a stimulus is no longer characterized by means of continuous spatial dimensions but by means of discrete dimensions or features (see chap. 16 for another account of these results). Hence, it is worthwhile to develop probabilistic choice models that are based on a representation of the choice objects in terms of features or discrete dimensions. In this section we present one probabilistic choice model that is based on an additive tree model. This model was recently developed by Carroll and De Soete (1990) and belongs to a general class of stochastic tree unfolding models proposed by Carroll, DeSarbo, and De Soete (1988, 1989). Currently, it is the only probabilistic tree unfolding model and method that meets all the requirements discussed in the first section. It is a moderate utility model (unlike the stochastic ultrametric tree model devised by DeSarbo, De Soete, Carroll, and Ramaswamy, 1988), and it does not require an a priori tree structure in order to be applicable (unlike the preference model proposed by Tversky and Sattath, 1979). The stochastic ultrametric tree model developed by DeSarbo et al. (1988) is based on Thurstone's LCJ Case V and is therefore a strong utility model. The PRETREE model of Tversky and Sattath (1979) is a moderate utility model, but requires an a priori tree structure reflecting the feature composition of the choice objects. In addition, it cannot represent differences between subjects or groups of subjects.

A tree is a connected graph with a unique path between any two nodes (i.e., a tree is a connected graph without cycles). An additive tree (also called a path length tree [Carroll, 1976], or a weighted free tree [Cunningham, 1978]), is a tree in which a nonnegative weight or length is attached to each link. The distance between any two nodes of an additive tree is defined as the sum of the weights attached to the links on the path connecting the two nodes. When using an additive tree to represent the similarity structure among objects, the links are assumed to correspond to discrete dimensions or features of the objects (cf. Sattath & Tversky, 1977). Furnas (1980) suggested that an additive tree model with its associated distance metric could be adopted for formulating an unfolding model much in the same way that Coombs (1964) relied on a spatial representation along with the Euclidean distance metric in his unfolding model. In such an additive tree unfolding model (cf. De Soete, Furnas, DeSarbo, & Carroll, 1984), both the subjects and the choice objects are represented by the terminal nodes of an additive tree. The additive tree distances between the object nodes and the subject nodes determine the utilities of the objects for the subjects. The smaller the additive tree distance between the nodes corresponding to object j and subject i, the larger is the utility of object j for that subject. An example of such an additive tree representation is given in Figure 3.6. The tree displayed in Figure 3.6 has five terminal nodes: two nodes represent subjects (i and i′), and three nodes represent objects (j, k and l). The links of the tree are arbitrarily numbered

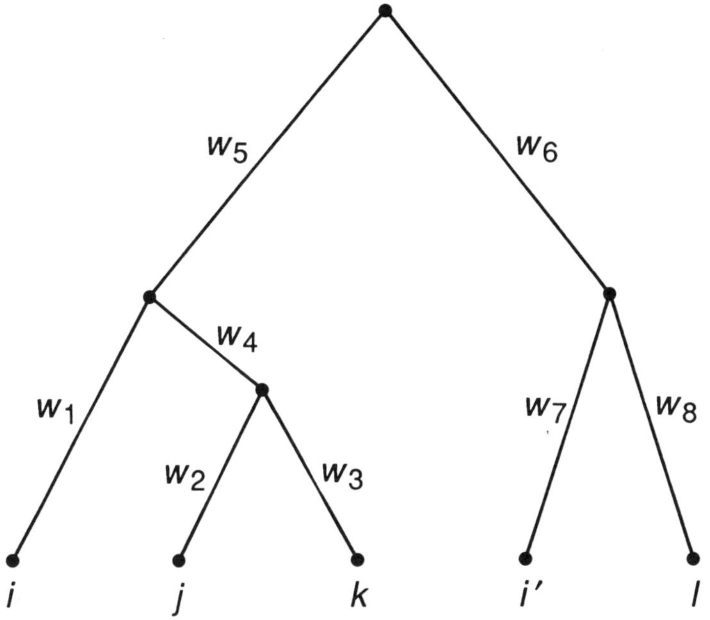

FIG. 3.6. Additive unfolding tree representing two subjects (i and i′) and three objects (j, k, l).

from 1 to 8, and the weight of a link q is denoted by w_q. The additive tree distance between the nodes representing subject i and object j is $w_1 + w_4 + w_2$, and the distance between i′ and k is $w_7 + w_6 + w_5 + w_4 + w_3$. The additive tree unfolding model proposed by Furnas (1980) is a deterministic model: both the topology of the tree and the weights assigned to the links are constant. The probabilistic additive tree unfolding model developed by Carroll and De Soete (1990), and presented in the next section, is based on a probabilistic formulation of this deterministic additive tree unfolding model. In the sequel, this model will be referred to as the PATU model (for probabilistic additive tree unfolding model).

Model Formulation

Given an additive tree with Q links and N + M terminal nodes representing N subjects and M choice objects, we can define an (N M) × Q indicator matrix **T** that indicates which links q (q = 1, . . . , Q) occur on the path between each subject node i (i = 1, . . . , N) and each object node j (j = 1, . . . , M) as follows: $t_{(ij)q}$, the element corresponding to row (i, j) and column q, is 1 if and only if link q is on the path connecting the nodes that represent subject i and object j, and 0 otherwise. The indicator matrix **T** that corresponds to the tree in Figure 3.6 is presented in Figure 3.7. In the PATU model, the weights attached to the links in the tree are no longer considered as constants (as in the deterministic additive tree unfolding model), but as random variables. Let **W** be the Q-dimensional random variable representing these branch weights. It is assumed that **W** follows a multivariate normal distribution

$$\mathbf{W} \sim N(\boldsymbol{\mu}, \boldsymbol{\Sigma}) , \tag{45}$$

with $\mu_q > 0$ for q = 1, . . . , Q. The distribution of the branch weights is here assumed to be identical for all subjects. Note, however, that **W** includes for each subject a component that is unique for that subject, namely the weight of the link connecting the subject node to the tree. The additive tree distance between the

Links

$$\begin{array}{c} \\ (i,j) \\ (i,k) \\ (i,l) \\ (i',j) \\ (i',k) \\ (i',l) \end{array} \begin{array}{c} \begin{array}{cccccccc} 1 & 2 & 3 & 4 & 5 & 6 & 7 & 8 \end{array} \\ \left[\begin{array}{cccccccc} 1 & 1 & 0 & 1 & 0 & 0 & 0 & 0 \\ 1 & 0 & 1 & 1 & 0 & 0 & 0 & 0 \\ 1 & 0 & 0 & 0 & 1 & 1 & 0 & 1 \\ 0 & 1 & 0 & 1 & 1 & 1 & 1 & 0 \\ 0 & 0 & 1 & 1 & 1 & 1 & 1 & 0 \\ 0 & 0 & 0 & 0 & 0 & 0 & 1 & 1 \end{array} \right] \end{array}$$

FIG. 3.7. Indicator matrix **T** associated with the additive unfolding tree in Figure 3.6.

nodes representing subject i and object j can now be written as $\mathbf{t}_{(ij)}\mathbf{W}$, where $\mathbf{t}_{(ij)}$ denotes the (ij)-th row of $\mathbf{T}$.

Each time a subject i is presented a pair of choice objects (j, k), a new sample $\mathbf{w}$ is drawn from $\mathbf{W}$, and subject i prefers object j to object k whenever the additive tree distance (in terms of the weights $\mathbf{w}$) between the nodes i and j is smaller than the additive tree distance (in terms of $\mathbf{w}$) between i and k, or whenever

$$\mathbf{t}_{(ij)}\mathbf{w} < \mathbf{t}_{(ik)}\mathbf{w} . \tag{46}$$

Thus, the probability that subject i prefers object j to k is

$$\begin{aligned} p_{ijk} &= \text{Prob}\{\mathbf{t}_{(ij)}\mathbf{W} < \mathbf{t}_{(ik)}\mathbf{W}\} \\ &= \text{Prob}\{(\mathbf{t}_{(ij)} - \mathbf{t}_{(ik)})\mathbf{W} < 0\} . \end{aligned} \tag{47}$$

Because of Equation 45, $(\mathbf{t}_{(ij)} - \mathbf{t}_{(ik)})\mathbf{W}$ is normally distributed,

$$(\mathbf{t}_{(ij)} - \mathbf{t}_{(ik)})\mathbf{W} \sim N((\mathbf{t}_{(ij)} - \mathbf{t}_{(ik)})\boldsymbol{\mu}, \delta^2_{ijk}) \tag{48}$$

with

$$\delta^2_{ijk} = (\mathbf{t}_{(ij)} - \mathbf{t}_{(ik)})\boldsymbol{\Sigma}(\mathbf{t}_{(ij)} - \mathbf{t}_{(ik)})' . \tag{49}$$

Note that δ_{ijk} is the generalized Euclidean distance between rows (ij) and (ik) of $\mathbf{T}$ in the metric $\boldsymbol{\Sigma}$. Equations 48–49 allow us to rewrite Equation 47 as

$$p_{ijk} = \Phi\left(\frac{(\mathbf{t}_{(ik)} - \mathbf{t}_{(ij)})\boldsymbol{\mu}}{\delta_{ijk}}\right) . \tag{50}$$

If we now assume, following the arguments in Edgell and Geisler (1980), that $\boldsymbol{\Sigma}$ is a diagonal matrix with diagonal elements

$$\sigma_{qq} = \alpha\mu_q , \tag{51}$$

where α is some positive constant, then δ^2_{ijk} reduces to

$$\delta^2_{ijk} = \alpha \sum_{q=1}^{Q} \mu_q(t_{(ij)q} - t_{(ik)q})^2 . \tag{52}$$

Equation 52 can be shown to be proportional to the additive tree distance in terms of the weights $\boldsymbol{\mu}$ between the nodes representing objects j and k (cf. Carroll & De Soete, 1990). (This property is easily verified in Figures 3.6 and 3.7.) If we write the additive tree distance in terms of $\boldsymbol{\mu}$ between any two nodes s and t as d_{st}, then we obtain

$$\delta^2_{ijk} = \alpha d_{jk} , \tag{53}$$

and Equation 50 becomes

$$p_{ijk} = \Phi\left(\frac{d_{ik} - d_{ij}}{\sqrt{\alpha d_{jk}}}\right) . \tag{54}$$

If we replace $\boldsymbol{\mu}$ by $\beta\boldsymbol{\mu}$, where β is an arbitrary positive constant, Equation 54 becomes

$$p_{\mathrm{ijk}} = \Phi\left(\frac{\beta(d_{\mathrm{ik}} - d_{\mathrm{ij}})}{\sqrt{\alpha\beta}\sqrt{d_{\mathrm{jk}}}}\right). \tag{55}$$

Without loss of generality, we can set β equal to α, so that Equation 54 reduces to

$$p_{\mathrm{ijk}} = \Phi\left(\frac{d_{\mathrm{ik}} - d_{\mathrm{ij}}}{\sqrt{d_{\mathrm{jk}}}}\right), \tag{56}$$

which defines the PATU model entirely in terms of additive tree distances. From Equation 56 it is apparent that the probability of preferring object j to object k is a strictly increasing function of the difference in tree distance between the subject node and the object nodes divided by a quantity that is a strictly increasing function of the distance between the two objects. Since δ_{ijk}, as defined in Equation 52, is a weighted Euclidean distance between rows (ij) and (ik) of $\mathbf{T}$, $\sqrt{d_{\mathrm{jk}}}$ is a distance metric and the PATU model is a moderate utility model of the form of Equation 10.

Parameter Estimation and Model Validation

Estimating the parameters of the PATU model is far more complicated than estimating the parameters in either the WV or WIP model. This is mainly because, in addition to the continuous parameters $\boldsymbol{\mu}$, the topology or discrete structure of the additive tree needs to be estimated. In principle, this involves a combinatorial optimization problem. However, as shown in the case of additive similarity trees by De Soete (1983a) and De Soete et al. (1984), such a combinatorial optimization problem can be approximated by a much more feasible continuous optimization problem.

Let $\mathbf{A}$ be a symmetric $(\mathrm{N} + \mathrm{M}) \times (\mathrm{N} + \mathrm{M})$ matrix containing the pairwise distances between all N + M terminal nodes of a probabilistic additive unfolding tree defined in terms of the weights $\boldsymbol{\mu}$; that is,

$$a_{\mathrm{st}} = \begin{cases} \text{distance between subject nodes s and t} & \text{iff s, t} \le \mathrm{N}, \\ \text{distance between subject node s and object node t} - \mathrm{N} & \text{iff s} \le \mathrm{N} \text{ and t} > \mathrm{N}, \\ \text{distance between object nodes s} - \mathrm{N} \text{ and t} - \mathrm{N} & \text{iff s, t} > \mathrm{N} \end{cases} \tag{57}$$

for s, t = 1, . . . , N + M. It is well known that such additive tree distances satisfy the so-called additive inequality or four-point condition:

$$a_{\mathrm{st}} + a_{\mathrm{uv}} \le \max(a_{\mathrm{su}} + a_{\mathrm{tv}}, a_{\mathrm{sv}} + a_{\mathrm{tu}}) \tag{58}$$

for all s, t, u, v = 1, . . . , N + M (cf., e.g., Dobson, 1974). This additive inequality is a necessary and sufficient condition for additive tree distances. This implies that whenever a distance matrix **A** satisfies Equation 58, it uniquely defines an additive tree, both in terms of its topology and the weights attached to the links. In fact, it is fairly easy to derive the tree topology and the branch weights from a matrix **A** that satisfies Equation 58 (cf. Dobson, 1974). Therefore, in order to obtain maximum likelihood estimates of the parameters in the PATU model, it suffices to maximize the likelihood function (Equation 33) with

$$p_{ijk} = \Phi\left(\frac{a_{i(N+k)} - a_{i(N+j)}}{\sqrt{a_{(N+j)(N+k)}}}\right), \tag{59}$$

with respect to the distance matrix **A** subject to the constraint that **A** satisfies Equation (58). This constrained (continuous) optimization problem can be solved by means of a mathematical programming technique, which is described and illustrated in Carroll and De Soete (1990).

Because of the presence of discrete parameters, it is not possible to state the degrees of freedom of the PATU model. This also implies that we cannot use a Likelihood Ratio Test to statistically compare the goodness of fit of the PATU model with the goodness of fit of a null model (as described in the second section), nor can we adopt any of the information criteria such as the AIC statistic. As an alternative approach to testing the goodness of fit of the PATU model statistically, we can resort to a Monte Carlo significance testing procedure proposed by Hope (1968). Denoting the maximum likelihood estimates of the parameters in the PATU model as derived from the data by $\hat{\mathbf{A}}$, this procedure involves randomly sampling K − 1 Monte Carlo data sets from the PATU model, with $\hat{\mathbf{A}}$ as population parameters and using the same numbers of replications F_{ijk} as in the real data. For each Monte Carlo data set, $-2\ log\ (\hat{L}_{PATU}/\hat{L}_{NULL})$ is computed, where $\hat{L}_{PATU}$ and $\hat{L}_{NULL}$, respectively, denote the maximum of the likelihood function under the PATU model and the null model. The null hypothesis that the PATU model gives an equally good account of the data as the saturated null model is rejected at significance level π, when the value of $-2\ log\ (\hat{L}_{PATU}/\hat{L}_{NULL})$ for the observed data exceeds $K(1 - \pi)$ of the values of $-2\ log\ (\hat{L}_{PATU}/\hat{L}_{NULL})$ for the Monte Carlo samples. A minimal value of K when using a significance level of $\pi = 0.05$ is 20, whereas larger values yield a more powerful test (see Hope, 1968).

A LATENT CLASS APPROACH

Introduction

As mentioned in the first section, the WV, WIP, and PATU models require replicated paired comparisons data in order to enable reliable parameter estimation. However, it is often not possible to obtain within-subject replications for each pair of choice objects. Suppose, instead, that the N subjects are presented all $\binom{M}{2}$ pairs of M objects only once. The data obtained in such a situation can be coded by means of indicator variables as follows:

$$y_{ijk} = \begin{cases} 1 & \text{iff subject i prefers object j to object k,} \\ 0 & \text{otherwise.} \end{cases}$$

In the sequel, the data of subject i will be denoted by the M(M − 1)/2-component column vector $\mathbf{y}_i = (y_{i21}, y_{i31}, y_{i32}, \ldots, y_{iM(M-1)})'$, and the total data set will be denoted by the N × $\binom{M}{2}$ matrix $\mathbf{Y} = (\mathbf{y}_1, \ldots, \mathbf{y}_N)'$. If we want to apply any of the models presented in the previous sections to such data, we must either treat the N subjects as replications of each other or group the N subjects into a small number of homogeneous groups. In the first approach, the N rows of **Y** are considered as replications of a single subject, and f_{1jk} and F_{1jk} are defined as

$$f_{1jk} = \sum_{i=1}^{N} y_{ijk}, \qquad F_{1jk} = N\ . \tag{60}$$

If indeed the subjects can be treated as replications of each other, this approach leads to a very parsimonious representation of **Y.** However, if there *are* some systematic differences among the N subjects, then the independence assumption on which Equation 33 is based will be violated and the resulting analysis will be incomplete, if not totally misleading. In the second approach, the subjects are a priori clustered into a small number of homogeneous groups, and the subjects within the same group are treated as replications of each other. Any of the previous models can then be applied to these reduced (replicated) data. Unfortunately, it is often not possible to partition the subjects into homogeneous subsets on an a priori basis.

An alternative approach, recently elaborated by De Soete (1990), extends the models in previous sections to enable simultaneous estimation of the homogeneous groups *and* the choice model parameters. This approach is based on a latent class formulation (Lazarsfeld & Henry, 1968) and is outlined in the next section.

General Formulation

Suppose there exist T (T ≪ N) latent classes or subpopulations. Each subject i (i = 1, . . . , N) belongs to one and only one latent class t (1 ≤ t ≤ T), but we do not know in advance the class to which a subject belongs. We now want to model the preference data for the T classes by means of a moderate utility model that incorporates some parameters that can capture the differences among the T classes. Thus, in addition to a set of parameters that are common for the T classes, denoted τ, the latent class choice model incorporates for each class t a set of class-specific parameters ζ_t. Consequently, $\boldsymbol{\theta}$, the vector comprising all the parameters in the choice model, now consists of the elements in

$$\tau \cup \bigcup_{t=1}^{T} \zeta_t \,. \tag{61}$$

The (unconditional) probability that a subject i belongs to latent class t is denoted λ_t, with, of course,

$$\sum_{t=1}^{T} \lambda_t = 1 \,. \tag{62}$$

The distribution of the data of a subject i can now be specified as a finite mixture of product-binomial distributions

$$\phi(\mathbf{y}_i|\boldsymbol{\theta}, \boldsymbol{\lambda}) = \sum_{t=1}^{T} \lambda_t \psi(\mathbf{y}_i|\tau, \zeta_t) \tag{63}$$

where $\boldsymbol{\lambda}$ is defined as $(\lambda_1, \ldots, \lambda_T)'$ and

$$\psi(\mathbf{y}_i|\tau, \zeta_t) = \prod_{j=2}^{M} \prod_{k=1}^{j-1} p_{tjk}^{y_{ijk}} (1 - p_{tjk})^{(1-y_{ijk})} \,, \tag{64}$$

where p_{tjk} denotes the probability that a subject in latent class t prefers choice object j to k.

For the latent class WV model, a separate vector is provided for each latent class. The terminus of the vector for latent class t is multivariate normally distributed with mean $\boldsymbol{\mu}_t$ and variance $\boldsymbol{\Sigma}_t$. The probability p_{tjk} is then defined as

$$p_{tjk} = \Phi\left(\frac{(\mathbf{x}_j - \mathbf{x}_k)'\boldsymbol{\mu}_t}{\sqrt{(\mathbf{x}_j - \mathbf{x}_k)'\boldsymbol{\Sigma}_t(\mathbf{x}_j - \mathbf{x}_k)}}\right) . \tag{65}$$

In this case, τ and ζ_t are defined as

$$\tau = \{\mathbf{x}_1, \cdots, \mathbf{x}_M\} \qquad \zeta_t = \{\boldsymbol{\mu}_t, \boldsymbol{\Sigma}_t\} \,.$$

In the latent class choice model based on the WIP model, each latent class is represented by a separate ideal point. The mean and variance of the ideal point for latent class t are $\boldsymbol{\mu}_t$ and $\boldsymbol{\Sigma}_t$, respectively. The choice probabilities predicted by the latent class WIP model are

$$p_{tjk} = \Phi\left(\frac{(\mathbf{x}_k'\mathbf{x}_k - \mathbf{x}_j'\mathbf{x}_j) - 2(\mathbf{x}_k - \mathbf{x}_j)'\boldsymbol{\mu}_t}{2\sqrt{\mathbf{x}_j - \mathbf{x}_k)'\boldsymbol{\Sigma}_t(\mathbf{x}_j - \mathbf{x}_k)}}\right) , \tag{66}$$

and the parameter sets τ and ζ_t consist of the same elements as in the latent class WV model. Finally, in the latent class PATU model, each latent class is represented by a separate terminal node. The probability that a subject belonging to latent class t prefers object j k is

$$p_{tjk} = \Phi\left(\frac{d_{tk} - d_{tj}}{\sqrt{d_{jk}}}\right), \tag{67}$$

where d_{tk} denotes the additive tree distance between the nodes corresponding to latent class t and object k, and d_{jk} denotes the additive tree distance between the nodes representing objects j and k. Here, the parameter sets τ and ζ_t are defined as

$$\tau = \{d_{jk} | 1 \le j < k \le M\} \qquad \zeta_t = \{d_{t1}, \cdots, d_{tM}\} .$$

Once estimates $\hat{\boldsymbol{\theta}}$ and $\hat{\boldsymbol{\lambda}}$ are obtained of the model parameter vectors $\boldsymbol{\theta}$ and $\boldsymbol{\lambda}$, the a posteriori probability that a subject i belongs to latent class t can be calculated by means of Bayes' theorem. This a posteriori probability, written as $h_{it}(\hat{\boldsymbol{\theta}}, \hat{\boldsymbol{\lambda}})$, is

$$\begin{aligned} h_{it}(\hat{\boldsymbol{\theta}}, \hat{\boldsymbol{\lambda}}) &= \text{Prob}\,(t|\mathbf{y}_i, \hat{\boldsymbol{\theta}}, \hat{\boldsymbol{\lambda}}) \\ &= \frac{\text{Prob}\,(t|\hat{\boldsymbol{\theta}}, \hat{\boldsymbol{\lambda}}) \times \text{Prob}\,(\mathbf{y}_i|t, \hat{\boldsymbol{\theta}}, \hat{\boldsymbol{\lambda}})}{\text{Prob}\,(\mathbf{y}_i|\hat{\boldsymbol{\theta}}, \hat{\boldsymbol{\lambda}})} \\ &= \frac{\lambda_t \psi(\mathbf{y}_i|\hat{\tau}, \hat{\zeta}_t)}{\phi(\mathbf{y}_i|\hat{\boldsymbol{\theta}}, \hat{\boldsymbol{\lambda}})} . \end{aligned} \tag{68}$$

A subject can then be assigned to the class for which the a posteriori membership probability is the largest. Thus, as a result of the analysis, we obtain, in addition to a representation of the preference structure of the T classes according to either the WV, WIP, or PATU model, a (fuzzy or probabilistic) clustering of the N subjects into T homogeneous groups.

Parameter Estimation and Model Validation

Maximum likelihood estimates of $\boldsymbol{\theta}$ and $\boldsymbol{\lambda}$ can be obtained by maximizing the likelihood

$$L_2(\boldsymbol{\theta}, \boldsymbol{\lambda}|\mathbf{Y}) = \prod_{i=1}^{N} \phi(\mathbf{y}_i|\boldsymbol{\theta}, \boldsymbol{\lambda}) \tag{69}$$

with respect to $\boldsymbol{\theta}$ and $\boldsymbol{\lambda}$ subject to Equation 62. Like most estimation problems with finite mixture models (cf. McLachlan & Basford, 1988), this optimization problem is most easily solved by means of a so-called EM Algorithm (Dempster, Laird, & Rubin, 1977). The EM algorithm for maximizing Equation 69 alternates between two steps: an E-step (expectation step) in which new provisional estimates of the conditional class membership probabilities are calculated based on provisional estimates of $\boldsymbol{\theta}$ and $\boldsymbol{\lambda}$, and an M-step (maximization step) in which new estimates of $\boldsymbol{\theta}$ and $\boldsymbol{\lambda}$ are computed on the basis of these provisional estimates of the conditional class membership probabilities. Let $\boldsymbol{\theta}^{(0)}$ and $\boldsymbol{\lambda}^{(0)}$ denote some initial estimates of $\boldsymbol{\theta}$ and $\boldsymbol{\lambda}$. Then new estimates of the class membership probabilities are obtained by evaluating $h_{it}(\boldsymbol{\theta}^{(0)}, \boldsymbol{\lambda}^{(0)})$ (cf. Equation 68). Defining (in analogy to f_{ijk} and F_{ijk})

$$f_{tjk} = \sum_{i=1}^{N} y_{ijk} h_{it}(\boldsymbol{\theta}^{(0)}, \boldsymbol{\lambda}^{(0)})$$

and

$$F_{tjk} = \sum_{i=1}^{N} h_{it}(\boldsymbol{\theta}^{(0)}, \boldsymbol{\lambda}^{(0)}) ,$$

we can obtain new estimates of $\boldsymbol{\theta}$ and $\boldsymbol{\lambda}$ in the M-step by maximizing

$$\sum_{t=1}^{T} \sum_{j=2}^{M} \sum_{k=1}^{j-1} [f_{tjk} \, log \, p_{tjk} + (F_{tjk} - f_{tjk}) \, log \, (1 - p_{tjk})]$$

by means of the Fisher scoring method outlined in the second section, and a new estimate of $\boldsymbol{\lambda}$ is computed by

$$\hat{\lambda} = \frac{\sum_{i=1}^{N} h_{it}(\boldsymbol{\theta}^{(0)}, \boldsymbol{\lambda}^{(0)})}{N} .$$

These new estimates of $\boldsymbol{\theta}$ and $\boldsymbol{\lambda}$ are then used to update the provisional estimates of the conditional class membership probabilities. These updated conditional class membership probabilities are subsequently used to arrive at new estimates of $\boldsymbol{\theta}$ and $\boldsymbol{\lambda}$, and other terms. This iterative process continues until the likelihood function (Equation 69) cannot be improved any more. Further details of this EM algorithm can be found in De Soete (1990) (see also De Soete & DeSarbo, 1991).

When applying latent class choice models to empirical data, we do not know in advance T, the required number of latent classes. The usual way for deciding on the required number of latent classes involves testing whether a solution with T + 1 latent classes gives a significantly better fit than a solution with T latent classes. If a (T + 1)-class solution does not significantly improve the T-class solution, T classes suffice to describe the data adequately. Unfortunately, as in most mixture distribution problems, the relevant likelihood ratio statistic for testing T versus T + 1 latent classes is *not* asymptotically distributed as a chi-square random variable with known degrees of freedom (McLachlan & Basford, 1988). However, instead of a classical Likelihood Ratio Test, one can apply the Monte Carlo significance testing procedure mentioned in the fourth section. An illustration of this approach is presented in De Soete (1990).

CONCLUSION

We reviewed some probabilistic models for paired comparisons data. All the models discussed are moderate utility models. In addition, they incorporate parameters for modeling differences between subjects or homogeneous groups of subjects. Finally, all the models are based on some kind of multidimensional representation of the choice objects. In the wandering vector model and the wandering ideal point models, a continuous spatial representation is used, whereas the probabilistic additive tree unfolding model is based on a discrete tree representation. For all models, however, this multidimensional representation of the choice objects is not required a priori but is derived from the paired comparisons data. For each model, we outlined an algorithm for obtaining maximum likelihood estimates of the model parameters, and we discussed methods for evaluating the goodness of fit of the model. In the last section, we showed how these probabilistic choice models can be extended in a latent class framework.

4 Multivariate Models of Preference and Choice

Ulf Böckenholt
University of Illinois at Urbana-Champaign

INTRODUCTION

This chapter presents a multivariate approach toward modeling preferential choice with a particular emphasis on the method of paired comparisons. Because the method of paired comparisons rests on a minimal number of assumptions, it proved to be applicable across a wide range of disciplines and, consequently, stimulated important work in the areas of experimental design, nonparametric statistics, as well as measurement and scaling. In general, this technique requires that pairs of objects are presented either simultaneously or successively to judges whose task is to indicate which member of the pair they prefer on a specific criterion. The criterion may be overall preference or any attribute that characterizes the choice objects. Judges are not always consistent when making these comparisons. During the last 80 years, several mathematical models were suggested for describing paired comparison responses on a single attribute and, in particular, explaining inconsistencies in pairwise judgments under seemingly identical conditions. David (1988) provides a recent comprehensive review of this research. In this chapter, multivariate counterparts of the proposed models are developed that describe paired comparison judgments with respect to multiple attributes.

In a *multivariate* paired comparison task, information about the choice pairs is obtained by asking subjects to compare objects with respect to *several* criteria. For example, in the first reported application of a multivariate paired comparison experiment, pharmaceutical products for children were scaled regarding their color, odor, and taste (Nakagami, 1961). Although multivariate paired comparison data may be examined by analyzing separately each set of paired comparison data corresponding to a criterion, such an approach neglects the correlations between the individual responses. These correlations may contain important information about judgmental processes underlying the comparison task. In particular, relationships among the paired comparison responses can be determined even if the sample as a whole is indifferent about the presented choice alternatives or the corresponding variations in the judged attributes. In addition to the analysis of the associations among the responses, scaling solutions determined for each paired comparison criterion may be projected onto the scaling representation obtained from the overall preference judgment. Thus, responses to an attribute may not only distinguish the objects but may also explain preference differences among them. As a result, a multivariate treatment of paired comparison responses may clarify interpretations regarding the perception of physical and psychological characteristics of the objects. Several examples will be presented that illustrate the usefulness of a multivariate analysis.

This chapter is organized as follows. First, several frequently applied probabilistic paired comparison models for univariate responses are reviewed. In particular, the Bradley-Terry-Luce model (BTL), Thurstone's Case V and Case III, and generalized Thurstonian models are presented. Detailed discussions about the latter class of models can be found in I. Böckenholt and Gaul (1986), Bradley (1984), DeSarbo, DeSoete, & Jedidi (1987), DeSoete and Carroll (1983), DeSoete, Carroll, and DeSarbo (1986), Heiser and DeLeeuw (1981), and Takane (1980, 1987). Next, these models are extended to handle multivariate paired comparison data. Because there is no unique multivariate extension of these paired comparison models, several multivariate formulations are considered and compared with each other. Estimation and inference issues are also examined.

BRIEF REVIEW OF UNIVARIATE CHOICE MODELS

Because the method of paired comparison is of great practical simplicity, it has led to many models describing the stochastic process underlying the paired comparison judgment. In the following selective review of paired comparison models, it is assumed that $t \geq 2$ distinct objects, $O_1, O_2, \ldots, O_t$, are presented pairwise to a group of judges. A judge is instructed to select the object of the pair O_i and O_j that is superior based on a prescribed criterion α. The outcome of the selection is written $(O_i \rightarrow O_j; \alpha)$, which denotes that object O_i is chosen over object O_j with respect to criterion α. In addition, it is assumed that each judge compares only one pair of objects. Thus, n_{ij} independent decisions are observed for each pairwise comparison with respect to the criterion α. Approaches based on comparisons of several pairs of objects by a judge are discussed in the last section.

The Bradley-Terry-Luce (BTL) Model

The paired comparison model suggested by Bradley and Terry (1952) and Luce (1959) provides a unidimensional representation of aggregated paired comparison data. The probability that object O_i is chosen over object O_j with respect to the criterion α is given by

$$P(O_i \rightarrow O_j; \alpha) = \frac{\pi_{i\alpha}}{\pi_{i\alpha} + \pi_{j\alpha}} = \{1 + exp -(ln\ \pi_{i\alpha} - ln\ \pi_{j\alpha})\}^{-1}$$

where $\pi_{i\alpha}$ represents the worth of the object on an underlying continuum that is relevant for the criterion α. The worth parameters are estimated under the constraint

$$\sum_{i=1}^{t} \pi_{i\alpha} = 1$$

and are nonnegative. Thus, $\binom{t}{2}$ pairwise choice probabilities are summarized by $t - 1$ parameters. The BTL model has received considerable attention in connection with the analysis of categorical data. Log-linear representations of the BTL model and various extensions of it have been suggested by Fienberg and Larntz (1976), Fienberg (1979), Koehler and Ridpath (1982), and Van Putten (1982). Similarly, Luce's choice axiom for modeling confusion data has also been formulated as a log-linear model (Smith, 1982). These representations of both the BTL model and the choice axiom have strongly profited from the work on log-linear models. In particular, maximum likelihood theory underlying log-linear models provides straightforward solutions to estimation and inference problems of these models.

However, by now it is well-known that the BTL model is too restrictive for adequately describing choices between similar choice alternatives (Debreu, 1960; Luce, 1977a, Rumelhart & Greeno, 1971; Tversky & Russo, 1969). For example, similarity relations between alternatives may lead subjects to treat them as substantially the same, and this in turn may lead to violations of the simple scalability assumption underlying the BTL model. In contrast, Thurstone's random utility model (Thurstone, 1927a) takes into account perceived dependencies between choice objects. Consequently, this model is richer in its descriptive features than the BTL model. Different members of this class of models are discussed in the next section.

Thurstone's Law of Comparative Judgment

Thurstone (1927a) assumed that judgments about an object O_i with respect to the criterion α are determined by discriminal processes and can be represented by a random variable $\nu_{i\alpha}$,

$$\nu_{i\alpha} = \mu_{i\alpha} + \epsilon_{i\alpha} ,$$

where $\mu_{i\alpha}$ is called the *affective value* of object i and corresponds to the modal response of a subject or a homogeneous group of subjects. Random components of the discriminal process are represented by the random variable $\epsilon_{i\alpha}$. Thurstone assumed that $\epsilon_{i\alpha}$ is normally distributed with mean 0 and variance $\sigma^2_{i\alpha}$. (Luce, 1977b provides an extensive discussion of these and other model features.) The probability of choosing object O_i over object O_j with respect to the criterion α is given by the difference process

$$P(O_i \rightarrow O_j, \alpha) = \frac{1}{\sqrt{2\pi}\,\sigma_{ij\alpha}} \int_0^\infty exp\left\{-\frac{1}{2}\left(\frac{u - (\mu_{i\alpha} - \mu_{j\alpha})}{\sigma_{ij\alpha}}\right)^2\right\} du ,$$

and the standard deviation of the mean comparison is

$$\sigma_{ij\alpha} = \sqrt{\sigma^2_{i\alpha} + \sigma^2_{j\alpha} - 2\,\kappa_{ij\alpha}\sigma_{i\alpha}\sigma_{j\alpha}} ,$$

with the correlation between the pair $(\epsilon_{i\alpha}, \epsilon_{j\alpha})$ denoted by $\kappa_{ij\alpha}$. To obtain the integral of the standard normal density function, we introduce a change of variable with $y = (u - (\mu_{i\alpha} - \mu_{j\alpha}))/\sigma_{ij\alpha}$, and

$$P(O_i \rightarrow O_j; \alpha) = \frac{1}{\sqrt{2\pi}} \int_{-(\mu_{i\alpha}-\mu_{j\alpha})/\sigma_{ij\alpha}}^\infty exp\left(-\frac{1}{2}y^2\right) dy$$

$$= \Phi\left(\frac{\mu_{i\alpha} - \mu_{j\alpha}}{\sigma_{ij\alpha}}\right) ,$$

where Φ denotes the standard normal distribution function. Because this paired comparison representation is not identifiable in its full form, several constraints on the joint distribution of the pair $(\epsilon_{i\alpha}, \epsilon_{j\alpha})$ were suggested by Thurstone. Two of these constraints he termed Case III and Case V. In Case III, the correlations are constrained to be equal for all choice pairs, however, the standard deviations, $\sigma_{i\alpha}$, may differ. Case V posits that, in addition to the equal correlation constraint of Case III, the variances are restricted to be equal for all choice objects. Both constraints reduce considerably the number of parameters to be estimated. In Case V, $t - 1$ scale values have to be determined; in Case III, $t - 1$ scale vales and $t - 1$ variances have to be estimated.

Halff (1976) showed that $\sigma_{ij\alpha}$ satisfies the metric axioms required of a distance measure. Consequently, the discriminability parameter $\sigma_{ij\alpha}$ can be interpreted to measure, at least partially, the dissimilarity between the objects O_i and O_j. Sjöberg (1980) obtained empirical support for this interpretation by reporting a strong relationship between independently elicited similarity judgments and $\sigma_{ij\alpha}$. These findings led to a class of new models, the so-called generalized Thurstonian models, which facilitate a multidimensional scaling of the choice objects. Three exemplars of this class are reviewed here. For simplicity, individual differences are assumed to be negligible.

Factorial Model

The "factorial" model was developed by Takane (1980) and Heiser and DeLeeuw (1981). These authors suggested approximating the covariance matrix $\mathbf{\Sigma}_\alpha$ with elements $(\kappa_{ij\alpha}\, \sigma_{i\alpha}\, \sigma_{j\alpha})$, by a matrix $\mathbf{X}_\alpha$, $\mathbf{\Sigma}_\alpha = \mathbf{X}'\mathbf{X}$ of rank k ($k \leq t$). Thus, the discriminability parameter is now represented as

$$\sigma_{ij\alpha} = \sqrt{(\mathbf{x}_{i\alpha} - \mathbf{x}_{j\alpha})'(\mathbf{x}_{i\alpha} - \mathbf{x}_{j\alpha})}\ ,$$

where $\mathbf{x}_{i\alpha}$ is the i-th column vector of the matrix of object coordinates $\mathbf{X}_\alpha$, and $\sigma_{ij\alpha}$ can be interpreted as the distance between objects O_i and O_j in a k-dimensional Euclidean space.

Wandering Vector Model

The wandering vector model introduced by Carroll (1980) and DeSoete and Carroll (1983) is a special case of the factorial model (De Soete, 1983b). This model facilitates a simultaneous representation of objects and subjects in a joint space. It assumes that the probability of preferring object O_i over object O_j can be modeled by additionally constraining the mean scale value $\mu_{i\alpha} = \mathbf{x}_{i\alpha}'\mathbf{v}_\alpha$. Thus, a scale value is obtained as a linear function of the object coordinates, where $\mathbf{v}_\alpha$ is the mean terminus of a k-dimensional random vector $\mathbf{u}_\alpha$ that is normally distributed with an identity covariance matrix. A respondent samples a vector realization $\mathbf{u}_\alpha$ and prefers O_i over O_j when $\mathbf{x}_{i\alpha}'\mathbf{u}_\alpha > \mathbf{x}_{j\alpha}'\mathbf{u}_\alpha$.

Wandering Ideal Point Model

The wandering ideal point model proposed by I. Böckenholt and Gaul (1986) and DeSoete et al. (1986) rests on assumptions similar to those of the vector model. This model assumes that $\mathbf{v}_\alpha$ is the mean of a k-dimensional random ideal point vector $\mathbf{u}_\alpha$. A respondent samples an ideal point realization $\mathbf{u}_\alpha$ and prefers O_i over O_j if the scale value of O_i is closer to the sampled ideal point; that is,

$$(\mathbf{x}_{i\alpha} - \mathbf{u}_\alpha)'\ \mathbf{W}_\alpha(\mathbf{x}_{i\alpha} - \mathbf{u}_\alpha) < (\mathbf{x}_{j\alpha} - \mathbf{u}_\alpha)'\ \mathbf{W}_\alpha(\mathbf{x}_{j\alpha} - \mathbf{u}_\alpha)\,,$$

where $\mathbf{W}_\alpha$ is a $k \times k$ diagonal weight matrix.

This presentation of the BTL, Thurstonian, and generalized Thurstonian models only highlights some of the characteristic features of these models. For more extensive discussions and applications of these models, Chapters 2 and 5 should be consulted. The next section deals with the multivariate extension of these paired comparison models.

MULTIVARIATE PREFERENCE MODELS

In many paired comparison experiments, it is common to collect preference judgments for several object attributes. For example, in a large-scale product optimization study (Böckenholt, 1988) consumers were asked the following three paired comparison questions: (a) Which cigarette do you prefer with respect to aroma? (b) Which cigarette do you prefer with respect to taste? (c) Which cigarette do you prefer with respect to lightness? One reason for the use of paired comparisons is that they may yield more accurate results than other techniques, such as rating scales. For example, respondents may be asked to rate their degree of preference on a scale ranging from "dislike extremely" to "like extremely." Although this method of recording the desirability of object attributes is convenient and easy for the respondent to understand, it has the disadvantage of mingling differences in the respondent's interpretation of the category labels with actual variation in preference for the object samples. More specifically, there is considerable evidence that rating scales are not interpersonally comparable and that respondents may define the categories relative to the type of stimuli they are rating (Farley, Katz, & Lehmann, 1978). This lack of invariance of rating scales limits their usefulness in preference studies involving objects with heterogeneous attributes. However, these sources of extraneous variation disappear when pairwise judgments are substituted for absolute judgments. Thus, the use of multivariate paired comparisons seems more appropriate because it may lead to more accurate judgments and to data that are comparable over different choice sets and samples.

In a complete multivariate paired comparison task, all possible pairs of objects are compared with respect to each of p criteria. Because every respondent gives a binary response, one may observe 2^p possible preference patterns per object pair. For instance, if the number of criteria is 2, then the preference patterns {(ii), (ij), (ji), (jj)} may be observed. The preference pattern (ii) denotes that O_i is chosen over O_j with respect to both criteria, the pattern (ij) indicates that O_i is chosen over O_j with respect to the first criterion, and that O_j is chosen over O_i with respect to the second criterion, and so forth.

The response vector $\mathbf{s} = (s_1, s_2, \ldots, s_p)$ represents one of the 2^p possible preference patterns, where $s_\alpha = \mathrm{i}$ if O_i is chosen over O_j and $s_\alpha = \mathrm{j}$ if O_j is chosen over O_i with respect to the criterion α. To introduce the multivariate approach, we now consider the simplest case (p = 2) is in some detail. The letters α and β are used to denote two different judgmental criteria, and $P(\mathbf{s} = \mathrm{ii}|\mathrm{ij})$ denotes the probability that O_i is chosen over O_j with respect to both criteria.

If the responses to both criteria are independent, then the joint probabilities can be computed as the product of the marginal or paired comparison probabilities,

$$P(\mathbf{s} = \mathrm{ii}|\mathrm{ij}) = P(O_i \rightarrow O_j;\, \alpha)P(O_i \rightarrow O_j;\, \beta) .$$

Clearly, the assumption of independence between responses is rather restrictive. Therefore several approaches are presented to model the associations among the responses. Models for analyzing associations between responses in multivariate paired comparison experiments were first suggested by Davidson and Bradley (1969, 1970). Their formulation of a multivariate paired comparison model is based on the Farlie-Gumbel-Morgenstern approach (Johnson & Kotz, 1975,

1977) and coincides with Bahadur's (1961) second-order approximation to multivariate distributions of binary random variables. As a result of their parametrization, the paired comparison data corresponding to each of the p attributes are described by BTL models. Davidson and Bradley selected the phi coefficient of correlation, φ, for a 2×2 table as a measure of association between two response variables. An extension of their approach to a choice situation that allows for ties was subsequently presented by Davoodzadeh and Beaver (1983). In the next section Bahadur's second-order approximation is adopted to develop a multivariate extension of Thurstonian models.

Fienberg and Larntz (1976) proposed a log-linear representation of the BTL model that simplifies estimation and test procedures because well-developed maximum likelihood methods can be applied. In the log-linear approach, the BTL model is fitted to the distribution obtained for each of the p attributes, and the associations among the responses are modeled simultaneously. The measure of association simplifies to a log-odds ratio in the case of two attributes. Beaver (1983) extended this approach to choice situations where subjects are allowed to express their indifference. Böckenholt (1988) presented a general logistic framework for analyzing multivariate paired comparison data (with ties) that facilitates testing design related effects, including order effects within object pairs, and group treatment effects.

In the following sections, multivariate extensions of the univariate paired comparison model reviewed in the previous section are presented. First, a multivariate formulation of the BTL model in a log-linear framework is outlined. This presentation draws on the work by Böckenholt (1988) and Fienberg and Larntz (1976). Because the BTL model is limited in its range of applicability, multivariate versions of Thurstonian models are discussed (Böckenholt, 1990). The first multivariate version assumes that the joint distribution of the responses is multivariate normal, and the second extension is based on Bahadur's (1961) second-order approximation of multivariate discrete distributions. Finally, the different multivariate approaches are compared regarding their various model features.

A Multivariate Extension of the BTL Model

For the following development of a multivariate BTL model, the simplest case with two objects and two judgmental criteria is considered and then extended to the case of t objects and p criteria. According to the BTL model, the joint probability $P_I(\mathbf{s} = \text{ii}|\text{ij})$ under independence for two criteria is given by

$$P_I(\mathbf{s} = \text{ii}|\text{ij}) = \frac{\pi_{i\alpha}}{\pi_{i\alpha} + \pi_{j\alpha}} \frac{\pi_{i\beta}}{\pi_{i\beta} + \pi_{j\beta}},$$

where the subscript I denotes that the responses are independent.

It is convenient to express $P_I(\mathbf{s} = \text{ii}|\text{ij})$ in logit form by using the transformation (Bock, 1975)

$$P_I(\mathbf{s} = \text{ii}|\text{ij}) = \frac{exp\,\{z_I(\mathbf{s} = \text{ii}|\text{ij})\}}{exp\,\{z_I(\mathbf{s} = \text{ii}|\text{ij})\} + exp\,\{z_I(\mathbf{s} = \text{ij}|\text{ij})\} + exp\,\{z_I(\mathbf{s} = \text{ji}|\text{ij})\} + exp\,\{z_I(\mathbf{s} = \text{jj}|\text{ij})\}},$$

where

$$z_I(\mathbf{s} = \text{ii}|\text{ij}) + z_I(\mathbf{s} = \text{ij}|\text{ij}) + z_I(\mathbf{s} = \text{ji}|\text{ij}) + z_I(\mathbf{s} = \text{jj}|\text{ij}) = 0\ .$$

Consequently, the relation between the worth parameters $\pi_{i\alpha}$, $\pi_{j\alpha}$, and $z_I(\mathbf{s}\,|\text{ij})$ has the simple form

$$z_I(\mathbf{s}|\text{ij}) = \frac{1}{2}\,(ln\ \pi_{s_\alpha \alpha} - ln\ \pi_{s_{\alpha'} \alpha}) + \frac{1}{2}\,(ln\ \pi_{s_\alpha \beta} - ln\ \pi_{s_{\alpha'} \beta})\ ,$$

where s_α = i or j when $s_{\alpha'}$ = j or i, respectively. The logistic approach provides a straightforward way for modeling the associations between the responses for the two criteria. The measure of association is the cross-product or log odds ratio, which is computed as

$$\tau_{ij\alpha\beta} = ln\left(\frac{P(\mathbf{s} = \text{ii}|\text{ij})P(\mathbf{s} = \text{jj}|\text{ij})}{P(\mathbf{s} = \text{ij}|\text{ij})P(\mathbf{s} = \text{ji}|\text{ij})}\right).$$

Note that the log-odds ratio is not dependent on the marginal distribution of the preference probabilities. It has a clear interpretation and runs from $-\infty$ to ∞. However, it can be easily standardized such that its upper/lower bound is ± 1. For example, Yule (1900) suggested the transformation

$$\frac{exp\ (\tau_{ij\alpha\beta}) - 1}{exp\ (\tau_{ij\alpha\beta}) + 1}\ .$$

The result of this transformation can be interpreted as the probability that O_i (O_j) is preferred over O_j (O_i) with respect to both criteria minus the probability that O_i (O_j) is preferred with respect to the first criterion but not the second criterion. Moreover, simulation studies by Digby (1983) and Becker and Clogg (1988) demonstrated that this transformation may produce coefficients that are quite similar to a tetrachoric correlation coefficient.

The log-odds ratio can be easily incorporated in the multinomial logit representation as a further additive component. The multivariate model for two criteria and the choice pair O_i and O_j is written as

$$z(\mathbf{s} = \text{ii}|\text{ij}) = \frac{1}{2}(ln\ \pi_{i\alpha} - ln\ \pi_{j\alpha}) + \frac{1}{2}(ln\ \pi_{i\beta} - ln\ \pi_{j\beta}) + \frac{1}{4}\,\tau_{ij\alpha\beta}\ ,$$

$$z(\mathbf{s} = \text{ij}|\text{ij}) = \frac{1}{2}(ln\ \pi_{i\alpha} - ln\ \pi_{j\alpha}) - \frac{1}{2}(ln\ \pi_{i\beta} - ln\ \pi_{j\beta}) - \frac{1}{4}\,\tau_{ij\alpha\beta}\ ,$$

$$z(\mathbf{s} = \mathrm{ji}|\mathrm{ij}) = -\frac{1}{2}(ln\ \pi_{i\alpha} - ln\ \pi_{j\alpha}) + \frac{1}{2}(ln\ \pi_{i\beta} - ln\ \pi_{j\beta}) - \frac{1}{4}\tau_{ij\alpha\beta}\ ,$$

$$z(\mathbf{s} = \mathrm{jj}|\mathrm{ij}) = -\frac{1}{2}(ln\ \pi_{i\alpha} - ln\ \pi_{j\alpha}) - \frac{1}{2}(ln\ \pi_{i\beta} - ln\ \pi_{j\beta}) + \frac{1}{4}\tau_{ij\alpha\beta}\ .$$

The generalization to $p \geq 3$ is straightforward. For example, the multinomial logit for preferring O_i over O_j with respect to p attributes is given by

$$z(\mathbf{s} = \mathrm{ii} \cdots \mathrm{i}|\mathrm{ij}) = \frac{1}{2}\sum_{\alpha=1}^{p}(ln\ \pi_{i\alpha} - ln\ \pi_{j\alpha}) + \frac{1}{4}\sum_{\alpha<\beta}^{p}\pi_{ij\alpha\beta}\ .$$

Similar expressions can be derived for the remaining response patterns. Note that this equation posits that the association between two responses may be different for each object pair. A simplified version of this equation is obtained by requiring the association coefficients to be the same for all pairwise comparisons, that is, $\tau_{ij\alpha\beta} = \tau_{\alpha\beta}$.

Thurstone's Model

Based on the assumption that each response variable is normally distributed, the multivariate normal distribution is a natural extension for describing the joint distribution of the multiple responses. Again, the simplest case of two judgment criteria is considered first. In the case of two criteria, the probability of preferring O_i over O_j under independence is given by

$$P_I(\mathbf{s} = \mathrm{ii}|\mathrm{ij}) = \Phi\left(\frac{\mu_{i\alpha} - \mu_{j\alpha}}{\sigma_{ij\alpha}}\right)\Phi\left(\frac{\mu_{i\beta} - \mu_{j\beta}}{\sigma_{ij\beta}}\right).$$

Under dependence we obtain

$$P(\mathbf{s} = \mathrm{ii}|\mathrm{ij}) =$$

$$\frac{1}{2\pi\ |\boldsymbol{\Sigma}|^{1/2}}\int_0^{\infty}\int_0^{\infty} exp\left\{-\frac{1}{2}(\mathbf{u} - (\boldsymbol{\mu}_i - \boldsymbol{\mu}_j))'\boldsymbol{\Sigma}^{-1}(\mathbf{u} - (\boldsymbol{\mu}_i - \boldsymbol{\mu}_j))\right\} d\mathbf{u}\ ,$$

where $\boldsymbol{\Sigma}$ is a covariance matrix with elements

$$\boldsymbol{\Sigma} = \begin{bmatrix} \sigma^2_{ij\alpha} & \rho_{\alpha\beta}\sigma_{ij\alpha}\sigma_{ij\beta} \\ \rho_{\alpha\beta}\sigma_{ij\alpha}\sigma_{ij\beta} & \sigma^2_{ij\beta} \end{bmatrix},$$

$\boldsymbol{\mu}_i = (\mu_{i\alpha}, \mu_{i\beta})'$, and $\boldsymbol{\mu}_j = (\mu_{j\alpha}, \mu_{j\beta})'$. The tetrachoric correlation coefficient between the responses to the criteria α and β is denoted by $\rho_{\alpha\beta}$.

Let Φ_2 denote the bivariate normal cumulative distribution function with integration limits $(\mu_{i\alpha} - \mu_{j\alpha})/\sigma_{ij\alpha}$, $(\mu_{i\beta} - \mu_{j\beta})/\sigma_{ij\beta}$ and correlation coefficient $\rho_{\alpha\beta}$. The probabilities associated with the four possible outcomes in a comparison of O_i and O_j can be written as

$$P(\mathbf{s} = \text{ii}|\text{ij}) = \Phi_2\left(\frac{\mu_{i\alpha} - \mu_{j\alpha}}{\sigma_{ij\alpha}}, \frac{\mu_{i\beta} - \mu_{j\beta}}{\sigma_{ij\beta}}; \rho_{\alpha\beta}\right),$$

$$P(\mathbf{s} = \text{ij}|\text{ij}) = \Phi_2\left(\frac{\mu_{i\alpha} - \mu_{j\alpha}}{\sigma_{ij\alpha}}, \frac{\mu_{j\beta} - \mu_{i\beta}}{\sigma_{ij\beta}}; -\rho_{\alpha\beta}\right),$$

$$P(\mathbf{s} = \text{ji}|\text{ij}) = \Phi_2\left(\frac{\mu_{j\alpha} - \mu_{i\alpha}}{\sigma_{ij\alpha}}, \frac{\mu_{i\beta} - \mu_{j\beta}}{\sigma_{ij\beta}}; -\rho_{\alpha\beta}\right),$$

$$P(\mathbf{s} = \text{jj}|\text{ij}) = \Phi_2\left(\frac{\mu_{j\alpha} - \mu_{i\alpha}}{\sigma_{ij\alpha}}, \frac{\mu_{j\beta} - \mu_{i\beta}}{\sigma_{ij\beta}}; \rho_{\alpha\beta}\right).$$

The generalization to $p \geq 3$ follows similar principles. For example, the probability of preferring O_i over O_j with respect to p attributes is given by

$$P(\mathbf{s} = \text{ii} \cdots \text{i}|\text{ij}) = \Phi_p\left(\frac{\mu_{i\alpha} - \mu_{j\alpha}}{\sigma_{ij\alpha}}, \frac{\mu_{i\beta} - \mu_{j\beta}}{\sigma_{ij\beta}}, \ldots, \frac{\mu_{ip} - \mu_{jp}}{\sigma_{ijp}}; \mathbf{R}\right),$$

where $\mathbf{R}$ is a $p \times p$ matrix with the correlations between the responses as elements. Unfortunately, the evaluation of the multivariate normal distribution is computationally difficult for more than three response variables. Therefore an approximation to multivariate distributions is derived in the next subsection.

Bahadur's Approach

Bahadur (1961) suggested a general procedure to represent the joint distribution of binary responses. His approach is reformulated here to provide a general framework for deriving multivariate representations of paired comparison models. Next, it is applied to extend the BTL model (Davidson and Bradley, 1969) and the Thurstonian model (Böckenholt, 1990).

Following the approach by Bahadur (1961), we model the probability of the response vector $\mathbf{s} = (s_1, s_2, \ldots, s_p)$ for the objects O_i and O_j by

$$P(\mathbf{s}\,|\text{ij}) = P_I(\mathbf{s}\,|\text{ij})h(\mathbf{s}\,|\text{ij}),$$

where $P_I(\mathbf{s}\,|\text{ij})$ is the joint probability of the responses when they are independent, and $h(\mathbf{s}\,|\text{ij})$ is a "correction factor" that accounts for the correlation among the responses. As shown, the joint probability of the responses under independence may be written as

$$P_I(\mathbf{s}|\text{ij}) = \prod_{\alpha=1}^{p} P(O_i \rightarrow O_j;\, \alpha)^{x_{ij\alpha}} P(O_j \rightarrow O_i;\, \alpha)^{1-x_{ij\alpha}}$$

$$= \prod_{\alpha=1}^{p} P(O_{s_\alpha} \rightarrow O_{s_{\alpha'}}; \alpha) ,$$

where $x_{ij\alpha} = 1$ if $s_\alpha = i$, and 0 otherwise. To account for departures from independence, Bahadur (1961) derived a correction factor as an additive combination of second-order and higher-order (up to p-th-order) correlation terms. To preserve symmetry with respect to the two objects O_i and O_j, we only consider a correction factor with a second-order correlation,

$$h(\mathbf{s}|ij) = 1 + \sum_{\alpha<\beta}^{p} \varphi_{\alpha\beta} z_{ij\alpha} z_{ij\beta} ,$$

where

$$z_{ij\alpha} = \frac{x_{ij\alpha} - P(O_i \rightarrow O_j; \alpha)}{\sqrt{P(O_i \rightarrow O_j; \alpha)\, P(O_j \rightarrow O_i; \alpha)}}$$

is a standardized variate. Thus, the complete model for multivariate paired comparison data is

$$P(\mathbf{s}|ij) = \prod_{\alpha=1}^{p} P(O_{s_\alpha} \rightarrow O_{s_{\alpha'}}; \alpha)$$

$$\times \left(1 + \sum_{\alpha<\beta}^{p} \varphi_{\alpha\beta} \frac{x_{ij\alpha} - P(O_i \rightarrow O_j; \alpha)}{\sqrt{P(O_i \rightarrow O_j; \alpha)\, P(O_j \rightarrow O_i; \alpha)}}\right.$$

$$\left. \times \frac{x_{ij\beta} - P(O_i \rightarrow O_j; \beta)}{\sqrt{P(O_i \rightarrow O_j; \beta)\, P(O_j \rightarrow O_i; \beta)}}\right) .$$

This general formulation of a multivariate paired comparison model may yield a proper distribution function only if certain conditions are satisfied. Bahadur discusses some of these conditions that ensure the nonnegative definiteness of the correlation matrix of the responses. Let **R** denote the correlation matrix with elements $\{\varphi_{\alpha\beta}\}$ and

$$l_\alpha = \max \left(\frac{P(O_i \rightarrow O_j; \alpha)}{P(O_j \rightarrow O_i; \alpha)}, \frac{P(O_j \rightarrow O_i; \alpha)}{P(O_i \rightarrow O_j; \alpha)} \right) .$$

Then a proper distribution function is obtained if

$$\lambda_{\min}(\mathbf{R}) \geq 1 - \frac{2}{\sum_{\alpha=1}^{p} l_\alpha} ,$$

where $\lambda_{min}(\mathbf{R})$ is the smallest eigenvalue of the matrix $\mathbf{R}$. When $p = 2$, one can show that the correlation coefficient $\varphi_{\alpha\beta}$ is Pearson's phi coefficient of correlation for a 2×2 table,

$$\varphi_{\alpha\beta} = \frac{P(\mathbf{s} = \mathrm{ii}|\mathrm{ij}) - P(O_i \to O_j;\, \alpha)P(O_i \to O_j;\, \beta)}{\sqrt{P(O_j \to O_i;\, \alpha)P(O_j \to O_i;\, \beta)P(O_i \to O_j;\, \alpha)P(O_i \to O_j;\, \beta)}},$$

and constrained to be in the interval

$$-\sqrt{\frac{P(O_i \to O_j;\, \alpha)P(O_i \to O_j;\, \beta)}{P(O_j \to O_i;\, \alpha)P(O_j \to O_i;\, \beta)}} \leq \varphi_{\alpha\beta} \leq \sqrt{\frac{P(O_i \to O_j;\, \alpha)P(O_j \to O_i;\, \beta)}{P(O_j \to O_i;\, \alpha)P(O_i \to O_j;\, \beta)}}.$$

Thus only if respondents prefer O_i over O_j to the same extent on both criteria, can $\varphi_{\alpha\beta}$ reach its upper bound of 1, and $\varphi_{\alpha\beta} = \pm 1$ if at least one of the $P(\mathbf{s}\,|\mathrm{ij})$ is zero.

In the next subsection, multivariate extensions of the BTL model and the Thurstonian models based on Bahadur's second-order approximation are developed. However, the approach is not limited to these two classes of models. Other univariate paired comparison models may be extended to the multivariate case in an analogous fashion.

Application to BTL Model

A detailed application of the second-order approximation for a multivariate representation of the BTL model is provided in Davidson and Bradley (1969). These authors define the standardized variate $z_{ij\alpha}$ of the multivariate BTL model as

$$z_{ij\alpha} = \frac{x_{ij\alpha} - \pi_{i\alpha}/(\pi_{i\alpha} + \pi_{j\alpha})}{\sqrt{\pi_{i\alpha}\pi_{j\alpha}}/(\pi_{i\alpha} + \pi_{j\alpha})},$$

and

$$P(\mathbf{s} = \mathrm{ii} \ldots \mathrm{i}|\mathrm{ij}) = \prod_{\alpha=1}^{p} \frac{\pi_{s_\alpha \alpha}}{\pi_{i\alpha} + \pi_{j\alpha}}$$

$$\left(1 + \sum_{\alpha<\beta}^{p} \varphi_{\alpha\beta} \frac{x_{ij\alpha} - \pi_{i\alpha}/(\pi_{i\alpha} + \pi_{j\alpha})}{\sqrt{\pi_{i\alpha}\pi_{j\alpha}}/(\pi_{i\alpha} + \pi_{j\alpha})} \times \frac{x_{ij\beta} - \pi_{i\beta}/(\pi_{i\beta} + \pi_{j\beta})}{\sqrt{\pi_{i\beta}\pi_{j\beta}}/(\pi_{i\beta} + \pi_{j\beta})}\right).$$

This second-order approximation yields nonnegative probabilities if

$$\lambda_{min}(\mathbf{R}) \geq 1 - \frac{2}{\Sigma_{\alpha=1}^{p} \max(\pi_{i\alpha}/\pi_{j\alpha},\, \pi_{j\alpha}/\pi_{i\alpha})}.$$

Under independence the second-order approximation and the multivariate logistic BTL model are identical. However, both approaches will generally differ in their predictions in the case of significant associations among the responses.

Application to Thurstonian Models

In the context of Thurstonian models, the standardized variate $z_{ij\alpha}$ may be written as

$$z_{ij\alpha} = \frac{x_{ij\alpha} - \Phi((\mu_{i\alpha} - \mu_{j\alpha})/\sigma_{ij\alpha})}{\sqrt{\Phi((\mu_{i\alpha} - \mu_{j\alpha})/\sigma_{ij\alpha})\Phi((\mu_{j\alpha} - \mu_{i\alpha})/\sigma_{ij\alpha})}}.$$

After some algebraic simplifications, the departure from independence, $h(\mathbf{s}\,|ij)$, can be represented as

$$1 + \sum_{\alpha<\beta}^{p} \delta(s_\alpha, s_\beta)\, \varphi_{\alpha\beta} \sqrt{\frac{\Phi(\mu_{ji\alpha}/\sigma_{ij\alpha})^{\delta(i,s_\alpha)}\, \Phi(\mu_{ji\beta}/\sigma_{ij\beta})^{\delta(i,s_\beta)}}{\Phi(\mu_{ij\alpha}/\sigma_{ij\alpha})^{\delta(i,s_\alpha)}\, \Phi(\mu_{ij\beta}/\sigma_{ij\beta})^{\delta(i,s_\beta)}}},$$

where $\mu_{ij\alpha} = \mu_{i\alpha} - \mu_{j\alpha}$ and $\delta(\cdot,\cdot) = 1$ if both arguments are equal and -1 otherwise. For example, in a comparison between two objects with respect to two criteria, the departure from independence is modeled as

$$h(\mathbf{s} = ii|ij) = 1 + \varphi_{\alpha\beta} \sqrt{\frac{\Phi(\mu_{ji\alpha}/\sigma_{ij\alpha})\, \Phi(\mu_{ji\beta}/\sigma_{ij\beta})}{\Phi(\mu_{ij\alpha}/\sigma_{ij\alpha})\, \Phi(\mu_{ij\beta}/\sigma_{ij\beta})}},$$

$$h(\mathbf{s} = ij|ij) = 1 - \varphi_{\alpha\beta} \sqrt{\frac{\Phi(\mu_{ji\alpha}/\sigma_{ij\alpha})\, \Phi(\mu_{ij\beta}/\sigma_{ij\beta})}{\Phi(\mu_{ij\alpha}/\sigma_{ij\alpha})\, \Phi(\mu_{ji\beta}/\sigma_{ij\beta})}},$$

$$h(\mathbf{s} = ji|ij) = 1 - \varphi_{\alpha\beta} \sqrt{\frac{\Phi(\mu_{ij\alpha}/\sigma_{ij\alpha})\, \Phi(\mu_{ji\beta}/\sigma_{ij\beta})}{\Phi(\mu_{ji\alpha}/\sigma_{ij\alpha})\, \Phi(\mu_{ij\beta}/\sigma_{ij\beta})}},$$

$$h(\mathbf{s} = jj|ij) = 1 + \varphi_{\alpha\beta} \sqrt{\frac{\Phi(\mu_{ij\alpha}/\sigma_{ij\alpha})\, \Phi(\mu_{ij\beta}/\sigma_{ij\beta})}{\Phi(\mu_{ji\alpha}/\sigma_{ij\alpha})\, \Phi(\mu_{ji\beta}/\sigma_{ij\beta})}},$$

A proper distribution function is obtained if

$$\lambda_{\min}(\mathbf{R}) \geq 1 - 2 \Big/ \sum_{\alpha=1}^{p} \max\left(\frac{\Phi(\mu_{ij\alpha}/\sigma_{ij\alpha})}{\Phi(\mu_{ji\alpha}/\sigma_{ij\alpha})}, \frac{\Phi(\mu_{ji\alpha}/\sigma_{ij\alpha})}{\Phi(\mu_{ij\alpha}/\sigma_{ij\alpha})}\right).$$

To keep this presentation general, we imposed no restrictions on the parameters of the Thurstonian models. However, to ensure identifiability, we must constrain the variances, covariances, and scale values of the various Thurstonian models. For example, a multivariate representation of Thurstone's Case III is obtained by setting the objects' covariances equal to zero. Similarly, a multivariate Thurstone's Case V representation results by additionally constraining the objects' variances to be the same. Moreover, by imposing the constraints on the objects' scale values and their variances and covariances discussed in the section on generalized Thurstonian models, we can obtain multivariate representations of this richer class of models.

COMPARISON OF MULTIVARIATE REPRESENTATIONS

Thurstonian Models

Multivariate Thurstonian models based on either Bahadur's approximation or the multivariate normal distribution extension share the same number of parameters for representing paired comparison data. The two approaches are identical when the responses are unrelated. However, in the case of dependencies among the responses, the approaches differ on two important factors. First, from a computational viewpoint, Bahadur's approximation is easier to determine because it requires only the evaluation of univariate integrals. Thus, the problem of parameter estimation is simplified considerably. This may prove to be a particular advantage for highly parametrized paired comparison models. Second, a major limitation of Bahadur's approximation concerns the association structure among the responses. It has been noted repeatedly in the literature that this approach yields a proper probability distribution only if correlations among the responses are small (Goodman, 1987; Holland, 1987; Lord, 1962). Moreover, there are problems with the interpretation of the phi coefficient, which is computed in the second-order approximation (Lord & Novick, 1968). In contrast, a tetrachoric correlation coefficient seems more appropriate if the normality assumptions are justified. However, these differences between both measures of association may be of little practical interest if the correlations between the responses are not too strong.

Both approaches share the important feature that their marginal probabilities are equal to the univariate preference probabilities when the responses are related. Although it is straightforward to prove this point, a numerical example is presented for illustrative purposes. The data in Table 4.1a were generated by a multivariate normal Thurstonian model with zero covariances and variances equal to $\frac{1}{2}$, scale values $\mu_{1\alpha} = -\frac{1}{2}$, $\mu_{2\alpha} = 0$, $\mu_{3\alpha} = \frac{1}{2}$, $\mu_{1\beta} = 0$, $\mu_{2\beta} = \frac{1}{2}$, $\mu_{3\beta} = -\frac{1}{2}$, and a tetrachoric correlation coefficient $\rho_{\alpha\beta} = -\frac{1}{4}$. The first row of Table 4.1a displays the outcomes of the comparison between object 1 and object 2. For example, 7 out of 100 hypothetical respondents prefer object 1 on both attributes, 24 respondents prefer object 1 on the first attribute α *and* object 2 on the second attribute β, and so forth. The second and third rows of Table 4.1a contain the results of the comparisons between object 1 and 3 and objects 2 and 3, respectively.

TABLE 4.1
Paired Comparison Cell Frequencies
(Multivariate Normal Thurstonian Model)

(a) $\rho_{\alpha\beta} = -0.25$

Pairs		Cell Frequencies			
i	*j*	*(ii)*	*(ij)*	*(ji)*	*(jj)*
1	2	7	24	24	45
1	3	9	60	7	24
2	3	24	60	7	9

(b) $\rho_{\alpha\beta} = +0.25$

1	2	13	18	18	51
1	3	13	56	3	28
2	3	28	56	3	13

The data in Table 4.1b were generated with the same variances and scale values but a tetrachoric correlation coefficient of $\frac{1}{4}$. Note that, although the cell frequencies differ, the marginal frequencies are equal to the marginal frequencies of Table 4.1a. For example, 31 respondents prefer object 1 over object 2 with respect to attribute β in Tables 4.1a and 1b. Thus, the (sign) change in the correlation coefficient does not affect the marginal preference frequencies. The same result holds for the Thurstonian model based on Bahadur's second-order approximation. When the paired comparison data in Table 4.2 were generated, the same variances and scale values were used. The Pearson phi correlation coefficient $\varphi_{\alpha\beta}$ was set equal to $-\frac{1}{4}$ in Table 4.2a and to $+\frac{1}{4}$ in the Table 4.2b.

TABLE 4.2
Paired Comparison Cell Frequencies
(Bahadur's Second-Order Representation)

(a) $\varphi_{\alpha\beta} = -0.25$

Pairs		Cell Frequencies			
i	*j*	*(ii)*	*(ij)*	*(ji)*	*(jj)*
1	2	4	27	27	42
1	3	7	62	9	22
2	3	22	62	9	7

(b) $\varphi_{\alpha\beta} = +0.25$

1	2	15	16	16	53
1	3	15	54	1	30
2	3	30	54	1	15

BTL Models

Most of the comments discussed in the previous subsection apply for the comparison between a multivariate logistic BTL model and a multivariate BTL model based on Bahadur's approach. Generally, the log-odds ratio may be considered superior to the phi coefficient when describing associations between responses (Goodman, 1987). Moreover, due to its simple structure, the logistic version of the BTL model is computationally more attractive than the version based on the Bahadur approximation. However, the logistic formulation of the BTL model does not possess the important feature that the marginal probabilities are equal to the univariate preference probabilities except in the case of independence. Thus, the scale values determined from the logistic BTL model may change considerably if the responses are highly correlated, and thus caution should be exercised when interpreting the scaling results. As discussed in the previous section, a paired comparison model based on Bahadur's approximation does not share this difficulty. Consequently, the logistic version of the BTL model seems to be most useful when a researcher is interested in modeling the association structure among the responses and is less concerned about the worth parameters of the multivariate BTL model.

MODEL ESTIMATION AND TESTS

Model parameters of a multivariate representation are estimated by maximum likelihood methods. Assuming random sampling of subjects for the paired comparisons, we specify the log-likelihood function as

$$ln\, L = \mathrm{c} + \sum_{\mathrm{i<j}}^{\mathrm{t}} \sum_{\mathrm{m=1}}^{2^{\mathrm{p}}} r(\mathbf{s}_{\mathrm{m}}|\mathrm{ij})\; ln\, P(\mathbf{s}_{\mathrm{m}}|\mathrm{ij}),$$

where a response pattern is indexed by m, and $r(\mathbf{s}_m|ij)$ is the frequency of respondents showing this pattern $\mathbf{s}_m$ in the comparison of the objects O_i and O_j, and c is a constant. By maximizing the log-likelihood function with respect to the model parameters, we generally obtain unique maximum likelihood estimates if the objects can be connected for each judgment criterion and appropriate constraints are imposed on the model parameters (Van Putten, 1982). The parameters of the multivariate logistic BTL model may be estimated from general programs for determining log-linear models. The remaining multivariate representations of paired comparison data cannot be estimated with canned computer packages. However, in applications, a Newton-Raphson Algorithm yielded rapid convergence when starting values of the parameter estimates were set equal to the maximum likelihood estimates obtained from separate analyses of the p paired comparison matrices (Böckenholt, 1990).

Large sample tests of fit of any of the specified models or submodels are available using the likelihood ratio (LR) chi-square statistic:

$$G^2 = 2 \sum_{i<j}^{t} \sum_{m=1}^{2^p} r(\mathbf{s}_m|ij)\; ln \left\{ \frac{r(\mathbf{s}_m|ij)}{r^e(\mathbf{s}_m|ij)} \right\},$$

where $r^e(\mathbf{s}_m|ij)$ are the "expected" frequencies under the model to be tested.

When one model is nested within another, differences between the likelihood ratio statistics can be computed to assess the importance of the contribution to the likelihood ratio statistic by the additional constraints imposed by the stronger model. This difference is asymptotically distributed as a chi-square statistic with the number of degrees of freedom equal to the difference between the number of parameters in the unrestricted and restricted models (see chap. 1 for more details). This approach provides further guidance in selecting a parsimonious model.

The full rank or saturated model has $2^p(\binom{t}{2} - 1)$ parameters. However, it may be sufficient to estimate $p(t - 1)$ location parameters and $p(p - 1)/2$ association parameters. For example, a multivariate Thurstone Case V model (or, equivalently, a multivariate BTL model) with an association parameter for each response pair may be tested with $2^p(\binom{t}{2} - 1) - p(2t + p - 3)/2$ degrees of freedom. More detailed tests are commonly concerned with examining differences in the location, scale, and association parameters. The equality of association coefficients may be examined by first estimating an association coefficient for each response pair and then restricting the association coefficients to be the same for all response pairs. Thus, the equality of association coefficients may be tested with $(\binom{t}{2} - 1)p(p - 1)/2$ degrees of freedom. Moreover, the hypothesis of no association between the attributes may be tested against the hypothesis of equal association coefficients with $p(p - 1)/2$ degrees of freedom.

To illustrate some of these tests, consider the hypothetical data set in Table 4.3. Suppose that criterion α is overall preference and that the criteria β and γ distinguish the objects O_1, O_2, and O_3 along some continua. In Tables 4.3 and 4.4 the symbol O is omitted and the objects are denoted by 1, 2, and 3. For example, in the comparison of O_1 and O_2, 17 respondents prefer O_1 with respect to all three criteria, 23 respondents select O_1 with respect to criteria α and β, and so forth.

TABLE 4.3
Observed Cell Frequencies (Hypothetical Example)

Pairs		*Cell Frequencies*							
i	*j*	*(iii)*	*(iij)*	*(iji)*	*(ijj)*	*(jii)*	*(jij)*	*(jji)*	*(jjj)*
1	2	17	23	4	4	6	7	18	21
1	3	20	18	7	6	6	2	15	26
2	3	17	5	20	6	7	15	4	26

TABLE 4.4
Correlation Coefficients Obtained from Thurstonian Model Based on Bahadur's Second-Order Representation

Pairs		*Correlations*		
i	*j*	$\hat{\varphi}_{\alpha\beta}$	$\hat{\varphi}_{\alpha\gamma}$	$\hat{\varphi}_{\beta\gamma}$
1	2	.56	−.02	−.04
1	3	.59	.11	.18
2	3	.04	.56	.11

Fitting a multivariate Thurstonian Case V model (based on Bahadur's approximation) with a correlation coefficient for each response pair yields a likelihood ratio statistic $G^2 = 25.74$ with 12 degrees of freedom. The number of degrees of freedom (df) of this statistic is the difference between the number of unconstrained cells (21) and the number of estimated parameters ($\varphi_{\alpha\beta}$, $\varphi_{\alpha\beta}$, $\varphi_{\beta\gamma}$; $\mu_{i\alpha}$, $\mu_{i\beta}$, $\mu_{i\gamma}$, $i = 1, 2, 3$) corrected for the number of constraints imposed on the parameters ($\Sigma\, \mu_{i\alpha} = \Sigma\, \mu_{i\beta} = \Sigma\, \mu_{i\gamma} = 0$). Clearly, this model does not provide a satisfactory fit of the data. Significant deviations from the data may occur as result of an inappropriate paired comparison model or an insufficient representation of the association structure. We investigate the adequacy of the paired comparison structure by estimating a parameter for each of the three pairwise comparisons with respect to the three criteria. This model test requires the estimation of three additional parameters, yet the likelihood ratio statistic $G^2 = 25.24$ (df = 15) is only slightly smaller than the one of the Thurstonian Case V model. Thus the difference in the likelihood ratio statistics $\Delta G^2 = 25.74 - 25.24 = 0.50$ with 3 degrees of freedom indicates that the Thurstone Case V representation is sufficient for the marginal distribution of the data.

In addition to testing the appropriateness of the paired comparison model representation, the association structure of the responses may be examined in more detail. For example, one may test the assumption that associations are the same for every object pair. By allowing for a different correlation coefficient for each choice pair (that is, $\varphi_{ij\alpha\beta} \neq \varphi_{ij\alpha\gamma} \neq \varphi_{ij\beta\gamma}$), we increase the number of parameters to be estimated by 6 and the estimated model has a $G^2 = 1.96$ with 6 degrees of freedom. This model test in combination with a further residual analysis indicates a satisfactory fit of the data. The estimated correlation coefficients are presented in Table 4. Clearly, the correlations between the three attributes vary for each object pair. While for the first and second choice pair the responses regarding the criteria α and β are strongly positively related ($\hat{\varphi}_{12\alpha\beta} = .56$; $\hat{\varphi}_{13\alpha\beta} = .59$), for the third choice pair the responses regarding the criteria α and γ are strongly positively ($\hat{\varphi}_{23\alpha\gamma} = .56$) related.

In general, an overall satisfactory fit of a multivariate paired comparison model is, of course, only a first step when analyzing the data. Additional detailed tests are necessary for models with many parameters before one can conclude that the selected model provides an appropriate representation of the data. In particular, separate tests of the paired comparison part, the association part, and other parts of the multivariate model structure are useful even when the overall fit seems satisfactory.

EMPIRICAL APPLICATIONS OF THE MULTIVARIATE PAIRED COMPARISON MODELS

Example 1: An Empirical Comparison of the Multivariate Models

We now consider an illustration of the multivariate BTL and Thurstonian paired comparison models. The selected data set is taken from Davidson and Bradley (1971). In a complete paired comparison design, three vanilla puddings were assessed by three independent groups of judges with respect to color (α), taste or flavor (β), and overall quality (γ). The data and the expected frequencies of the best-fitting model are displayed in Table 4.5.

The results of the analysis are presented for each multivariate representation separately. The model tests are based on the likelihood ratio goodness-of-fit statistic which is compared to a χ^2 distribution. However, this comparison should be interpreted with caution because the expected frequencies under any of the following paired comparison models are quite small.

Table 4.6 shows several tests of the multivariate BTL model based on the logistic distribution extension and Bahadur's approximation. The BTL model has a likelihood ratio goodness-of-fit statistic of $G^2 = 12.99$. Clearly, this model with 12 degrees of freedom provides a satisfactory fit to the data. Due to the specific parametrization of the model, it is straightforward to test various hypotheses about the model parameters. For example, a hypothesis test of zero associa-

TABLE 4.5
Observed and Expected Cell Frequencies (Example 1)
(expected frequencies given in parentheses)

Pairs		*Cell Frequencies*							
i	*j*	*(iii)*	*(iij)*	*(iji)*	*(ijj)*	*(jii)*	*(jij)*	*(jji)*	*(jjj)*
1	2	6	2	1	1	1	1	0	8
		(7.4)	(0.9)	(0.9)	(0.9)	(0.9)	(0.9)	(0.9)	(7.4)
1	3	3	2	1	1	1	2	1	11
		(8.1)	(1.0)	(1.0)	(1.0)	(1.0)	(1.0)	(1.0)	(8.1)
2	3	12	2	0	0	0	1	0	8
		(8.5)	(1.0)	(1.0)	(1.0)	(1.0)	(1.0)	(1.0)	(8.5)

TABLE 4.6
Goodness-of-Fit Statistics of Multivariate BTL Models Based on Multivariate Logistic Extension and Bahadur's Representation

Model Tests	*Logistic* G^2	*df*	*Bahadur* G^2
A. Multivariate BTL	12.99	12	13.36
B. Zero associations	80.58	15	80.58
C. Equal preferences	19.36	18	19.36
D. Equal preferences, common association	20.22	20	20.22

tion between the three response pairs ($\tau_{\alpha\beta} = \tau_{\alpha\gamma} = \tau_{\beta\gamma} = 0$) indicates that the responses are not independent (model test B). This hypothesis is tested by computing the difference between the likelihood ratio statistic for the model with zero associations ($G^2 = 80.58$, df = 15) and the model with arbitrary correlations ($G^2 = 12.99$, df = 12), $\Delta G^2 = 80.58 - 12.99 = 67.59$. This statistic is compared to a χ^2 distribution with 3 degrees of freedom. In contrast, tests for equal preferences indicate that taste, color, and overall quality differences are quite small for the three puddings. This hypothesis (model test C) posits that ($\pi_{i\alpha} = \pi_{i\beta} = \pi_{i\gamma} = \frac{1}{3}$ for i = 1, 2, 3). A test of this hypothesis yields a $\Delta G^2 = 6.37$ on 6 degrees of freedom. In fact, only one parameter is required to adequately represent the paired comparison data, a common association coefficient ($\hat{\tau} = 2.14$) for the three response pairs (model test D). This model has a likelihood ratio statistic of $G^2 = 20.22$ with degrees of freedom equal to 20.

The second column of Table 4.6 shows the model test obtained when fitting a multivariate BTL model based on Bahadur's approximation. The likelihood ratio chi-square statistic of a multivariate paired comparison model with BTL marginals and three association coefficients (model test A) has a value of $G^2 = 13.36$, indicating a satisfactory fit when compared to the χ^2 distribution with 12 degrees of freedom. Nine parameters, three association coefficients (φ_{12}, φ_{13}, φ_{23}), and six worth parameters ($\pi_{i\alpha}$, $\pi_{i\beta}$, $\pi_{i\gamma}$, i = 1, 2) are estimated under the constraints $\Sigma\, \pi_{i\alpha} = \Sigma\, \pi_{i\beta} = \Sigma\, \pi_{i\gamma} = 1$. A test of zero associations ($\varphi_{\alpha\beta} = \varphi_{\alpha\gamma} = \varphi_{\beta\gamma} = 0$) yields a likelihood ratio statistic of $\Delta G^2 = 80.58 - 13.36 = 67.22$ on 3 degrees of freedom (model test B). A test of preference differences (model test C) yields a $\Delta G^2 = 6.0$ on 6 degrees of freedom. Again, only one parameter is required to adequately represent the paired comparison data. Model D with a common association coefficient ($\hat{\varphi} = 0.65$) for the three response pairs has a likelihood ratio statistic of $G^2 = 20.22$ with 20 degrees of freedom.

The results of the corresponding Thurstonian model tests based on the multivariate normal distribution and Bahadur's approximation are identical to the ones obtained from the multivariate BTL model and the BTL model based on Bahadur's approximation, respectively. For example, model tests A* (Case V marginals and three correlation coefficients) yield values of $G^2 = 12.99$ and G^2

= 13.36 for the former and latter Thurstonian representation, respectively. Again, modeling the full joint distribution of the responses has little impact on the fit of the models. The common association coefficient of the multivariate normal Thurstonian model has a value of $\hat{\rho} = 0.85$.

In summary, the results obtained when applying the four formulations of multivariate paired comparison models are quite similar. Only for model tests A and A* did the multivariate logistic BTL model and the multivariate normal Thurstonian model provide slightly better fits, presumably because these models are more flexible in modeling the associations between the responses in the case of preference differences. Although a substantive interpretation of the results is not possible because background information about this data set is not available, it is clear that the sample in this study did not show preference differences among the three pudding brands along any of the attributes flavor, color, and overall quality. However, it is important to note that it was possible to estimate a rather large and equal correlation between response variable pairs. Thus, one can reliably determine the perceived dependencies among the object attributes, even if the sample as a whole is indifferent about the variations in the object attributes.

Example II: Application of the Multivariate Generalized Thurstonian Models

The following data set was extracted from an unpublished study by the author in which each respondent was asked, among other things, to express his or her preference for one of two cookies with respect to the criteria overall preference (*P*), sweetness (*S*), and crispness (*C*). The choice set consisted of the cookie brands Oreo (1), Nutter Butter (2) Chips Ahoy (3), Ginger Snaps (4), Nilla Wafers (5), Graham Cookies (6), and Animal Crackers (7). The data obtained from 100 subjects are displayed in Table 4.7. The first row of this table contains the outcomes of a comparison between the brands Oreo and Nutter Butter. For example, Oreo was selected first by 36 respondents on all three criteria and by 19 respondents on the criteria overall preference and sweetness. As in the previous applications, model tests are based on the likelihood ratio goodness-of-fit statistic. However, because every subject compared all possible cookie pairs, significance tests of this statistic may be biased.

In the following analyses, the Bahadur representation for multivariate normal paired comparison data was applied because of its computational simplicity. A multivariate Thurstone Case V model with three correlation coefficients to describe the relationship between the response variables was fitted to the data. This model requires the estimation of 21 parameters [$p(t - 1) = 18$ scale values and 3 correlation coefficients]. The likelihood ratio statistic of $G^2 = 206.03$ with 126 degrees of freedom strongly rejects this model. Further analyses showed that a

TABLE 4.7
Observed Cell Frequencies (Example 2)

Pairs		*Cell Frequencies*							
i	*j*	*(iii)*	*(iij)*	*(iji)*	*(ijj)*	*(jii)*	*(jij)*	*(jji)*	*(jjj)*
1	2	36	19	9	4	20	3	6	3
1	3	20	39	13	12	3	4	0	9
1	4	6	70	0	5	1	18	0	0
1	5	36	39	2	9	5	8	1	0
1	6	12	69	0	3	3	12	0	1
1	7	21	57	2	2	3	15	0	0
2	3	1	15	2	34	2	8	8	30
2	4	1	61	0	17	1	11	1	8
2	5	15	43	6	17	2	11	2	4
2	6	1	67	0	8	1	1	0	6
2	7	9	58	1	9	1	16	1	5
3	4	14	57	2	9	4	13	1	0
3	5	34	27	2	4	18	9	6	0
3	6	15	62	1	6	4	9	1	2
3	7	27	49	4	4	7	7	1	1
4	5	16	0	14	0	24	1	40	5
4	6	20	14	6	4	22	6	17	11
4	7	29	14	11	0	14	4	21	7
5	6	4	41	1	28	3	7	2	14
5	7	16	39	6	19	1	11	6	2
6	7	19	17	16	4	12	8	15	9

Thurstone Case V representation may be appropriate for the response variables sweetness and crispness. However, the representation of the overall preference responses required a less restrictive model. Based on the various Thurstonian models that were tested, a two-dimensional Wandering Vector model provided the most adequate description of the overall preference data. Thus, a model with a Thurstone Case V representation for the criteria sweetness and crispness and a two-dimensional Wandering Vector representation for the criterion overall preference yielded a likelihood ratio statistic of $G^2 = 145.7$ with 120 degrees of freedom. The degrees of freedom were computed as the difference between the unconstrained cell probabilities (147) and the model parameters (12 scale vales for the sweetness and crispness attributes, 12 parameters for the Wandering Vector model, and 3 correlation coefficients). A further examination of the scaling results showed that the two-dimensional solution obtained from the Wandering Vector representation is similar to the scale values obtained from the two Case V solutions. Consequently, in the next model the two-dimensional representation of the Wandering Vector model was restricted to be equal to the scale values of the Case V representations. Thus, the probability that O_i is preferred to O_j with respect to attributes P, S, and C was modeled as

$P(\mathbf{s} = \text{iii}|\text{ij})$

$$= \Phi\left(\frac{\mu_{ijP}}{\sigma_{ijP}}\right) \Phi\left(\frac{\mu_{ijS}}{\sqrt{2}}\right) \Phi\left(\frac{\mu_{ijC}}{\sqrt{2}}\right)\left(1 + \varphi_{PS}\sqrt{\frac{\Phi(\mu_{jiP}/\sigma_{ijP})}{\Phi(\mu_{ijP}/\sigma_{ijP})}\frac{\Phi(\mu_{jiS}/\sqrt{2})}{\Phi(\mu_{ijS}/\sqrt{2})}}\right.$$

$$\left. + \varphi_{PC}\sqrt{\frac{\Phi(\mu_{jiP}/\sigma_{ijP})}{\Phi(\mu_{ijP}/\sigma_{ijP})}\frac{\Phi(\mu_{jiC}/\sqrt{2})}{\Phi(\mu_{ijC}/\sqrt{2})}} + \varphi_{SC}\sqrt{\frac{\Phi(\mu_{jiS}/\sqrt{2})}{\Phi(\mu_{ijS}/\sqrt{2})}\frac{\Phi(\mu_{jiC}/\sqrt{2})}{\Phi(\mu_{ijC}/\sqrt{2})}}\right),$$

where

$$\mu_{ijP} = \mu_{ijS}v_S + \mu_{ijC}v_C \quad \text{and} \quad \sigma_{ijP} = \sqrt{\mu_{ijS}^2 + \mu_{ijC}^2}\,.$$

This model produced a goodness-of-fit statistic of $G^2 = 156.5$ with 131 degrees of freedom. Due to the constraints imposed on this particular Wandering Vector representation, the number of model parameters to be estimated decreased by 11. Finally, a multivariate normal Thurstonian model with the same number of parameters was fitted to the data set. It yielded a somewhat better goodness-of-fit statistic of $G^2 = 149.4$ with 131 degrees of freedom. The correlations between the responses are $\hat{\rho}_{SC} = -0.03$, $\hat{\rho}_{SP} = 0.24$, and $\hat{\rho}_{CP} = -0.09$, which indicates that the sweetness and crispness responses are only weakly related. A test of the hypothesis $\rho_{SC} = 0$ yields a $\Delta G^2 = 0.26$ with df $= 1$ and indicates that the null hypothesis cannot be rejected. However, tests of the hypotheses $\rho_{CP} = 0$ and $\rho_{SP} = 0$ yield $G^2 = 4.4$ and $G^2 = 30.7$, respectively. Thus, the relationships between these responses and the overall preference response are substantial but in opposite directions. This correlational pattern provides further evidence that the subjects in this sample may have based their overall preference judgment on the preferred sweetness and crispness level of the cookies. A graphical representation of the two-dimensional solution obtained from the multivariate Thurstonian model with $\rho_{SC} = 0$ is depicted in Figure 4.1. The arrow corresponds to the mean vector $\mathbf{v}_P = (v_C, v_S)$. This vector describes the directions most preferred by the subjects. Projections of the alternatives' coordinates on the mean vector determine the preference order of the cookies.

In summary, subjects not only distinguished among the different attributes of the cookies, but it seems likely that they also used this information to form their overall preference judgments. This conclusion is strongly supported by the correlational structure between the response variables and the high similarity between the scaling solutions obtained from the Wandering Vector model for the overall preference data and the Case V representations for the sweetness and crispness data.

DISCUSSION

The multivariate extensions presented in this chapter do not explicitly take into account individual differences because it is assumed that every respondent com-

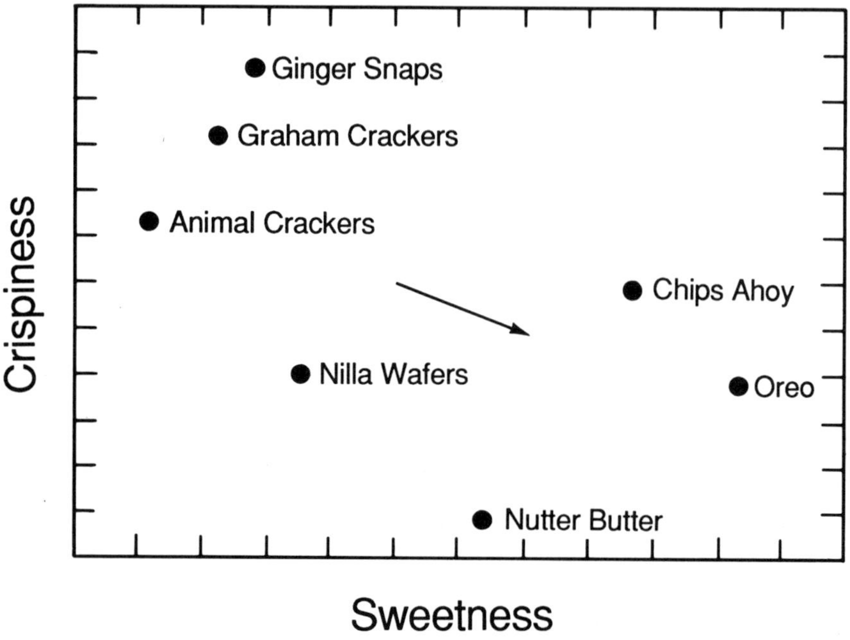

FIG. 4.1. Graphical representation of two-dimensional solution of Example 2.

pares only one pair of objects with respect to the p criteria. Frequently, however, respondents may be asked to compare all pairs or a subset of object pairs. In this case, it is desirable to distinguish two different dependency types among the responses. While the first type of dependency is a result of an individual comparing several pairs of objects, the second type is a result of an individual comparing the same object pair with respect to several attributes. The multivariate approach presented here accounts for the latter type of dependency. The former type requires a more complex methodology. Takane (1987) developed a general Analysis of Covariance Structures (ACOVS) approach to model explicitly the between and within subject sources of variation in a multiple-judgment sampling situation for Thurstonian and generalized Thurstonian models. Thus, a promising extension of the multivariate normal paired comparison model is to combine it with Takane's ACOVS representation to account for systematic individual difference components.

Testing the suitability of a multivariate paired comparison model is only a first step in the analysis of preference data. In almost all applications, it is useful to include external information about the objects and design-related effects. The simple structure of the multivariate models presented here facilitates straightforward and flexible analyses of the effect of concomitant variables. Moreover, the approach of separating the multivariate model structure into two components, one for modeling the response variables under independence, and one for modeling the association structure among the responses, is not limited to paired comparison data. Böckenholt (1992) applied this approach to derive multivariate models for the analysis of ranking and first choice data. Other important applications may include the modeling of multivariate data obtained in a signal detection experiment (Ashby, 1988; Ashby & Townsend, 1988) or in a multiple choice task (Böckenholt & Böckenholt, 1990). In general, a multivariate analysis is often much more effective than a univariate approach and facilitates many additional tests that are helpful in understanding the perceptual processes governing choice.

ACKNOWLEDGMENTS

Requests for reprints should be sent to Ulf Böckenholt, Department of Psychology, University of Illinois at Urbana-Champaign, Champaign, Il 61820, U.S.A. The author is grateful to F. Gregory Ashby and to an anonymous reviewer for helpful comments on the presentation of the material.

5 A General Probabilistic Model for Triad Discrimination, Preferential Choice, and Two-Alternative Identification

Daniel M. Ennis
Philip Morris Research Center and Department of Physiology
Medical College of Virginia

Kenneth Mullen
Department of Mathematics and Statistics
University of Guelph

From a mathematical modeling viewpoint, there are very close parallels between triad discrimination, preferential choice, and two-alternative identification under certain assumptions concerning the decision rules employed. The purpose of this chapter is to introduce a very general probabilistic model in a computationally simple form that can be used to model results obtained from several different types of psychological tasks. Chapter 11 contains a discussion of a number of probabilistic models of identification. One of these models, based on ordinal decision rules, will be covered in this chapter.

It might be useful to begin by providing a general overview of tasks involving three alternatives. First consider the situation in which all three alternatives are stimuli. Depending on the instructions, these tasks are variants of the Method of Triads. Two methods have been commonly discussed in the literature. Torgerson (1958) refers to one of them as the "complete method of triads," which we call Torgerson's Method of Triads, and the other as "Richardson's method of triadic combinations" (1938), which we call Richardson's Method of Triads. In Torgerson's Method of Triads, the three stimuli are presented to the subject in each of three independent trials. On each trial, one stimulus is designated as the standard. The subject's task is to select from the remaining two stimuli, the stimulus most similar to the standard. Each stimulus serves as the standard for one of the three trials. For instance, in the first trial, the subject's task might be to select which of $\mathbf{S}_j$ or $\mathbf{S}_k$ is most similar to $\mathbf{S}_i$. The symbol ${}_iP_{jk}$ is the probability that $\mathbf{S}_i$ is more similar to $\mathbf{S}_j$ than $\mathbf{S}_k$. The three trials are independent and may give rise to different psychological magnitudes from trial to trial for the same stimulus. Richardson's Method of Triads involves a single presentation of the three stimuli and the subject's task is to judge which two objects are most alike perceptually and which two are most different. It is important to point out that most tristimulus models assume that the psychological magnitudes remain at *fixed values* during a trial for both Torgerson's and Richardson's methods. If this is not the case (which is not unlikely for Richardson's method because two decisions are required per trial), the same two objects may appear to be most alike *and* most different. A model for this kind of result has been derived and is given in Ennis, Mullen, Frijters, and Tindall (1989). A very common practice in the sensory evaluation of foods and beverages is to present three stimuli, two of which are (presumptively) physically identical. Three methods are commonly used: the Duo-Trio Method, the **ABX** Method, and the Triangular Method. In the Duo-Trio Method, one of the two "identical" stimuli is chosen as a standard, and the subject's task is to decide which of the other two stimuli is most like the standard. In the **ABX** Method, the two "different" stimuli are chosen as standards (**A** and **B**), and the task is to pick the standard which is most like the third stimulus (**X**). The Duo-Trio Method and the **ABX** Method are variants of Torgerson's Method of Triads. The third method, called the Triangular Method, involves the selection of "the most different" stimulus and is a special case of Richardson's Method of Triads.

The three alternatives just discussed need not be physical stimuli presented during a trial. They could be the subject's memory of stimuli presented at some earlier time or the subject's conception of objects that were never experienced materially. For example, one alternative might be the subject's conception of an ideal stimulus. Tasks that make use of the idea of memory representations occur in identification and categorization experiments. The concept of the ideal stimulus is used in preference modeling. In a two-alternative identification experiment, a subject might be assumed to compare a stimulus representation with two memory representations and to "identify" the stimulus by naming the memory representation most similar to the stimulus. A model for paired preference might be based on the assumption that the preferred stimulus, of two, is the one most similar to an ideal stimulus.

Due to the many applications for a viable model involving the comparison of three alternatives, a computationally tractable form would seem to be highly desirable. This model could then unify many special cases dealing with a variety of experimental methods under one umbrella.

In a previous paper (Ennis, Palen, & Mullen, 1988), it was mentioned that the wandering ideal point (WIP) model (De Soete, Carroll, & DeSarbo, 1986; see also chap. 2) is closely related to a Thurstonian variant of Torgerson's Method of Triads (Ennis, Mullen, & Frijters, 1988). The WIP model is a probabilistic interpretation of Coombs' (1964) preference unfolding model. In the WIP model one assumes that the mental representation of the stimuli is a set of fixed points and that the representation of the ideal stimulus "wanders". This latter assumption is achieved by assuming that the momentary ideal stimulus values within each trial in a preference task are drawn at random from a multivariate normal distribution. The preference decision depends on the Euclidean distances between the ideal stimulus value and the stimulus values. The subject chooses the stimulus closest (smallest Euclidean distance) to the ideal stimulus when making a preference judgment. In a different context, Hefner (1958) postulated multivariate normal distributions (with identity covariance matrices) for momentary psychological values for stimuli. If, unlike the WIP model, it is assumed that psychological values for both the stimuli and the ideal stimulus are drawn from multivariate normal distributions (for which the covariance matrix need not be the identity matrix), then the resulting choice model is more general than the WIP model and also more general with regard to the stimulus distributions than Hefner's model or the model of Zinnes and Griggs (1974), where it was assumed that the stimulus distribution variances are equal.

Consider the decision process specified in Torgerson's Method of Triads. The subject is presented with three stimulus objects, $\mathbf{S}_i$, $\mathbf{S}_j$, and $\mathbf{S}_k$, and, given $\mathbf{S}_i$ as the standard, for instance, is asked to decide which of $\mathbf{S}_j$ or $\mathbf{S}_k$ is most like $\mathbf{S}_i$. If $\mathbf{S}_i$ is assumed to be the ideal stimulus, then the probability of selecting $\mathbf{S}_j$ instead of $\mathbf{S}_k$ is the probability of preferring $\mathbf{S}_j$ over $\mathbf{S}_k$. This decision is based on the Euclidean distances between the momentary values. An equation for computing the probability of this event, called ${}_iP_{jk}$, is given in Ennis, Mullen, and Frijters (1988) for the unidimensional case. In an identification experiment, $\mathbf{S}_i$ might represent a probe and $\mathbf{S}_j$ and $\mathbf{S}_k$ might represent the memory of stimuli $\mathbf{S}_j$ and $\mathbf{S}_k$ that have been established through training. An identification decision based on the distance between momentary values corresponding to $\mathbf{S}_i$ and $\mathbf{S}_j$, and $\mathbf{S}_i$ and $\mathbf{S}_k$ could be modeled in exactly the same way as triad discrimination and preferential choice. Consequently, these three psychological tasks—triad discrimination, preferential choice, and two-alternative identification—have exactly the same mathematical model under appropriate assumptions.

MODEL ASSUMPTIONS

Multidimensional tristimulus models for the Duo-Trio and Triangular Methods have recently been developed (Ennis & Mullen, 1986a,b; Kapenga, de Doncker, Mullen, & Ennis, 1987; Mullen, Ennis, de Doncker, & Kapenga, 1988). The models all assume that the momentary effects of each choice alternative can be represented as a multivariate probability distribution. A useful starting point in developing a multidimensional extension of Torgerson's Method of Triads is to begin with a special case, the Duo-Trio Method.

In the Duo-Trio Method, the multidimensional tristimulus models assume that the distributions for two of the stimuli are identical. For instance, the distributions corresponding to $\mathbf{S}_i$ and $\mathbf{S}_j$ might be identical, and one of these stimuli, say $\mathbf{S}_i$, is designated as a standard. The subject's task is to decide which of $\mathbf{S}_j$ or $\mathbf{S}_k$ is most like $\mathbf{S}_i$. The means of the distributions corresponding to the three stimuli are $\boldsymbol{\mu}_i$, $\boldsymbol{\mu}_j$ and $\boldsymbol{\mu}_k$ and $\boldsymbol{\mu}_i = \boldsymbol{\mu}_j$; their covariance matrices are $\boldsymbol{\Sigma}_i$, $\boldsymbol{\Sigma}_j$, and $\boldsymbol{\Sigma}_k$, and $\boldsymbol{\Sigma}_i$

$= \Sigma_j$. If $\mathbf{x}_i$ and $\mathbf{x}_j$ are the momentary psychological values corresponding to two stimuli S_i and S_j, and $\mathbf{x}_k$ represents the corresponding magnitudes for a third stimulus S_k, then in a particular trial a correct overt response (with probability ${}_iP_{jk}$,) will be obtained if

(i) $|\mathbf{x}_i - \mathbf{x}_j| < |\mathbf{x}_i - \mathbf{x}_k|$ when S_i is the standard, or

(ii) $|\mathbf{x}_i - \mathbf{x}_j| < |\mathbf{x}_j - \mathbf{x}_k|$ when S_j is the standard.

Cases (i) and (ii) give identical results, so the following discussion will focus on case (i).

MATHEMATICAL FORMS

Let $(\mathbf{x}_i - \mathbf{x}_j) = \mathbf{u}$ and $(\mathbf{x}_i - \mathbf{x}_k) = \mathbf{v}$. As shown in Mullen and Ennis (1987), ${}_iP_{jk}$ corresponds to the probability density content of the hypervolume inside the n-dimensional hypersphere $|\mathbf{u}| = R$ centered at 0 (where $R = |\mathbf{v}|$), or

$$ {}_iP_{jk} = \int_C f(\mathbf{u}, \mathbf{v})\, d\mathbf{u}\, d\mathbf{v} \,, \tag{1} $$

where C is the region for which $|\mathbf{u}| < |\mathbf{v}|$ and

$$ f(\mathbf{u}, \mathbf{v}) = \frac{exp\,\{-0.5(\mathbf{z} - \boldsymbol{\mu})'\, \Sigma^{-1}(\mathbf{z} - \boldsymbol{\mu})\}}{(2\pi)^n |\Sigma|^{1/2}} \,, $$

$$ \mathbf{z} = (\mathbf{u}, \mathbf{v}) \,, $$

$$ \boldsymbol{\mu} = [(\boldsymbol{\mu}_i - \boldsymbol{\mu}_j), (\boldsymbol{\mu}_i - \boldsymbol{\mu}_k)] \,, $$

$$ \Sigma = \begin{bmatrix} \Sigma_1 & \Sigma_2 \\ \Sigma_2 & \Sigma_3 \end{bmatrix}, \qquad \text{with } \Sigma_1 = \Sigma_i + \Sigma_j, \quad \Sigma_2 = \Sigma_i \quad \text{and} \quad \Sigma_3 = \Sigma_i + \Sigma_k $$

When Equation 1 is used to model the Duo-Trio Method, $\boldsymbol{\mu}_i = \boldsymbol{\mu}_j$ and $\Sigma_i = \Sigma_j$. However, this need not be the case. If we assume that the distributions corresponding to S_i and S_j are *not* the same, then Equation 1 models the multidimensional Thurstonian variant of Torgerson's Method of Triads. Recalling that the probability of selecting S_j instead of S_k as the stimulus most similar to S_i is identical to the probability of preferring S_j to S_k if S_i represents the ideal stimulus, it can be seen that Equation 1 also predicts preference probabilities. Note also that if $\boldsymbol{\mu}_i$ and Σ_i are the mean vector and covariance matrix of the probe's distribution, then Equation 1 is also an identification model with $\boldsymbol{\mu}_j$, $\boldsymbol{\mu}_k$, Σ_j, and Σ_k representing the memory distributions.

Equation 1 can be transformed to constant limits of integration as shown in Mullen et al. (1988), but still requires the evaluation of a 2n-fold integral. The 2n-fold integral given in Equation 1 can be simplified significantly by defining the integral in terms of an indefinite quadratic form (Mullen & Ennis, 1991), which leads to a single integral, irrespective of the dimensionality of the vector space of psychological magnitudes. From Equation 1,

$$ {}_iP_{jk} = \int_{C<0} \frac{exp\,\{-0.5(\mathbf{z} - \boldsymbol{\mu})'\boldsymbol{\Sigma}^{-1}(\mathbf{z} - \boldsymbol{\mu})\}}{(2\pi)^n|\boldsymbol{\Sigma}|^{1/2}}\, dz $$

$$ C = \mathbf{u} \cdot \mathbf{u} - \mathbf{v} \cdot \mathbf{v} = \mathbf{z}'\mathbf{J}\mathbf{z} \,. $$

where

$$ \mathbf{J} = \begin{bmatrix} \mathbf{I} & \mathbf{0} \\ \mathbf{0} & -\mathbf{I} \end{bmatrix} . $$

The goal of the following linear algebra steps is to reduce Equation 1 to a standard canonical form (i.e., with a diagonal matrix in the limit of integration) for which there is a known computationally simple solution. This reduction to a standard form is achieved in two stages: (a) Cholesky Factorization to transform the density function to a standard multivariate normal (see chap. 1) and (b) diagonalization of the matrix in the quadratic form that defines the limits of integration.

The first step involves Cholesky Factorization. Let $\mathbf{A}$ be a nonsingular lower triangular matrix defined by $\mathbf{AA}' = \boldsymbol{\Sigma}$. Let $\mathbf{z}^* = \mathbf{A}^{-1}(\mathbf{z} - \boldsymbol{\mu})$. Then

$$ {}_iP_{jk} = \int_{D<0} \frac{exp\,(-0.5\mathbf{z}^* \cdot \mathbf{z}^*)}{(2\pi)^n}\, d\mathbf{z}^* \,, $$

where

$$ D = (\mathbf{z}^* + \boldsymbol{\xi})'\mathbf{A}'\mathbf{J}\mathbf{A}(\mathbf{z}^* + \boldsymbol{\xi}) \qquad \text{with } \boldsymbol{\xi} = \mathbf{A}^{-1}(\boldsymbol{\mu}) \,. $$

The next stage achieves the desired diagonalization.

$$ \boldsymbol{\omega} = \mathbf{P}'(\mathbf{z}^*) \qquad \text{and} \qquad \mathbf{d} = -\mathbf{P}'(\boldsymbol{\xi}) \,, $$

where $\mathbf{P}$ is the matrix of normalized eigenvectors of $\mathbf{A}'\mathbf{J}\mathbf{A}$.

$$ \begin{aligned} D &= (\boldsymbol{\omega} - \mathbf{d})'\mathbf{P}'\mathbf{A}'\mathbf{J}\mathbf{A}\mathbf{P}(\boldsymbol{\omega} - \mathbf{d}) \\ &= (\boldsymbol{\omega} - \mathbf{d})'\Delta(\boldsymbol{\omega} - \mathbf{d}) \,, \end{aligned} $$

$$ {}_iP_{jk} = \int_{D<0} \frac{exp\,(-0.5\boldsymbol{\omega} \cdot \boldsymbol{\omega})}{(2\pi)^n}\, d\boldsymbol{\omega} $$

$$ = \Pr\left[\sum_{i=1}^{2n} \delta_i(\omega_i - d_i)^2 < 0 \right] $$

$$= \Pr\left[\sum_{i=1}^{r} \delta_i \chi^2_{m_i, d_i} < 0\right],$$

where

$$\delta_i = \text{eigenvalues of } \boldsymbol{\Sigma} \begin{bmatrix} \mathbf{I} & \mathbf{0} \\ \mathbf{0} & -\mathbf{I} \end{bmatrix}$$

m_i = degrees of freedom of the i-th noncentral chi square

d_i = noncentrality parameter of the i-th chi square

r = number of distinct eigenvalues

In this form, from the work of Imhof (1961), the probability of choosing $\mathbf{S}_j$ or $\mathbf{S}_k$ is

$${}_iP_{jk} = 0.5 - \frac{1}{\pi}\int_0^{\infty} \frac{\sin\theta(t)}{t\rho(t)}\, dt\,, \tag{2}$$

where

$$\theta(t) = 0.5 \sum_{i=1}^{r} [m_i \tan^{-1}(\delta_i t) + d_i^2 \delta_i t(1 + \delta_i^2 t^2)^{-1}]\,,$$

$$\rho(t) = \left[\prod_{i=1}^{r} (1 + \delta_i^2 t^2)^{m_i/4}\right] \exp\left\{0.5 \sum_{j=1}^{r} \frac{(d_j \delta_j t)^2}{1 + \delta_j^2 t^2}\right\}.$$

RELATIONSHIPS AMONG TRIAD AND PREFERENCE MODELS

Figure 5.1 summarizes the relationships between the model formulated in Equation 1 and other triad and preference models. It can be seen that the model presented in this chapter is the general case for any model that specifies that a subject will choose between two alternatives, the one whose momentary psychological effect has the smaller Euclidean distance to the momentary effect of a third alternative when the distributions of all momentary effects are assumed to be multivariate normal. The model includes the following special cases: the Thurstonian variant of Torgerson's Method of Triads, the Duo-Trio Method model, the wandering ideal point model, the preference model of Zinnes and Griggs (1974), and Coombs' (1964) preference unfolding model. Also included is the two-alternative identification model based on a comparison of distances between a probe and the memory representations.

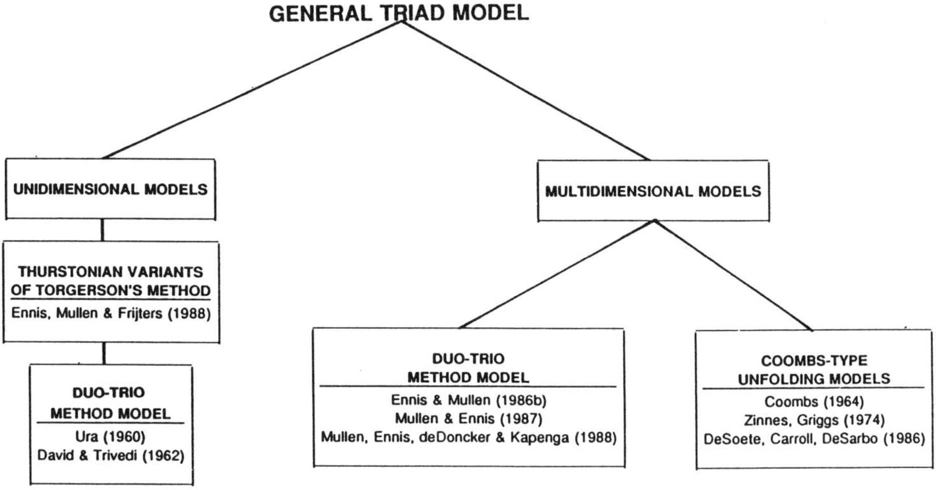

FIG. 5.1. Relationship among triad and preference choice models as special cases of the general triad model.

COMPUTING

Numerical integration and parameter estimation techniques for equations such as Equations 1 and 2 have been discussed in Mullen and Ennis (1987), Mullen et al. (1988), and Ennis, Palen, and Mullen (1988). The numerical evaluation of Equation 1 is fairly computationally intense, partly because it involves the numerical evaluation of a $2n$-fold integral, where n is the number of dimensions. A comparison of the computational efficiency of Equations 1 and 2, on a Gould 32/97 computer when $n = 2$, revealed that Equation 2 could be computed 10^3 to 10^4 times faster (to the same accuracy) than adaptive numerical integration of Equation 1, depending on the specific parameters chosen. When n is larger than 2, the relative efficiency of Equation 2 should become even greater because the computing time will be directly proportional to n rather than a function involving n as an exponent.

Parameters of the distributions corresponding to $\mathbf{S}_i$, $\mathbf{S}_j$, and $\mathbf{S}_k$ can be estimated by using Nonlinear Least Squares as outlined in Chapter 11. It would be interesting to simultaneously fit triad and preference matrices with Equation 2 for an ensemble of stimuli.

CONCLUDING REMARKS

Triad discrimination, preferential choice, and two-alternative identification share a common mathematical model. This model is based on the assumption that subjects make choices between stimuli or memory representations based on Euclidean distances between stimuli, stimuli and ideal stimuli, or probes and memory representations. These ideas were presented in the context of a probabilistic model that assumes multivariate normal probability density functions for stimuli, ideal stimuli, or memory representations. A computationally simple form to compute decision probabilities has been given.

6 Uniting Identification, Similarity and Preference: General Recognition Theory

Nancy A. Perrin
Portland State University

Psychology has a long history of investigating identification, similarity, and preference judgments. However, until recently no theory attempted to account for all three of these judgments simultaneously, despite the fact that they appear to be strongly related. For example, in making a preference judgment the items in the choice set may first be identified, next the similarity between the different items in the choice set might be estimated, and finally preference can be determined. In 1986, General Recognition Theory (GRT) (Ashby & Perrin, 1988; Ashby & Townsend, 1986; Perrin, 1986) was introduced. One of the strengths of this theory is that it attempts to unify research in identification, similarity, and preference by using a common psychological space to model all three types of responses. Therefore, GRT offers a framework to better understand the perceptual processes associated with these judgments.

In an identification experiment, the stimulus set consists of two or more stimuli, and the subject is shown a stimulus and asked to name or identify it. Feedback as to the correct response is often given. Each stimulus is presented many times, and a confusion matrix is used to summarize the responses. The elements of the matrix are the number of times the column stimulus was identified as the row stimulus. In a similarity experiment, subjects are shown two stimuli simultaneously or consecutively and are asked to judge the similarity or dissimilarity of the stimuli. Subjects are shown all possible pairs of the stimuli, and the response scale for the similarity judgment is typically a rating scale. The responses are summarized in a similarity matrix, with each element representing the judged similarity of the row and column stimuli. Finally, in a preference experiment, subjects are asked to select the stimulus they most prefer. The most common preference experiment involves paired comparisons in which subjects are shown a pair of stimuli and asked which of the two they most prefer. All possible pairs are presented, and the data are summarized in a matrix where the elements are the number of times the row stimulus was preferred over the column stimulus.

There have been numerous attempts to combine existing models of similarity and identification. The most successful of these are based on the biased-choice model (Luce, 1963a; Shepard, 1957). In this identification model, the probability of responding $\mathbf{R}_j$ when stimulus $\mathbf{S}_i$ is presented, $P(\mathbf{R}_j|\mathbf{S}_i)$, is a function of the similarity of stimuli $\mathbf{S}_i$ and $\mathbf{S}_j$, denoted η_{ij}, and the bias toward response $\mathbf{R}_j$, denoted β_j. Specifically,

$$P(\mathbf{R}_j|\mathbf{S}_i) = \frac{\beta_j \eta_{ij}}{\sum_m \beta_m \eta_{im}} . \tag{1}$$

When applying this model, it is usually assumed that similarity is symmetric so that $\eta_{ij} = \eta_{ji}$. Although the empirical validity of this assumption has been questioned (Krumhansl, 1978; Tversky, 1977), the biased-choice model was the most successful identification model for more than 25 years (e.g., J. E. Smith, 1982; Townsend & Ashby, 1982).

Many attempts to unify similarity and identification have involved some version of the biased-choice model. In Shepard's (1957) original formulation of the model, he assumed $\eta_{ij} = exp\ (-d_{ij})$, where d_{ij} is the distance between the perceptual representations of stimuli $\mathbf{S}_i$ and $\mathbf{S}_j$, in some low-dimensional psychological space. The resulting model, known as the multidimensional scaling (MDS)-choice model, has been generalized in one form or another by several researchers (see chaps. 13–15). A version based on simple Euclidean distances was proposed by Shepard (1958b) and investigated by Takane and Shibayama (1985; see also chap. 13) and Nosofsky (1984, 1985b, 1986, 1987; see also chap. 14). In a similar vein, Nakatani (1972) derived the confusion-choice model, which uses simple Euclidean distance but assumes that computation of the distances is noisy. Instead of using distance, Keren and Baggen (1981) replaced the η_{ij} of Equation 1 with the dissimilarity measure of Tversky's (1977) feature-contrast model, thereby creating the unique-feature model.

None of these attempts have been completely successful. First, since each of these models is a special case of the biased-choice model, it cannot fit a set of identification data better than the biased-choice model. Although the biased-choice model often provides excellent fits to identification confusion matrices, this is not always the case (e.g., Ashby & Lee, 1991; Ashby & Perrin, 1988). Second, the MDS-choice models and Nakatani's model are based on geometric models of similarity and thus are constrained to predict that perceived dissimilarity satisfies some or all of the distance axioms. Although some geometric models can predict violations of the triangle inequality (e.g., weighted MDS-choice model; Nosofsky, 1987), several researchers have argued that every (or at least most) distance axiom is inappropriate (Krumhansl, 1978; Tversky, 1977).

There have also been attempts to unite similarity and preference judgments. Many of these begin with an MDS model of similarity and then assume that the most preferred item is the one most similar (i.e., nearest) to the subject's hypothetical ideal item (as in Coombs, 1950, unfolding model). Different models represent the subject's ideal item as a subject vector (Tucker, 1960), a point (Carroll, 1972; Tucker, 1972), or a probability distribution (DeSarbo, Oliver, & De Soete, 1986; De Soete, Carroll, & DeSarbo, 1986; see chaps. 2–5 for more details). Ramsay (1980) suggested a method for jointly estimating dissimilarity and pairwise preferences based on the ideal point model. Like the MDS-choice models, these models all are constrained by some or all of the distance axioms.

General Recognition Theory offers a rich framework within which to account for identification, similarity, and preference judgments while correcting some of the shortcomings encountered in other models. As we shall see, GRT of preference is not constrained by the distance axioms. Additionally, some of the current similarity and preference models are contained in GRT as special cases. This in turn provides a framework to explore the relationships between these models.

GENERAL RECOGNITION THEORY

Consider a set of stimuli constructed by varying the level of two physical dimensions X and Y. GRT assumes that the percepts of any single presentation of such a stimulus can be represented as a point in a multidimensional space. Suppose the space has dimensions x and y.

It is also assumed that repeated presentation of the same stimulus produces a distribution of perceptual effects (i.e., so that $\boldsymbol{x}$ and $\boldsymbol{y}$ are random variables) with probability density function $f(x, y)$. In an identification task with stimuli $\mathbf{S}_A$ and $\mathbf{S}_B$, each varying on two dimensions, GRT postulates that the subject divides the perceptual space into two regions. All perceptual effects falling in one region elicit an $\mathbf{R}_A$ response, and all effects in the other region elicit response $\mathbf{R}_B$. The decision bound is the line or curve that separates the two regions. Figure 6.1 illustrates the contours of equal likelihood and decision bound associated with such a case. Each contour of equal likelihood is characterized by a covariance matrix and mean vector of the form (see chap. 1)

$$\boldsymbol{\Sigma} = \begin{bmatrix} \sigma_x^2 & \rho_{xy}\sigma_x\sigma_y \\ \rho_{xy}\sigma_x\sigma_y & \sigma_y^2 \end{bmatrix}, \qquad \boldsymbol{\mu} = \begin{bmatrix} \mu_x \\ \mu_y \end{bmatrix}.$$

Different versions of GRT can be constructed by making different assumptions about how the subject places the decision bound (see chap. 16). The response boundary in Figure 6.1 maximizes the probability of a correct response. This optimal boundary is the set of points satisfying

$$l(x, y) = \frac{f_A(x, y)}{f_B(x, y)} = 1 \,. \tag{2}$$

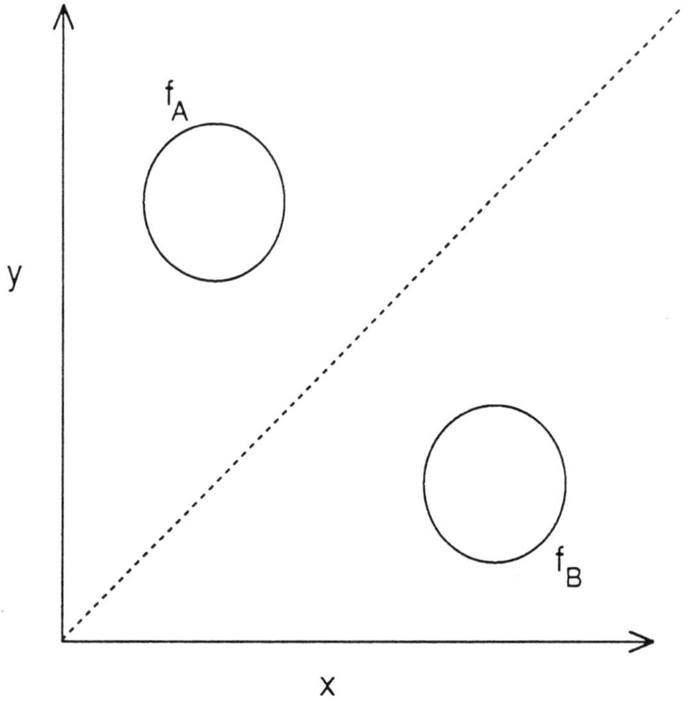

FIG. 6.1. Contours of equal probability and decision boundary for a two-stimulus recognition task.

Ashby and Gott (1988) and Ashby and Maddox (1990) presented empirical evidence that subjects can place the boundary so that performance in terms of response accuracy is approximately maximized, at least in a categorization task (see also chap. 16). In doing so, the subjects exhibited relatively little variability in their response process.

A response bias occurs if the subject places the boundary such that $l(x, y) = \mathrm{b}$, where $\mathrm{b} \neq 1$. In this case the subject's decision rule may maximize something other than accuracy, such as payoffs.

According to GRT, on any given trial, the presentation of the stimulus will elicit a perceptual effect that may fall anywhere in the perceptual space. Stimulus $\mathbf{S}_A$ is confused with stimulus $\mathbf{S}_B$ if the perceptual effect of $\mathbf{S}_A$ falls in the response region associated with $\mathbf{R}_B$. In this case, an error in identification occurs. In the two-dimensional case, the probability of confusing $\mathbf{S}_B$ for $\mathbf{S}_A$ is given by

$$P(\mathbf{R}_B|\mathbf{S}_A) = \int_{r_B}\int f_A(x, y)\, dx\, dy\ , \tag{3}$$

where r_B is the region in the (x,y) place associated with response $\mathbf{R_B}$. Any factor that decreases the proportion of the $\mathbf{S_A}$ distribution falling in the $\mathbf{R_B}$ response region will decrease confusability between the two stimuli. One way to do this is to increase the distance between the means of the two distributions; however, decreasing the relevant variances will also decrease confusability. Therefore, the probability of a correct identification is not necessarily monotonic with inter-mean distance in GRT.

The most familiar version of GRT assumes the perceptual distributions are multivariate normal. This special case, called the general Gaussian recognition model, is related to Thurstone's Law of Categorical Judgment (Thurstone, 1927a; see also Ennis, 1988a; Ennis & Mullen, 1986a; Hefner, 1958; Torgerson, 1958; Zinnes & MacKay, 1983), or it can be viewed as a multidimensional generalization of Signal Detection Theory (see, e.g., Graham, Kramer, & Yager, 1987; Green & Swets, 1974; Nakatani, 1972; Tanner, 1956; Wandell, 1982).

GRT can be generalized to account for data from identification experiments with any number of stimuli varying along any number of dimensions. For example, consider a stimulus ensemble containing four stimuli that are created by factorially combining two levels of each of two dimensions. For example, the stimuli might be plastic blocks that vary in size (with two levels: $\mathbf{A}_1$ = small, $\mathbf{A}_2$ = large) and weight (with two levels: $\mathbf{B}_1$ = light and $\mathbf{B}_2$ = heavy). Figure 6.2 shows the contours of equal likelihood representing each of the stimuli and some hypothetical decision boundaries. In this case there are four possible responses: $\mathbf{A}_1\mathbf{B}_1$, $\mathbf{A}_1\mathbf{B}_2$, $\mathbf{A}_2\mathbf{B}_1$, $\mathbf{A}_2\mathbf{B}_2$. An optimal response function in terms of accuracy selects the response associated with the stimulus most likely to have produced the perceptual effect. In the case of Figure 6.2, this divides the perceptual space into four regions. In effect, the subject uses the X_0 criterion for deciding the level of component **A** and the Y_0 criterion for deciding the level of component **B**.

Accounting for Identification Data

Using the GRT framework, data from identification experiments can be tested directly for a number of decisional and perceptual properties. The most popular of these are perceptual independence, decisional separability, and perceptual separability (Ashby & Townsend, 1986). The results of these tests lead to a better understanding of how the subject perceives the stimuli, and they allow one to simplify the GRT models.

Perceptual independence of components **A** and **B** holds if and only if the perceptual effects of **A** and **B** are statistically independent; that is, for stimulus $\mathbf{A}_i\mathbf{B}_j$ if and only if

$$f_{\mathbf{A}_i\mathbf{B}_j}(x,y) = g_{\mathbf{A}_i\mathbf{B}_j}(x)\, g_{\mathbf{A}_i\mathbf{B}_j}(y)$$

for all x and y, where, for example, $g_{\mathbf{A}_i\mathbf{B}_j}(x)$ is the marginal distribution on

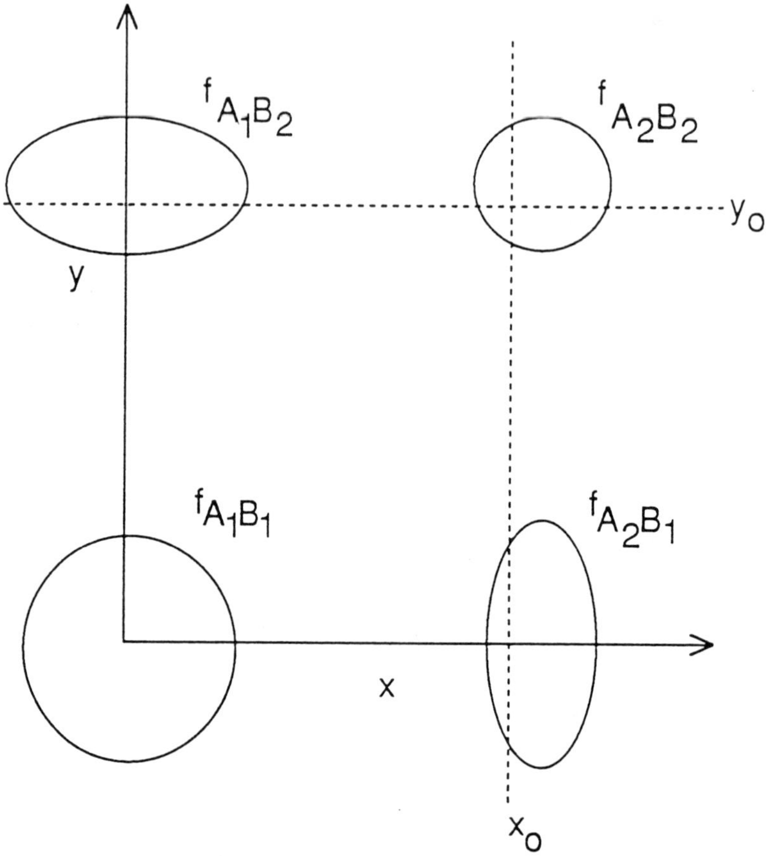

FIG. 6.2. Contours of equal probability and decision boundaries for a four-stimulus recognition task.

dimension $\boldsymbol{x}$ when the stimulus is $\mathbf{A}_i\mathbf{B}_j$ (see Definition 1.1). Perceptual independence implies all covariance terms are zero.

Perceptual separability holds if and only if the marginal perceptual distribution of each level of a given component does not depend on the level of the other component; that is, if and only if for i = 1 and 2,

$$g_{\mathbf{A}_i\mathbf{B}_1}(x) = g_{\mathbf{A}_i\mathbf{B}_2}(x) \qquad \text{for all } x \; , \tag{4}$$

and for j = 1 and 2,

$$g_{\mathbf{A}_1\mathbf{B}_j}(y) = g_{\mathbf{A}_2\mathbf{B}_j}(y) \qquad \text{for all } y \; . \tag{5}$$

Finally, decisional separability holds if and only if the decision bounds are parallel to the coordinate axes (as in Figure 6.2). A more detailed discussion of these concepts can be found in Ashby and Townsend (1986; see also chaps. 7–9).

Ashby and Townsend (1986) used GRT and data from a complete identification experiment reported by Townsend, Hu, and Ashby (1980, 1981) to test for perceptual independence and separability. In the Townsend et al. (1980, 1981) experiment, two levels of two stimulus components were factorially combined. The components were a horizontal line segment and a vertical line segment joined at an upper left corner. The two levels were component presence and absence. This leads to a four-stimulus identification task like the one associated with Figure 6.2. On each trial, one of these four stimuli was randomly selected and tachistoscopically shown to the subject, who was asked to make an identification response.

Using tests that they developed, Ashby and Townsend (1986) concluded that: (a) the perceptual effects of the vertical and horizontal components are statistically independent (i.e., perceptual independence), (b) the perceptual effects of a given level of one component do not depend on the level of the other component (i.e., perceptual separability), and (c) the decision about which level of a given component is contained in the stimulus does not depend on the perceptual effect of the other component or that the data satisfy decisional separability.

Ashby and Perrin (1988) fitted the general Gaussian recognition model to the Townsend et al. (1980, 1981) data, using the results previously discussed to reduce the number of free parameters. The fits were then compared with the biased-choice model, a city-block MDS choice model with an exponential similarity function, a Euclidean MDS-choice model with a Gaussian similarity function [i.e., $\eta_{ij} = exp\ (-d_{ij}^2)$], and the unique-feature model. The best-fitting general Gaussian recognition model fits the data about as well as the biased-choice model (Luce, 1963a; Shepard, 1957). The city-block MDS choice model and the Euclidean MDS-choice model with a Gaussian similarity function also provided good fits to the data.

Ashby and Lee (1991) provided further evidence of GRT's ability to account for identification data. Using semicircles with a line projecting from the center to the rim as stimuli, subjects were asked to make identification and similarity judgments. In this case, the general Gaussian recognition model fit the identification data substantially better than the biased-choice model, an exponential/city-block MDS choice model, a Gaussian/Euclidean MDS-choice model, or an exponential/Euclidean MDS-choice model.

At least with certain kinds of data, then, GRT can fit as well or better than the biased-choice model. In addition, extra information about the perceptual space can be found by examining the parameter values of the best-fitting GRT model. For example, it was found with the Townsend et al. (1980, 1981) data that when a component was present its perceptual variance was significantly smaller than when the component was absent. Therefore, when the component was absent, perceptual noise was sometimes great enough to cause subjects to mistakenly perceive its presence. In the letter recognition literature these misperceptions are called ghost features (Townsend & Ashby, 1982). It was also found that the decision criteria were very large. Subjects consistently used high thresholds on both dimensions. This, too, is consistent with the letter recognition literature (Rumelhart, 1971). In addition, although the components of the circular stimuli in the Ashby and Lee (1991) study had been previously thought to be separable, the fits of the various GRT models strongly indicated an asymmetric integrality. The perceived size of the circles did not depend on the orientation of the line segment, but perceived orientation did depend on circle size.

Another interesting aspect of the GRT fits to identification confusion matrices are the perceived similarities predicted from the resulting parameter estimates. Unlike the biased-choice model and the MDS-choice models, GRT can predict similarities that are not constrained by any of the distance axioms. The next section introduces the GRT of similarity.

GENERAL RECOGNITION THEORY OF SIMILARITY

To account for perceived similarity, Ashby and Perrin (1988) assumed that in the absence of response bias, similarity, and confusability are proportional. If no response bias exists, the decision boundary is placed where the likelihood ratio $l(x,y)$ equals unity, and, therefore, in the two-dimensional case a measure of the perceived similarity of $\mathbf{S}_A$ to $\mathbf{S}_B$ is

$$s(\mathbf{S}_A, \mathbf{S}_B) = k \int_{r_B} \int f_A(x, y)\, dx\, dy, \qquad \text{when } l(x, y) = 1\,, \tag{6}$$

where k is some positive constant. Thus, in GRT, the similarity of stimulus $\mathbf{S}_A$ to $\mathbf{S}_B$ is naturally defined as the proportion of the $\mathbf{S}_A$ perceptual distribution falling in the response region assigned to $\mathbf{R}_B$ in an unbiased two-choice identification task (when $k = 1$). The constant k acts like the unit of measurement in a ratio scale and so can be set to 1 without loss of generality.

The GRT similarity model can be formulated in two ways, depending on whether stimulus context is considered (Ashby & Perrin, 1988). When three or more stimuli are in the ensemble, the decision boundaries can be placed in the perceptual space by considering any two stimuli in isolation and ignoring the third stimulus or by considering the entire ensemble at once. The former is a context-free similarity model, and the latter is a context-sensitive similarity model.

GRT and Multidimensional Scaling

Ashby and Perrin (1988) showed that traditional multidimensional scaling models that employ a Euclidean distance metric are a special case of the context-free general Gaussian recognition model of similarity. The MDS models relate perceived similarity to distance in a psychological space. The perceptual effects of the stimuli are represented as points in the space, and similarity is inversely related to the Euclidean distance between the points.

The MDS models vary in how the dimensions of the psychological space are combined. The general Euclidean scaling model (Carroll & Chang, 1972; Carroll & Wish, 1974; Tucker, 1972) allows subjects to differentially weight potentially oblique dimensions. The angle between dimensions and the weights for each dimension can vary across subjects, but all subjects are assumed to use the same stimulus coordinates. The general Euclidean scaling model defines perceived dissimilarity of $\mathbf{S}_A$ to $\mathbf{S}_B$ for subject i as

$$\delta_i(\mathbf{S}_A,\mathbf{S}_B) = [w_{xi}^2(x_A - x_B)^2 + w_{yi}^2(y_A - y_B)^2 + 2w_{xi}w_{yi}\, cos\, \theta_i(x_A - x_B)(y_A - y_B)]^{1/2}\,, \quad (7)$$

where θ_i is the angle between dimensions x and y for subject i; w_{xi}, for example, is the weight associated with the x dimension for subject i, and x_A, for example, is the coordinate on the x dimension for stimulus $\mathbf{S}_A$. The following result establishes the relation between the general Euclidean scaling model and GRT.

Proposition 6.1 (Ashby & Perrin 1988): If the following restrictions are placed on the general Gaussian recognition model, it makes similarity predictions identical to those of the general Euclidean scaling model.

1. Perceived similarity is context-free.
2. Similarity and dissimilarity are related by $d(\mathbf{S}_A, \mathbf{S}_B) = -2\Phi^{-1}[s(\mathbf{S}_A, \mathbf{S}_B)]$, where Φ is the normal cumulative distribution function.
3. All subjects have the same configuration of perceptual means.
4. For each subject, all stimuli have the same associated perceptual covariance matrix.

The general Gaussian recognition model that is equivalent to the general Euclidean scaling model has a perceptual distribution centered at each stimulus point (x_i,y_j), and the covariance matrix associated with every perceptual distribution of subject i equals

$$\mathbf{\Sigma}_i = \begin{bmatrix} \dfrac{1}{w_{xi}^2\, sin^2\, \theta_i} & \dfrac{-cos\, \theta_i}{w_{xi}w_{yi}\, sin^2\, \theta_i} \\ \dfrac{-cos\, \theta_i}{w_{xi}w_{yi}\, sin^2\, \theta_i} & \dfrac{1}{w_{yi}^2\, sin^2\, \theta_i} \end{bmatrix}.$$

Thus, in this model, all perceptual covariance matrices are equal within each subject's perceptual space. Because the general Euclidean scaling model allows each subject to have unique values for θ, w_x, and w_y, the equivalence mapping allows GRT to postulate different covariance matrices for different subjects.

GRT also contains the more restrictive weighted Euclidean scaling model (Carroll & Chang, 1970; Horan, 1969) as a special case. This model restricts the dimensions to be orthogonal and so eliminates the last term in Equation 7. The general Gaussian recognition model that is equivalent to the weighted Euclidean model has a perceptual distribution centered at each stimulus point and a covariance matrix associated with every perceptual distribution equal to

$$\mathbf{\Sigma}_i = \begin{bmatrix} \frac{1}{w_{xi}^2} & 0 \\ 0 & \frac{1}{w_{yi}^2} \end{bmatrix}.$$

Once again the perceptual covariance matrices are allowed to vary across subjects but not stimuli. Finally, the simple Euclidean scaling model (McGee, 1968) does not allow for differential weighting of dimensions and restricts the dimensions to be orthogonal. In the equivalent general Gaussian recognition model, the covariance matrices equal the identity for all subjects and all stimuli.

Figure 6.3 illustrates the relationship between GRT and the MDS models. The top panel is a possible stimulus representation of four stimuli varying on two physical dimensions. The center panel illustrates four possible perceptual representations according to GRT. The bottom panel presents the MDS representations that correspond to the foregoing GRT representations. The first GRT representation describes a case where each stimulus has a different associated covariance matrix. For example, when stimulus **A** is presented, the perceptual dimensions x and y are perceived independently, but when stimulus **B** is presented x and y exhibit a negative dependence. There is no corresponding MDS representation in this case. In the second GRT representation, the stimuli all have the same associated covariance matrix, and x and y exhibit a negative dependence. This corresponds to the general Euclidean scaling model with oblique axes and differential weighting of dimensions. In the next representation, all stimuli have the same associated covariance matrix, and x and y are perceived independently. The corresponding MDS model is the weighted Euclidean scaling model with differential weighting of the dimensions and orthogonal dimensions. Greater weight is placed on the u dimension because there is greater variability along the y dimension in the corresponding GRT representation. Finally, in the last representation, all stimuli have covariance matrices equal to the identity. The corresponding MDS representation has orthogonal axes and equal weighting of the dimensions.

Predicting Violations of the Distance Axioms

Because of their reliance on distance, MDS similarity, identification, and preference models predict perceived dissimilarities to satisfy some or all of the distance axioms. The empirical validity of all these axioms has been questioned, and a

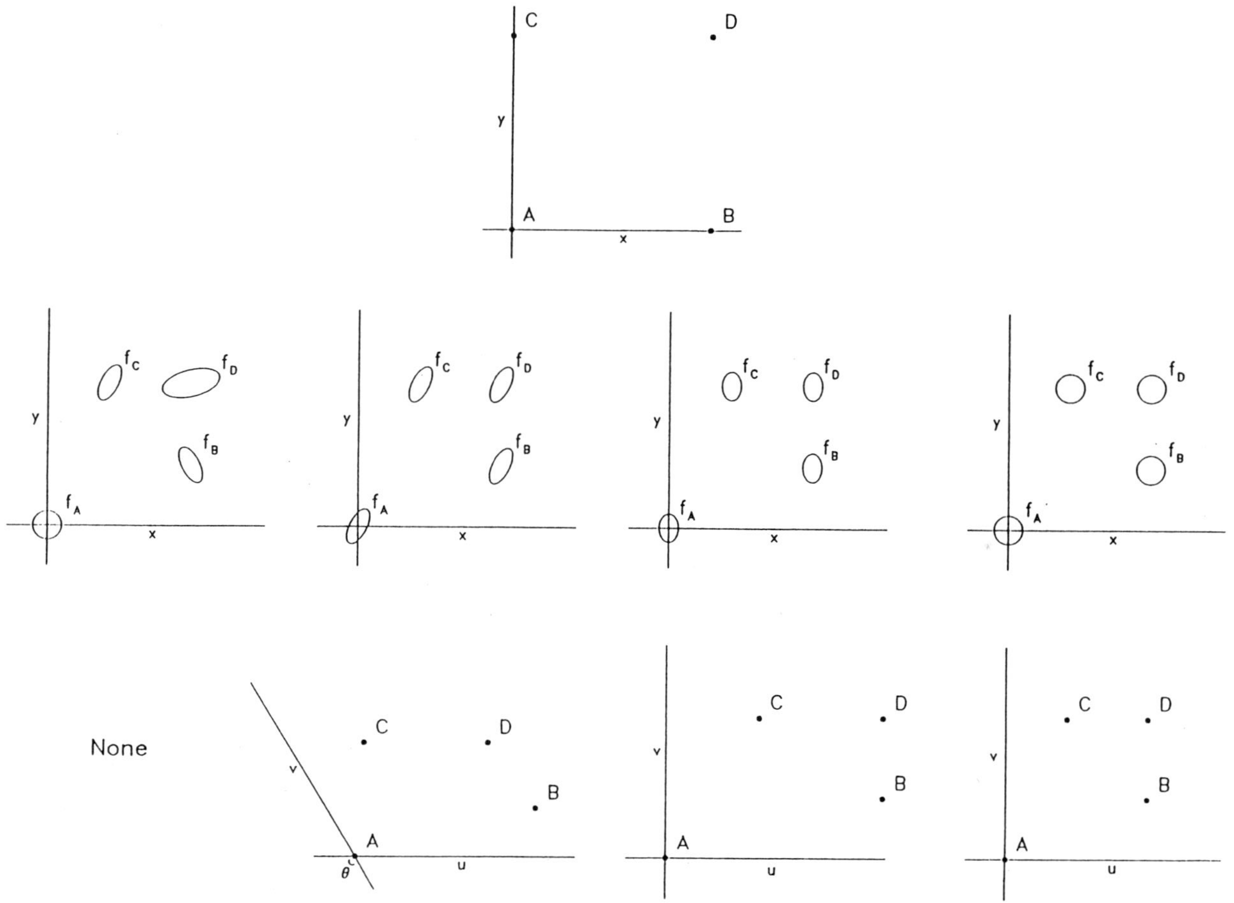

FIG. 6.3. Possible GRT representations for four stimuli and the corresponding MDS representations.

complete theory of similarity, identification, or preference should be able to predict violations of any of these axioms (e.g., Krumhansl, 1978; Tversky, 1977).

The first axiom asserts that all self-dissimilarities are equal. Thus, for all items $\mathbf{S}_A$ and $\mathbf{S}_B$,

$$\delta(\mathbf{S}_A, \mathbf{S}_A) = \delta(\mathbf{S}_B, \mathbf{S}_B) . \quad (8)$$

Krumhansl (1978) argued that stimuli having few features in common with other objects in the stimulus domain have a smaller perceived self-dissimilarity. Ashby and Perrin (1988) showed that the contours of equal probability in Figure 6.4 lead to a violation of equal self-dissimilarity because the proportion of the $\mathbf{S}_A$ perceptual distribution lying in its response region is smaller than the proportion of the $\mathbf{S}_B$ perceptual distribution lying in its own response region.

The second distance axiom, minimality, states that two stimuli are always at least as dissimilar as either stimulus is to itself. Thus, for all stimuli $\mathbf{S}_A$ and $\mathbf{S}_B$,

$$\delta(\mathbf{S}_A, \mathbf{S}_B) \geq \delta(\mathbf{S}_A, \mathbf{S}_A) . \quad (9)$$

Tversky (1977) argued that this weak assumption may sometimes be inappropriate. GRT predicts that violations of minimality must be due to context effects. Even in the presence of context, GRT predicts minimality to be only rarely violated. A violation implies that some stimulus $\mathbf{S}_B$ must be more similar to $\mathbf{S}_A$ than $\mathbf{S}_A$ is to itself. For this to happen, there must be more than two stimuli in the

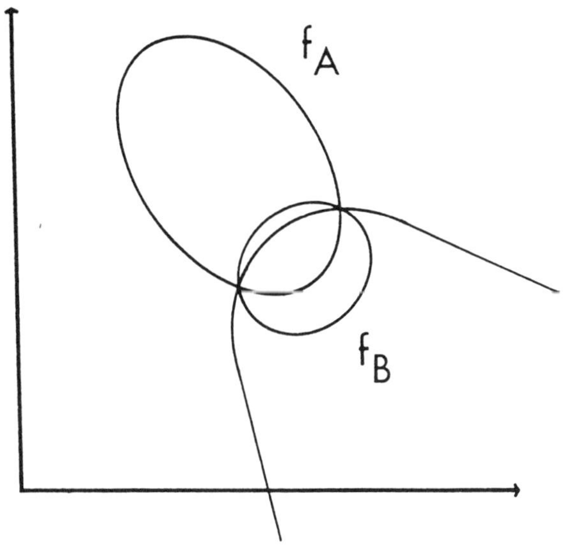

FIG. 6.4. Contours of equal probability for a case in which GRT predicts a violation of self-dissimilarity.

ensemble and they must be highly similar. Such a case might arise if the stimuli are three monochromatic lights differing only in intensity. If the three intensities are all near threshold and very close together, then identification of the middle intensity will be very difficult. This may cause the center light to be misidentified as one of the end lights more frequently than it is correctly identified as itself. These misidentifications cause the similarity of the center light and end light to be greater than the similarity of the center light to itself.

The third axiom, symmetry, states that the dissimilarity of $\mathbf{S}_A$ to $\mathbf{S}_B$ must equal the dissimilarity of $\mathbf{S}_B$ to $\mathbf{S}_A$, or that

$$\delta(\mathbf{S}_A, \mathbf{S}_B) = \delta(\mathbf{S}_B, \mathbf{S}_A) \ . \tag{10}$$

This axiom is assumed by the biased-choice model. Tversky's well-known example of asymmetric similarity is that most subjects judge the similarity of North Korea to Red China to be greater than the similarity of Red China to North Korea. GRT predicts that symmetry will be violated with the contours of equal likelihood illustrated in Figure 6.4. The overlap of the $\mathbf{S}_A$ perceptual distribution into the $\mathbf{R}_B$ response region is greater than the overlap of the $\mathbf{S}_B$ distribution in the $\mathbf{R}_A$ response region, and so GRT predicts the dissimilarity of $\mathbf{S}_B$ to $\mathbf{S}_A$ to be greater than the dissimilarity of $\mathbf{S}_A$ to $\mathbf{S}_B$.

According to GRT, symmetry fails whenever a difference exists between the perceptual covariance structure associated with a pair of stimuli. This may take the form of a difference in the amount of perceptual variability along a given dimension or of a difference in the amount of some perceptual dependence. Symmetry also may be violated due to context effects. These factors offer one explanation for the reported asymmetry between the concepts of North Korea and Red China. North Korea is a more vague and poorly defined concept than Red China, and so the variability associated with the mental representation of North Korea should be greater than the variability associated with the concept of Red China.

The last distance axiom is the triangle inequality, which states that for any three stimuli $\mathbf{S}_A$, $\mathbf{S}_B$, and $\mathbf{S}_C$,

$$\delta(\mathbf{S}_A, \mathbf{S}_C) \leq \delta(\mathbf{S}_A, \mathbf{S}_B) + \delta(\mathbf{S}_B, \mathbf{S}_C) \ . \tag{11}$$

Numerous examples in which the triangle inequality seems to be violated have been cited (Tversky, 1977; Tversky & Gati, 1982) with some dating back to the time of William James (1890). Both the weighted and general MDS models can predict violations of the triangle inequality. However, the weighted model must allow the dimension weights to change with context. Figure 6.2 illustrates contours of equal likelihood for which GRT predicts a violation of the triangle inequality. In this case, $\mathbf{A}_2\mathbf{B}_1$ and $\mathbf{A}_2\mathbf{B}_2$ are very similar and $\mathbf{A}_2\mathbf{B}_2$ and $\mathbf{A}_1\mathbf{B}_2$ are very similar; yet in disagreement with the triangle inequality, $\mathbf{A}_1\mathbf{B}_2$ and $\mathbf{A}_2\mathbf{B}_1$ are very dissimilar.

Other models of similarity based upon Euclidean distances can account for violations of some of the distance axioms. MacKay and Zinnes (1981; Zinnes & MacKay, 1983; chap. 2) and Ennis (Ennis & Mullen, 1986a; Ennis, Palen, & Mullen, 1988; chaps. 5 and 11) derived probabilistic versions of MDS. These models assume that the perceptual representation of each stimulus is a multivariate normal distribution. Similarity is assumed to be inversely related to the distance between momentary perceptual effects. However, since the percepts vary from trial to trial, dissimilarity is not necessarily monotonically related to distance between the means of the distributions. The probabilistic MDS models propose exactly the same perceptual representation as GRT. The two approaches differ only in their assumptions about how the subject uses the perceptual information to judge similarity. At this point, the empirical evidence is insufficient to determine which approach is more valid. One possibility is that both approaches are valid but they apply in different situations. When the subject is making judgments about unfamiliar stimuli, he or she may compute distance because of an unfamiliarity with the stimulus distributions. In this case, a probabilistic MDS model is more valid. However, when the subject is making judgments about familiar stimuli, the distributions are more likely to be known and so overlap could be computed. In this case, GRT would be more appropriate.

Other Predictions with Similarity Data

When examining similarity models, the predictions of another powerful model, the feature-contrast model (Tversky, 1977), must be considered. The feature-contrast model characterizes stimuli as sets of features, and dissimilarity is based on a feature-matching function that weights common and distinct features. Dissimilarity of $\mathbf{S}_A$ to $\mathbf{S}_B$ is given by

$$\delta(\mathbf{S}_A, \mathbf{S}_B) = \alpha g(\mathbf{S}_A - \mathbf{S}_B) + \beta g(\mathbf{S}_B - \mathbf{S}_A) - \theta g(\mathbf{S}_A \cap \mathbf{S}_B)\,, \tag{12}$$

where α, β, and θ are nonnegative free parameters, and g is a measure of the salience of a set of features. The first term represents the weighted salience of the features contained in $\mathbf{S}_A$ but not $\mathbf{S}_B$, the second term represents the weighted salience of the features contained in $\mathbf{S}_B$ but not $\mathbf{S}_A$, and the last term represents the weighted salience of the features contained in both stimuli.

Since the feature-contrast model assumes a psychological space composed of discrete features and GRT assumes a continuous psychological space, a direct comparison of the two theories is difficult. Even so, comparisons are possible.

Tversky and Gati (1982; Gati & Tversky, 1982) identified three ordinal properties that characterize what they called a "monotone proximity structure." These axioms were originally proposed as further constraints on MDS models of similarity, but Proposition 6.2 shows that under certain conditions two of these also constrain the feature-contrast model. On the other hand, Ashby and Perrin (1988) showed that none of these properties constrain GRT.

The first property is dominance, which states that

$$\delta(ap, bq) > \max\,[\delta(ap, aq)\ ,\ \delta(aq, bq)]\ , \tag{13}$$

where $\delta(ap,bp)$ is the dissimilarity between a pair of stimuli, *ap* and *bp*, varying on two features. The first stimulus has a value of *a* on the first feature and a value of *p* on the second feature. Dominance states that the two-dimensional dissimilarity must exceed both of the one-dimensional dissimilarities.

Figure 6.5 shows contours of equal likelihood that lead to a violation of the dominance axiom. Notice that these contours all exhibit a positive covariance. Perrin and Ashby (1991) showed that a violation of the dominance axiom is expected whenever the perceptual dimensions are not perceived independently. Therefore, dominance is a good test of perceptual independence for dissimilarity data. Perceptual dependencies are expected in several cases. For example, consider the relationship between size and weight. When two objects are the same mass but differ in size, the larger object appears heavier because of the size-weight illusion. Figure 6.5 might represent three stimuli varying in size and weight. The two stimuli that differ only on one dimension may appear more dissimilar than two stimuli differing on both dimensions because of the effect of

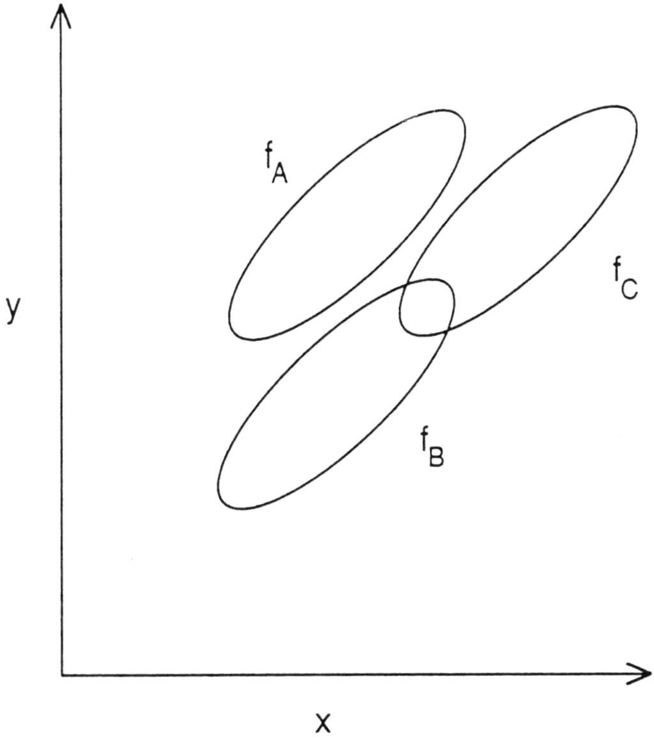

FIG. 6.5. Contours of equal probability for a case in which GRT predicts a violation of dominance.

the illusion. In support of this hypothesis, Perrin and Ashby found frequent violations of dominance with similarity data collected on plastic blocks varying in size and weight.

The second property is called consistency and states that

$$\begin{aligned} \delta(ap, bp) > \delta(cp, dp) \quad & \text{iff } \delta(aq, bq) > \delta(cq, dq)\ , \\ \delta(ap, aq) > \delta(ar, as) \quad & \text{iff } \delta(bp, bq) > \delta(br, bs) \end{aligned} \tag{14}$$

for all values of a, b, c, d, p, q, r, and s. In other words, the dissimilarity of two pairs of stimuli differing on one dimension does not depend on the level of the other fixed dimension. Although this axiom has rarely been tested, MacAdam (1942) reported results that suggest violations may be possible. He estimated the variance of the wavelengths of the indiscriminable colors in a two-color discrimination task and found that as more white is added to indigo the variance increases, but that as more white is added to green the variance decreases. GRT predicts that, because of the different pattern of variances across stimuli, consistency will be violated with these stimuli. Maddox (chap. 7) shows that violations of consistency are expected when perceptual separability is violated.

The following result establishes the conditions under which the aforementioned axioms are predicted by the feature-contrast model. The proof is given in Appendix A.

Proposition 6.2: When the stimulus features are unique and can be identified and experimentally manipulated, the feature-contrast model predicts that consistency holds. If, in addition, the feature saliency function is nonnegative and nondecreasing, the feature-contrast model predicts that dominance holds.

The nondecreasing assumption eliminates the possibility of certain severe interactions between stimulus features (i.e., $g(ap) \geq \max[g(a), g(p)]$). In other words, the saliency of a pair of features cannot be less than the saliency of either feature by itself. The nonnegative assumption requires $g(a) \geq 0$ for any a.

Since GRT is not constrained to predict the preceding properties in dissimilarity data and it can predict violations of the distance axioms in dissimilarity data, in one sense, at least, it has more flexibility in explaining similarity judgments than either the feature-contrast model or the MDS models. Several studies support the need for these more general predictions to account for similarity judgments.

Studies Supporting GRT Similarity Predictions

Ashby and Perrin (1988) reported the results of an experiment that tested the different predictions of traditional MDS models and GRT. In the experiment, subjects first assigned rectangular stimuli to one of two experimenter-defined categories. Each category was defined by a bivariate normal distribution. After a block of categorization trials, subjects judged the similarity of the two categories. The overlap of the two category distributions varied across three conditions, but the means remained invariant. Any model that assumes dissimilarity is a function of intermean distance only, thus predicts the dissimilarities to be the same for the three conditions. GRT predicts the dissimilarities to vary across the three conditions, since the variance and covariances change.

Ashby and Perrin (1988) found that the categorization results and similarity results agreed with the predictions of GRT. Specifically, categorization accuracy decreased as overlap increased and similarity increased as overlap increased, even though intermean distance is constant across the three conditions. This study shows that similarity is not solely a function of intermean distance, but that subjects also take variances and covariances into consideration when judging similarity.

Further support for the GRT representation of similarity came from Ashby and Lee (1991), who had the same subjects participate in an identification experiment and in a similarity study. In both tasks, stimuli were semicircles of varying radii that contained a line of varying orientation. In the first step of the data analysis, the biased-choice model, three versions of the MDS-choice model, and a GRT model (along with several special cases) were fit to the identification confusion matrices. As noted before, the GRT model provided the best fit. Next, with the parameter estimates from the identification data, similarity judgments were predicted from each model. In addition, each model was allowed one free attention parameter, which measured the subject's allocation of attention to the two stimulus dimensions. When the rank orderings of the predicted similarities were compared with the observed similarity judgments, the GRT model was found to provide the best fit to the data of both subjects. Even more impressively, the GRT model (with one free parameter) accounted for the similarity judgments almost as well as an MDS model (with 14 free parameters) fit directly to the similarity data.

These results support the hypothesis that subjects allocated attention to the dimensions differently in the identification and similarity tasks. In the identification task, the dimensions were given equal attention, which maximizes accuracy. The attention parameter was needed to adequately fit the similarity data because in the similarity task subjects allocated most of their attention to the more salient size dimension. When judging similarity, there is no correct response, so subjects may conserve energy by attending to one dimension more than the other.

The fact that the GRT model with one attention parameter fit about as well as the MDS similarity model is very striking, considering the difference in the number of free parameters (i.e., 1 versus 14). This result is possible only if there is a close relationship between similarity and identification and if distributional overlap is a more accurate measure of perceived similarity than is Euclidean distance. The next step is to generalize these findings to account for preference judgments.

GENERAL RECOGNITION THEORY OF PREFERENCE

In explaining preference judgments, GRT borrows the concept of an ideal stimulus from the unfolding MDS preference models (Bennett & Hays, 1960; Carroll, 1972; Coombs, 1950; Tucker, 1972). Like the unfolding models, GRT of preference hypothesizes that, when selecting a most preferred item from the choice set, subjects consider the similarity of each item to some hypothetical personal ideal item. MDS models characterize the items and the ideal as points in the multidimensional space. GRT represents the items and the ideal as distributions in the perceptual space. This is the same space used to explain identification and similarity judgments, although the weighting of the dimensions may vary across the three types of tasks (Ashby & Lee, 1991). The item with the greatest distributional overlap with the ideal is selected as most preferred.

Perrin (1986) described the process of selecting an item from the choice set as a series of identification and similarity judgments. When a choice set is presented, each item is first identified. Next, the similarity of each item in the choice set to the ideal item is computed as defined by the GRT similarity model in a context-sensitive perceptual space. An unbiased decision boundary for each item is placed in the perceptual space so that similarity between the item and the ideal can be computed. The integration is under the choice item distribution throughout the response region associated with the ideal item. In the two-dimensional case each item-ideal similarity is defined as

$$s(\mathbf{S}_A, \mathbf{S}_I) = \int_{r_I}\int f_A(x, y)\, dx\, dy \qquad \text{where } l(x, y) = 1 . \tag{15}$$

The item with the greatest similarity to the ideal is selected as the most preferred item in the choice set. This provides an ordering of preference on a ratio scale that ordinally agrees with judged preference.

The parameters of the ideal distribution have special meaning. In particular, the mode (or modes) on each dimension is the amount, aspect, or element the subject is most likely to imagine as his or her ideal for that dimension. For example, if one dimension of selecting a car was price, the mode would reflect the most likely amount one would prefer to spend. If another aspect of selecting a car was size (i.e., compact, sedan, station wagon) the mode on that dimension would correspond to the most likely desired car size.

The variances associated with each dimension are determined by the importance of that dimension—the more important a dimension, the smaller the variance. The less important a dimension, the harder an ideal value is to locate in the perceptual space. Therefore, when repeated samples of the ideal are taken, values corresponding to less important dimensions will tend to vary more because there is a wider range of acceptable values associated with the ideal on that dimension. Thus, less important dimensions have larger variances. Large variances allow for greater overlap of the ideal and stimulus distributions, increasing their similarity.

Covariances can be interpreted as trade-offs between different dimensions of the choice items. If one is willing to pay a higher price for a car with air conditioning, a nonzero covariance arises between the price and air conditioning dimensions.

In the GRT preference model, variability in performance can occur because of an error in computing the similarities and also because of misidentification of the items in the choice set. This first source of response variability is common to all preference models based on the unfolding principle, but the latter source is unique to GRT. In GRT, before a preference judgment can be made, each item in the choice set must be identified. The confusability between the choice items may influence the item-ideal similarity judgments and the resulting preference order. For example, if during the recognition process a perceptual sample from the $\mathbf{S}_A$ distribution falls into the response region associated with $\mathbf{S}_B$, $\mathbf{S}_A$ is confused as $\mathbf{S}_B$. The subject in this case may believe that two $\mathbf{S}_B$'s are presented. The similarity to the ideal is then judged with respect to $\mathbf{S}_B$ instead of $\mathbf{S}_A$ for both stimuli. These errors in identification will in turn influence preference, since they may cause shifts in the ordering of the $s(\mathbf{S}_j, \mathbf{S}_I)$ for all items j in the choice set.

Through a series of Monte Carlo investigations, Perrin (1986) showed that errors in identification cause changes in the preference ordering. When two items are often confused and both are similar to the ideal, the preference for the item that is most often misidentified is reduced. If $\mathbf{S}_B$ is often confused as $\mathbf{S}_A$, for example, the preference for $\mathbf{S}_B$ will decrease.

The error model associated with preference judgments assumes that identification precedes preference and that identification errors are a potential source of variability in preference judgments. For this to be true, it must also be assumed that the person making the judgment is familiar with the stimuli. However, it is not always the case that the stimuli are familiar (nor do they need to be in order to make a preference judgment).

Another case in which an identification error is unlikely to occur is when the items in the choice set are identified by labels. For example, when subjects are asked whether they prefer Coke or Pepsi, an error in identification is unlikely. However, if subjects are given a taste of each drink from an unmarked container and asked which they prefer, an identification error may occur if one drink is misperceived as the other. GRT is one of the few theories that predicts possible preference reversals across these two methods of stimulus presentation.

Relationship Between GRT Preference Model and MDS Unfolding Models

The traditional Euclidean MDS unfolding models (Carroll, 1972) hypothesize that the perceptual space used in making preference judgments contains a point for each item in the choice set and a point corresponding to the person's ideal item. Preference is a function of the Euclidean distance between items and the ideal. The item nearest to the ideal is considered the most preferred. These unfolding models predict single-peaked preference functions; that is, they postulate that there exists a single point in the multidimensional space for which preference increases as the point is approached from any direction.

The general Euclidean unfolding model (Carroll, 1972) is the most general of the completely deterministic MDS preference models. It represents each subject's ideal as a point in a multidimensional space and uses the general Euclidean scaling model (i.e., Equation 7) to compute similarity. The weighted Euclidean unfolding model and the simple Euclidean unfolding model can be derived by restricting the Equation 7 similarity measure (i.e., first by setting all θ_i to 90° and then by setting all w to 1.0).

The relationship between the MDS unfolding models and the GRT preference model mirrors the relationship between the MDS similarity models and the GRT similarity model. In GRT and in the general Euclidean unfolding model, the basic measure of preference is the similarity between each item in the choice set and the ideal. Therefore, in the absence of identification errors, if the two models make the same similarity predictions they will be completely equivalent. Proposition 6.1 established the conditions under which such equivalence occurs. The three unfolding models are therefore all special cases of the GRT of preference in the same way that the three similarity models are special cases. Thus, the GRT preference model is more general than the traditional Euclidean unfolding models in at least two respects: (a) it does not assume context-free responding; (b) unlike the special case of GRT that is equivalent to the MDS unfolding models, in general, GRT does not require all perceptual distributions to have equal covariance matrices.

There are two other advantages of GRT over the general Euclidean unfolding models. First, GRT allows for violations of all the distance axioms. Like the MDS similarity models, an unfolding model solution for preference data leads to a configuration of the items and the ideal in the perceptual space that will always satisfy some of the distance axioms. Second, the GRT preference model is not restricted to predicting single-peaked preference functions in which preference increases as a single point in the multidimensional perceptual space is approached. When the distributions are not constrained to be normal, GRT of preference can predict other preference functions (Perrin, 1986). For some distributions the preference function will not even be single-peaked. For example, bimodal ideal distributions lead to double-peaked preference functions, where preference increases as two separate points in the space are approached. One interpretation of bimodal ideal distributions is that they reflect the fact that more than one ideal exists. MDS unfolding models assume that only one ideal point exists, although they could be generalized in a similar fashion to include more than one ideal.

Relationship Between GRT Preference Model and Probabilistic MDS Preference Models

De Soete et al. (1986; see chap. 3) hypothesized an unfolding model in which the ideal point for each subject has a multivariate normal distribution. This model, which is called the wandering ideal point model, represents the items in the choice set as fixed points in the multidimensional space. No restrictions are placed on the covariance matrix associated with the ideal. Preference is based on the Euclidean distance between the item and the momentary sample of the ideal. This model leads to single-peaked preference functions and is constrained by some of the distance axioms.

Mullen and Ennis (1991; see also chap. 5) extended the wandering ideal point model to include independent normal distributions for the items in the choice set as well as the ideal item. Preference is determined by the distances between the momentary samples of each stimulus and the momentary sample of the ideal. This model can account for violations of many of the distance axioms (except symmetry). Mullen and Ennis' model and GRT make essentially the same representation assumptions; however, they differ in other respects. The Mullen and Ennis model is not context-sensitive and is less sensitive to perceptual dependence (Ennis & Ashby, 1991). Whether such sensitivity is desirable is an unanswered empirical question.

As with the Ennis et al. (1988) similarity model and GRT, it is possible that these distance-based preference models are more appropriate when subjects are making judgments about unfamiliar stimuli. When the distribution associated with each item is unfamiliar, subjects may choose to compute distance between momentary samples of the item and the ideal. On the other hand, when the items are familiar, both an identification process and computation of overlap between the item and ideal distributions could be carried out by the subject.

It is interesting to compare predictions of the wandering ideal point model (De Soete et al., 1986), the Mullen and Ennis (1991) model, and the GRT preference model. The situation in which the predictions of the GRT preference model are most likely to differ from the predictions of the other two models is when a covariance term exists. In order to test this hypothesis, a series of computer simulations were run to determine which item in a two-item choice set is most preferred according to each of the three models. The means of the item perceptual distributions were (7,10) for item **A** and (8,7) for item **B**. Both distributions had variances of 1 on both dimensions and covariances of 0.5. The ideal distribution was given a mean of (10,10) with the same associated covariance matrix.

To estimate which of the two items would be most preferred according to the wandering ideal point model, 1,000 points were randomly selected from the ideal distribution. For each of these points, a pair of distances was computed, one to the mean of the **A** distribution and one to the mean of the **B** distribution. The item most often associated with the smaller distance was considered the most preferred. For the parameters cited, item **A** was preferred over item **B** (**A** had the smaller distance 621 times).

To determine which of the two items is most preferred according to Mullen and Ennis' model, 1000 random samples were taken from each of the ideal, item **A**, and item **B** distributions. Next, the distance between the samples from the ideal and item **A** distributions was computed as well as the distance between the samples from the ideal and item **B** distributions. For the same parameters, item **A** was more frequently preferred than item **B** (**A** had the smaller distance 566 times).

In the case of the GRT preference model, the similarity of the item to the ideal was computed by taking 1,000 samples from each of the item distributions. Next the proportion of the samples falling in the response region of the ideal stimulus was determined for each item. This leads to estimates of the similarity between the items and the ideal. The item with the greatest similarity to the ideal was considered the most preferred. With the same parameters, item **B** was preferred over item **A** (the similarity of item **A** and the ideal was 0.046 and the similarity of item **B** and the ideal was 0.061). Therefore, in this example, the GRT preference model predicts a different preference ordering than both of the probabilistic unfolding models.

If there is no covariance between the perceptual dimensions, then the three models are more likely to make the same predictions. In fact, when a computer simulation was run using these parameters but changing the covariances to zero, all three models predicted item **A** to be most preferred.

Recall that one plausible hypothesis suggests that the probabilistic MDS models may provide a better representation of the preference process when the stimuli are unfamiliar, and GRT may be a better model when the stimuli are familiar. In the GRT preference model, covariances represent trade-offs between dimensions. In addition, the probabilistic MDS unfolding models are apparently less sensitive to covariation than the GRT models. Therefore, this hypothesis makes the interesting prediction that when the items in the choice set are unfamiliar, trade-offs between dimensions and perceptual dependencies will have less effect on preference than when the items in the choice set are familiar.

The GRT preference model has a large number of parameters. Like the Mullen and Ennis (1991) model, there is a mean and variance on each dimension as well as a covariance term for each pair of dimensions for each item in the choice set and for the ideal. However, by combining the results of Ashby and Townsend (1986), Ashby and Perrin (1988), and Perrin (1986), we can test assumptions such as perceptual independence, decisional separability, and perceptual separability. If identification data are available, the parameters of each item's perceptual distribution can be estimated, and then paired choice probabilities could be used to estimate parameters of the person's ideal distribution. Alternatively, all parameters could be estimated simultaneously. With a two-dimensional representation, the most general version of the GRT preference model has five parameters per stimulus and five for the ideal. For one distribution, both means can be set arbitrarily to 0 and both variances to 1. Therefore, with n stimuli there are 5n + 1 free parameters. There are also n(n − 1)/2 df in a paired comparison experiment. Thus, the model is testable if n(n − 1)/2 > 5n + 1, which holds whenever n > 11.

Summary

GRT is capable of predicting identification judgments as well as or better than the biased-choice model (Luce, 1963a). However, GRT need not assume that similarity is symmetric. In terms of similarity, GRT contains the traditional Euclidean scaling models as special cases, but is not constrained by any of the distance axioms. It can also predict violations of the dominance and consistency axioms that constrain many versions of the feature-contrast model (Tversky, 1977). As a theory of preference, it contains the traditional Euclidean unfolding models as special cases, yet is more general than these models in several respects. For example, the GRT preference model is not restricted to predicting single-peaked preference functions and is not constrained by any distance axioms.

The value of GRT is that the theory unifies several separate research areas in perceptual and cognitive psychology. The theory allows for exploration of the relationships between identification, similarity, preference, and categorization (see chap. 16). GRT offers a deeper interpretation of the psychological processes underlying these judgments while avoiding some of the problems associated with other models of identification, similarity, and preference.

APPENDIX A

Proof of Proposition 6.2:

1. The dominance axiom states that

$$\delta(ap,bq) > \max[\delta(ap,aq),\ \delta(aq,bq)].$$

Rewriting the dissimilarities in terms of the feature-contrast model, we have for the inequality:

$$\begin{aligned}&\alpha g(ap) + \beta g(bq) - \theta g(\emptyset)\\ &\quad > \max[\alpha g(p) + \beta g(q) - \theta g(a)\ ,\ \alpha g(a) + \beta g(b) - \theta g(q)]\ ,\end{aligned}$$

which will hold when the saliency function is nondecreasing and nonnegative or when

$$g(ap) > g(p)\ ,\quad g(ap) > g(a)\ ,\quad g(bq) > g(q)\ ,\quad \text{and}\quad g(bq) > g(b)\ .$$

2. The consistency axiom states that

$$\delta(ap,bp) > \delta(cp,dp) \quad \text{iff} \quad \delta(aq,bq) > \delta(cq,dq)$$

and

$$\delta(ap,aq) > \delta(ar,as) \quad \text{iff} \quad \delta(bp,bq) > \delta(br,bs) \ .$$

Rewriting the antecedent condition in terms of the feature-contrast model, the inequality becomes

$$\alpha g(a) + \beta g(b) - \theta g(p) > \alpha g(c) + \beta g(d) - \theta g(p) \ ,$$

which reduces to

$$\alpha g(a) + \beta g(b) > \alpha g(c) + \beta g(d) \ .$$

Rewriting and reducing the consequent condition yields this same inequality. A similar proof can be derived for the other dimension.

II INTERACTIONS BETWEEN PERCEPTUAL DIMENSIONS

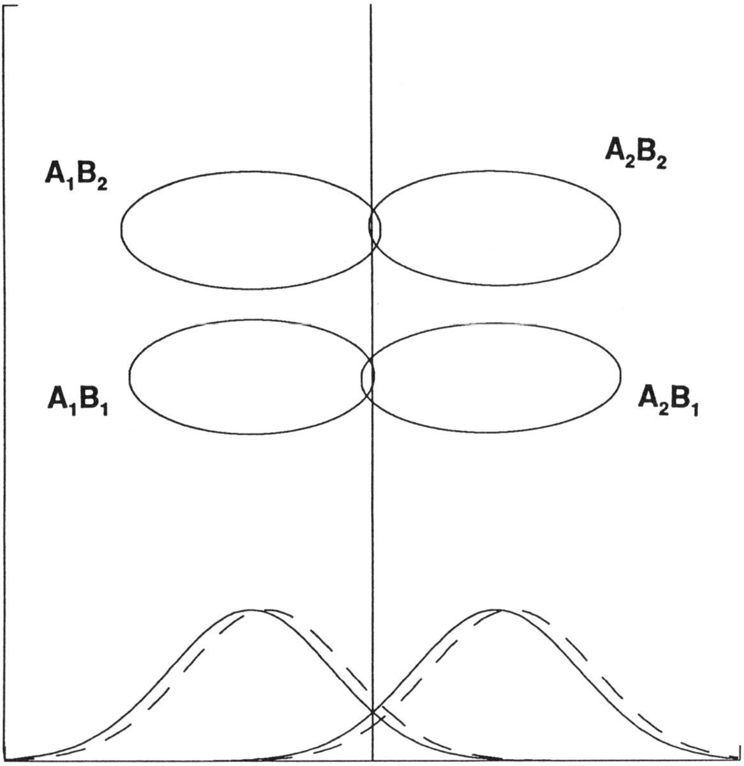

7 Perceptual and Decisional Separability

W. Todd Maddox
University of California at Santa Barbara

A fundamental issue in human perception is to determine how different stimulus dimensions interact during perceptual processing (e.g., Ashby & Townsend, 1986; Garner, 1970, 1974). Two main classes of stimulus dimensions have been identified. These have been variously termed unitary and analyzable (Shepard, 1964), integral and nonintegral (Lockhead, 1966), or integral and separable (Garner, 1974).[1] This chapter adopts Garner's (1974) terminology. The traditional distinction between integral and separable stimulus dimensions emerges from the results of a series of experimental tasks (Garner, 1974; Garner, Hake, & Eriksen, 1956) that purport to assess the extent to which a stimulus is processed by its dimensional values as opposed to as a unitary whole. If the results of these tasks suggest independent processing by dimensions, the stimulus dimensions are termed *separable,* if the results indicate processing as an unanalyzable whole, the dimensions are termed *integral* (e.g., Garner, 1974; Lockhead, 1966; however, see Cheng & Pachella, 1984, and J. D. Smith & Kemler-Nelson, 1984, for alternative processing theories; see also L. B. Smith, 1989, for a developmental processing theory). Prototypical separable dimensions are hue and shape (e.g., Garner, 1977). Prototypical integral dimensions are hue and brightness (e.g., Garner & Felfoldy, 1970; Hyman & Well, 1968).

This chapter examines four operational tests of separability: (a) the Filtering Task, (b) the Redundancy Task, (c) Direct Dissimilarity Scaling, and (d) the

[1]Integrality and separability refer to *pairs* of stimulus dimensions. For example, hue and brightness may be integral, but size and brightness may not. Strictly speaking, then, a more appropriate term would be *stimuli that are composed of integral dimensions;* however, the term *integral dimensions* is more common.

Restricted Classification Task. Although these tasks have proven useful, as originally proposed they were operational and lacked a rigorous theoretical basis. A theoretical foundation can be provided by incorporating them into General Recognition Theory (GRT; Ashby, 1988, 1989; Ashby & Gott, 1988; Ashby & Maddox, 1990, 1991b, 1991c, 1992, in press; Ashby & Perrin, 1988; Ashby & Townsend, 1986; Kadlec & Townsend, 1992), which rigorously defines two types of separability—*perceptual* and *decisional*—and several related concepts, such as perceptual independence.

In the first half of the chapter, the Filtering and Redundancy Tasks are investigated. To facilitate the theoretical development of these two response time (RT) tests of separability, a recent extension of GRT is introduced; namely that processing time (RT) is inversely related to the distance from the perceptual effect of a stimulus to the nearest decision bound (Ashby & Maddox, 1991c). This *RT-distance hypothesis* leads to a powerful RT theory of perceptual separability that will be used to critically examine the Filtering and Redundancy Tasks. In the second half of the chapter, two unspeeded operational tests of separability are examined. The chapter concludes with a short section on other methods of investigating perceptual separability, such as modeling data from a Complete Identification Experiment.

To avoid confusing the operationally defined terms of separability and integrality with the theoretically defined terms of perceptual separability, perceptual integrality, decisional separability, and decisional integrality, we use the terms *separability* and *integrality* when referring to the operational definitions. When the potential for confusion is great, the terms *Garnerian separability* and *Garnerian integrality* will be used to refer to the operational definitions.

FOUR OPERATIONAL TESTS OF SEPARABILITY

The results of several experimental tasks have been used to classify stimulus dimensions as integral or separable (Garner, 1974). One of the most popular is *Speeded Classification*. Here the stimulus set consists of four stimuli that are created by factorially combining two levels of two physical components. Call the components **A** and **B**. Then the four stimuli can be denoted by $\mathbf{A}_1\mathbf{B}_1$, $\mathbf{A}_2\mathbf{B}_1$, $\mathbf{A}_1\mathbf{B}_2$, and $\mathbf{A}_2\mathbf{B}_2$. For example, suppose component **A** is shape and its two levels are circle ($\mathbf{A}_1$) and triangle ($\mathbf{A}_2$), and that component **B** is hue with levels blue ($\mathbf{B}_1$) and green ($\mathbf{B}_2$). Then the four stimuli are a blue circle ($\mathbf{A}_1\mathbf{B}_1$), a green circle ($\mathbf{A}_1\mathbf{B}_2$), a blue triangle ($\mathbf{A}_2\mathbf{B}_1$), and a green triangle ($\mathbf{A}_2\mathbf{B}_2$). In the *filtering condition* (Posner, 1964), the subject is presented with one of the four stimuli on each trial and is asked to categorize, *as quickly as possible,* the level of component **A** (or **B**). In other words, the subject determines whether the shape is circle or triangle. Although hue is irrelevant in this case, the hue of the stimulus still varies from trial to trial. In the *control condition,* the subject's task is identical;

however, there is now no variation along the irrelevant dimension. For example, if the subject is asked to classify by shape, the stimulus ensemble might include the green circle and the green triangle. If the mean RT in the filtering condition is longer than in the control condition, the irrelevant dimension is said to *interfere* with efficient processing of the relevant dimension, and the stimulus dimensions are classified as integral. If no mean RT difference emerges, there is no interference and the dimensions are classified as separable. This experimental procedure is referred to as the Filtering Task because the subject's task is to "filter out" information from the irrelevant dimension. The assumption is that *selective attention* to one of two separable dimensions is easy, whereas selective attention to one of two integral dimensions is difficult.

Another popular Speeded Classification Task is the *Redundancy Task* (Garner, 1974). In the redundancy condition only two of the original four stimuli are utilized: either $\mathbf{A}_1\mathbf{B}_1$ and $\mathbf{A}_2\mathbf{B}_2$ or $\mathbf{A}_1\mathbf{B}_2$ and $\mathbf{A}_2\mathbf{B}_1$. In this condition, the values along the two dimensions are correlated in the sense that correct identification of the level of one component allows the subject to infer the correct level of the other component. On each trial the subject is presented with one of the two stimuli and is again asked to determine, as quickly as possible, the level of component **A** (or **B**). If mean RT is shorter in this condition than in the control condition (described earlier), a *redundancy gain* is said to result and the stimulus dimensions are classified as integral. If no redundancy gain is found, the dimensions are classified as separable.

Direct Dissimilarity Scaling of multidimensional stimuli has also been used to classify stimulus dimensions as integral or separable (e.g., Attneave, 1950; Shepard, 1964; Torgerson, 1958). In this procedure a set of stimuli are created by factorially combining several levels of two stimulus dimensions. The subject is then presented with all possible pairs of stimuli, one pair at a time, and is asked to rate the dissimilarity of the two stimuli on a scale from, say, 1 to 10. These dissimilarity ratings are then submitted to a Multidimensional Scaling program that represents each stimulus as a point in a perceptual space of low dimensionality with the constraint that the ordinal relation between the interpoint distances and the dissimilarity ratings agree as closely as possible. If the Euclidean distance metric fits the data best, the dimensions are assumed to be integral. If the city-block metric fits best, the dimensions are assumed to be separable (Attneave, 1950; Handel & Imai, 1972; Hyman & Well, 1967, 1968; however, see Dunn, 1983, and Ronacher & Bautz, 1985). The idea is that the dimensional structure of separable dimensions is readily apparent, and so the dissimilarity between two stimuli is determined by adding the dissimilarities along each individual dimension, which is analogous to assuming city-block distance. When the stimulus dimensions are integral, however, the dimensional structure is not readily apparent, so dissimilarity is assumed to be a function of the Euclidean distance between stimuli.

The *Restricted Classification Task* (e.g., Burns & Shepp, 1988; Burns, Shepp,

McDonough, & Weiner-Ehrlich, 1978; Grau & Kemler-Nelson, 1988) has also been used to determine stimulus integrality or separability. In Restricted Classification, three stimuli that vary along two physical dimensions are presented to the subject and the subject's task is to decide which two "go together best." Two of the three stimuli share a value along one physical dimension, but are very dissimilar along the other, whereas another pair are quite similar overall but do not share any dimensional values. If the pair that are more similar overall tend to be chosen as the two that go together best, the dimensions are classified as integral. If the pair that share a dimensional value are most often chosen, then the dimensions are assumed to be separable.

This set of converging operations has been taken as an operational definition of separability (Garner, 1974). Operationally, stimulus dimensions that show a redundancy gain and interference in Speeded Classification (e.g., Garner & Felfoldy, 1970), classification based on overall similarity in Restricted Classification (e.g., Handel & Imai, 1972), and produce a Euclidean metric in Dissimilarity Scaling (e.g., Hyman & Well, 1967) are termed integral. Stimulus dimensions that show no redundancy gain or interference in Speeded Classification (e.g., Garner & Felfoldy, 1970), classification based on dimensional relations (e.g., Burns et al., 1978) and produce a city-block metric in Dissimilarity Scaling (e.g., Shepard, 1964) are termed separable.

These four operational tests of separability have been applied to numerous stimulus dimensions. A majority of the work has been conducted with dimensions that are processed *visually,* for example, length and width of rectangles (e.g., Dunn, 1983; Felfoldy, 1974; Krantz & Tversky, 1975; Schönemann, 1977; Weiner-Ehrlich, 1978; Weintraub, 1971), and size of a circle and orientation of a radial line (e.g., Garner & Felfoldy, 1970; Shepard, 1964). Other stimulus modalities have also been investigated. These include *auditory* dimensions, such as pitch and timbre (e.g., Grau & Kemler-Nelson, 1988; Melara & Marks, 1990a; Wood, 1974) and pitch and loudness (e.g., Melara & Marks, 1990b), and stimulus dimensions that can be extracted *haptically,* such as shape, texture, and hardness (e.g., Klatzky, Lederman, & Reed, 1987, 1989; Reed, Lederman, & Klatzky, 1990). *Cross-modal* dimensions, such as color and pitch (e.g., Melara, 1989a) and position and pitch (e.g., Melara & O'Brien, 1987), have also been examined.

In many cases the results of all four tests converge, and the stimulus dimensions are unambiguously classified as, say, integral. Frequently, however, one operational test will indicate integrality and another test will indicate separability. For example, in Speeded Classification, a redundancy gain has been found for size and brightness (Biederman & Checkosky, 1970; Levy & Haggbloom, 1971), a result indicative of integrality. In the Filtering Task, however, these dimensions showed no interference effect (e.g., Gottwald & Garner, 1975), as expected from separable dimensions. Another frequent occurrence is for the pattern of results to suggest integrality, but for the degree of interference and/or redundancy gain to differ from that for other integral dimensions. For example, when Garner and Felfoldy (1970) compared speeded classification results for value and chroma of a single Munsell color chip with those for the horizontal and vertical locations of a single dot on a card, they found the redundancy gain to be comparable for the two pairs of dimensions; however, value and chroma caused approximately five times as much interference in the Filtering Task. These inconsistent results led Garner (1970, 1974) to postulate a continuum of integrality. One goal of this chapter is to propose an explanation that unifies these inconsistent results.

Several other operational tests of separability have been introduced in the literature. These included the Same-Different Task (Dixon & Just, 1978; Garner, 1988; Melara, 1989b), the Privileged Axes Task (J. D. Smith & Kemler-Nelson, 1984; L. B. Smith & Kemler, 1978), the Complexity Judgment Task (Foard & Kemler-Nelson, 1984), the Absolute Identification Task (Lockhead, 1966), the Dimensional Withdrawal Task (Klatzky et al., 1989; Reed et al., 1990), the Texture Segregation Task (Beck, 1966; Callaghan, 1984, 1989; Callaghan, Lasaga, & Garner, 1986) and the Multiclass Procedures (Melara & Marks, 1990a, 1990b). Unfortunately, a critical examination of each of these tests is beyond the scope of this chapter. Instead, the focus is on the four popular separability tests described.

GENERAL RECOGNITION THEORY

The basic assumptions and definitions of General Recognition Theory (GRT) are briefly introduced here. For a more thorough review see Ashby and Townsend (1986; see also chaps. 6, 8, and 16). A stochastic version of the theory was introduced by Ashby (1989).

In short, GRT is a multidimensional extension of Signal Detection Theory (e.g., Graham, Kramer, & Yager, 1987; Green & Swets, 1974; Tanner, 1956; Wandell, 1982). It assumes that the perceptual effect of a stimulus is random and can be represented by a point in a multidimensional space. The distribution of percepts over trials is described by a multivariate probability distribution.

Ashby and Townsend (1986) distinguished between two types of separability: perceptual separability and decisional separability. Consider an Identification Experiment with the four stimuli $\mathbf{A}_1\mathbf{B}_1$, $\mathbf{A}_1\mathbf{B}_2$, $\mathbf{A}_2\mathbf{B}_1$, and $\mathbf{A}_2\mathbf{B}_2$ and the corresponding hypothetical contours of equal likelihood shown in Figure 7.1a. *Perceptual separability* occurs if the perceptual effect of a particular component is unaffected by the level of the other component. In other words, if component **A** is perceptually separable from component **B**, then the distribution of percepts associated with component **A** should be the same for, say, stimuli $\mathbf{A}_1\mathbf{B}_1$ and $\mathbf{A}_1\mathbf{B}_2$. If **A** is perceptually separable from **B** and **B** is perceptually separable from **A**, then **A** and **B** are said to be *mutually* perceptually separable. More formally, mutual perceptual separability holds if

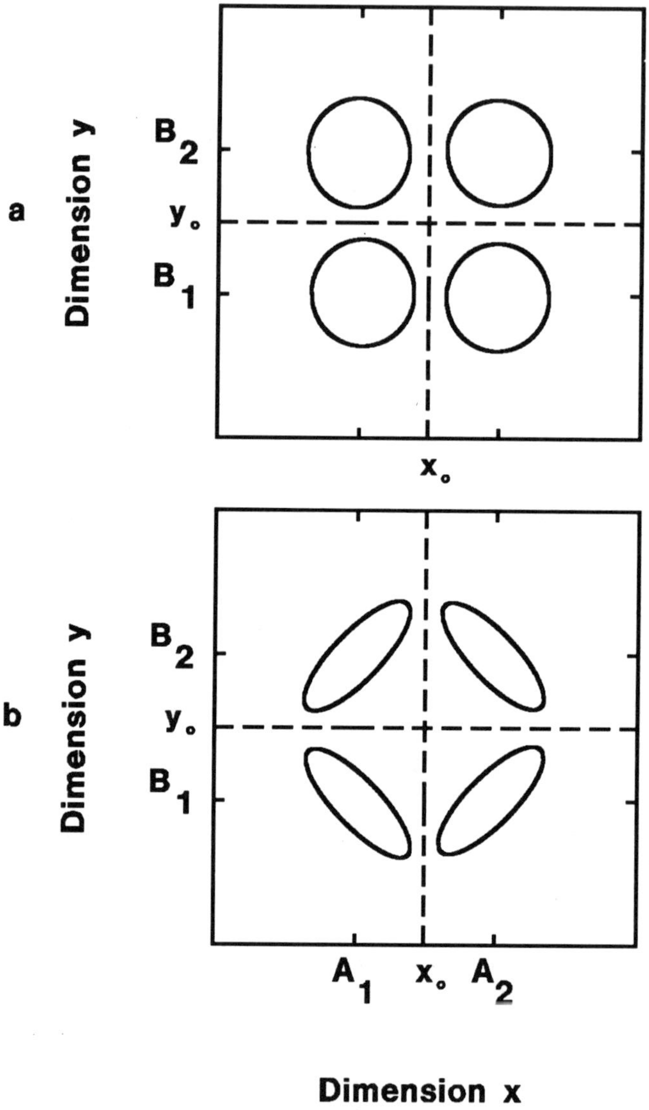

FIG. 7.1. Schematic illustrating the contours of equal likelihood associated with the stimuli $\mathbf{A_1B_1}$, $\mathbf{A_1B_2}$, $\mathbf{A_2B_1}$, and $\mathbf{A_2B_2}$. (a) With this stimulus ensemble perceptual independence, perceptual separability, and decisional separability are satisfied. (b) With this stimulus ensemble perceptual and decisional separability hold, but perceptual independence is violated.

$$g_{1j}(y) = g_{2j}(y) \qquad \text{for j} = 1 \text{ and } 2 \tag{1}$$

and if

$$g_{i1}(x) = g_{i2}(x) \qquad \text{for i} = 1 \text{ and } 2 \tag{2}$$

for all values of x and y (Ashby & Townsend, 1986). If **A** is perceptually separable from **B**, but **B** is *not* perceptually separable from **A**, then an *asymmetric* perceptual separability is said to exist (i.e., Equation 2 is satisfied, but Equation 1 is not). Note that perceptual separability is a property of a group of stimuli. Mutual perceptual separability holds in Figure 7.1a.

Decisional separability holds if the *decision* about the level of a dimension does not depend on the perceptual effect of the other dimension. Consider, for example, the four-stimulus Identification Experiment described in Figure 7.1a. Decisional separability holds along dimension x because the subject has set a criterion x_0 on dimension x and always responds either $\mathbf{A_2B_1}$ or $\mathbf{A_2B_2}$ when the percept is above x_0 and either $\mathbf{A_1B_1}$ or $\mathbf{A_1B_2}$ when the percept is below x_0, regardless of the perceptual effect for dimension y. Analogously, decisional separability holds for dimension **B** when the subject uses the criterion y_0 regardless of the value of x. Decisional separability is associated with decision bounds that are parallel to the coordinate axes, as in Figure 7.1a.

Although we might expect perceptual and decisional separability to be empirically correlated, they are logically unrelated (Ashby & Townsend, 1986). In a series of categorization experiments, Ashby and his colleagues found that subjects can utilize decisional separability with Garnerian integral dimensions (Ashby & Gott, 1988) and decisional integrality with Garnerian separable dimensions (Ashby & Maddox, 1990, 1992). In fact, the general finding was that subjects utilized the decision strategy that was most nearly optimum (i.e., maximized accuracy) even when this required integrating information from separable stimulus dimensions or selective attention with integral dimensions (see chap. 16). Because of findings such as these, it is important to distinguish carefully between perceptual and decisional separability when critically reviewing the operational tests of separability.

Another important and related concept is perceptual independence. *Perceptual independence* holds for stimulus $\mathbf{A_iB_j}$ if and only if the perceptual effects for dimensions **A** and **B** are statistically independent—more specifically, if and only if

$$f_{ij}(x, y) = g_{ij}(x)g_{ij}(y)$$

for all values of x and y (Ashby & Townsend, 1986; see also Ashby & Maddox, 1991b for a recently developed RT theory of perceptual independence). If the perceptual effects are normally distributed, then perceptual independence holds if and only if the perceptual effects of components **A** and **B** are uncorrelated. Note that perceptual independence is a property of a single stimulus. Although perceptual independence may hold for stimulus $\mathbf{A}_1\mathbf{B}_1$, it may be violated for $\mathbf{A}_2\mathbf{B}_2$. Perceptual independence is satisfied for all stimuli in Figure 7.1a and is violated for all stimuli in Figure 7.1b.

Note that perceptual separability and perceptual independence are logically unrelated. This is true because perceptual separability is a relation that holds only for the marginal perceptual distributions [i.e., $g_{ij}(x)$], whereas perceptual independence is a relation that holds between the joint [i.e., $f_{ij}(x, y)$] and marginal perceptual distributions. For example, note that although perceptual independence is violated for all stimuli in Figure 7.1b, perceptual separability holds along both dimensions. Despite this fact, violations of perceptual independence can have a strong influence on the shape of the optimal decision bound (e.g., whether decisional separability is satisfied). As we will see shortly, violations of decisional separability may seriously undermine the validity of some operational separability tests.

SPEEDED CLASSIFICATION: FILTERING AND REDUNDANCY TASKS

Ashby and Townsend (1986) proposed several quantitative tests of separability that can be applied to accuracy data from a Complete Identification Experiment (see section entitled "Alternative Methods for Testing Perceptual Separability"); no tests were proposed that use response time (RT) as data. To provide a theoretical foundation for the Filtering and Redundancy Tasks within GRT, processing time assumptions must be incorporated into GRT. The most common processing assumption of univariate Signal Detection Theory (e.g., Green & Swets, 1974) is that processing time is inversely related to the distance from the perceptual effect to the decision criterion (Bindra, Donderi, & Nishisato, 1968; Bindra, Williams, & Wise, 1965; Emmerich, Gray, Watson, & Tanis, 1972; E. E. Smith, 1968). The multivariate generalization of this assumption, which Ashby and Maddox (1991c) called the *RT-distance hypothesis,* states that processing time is inversely related to the distance from the perceptual effect to the nearest decision bound.

The RT-distance hypothesis does not specify the exact relation between processing time and distance to the nearest bound, only that processing time is a monotonically decreasing function of distance. Although no direct support for the RT-distance hypothesis exists from identification data, a number of categorization (e.g., Bornstein & Monroe, 1980; Cartwright, 1941) and recognition memory studies (Murdock, 1985; Murdock & Anderson, 1975) provide support for the hypothesis (see Ashby & Maddox, 1991b, 1991c for a more detailed discussion of the empirical validity of the RT-distance hypothesis).

Theoretical Analysis

Denote the observed RT to categorize dimension **A** at level i by $\boldsymbol{RT}_{\mathbf{A}i}$. Ashby and Maddox (1991c) assumed that observed RT is the sum of two separate subprocesses: the time to perform the categorization process, $\boldsymbol{T}_{\mathrm{Ai}}$, and the time for all other processing (e.g., motor time), $\boldsymbol{T}_{\mathrm{m}}$. Thus,

$$\boldsymbol{RT}_{\mathbf{Ai}} = \boldsymbol{T}_{\mathbf{Ai}} + \boldsymbol{T}_{\mathrm{m}} , \tag{3}$$

where $\boldsymbol{T}_{\mathbf{Ai}}$ and $\boldsymbol{T}_{\mathrm{m}}$ are assumed to be statistically independent.

Perceptual Separability

Ashby and Maddox (1991c) showed that when perceptual *and* decisional separability are satisfied across conditions and the RT-distance hypothesis holds, then for i = 1 and 2 and for all t > 0,

$$P_{\mathrm{C}}(\boldsymbol{RT}_{\mathbf{Ai}} \leq \mathrm{t} |\ \mathbf{A}_{\mathrm{i}}\mathbf{B}_{1}) = P_{\mathrm{R}}(\boldsymbol{RT}_{\mathbf{Ai}} \leq \mathrm{t} |\ \mathbf{A}_{\mathrm{i}}\mathbf{B}_{1}) = P_{\mathrm{R}}(\boldsymbol{RT}_{\mathbf{Ai}} \leq \mathrm{t} |\ \mathbf{A}_{\mathrm{i}}\mathbf{B}_{2}) \tag{4a}$$

and

$$P_{\mathrm{C}}(\boldsymbol{RT}_{\mathbf{Ai}} \leq \mathrm{t} |\ \mathbf{A}_{\mathrm{i}}\mathbf{B}_{1}) = P_{\mathrm{F}}(\boldsymbol{RT}_{\mathbf{Ai}} \leq \mathrm{t} |\ \mathbf{A}_{\mathrm{i}}\mathbf{B}_{1}) = P_{\mathrm{F}}(\boldsymbol{RT}_{\mathbf{Ai}} \leq \mathrm{t} |\ \mathbf{A}_{\mathrm{i}}\mathbf{B}_{2}) , \tag{4b}$$

where the subscripts C, F, and R represent the control, filtering, and redundancy conditions, respectively.[2] When Equations 4 are satisfied, mean RTs in the control, filtering, and redundancy conditions will be equal and no interference effect or redundancy gain will occur. Under these conditions the Filtering and Redundancy Tasks provide good tests of perceptual separability.

To see why this result holds, consider Figures 7.1a and 7.2a, which illustrate hypothetical contours of equal likelihood for a typical Filtering and Redundancy Task, respectively. In both examples, mutual perceptual separability is satisfied because the marginal perceptual distribution for each level of both dimensions is unaffected by the level of the other dimension. Decisional separability is also satisfied because the decision bounds are parallel to the coordinate axes. Suppose the perceptual effect associated with the presentation of stimulus $\mathbf{A}_{\mathrm{i}}\mathbf{B}_{\mathrm{j}}$ is (x, y). Because of decisional separability and the RT-distance hypothesis, RT on trials when the subject is asked to categorize by the level of component **A** is completely determined by the distance from the perceptual effect associated with component **A**, x, and the decision bound, x_c, which in turn is completely determined by the marginal perceptual distribution of component **A**. Thus, if perceptual separability holds, then Equation 4 follows.

Note that this result makes no assumptions about perceptual independence. For example, Figure 7.1b depicts hypothetical contours of equal likelihood for a Filtering Task where perceptual and decisional separability hold but perceptual independence is violated. Even though perceptual independence is violated, if

[2]Empirically, it is possible for the second equality of Eqs. 4a & 4b to be satisfied but for the first to be violated. This is especially likely for the Filtering Task (i.e., Eq. 4b) because four stimuli are possible in the filtering condition whereas only two are possible for the control condition. Ashby and Maddox (1991c) develop a test of perceptual separability that requires only the first inequality to hold.

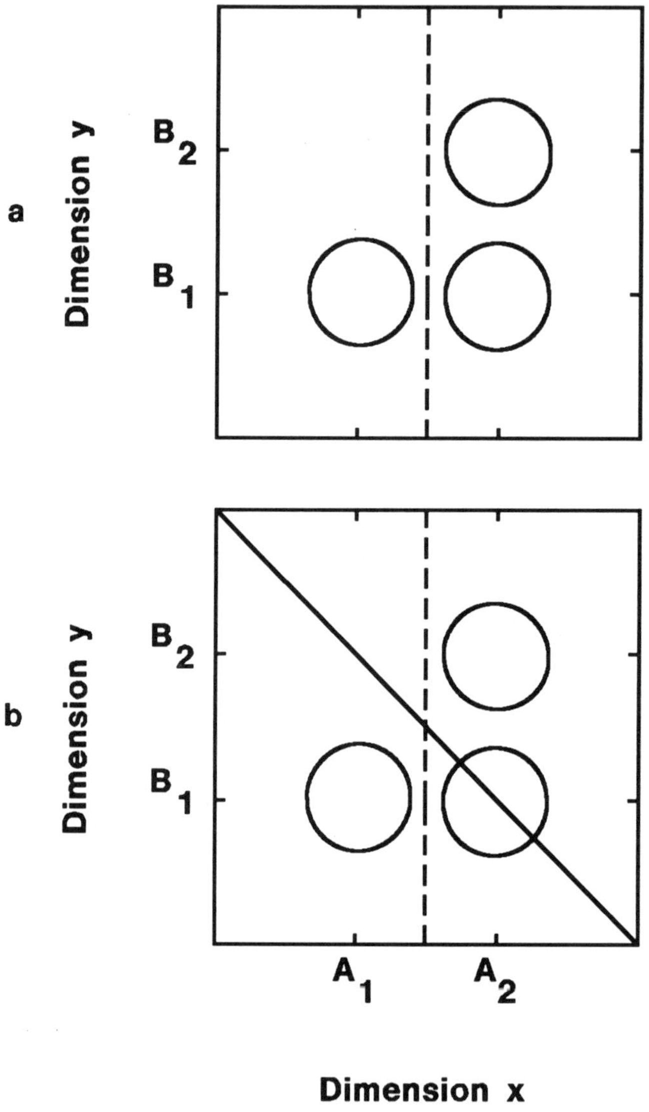

FIG. 7.2. Contours of equal likelihood for stimuli $\mathbf{A_1B_1}$, $\mathbf{A_2B_1}$ and $\mathbf{A_2B_2}$: (a) the broken line represents the decisional separability decision bound; (b) the broken line represents the decisional separability decision bound, and the solid line represents the optimal decision bound for the redundancy condition (i.e., with stimuli $\mathbf{A_1B_1}$ and $\mathbf{A_2B_2}$).

the RT-distance hypothesis holds then no interference effect will occur. This is because a perceptual dependence has no effect on the marginal perceptual distributions.

The theoretical analysis to this point shows that the results of the Filtering and Redundancy Tasks, which have been used to operationally define Garnerian separability, can be used to test perceptual separability with one major caveat: *decisional separability must also be satisfied.* It is critical then to determine under what conditions a separable decision strategy is reasonable.

Ashby and Maddox (1991c) showed that when the perceptual distributions are multivariate normal and perceptual separability and independence hold, the ideal observer utilizes a separable decision strategy in the filtering condition but violates decisional separability in the redundancy condition. With the additional constraint that all perceptual variances are equal (as in Figure 7.2), Ashby and Maddox (1991c) show that a redundancy gain will occur in the redundancy condition.

As Figure 7.2b shows, because only stimuli $\mathbf{A}_1\mathbf{B}_1$ and $\mathbf{A}_2\mathbf{B}_2$ are used in the redundancy condition, the optimal responder violates decisional separability and instead uses the solid line bound in Figure 7.2b, which yields a redundancy gain. In the filtering condition, however, all four stimuli are included, so the optimal responder adopts decisional separability (see Figure 7.1a).

These results make clear the importance of distinguishing between perceptual separability and decisional separability. If decisional separability holds for stimuli that are perceptually separable and if the marginal perceptual distributions do not differ across conditions, then the results of the Filtering and Redundancy Tasks, which have traditionally been used as operational definitions of Garnerian separability, can be used to test perceptual separability. If, however, decisional separability does *not* hold, then there is no guarantee that mean RTs in the control, filtering, and redundancy conditions will all be equal, so the Filtering and Redundancy Tasks should not be used as tests of perceptual separability. Even so, the optimal responder is more likely to adopt decisional separability in the Filtering Task, a fact that makes the Filtering Task a more powerful test of perceptual separability than the Redundancy Task.

Perceptual Integrality

If a perceptual integrality exists, then decisional separability will not be generally optimal, even in the filtering conditions. Even so, it is plausible to expect a naive subject to adopt decisional separability in both the Filtering and Redundancy Tasks, regardless of whether the components are perceptually separable.

Perceptual integrality is difficult to study because of the many different forms that integrality can take. A particularly simple form is illustrated in Figure 7.3. Perceptual integrality exists because increasing the level of component **B** tends to increase the perceived value of component **A** (and vice versa). The integrality is

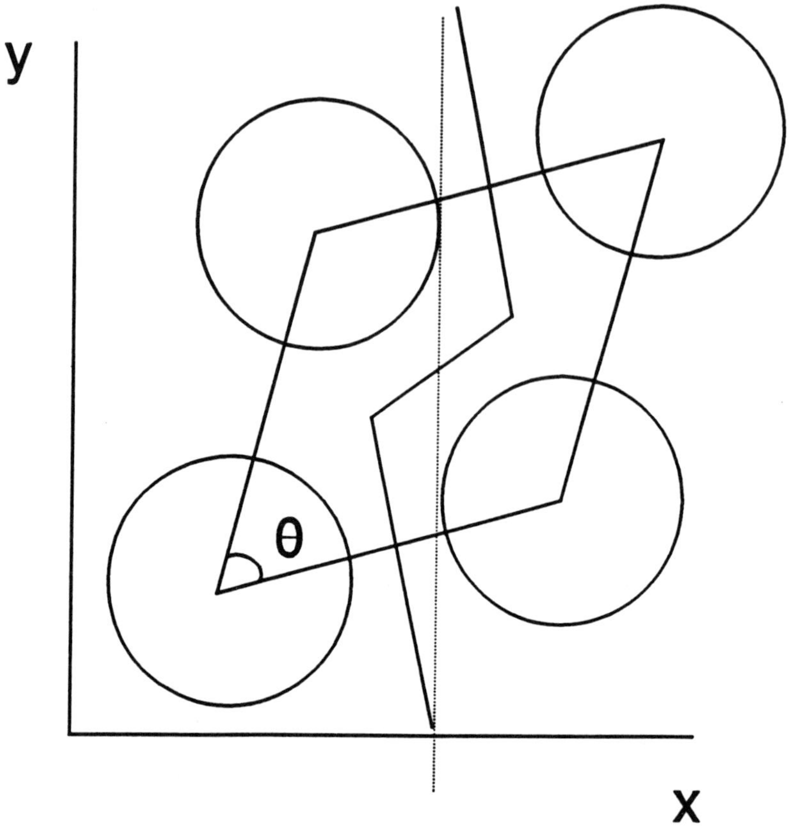

FIG. 7.3. Contours of equal likelihood illustrating a mean-shift integrality.

of a simple form because, for example, the $\mathbf{A}_1\mathbf{B}_1$ and $\mathbf{A}_1\mathbf{B}_2$ marginal distributions on dimension x have the same variance but different means. Therefore, this will be referred to as a *mean-shift integrality*. Note that the degree of integrality is determined by the angle θ. Without loss of generality, we shall restrict discussion to cases for which $\theta < 90°$. (Perceptual separability holds when $\theta = 90°$.) In other forms of integrality, the $\mathbf{A}_i\mathbf{B}_1$ and $\mathbf{A}_i\mathbf{B}_2$ marginals on dimension x might have the same means but different variances, but in the most general case, both the means and variances could be different.

When a mean-shift integrality exists, no firm predictions can be made about the Filtering Test. On the other hand, definite conclusions can be made about the Redundancy Test. Ashby and Maddox (1991c) showed that when the perceptual distributions are multivariate normal, all perceptual variances are equal, perceptual independence holds, and subjects respond optimally or else decisional separability holds then a redundancy gain will occur. If decisional separability holds then a redundancy loss will occur in the negative redundancy condition where stimuli $\mathbf{A}_2\mathbf{B}_1$ and $\mathbf{A}_1\mathbf{B}_2$ are utilized. If the subject responds optimally and the components are equally discriminable, then a redundancy gain occurs in the negative redundancy condition when the angle $\theta > 60°$ and a redundancy loss occurs when $\theta < 60°$. If θ exactly equals 60°, then no redundancy gain or loss results.

This result provides further support for the Speeded Classification Tests of separability. If the components are integral, then in general, redundancy effects are expected regardless of whether the subject uses optimal decision bounds or bounds that satisfy decisional separability. The results of the last two sections are summarized in Table 1, which paints a fairly complete picture of the effects of perceptual separability and one simple form of integrality on the outcomes of the Filtering and Redundancy Tests. One gap remains, however; namely, the effects on the Filtering Test of a mean-shift integrality. Ashby and Maddox (1991c) investigated this issue through Monte Carlo simulation.

Monte Carlo Simulations

Since the RT-distance hypothesis assumes only an inverse relationship between distance and RT, a specific monotonic function relating RT and distance to the decision bound is needed before the Filtering Task can be simulated. Murdock (1985) argued that a plausible function is of the form

$$RT = \alpha\, e^{-\beta D} + \gamma\,, \tag{5}$$

where D is the distance from the percept to the decision bound and α, β, and γ are constants. To determine numerical values of these three constants, Ashby and Maddox fit Equation 5 to categorization RTs collected by Ashby and Maddox (1990). A good fit was obtained with $\alpha = 354$, $\beta = .00377$, and $\gamma = 881$. To make their conclusions as general as possible, Ashby and Maddox also conducted simulations with $\alpha = 100$ and $\alpha = 500$, and with $\beta = .001$, $\beta = .005$, and $\beta = .01$. In addition, 12 different levels of discriminability were selected for each choice of α, β, γ. In each simulation, 30,000 random samples were drawn from each perceptual distribution and the distance was computed from each sample to the decision bound. Finally, Equation 5 was used to determine RT.

Figure 7.3 shows sample contours of equal likelihood from Filtering Condition A. The solid line is the optimal decision bound and the dotted line bound satisfies decisional separability. Note that perceptual separability is violated on both dimensions. The angle θ, which determines the degree of integrality, was set to $\theta = 60°$, $\theta = 45°$, and $\theta = 30°$.

Because a perceptual integrality exists, a conventional application of the Filtering Test predicts an RT interference. An examination of the results (summarized in Table 7.1) revealed four conclusions. First, an interference does

TABLE 7.1
Predicted Outcomes of Filtering and Redundancy Tests

		Perceptual Separability	Mean-Shift Integrality
Filtering	DS	RT Invariance	Facilitation (at low discriminability) Interference (at high discriminability)
	OP	RT Invariance	RT Invariance (for moderate integralities) Interference (for extreme integralities)
Redundancy	DS	RT Invariance	Redundancy Gain (in + Condition) Redundancy Loss (in − Condition)
	OP	Redundancy Gain	Redundancy Gain (in + Condition and in − Condition if $\theta > 60°$) Redundancy Loss (in − Condition if $\theta < 60°$)

Note: DS = decisional separability, OP = optimal responding

occur, but not at all levels of discriminability. In general, the interference is largest at moderately high levels of discriminability. In fact, when decisional separability holds, a facilitation actually occurs at low levels of discriminability. Second, at extremely high levels of discriminability the interference begins to disappear. This latter result is due to a ceiling effect. As discriminability increases, at some point it becomes so high that almost all RT variability is due to variability in response execution time. Third, the magnitude of the interference depends heavily on the exact values of α, β, and γ. In some cases, the interference never gets larger than 2 msec. Finally, an interesting interaction occurs between the degree of integrality and the type of decision bound used by the subject. At low and moderate levels of integrality (i.e., when $90° > \theta > 60°$) the interference is smaller or nonexistent when optimal decision bounds are used. However, when the integrality is extreme (i.e., $\theta \leq 45°$), the interference is larger when the decision bounds are optimal.

Empirical Analysis

Ashby and Maddox (1991c) conducted two experiments to determine whether experienced subjects show a redundancy gain with stimulus dimensions that have been found to be Garnerian separable. In Experiment 1, the stimuli used were semicircles that varied in size with a spoke radiating from the center that varied in orientation. Six subjects participated in the experiment and completed several experimental sessions. In Experiment 2 the stimuli were rectangles that varied in shape and brightness. Four subjects participated and completed 15 experimental sessions. It was hypothesized that no redundancy gain would be found in the data from the first experimental sessions, but that a redundancy gain would emerge in the data from the last experimental sessions.

The results strongly supported this hypothesis. For size and orientation classification, mean control and redundancy condition RTs from the first experimental session were not significantly different. By the final experimental session, however, significant redundancy gains ($p < 0.01$) had emerged for both size and orientation classification. For brightness classification no redundancy gain was found during Days 1 and 2, however, a significant redundancy gain was found for shape classification. During the last two days, significant redundancy gains were found for both shape and brightness classification (see Ashby & Maddox, 1991c for more details). If, as these data suggest, experienced subjects violate decisional separability, then the redundancy task should not be used as a test of perceptual separability when the subjects are experienced. Novice subjects may be more likely to utilize decisional separability; however, the rate at which subjects shift from decisional separability to a more optimal decision strategy may differ across subjects. Researchers might consider utilizing three stimuli in the redundancy condition, such as $\mathbf{A}_1\mathbf{B}_1$, $\mathbf{A}_2\mathbf{B}_1$, and $\mathbf{A}_2\mathbf{B}_2$, because decisional separability would be more likely in this condition.

Degrees of Integrality

In a review of speeded classification results, Garner (1970, 1974) noted that the magnitude of the interference and/or redundancy gain frequently differed across stimulus dimensions. This result led Garner (1970, 1974) to suggest that a continuum of integrality might exist.

Although a continuum of integrality may exist, the Monte Carlo simulations just discussed offer alternative explanations for the fact that the magnitude of interference effects and redundancy gains differ across stimulus dimensions. The form of the subject's RT-distance function affects the absolute magnitude of redundancy gains and interference effects. Empirical evidence from Garner and Felfoldy (1970) corroborates this finding. They found the magnitude of interference effects and redundancy gains to vary significantly across subjects for several different stimulus dimensions.

Discriminability differences also impart a strong effect on the magnitude of redundancy gains and interference effects. Clearly, before the results of these operational tests of separability can be used to argue for a continuum of integrality, it is important to control variation in the subject's level of experience with the stimulus dimensions (see Ashby & Maddox, 1991c), individual differences in the subject's particular RT-distance function, and dimensional discriminability differences within and across stimulus dimensions.

DIRECT DISSIMILARITY SCALING

A very different operational test of Garnerian separability relies on data collected from a Direct Dissimilarity Scaling Experiment. Here, subjects are presented with pairs of stimuli and are asked to rate their dissimilarity on a scale from, say, 1 to 10. The stimuli are generally chosen from an ensemble that varies systematically along two physical dimensions (e.g., hue and brightness of Munsell color chips). The fundamental assumption is that each stimulus can be represented perceptually as a point in a multidimensional psychological space. The psychological distance between points is assumed to be monotonically related to perceived dissimilarity, with widely separated stimuli being more dissimilar than neighboring stimuli.

The crucial test is to determine how subjects ascertain the dissimilarity between stimulus pairs that differ along both dimensions. Consider the perceptual representations of the two stimuli, **A** and **B**, in Figure 7.4. One possibility is that the perceived dissimilarity between stimuli **A** and **B**, denoted $d(\mathbf{A},\mathbf{B})$, is equivalent to the sum of the two unidimensional dissimilarities, $d_x(\mathbf{A}, \mathbf{B})$ and $d_y(\mathbf{A}, \mathbf{B})$. In other words,

$$d(\mathbf{A}, \mathbf{B}) = d_x(\mathbf{A}, \mathbf{B}) + d_y(\mathbf{A}, \mathbf{B}) .$$

In this case $d(\mathbf{A},\mathbf{B})$ conforms to the city-block distance metric. Another possibility is that subjects ignore the dimensional structure of the stimulus. In this case,

$$d(\mathbf{A}, \mathbf{B}) = [d_x(\mathbf{A}, \mathbf{B})^2 + d_y(\mathbf{A}, \mathbf{B})^2]^{1/2} ,$$

which conforms to the Euclidean distance metric. Operationally, stimulus dimensions that are combined by using a Euclidean distance metric are classified as integral, whereas stimulus dimensions that are combined by using a city-block distance metric are classified as separable (e.g., Garner, 1974; Hyman & Well, 1968; Shepard, 1964).[3]

Assumptions

The use of Direct Dissimilarity Scaling as an operational test of Garnerian integrality and separability is only valid if psychological distance, and in particu-

[3]Experimental paradigms other than Direct Dissimilarity Scaling can be used to determine the best-fitting distance metric for a set of multidimensional stimuli. For example, researchers interested in perceptual identification and categorization use identification errors to determine the best-fitting distance metric (e.g., Nosofsky, 1985b, 1986). This approach may be better than Dissimilarity Scaling, because identification data are usually less noisy.

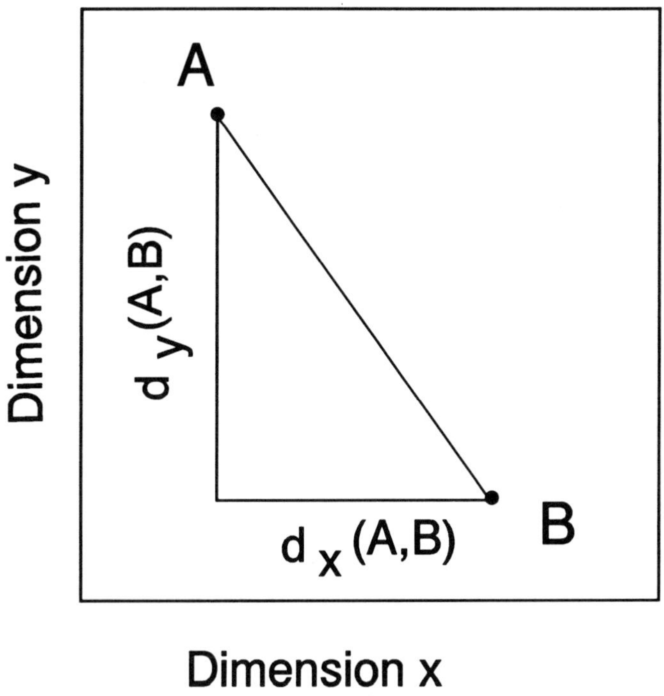

FIG. 7.4. Schematic illustrating two ways subjects can compute dissimilarity in a metric space.

lar the city-block or Euclidean distance metric, provides a good model of perceived dissimilarity. At the most general level, this requires that perceived dissimilarity satisfy certain distance axioms, the empirical validity of which has been questioned. Because the relation between judged dissimilarity and perceived dissimilarity is assumed to be ordinal, some of these axioms (i.e., the triangle inequality) cannot be tested directly on the judged dissimilarity data. A number of the axioms, however, are empirically testable.

Distance Axioms

The first requirement is that all perceived self-dissimilarities are equal. Specifically,

$$d(\mathrm{i}, \mathrm{i}) = d(\mathrm{j}, \mathrm{j})$$

for all stimuli i and j. Empirical evidence against this axiom is reviewed by Krumhansl (1978). Krumhansl argued that unique stimuli—that is, stimuli that are very dissimilar from most other stimuli in the ensemble—have smaller perceived self-dissimilarities, whereas stimuli that are very similar to a large number of other stimuli in the ensemble have higher perceived self-dissimilarities.

The second axiom, minimality, states that the perceived dissimilarity between two different stimuli is at least as great as the perceived dissimilarity of either stimulus to itself. In other words,

$$d(\mathrm{i}, \mathrm{j}) \geq d(\mathrm{i}, \mathrm{i}) \qquad \text{and} \qquad d(\mathrm{i}, \mathrm{j}) \geq d(\mathrm{j}, \mathrm{j})$$

for all stimuli i and j. Tversky (1977) argued against this axiom.

The third axiom, symmetry, states that the perceived dissimilarity between stimuli i and j equals the perceived dissimilarity between j and i, or

$$d(\mathrm{i}, \mathrm{j}) = d(\mathrm{j}, \mathrm{i}) \ .$$

Several violations of this assumption have been noted (e.g., Krumhansl, 1978; Tversky, 1977). For example, subjects rated the dissimilarity of China to North Korea to be greater than the dissimilarity of North Korea to China (Tversky, 1977).

The fourth axiom is called the triangle inequality. For any three stimuli i,j, and k the triangle inequality holds if

$$d(\mathrm{i}, \mathrm{j}) + d(\mathrm{j}, \mathrm{k}) \geq d(\mathrm{i}, \mathrm{k}) \ .$$

This axiom is empirically difficult to test, since judged dissimilarity need only be monotonically related to perceived dissimilarity. Tversky and Gati (1982) proposed an empirically testable axiom, called the corner inequality, that captures the spirit of the triangle inequality. Tversky and Gati (1982) tested the corner inequality and found severe violations for separable stimulus dimensions.

When the distance axioms are violated in dissimilarity data, psychological distance does not provide a good model of perceived similarity and the Euclidean versus city-block test of separability is invalid. Suppose, however, that for a given set of data the distance axioms are satisfied. This implies that, for this data, perceived dissimilarity can be modeled by *some* distance metric, although not necessarily by city-block or Euclidean distance.

The city-block and Euclidean metrics are both special cases of the Minkowski-*R* distance metric,

$$d_{\mathrm{ij}} = \left[\sum_{\mathrm{k}=1}^{\mathrm{n}} |x_{\mathrm{ik}} - x_{\mathrm{jk}}]^{R} \right]^{1/R} , \tag{6}$$

where d_{ij} is the distance between stimuli i and j, n equals the number of stimulus dimensions, x_{ik} represents the coordinate of stimulus i on dimension k, and $R \geq 1$. The city-block metric results when $R = 1$ and the Euclidean metric when R = 2.

In addition to the distance axioms, the Minkowski-R distance metric requires other relations to hold, namely interdimensional additivity and intradimensional subtractivity (Beals, Krantz, & Tversky, 1968; Tversky & Krantz, 1970; see also Suppes, Krantz, Luce, & Tversky, 1989). Briefly, interdimensional additivity states that the dissimilarity between any two stimuli is some additive function of the unidimensional dissimilarities. Intradimensional subtractivity states that the dissimilarity between two stimuli along one dimension depends on the absolute difference between their coordinate values along that dimension (see Beals et al., 1968, and Suppes et al., 1989, for methods of testing these relations).

Like the distance axioms, empirical violations of interdimensional additivity and intradimensional subtractivity are well documented. For example, Krantz and Tversky (1975; see also Burns et al., 1978; Weiner-Ehrlich, 1978) found large violations for height and width of rectangles. Similar results have been found for hue and chroma of Munsell color chips (Burns et al., 1978).

It is meaningful to determine the value of R (see Equation 6) that provides the best account of a set of dissimilarity data, only if interdimensional additivity, intradimensional subtractivity, and the distance axioms are all satisfied. However, even if all these axioms are valid, it may turn out that some value of R other than 1 or 2 provides the best fit. Ronacher and Bautz (1985), for example, collected dissimilarity ratings for stimuli varying in size and brightness and found several subjects whose data was best fit by values of R around 1.4. Tversky and Gati (1982, Study 6) found similar results for color patches varying in hue and chroma. Values of $R < 1$ violate the triangle inequality and invalidate a distance-based interpretation of the perceptual space. Tversky and Gati (1982) found values of $R < 1$ to fit best for five different sets of separable stimuli, supporting their claim that a distance-based model of the subject's perceptual space is inappropriate when the stimulus dimensions are separable.

In summary, there is ample evidence disconfirming the validity of the Minkowski-R metric as a model of perceived dissimilarity. Because it is dangerous to interpret parameter estimates from an invalid model, conclusions about the separability of a pair of stimulus dimensions drawn on the basis of the city-block versus Euclidean test should be interpreted with caution. Even so, the argument motivating the test has a beguiling appeal. Therefore, it is reasonable to ask if the argument can be couched within a more powerful model of similarity, that is, one that is not constrained by the distance axioms, by interdimensional additivity, or by intradimensional subtractivity. In the next section, such a model is developed.

General Recognition Theory of Similarity

The fundamental assumption of the MDS theory of similarity is that perceived similarity is inversely related to distance in some multidimensional perceptual space. Perceived similarity in General Recognition Theory is proportional to the probability of a confusion in an unbiased identification task (Ashby & Perrin, 1988; see also chap. 6). If the stimuli **A** and **B** are two-dimensional, this implies

$$s(\mathbf{A}, \mathbf{B}) = \iint_{R_\mathbf{B}} f_\mathbf{A}(x, y)\, dx\, dy\ , \qquad (7)$$

where $s(\mathbf{A}, \mathbf{B})$ denotes the similarity of stimulus **A** to stimulus **B**, $f_\mathbf{A}(x, y)$ represents the distribution of perceptual effects for stimulus **A**, and $R_\mathbf{B}$ is the region in the (x, y) plane associated with response **B** in an unbiased identification task (Ashby & Perrin, 1988).[4] The interpretation of Equation 7 is straightforward when there are only two stimuli in the ensemble. When the ensemble contains three or more stimuli, the interpretation is less clear. Consider the hypothetical contours of equal likelihood for the three stimuli in Figure 7.5. When asked to judge the similarity of stimulus **A** to stimulus **B**, which decision bounds will the subject use? One possibility is that subjects utilize the solid-line decision bounds, because these are the optimal decision bounds for an identification task. Another possibility is that subjects ignore the fact that stimulus **C** is in the ensemble and use the decision bound separating only distributions **A** and **B** (represented by the vertical line). When all stimuli in the ensemble are considered, the model is *context-sensitive*. When only the immediately relevant stimuli are considered, the model is *context-free* (see Ashby & Perrin, 1988, p. 130, for more details).[5]

The GRT similarity model can predict and account for violations of each of the distance axioms (Ashby & Perrin, 1988). The model also offers an explanation for the frequent finding that the city-block and Euclidean distance metrics provide the best fit for separable and integral stimulus dimensions, respectively, by postulating the use of different *decision bounds* for integral and separable dimensions.

Ashby and Perrin (1988, Lemma 1; see also chap. 6) showed that the simple Euclidean MDS model is a special case of the context-free GRT similarity model in which all perceptual distributions are normal with covariance matrices equal to the identity, and in which similarity and dissimilarity are related by the function

$$d(\mathbf{S_A}, \mathbf{S_B}) = -2\Phi^{-1}[s(\mathbf{S_A}, \mathbf{S_B})] \ ,$$

where Φ represents the standard normal cumulative distribution function. In other words, under these conditions, the GRT similarity model predicts that the dissimilarity between stimuli **A** and **B** is equal to the distance between the mean percepts of stimuli **A** and **B.** As the next result shows, a perfect rank order correlation between intermean distance and dissimilarity is still preserved if the covariance matrices for the perceptual distributions are allowed to be scalar multiples of the identity matrix and if similarity and dissimilarity are related by any monotonically decreasing function.[6]

---

[4]The decision bounds separating response regions **A** and **B** in an unbiased identification experiment are placed where the likelihood ratio $f_\mathbf{A}/f_\mathbf{B} = 1$.

[5]The MDS theory of similarity is context-free in the sense that the similarity between two stimuli is determined only by their interpoint distance and is unaffected by other stimuli in the ensemble. Tversky (1977) presents data showing marked context effects on similarity judgments.

[6]Two functions are currently popular: the exponential decay similarity function, where similarity s and dissimilarity d are related by

$$s = exp\ (-d) \ ,$$

and the Gaussian similarity function, where

$$s = exp\ (-d^2) \ .$$

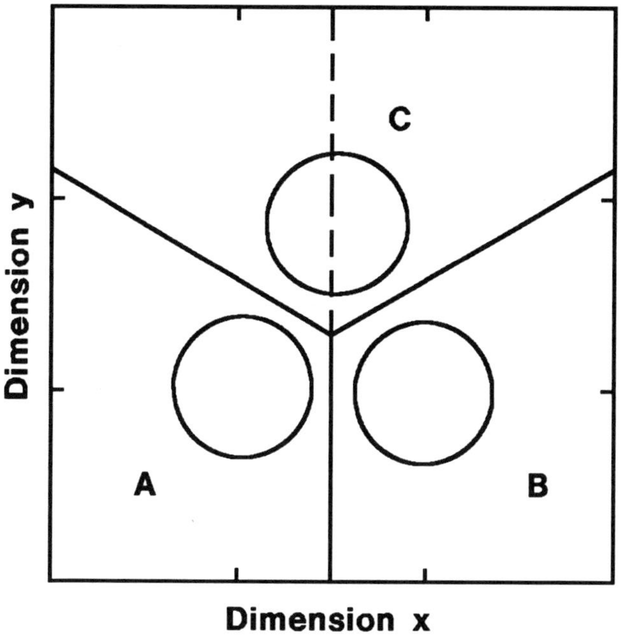

FIG. 7.5. Hypothetical contours of equal likelihood for stimuli **A, B,** and **C.** The solid lines represent the decision bounds used under the context-sensitive version of GRT. The dashed line represents the decision bound separating stimuli **A** and **B** under the context-free version of GRT.

Proposition 7.1: Consider any two stimuli $\mathbf{S_A}$ and $\mathbf{S_B}$ with mean perceptual effects $\boldsymbol{\mu}_\mathbf{A}$ and $\boldsymbol{\mu}_\mathbf{B}$ and covariance matrices $\boldsymbol{\Sigma}_\mathbf{A} = \boldsymbol{\Sigma}_\mathbf{B} = \sigma^2 \mathbf{I}$, where $\mathbf{I}$ is the identity matrix. Let $d_{\mathbf{AB}}$ be the Euclidean distance between $\boldsymbol{\mu}_\mathbf{A}$ and $\boldsymbol{\mu}_\mathbf{B}$, and let $d(\mathbf{A}, \mathbf{B})$ be the perceived dissimilarity of stimulus **A** to stimulus **B.** If similarity is computed by using the context-free GRT similarity model, and if dissimilarity is related to similarity by any monotonically decreasing function, then the rank order correlation between $d_{\mathbf{AB}}$ and $d(\mathbf{A}, \mathbf{B})$ is perfect.

Proof: See Appendix A.

Proposition 7.1 assumes that the subject uses the optimal decision bound (i.e., the decision bound that maximizes accuracy) to separate the two response regions. In most cases this requires integrating information from the individual stimulus dimensions (Ashby & Gott, 1988). Information integration is assumed automatic for Garnerian integral dimensions,[7] so it seems plausible that this

[7]The *optimality* of this integration remains to be tested. However, when the dimensions are measured in the same units (e.g., length), there is evidence that information integration is nearly optimal (i.e., maximizes accuracy) for Garnerian integral dimensions (e.g., Ashby & Gott, 1988; Ashby & Maddox, 1992).

condition is met for Garnerian integral dimensions. Thus, the common finding that dissimilarity ratings for integral dimensions are best fit by a Euclidean metric is compatible with the GRT similarity model.

Information integration is assumed to be more difficult for separable dimensions (e.g., Garner, 1974), so, in this case, the assumption of optimal decision bounds seems less likely to hold. Instead, with separable dimensions subjects may choose boundaries that are parallel to the coordinate axes (i.e., that satisfy decisional separability). Although Ashby and Maddox (1990, 1992) showed that *experienced* subjects can integrate information with separable dimensions in an approximately optimal fashion, decisional separability might be easier. When judging similarity there is no objectively correct response, so a reasonable hypothesis is that subjects choose decision bounds that are easy to implement. If a relation similar to Proposition 7.1 holds between city-block distance and the GRT similarity measure when *decisional separability* is satisfied, then GRT would also account for the finding that with separable dimensions dissimilarities are frequently well described by the city-block distance metric.

As it turns out, the rank order correlation between city-block distance and the GRT dissimilarity measure is not perfect. Examples can be found in which city-block distance increases, but GRT dissimilarity decreases. To determine the magnitude of this correlation, Monte Carlo simulations were conducted.

In each simulation, the similarity between 25 hypothetical two-dimensional stimuli was computed. The perceptual means on each dimension were uniformly distributed over the set $\{1, 2, 3\}$. Each perceptual distribution had covariance matrix $\mathbf{I}$ (the identity matrix). The following values were computed: (a) city-block and Euclidean intermean distances, and (b) similarity using both the decisional separability and the optimal decision bounds. Similarities were converted to dissimilarities via either the exponential decay similarity function

$$s = exp\ (-d)$$

or the Gaussian function

$$s = exp\ (-d^2)\ ,$$

where s and d represent similarity and dissimilarity, respectively. The exponential decay similarity function is frequently used with separable dimensions, and the Gaussian function is often used with integral dimensions (e.g., Nosofsky, 1985b; Shepard, 1957). Accordingly, the exponential decay function was used for the decisional separability simulations, and the Gaussian similarity function was used for the optimal bound simulations.[8] This procedure was replicated three times, and the average results are presented in Table 7.2.

Although all correlations are high, note that the correlations between city-

[8]The simulations were repeated with the opposite pairings and yielded similar results.

TABLE 7.2
Correlations Between City-Block and Euclidean Distances and Dissimilarity Derived from Decisional Separability and the Optimal Model

Set	*C-B/DS*	*E/DS*	*C-B/O*
1	.999	.982	.977
2	.998	.990	.979
3	.996	.989	.975

Note: Columns denote the rank order correlation between city-block distance and dissimilarity measured using the decisional separability bounds (C-B/DS), Euclidean distance and dissimilarity measured using the decisional separability bounds (E/DS), city-block distance and dissimilarity measured using the optimal bound (C-B/O).

block distance and dissimilarity computed from the decisional separability bounds are all greater than 0.995. In addition, note that the smallest of these correlations is larger than the largest correlation between Euclidean distance and dissimilarity measured by using the decisional separability bounds or between city-block distance and dissimilarity measured by using the optimal bounds.

The implication of Proposition 7.1 and the simulations is that subjects may not be computing distance when asked to make a dissimilarity judgment, but they may rather be computing overlap of one perceptual distribution into another response region (Ashby & Perrin, 1988), with the boundaries between regions differing for integral and separable dimensions. This hypothesis[9] predicts that the Euclidean model should be the best version of MDS when the dimensions are integral, and the city-block MDS models should fit better than the Euclidean MDS model when the dimensions are separable. At the same time it offers a theory of the subject's behavior that does not require the distance axioms to hold, which is not true for the MDS approach to similarity.

Despite the fact that the Euclidean versus city-block test of separability is invalid when dissimilarity data violate the distance axioms, other tests of dissimilarity data can be constructed that do provide useful information about perceptual separability. The next result shows that an axiom called consistency (Tversky & Gati, 1982) is strongly related to perceptual separability.

Consider the case where stimuli are two-dimensional and can take on one of n levels on each dimension **A** and **B**. Let $d(\mathbf{A}_1\mathbf{B}_1, \mathbf{A}_2\mathbf{B}_2)$ be an ordinal measure of

[9]This hypothesis was proposed by F. G. Ashby (personal communication, September 1989).

the dissimilarity between stimuli $\mathbf{A}_1\mathbf{B}_1$ and $\mathbf{A}_2\mathbf{B}_2$. Consistency is satisfied when

$$\begin{aligned} & d(\mathbf{A}_1\mathbf{B}_1, \mathbf{A}_2\mathbf{B}_1) > d(\mathbf{A}_3\mathbf{B}_1, \mathbf{A}_4\mathbf{B}_1) \\ \text{iff} \quad & d(\mathbf{A}_1\mathbf{B}_2, \mathbf{A}_2\mathbf{B}_2) > d(\mathbf{A}_3\mathbf{B}_2, \mathbf{A}_4\mathbf{B}_2) \end{aligned} \tag{8}$$

and

$$\begin{aligned} & d(\mathbf{A}_1\mathbf{B}_1, \mathbf{A}_1\mathbf{B}_2) > d(\mathbf{A}_1\mathbf{B}_3, \mathbf{A}_1\mathbf{B}_4) \\ \text{iff} \quad & d(\mathbf{A}_2\mathbf{B}_1, \mathbf{A}_2\mathbf{B}_2) > d(\mathbf{A}_2\mathbf{B}_3, \mathbf{A}_2\mathbf{B}_4) \ . \end{aligned} \tag{9}$$

In other words, consistency holds when the dissimilarity between two levels of one dimension is constant across levels of the other dimension.

> *Proposition 7.2:* Consider the case where stimuli vary along two physical dimensions and can take on one of n levels on each dimension. If the context-free GRT similarity model holds, then when perceptual and decisional separability are satisfied along one physical dimension, consistency must also hold for that dimension.

Proof: See Appendix A.

Note that Proposition 7.2 makes no assumptions about perceptual independence. Perceptual separability and decisional separability are all that is required for consistency to hold. Although consistency does not directly imply perceptual separability and decisional separability, if consistency is violated then perceptual separability and/or decisional separability must be violated.

Perrin and Ashby (1991) showed that dominance, another relation that can be tested on dissimilarity data, provides information about perceptual dependencies between stimulus dimensions. Dominance holds when

$$d(\mathbf{A}_1\mathbf{B}_1, \mathbf{A}_2\mathbf{B}_2) > \max[d(\mathbf{A}_1\mathbf{B}_1, \mathbf{A}_1\mathbf{B}_2), d(\mathbf{A}_1\mathbf{B}_2, \mathbf{A}_2\mathbf{B}_2)] \ .$$

In other words, when the two-dimensional dissimilarity is greater than either one-dimensional dissimilarity. In short, violations of dominance suggest violations of perceptual independence. Within the present discussion, this test is useful because the Minkowski-R metric predicts dominance. If dominance is violated, then testing whether the city-block or Euclidean metric fits the data best is inappropriate.

Testing dominance and consistency on the same set of similarity ratings could also shed light on the empirical relation between perceptual independence and perceptual separability.[10] Although perceptual independence and perceptual separability are logically unrelated, little is known about the empirical correlation between the two.

---

[10]This idea was suggested by F. G. Ashby (personal communication, August 1990).

RESTRICTED CLASSIFICATION

In the typical Restricted Classification Task, subjects are presented with three stimuli and are asked to decide which two "go together best" or "belong in the same group." A typical stimulus configuration is shown in Figure 7.6a. Two stimuli (**A** and **B**) share a level on one physical dimension, but are very different along the other. Another pair of stimuli (**B** and **C**) differ on both physical dimensions, but are quite similar overall. The third pair (**A** and **C**) differ on both dimensions and are very dissimilar overall. With physical dimensions that have been classified as separable (based on the results of other operational tests of separability), subjects frequently respond that stimuli **A** and **B** go together best. With integral dimensions, stimuli **B** and **C** are most often chosen. In other words, separable dimensions tend to be classified by shared dimensions, whereas integral dimensions tend to be classified by overall similarity. These results have led some researchers to include the Restricted Classification Task as an operational test of Garnerian separability.

The main assumption of this approach is that subjects group stimuli by shared dimensional value when the dimensions are separable and by overall similarity when the dimensions are integral. This assumes, of course, that stimuli **A** and **B** share a dimensional value and that stimuli **B** and **C** are the most similar. The experimenter typically can guarantee these properties in the *physical space,* but they must also hold in the subject's *perceptual space.*

The assumption that stimuli **B** and **C** are perceived to be the most similar of the three pairs is usually verified on the basis of dissimilarity data (e.g., Burns et al., 1978). A better method, however, would be to use the method of triads (e.g., Ennis, Mullen, & Frijters, 1988; Richardson, 1938; Torgerson, 1958; see chap. 5), where three stimuli are presented simultaneously and the subjects' task is to determine which two are most similar and which two are least similar. This would guarantee that **B** and **C** are more similar than **A** and **B** when all three stimuli are present.[11]

It must also be confirmed that stimuli **A** and **B** share a dimensional value *perceptually.* If GRT is correct, then this condition is ambiguous. Even if perceptual separability holds, so that **A** and **B** have equal marginal distributions on dimension x, the probability that **A** and **B** will be perceived to have equal values on a dimension on any single trial is zero. As an operational definition of this condition, one might assume that the mean perceptual effects for stimuli **A** and **B**

[11]Although MDS stimulus representations assume the similarity between two stimuli is unaffected by the presence of a third stimulus, other theories of similarity, such as the context-sensitive General Recognition Theory, predict that the similarity between two stimuli can change when another stimulus is present (Ashby & Perrin, 1988; see also Tversky, 1977). In fact, this approach predicts that if $s(\mathbf{B}, \mathbf{C}) > s(\mathbf{A}, \mathbf{B})$ when the stimuli are presented as pairs, then frequently $s(\mathbf{A}, \mathbf{B}) > s(\mathbf{B}, \mathbf{C})$ when the triple is presented.

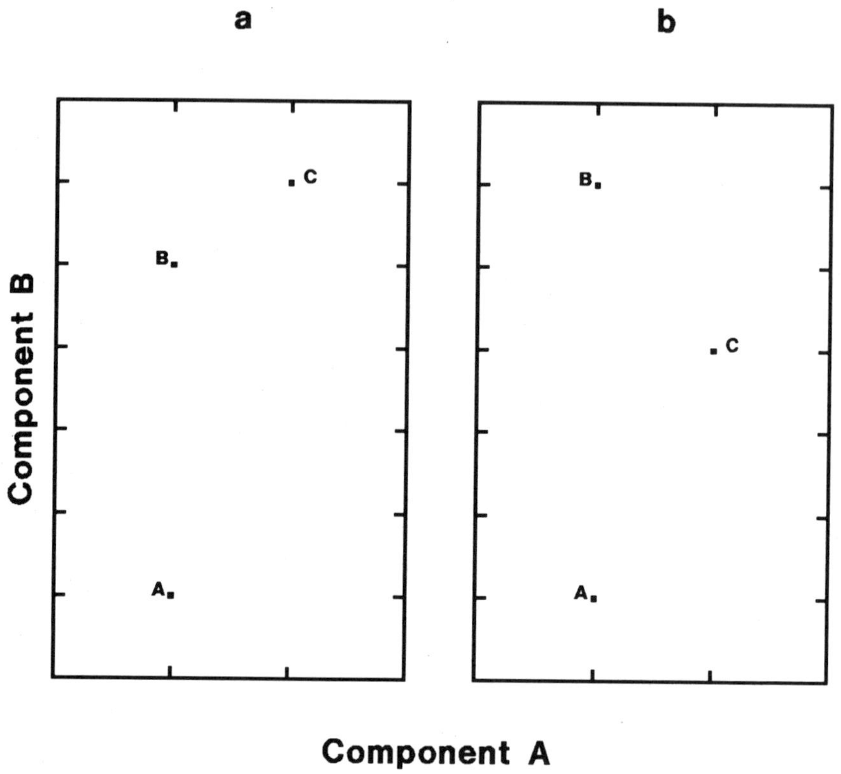

FIG. 7.6. (a) A typical stimulus configuration for the restricted classification task. (b) Alternative stimulus configuration.

are the same along one dimension. One possible test of this assumption is to simply ask subjects whether pairs of two-dimensional stimuli differ in one or two ways (Foard & Kemler-Nelson, 1984). Of course, the effects of perceptual noise could make data of this sort difficult to interpret. Another possibility is to examine MDS solutions obtained from similarity judgments on the set of stimuli, but the assumptions of this procedure have been seriously questioned. Clearly more work is needed in this area.

Stimulus, Task, and Observer Factors

The validity of Restricted Classification as a test of separability relies on the soundness of the assumptions just described. Even if these requirements are usually met, a review of the empirical data suggests that this task is far from providing an unequivocal test of separability. In fact, of the four tasks reviewed, the Restricted Classification Task appears the most susceptible to variation in other factors.

Burns and Shepp (1988; Burns et al., 1978) found the frequency of dimensional and similarity classifications to be strongly influenced by the nature of the stimulus configuration. For example, fewer dimensional classifications were found for the Figure 7.6b stimulus configuration than for the Figure 7.6a configuration.

Task factors also influence restricted classification results. Subjects under speed stress produce more overall similarity classifications than subjects not under speed stress (Ward, 1983, experiment 2). Subjects asked to give their "first impression" give significantly more overall similarity classifications than subjects asked to be "meticulous" (J. D. Smith & Kemler-Nelson, 1984, experiment 5; Ward, Foley, & Cole, 1986).

Individual and developmental differences are also prevalent. Ward and his colleagues (1983, 1985, 1986) found a high correlation between response tempo (i.e., rate of responding) and the number of similarity classifications across a wide variety of stimulus dimensions, with fast responders making more overall similarity classifications. In addition, children tend to classify by similarity more than by dimension (L. B. Smith, 1989; L. B. Smith & Kemler, 1977, 1978; Ward, 1983).

Theoretical Analysis

In this section, a model is developed of a subject's performance in the Restricted Classification Task. The model is flexible enough to account for many of the stimulus, task, and observer factors described earlier, yet rigorous enough to provide a strong theoretical link between the Restricted Classification Task and perceptual separability.

First, assume that subjects choose a response on the basis of similarity computations and that the two stimuli that go together best are the two that are most similar. A powerful theory of similarity that is especially appropriate for the Restricted Classification Task was developed by Ennis, Palen, and Mullen (1988; see also chaps. 5 and 11). The theory assumes the same perceptual representation as GRT. For example, the stimulus configuration in Figure 7.6a could be represented by the contours of equal likelihood shown in Figure 7.7a. On a given trial, the subject is presented with three stimuli, such as those in Figure 7.6a, which may lead to the perceptual effects a, b, and c in Figure 7.7a. The subject is assumed to compute the distance between the points and to choose the two that are closest (i.e., the most similar) as the two that go together best. The Ennis et al. model can be extended by allowing subjects to differentially weight (i.e., selectively attend to) certain stimulus dimensions. One way to implement this model is to assume that subjects selectively attend to a dimension if the percep-

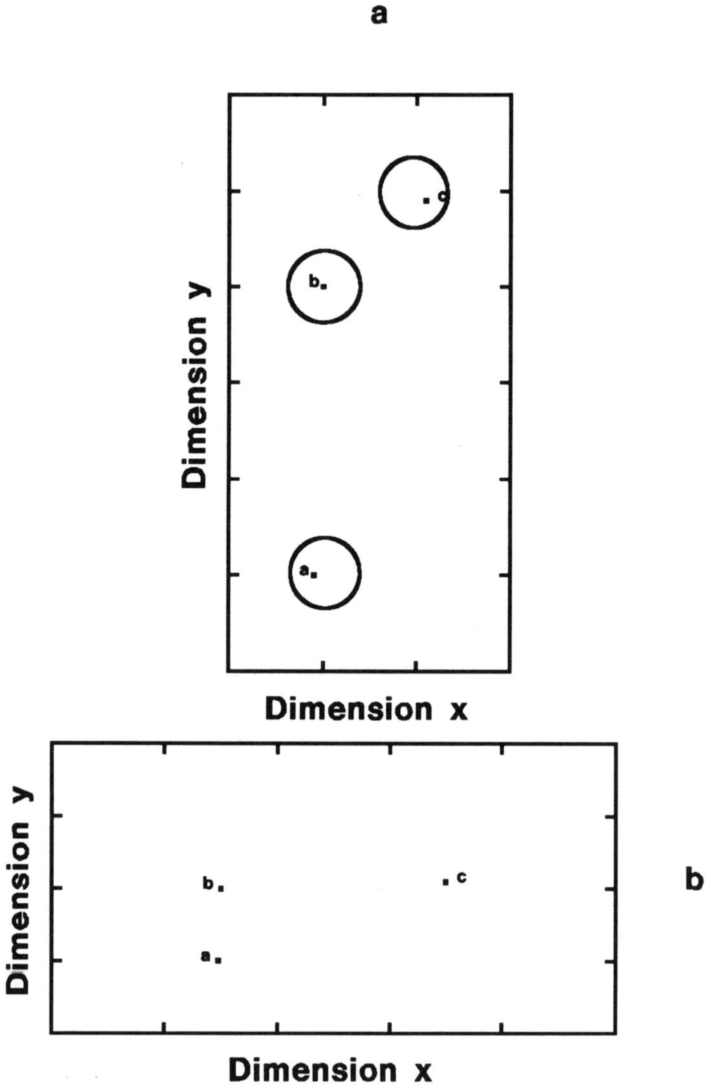

FIG. 7.7. (a) Hypothetical contours of equal likelihood for this configuration and three hypothetical perceptual effects. (b) Hypothetical locations of the three perceptual effects with selective attention to dimension *x*.

tual effects for two stimuli along that dimension fall within some small range. This strategy is reasonable because selective attention to a dimension can maximize the *similarity* between one pair of stimuli (e.g., **AB**) and maximize the *dissimilarity* between the other pairs (e.g., **AC** and **BC**). This strategy makes intuitive sense, because the subject's task is to find the two that go together best. The idea of selective attention to dimensions is not new and in fact forms the basis of the weighted Euclidean scaling model (Carroll & Chang, 1970; see also chaps. 6 and 14). It has also been advanced to account for developmental effects in the restricted classification task (see L. B. Smith, 1989).

What kind of predictions does this model make? Consider a case where perceptual separability is satisfied, as in Figure 7.7a. Because a and b have nearly identical values along dimension *x*, the subject attends more heavily to that dimension. This shrinks the *y* dimension and stretches the *x* dimension, causing the similarity between a and b to be maximized (see Figure 7.7b). Thus, when perceptual separability holds, the subject frequently classifies by dimensions. Note that this model also predicts the small number of overall similarity classifications that are often observed for separable dimensions. These classifications occur on the few trials where random fluctuation causes the percepts a and b to differ considerably along the *x* dimension. If the difference is great enough, the subject will not selectively attend to dimension *x*. When this happens, percepts b and c are most similar and an overall similarity classification prevails.

Now consider a case such as in Figure 7.8, in which perceptual separability is violated. Again consider the hypothetical percepts a, b, and c. In this case, percepts a and b differ considerably along dimension *x*, and percepts b and c differ considerably along dimension *y*. The model predicts no selective attention (i.e., neither dimension is stretched). Because percepts b and c are the nearest neighbors, stimuli **B** and **C** are most similar, so we get the predicted result; that is, the subject classifies by overall similarity. Note that this model also predicts at least a few dimensional classifications. At times, percepts a and b will be very similar along dimension *x*, and a dimensional classification will occur.

This model also accounts for many of the stimulus, task, and observer effects described in the previous section. For example, subjects asked to respond with their "first impression," as well as subjects who rate high in response tempo, would be less likely to differentially attend to a dimension even when perceptual separability holds. With equal attention allocated to the two stimuli dimensions, stimuli **B** and **C** are most similar. If selective attention to dimensions develops with age, as suggested by L. B. Smith (1989), then this approach can also account for the developmental shift from overall similarity to dimensional classification. If young children cannot differentially attend to dimensions, then overall similarity classifications will be more frequent.

The model makes other testable predictions. For example, any experimental manipulation that increases perceptual noise, such as tachistoscopic presentation or masking, should increase the frequency of overall similarity classifications

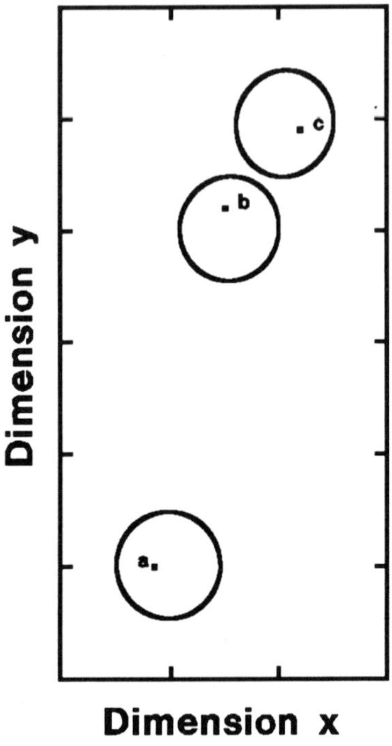

FIG. 7.8. Hypothetical contours of equal likelihood and three perceptual effects for a case where perceptual separability is violated.

when perceptual separability is satisfied. This is because as perceptual noise increases the probability that percepts a and b will fall within a small range on dimension x decreases, and thus selective attention is less likely to occur. It is possible, however, that in such a situation the subject would increase the size of the critical range; that is, he or she would relax the criteria under which selective attention is invoked.

ALTERNATIVE METHODS FOR TESTING PERCEPTUAL SEPARABILITY

Data collected in identification experiments have been frequently used to compare models of human information processing (e.g., Townsend, 1971). Such data also offer several powerful tests of perceptual separability.

Ashby and Townsend (1986, Theorem 5) developed several quantitative tests of separability that can be applied to accuracy data from a Complete Identification Experiment (i.e., a feature complete factorial design), in which stimuli are constructed by factorially combining several levels of two or more stimulus components. The subject's task is to correctly identify the stimulus presented on each trial. To test for separability, one can compare the probability of correctly identifying the level of one component across different levels of a second component. Consider the hypothetical contours of equal likelihood illustrated in Figure 7.1a (or 7.1b). Ashby and Townsend (1986) showed that if perceptual and decisional separability hold for components **A** and **B**, then, for i = 1 and 2,

$$P(a_ib_1|\mathbf{A}_i\mathbf{B}_1) + P(a_ib_2|\mathbf{A}_i\mathbf{B}_1) = P(a_ib_1|\mathbf{A}_i\mathbf{B}_2) + P(a_ib_2|\mathbf{A}_i\mathbf{B}_2)\ , \qquad (10)$$

and for j = 1 and 2,

$$P(a_1b_j|\mathbf{A}_1\mathbf{B}_j) + P(a_2b_j|\mathbf{A}_1\mathbf{B}_j) = P(a_1b_j|\mathbf{A}_2\mathbf{B}_j) + P(a_2b_j|\mathbf{A}_2\mathbf{B}_j)\ . \qquad (11)$$

This condition (i.e., Equations 10 and 11) is called *marginal response invariance* (see chap. 8 for a more thorough discussion of marginal response invariance and related tests).

Perceptual separability and decisional separability are also related to measures derived from information theory (e.g., Ashby & Townsend, 1986; Attneave, 1959; Garner, 1962; Kadlec & Townsend, 1992). For example, Ashby and Townsend (1986, Theorem 6) showed that if perceptual separability and decisional separability hold for components **A** and **B**, then the partial contingent uncertainties $T_\mathbf{B}(\mathbf{A}, \text{b})$ and $T_\mathbf{A}(\mathbf{B}, \text{a})$, equal zero, where $T_\mathbf{B}(\mathbf{A}, \text{b})$ is defined as the contingent uncertainty between stimulus dimension **A** and response dimension b with stimulus dimension **B** partialed out (see also Wickens & Olzak, 1989, section A-4).

Another way to test for perceptual separability is to use the errors from an identification task to estimate the parameters of the perceptual distribution for each stimulus. Comparing fits between general models that allow for perceptual integrality with more restricted models that assume perceptual separability allows the researcher to determine whether perceptual separability is a reasonable assumption for a given pair of stimulus dimensions. Recently, Ashby and Lee (1991) did just this with semicircles that varied in diameter and in the orientation of a radial line. Although these dimensions have been operationally classified as separable (e.g., Burns et al., 1978), Ashby and Lee (1991) found consistent violations of perceptual separability along the orientation dimension.

Data collected in a concurrent ratings task (e.g., Graham, 1989; Olzak, 1986) can also be used to investigate the properties of perceptual distributions. In this task, two or more levels of two or more stimulus components are factorially combined to create a set of n-dimensional stimuli. On each trial, one stimulus is presented to the subject, and the subject is asked to make a separate judgment about each stimulus component. Each judgment indicates the subject's confidence that the associated component was presented at the highest level. Wickens and Olzak (see chap. 9) successfully used data collected in the concurrent ratings task to study the perceptual properties of horizontal and vertical sine-wave gratings that vary in frequency and contrast (see also Ashby, 1988).

SUMMARY AND CONCLUSIONS

Any psychological task that demands an overt response requires some decision process. Although the four operational tests of separability discussed in this chapter purport to assess perceptual processes *only*, each task requires an overt response and so some decision process is required. The goal of this chapter was to point out the effects of different decision processes on the results of the Filtering, Redundancy, Direct Dissimilarity Scaling, and Restricted Classification Tasks.

Perceptual separability and integrality are properties of particular pairs of stimulus dimensions and their interaction within the perceptual system, whereas decisional separability and integrality are not. Rather, decisional separability and integrality are under the subject's volitional control. As such, they are influenced by the subject's motivation and by the design of the experiment. In one experimental condition, decisional separability may be optimal, whereas in another it may not.

When perceptual *and* decisional separability are satisfied and the RT-distance hypothesis holds, no redundancy gain or interference effect will occur, and, thus, under these conditions the Redundancy and Filtering Tasks provide valid tests of perceptual separability. If, however, decisional separability is violated with perceptually separable dimensions, then redundancy gains are likely and interference effects are possible, thus invalidating the use of the Filtering and Redundancy Tasks as tests of perceptual separability. Nevertheless, the Filtering Task provides a better test of perceptual separability because the ideal observer is much more likely to use decisional separability in the Filtering task than in the Redundancy Task.

The distinction between perceptual separability and decisional separability is also important when examining the Direct Dissimilarity Scaling Task. The frequent empirical correlation between the city-block (Euclidean) distance metric and separable (integral) dimensions can be explained by assuming decisional separability for perceptually separable dimensions and decisional integrality for perceptually integral dimensions (see Proposition 7.1).

Decision processes play a central role in the Restricted Classification Task as well. A similarity-based model of the Restricted Classification Task is developed, whose fundamental assumption is that subjects will selectively attend to a particular stimulus dimension when the percepts of at least two of the three stimuli have values on that dimension less than a criterial distance apart. The model predicts that selective attention will be prevalent when the stimulus dimensions are perceptually separable and that selective attention leads to more dimensional classifications.

What recommendations does this chapter offer for the researcher interested in studying perceptual separability? Which experimental paradigms are valid and under what conditions? The Restricted Classification and Redundancy Tasks appear the weakest of the four operational tasks discussed. The assumptions of the Restricted Classification Task are not easily tested, and, even if satisfied, the task is too susceptible to extraneous effects (e.g., stimulus, task, and observer). The Redundancy Task is also susceptible to extraneous variables, such as the subject's level of experience with the task. In addition, the ideal observer frequently violates decisional separability in the redundancy condition, thereby invalidating the Redundancy Task as a test of perceptual separability. The assumptions of Direct Dissimilarity Scaling are more easily tested, but have weak empirical validity (e.g., Tversky, 1977). Despite this fact, consistency, a relation that can be tested on dissimilarity data, is related to perceptual separability and decisional separability (see Proposition 7.2). Of the four operational tests reviewed in this chapter, the Filtering Task provides the best test of perceptual separability, because the ideal observer frequently utilizes decisional separability in the filtering condition.

Data from an identification task provide the most rigorous tests of perceptual separability because converging evidence from several quantitative tests (e.g., marginal response invariance or transmitted information) can be obtained. In addition, the parameters of each perceptual distribution can be estimated, and fits between general and more constrained models can be compared.

APPENDIX A

Proof of Proposition 7.1: The first several steps of the proof are identical to those of Ashby and Perrin (1988, Theorem 1) and will not be repeated. Begin with their equation stating

$$s(\mathbf{A}, \mathbf{B}) = \Phi\{-\tfrac{1}{2}[\boldsymbol{\mu}_\mathbf{A} - \boldsymbol{\mu}_\mathbf{B})'\boldsymbol{\Sigma}^{-1}(\boldsymbol{\mu}_\mathbf{A} - \boldsymbol{\mu}_\mathbf{B})]^{1/2}\}\,, \tag{A1}$$

where Φ represents the standard normal cumulative distribution function. Now, since $\boldsymbol{\Sigma} = \sigma^2\mathbf{I}$, $s(\mathbf{A}, \mathbf{B}) = \Phi(-d_{\mathbf{AB}}/2\sigma^2)$, where $d_{\mathbf{AB}}$ is the Euclidean distance between means.

Denote the monotonically decreasing function that relates dissimilarity and similarity by g. Then

$$d(\mathbf{A}, \mathrm{B}) = g[s(\mathbf{A}, \mathrm{B})] = g\left[\Phi\left(\frac{-d_{\mathbf{AB}}}{2\sigma^2}\right)\right]. \tag{A2}$$

As $d_{\mathbf{AB}}$ increases, $\Phi(-d_{\mathbf{AB}}/2\sigma^2)$ decreases, so $g[\Phi(-d_{\mathbf{AB}}/2\sigma^2)]$ is increasing, which proves the theorem.

Proof of Proposition 7.2: For simplicity, I derive only Equation 8. The proof for Equation 9 follows analogously. If components **A** and **B** are perceptually separable, then

$$g_{i1}(x) = g_{i2}(x)$$

for all x and for i = 1, 2, 3, and 4.

Let x_{12} be the criterion between the representations of $\mathbf{A}_1$ and $\mathbf{A}_2$. Because decisional separability holds and responding is context-free, the similarity of stimulus $\mathbf{A}_1\mathbf{B}_j$ to stimulus $\mathbf{A}_2\mathbf{B}_j$ is found from Equation 7 to be

$$\begin{aligned} s(\mathbf{A}_1\mathbf{B}_1, \mathbf{A}_2\mathbf{B}_1) &= \int_{-\infty}^{\infty}\int_{x_{12}}^{\infty} f_{11}(x, y)\,dx\,dy \\ &= \int_{x_{12}}^{\infty} g_{11}(x)\,dx \\ &= \int_{x_{12}}^{\infty} g_{12}(x)\,dx \\ &= \int_{-\infty}^{\infty}\int_{x_{12}}^{\infty} f_{12}(x, y)\,dx\,dy \\ &= s(\mathbf{A}_1\mathbf{B}_2, \mathbf{A}_2\mathbf{B}_2)\ . \end{aligned}$$

In a similar fashion, it can be shown that $s(\mathbf{A}_3\mathbf{B}_1, \mathbf{A}_4\mathbf{B}_1) = s(\mathbf{A}_3\mathbf{B}_2, \mathbf{A}_4\mathbf{B}_2)$. Without loss of generality, assume $s(\mathbf{A}_3\mathbf{B}_1, \mathbf{A}_4\mathbf{B}_1) > s(\mathbf{A}_1\mathbf{B}_1, \mathbf{A}_2\mathbf{B}_1)$. If the function relating similarity and dissimilarity is monotonically decreasing, then

$$\begin{aligned} &d(\mathbf{A}_1\mathbf{B}_1, \mathbf{A}_2\mathbf{B}_1) > d(\mathbf{A}_3\mathbf{B}_1, \mathbf{A}_4\mathbf{B}_1) \\ \text{iff}\quad &d(\mathbf{A}_1\mathbf{B}_2, \mathbf{A}_2\mathbf{B}_2) > d(\mathbf{A}_3\mathbf{B}_2, \mathbf{A}_4\mathbf{B}_2)\ . \end{aligned}$$

Therefore, consistency holds.

ACKNOWLEDGMENTS

This research was supported in part by a National Science Foundation Grant BNS88-19403 to F. Gregory Ashby and a Social Science-Humanities Grant to W. Todd Maddox. I especially wish to thank Greg Ashby for help at all stages of this research. I would also like to thank Helena Kadlec, Rich Ivry, Jack Loomis, and John Cotton for helpful comments on an earlier version of this manuscript and Bill Lee, Jerry Balakrishnan, and Geoff Boynton for many helpful discussions.

Correspondence concerning this article should be addressed to W. Todd Maddox, Department of Psychology, University of California, Santa Barbara, CA 93106.

8 Signal Detection Analyses of Dimensional Interactions

Helena Kadlec
Purdue University

James T. Townsend
Indiana University

INTRODUCTION

This chapter traces the development and impact of Signal Detection Theory in the study of perception. Emphasis is on the extension of Signal Detection Theory to visual perception in two-dimensional perceptual spaces, although the results presented here are general and not restricted to the visual domain or the two-dimensional case. Within the context of General Recognition Theory (GRT; Ashby & Townsend, 1986; see also chaps. 6 and 16 in this volume), theoretical relationships exist between the unobservable notions of perceptual separability and perceptual independence and the observable (and estimable) concepts of sampling independence, marginal response invariance, and two sets of signal detection parameters (Kadlec & Townsend, 1992). These relationships and their applications will be presented.

A procedure for testing perceptual independence and perceptual and decisional separabilities follows from these theoretical results. We illustrate it with three sets of data. The first data set is a direct application of the results in a two-dimensional space where the stimuli have two components each at one of two possible levels of presentation. The second data set illustrates the generalization to a situation where stimuli are composed of four components each at one of two possible levels. The third data set generalizes the procedure to a case where stimuli are two-dimensional, but each component has one of four possible levels of presentation. Some issues related to these generalizations of Signal Detection Theory to more than one and two dimensions will be discussed.

The organization of the chapter is as follows. In the first section we briefly review unidimensional Signal Detection Theory and some of its applications and extensions. In the second section we discuss perceptual dimensions, the definitions, and some ways in which they have been studied. In the third section, the GRT framework is briefly reviewed, and two sets of signal detection parameters based on generalization of signal detection theory to the multidimensional case are introduced. The various notions of "perceptual independence" are explicitly defined within the GRT framework in the fourth section, and in the next section the major results of Ashby and Townsend (1986) and Kadlec and Townsend (1992) relating various notions of "perceptual independence" with each other and the two sets of signal detection parameters are presented. (Note that we use "perceptual independence" in quotation marks to refer to the general sense of independence as used in the literature with its various connotations, and we reserve perceptual independence without quotation marks for the notion precisely defined in the fourth section.) These theoretical results lead to a method of testing perceptual separability and independence, which is presented and illustrated with three sets of data in the sixth section. In the final section of the chapter, some future directions and extensions are discussed. We attempted to make each section self-contained; thus, readers familiar with the material in any of the sections may skip to the next.

SIGNAL DETECTION THEORY AND ITS IMPACT ON THE STUDY OF PERCEPTION

Historically, Signal Detection Theory stemmed from the direct application of Statistical Decision Theory to the detection of auditory signals embedded in noise (Peterson & Birdsall, 1953). It was immediately recognized that this approach could be easily applied to other sensory domains, particularly the detection of visual stimuli (Tanner & Swets, 1954; see also Green & Swets, 1974), and this unidimensional approach could be generalized to the recognition of more than one stimulus, for example, two different auditory stimuli or color stimuli (Tanner, 1956), and the detection of various components of complex auditory signals (Green, 1958).

The traditional experimental paradigm was a simple judgment task where on a given trial the observer responded yes or no, depending on whether he or she detected a signal embedded in some noise that could potentially mask the true signal. Many such trials (usually hundreds) would be presented to obtain estimates of two probabilities: the probability of a *hit* calculated as the proportion of trials on which the observer correctly responded that the signal was present, and the probability of a *false alarm* estimated as the proportion of trials on which the observer incorrectly reported that he or she detected the signal when it was not presented.

The basic underlying assumption is that over trials a given stimulus (whether a signal in noise or noise alone) produces a distribution of perceptual effects, denoted here as $g_s(x)$ and $g_n(x)$ for the signal + noise and noise-alone distributions, respectively. These underlying distributions, one for each type of trial, are then used along with the estimated probabilities of hits and false alarms to calculate the sensitivity estimate d' and an estimate of the response bias β from the following relations:

$$P(\text{hit}) = P(\text{signal reported} \mid \text{signal present}) = \int_c^{\infty} g_s(x)\, dx$$

and

$$P(\text{false alarm}) = P(\text{signal reported} \mid \text{signal absent}) = \int_c^{\infty} g_n(x)\, dx\ ,$$

where c is the decision criterion such that if the perceptual effect x falls above c the observer responds that he or she detected the signal, and if the perceptual effect falls below c the observer responds that he or she did not detect the signal. The two parameters are defined as follows: the d', or sensitivity parameter, represents the (standardized) distance between the means of the noise and the signal + noise densities,

$$d' = \frac{\mu_s - \mu_n}{\sigma_n}\ ,$$

and β, the response bias parameter, is the ratio of the two densities at the criterion point c,

$$\beta = \frac{g_s(c)}{g_n(c)}\ .$$

The usual assumptions are that both densities are normal and that the noise distribution has a mean of 0 ($\mu_n = 0$) and standard deviation of 1 ($\sigma_n = 1$).

Since the introduction of Signal Detection Theory, its applications have flourished in various research domains. These research areas will not be reviewed here, but to give the reader a flavor of the variety of applications, we give two examples: (a) multimodal signal detection was used to evaluate the degree to which the visual and auditory perceptual systems interact and share capacity (e.g., Eijkman & Vendrik, 1965; Fidell, 1970; Taylor, Lindsay, & Forbes, 1967); and (b) examination of selective influence of various experimental factors on the two (d' and β) parameters, for example, stimulus intensity on the sensitivity parameter d', and payoffs or cost effects on the response bias parameter β. The typical experimental paradigms in which Signal Detection Theory has been used include detection of stimuli presented very briefly or at sensory threshold using yes-no judgment tasks or two- or four-interval forced-choice tasks, and discrimination between (or identification of) highly confusable stimuli.

A third example, and one that is directly relevant to our discussion, involves application of Signal Detection Theory to evaluate "independence" (sometimes also referred to as separability or orthogonality) of perceptual dimensions representing the stimulus components in multiattribute stimuli. This includes studies on whether the "processing channels" for each of the stimulus components operate independently in some sense. Two examples in the auditory domain involve questions of whether the components of two-dimensional stimuli (e.g., two tones at different frequencies presented simultaneously) can be recognized "independently" of each other (e.g., Corcoran, 1967), and whether the perceptual dimensions of pitch and loudness are "independent" (e.g., Zagorski, 1975). Similarly in vision, Signal Detection Theory has been employed to examine whether the various spatial frequency "channels" operate "independently" (e.g., Graham, 1989; Hirsch, Hylton, & Graham, 1982; Olzak, 1986).

Most studies that evaluate the "independence" of stimulus components in multiattribute stimuli employ a form of *feature-complete factorial designs*. In these designs, the stimulus set is formed by combining each level of each component factorially with every level of every other component. Ashby and Townsend (1986) called such designs *complete identification* designs. When confidence judgments on each component are required with such a stimulus set, it is called the *concurrent experiment* (e.g., Ashby, 1988; Graham, 1989; Olzak, 1986). In each of these designs, performance on a given component at a fixed level is then compared across levels of the other component(s).

The various applications of Signal Detection Theory were paralleled by some theoretical developments, for example, to the detection of a number of equally detectable orthogonal signals (Green & Birdsall, 1978; Nolte & Jaarsma, 1967). However, little in the way of formal development of multidimensional Signal Detection Theory was accomplished. This could primarily be due to the problem of generalizing the decision criteria of Signal Detection Theory to two- and higher-dimensional perceptual space (see end of the third section on GRT).

PERCEPTUAL DIMENSIONS AND THEIR "SEPARABILITY"

Around the same time as Signal Detection Theory was introduced in the study of psychophysics (mid-1960s to early 1970s), psychologists studying perception began to devote attention to the issue of whether and which perceptual dimensions are perceived "independently" using various response time paradigms. Based on earlier work by Attneave (1950), Garner and his co-workers, as well as others since then (e.g., Burns & Shepp, 1988; Melara & Marks, 1990a, 1990b; Shepard, 1964), have been interested in determining how a number (usually two) of different stimulus components are perceived when viewed in combination with each other in the same stimulus. In general, if one component does not have any influence on the perception of the other, the components are said to be separable (Garner, 1974); conversely, if the perception of one component is influenced by the other, the two are said to be integral (Lockhead, 1966). Much earlier work in this area is summarized in Garner (1974). (See also chap. 7.)

In most of this work, the experimental paradigms used response times as the dependent measure and included speeded classification tasks (e.g., Cheng & Pachella, 1984; Lockhead & King, 1977; Melara & Marks, 1990a, 1990b), same-different judgment tasks (e.g., Dixon & Just, 1978), and absolute judgment tasks (e.g., Weintraub, 1971). Taken together, these paradigms were to provide converging evidence about the separability or integrality of numerous perceptual dimensions.

Separability in Garner's sense is defined operationally without much theoretical basis. This has sometimes resulted in debates about what separability and integrality mean. For example, some investigators believe that separability and integrality are not dichotomous, but represent two extremes of a continuum (e.g., Cheng & Pachella, 1984; Grau & Kemler-Nelson, 1988; Smith & Kemler, 1978). Within such a continuum, Cheng and Pachella (1984) interpreted separability in terms of a correspondence of physical dimensions of a stimulus to a finite number of psychological attributes that can be selectively attended to; those physical dimensions that have such a correspondence to a psychological attribute are defined as separable. Lockhead and his co-workers (Lockhead & King, 1977; Monahan & Lockhead, 1977), on the other hand, have claimed that performance on classification and identification of integral stimuli can best be predicted based on psychological distances between stimuli in a similarity space. In fact, the traditional view was that stimuli composed of integral dimensions are not (psychologically) perceived as dimensions at all, but rather as dimensionless "blobs" (Garner, 1974; Lockhead, 1979; but see Melara & Marks, 1990a). It is difficult to resolve such definitional problems in a theory-free perspective.

Within GRT, perceptual separability has a clearly defined meaning (see section on Various Concepts of "Perceptual Independence"). Although perceptual separability is defined in somewhat different terms in the two approaches, there is hope that at least some of the psychological substrate that is pertinent to the Garner train of research will overlap with that of Ashby and Townsend (1986). Ashby and Maddox (see chap. 7) have begun to link Garner's definition of separability with the theoretical notion of perceptual separability defined in GRT. More evidence on this question, however, is critically needed.

The method for testing perceptual separability based on multidimensional Signal Detection Theory that we present in this chapter involves an identification-discrimination paradigm with accuracy measures as the dependent variable, thus providing another line of investigation on perceptual separability. Whereas Multidimensional Scaling and Factor Analysis are methods specifically designed to uncover underlying psychological or perceptual dimensions, investigators studying perceptual separability in multiattribute stimuli typically assume, or concretely specify, what the perceptual dimensions are. Once established by the investigator, the question then becomes whether these dimensions interact, and if so how. The method based on the GRT perspective developed here is of the latter genre. It is more general, however, as GRT encompasses and unifies many different paradigms, such as perceived similarity (Ashby & Perrin, 1988), preference (see chap. 6), and a number of models of decision making (Ashby & Gott, 1988). Additionally, our hope is that the method we present will be extended to make it useful also for identifying perceptual dimensions. Results of new tests and modeling may thus be able to provide support for, or refute, existing notions of what constitutes a given set of perceptual dimensions. A method that could serve both of these functions, to find the relevant perceptual dimensions and to examine how they are perceived, would be very useful and would provide an interesting alternative to Multidimensional Scaling.

Perhaps the single most important issue when studying perception from this "dimensional" perspective concerns the definition of perceptual dimensions. Tversky and Krantz (1970) have defined perceptual dimensions as the organizing principles or factors along which stimuli are perceived and structured. These perceptual dimensions are contrasted with physical attributes that characterize the stimuli or dimensions derived from Factor Analysis or Multidimensional Scaling. For example, physical attributes (or physical dimensions) may be stimulus intensity, hue, or line orientation for visual stimuli, and frequency and amplitude of sound waves for auditory stimuli. A perceptual dimension, on the other hand, may be the strength with which a given feature is represented in the perceptual space (e.g., Wickelgren, 1967), possibly realized in the nervous system by the frequency of firing of neurons or the number of neurons firing in a specific cortical area. This is the sense of perceptual dimension that we employ here. Tversky and Krantz (1970), however, assume that perceptual dimensions are by definition "independent", which we do not, since one of the goals of our investigation is to specifically examine their "independence" (in the various senses of the word, as defined later).

The identification of perceptual dimensions in the different sensory domains has met with mixed success. In the case of audition, the perceptual dimensions of loudness, pitch, and timbre correspond best to the physical stimulus dimensions of amplitude, frequency, and waveform shape, respectively, of a sound wave. (Note that there does not necessarily need to be a one-to-one mapping between physical and perceptual values.) In two recent studies, Melara and Marks (1990a, 1990b) introduced two interesting distinctions among perceptual dimensions for auditory stimuli, although presumably these would also hold for other senses. The first involves a distinction between "primary" versus "nonprimary" perceptual dimensions (Melara & Marks, 1990a). It employs an experimental paradigm where the axes of the physical dimensions, from which the compound stimuli are constructed, are experimentally rotated. That orientation that results in separability in Garner's sense, and thus in dimensions that are perceived as the most salient without suffering performance deficits, then corresponds to the "primary" dimensions (Melara & Marks, 1990a).

The second distinction (Melara & Marks, 1990b), "hard" versus "soft" dimensions, concerns the contextual effects of one dimension on the other. The assertion is that in a feature-complete factorial design, two types of contexts operate simultaneously to affect perception of the individual components. In classifying stimuli on one dimension, *intraclass context* is defined as variation along an unattended dimension that interferes with classification on the attended dimension because the attended dimension itself may now be perceived as varying. In classification of pairs of stimuli when the two dimensions are correlated, for example, classifying stimuli that are "high" (or "low") on both dimensions (in this case positively correlated dimensions), this *redundant context* may make the stimuli more discriminable and thereby facilitate performance. Melara and Marks found that auditory perceptual dimensions can be distinguished on the basis of effects of intraclass context; pitch and timbre are "hard" perceptual dimensions because they resist intraclass context and profit from redundant context, whereas loudness is a "soft" perceptual dimension since both contexts affect its perception.

Both of these distinctions are interesting extensions of Garner's research and enhance our understanding of perceptual dimensions. As discussed before, this work was primarily done in the auditory domain, since auditory perceptual dimensions seem to be more clearly specified. Applying such paradigms to other senses should provide many fruitful insights.

In vision, the picture for perceptual dimensions seems more complex. Various "modules" for processing different aspects of visual perception, such as motion, color, texture, depth, and contour (or form), have been proposed, and questions have been raised whether these are or can be processed "independently" (e.g., Livingstone & Hubel, 1988; Marr, 1982; Nakayama & Silverman, 1986; Treisman & Gelade, 1980; Treisman & Gormican, 1988). The dimensions for some of these modules have been proposed and effectively studied. For example, color perception involves the three perceptual dimensions brightness, hue, and saturation, which correspond to the physical stimulus attributes amplitude, frequency (or wavelength), and purity of light waves, respectively (e.g., Burns & Shepp, 1988; Krantz, 1974). For texture perception, Julesz (1981, 1985) has an extensive theory based on what he calls "textons" whose first- and higher-order statistical characteristics have different perceptual qualities.

For pattern or form perception, however, there is no general agreement on what the basic perceptual dimensions are. A classic example, involving dissimilarity ratings of rectangles, illustrates this problem of defining the relevant perceptual dimensions. Whereas some subjects judge dissimilarity of rectangles based on the dimensions of height and width, others use the dimensions of area and shape (e.g., Krantz & Tversky, 1975; Lazarte & Schönemann, 1991). Note that this may be a decisional and not necessarily perceptual effect; nevertheless the question of how to define the relevant perceptual dimensions remains.

The discovery of cortical columns in visual areas of the brain that preferentially respond to lines and edges of specific orientations (e.g., Hubel, 1982; Hubel & Livingstone, 1985; Hubel & Weisel, 1959, 1968) led to speculation that these simple orientation lines and edges could represent the perceptual dimensions of which all patterns were subsequently composed. Other investigators, however, argue that the brain analyzes a visual scene in terms of spatial frequency components contained in the scene, and that each frequency component is subserved by its own processing "channel" (e.g., De Valois & De Valois, 1988; Graham, 1981, 1989; Watson, 1983). Evidence from primates also seems to support this latter view; visual cortical cells do preferentially respond to different spatial frequencies (e.g., K. De Valois & Tootell, 1983; R. De Valois, Albrecht, & Thorell, 1982).

Some studies have attempted to test these two alternative hypotheses—whether bars and edges or spatial frequency components are the relevant physiological stimuli. The results suggest that spatial frequency information is physiologically more relevant than the more simple (but spectrally much more complex) bars and edges (see, e.g., De Valois & De Valois, 1988, pp. 206–211). The two views, however, have not yet been resolved to everyone's satisfaction, and they may not be antithetic, since neural responses depend on frequency and orientation of the stimulus, as well as other factors such as motion, direction of motion, and end stopping (R. De Valois, Yund, & Hepler, 1982; Webster & R. De Valois, 1985). It is also a big leap to suggest that perceptual dimensions are the same as the stimulus attributes that drive *single* cortical cells. In order to specify the relevant perceptual dimensions, much work is yet needed on all fronts and particularly with respect to merging "top-down" approaches of perception with the "bottom-up" approach of physiology.

GENERAL RECOGNITION THEORY AND SIGNAL DETECTION MACRO- AND MICROANALYSES

With the different experimental paradigms employed to investigate interactions of perceptual dimensions, the terminology regarding "perceptual independence" of dimensions has become quite perplexing. Within the context of GRT, however, Ashby and Townsend (1986) defined and interrelated many of the various terms that now connote "perceptual independence"; these definitions will be presented in the next section. In this section, we briefly review GRT and introduce the two sets of parameters of signal detection macroanalyses and microanalyses. (See chaps. 6, 7, and 16 for other results and extensions of GRT.)

In the notation of Chapter 1, in GRT a stimulus that is constructed from two components is represented as $\mathbf{A}_i\mathbf{B}_j$, i = 1, . . . , n, j = 1, . . . , m, where **A** and **B** denote the (physical) stimulus components (e.g., intensity, line length, etc.), each of which is represented by a dimension in the perceptual space (denoted X and Y, respectively). More generally, a stimulus may have more than two components, for example, components **A**, **B**, . . . , **N**, each represented by a perceptual dimension and each with its own levels. The subscripts represent the levels of the corresponding components in the presented stimulus. It has sometimes been mistakenly assumed that when only two levels are included in the design they imply feature presence or absence. In fact, Garner and Haun (1978) defined "features" as perceptual dimensions that are either present or absent. However, it is worth stressing that in our usage the component or feature levels can take on *any* values, although we sometimes use feature presence and absence in our examples.

GRT views perception as a two-stage process. When a stimulus $\mathbf{A}_i\mathbf{B}_j$ is presented, perceptual processes of the system operate on it to produce a perceptual effect (x,y). Based on this effect, the decisional processes then choose the response that the system will make. The theory assumes that the perceptual effect of any given stimulus (specifically of each component of the stimulus) is not constant over trials but has some (usually continuous) distribution. This allows us to represent each stimulus by a joint probability density of the perceptual effects of the constituent features in the perceptual space. In the case where there are two stimulus components, a bivariate density, $f_{ij}(x,y)$, represents the distribution of perceptual effects of stimulus $\mathbf{A}_i\mathbf{B}_j$. For example, in a feature-complete factorial design with two components each with two levels (e.g., i = 1, 2 and j = 1, 2 with 1 denoting feature absence and 2 denoting feature presence), we have four bivariate densities in the perceptual space: one for the blank stimulus, one for each of the stimuli composed of each feature individually, and one for the stimulus containing both features. Equal probability contours representing these four stimuli are shown as circles and ellipses in the upper left part of Figure 8.1 (the other parts of this figure will be explained in more detail later).

For the decision process, it is assumed that the observer sets up decision criteria that divide the perceptual space into different response regions. Each component usually has its own criterion (lines labeled $c_{\mathbf{A}}$ and $c_{\mathbf{B}}$ in Figure 8.1). A stimulus presentation on a given trial results in a percept represented by a single point in this perceptual space. The subject's response then corresponds to the region in the perceptual space where the percept falls in relation to the decision criterion for each component. For example, if the percept falls above the criterion for component **A** ($c_{\mathbf{A}}$ on Figure 8.1) and below the criterion for component **B** ($c_{\mathbf{B}}$), the subject responds that feature **A** was present and feature **B** was absent. Stated this way, GRT is completely general and does not assume any particular form for the densities. We will, however, employ the Gaussian version of GRT and estimate signal detection parameters based on Gaussian densities.

Each joint density has associated with it its corresponding marginal densities.

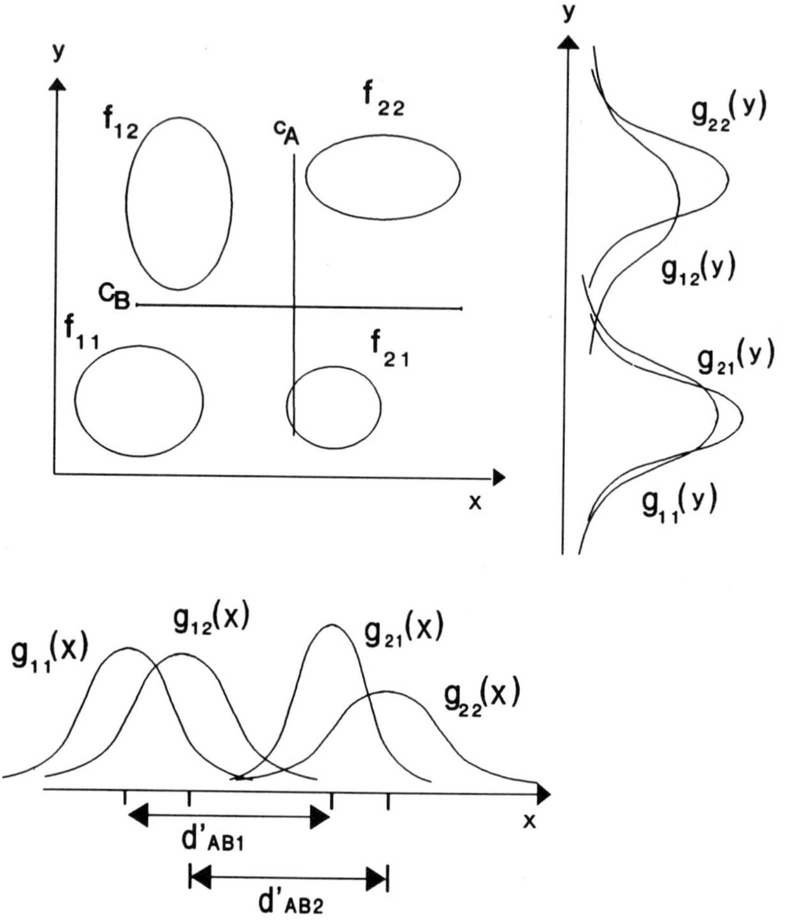

FIG. 8.1. Equal-density contours of the joint densities representing the perceptual effects of four stimuli constructed from two dimensions, with two levels on each dimension (upper left). For each stimulus, marginal densities, $g_{ij}(x)$ (bottom of figure) and $g_{ij}(y)$ (right-hand side), result after integrating out $\boldsymbol{Y}$ and $\boldsymbol{X}$, respectively. These marginal densities are then used for computing the marginal d''s and β's. See text for further explanation.

In the two-dimensional case, for each stimulus $\mathbf{A}_i\mathbf{B}_j$ we have one marginal density for the perceptual effect of component **A** ($\boldsymbol{X}$), denoted by $g_{ij}(x)$ (see bottom of Figure 8.1), and a marginal density for $\boldsymbol{Y}$ (component **B**), $g_{ij}(y)$ (see the right side of Figure 8.1). According to this multidimensional point of view, two sets of signal detection parameters can be defined (Townsend, Hu, and Evans, 1984; Townsend, Hu, and Kadlec, 1988). The mathematical definitions are given in Appendix A.

Signal detection macroanalyses use the marginal densities, resulting in d''s and β's for each component, at each level of the other component. For example, in the four-stimulus case in Figure 8.1, we have one d' and β for component **A** at the first level of component **B**, denoted $d'_{\mathbf{AB}1}$, and one d' and β at the second level of component **B**, $d'_{\mathbf{AB}2}$ (see bottom of Figure 8.1). The d''s and β's for component **B** at each of the levels of component **A** are defined analogously and would appear along the y-axis. Investigations of perceptual "independence" using Signal Detection Theory have usually employed these *marginal* estimates (e.g., Graham, Kramer, & Haber, 1985; Olzak, 1986; Wickelgren, 1967).

The second set of signal detection parameters are obtained from *signal detection microanalyses* (Townsend et al., 1984, 1988). These *conditional* signal detection parameters are obtained for each component at each level of another component, *within the same stimulus,* by conditioning on how the other component in the stimulus was perceived. In the two-dimensional example, two pairs of parameters are obtained for each component: (a) by conditioning on whether the second component was a "hit" (correctly reported as present) or a "miss" (incorrectly reported as absent), both of which imply that the second component was present in the stimulus, and (b) by conditioning on whether the second component was a "correct rejection" (correct report that it was absent) or a "false alarm" (incorrect report that it was present), which indicates that the second component was not in the stimulus. Please note that we keep this nomenclature ("hits", "miss", etc.) even in the more general case when there are more than two levels of each component, even though these terms will then actually stand for conditioning above or below a given criterion. These conditional estimates were employed by Sorkin, Pohlmann, and Gilliom (1973) in an innovative feature-complete factorial design with two auditory stimuli.

The conditional parameters for a given component are based on the densities that result from the joint densities after we condition on the particular response made for the other component (see Figure 8.2 and Appendix A). Consider the d' for component **A** conditioned on the hit of component **B**, $d'(\mathbf{A}|\mathbf{B}\text{ hit})$, in our binary-valued two-dimensional example. The hit of **B** implies that **B** was present in the stimulus; thus, we use those portions of $f_{12}(x, y)$ and $f_{22}(x, y)$ that fall *above the* $c_\mathbf{B}$ *criterion* to obtain $d'(\mathbf{A}|\mathbf{B}\text{ hit})$. To obtain $d'(\mathbf{A}|\mathbf{B}\text{ miss})$, we use those portions of $f_{12}(x, y)$ and $f_{22}(x, y)$ falling *below* the $c_\mathbf{B}$ criterion.

A critical problem in generalizing Signal Detection Theory to two or more dimensions is the generalization of the response bias parameter β when a decision criterion is not parallel to the axis. In one dimension, the criterion is a point on the axis representing the perceptual effect such that, if the percept on a given trial falls above the criterion, the decision is to report the feature (signal) as present, and if the percept falls below the criterion it is reported as absent. In two dimensions, however, the criterion becomes a line or, more generally, a curve. When the criterion, say $c_\mathbf{A}$, is not parallel to the perceptual y-axis, there does not exist a unique point to represent the "average" criterion for **A** such that the

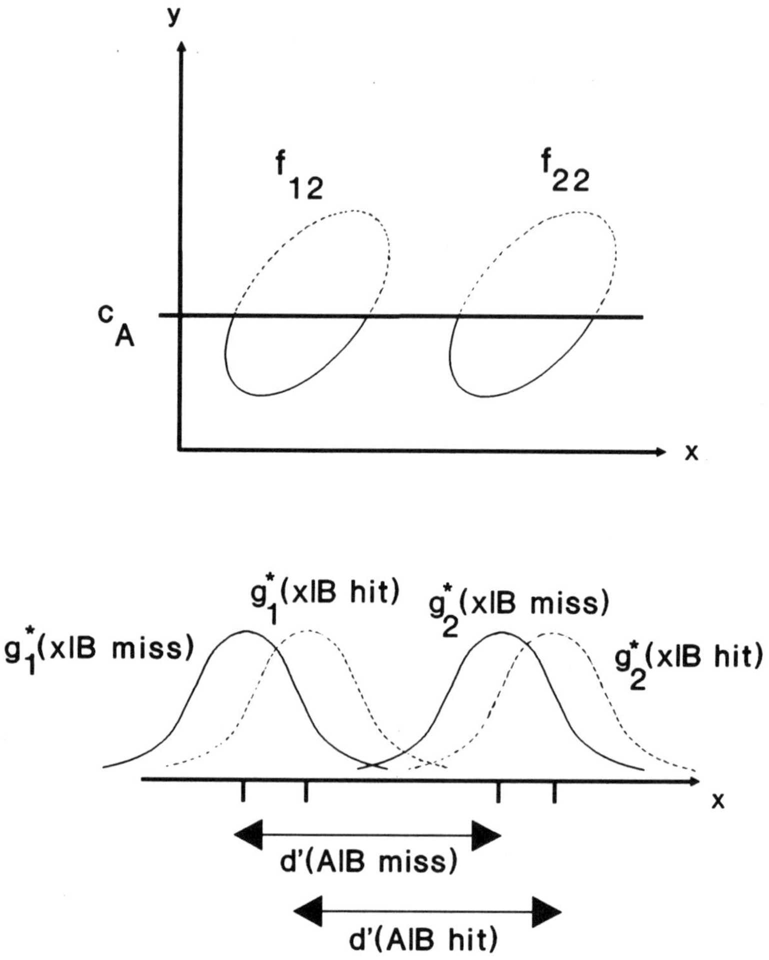

FIG. 8.2. Illustration of conditional d''s. Joint densities for only two stimuli, with feature **B** at the second level, are shown (upper figure); after normalization, the dashed portions of the contours, above the c_B criterion, are used to obtain marginal densities for computing d'(**A**|**B** hit), and the solid portions give d'(**A**|**B** miss) (bottom figure).

probabilities of hits and false alarms are preserved when mapping from the two-dimensional space to one (the marginal x) dimension. The definition of β thus becomes more complex, since it would depend on how component **B** was perceived (it would be a function of y). Similar complexities plague the conditional densities on which the conditional parameters are based. In many of the theorems, we therefore assume parallel decision criteria.

VARIOUS CONCEPTS OF "PERCEPTUAL INDEPENDENCE"

Different notions connoting "perceptual independence" have been defined within the GRT framework (Ashby & Townsend, 1986). The three theoretical definitions we consider here are perceptual independence, perceptual separability, and decisional separability. Two additional concepts of "independence", sampling independence and marginal response invariance, are empirically observable conditions that are closely related to the former ones.

To make these definitions more explicit, consider the following example. Suppose the stimulus set is composed of a feature-complete factorial combination of (some of) the following components and levels: component **A**—geometric shapes (circles, squares, triangles); component **B**—colors (red, blue, green); component **C**—sizes (small, large); and component **D**—brightness (dim, bright).[1] The simplest feature-complete factorial design with components **A** and **B**, each with two levels, has four stimuli in the ensemble (red circle, blue circle, red square, and blue square), and each stimulus is represented by a bivariate density in a two-dimensional perceptual space.

For each concept, we first give the formal definition, explain it in terms of our previous example, and then discuss the generalizations to (a) two-dimensional cases with more than two levels for each component, and (b) higher-dimensional cases. We begin with the theoretical definitions.

Perceptual Independence

Definition 8.1: Perceptual independence (this is Definition 1.1) of components **A** and **B** in a feature-complete factorial design holds in stimulus $\mathbf{A}_i\mathbf{B}_j$ if and only if the perceptual effects of **A** and **B** are statistically independent, that is, if and only if

$$f_{ij}(x, y) = g_{ij}(x)g_{ij}(y), \qquad \text{for all } x \text{ and } y .$$

This condition signifies that within a given stimulus, say a blue square, the perceptual effect of one component (blue) does not influence the perceptual effect of the other component (square), no matter where in the perceptual space the overall percept may fall. Thus, on every trial where a given stimulus is presented, if perceptual independence holds in that stimulus one component will not affect the other. Note that for Gaussian densities, this amounts to a zero correlation between the perceptual effects of the two components.

Generalizing this definition to more than two levels on each of two compo-

[1]These stimulus components are chosen merely for illustrative purposes. The fact that each component may itself have multidimensional perceptual representations should not cause confusion.

nents is straightforward: simply replace the corresponding values for i and j. In this two-dimensional case with m levels on each dimension, Ashby (1988) has shown how a generalization of the tetrachoric r can be employed to test for perceptual independence.

When more than two dimensions are present, the generalization becomes more interesting, since alternative definitions exist. We define *mutual* perceptual independence of *all* components simultaneously. For example, in the four-dimensional case, mutual perceptual independence of all four components in stimulus $\mathbf{A}_i\mathbf{B}_j\mathbf{C}_p\mathbf{D}_q$ holds when

$$f_{ijpq}(x, y, z, w) = g_{ijpq}(x)g_{ijpq}(y)g_{ijpq}(z)g_{ijpq}(w)$$

for all x, y, z, and w.

Alternatively, *joint* (pairwise) perceptual independence is defined for pairs of components at each *fixed* combination of levels of the other component(s), essentially conditioning on the levels of the other component(s). For example, in stimulus $\mathbf{A}_i\mathbf{B}_j\mathbf{C}_p\mathbf{D}_q$, pairwise joint independence of components **A** and **B**, at given values of $\mathbf{Z}$ and $\mathbf{W}$, representing the perceptual effects of components **C** and **D**, respectively, holds when

$$f_{ijpq}(x, y|\mathbf{Z}=z, \mathbf{W}=w) = g_{ijpq}(x|\mathbf{Z}=z, \mathbf{W}=w)g_{ijpq}(y|\mathbf{Z}=z, \mathbf{W}=w)$$

for all x and y, where $g_{ijpq}(x|\mathbf{Z}=z, \mathbf{W}=w)$, for example, is the marginal density of the *three* perceptual effects $\mathbf{X}$, $\mathbf{Z}$, and $\mathbf{W}$, with $\mathbf{Z}$ fixed at z and $\mathbf{W}$ fixed at w. More concretely, shape (**A**) and color (**B**) are jointly pairwise independent in a given stimulus, but only at particular values of $\mathbf{Z}$ and $\mathbf{W}$, that is, only when the percept of the stimulus falls in a particular region of the perceptual space on the **C** (size) and **D** (brightness) dimensions (e.g., when it appears larger and brighter, but not when it appears smaller and dimmer). Note that mutual perceptual independence of all components implies the joint perceptual independence of the subsets of components.

Similarly, for four or more components, we can also define joint three-way independence between, say, components **A**, **B**, and **D** at a given value of $\mathbf{Z}$ representing the perceptual effect associated with component **C** in the given stimulus. Here we have

$$f_{ijpq}(x, y, w|\mathbf{Z}=z) = g_{ijpq}(x|\mathbf{Z}=z)g_{ijpq}(y|\mathbf{Z}=z)g_{ijpq}(w|\mathbf{Z}=z) ,$$

for all x, y, and w, where $g_{ijpq}(x|\mathbf{Z}=z)$, for example, is the marginal density of the *two* perceptual effects $\mathbf{X}$ and $\mathbf{Z}$, with $\mathbf{Z}$ fixed at z. In this example, the components of shape, color, and brightness are jointly (three-way) independent, but depend on the particular value of $\mathbf{Z}$ (size).

These definitions clearly indicate that perceptual independence is concerned with *within*-stimulus effects. Thus, it may be that in the same experiment perceptual independence of the components may hold in one stimulus (e.g., in the blue square) but not in another (e.g., the red square). Perceptual and decisional separabilities, on the other hand, describe the effects that the components have on each other *across* different stimuli. These definitions are given next.

Perceptual and Decisional Separabilities

Definition 8.2: In a feature-complete factorial design with stimuli $\mathbf{A}_i\mathbf{B}_j$, i = 1,2, j = 1,2, component **A** is *perceptually separable* from component **B** if and only if the perceptual effect of component **A** does not depend on the level of component **B**—that is, if and only if

$$g_{i1}(x) = g_{i2}(x), \qquad i = 1,2 .$$

Similarly, component **B** is *perceptually separable* from component **A** if and only if the perceptual effect of component **B** does not depend on the level component **A**—that is, if and only if

$$g_{1j}(y) = g_{2j}(y), \qquad j = 1,2$$

Definition 8.3: In a feature-complete factorial design with stimuli $\mathbf{A}_i\mathbf{B}_j$, i = 1,2, j = 1,2, component **A** (**B**) is *decisionally separable* if and only if the decision about component **A** (**B**) does not depend on the level of component **B** (**A**)—that is, if the decision bound for component **A** (**B**) in the GRT representation is parallel to the *Y*-axis (*X*-axis).

In our two-dimensional example, if shape is perceptually separable from color, it means that when we average across colors the two densities for shape will be identical. In other words, the perceptual effect of the square will have the same distribution (across trials) whether it is obtained from the red-square stimulus trials or from the blue-square stimulus, and similarly for the perceptual effects of the circle stimuli. In yet other words, the level of the color component has no effect on the perception of the shape across trials. The same interpretation is given to decisional separability of one component across levels of the other.

In the definitions of perceptual and decisional separabilities, note that one feature may be perceptually or decisionally separable from the other while the other need not be perceptually or decisionally separable from the first. This is an important point, since in some of our theorems separability of one feature is sufficient, whereas in other theorems both components must be separable.

To generalize perceptual separability to more than two levels is straightforward. The requirement is that all marginal densities for each level of a given component be identical across *all* levels of the other component; for example, for components **A** and **B** with n and m levels, respectively, component **A** is perceptually separable from **B** when

$$g_{i1}(x) = g_{i2}(x) = \cdots = g_{im}(x), \qquad \text{for } i = 1,2, \cdots ,n ,$$

and component **B** is perceptually separable from **A** when

$$g_{1j}(y) = g_{2j}(y) = \cdots = g_{nj}(y), \qquad \text{for } j = 1,2, \cdots, m \,.$$

In other words, the level on one component does not affect how the other component is perceived.

For more than two dimensions, we again have alternative definitions: joint perceptual separability and single-component perceptual separability. A pair of components, say **A** and **B,** are *jointly* (pairwise) perceptually separable from component **C** when the joint densities for perceiving components **A** and **B** are equivalent across levels of **C**: that is,

$$g_{ij1}(x, y) = g_{ij2}(x, y), \qquad \text{for } i = 1,2 \text{ and } j = 1,2 \,.$$

This means, for example, that the density for the blue square is identical whether it is large or small, and similarly for the other color-shape combinations.

Single-component perceptual separability, for example for component **A** (from components **B** and **C**), holds when

$$g_{i11}(x) = g_{i12}(x) = g_{i21}(x) = g_{i22}(x), \qquad \text{for } i = 1,2 \,.$$

Note that equality of the first two terms alone indicates separability of **A** across **C** at the first level of **B**, whereas equality of the third and fourth terms indicates separability of **A** across **C** at the second level of **B**. Similarly, equality of the first and third terms signifies separability of **A** across **B** at the first level of **C**, and the second and fourth terms denote separability of **A** across **B** at the second level of **C**. Single-component perceptual separability, even for all components, does not imply joint (pairwise) perceptual separability, nor vice versa, since different marginal densities are involved in the two types of definitions.

Generalizing decisional separability to more levels, we simply require that all the decision bounds, between all the levels on each dimension, be parallel to the perceptual axes. In higher-dimensional spaces, each of the decision bounds (in general now hyperplanes) must be parallel to its perceptual axis.

These then are the theoretical notions of "independence" defined within the GRT framework. The following two senses of independence are operational definitions. Both concern overall probabilities (corresponding to areas and volumes under the densities in GRT) rather than conditions that must hold at all perceptual values (x,y), and, thus, in this sense are weaker than the theoretical concepts defined before. Sampling independence is the global analog of perceptual independence and is a within-stimulus outcome. Marginal response invariance is analogous to perceptual separability.

Sampling Independence

Definition 8.4: If a and b denote the events that components **A** and **B**, respectively, are reported, then *sampling independence* in stimulus $\mathbf{A}_i\mathbf{B}_j$ holds if and only if

$$P(a_2b_2|\mathbf{A}_i\mathbf{B}_j) = P(\mathbf{A} \text{ is sampled } |\mathbf{A}_i\mathbf{B}_j) \times P(\mathbf{B} \text{ is sampled } |\mathbf{A}_i\mathbf{B}_j)$$
$$= [P(a_2b_1|\mathbf{A}_i\mathbf{B}_j) + P(a_2b_2|\mathbf{A}_i\mathbf{B}_j)] \times [P(a_1b_2|\mathbf{A}_i\mathbf{B}_j) + P(a_2b_2|\mathbf{A}_i\mathbf{B}_j)] \, .$$

In other words, sampling independence holds in stimulus $\mathbf{A}_i\mathbf{B}_j$ if and only if the probability that both features are reported is equal to the probability that feature **A** is reported (regardless of the level reported for the level of feature **B**) times the probability that feature **B** is reported (regardless of the level reported for feature **A**). This is simply that the joint probability of two events, a_2 and b_2, equals the product of the two marginal probabilities for each event.

In our example, this means that when a blue square, say, is presented to the observer, the probability that he or she will respond, for example, "red square" is equal to the probability of reporting "red" (regardless of shape or, in other words, the probability of reporting red squares plus the probability of reporting red circles) times the probability of reporting "square" (regardless of color, which is the probability of reporting red squares plus the probability of reporting blue squares). All other conditional response probabilities are defined similarly; that is, for each stimulus $\mathbf{A}_i\mathbf{B}_j$ we can define $P(a_pb_q|\mathbf{A}_i\mathbf{B}_j)$, where the subscripts p and q can take on any of the values of i and j, respectively. In the previous example, on trials when blue squares were presented, sampling independences of the color and shape components are determined for red squares (as before), as well as for red circles, blue squares, and blue circles, by using this expression with the appropriate subscripts.

In the more general two-component case where there are n levels of component **A** and m levels of component **B**, sampling independence is defined as

$$P(a_2b_2|\mathbf{A}_i\mathbf{B}_j) = \left[\sum_{k=1}^{m} P(a_2b_k|\mathbf{A}_i\mathbf{B}_j)\right] \times \left[\sum_{k=1}^{n} P(a_kb_2|\mathbf{A}_i\mathbf{B}_j)\right] .$$

As before, this simply states that one joint probability equals the product of the two marginals, except now the marginal probabilities for each component level are computed across all the possible levels of the other component. To make this more concrete, consider components **A** and **B** each with three levels. On trials when blue squares, say, are presented, sampling independence of red squares holds if, as before, the probability of reporting red squares is equal to the probability of reporting red (now the probability of reporting red squares, red circles, plus red triangles) times the probability of reporting squares (red, blue, and green).

Generalizing sampling independence to cases where there are more than two components, we again define *joint* (pairwise) sampling independence for pairs of components at each *fixed* combination of levels of the other component(s). For example, in our three-dimensional scenario suppose we have joint pairwise sampling independence for components **A** (shape) and **C** (size), holding **B** (color) constant, in stimulus $\mathbf{A}_i\mathbf{B}_j\mathbf{C}_k$. Joint sampling independence of **A** and **C** holds (when red [b_1] is reported) if the joint probability of reporting large (c_2) squares (a_2) equals the product of the marginal probabilities, or

$$P(a_2b_1c_2|\mathbf{A}_i\mathbf{B}_j\mathbf{C}_k) = \left[\sum_{r=1}^{m} P(a_2b_1c_r|\mathbf{A}_i\mathbf{B}_j\mathbf{C}_k)\right] \times \left[\sum_{p=1}^{n} P(a_pb_1c_2|\mathbf{A}_i\mathbf{B}_j\mathbf{C}_k)\right].$$

Note that b_1 is constant in this expression: We could obtain sampling independence of shape and size when the stimuli are red but not when they are blue. In four (and higher) dimensions, intermediate cases again arise. For example, three-way joint sampling independence is defined for three components as before, across the fixed levels of the fourth (and higher) component(s).

Mutual sampling independence is defined to hold when the joint probability of all components equals the product of all marginal probabilities. For example, in stimulus $\mathbf{A}_i\mathbf{B}_j\mathbf{C}_k$, mutual sampling independence holds when the probability of reporting a large (c_2) red (b_1) square (a_2) equals the product of marginal probabilities of reporting large, of reporting square, and of reporting blue; that is,

$$P(a_2b_1c_2|\mathbf{A}_i\mathbf{B}_j\mathbf{C}_k) = \left[\sum_{q=1}^{n}\sum_{r=1}^{s} P(a_2b_qc_r|\mathbf{A}_i\mathbf{B}_j\mathbf{C}_k)\right] \times \left[\sum_{p=1}^{m}\sum_{r=1}^{s} P(a_pb_1c_r|\mathbf{A}_i\mathbf{B}_j\mathbf{C}_k)\right] \times \left[\sum_{p=1}^{m}\sum_{q=1}^{n} P(a_pb_qc_2|\mathbf{A}_i\mathbf{B}_j\mathbf{C}_k)\right].$$

Since these are probabilities of events, mutual sampling independence of all components implies pairwise (and three-way, etc.) independence of the components (e.g., Hogg & Craig, 1978, p. 87). (In the Gaussian case, pairwise independence for *all* pairs also implies mutual independence.) This suggests a hierarchical testing procedure, beginning with the examination of mutual independence of all components and, if dependence is found working "down," determining where the dependencies originate.

Marginal Response Invariance

Definition 8.5: In a feature-complete factorial design with stimuli $\mathbf{A}_i\mathbf{B}_j$, $i = 1,2$, $j = 1,2$, *marginal response invariance* for feature **A** holds across the two levels of feature **B** if and only if

$$P(a_ib_1|\mathbf{A}_i\mathbf{B}_1) + P(a_ib_2|\mathbf{A}_i\mathbf{B}_1) = P(a_ib_1|\mathbf{A}_i\mathbf{B}_2) + P(a_ib_2|\mathbf{A}_i\mathbf{B}_2),$$
$$\text{for } i = 1,2 \text{ .}$$

Similarly, marginal response invariance holds for feature **B** across the two levels of feature **A** if and only if

$$P(a_1b_j|\mathbf{A}_1\mathbf{B}_j) + P(a_2b_j|\mathbf{A}_1\mathbf{B}_j) = P(a_1b_j|\mathbf{A}_2\mathbf{B}_j) + P(a_2b_j|\mathbf{A}_2\mathbf{B}_j),$$
$$\text{for } j = 1,2 \text{ .}$$

In other words, marginal response invariance holds for one component (say **A**) across the two levels of the second component (**B**) if and only if the probability of correctly recognizing component **A** does not depend on the level of component **B**. In terms of our hypothetical example, marginal response invariance for shape across colors means that the probability of correctly recognizing the shape as a square or a circle does not depend on the color of the stimulus.

To generalize marginal response invariance to more than two levels on two dimensions is again straightforward (see also Ashby, 1988). Marginal response invariance holds for component **A** (at level i) across levels of component **B** if

$$\sum_{j=1}^{n} P(a_ib_j|\mathbf{A}_i\mathbf{B}_1) = \sum_{j=1}^{n} P(a_ib_j|\mathbf{A}_i\mathbf{B}_2) = \cdots = \sum_{j=1}^{n} P(a_ib_j|\mathbf{A}_i\mathbf{B}_n),$$

$$\text{for } i = 1, \ldots, m;$$

and for component **B** (at level j) across levels of component **A** if

$$\sum_{i=1}^{m} P(a_ib_j|\mathbf{A}_1\mathbf{B}_j) = \sum_{i=1}^{m} P(a_ib_j|\mathbf{A}_2\mathbf{B}_j) = \cdots = \sum_{i=1}^{m} P(a_ib_j|\mathbf{A}_m\mathbf{B}_j),$$

$$\text{for } j = 1, \ldots, n;$$

Again, generalizations to more than two components result in two definitions. For example, in the three-dimensional case where each component has two levels, components **A** and **B** (at levels i and j, respectively) are *jointly* (pairwise) marginally invariant across levels of component **C** when

$$\sum_{k=1}^{2} P(a_ib_jc_k|\mathbf{A}_1\mathbf{B}_j\mathbf{C}_1) = \sum_{k=1}^{2} P(a_ib_jc_k|\mathbf{A}_i\mathbf{B}_j\mathbf{C}_2)$$

$$\text{for } i = 1,2 \text{ and } j = 1,2.$$

Another way of interpreting joint marginal response invariance is as the marginal response invariance of component **A** (at level i) across levels of component **C**, holding component **B** fixed at level j.

Single-component marginal response invariance is defined as the probability of correctly recognizing a given component regardless of the levels of *all other* components. For example, component **A** (at level i, for i = 1 and 2) is marginally invariant across components **B** and **C** if

$$\sum_{j=1}^{2}\sum_{k=1}^{2} P(a_i b_j c_k|\mathbf{A}_i\mathbf{B}_1\mathbf{C}_1) = \sum_{j=1}^{2}\sum_{k=1}^{2} P(a_i b_j c_k|\mathbf{A}_i\mathbf{B}_1\mathbf{C}_2)$$

$$= \sum_{j=1}^{2}\sum_{k=1}^{2} P(a_i b_j c_k|\mathbf{A}_i\mathbf{B}_2\mathbf{C}_1)$$

$$= \sum_{j=1}^{2}\sum_{k=1}^{2} P(a_i b_j c_k|\mathbf{A}_i\mathbf{B}_2\mathbf{C}_2) .$$

Unlike sampling and perceptual independence, however, joint marginal response invariance of all pairs of components does not imply single-component marginal response invariance, nor does single-component marginal response invariance for all components imply joint marginal response invariance for all pairs. Examples of confusion matrices where one holds and the other fails can be easily constructed. This also differs from conjoint measurement theory, where joint independence for all pairs of factors implies independence of all single factors (Krantz & Tversky, 1971).

In our present work, it seems more informative and relevant to use the more local, detailed (pairwise) definitions already given, which involve conditioning on the fixed levels of all other components. Essentially, we are interested in examining the separabilities of each perceptual dimension from every other dimension, and this may or may not depend on the levels of the third, or higher, dimensions in the stimulus set. This latter way of generalizing is also consistent with our evaluations of the pairwise d''s in the multidimensional perceptual space. In other words, we are not so much interested here in the overall pooled effects of the other dimensions on a given dimension (i.e., single-component marginal response invariance or mutual perceptual or sampling independence), by evaluating one dimension without regard to the levels on the other dimensions.

THEORETICAL RESULTS FOR PERCEPTUAL AND DECISIONAL SEPARABILITIES AND PERCEPTUAL INDEPENDENCE

In this section we review the major theoretical results relating perceptual and decisional separabilities and perceptual independence with the observable (and testable) properties of sampling independence and marginal response invariance and the two sets of signal detection parameters. Within GRT, Ashby and Townsend (1986) related many of these concepts (as well as others) to each other and showed how some yield useful tests of perceptual separability and independence. We present three of their theorems here, as they are directly related to, and complement, our later results. The subsequent six theorems show the relationships among the signal detection macro- and microanalytic parameters with perceptual separability and independence (the proofs are given in Kadlec & Townsend, 1992). All theorems pertain to feature-complete factorial designs with two dimensions and two levels on each dimension; however, extensions of the results to higher-dimensional spaces and/or to more than two levels are direct (given the generalized definitions presented earlier). Where the result is stated only for component **A,** an analogous result also holds for component **B** simply by interchanging the roles of **A** and **B**.

General Theorems Relating Sampling Independence, Perceptual Independence, Perceptual Separability, Decisional Separability, and Marginal Response Invariance: Theorems 8.1–8.3

The first theorem relates sampling independence and perceptual independence (Theorem 1 in Ashby & Townsend, 1986).

> *Theorem 8.1:* 1. Sampling independence of components **A** and **B** in stimulus $\mathbf{A}_i\mathbf{B}_j$ occurs if perceptual independence and decisional separability hold for both components.
>
> 2. Perceptual independence of components **A** and **B** in stimulus $\mathbf{A}_i\mathbf{B}_j$ occurs if sampling independence holds on components **A** and **B** for differing decision criteria and if decisional separability holds for both components.
>
> 3. If decisional separability fails, then sampling independence is logically unrelated to perceptual independence.

Notice that sampling independence and perceptual independence are logically related only when decisional separability holds. In addition, this theorem does not assume specific distributions and, therefore, holds for the general GRT case. In part 2 of Theorem 8.1, the stipulation that sampling independence holds for differing decision criteria is necessary to ensure that the identification process is not simply due to some idiosyncratic placement of the decision bounds, but that it holds no matter where the (parallel) decision bounds are placed.

The next theorem relates perceptual and decisional separability to perceptual independence (Theorem 4 in Ashby & Townsend, 1986).

> *Theorem 8.2:* Perceptual separability and decisional separability together imply perceptual independence of components **A** and **B** within each stimulus if both of the following conditions hold:
>
> (i) The perceptual representations of all stimuli are Gaussian.
>
> (ii) The subject is responding optimally (in the sense of maximizing probability of correct responses).

The third theorem relates perceptual and decisional separability with marginal response invariance. The first part of this theorem was presented in Ashby and Townsend (1986, Theorem 5) and concerns the general, distribution-free case; the second part was discovered by Kadlec and Townsend (1992) and applies to the Gaussian version of GRT only.

Theorem 8.3: 1. In the general distribution-free case, if perceptual and decisional separabilities hold for components **A** and **B**, then marginal response invariance holds for both components.

2. In the case where all densities are Gaussian and decisional separability holds for components **A** and **B**, perceptual separability holds for component **A** if both of the following conditions are satisfied:

(i) The marginal variances for component **A** are equal across levels of component **B**.

(ii) Marginal response invariance holds for component **A**.

The first part of this theorem indicates that both separabilities together are sufficient for marginal response invariance, but that neither alone is sufficient. Part 2 shows that marginal response invariance provides a useful test of perceptual separability in the Gaussian case under the assumptions that decisional separability holds and that the variances are equal across levels. The latter assumption does not mean that *all* variances need to be equal; in particular, it is not true that the variances of the noise and signal + noise distributions need to be equal. These three theoretical relationships are summarized in Figure 8.3.

Theorems Relating Perceptual and Decisional Separabilities with Signal Detection Parameters

We have recently extended the theoretical relationships from the multidimensional signal detection point of view (Kadlec & Townsend, 1992). The wealth of theoretical results yielded by this approach provides additional observability of perceptual independence and perceptual and decisional separability by the two sets of signal detection parameters. The two sets of parameters—the macroanalytic (marginal) and microanalytic (conditional) d''s and β's—are tied very closely to the GRT representation of the perceptual space in feature-complete factorial designs. Again, these results were shown for the case where there are two components, each with two possible levels, but they readily generalize to more components as well as to more levels. The assumption that each stimulus is represented by a multivariate Gaussian density underlies each of these theorems.

In some of the following theorems, we often need to make assumptions regarding the equality of variances of the marginal densities. However, there are two versions of this assumption. In the weaker case, the assumption of equal marginal variances *across levels of the other component* denotes that the variances of the marginal densities of one component do not change across levels of the other component. However, the variances of the noise and signal + noise densities under consideration need *not* be equal, even for the same component.

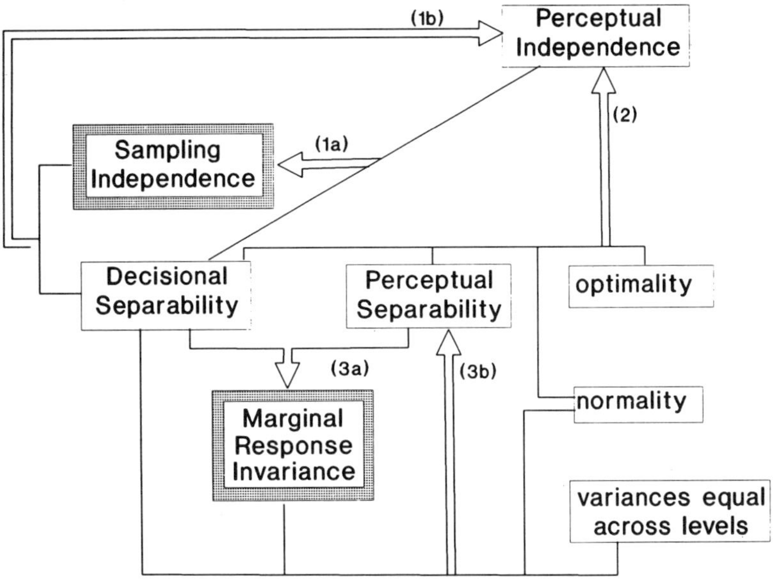

FIG. 8.3. Summary of theoretical relationships in Theorems 8.1 to 8.3 (adapted from Figure 11 in Ashby & Townsend, 1986). Note that these relationships hold in distribution-free cases, except where normality is also required. (Double arrows indicate the direction of an implication, and single lines connect the sufficient conditions. The shaded double boxes indicate observable conditions; conditions in single boxes are unobservable.)

We have already seen this assumption in part 2 of Theorem 8.3. The second, stronger assumption is that *all* marginal variances are equal, across levels of a component as well as the variances of the noise and signal + noise densities, for each component. We will make explicit which assumption is required in each of the theorems.

The next three theorems relate macroanalytic signal detection parameters with perceptual separability. Theorems 8.7 to 8.9 involve perceptual independence and the microanalytic signal detection parameters. For the theorems stated for component **A** across component **B**, the same results also hold for component **B** across component **A**.

Perceptual Separability, Decisional Separability, and Signal Detection Macroanalytic Parameters: Theorems 8.4–8.6

Theorem 8.4 concerns marginal d''s and perceptual separability.

Theorem 8.4: 1. If component **A** is perceptually separable from component **B**, then the marginal d''s for component **A** will be equal across levels of component **B**.

2. Equal marginal d''s for component **A** alone do not imply perceptual separability for component **A**.

3. Perceptual separability for *both* components holds if and only if the following three conditions hold:

(i) The variances of the marginal densities for each component are equal across levels of the other component.

(ii) The marginal d''s for one component are equal across levels of the other component for both components (i.e., $d'_{\mathbf{A1B}} = d'_{\mathbf{A2B}} = d'_{\mathbf{A}}$ and $d'_{\mathbf{AB1}} = d'_{\mathbf{AB2}} = d'_{\mathbf{B}}$).

(iii) $d'_{\mathbf{AB}} = \sqrt{d'^2_{\mathbf{A}} + d'^2_{\mathbf{B}}}$, where $d'_{\mathbf{AB}}$ is the diagonal d' between the densities f_{11} and f_{22} (we call this the Euclidean diagonal condition).

This theorem is particularly useful for two reasons; it does not depend on decisional separability, and part 3 gives the sufficient as well as the necessary conditions for mutual perceptual separability of two components. This allows us to draw conclusions about the unobservable perceptual separability from a number of testable conditions. Note that conditions (i) and (ii) in part 3 must hold for *both* components. Conditions (ii) and (iii) together indicate that the mean vectors (centers of the densities in Figure 8.1) form a rectangular configuration.

The diagonal d', however, cannot be accurately estimated from feature-complete factorial designs where *all* stimuli are presented to the observer in the same blocks of trials. On any one trial in such an experiment with two components each with two levels, one of four possible stimuli is presented and the observer responds with one of four possible responses. For the diagonal d', the estimate of the probability of a hit is the proportion of trials, when the two-component stimulus is presented, on which both features are correctly reported as present. (Similarly, the probability of a false alarm is the proportion of trials, when the blank stimulus is presented, on which both features are incorrectly reported as present.) However, since four responses are possible, if, on a two-component trial, an observer reports that he or she saw one component, thereby getting a hit on one component but a miss on the other, should this trial be included in the estimate of the probability of a hit? It is not clear whether such trials should be excluded from the estimates, thereby underestimating the probabilities, or included. We have thus suggested (Kadlec & Townsend, 1992) that a slightly different experimental design be used to test this condition. As in the "standard" feature-complete factorial design, in addition to blocks of trials with all stimuli, present separate blocks of trials with only the subset of stimuli necessary to estimate the diagonal d'. The studies discussed later in this chapter have not used this modified design, but this condition should be tested as soon as possible.

The next theorem states the relationships between perceptual and decisional separability and marginal β's:

Theorem 8.5: 1. If decisional separability holds for both components and perceptual separability holds for component **A**, then the marginal β's for component **A** will be equal across levels of component **B**.

2. If decisional separability holds for both components but perceptual separability fails for component **A**, then it does not logically follow that marginal β's for component **A** will be equal.

3. If decisional separability holds for both components and marginal β's for component **A** are equal, then it does not necessarily follow that perceptual separability will hold for component **A** (even when all marginal variances are equal).

This theorem simply states that under the assumption that decisional separability holds for both components, knowing that the marginal β's are equal does not give direct information about perceptual separability. The best we can do when we have support for perceptual separability from the marginal d' results is to obtain additional, but indirect, support for perceptual separability from the equal marginal β's. Conversely, if marginal d''s support perceptual separability (by being equal and satisfying the Euclidean diagonal d' condition), but the marginal β's are not equal, then the contrapositive of part 1 implies that decisional separability must have failed. In the absence of perceptual separability, part 2 states that the marginal β's can be anything, even when decisional separability holds.

Theorem 8.6 sheds more light on decisional separability with the relationships between the marginal response invariance and marginal signal detection parameters.

Theorem 8.6: 1. Marginal d''s for component **A** will be equal across levels of component **B** if all three of the following conditions are satisfied:

(i) Decisional separability holds for both components.
(ii) Marginal response invariance holds for component **A** across levels of component **B**.
(iii) The variances of the marginal densities for component **A** are equal across levels of component **B**.

2. Marginal β's for component **A** will be equal across levels of component **B** if both of the following conditions are satisfied:

(i) Decisional separability holds for both components.
(ii) Marginal response invariance holds for component **A** across levels of component **B** (without any assumptions about the marginal variances).

3. Marginal response invariance holds for component **A** if all four of the following conditions are satisfied:

(i) Decisional separability holds for both components.
(ii) Marginal d''s for component **A** are equal across levels of **B**.
(iii) Marginal β's for component **A** are equal across levels of **B**.
(iv) *All* marginal variances are equal.

In this theorem, decisional separability is required in each part of the theorem. Also note that under the strongest assumption about the variances (that they are *all* equal) and when decisional separability holds, marginal response invariance holds if and only if marginal d''s and marginal β's are equal. This theorem provides a stronger test of decisional separability, since equality of the variances is also potentially testable. If all the variances are found to be equal, but marginal response invariance, equal d''s, or equal β's are *not all* either supported or rejected, then decisional separability is logically falsified. If the marginal variances are equal for one component across levels of the other, decisional separability is weakly supported if marginal response invariance holds and marginal d''s are equal (part 1). But even if marginal variances are not equal, some support for decisional separability is obtained when marginal response invariance holds and marginal β's are equal (part 2).

These relationships between the marginal signal detection parameters, marginal response invariance, and the two separabilities are summarized in Figure 8.4.

Perceptual Independence, Decisional Separability and Signal Detection Microanalytic Parameters: Theorems 8.7–8.9

The next set of theorems relates the conditional d''s and β's with perceptual independence. Each theorem assumes that decisional separability holds for both components. These theorems also apply in the feature-complete factorial case,

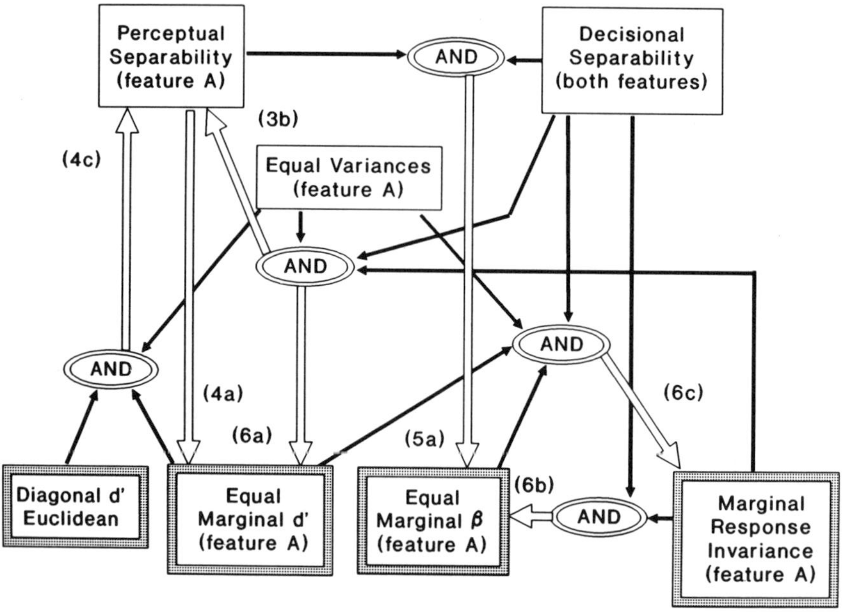

FIG. 8.4. Summary of theoretical relationships in Theorems 8.4 to 8.6 (marginal results). These hold in the Gaussian case. (Double arrows indicate the direction of an implication; solid arrows connect the sufficient conditions. Double-shaded boxes indicate observable conditions; single boxes denote unobservable conditions.)

but since perceptual independence is a within-stimulus property the results pertain to pairs of stimuli. Recall also that the terminology we use is strictly for convenience, and that feature "absence" refers to that portion of the perceptual space below a given criterion and feature "presence" to that above the criterion. For each theorem the results are given for component **A** conditional on component **B**; however, analogous results hold for component **B** conditional on component **A** by interchanging the roles of **A** and **B** in the conditional parameters as well as in the corresponding pairs of stimuli.

Perceptual independence is related with conditional d''s in Theorem 8.7 and with conditional β's in Theorem 8.8. Because these results are quite similar, we first state both, and then discuss them together.

Theorem 8.7: When decisional separability holds for both components, if perceptual independence holds in stimuli $\mathbf{A}_1\mathbf{B}_2$ and $\mathbf{A}_2\mathbf{B}_2$ ($\mathbf{A}_1\mathbf{B}_1$ and $\mathbf{A}_2\mathbf{B}_1$), then the d' for component **A** conditional on the hit (false alarm) of component **B** (above $c_{\mathbf{B}}$) will be equal to the d' for component **A** conditional on the miss (correct rejection) of component **B** (below $c_{\mathbf{B}}$), and these will equal the marginal d' for component **A** at the second (first) level of component **B**.

Theorem 8.8: When decisional separability holds for both components, if perceptual independence holds in stimuli $\mathbf{A}_1\mathbf{B}_2$ and $\mathbf{A}_2\mathbf{B}_2$ ($\mathbf{A}_1\mathbf{B}_1$ and $\mathbf{A}_2\mathbf{B}_1$), then β for component **A** conditional on the hit (false alarm) of component **B** will be equal to β for component **A** conditional on the miss (correct rejection) of component **B**, and these will equal the marginal β for component **A** at the second (first) level of component **B**.

These results are intuitively apparent from the definition of perceptual independence, since if two variables are independent the behavior of one does not influence the other. This fact was one of the original rationales for using the conditional d' and β analyses in the studies by Townsend et al. (1984, 1988). However, the implications in both of these theorems go from the unobservable perceptual independence to the conditional parameters. The converses of these theorems are not true. Thus, as far as support for perceptual independence goes, the best we can hope for by using the microanalyses is to accrue indirect evidence for it. However, data can falsify perceptual independence.

The final theorem relates conditional d''s and β's to sampling independence.

Theorem 8.9: When decisional separability holds for both components:

1. If sampling independence holds in stimuli $\mathbf{A}_1\mathbf{B}_2$ and $\mathbf{A}_2\mathbf{B}_2$ ($\mathbf{A}_1\mathbf{B}_1$ and $\mathbf{A}_2\mathbf{B}_1$), then the d' for component **A** conditional on the hit (false alarm) of component **B** will be equal to the d' for component **A** conditional on the miss (correct rejection) on component **B**.

2. If sampling independence holds in stimuli $\mathbf{A}_1\mathbf{B}_2$ and $\mathbf{A}_2\mathbf{B}_2$ ($\mathbf{A}_1\mathbf{B}_1$ and $\mathbf{A}_2\mathbf{B}_1$), then the β for component **A** conditional on the hit (false alarm) of component **B** will be equal to the β for component **A** conditional on the miss (correct rejection) of component **B**.

Parts 1 and 2 of this result follow directly from Theorems 8.1 and 8.7, and 8.1 and 8.8, respectively. In both parts, the relationships are among two testable conditions under the assumption of decisional separability. This theorem, therefore, provides a clear-cut test of decisional separability; decisional separability will be violated if either (a) sampling independence holds and either conditional d''s or β's fail to be constant, or (b) sampling independence fails and both conditional d''s or β's are constant.

The microanalytic relationships presented in Theorems 8.7 to 8.9 are summarized in Figure 8.5.

Summary and Procedures for Testing Perceptual Separability, Decisional Separability, and Perceptual Independence

The marginal signal detection parameters are related to perceptual and decisional separabilities (Figure 8.4), and the conditional parameters are primarily tied to perceptual independence (Figure 8.5). In Figure 8.4, the implication (4c) corresponding to Theorem 8.4, part 3 is a biconditional implication between perceptual separability for *both* features, equality of the marginal d''s, and variances for *both* features plus the Euclidean diagonal condition. In other words, if marginal d''s and variances are found to be equal for both features and the Euclidean diagonal condition holds, then perceptual separability is logically implied for both features. The importance of this result is that it allows us to draw a strong conclusion about perceptual separability.

These relationships can be used to test for the separabilities and independence of perceptual dimensions. Probabilities for testing sampling independence and marginal response invariance are directly obtainable from confusion matrices from feature-complete factorial designs. Marginal and conditional d''s and β's are also estimable from probabilities contained in confusion matrices. Along with the theoretical relationships presented, these can be used to draw conclusions about perceptual and decisional separability and perceptual independence. The conclusions one can draw from the various combinations of observed marginal and conditional results are shown in truth table format in Tables 8.1 and 8.2, and in flowchart form in Figures 8.6 and 8.7, respectively. Conclusions are presented only for component **A**; however, by interchanging the roles of **A** and **B**, we obtain the same information for component **B**. We should stress that these tables and figures do not include the test of the Euclidean diagonal d' condition, since we cannot test for it in the present data (see discussion following Theorem

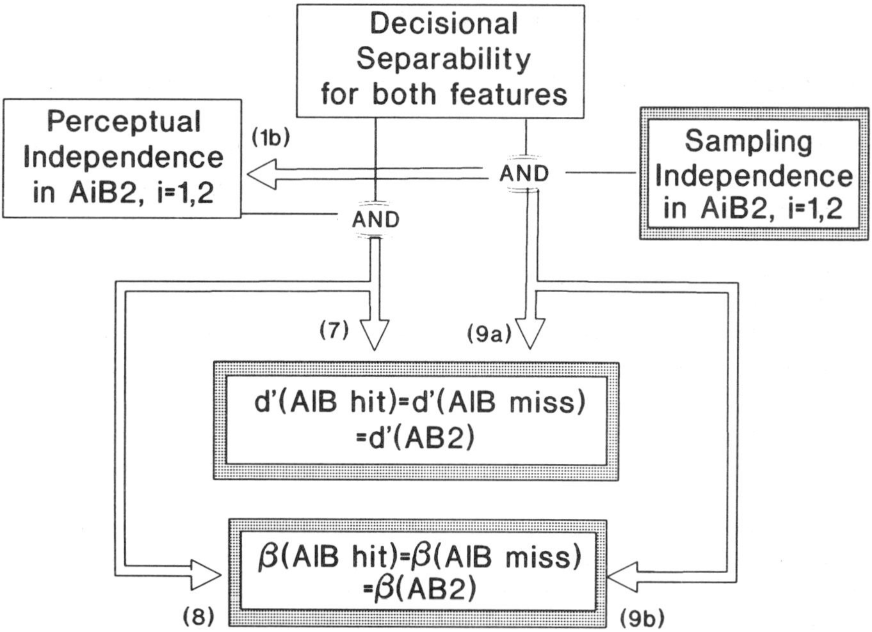

FIG. 8.5. Summary of theoretical relationships in Theorems 8.7 to 8.9 (conditional results). These hold in the Gaussian case. (Double arrows indicate the direction of an implication; solid arrows connect the sufficient conditions. Double-shaded boxes indicate observable conditions; single boxes denote unobservable conditions.)

8.4).[2] The conclusions would change only for perceptual separability when the marginal d''s were equal for both components but the Euclidean diagonal condition did not hold.

In all but one theoretical relationship (Theorem 8.4 part 3), the logical implications go from the unobservable (perceptual separability or perceptual independence) to the observable signal detection parameters. Positive empirical verification of the theoretical concepts thus cannot be directly obtained; however, data may be used in the contrapositive form of the implications to logically imply their failure. For example, equal marginal d''s for component **A** across levels of component **B** provide indirect support for perceptual separability in the sense that the data do not falsify it. However, *unequal* marginal d''s for component **A** across levels of **B** logically imply that perceptual separability has failed. The

[2]In the following section where we illustrate the method, we assume the Euclidean diagonal d' condition is also satisfied whenever we obtain evidence for equal marginal d''s for *both* components, and thereby that the means form a rectangular configuration. We only assume this for illustrative purposes, and we stress that this assumption should be tested as soon as possible. Following such a test, some conclusions we draw in the examples in the following section may change.

TABLE 8.1
Truth Table for Combinations of Observed Marginal Results and the Corresponding Conclusions

Observed Results			*Conclusions*		
Marginal Response Invariance for **A** *?*	*Marginal* d'_A *Equal ?*	*Marginal* β_A *Equal ?*	*Decisional Separability for* **A** *and* **B**	*Perceptual Separability for* **A**	*Equal Marginal Variances for* **A**
T	T	T	w-support (6b)	w-support (4a, 5a)[a]	w-support (6a)
T	T	F	s-failed for one or both (5a, 6b)	w-support (4a)	?
T	F	T	w-support (6b)	s-failed (4a)	s-failed (6a, 3b)
T	F	F	s-failed for one or both (6b)	s-failed (4a)	?
[b]F	T	T	s-failed[b] (6c)	w-support (4a, 5a)	s-failed[b] (6c)
F	T	F	s-failed for one or both (5a)	w-support (4a)	?
F	F	T	?	s-failed (4a)	?
F	F	F	?	s-failed (4a)	?

[a]If the same pattern of results is also found for **B** and the Euclidean diagonal d' condition is supported, then perceptual separability is s-supported for **A** and **B**.

[b]In this case, either decisional separability has failed or the marginal variances are not equal, or both. This will be denoted by ?(no).

former weak sense of empirical support will be indicated as w-support to distinguish it from the stronger s-support (or s-failure) resulting from a logical implication.

ILLUSTRATION OF THE TESTS FOR SEPARABILITIES AND PERCEPTUAL INDEPENDENCE

The testing procedure discussed and summarized in Figures 8.6 and 8.7 and Tables 8.1 and 8.2 is illustrated in this section. A directly applicable example (two components with two levels) is presented first. This will be followed by analyses to illustrate the two ways of generalizing to more than two dimensions and to more than two levels on each of two components.

TABLE 8.2
Truth Table for Combinations of Observed Conditional Results and the Corresponding Conclusions

Observed Results				*Conclusions*		
d′ for **A** *Conditional on*	*β for* **A** *Conditional on*	*Sampling Independence in Stimuli*		*Decisional Separability for* **A** *and* **B**	*Perceptual Independence in Stimuli*	
B *hit* = **B** *miss* (**B** *cr* = **B** *fa*)		A_1B_2 (A_1B_1)	A_2B_2 (A_2B_1)		A_1B_2 (A_1B_1)	A_2B_2 (A_2B_1)
T	T	T or F	T or F	w-support (7 & 8)	w-support (7 & 8)	
T	F	T	T	s-failed	?	?
F	T	T	T		(possibly w-supported)	
F	F	T	T			
T	F	F	F	Either DS failed or PI failed in at least one stimulus, or both. If DS supported (in marginal results), then PI s-failed in at least one of these stimuli.		
F	T	F	F			
F	F	F	F			

Two-Dimensional Case with Two Levels on each Dimension

An experiment by Townsend, Hu, and Ashby (1981; abbreviated THA 1981) used a feature-complete factorial design with a vertical line (|) and a horizontal line (—), each either present or absent (see Table 8.3). There were two experimental conditions in this study, a gap and a connected condition, but we will consider data only from the connected condition.

Some of the estimates of marginal response invariance and sampling independence probabilities and marginal and conditional d''s and β's for each of the two components across levels of the other component were reported previously (Ashby & Townsend, 1986; Kadlec & Townsend, 1992; Townsend et al., 1981) and will not be presented here (but are available from the authors upon request). The conclusions of these tests are shown in Table 8.4. Because of the variability in the patterns of results for the individual observers, we will describe the conclusions in detail only for observer 1, and leave the others to the reader to verify.

For observer 1, marginal response invariance held for each component across levels of the other component. In addition, marginal d' and β estimates were found to be equal for both components across levels of the other component. The path leading to the top of Figure 8.6 (or the top row of Table 8.1) thus applies for

Condition		Conclusions
MRI holds for feature A		
marginal d' and β EQUAL for feature A	⇒	DS w-supported for both features (6b) EQUAL VARIANCES w-supported for feature A (6a) PS supported for feature A (3b, 4a, 5a)
marginal d' EQUAL & marginal β NOT EQUAL for feature A	⇒	DS s-failed for one or both features (6b) PS w-supported for feature A (4a) no conclusions about VARIANCES
marginal d' NOT EQUAL & marginal β EQUAL for feature A	⇒	DS w-supported for both features (6b) PS s-failed for feature A (4a) VARIANCES for feature A not equal (6a, 3b)
marginal d' & β NOT EQUAL for feature A	⇒	DS s-failed for one or both features (6b) PS s-failed for feature A (4a) no conclusions about VARIANCES for feature A
MRI does not hold for feature A		
marginal d' & β EQUAL for feature A	⇒	either DS or EQUAL VARIANCES s-failed (6c) PS w-supported for feature A (4a, 5a)
marginal d' EQUAL & marginal β NOT EQUAL for feature A	⇒	PS w-supported for feature A (4a) DS s-failed for one or both features (5a) no conclusions about VARIANCES
marginal d' NOT EQUAL & marginal β EQUAL for feature A	⇒	PS s-failed for feature A (4a) no conclusions about DS no conclusions about VARIANCES
marginal d' & β NOT EQUAL for feature A	⇒	PS s-failed for feature A (4a) no conclusions about DS no conclusions about VARIANCES for feature A

FIG. 8.6. Flowchart for testing perceptual and decisional separabilities and the equal variance assumption from observed marginal results. See also Table 8.1 for an alternative presentation.

both features, indicating w-support for perceptual separability[3] and w-support for decisional separability.

From the conditional results, however, we find that, although sampling independence held in each stimulus, for each pair of stimuli either the conditional d''s or the conditional β's or both failed to be equivalent. The lower path in Figure 8.7 (alternatively the second set of rows in Table 8.2) should be consulted in this case, and we conclude that decisional separability has s-failed. This is a logical consequence and thus overrides our previous w-support of decisional separability. Our overall conclusion is then that decisional separability has s-failed for this observer, and no strong conclusions can be drawn about perceptual independence. However, the conclusion that perceptual separability holds for both components across levels of the other component remains viable.

This data set was also analyzed by Ashby and his colleagues in previous reports. Ashby and Townsend (1986) applied their test of the separabilities and

[3]We remind the reader that if we had a test of the Euclidean diagonal d' condition for these data, and it was empirically supported, then perceptual separability would be logically implied and thus s-supported.

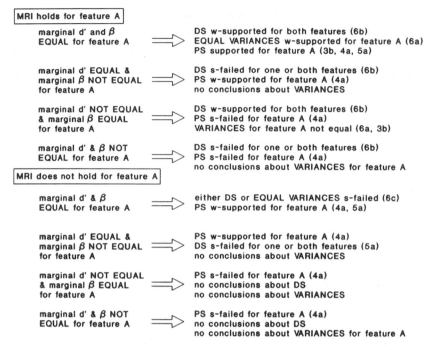

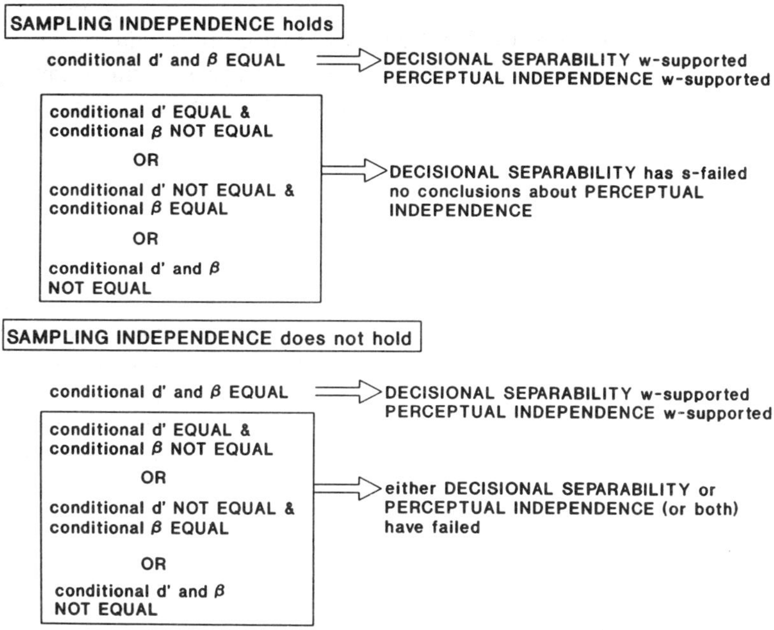

FIG. 8.7. Flowchart for testing perceptual independence and decisional separability from observed conditional results. See also Table 8.2 for an alternative presentation.

perceptual independence (based on Theorems 8.1 and 8.3, which relate sampling independence and marginal response invariance with the separabilities; see Figure 12 in Ashby & Townsend, 1986, p. 173), and concluded that the null hypothesis of perceptual and decisional separabilities could not be rejected for any of the observers in this study. Because sampling independence was tested only on $\mathbf{A}_2\mathbf{B}_2$ trials (see Townsend et al., 1981), Ashby and Townsend tested marginal response invariance for each component only at the second level and concluded

TABLE 8.3
Stimulus Components and Their Levels in the Three Studies Discussed

Study	*Stimulus Components*	*Levels of Components*
THA 1981	— (**A**)	0, 1 (absent, present)
	— (**B**)	0, 1
Nosofsky 1986	Angle of radial line (**A**)	50°, 53°, 56°, 59°
	Size of semicircle (**B**)	.478, .500, .522, .544 cm
THE 1984	| (**A**)	0, 1 (absent, present)
	— (**B**)	0, 1
	\ (**C**)	0, 1
	⊂ (**D**)	0, 1

TABLE 8.4
Summary of Results and Conclusions for THA 1981 Data

	O_1	O_2	O_3	O_4
MACROANALYSES				
Testing **A**(—) across **B**(|)				
Marginal response invariance?	Yes	No	Yes	No
Marginal *d′* equal?	Yes	No	Yes	Yes
Marginal β equal?	Yes	Yes	Yes	Yes
Testing **B**(|) across **A**(—)				
Marginal response invariance?	Yes	Yes	Yes	No
Marginal *d′* equal?	Yes	Yes	Yes	Yes
Marginal β equal?	Yes	Yes	No	No
Perceptual separability for **A**	Yes	No	w-yes	w-yes
Equal variances for **A**	w-yes	?	w-yes	? (no)
Perceptual separability for **B**	Yes	w-yes	w-yes	w-yes
Equal variances for **B**	w-yes	w-yes	?	?
Decisional separability for both (from marginal results)	w-yes	w-yes	No	No
MICROANALYSES				
Sampling independence holds in				
A1**B**1 ( )?	Yes	Yes	Yes	Yes
A1**B**2 (|)?	Yes	Yes	Yes	Yes
A2**B**1 (—)?	Yes	Yes	Yes	Yes
A2**B**2 (□)?	Yes	Yes	Yes	Yes
Conditional *d′*s equal for				
— given | hit vs. miss?	Yes	No	Yes	Yes
— given | cr vs. fa?	Yes	No	No	No
| given — hit vs. miss?	No	No	Yes	No
| given — cr vs. fa?	No	No	No	No
Conditional β's equal for				
— given | hit vs. miss?	No	Yes	Yes	Yes
— given | cr vs. fa?	No	Yes	No	No
| given — hit vs. miss?	No	Yes	Yes	No
| given — cr vs. fa?	No	No	No	No
Decisional separability (overall conclusions)	No	No	No	No
Perceptual independence				
in $\mathbf{A}_1\mathbf{B}_2$ and $\mathbf{A}_2\mathbf{B}_2$	?	?	w-yes	w-yes
in $\mathbf{A}_1\mathbf{B}_1$ and $\mathbf{A}_2\mathbf{B}_1$	?	?	?	?
in $\mathbf{A}_2\mathbf{B}_1$ and $\mathbf{A}_2\mathbf{B}_2$	?	?	w-yes	?
in $\mathbf{A}_1\mathbf{B}_1$ and $\mathbf{A}_1\mathbf{B}_2$	?	?	?	?

that marginal response invariance held for each observer. Here we tested sampling independence in each of the four stimuli, as well as marginal response invariance for each component at both levels, and found that marginal response invariance failed at the first level for observers 2 and 4. Our conclusions from the macroanalyses are thus slightly different, particularly with respect to decisional separability.

Ashby and Perrin (1988, experiment 3) also used this data set to fit two versions of the Gaussian general recognition model. Both models assumed perceptual independence, decisional separability, and constant density means for each component across levels of the other component, but differed in the assumptions made for the variances. In the six-parameter model, they assumed perceptual separability by estimating only the variances for the vertical and horizontal components, regardless of the level of the other component. In the 10-parameter model, however, the variances for the vertical and horizontal components were allowed to vary for each component across levels of the other component, thus allowing a weak violation of perceptual separability. For the observers in the connected condition, Ashby and Perrin found that the 10-parameter model significantly improved the fit over the 6-parameter model only for observer 4; but both models were still rejected for this observer. Both models were also rejected for observer 1, but both fit observers 2 and 3. Consistently with these results, our analyses also show that observer 4 was the only one that violated the equal-variance assumption. Our conclusions indicate that, although perceptual separability was supported for both components for observers 1 and 4, these two observers obtained the largest number of unequal conditional d' and β estimates, indicating failure of perceptual independence in at least some of the stimuli. In addition, we found that decisional separability has failed for each observer. Although the relative importance of decisional separability and perceptual independence is unknown, it appears that failure of perceptual independence may have contributed to the poorer fit of the models of Ashby and Perrin.

Two-Dimensional Case with Four Levels on each Dimension

The generalization of the analyses to a situation with more than two levels on each dimension will be demonstrated with data from Nosofsky (1986). Nosofsky used a feature-complete factorial design of stimuli with two components, a semicircle and a radial line, each at one of four possible levels (see Table 8.3). Because of the large amount of data, we will discuss only one of the two observers in this study. Table 8.5 gives the estimates for the marginal response invariance probabilities and marginal d''s and β's for observer 1.

The relevant comparisons are across the four rows within each column. Marginal response invariance holds for angle of radial line (component **A**) across semicircle sizes (**B**) at all levels of angle except the largest; marginal d''s are constant, but marginal β's are not equal. This implies w-support for perceptual separability and s-failure of decisional separability for angle across semicircle sizes. Marginal response invariance fails for all levels of semicircle sizes (**B**) across angle of radial line (**A**), marginal d''s remain constant, but marginal β's are not equal, a pattern of results also indicating w-support for perceptual separability and s-failure for decisional separability for component **B** across levels of

TABLE 8.5
Macroanalyses for Observer 1 in Nosofsky (1986)

Dimension **A** *(Angle of Radial Line) Across* **B** *(Size of Semicircle)*

	A_1B_j		A_2B_j		A_3B_j		A_4B_j
Marginal response invariance[a]							
j = 1 (.478 cm)	.761		.581		.634		.630*
j = 2 (.500 cm)	.796		.518		.609		.684
j = 3 (.522 cm)	.800		.561		.560		.701
j = 4 (.544 cm)	.764		.592		.593		.730*
Marginal *d′* estimates[b]							
j = 1 (.478 cm)		1.68		1.83		1.63	
j = 2 (.500 cm)		1.46		1.63		1.62	
j = 3 (.522 cm)		1.59		1.60		1.54	
j = 4 (.544 cm)		1.59		1.57		1.58	
Marginal β estimates[c]							
j = 1 (.478 cm)		0.35#		0.63#		1.27#	
j = 2 (.500 cm)		0.59		0.87		1.72	
j = 3 (.522 cm)		0.63		1.22		1.94	
j = 4 (.544 cm)		0.83#		1.37		2.46#	

Dimension **B** *(Size of Semicircle) Across* **A** *(Angle of Radial Line)*

	A_iB_1		A_iB_2		A_iB_3		A_iB_4
Marginal response invariance[a]							
i = 1 (50°)	.583		.775		.709		.748
i = 2 (53°)	.643		.628		.689		.682
i = 3 (56°)	.693		.682		.635		.632
i = 4 (59°)	.739		.650		.631		.588
Marginal *d′* estimates[b]							
i = 1 (50°)		1.65		1.76		1.09	
i = 2 (53°)		1.77		1.65		1.11	
i = 3 (56°)		1.80		1.73		1.04	
i = 4 (59°)		1.80		1.79		1.18	
Marginal β estimates[c]							
i = 1 (50°)		0.83		0.72#		1.26#	
i = 2 (53°)		0.91		0.59		1.09	
i = 3 (56°)		0.90		0.65		0.99	
i = 4 (59°)		0.73		0.61		0.97	

Notes: [a]* indicates a significant difference.

[b]* indicates a *d′* greater than 2 standard deviations from the column mean, using Grier's (1971) nonparametric test.

[c]# indicates that the **B** index (Grier, 1971) of the β varied by more than 10% from the other β's.

A. No conclusions about the marginal variances can be drawn for either dimension.

Regarding the perceptual versus decisional effects on identification performance, Nosofsky (1985b, 1986) reached similar conclusions for this observer by fitting various Multidimensional Scaling–similarity choice models. The best Multidimensional Scaling solution showed the 16 stimuli arranged in a regular rectagular configuration. In a perceptual space this would correspond to perceptual separability of both components, if equal variances are assumed. In addition, Nosofsky found that this observer's decisions on one component were *not* independent of the level of the other component. In particular, Nosofsky (1985b, p. 426) reports that this observer was biased against making identical responses for both components in a given stimulus [e.g., (3,3)]. This is also consistent with our conclusion that decisional separability has failed for this observer.

Sampling independence probabilities are given in Table 8.6, and the conditional d' and β estimates for each pair of stimuli are shown in Table 8.7. Sampling independence was found in all stimuli; thus, the top two rows of Table 8.2 or the top path in Figure 8.7 apply. The conclusions regarding perceptual independence and decisional separability from these conditional results are given in the last two columns of Table 8.7. From these results we again conclude that overall decisional separability has failed for both dimensions. For perceptual independence, since the test is for pairs of stimuli, for a given stimulus we must compare the results obtained from each test that involves that stimulus. For example, stimulus $\mathbf{A_1B_2}$ appears in the first two rows under the heading dimension **A** as well as in the fourth row under dimension **B**. Since the test for $\mathbf{A_1B_2}$ and $\mathbf{A_1B_3}$, however, indicated that perceptual independence was w-supported for both of these stimuli, the result for $\mathbf{A_1B_2}$ is that perceptual independence is w-supported. Perceptual independence in $\mathbf{A_1B_1}$ may remain in question, however, since the only other test involving $\mathbf{A_1B_1}$ is also questionable w-support. From these analyses we conclude that only the stimuli $\mathbf{A_1B_1}$, $\mathbf{A_2B_2}$, and $\mathbf{A_4B_3}$

TABLE 8.6
Sampling Independence for Observer 1 in Nosofsky (1986) Data

Stimulus	*P(x,y)*	*P(x)P(y)*	*Stimulus*	*P(x,y)*	*P(x)P(y)*
$\mathbf{A_1B_1}$	.424	.444	$\mathbf{A_1B_3}$	.572	.567
$\mathbf{A_2B_1}$	.402	.376	$\mathbf{A_2B_3}$	.403	.387
$\mathbf{A_3B_1}$	.436	.439	$\mathbf{A_3B_3}$	.351	.356
$\mathbf{A_4B_1}$	.488	.466	$\mathbf{A_4B_3}$	.420	.442
$\mathbf{A_1B_2}$	.545	.538	$\mathbf{A_1B_4}$	.561	.571
$\mathbf{A_2B_2}$	.332	.325	$\mathbf{A_2B_4}$	.426	.404
$\mathbf{A_3B_2}$	.411	.415	$\mathbf{A_3B_4}$	.400	.375
$\mathbf{A_4B_2}$	.450	.445	$\mathbf{A_4B_4}$	.416	.429

Note: None of the probabilities were significantly different on a two-tailed *Z* test at $\alpha = .25$ level.

TABLE 8.7
Conditional d' and β Estimates for Perceptual Independence for Observer 1 in Nosofsky (1986)

Stimuli	d' (>c)[a]		d' (<c)	β (>c)		β (<c)	*PI?*[b]	*DS?*
Dimension **A** *(angle of radial line), conditional on* **B** *(semicircle size)*								
A_1B_1 and A_1B_2	1.60		1.71	0.56	#	0.29	?(w-yes)	s-no
A_1B_2 and A_1B_3	1.84		1.80	0.61		0.72	w-yes	w-yes
A_1B_3 and A_1B_4	1.59		1.74	1.30		1.11	w-yes	w-yes
A_2B_1 and A_2B_2	1.44	*	2.09	0.69	#	0.11	?(w-yes)	s-no
A_2B_2 and A_2B_3	1.63		1.63	0.93	#	0.63	?(w-yes)	s-no
A_2B_3 and A_2B_4	1.68		1.31	1.73		1.68	w-yes	w-yes
A_3B_1 and A_3B_2	1.56		1.77	0.65	#	0.51	?(w-yes)	s-no
A_3B_2 and A_3B_3	1.59		1.73	1.30	#	0.74	?(w-yes)	s-no
A_3B_3 and A_3B_4	1.51		1.78	1.99		1.68	w-yes	w-yes
A_4B_1 and A_4B_2	1.56		1.53	0.95	#	0.63	?(w-yes)	s-no
A_4B_2 and A_4B_3	1.56		1.66	1.67	#	0.88	?(w-yes)	s-no
A_4B_3 and A_4B_4	1.61		1.56	2.74	#	1.96	?(w-yes)	s-no
Dimension **B** *(semicircle size), conditional on* **A** *(angle of radial line)*								
A_1B_1 and A_2B_1	1.72		1.46	0.64	#	1.08	?(w-yes)	s-no
A_2B_1 and A_3B_1	1.75		1.76	0.72		0.70	w-yes	w-yes
A_3B_1 and A_4B_1	1.16		0.90	1.22		1.36	w-yes	w-yes
A_1B_2 and A_2B_2	1.71	*	2.37	1.03	#	0.14	?(w-yes)	s-no
A_2B_2 and A_3B_2	1.70	*	1.41	0.63	#	0.42	?(w-yes)	s-no
A_3B_2 and A_4B_2	1.07		1.27	1.12		0.91	w-yes	w-yes
A_1B_3 and A_2B_3	1.77		1.87	0.96	#	0.67	?(w-yes)	s-no
A_2B_3 and A_3B_3	1.74		1.66	0.76	#	0.38	?(w-yes)	s-no
A_3B_3 and A_4B_3	1.04		1.05	1.12	#	0.70	?(w-yes)	s-no
A_1B_4 and A_2B_4	1.82		1.79	0.65	#	0.92	?(w-yes)	s-no
A_2B_4 and A_3B_4	1.76		1.85	0.69	#	0.46	?(w-yes)	s-no
A_3B_4 and A_4B_4	1.29		1.00	1.14		1.28	w-yes	w-yes

Notes: See notes to Table 8.5 for significance criteria.

[a]The notation d' (>c) means d' conditional above the criterion between the given pairs of stimuli, and d' (<c) stands for d' conditional below the criterion. Similar notation is used for the conditional β's.

[b]PI stands for perceptual independence, DS for decisional separability.

have at best uncertain w-support; for all other stimuli at least one of the tests in which they appeared indicated w-support for perceptual independence.

Four-Dimensional Case with Two Levels on each Dimension

Townsend, Hu, and Evans (1984; abbreviated THE 1984) used stimuli similar to those of Townsend et al. (1981), but with four components each either present or absent: a vertical line (|), horizontal line (—), a diagonal line (\), and a curved line (⊂) (see Table 8.3). This data set will illustrate how the analyses can be generalized to stimuli with a four-dimensional representation. Marginal response invariance probabilities, marginal d''s and marginal β's, as well as the conclusions about perceptual and decisional separabilities and marginal variances are presented in Table 8.8 for one of the four observers in this study. (Again because of the large volume of results, only those for observer 3 are shown.)

The results are given for each component across levels of one other component, at fixed levels of the third and fourth components (see discussion at end of the third section for our rationale). Conclusions for the separabilities and marginal variances reached by these analyses are given in the last three columns of Table 8.8. Perceptual separability was w-supported in most cases, failing in only three cases all of which involved component **A** (vertical line). Decisional separability s-failed in all but four tests; in three of the four tests where decisional separability was w-supported, the stimulus contained only two components. Finally, no conclusions could be drawn about the equality of the marginal variances in many cases.

Probabilities for testing sampling independence are given in Table 8.9. Begin-

TABLE 8.8
Observed Marginal Estimates and Summary of Separability Results
for Observer 3 THE 84

	MRI		*Marginal*		*Marginal*				*Marginal* σ^2
Component	P_1	P_2	d'_1	d'_2	β_1	β_2	*PS?*[a]	*DS?*	*Equal?*
A_2 across **B**									
at C_1D_1	.636	.560*	2.29	1.89	3.82	2.41*	w-yes	no	?
at C_1D_2	.577	.483*	1.61	1.35	1.09	1.23	w-yes	?(no)	?(no)
at C_2D_1	.524	.527	2.15	1.85	3.37	1.76*	w-yes	no	?
at C_2D_2	.404	.446*	1.20	2.36*	1.35	3.66*	no	?	?
A_2 across **C**									
at B_1D_1	.623	.584*	2.29	2.15	3.82	3.37	w-yes	? (no)	? (no)
at B_1D_2	.614	.477*	1.61	1.20	1.09	1.35*	w-yes	no	?
at B_2D_1	.517	.547	1.89	1.85	2.41	1.76*	w-yes	no	?
at B_2D_2	.456	.500*	1.35	2.36*	1.23	3.66*	no	?	?
A_2 across **D**									
at B_1C_1	.606	.604	2.29	1.61	3.82	1.09*	w-yes	no	?
at B_1C_2	.500	.427*	2.15	1.20*	3.37	1.35*	no	?	?
at B_2C_1	.500	.436*	1.89	1.35	2.41	1.23*	w-yes	no	?
at B_2C_2	.467	.416*	1.85	2.36	1.76	3.66*	w-yes	no	?
B_2 across **A**									
at C_1D_1	.463	.594*	1.88	2.17	2.56	2.51	w-yes	? (no)	? (no)
at C_1D_2	.557	.500*	2.10	1.83	1.73	2.02	w-yes	? (no)	? (no)
at C_2D_1	.526	.527	2.01	1.83	2.82	1.68*	w-yes	no	?
at C_2D_2	.404	.466*	1.56	2.10	1.26	2.27*	w-yes	no	?

(continued)

TABLE 8.8 (*Continued*)

Component	MRI		Marginal		Marginal				Marginal
	P_1	P_2	d'_1	d'_2	β_1	β_2	PS?[a]	DS?	σ^2 Equal?
B_2 across C									
at A_1D_1	.566	.593	1.88	2.01	2.56	2.82	w-yes	w-yes	w-yes
at A_1D_2	.503	.514	2.10	1.56	1.73	1.26*	w-yes	no	?
at A_2D_1	.517	.547	2.17	1.83	2.51	1.68*	w-yes	no	?
at A_2D_2	.456	.500*	1.83	2.10	2.02	2.27	w-yes	? (no)	? (no)
B_2 across D									
at A_1C_1	.466	.570*	1.88	2.10	2.56	1.73*	w-yes	no	?
at A_1C_2	.496	.480	2.01	1.56	2.82	1.26*	w-yes	no	?
at A_2C_1	.500	.436*	2.17	1.83	2.51	2.02	w-yes	? (no)	? (no)
at A_2C_2	.467	.416*	1.83	2.10	1.68	2.27	w-yes	? (no)	? (no)
C_2 across A									
at B_1D_1	.697	.590*	2.02	2.03	1.76	2.47*	w-yes	no	?
at B_1D_2	.480	.514	1.70	1.57	1.69	1.20*	w-yes	no	?
at B_2D_1	.526	.527	1.62	1.80	1.28	1.51*	w-yes	no	?
at B_2D_2	.404	.466*	1.67	1.79	1.84	2.03	w-yes	? (no)	? (no)
C_2 across B									
at A_1D_1	.713	.660*	2.02	1.62	1.76	1.28*	w-yes	no	?
at A_1D_2	.497	.504	1.70	1.67	1.69	1.84	w-yes	w-yes	w-yes
at A_2D_1	.524	.527	2.03	1.80	2.47	1.51*	w-yes	no	?
at A_2D_2	.467	.446	1.57	1.79	1.20	2.03*	w-yes	no	?
C_2 across D									
at A_1B_1	.703	.493*	2.02	1.70	1.76	1.69	w-yes	? (no)	? (no)
at A_1B_2	.496	.480	1.62	1.67	1.28	1.84*	w-yes	no	?
at A_2B_1	.500	.427*	2.03	1.57	2.47	1.20*	w-yes	no	?
at A_2B_2	.467	.416*	1.80	1.79	1.51	2.03*	w-yes	no	?
D_2 across A									
at B_1C_1	.590	.590	2.02	2.24	3.04	2.51	w-yes	w-yes	w-yes
at B_1C_2	.480	.514	2.12	2.00	2.44	1.79*	w-yes	no	?
at B_2C_1	.557	.500*	1.89	2.02	2.03	1.66*	w-yes	no	?
at B_2C_2	.404	.466*	2.39	2.41	3.26	2.35*	w-yes	no	?
D_2 across B									
at A_1C_1	.540	.567	2.02	1.89	3.04	2.03*	w-yes	no	?
at A_1C_2	.497	.404*	2.12	2.39	2.44	3.26*	w-yes	no	?
at A_2C_1	.577	.483*	2.24	2.02	2.51	1.66*	w-yes	no	?
at A_2C_2	.467	.446	2.00	2.41	1.79	2.35*	w-yes	no	?
D_2 across C									
at A_1B_1	.527	.507	2.02	2.12	3.04	2.44	w-yes	w-yes	w-yes
at A_1B_2	.503	.514	1.89	2.39	2.03	3.26	w-yes	no	?
at A_2B_1	.614	.477*	2.24	2.00	2.51	1.79*	w-yes	no	?
at A_2B_2	.456	.500*	2.02	2.41	1.66	2.35*	w-yes	no	?

Notes: See notes to Table 8.5 for significance criteria.

[a]PS stands for perceptual separability, DS stands for decisional separability, and MRI for marginal response invariance.

TABLE 8.9
Sampling Independence for Observer 3 in THE 84 Study

4-Way Sampling Independence

Stimulus	*P(x,y,z,w)*	*P(x)P(y)P(z)P(w)*
$A_2B_2C_2D_2$	.373	.304*

3-Way Sampling Independence

Stimulus	*P(x,y,z)*	*P(x)P(y)P(z)*
$A_2B_2C_2$ at D_1	.467	.406*
at D_2	.416	.379*
$A_2B_2D_2$ at C_1	.456	.381*
at C_2	.500	.440*
$A_2C_2D_2$ at B_1	.467	.364*
at B_2	.446	.408*
$B_2C_2D_2$ at A_1	.404	.380
at A_2	.466	.414*

2-Way Sampling Independence

Stimulus	*P(x,y)*	*P(x)P(y)*	*Stimulus*	*P(x,y)*	*P(x)P(y)*
A_2B_2 at C_1D_1	.550	.512*	B_2C_2 at A_1D_1	.549	.514*
at C_1D_2	.519	.491	at A_1D_2	.507	.502
at C_2D_1	.597	.541*	at A_2D_1	.577	.553
at C_2D_2	.566	.548	at A_2D_2	.556	.516*
A_2C_2 at B_1D_1	.557	.498*	B_2D_2 at A_1C_1	.593	.564
at B_1D_2	.507	.479	at A_1C_2	.564	.559
at B_2D_1	.567	.551	at A_2C_1	.596	.545*
at B_2D_2	.502	.509	at A_2C_2	.616	.598
A_2D_2 at B_1C_1	.671	.587*	C_2D_2 at A_1B_1	.570	.522*
at B_1C_2	.574	.485*	at A_1B_2	.548	.516
at B_2C_1	.603	.543*	at A_2B_1	.617	.571*
at B_2C_2	.643	.589*	at A_2B_2	.582	.555

Note: * indicates a significant difference at the $\alpha = .25$ level (two-tailed Z test).

ning with the mutual sampling independence of all four components (top of Table 8.9), we see that it has failed. Three-way sampling independence, however, was found to hold for components **B** (horizontal), **C** (diagonal), and **D** (curve) at the first level of **A** (when the vertical feature was absent). This must imply pairwise independence of these three components at the first level of **A** (**B** and **C** at $\mathbf{A_1D_2}$, **B** and **D** at $\mathbf{A_1C_2}$, and **C** and **D** at $\mathbf{A_1B_2}$), and, in fact, we find that this is so. For all other three-way combinations of the components, sampling independence has failed, and examination of the pairwise tests will indicate where the dependencies occurred.

Conditional signal detection estimates for testing pairwise perceptual independence of components **A** and **B**, at all possible combinations of levels of **C** and **D**, are presented in Table 8.10 (refer to Table 8.2 or Figure 8.7 for the conclusions). Similar analyses would be done for each pair of components, but because of numerous possible combinations (see Table 8.9), we feel it is more instructive to show fewer results with greater clarity.

As with the two-dimensional example with four levels, we test pairs of stimuli at a time. Perceptual independence for a given stimulus can only be concluded when none of the tests that involve that stimulus show failure of perceptual independence that cannot be attributed to another stimulus.

SUMMARY AND FUTURE DIRECTIONS

Human perception of visual patterns has often been studied from a "dimensional" perspective, whereby a stimulus is assumed to be decomposed by the perceptual system into a number of individual components. By varying the composition of the physical stimuli, we can investigate various influences of one component on the other. In this chapter, we have employed the framework of GRT to define and interrelate five notions of "perceptual independence" that have appeared in the literature to connote that one component does not influence another. We have given theoretical results that relate multidimensional Signal Detection Theory to the various notions of "independence" within GRT and that allow us to test these various "independencies." The method based on these theoretical results was illustrated with three examples from the literature.

TABLE 8.10
Perceptual Independence Tests for Components **A** and **B** Using Estimates of Conditional d' and β for Observer 3 in THE 1984

Components **C** and **D**	C_1D_1	C_1D_2	C_2D_1	C_2D_2
Sampling Independence of A_2 and B_2?	No	Yes	No	Yes
d' $(A_2\|B_2)$	1.94	1.43	2.07	1.80
d' $(A_2\|B_1)$	1.72	1.28	1.35*	1.40
β $(A_2\|B_2)$	1.93	1.11	1.38	1.43
β $(A_2\|B_1)$	3.76#	1.63#	2.33#	1.46
Perceptual independence in A_2B_2 and A_1B_2	? (w-yes)	? (w-yes)	? (w-yes)	w-yes
d' $(B_2\|A_2)$	2.26	2.04	2.17	1.66
d' $(B_2\|A_1)$	2.13	1.31*	1.11*	1.30
β $(B_2\|A_2)$	1.88	2.13	1.53	1.16
β $(B_2\|A_1)$	4.89#	1.66#	1.71	1.26
Perceptual independence in A_2B_2 in A_2B_1	? (no)	? (w-yes)	? (no)	w-yes
Decisional separability	? (no)	s-no	? (no)	w-yes

See notes to previous tables for significance criteria.

At the present time, these results have been employed only in feature-complete factorial designs with accuracy measures as the dependent variable. But the method is quite new, and there are extensions that could further strengthen it or render it more broadly applicable.

Many of the theorems for the marginal results assume that the marginal (or all) variances are equal. An experimental design that could simultaneously test this assumption along with the tests of the separabilities would therefore be desirable. There are two possible ways such a test may be incorporated, both of which involve the construction of a receiver operating characteristic (ROC) curve. This curve simply plots the probability of false alarms as a function of the probability of hits. From an isosensitivity curve, which results when all the d''s are equivalent (a testable condition that we already employ), an estimate of the "signal" variance can be obtained. The feature-complete factorial designs we discussed here provide only one point in the ROC space, which is insufficient to obtain an isosensitivity curve *and* an estimate of the "signal" variance. The two ways of obtaining more points for the ROC curve are by using confidence ratings rather than straight identification of each component-level, or awarding differential payoffs for different components in the stimulus set. Along with a test of the Euclidean diagonal condition (see discussion following Theorem 8.4). a strong test of perceptual separability would be achieved. Confidence ratings have been used by other investigators in developing and using methods somewhat similar to ours for testing "independence" of components (Ashby, 1988; Wickens & Olzak, 1989).

An interesting and direct application of the method presented here is to the kind of feature-complete factorial designs that Melara and Marks (1990a) used in their studies on uncovering "primary" perceptual dimensions. This involves different orientations of axes of the physical dimensions from which the stimuli are constructed. Although Melara and Marks used response times, the same stimuli could be used with accuracy measures. Presumably, there will be a most preferred orientation where perceptual and decisional separabilities will hold but fail at other orientations. As for perceptual independence of dimensions in a given stimulus, if the variances are equal in both dimensions and perceptual independence holds in one orientation, then perceptual independence should hold at all orientations. These analyses could provide interesting results for identifying "primary" perceptual dimensions in the visual domain, as well as other sensory arenas.

APPENDIX

The first part of this appendix defines marginal d' and β parameters of signal detection macroanalyses; in the second part, conditional d' and β of signal detection microanalyses are defined.

Signal Detection Macroanalyses

The d' and β parameters of signal detection macroanalysis are based on the marginal densities (see Figure 8.1). Theoretically these are obtained by integrating the joint densities in the perceptual space over the variable *not* of interest. These marginal densities are then used as the "noise" (that density where the feature was absent from the stimulus) and signal + noise (where the feature was present in the stimulus) densities, as in Signal Detectability Theory of Green and Swets (1974), to obtain the d' and β parameters. The theoretical formulas that follow correspond to the methods of estimation of these parameters used by Townsend et al. (1984, 1988).

We denote the mean vector and covariance matrix of density $f_{ij}(x, y)$ by

$$\boldsymbol{\mu}_{ij} = \begin{bmatrix} \mu_{Xij} \\ \mu_{Yij} \end{bmatrix} \quad \text{and} \quad \boldsymbol{\Sigma}_{ij} = \begin{bmatrix} \sigma^2_{Xij} & \sigma_{XYij} \\ \sigma_{XYij} & \sigma^2_{Yij} \end{bmatrix},$$

respectively. Note that for a normal density, the covariance term is $\sigma_{XYij} = \rho_{ij}\sigma_{Xij}\sigma_{Yij}$, where ρ_{ij} is the correlation coefficient between X and Y in density f_{ij}. The marginal d''s for feature **A** at the j-th level of feature **B** can then be written as

$$d'_{\mathbf{AB}j} = \frac{\mu_{X2j} - \mu_{X1j}}{[(\sigma^2_{X2j} + \sigma^2_{X1j})/2]^{1/2}}, \qquad j = 1,2 .$$

Similarly,

$$d'_{\mathbf{A}i\mathbf{B}} = \frac{\mu_{Yi2} - \mu_{Yi1}}{[(\sigma^2_{Yi2} + \sigma^2_{Yi1})/2]^{1/2}}, \qquad i = 1,2 .$$

are the marginal d''s for the detection of feature **B** at the i-th level of feature **A.**

As in Signal Detectability Theory, the marginal β's are defined as the likelihood ratios of the marginal densities, evaluated at the corresponding criterion values, $c_{\mathbf{A}}$ (criterion for presence of feature **A**) or $c_{\mathbf{B}}$ (criterion for presence of feature **B**), respectively. Thus, with analogous notation as for the marginal d''s, we define the marginal β's as

$$\beta_{\mathbf{AB}j} = \frac{g_{2j}(c_{\mathbf{A}})}{g_{1j}(c_{\mathbf{A}})}, \qquad j = 1,2 ;$$

and

$$\beta_{\mathbf{A}i\mathbf{B}} = \frac{g_{i2}(c_{\mathbf{B}})}{g_{i1}(c_{\mathbf{B}})}, \qquad i = 1,2 .$$

Signal Detection Microanalyses

In this section we consider the *conditional* d' and β parameters. As for the macroanalyses, the following theoretical formulas correspond to the methods of estimation in earlier experimental papers (Townsend et al., 1984, 1988). Note that these derivations demand that decisional separability holds—that is, that the criteria be parallel to the coordinate axes.

Recall that $\boldsymbol{X}$ is the random variable representing the perceptual effect resulting from the visually degraded presentation of feature **A**, and $\boldsymbol{Y}$ is the random variable analogously defined for feature **B**. We now wish to derive a joint density of $\boldsymbol{X}$ and $\boldsymbol{Y}$ when we condition, for example, on the hit or miss of feature **B**. The hit or miss on feature **B** demands that **B** was actually present in the stimulus; thus, we are concerned with the two densities f_{i2}, i = 1,2. The normalized joint densities for conditioning on the hit of feature **B**, for i = 1 and 2, are written as

$$f_i^*(x, y|\mathbf{B}\text{ hit}) = f_{i2}(x, y) \Big/ \int_{c_\mathbf{B}}^{\infty}\int_{-\infty}^{\infty} f_{i2}(x, y)\, dx\, dy$$

$$= \begin{cases} f_{i2}(x, y) \Big/ \int_{c_\mathbf{B}}^{\infty} g_{i2}(y)\, dy, & \text{for all real } x; \quad y > c_\mathbf{B}\ , \\ 0, & \text{elsewhere}\ , \end{cases}$$

and similarly when we condition on the miss of feature **B**, for i = 1,2,

$$f_i^*(x, y|\mathbf{B}\text{ miss}) = f_{i2}(x, y) \Big/ \int_{-\infty}^{c_\mathbf{B}}\int_{-\infty}^{\infty} f_{i2}(x, y)\, dx\, dy$$

$$= \begin{cases} f_{i2}(x, y) \Big/ \int_{-\infty}^{c_\mathbf{B}} g_{i2}(y)\, dy, & \text{for all real } x; \quad y < c_\mathbf{B}\ , \\ 0, & \text{elsewhere}\ , \end{cases}$$

Here $c_\mathbf{B}$ is the (y-coordinate) value of the decision criterion for feature **B**, $\boldsymbol{X}$ ranges over the real line in both densities, and $\boldsymbol{Y}$ ranges from the criterion $c_\mathbf{B}$ to infinity when conditioning on **B** hit and from negative infinity to $c_\mathbf{B}$ when we condition on **B** miss.

Using these densities, we obtain the corresponding marginal densities for $\boldsymbol{X}$ or $\boldsymbol{Y}$. The "marginal" conditional density for $\boldsymbol{X}$ conditioned on the hit of feature **B** is obtained by integrating over all possible y values; thus,

$$g_i^*(x|\mathbf{B}\text{ hit}) = \int_{c_\mathbf{B}}^{\infty} f_i^*(x, y|\mathbf{B}\text{ hit})\, dy$$

$$= \int_{c_\mathbf{B}}^{\infty} f_{i2}(x, y)\, dy \Big/ \int_{c_\mathbf{B}}^{\infty} g_{i2}(y)\, dy\ .$$

Similarly, the density for $\boldsymbol{X}$ conditional on the miss of feature **B** is

$$g_i^*(x|\mathbf{B}\text{ miss}) = \int_{-\infty}^{c_\mathbf{B}} f_{i2}(x, y)\, dy \Big/ \int_{-\infty}^{c_\mathbf{B}} g_{i2}(y)\, dy .$$

Analogous definitions hold for the marginal densities of the random variable Y conditioned on the hit or miss of feature **B** by integrating the joint densities over all possible x values. Using densities $f_{i1}(x, y)$, i = 1,2 in the integrals gives the joint and marginal densities for conditioning on the false alarm of feature **B** (those that are above $c_\mathbf{B}$) or conditioning on the correct rejections of feature **B** (those below $c_\mathbf{B}$).

By exchanging the roles of **A** and **B**, we also obtain the corresponding definitions for feature **B** conditioned on: (a) the hit or miss of feature **A** by employing joint densities f_{2j}, j = 1,2; or (b) the correct rejection or false alarm of feature **A** with densities f_{1j}, j = 1,2. In these cases, integration is over X, either above or below $c_\mathbf{A}$.

Using these densities, the conditional d''s are defined analogously to the d' parameter of Signal Detectability Theory. For example, the d' value for feature **A** conditional on the hit of feature **B** is given by

$$d'(\mathbf{A}|\mathbf{B}\text{ hit}) = \frac{E\,[X|\mathbf{B}\text{ hit}, \mathbf{A}_2\mathbf{B}_2] - E\,[X|\mathbf{B}\text{ hit}, \mathbf{A}_1\mathbf{B}_2]}{[\frac{1}{2}(Var\,[X|\mathbf{B}\text{ hit}, \mathbf{A}_2\mathbf{B}_2] + Var\,[X|\mathbf{B}\text{ hit}, \mathbf{A}_1\mathbf{B}_2])]^{1/2}} ,$$

where $E\,[X|\mathbf{B}\text{ hit}, \mathbf{A}_i\mathbf{B}_2]$ and $Var\,[X|\mathbf{B}\text{ hit}, \mathbf{A}_i\mathbf{B}_2]$ are the expected value and variance of X, respectively, given that feature **B** was a hit and stimulus $\mathbf{A}_i\mathbf{B}_2$ was presented. The expected values, for i = 1 and 2, are defined by

$$E\,[X|\mathbf{B}\text{ hit}, \mathbf{A}_i\mathbf{B}_2] = \int_{-\infty}^{\infty} x g_i^*(x|\mathbf{B}\text{ hit})\, dx$$

$$= \int_{c_\mathbf{B}}^{\infty} g_{i2}(y) E\,[X|Y = y, \mathbf{A}_i\mathbf{B}_2]\, dy \Big/ \int_{c_\mathbf{B}}^{\infty} g_{i2}(y)\, dy .$$

But for two random variables, X and Y, having a bivariate normal distribution, the conditional mean of X at a given y value is

$$E\,[X|Y = y] = \mu_X + (y - \mu_Y)\,\rho\,\frac{\sigma_X}{\sigma_Y} ,$$

where ρ is the correlation coefficient of the bivariate normal density, μ_X and σ_X^2 are the mean and variance of the marginal density of X, respectively, and similarly for μ_Y and σ_Y^2. Substituting this into the preceding integral and simplifying gives

$$E\,[X|\mathbf{B}\text{ hit}, \mathbf{A}_i\mathbf{B}_2] = \mu_{Xi2} - \rho_{i2}\,\frac{\sigma_{Xi2}}{\sigma_{Yi2}}\,(\mu_{Yi2} - E\,[Y|\mathbf{B}\text{ hit}, \mathbf{A}_i\mathbf{B}_2]) ,$$

where

$$E\,[Y|\mathbf{B}\text{ hit},\ \mathbf{A}_i\mathbf{B}_2] = \int_{c_\mathbf{B}}^{\infty} y g_i^*(y|\mathbf{B}\text{ hit})\,dy$$

$$= \int_{c_\mathbf{B}}^{\infty} y g_{i2}(y)\,dy \Big/ \int_{c_\mathbf{B}}^{\infty} g_{i2}(y)\,dy\,.$$

For the denominator of $d'(\mathbf{A}|\mathbf{B}\text{ hit})$,

$$Var\,[X|B\text{ hit},\ \mathbf{A}_i\mathbf{B}_2] = E\,[X^2|\mathbf{B}\text{ hit},\ \mathbf{A}_i\mathbf{B}_2] - \{E\,[X|\mathbf{B}\text{ hit},\ \mathbf{A}_i\mathbf{B}_2]\}^2\,,$$

with

$$E\,[X^2|\mathbf{B}\text{ hit},\ \mathbf{A}_i\mathbf{B}_2] = \int_{-\infty}^{\infty} x^2 g_i^*(x|\mathbf{B}\text{ hit})\,dx$$

$$= \int_{c_\mathbf{B}}^{\infty} g_{i2}(y) E\,[X^2|Y = y,\ \mathbf{A}_i\mathbf{B}_2]\,dy \Big/ \int_{c_\mathbf{B}}^{\infty} g_{i2}(y)\,dy$$

and $E\,[X|\mathbf{B}\text{ hit},\ \mathbf{A}_i\mathbf{B}_2]$ as before. But $E\,[X^2|Y = y,\ \mathbf{A}_i\mathbf{B}_2] = Var\,[X|Y = y,\ \mathbf{A}_i\mathbf{B}_2] + \{E\,[X|Y = y,\ \mathbf{A}_i\mathbf{B}_2]\}^2$, and $Var\,[X|Y = y] = \sigma_X^2\,(1 - \rho^2)$, so

$$Var\,[X|\mathbf{B}\text{ hit},\ \mathbf{A}_i\mathbf{B}_2] = \sigma_{Xi2}^2\,[1 - \rho_{i2}^2] + \rho_{i2}^2 \frac{\sigma_{Xi2}^2}{\sigma_{Yi2}^2} Var\,[Y|\mathbf{B}\text{ hit},\ \mathbf{A}_i\mathbf{B}_2]\,.$$

Similar expressions are defined for all conditional d''s. For example,

$$d'(\mathbf{A}|\mathbf{B}\text{ miss}) = \frac{E\,[X|\mathbf{B}\text{ miss},\ \mathbf{A}_2\mathbf{B}_2] - E\,[X|\mathbf{B}\text{ miss},\ \mathbf{A}_1\mathbf{B}_2]}{[\frac{1}{2}(Var\,[X|\mathbf{B}\text{ miss},\ \mathbf{A}_2\mathbf{B}_2] + Var\,[X|\mathbf{B}\text{ miss},\ \mathbf{A}_1\mathbf{B}_2])]^{1/2}}\,,$$

where $E\,[X|\mathbf{B}\text{ miss},\ \mathbf{A}_i\mathbf{B}_2]$ and $Var\,[X|\mathbf{B}\text{ miss},\ \mathbf{A}_i\mathbf{B}_2]$ are defined identically to $E\,[X|\mathbf{B}\text{ hit},\ \mathbf{A}_i\mathbf{B}_2]$ and $Var\,[X|\mathbf{B}\text{ hit},\ \mathbf{A}_i\mathbf{B}_2]$ (using "**B** miss" in place of "**B** hit"). Analogous definitions are obtained for d''s conditional on correct rejections and false alarms by using the appropriate densities.

The definitions for the conditional β's are easier to derive. Using the "marginal" conditional densities, we simply write the conditional β for feature **A** given the hit or miss of feature **B** as the ratio

$$\beta(\mathbf{A}|\mathbf{B}\text{ hit}) = \frac{g_2^*(c_\mathbf{A}|\mathbf{B}\text{ hit})}{g_1^*(c_\mathbf{A}|\mathbf{B}\text{ hit})}$$

and

$$\beta(\mathbf{A}|\mathbf{B}\text{ miss} = \frac{g_2^*(c_\mathbf{A}|\mathbf{B}\text{ miss})}{g_1^*(c_\mathbf{A}|\mathbf{B}\text{ miss})}\,,$$

where $c_\mathbf{A}$ is the x coordinate of the criterion for reporting feature **A**.

9 Three Views of Association in Concurrent Detection Ratings

Thomas D. Wickens
Lynn A. Olzak
University of California, Los Angeles, CA 90024

The ultimate goal of psychophysical research is to explain the behavioral responses of observers to multidimensional, real-world stimuli. This straightforward objective is exceedingly difficult to achieve. A full analysis must not only provide a physiologically based model of sensory information processing along each relevant dimension, but also a model of how multiple information sources within and across dimensions are combined or otherwise interact. Finally, the model must separate and account for the higher-level cognitive processes involved in attentional and decisional behaviors.

As we currently understand human perceptual processes, sensory information is processed simultaneously by many systems and subsystems. Along various dimensions, sensory information is first analyzed into a series of fundamental components. In later stages of processing these components are combined within and across senses to create a coherent representation of the world. Our understanding of the initial analysis process is based largely on experiments designed to test whether two stimuli are processed by independent subsystems. Traditional approaches to this question use experiments in which the effects of a secondary stimulus on the perception of a test stimulus are assessed. They include masking, adaptation and subthreshold summation paradigms. A more recent modification of the traditional approach involves comparisons of simple detection and identification performance when the two tasks are performed simultaneously (see chap. 10).

From traditional experiments, we know that at the grossest level, separate sensory systems respond in parallel to stimulation in different modes—air pressure, light, chemicals, and so forth. Within each system, a more refined analysis may take place, with subsystems again acting in parallel to extract different dimensions of the stimulus. In visual processing, which is among the better-understood sensory systems, these dimensions include color, spatial dimensions (e.g., location, orientation, and size or spatial frequency), and motion information. At the finest level of analysis, information about the value of the stimulus along each dimension within a sensory system may be signaled in parallel by multiple collections of neurons tuned to limited ranges of that dimension. Thus, the color system in vision signals color via three cone types selective to wavelength, the spatial system signals spatial frequency via a small number of mechanisms, each spanning about an octave in spatial frequency, and motion is signaled by mechanisms that may respond to motion only in a particular direction.

Although they are extremely fruitful in advancing our understanding of the analysis process, traditional psychophysical experiments are limited in the information they can provide when two stimuli are not processed independently. Furthermore, it is often difficult to identify the source of dependence from these types of studies and to separate sensory interactions from decisional biases or the effects of selective attention. Because processing dependence may occur at any level of processing—cross-modally, across dimensions within sense, or across tuned mechanisms within a dimension—many fundamental questions about the synthesis of sensory information across or within sensory systems remain unanswered.

In this chapter, we describe an experimental paradigm designed to provide the type of information needed to answer questions about the processing of complex stimuli—those that contain more than a single attribute upon which psychophysical decisions are based. In the concurrent rating task, two (or more) stimulus attributes, each of which can take on two (or more) values are varied in factorial combination. On each trial, the observer makes two (or more) psychophysical rating judgments reflecting the degree of certainty about the value of each attribute. The frequency with which each category is used is tallied in a series of contingency matrices to provide the raw data for analysis. Thus, unlike traditional studies in which information is gathered about the perception of a single stimulus as a function of the value of another stimulus, this paradigm efficiently provides information about the simultaneous influence of each stimulus component both on the response to itself and on the responses to the other component. Furthermore, if the sensory processes mediating the responses are well understood, the data can provide information about response bias, selective attention, and higher cognitive processes involved in the decision process.

We illustrate three approaches to the analysis of concurrent rating data, each of which provides a somewhat different perspective on associations found in data matrices. Each requires different assumptions about the underlying sensory and cognitive processes. As an example, we use data from a visual detection task designed to investigate interactions across mechanisms tuned to spatial frequency. However, the techniques we describe apply to any sensory modality, to tasks other than detection (for example, discrimination), and to any level of sensory processing.

THE CONCURRENT RATING TASK

As an example, we consider data from an experiment by Olzak & Kramer (1984) on the detection of compound spatial gratings (see also Olzak, 1986). The stimuli were vertical sinusoidal gratings, presented as near-threshold modulations of a constant background luminance. The modulations were of high and low spatial frequency (12 and 3 cycles per degree). These frequencies were chosen to be sufficiently far apart that conventional analysis has deemed them processed by separate channels, although some suggestions of interaction have been reported (Hirsch, Hylton, & Graham, 1982; Olzak, 1985; Olzak & Thomas, 1981; see also Graham, 1989). With the two grating frequencies, four stimulus types were formed: background alone, low-frequency modulation only, high-frequency modulation only, and both modulations combined, types denoted by ($\mathbf{N}_H$, $\mathbf{N}_L$), ($\mathbf{N}_H$, $\mathbf{S}_L$), ($\mathbf{S}_H$, $\mathbf{N}_L$), and ($\mathbf{S}_H$, $\mathbf{S}_L$), respectively. Contrast levels were chosen to yield approximately equal performance in single-stimulus discrimination. The composite stimuli were presented to the observer for 100 ms in a 3° area in the center of the visual field. The observer's task was to decide when either of the two components was present. Ratings were obtained for both components as a pair of six-level confidence ratings. Each of the four stimulus conditions was rated 350 times. Table 9.1 shows the data from one subject, which are used as an example throughout this chapter.

The data in Table 9.1 form a four-way contingency table. Two dimensions in this table, H and L, are fixed classifications determined by the investigator; the other two dimensions, X and Y, are response classifications produced by the observer. The X response is appropriate for the H signal, the Y response for the L signal.[1] Entries in Table 9.1 indicate the number of times that each response combination occurred; for example, on 44 of the 350 trials on which the stimulus ($\mathbf{N}_H$, $\mathbf{N}_L$) was presented, the subject responded with ratings of 1 to both signals. The numerical frequencies in Table 9.1 are indexed by four subscripts and are denoted by f_{hlxy}, where the subscripts h and l take the two values 0 and 1, indicating *absent* and *present*, respectively, and the subscripts x and y take values from 1 through 6. Thus, capital letters refer to the factors or dimensions of the table in general and lowercase letters to particular values.

The cells with responses (1,1) in the four subtables of Table 9.1 require special comment. As we have noted in other work (Olzak & Wickens, 1983; Wickens, 1992; Wickens & Olzak, 1989), the frequencies in these cells exceed the predictions of most simple models fitted to the remainder of the data. The relative overuse of this response category has many explanations, ranging from fundamental perceptual processes through various cognitive or response strat-

[1]Note that X and Y are in the same alphabetic order as H and L. Throughout our assignment of parameters (with the exception of ξ_x and η_y), we preserve this order, keeping a parameter associated with the high-frequency signal alphabetically before the comparable parameter associated with the low-frequency signal.

TABLE 9.1
Data from a Single Observer Detecting Two Spatial Frequency Signals in a Concurrent Detection Task (Olzak & Kramer, 1984)

		Low-Frequency Signal											
High-Frequency Signal		*Absent (y)*						*Present (y)*					
	x	*1*	*2*	*3*	*4*	*5*	*6*	*1*	*2*	*3*	*4*	*5*	*6*
Absent	1	44	13	9	16	5	3	8	5	8	12	12	31
	2	4	30	23	17	4	3	2	5	10	17	17	29
	3	9	20	17	10	9	0	2	5	7	15	19	25
	4	7	8	17	20	10	1	1	5	4	13	18	24
	5	6	14	3	2	4	4	0	5	1	2	10	12
	6	7	7	0	2	0	1	4	3	1	2	4	12
Present	1	7	5	6	4	2	0	4	0	1	4	3	11
	2	4	7	7	12	3	0	1	4	3	4	12	8
	3	5	13	8	5	1	1	2	0	3	8	8	12
	4	5	15	10	13	1	1	0	1	7	17	11	11
	5	14	38	10	6	3	1	4	8	8	12	20	12
	6	69	37	15	14	5	3	37	25	15	21	20	33

Note: Data from T. D. Wickens and L. A. Olzak (1989), The statistical analysis of concurrent detection ratings, *Perception and Psychophysics, 45,* p. 515. Copyright Psychonomic Society, 1989.

egies. Without inquiring yet as to the particular interpretation of the excess frequency, we do not wish these cells to compromise the description of the balance of the table, so we exclude them from influencing many of the fitting procedures here. The same effect can be produced by including special parameters to fit these cells in our models.

In the remainder of this chapter we apply three probabilistic models to these data. The models form a series starting with a specific and restricted Gaussian model and ending with a general log-linear model. Each model, we show, is best suited to answering certain types of questions; together they give the foundation of a statistical approach to data of this type in any branch of perceptual studies.

THE BIVARIATE GAUSSIAN MODEL

The strongest model that is appropriate to apply to these data is of a latent bivariate Gaussian (normal) distribution. This model combines the rating scale model of Signal Detection Theory (e.g., Green & Swets, 1974; Swets & Picket, 1982; Tanner, 1956) with the representation of a contingency table as a categorized bivariate distribution (in essence, the model underlying the polychoric correlation coefficient of Pearson, 1901; see also Wickens, 1989, section

13.6). It is also the Gaussian version of General Recognition Theory, as defined by Ashby & Townsend (1986) and discussed by Kadlec & Townsend (chap. 8). If the assumption of the Gaussian distribution is allowed, then the estimates of its parameters allow direct examination of the various types of interaction defined by this theory.

Consider the results from a single stimulus condition. Under the bivariate Gaussian detection model, each 6 × 6 subtable of frequencies is the result of categorizing an unobserved bivariate Gaussian distribution using a fixed series of cutpoints. The probability of a particular bivariate response is the probability that an observation from this distribution falls in the region bounded by two pairs of orthogonal criteria. Specifically, suppose that an I × J table of responses has been recorded. Let (X, Y) be a continuous bivariate Gaussian random variable with means μ and ν, variances σ^2 and τ^2, and correlation ρ, and let $\xi_1, \xi_2, \ldots, \xi_{I-1}$ and $\eta_1, \eta_2, \ldots, \eta_{J-1}$ be two series of cutpoints. For notational convenience put $\xi_0 = \eta_0 = -\infty$ and $\xi_I = \eta_J = \infty$. Based on this distribution and the cutpoints ξ_x and η_y, the probability of an observation in cell (x, y) is

$$P(\xi_{x-1} \leq X < \xi_x, \eta_{y-1} \leq Y < \nu_y) =$$

$$\int_{\xi_{x-1}}^{\xi_x} \int_{\eta_{y-1}}^{\eta_y} \phi_2\left(\frac{u-\mu}{\sigma}, \frac{v-\nu}{\tau}; \rho\right) dv\, du\ , \tag{1}$$

where $\phi_2(x, y; \rho)$ is the standard bivariate Gaussian density function with zero means, unit variances, and correlation ρ,

$$\phi_2(x, y; \rho) = \frac{1}{2\pi\sqrt{1-\rho^2}}\, exp\left(-\frac{x^2 - 2\rho xy + y^2}{2(1-\rho^2)}\right). \tag{2}$$

The bivariate Gaussian response model is extended to account for the response to several stimulus types in the same way that a univariate Gaussian representation accounts for responses to signal and noise in the signal detection analysis of single-response rating studies. Equation 1 is used to generate probabilities for each stimulus type, for a fixed set of cutpoints ξ_x and η_y, but allowing the parameters of the distribution to depend on the stimulus. So, the data in Table 9.1 require four Gaussian distributions, indexed by the four stimulus conditions $(\mathbf{N}_H, \mathbf{N}_L)$, $(\mathbf{N}_H, \mathbf{S}_L)$, $(\mathbf{S}_H, \mathbf{N}_L)$, and $(\mathbf{S}_H, \mathbf{S}_L)$, each specified by a quintuplet of parameters, μ_{hl}, σ_{hl}, ν_{hl}, τ_{hl}, and ρ_{hl}. Under this model the expected frequency in a cell is

$$E\,(f_{hlxy}) = f_{hl} \int_{\xi_{x-1}}^{\xi_x} \int_{\eta_{y-1}}^{\eta_y} \phi_2\left(\frac{u-\mu_{hl}}{\sigma_{hl}}, \frac{v-\nu_{hl}}{\tau_{hl}}; \rho_{hl}\right) dv\, du\ , \tag{3}$$

where f_{hl} is the number of observations in table hl, that is, the hl marginal of the table of f_{hlxy}. In the most general of these models, all five parameters can differ from one subtable to another, and the response frequencies are tied together only by the common values of the criteria ξ_x and η_y.

The latent Gaussian distributions are hypothetical, so the center and scale of the entire configuration of distributions is indeterminate. To identify the model two restrictions are placed on the X and Y dimensions. A convenient way to do so is to assert a standard form (i.e., zero mean and unit variance) for the distribution underlying the table of the ($\mathbf{N}_H$, $\mathbf{N}_L$) stimulus, an operation that is equivalent to assuming a standard distribution for the noise-only signal in the univariate signal detection analysis. If orthogonal axes are assumed, the full set of correlations is identifiable.

The bivariate Gaussian model can be generalized by changing the form of the criteria used to determine the responses. The model as described has criteria that are parallel to the axes and orthogonal to each other. In the terminology of General Recognition Theory, it shows *decisional separability* (see chaps. 7 and 8). Many modifications of the bivariate Gaussian model that are not decisionally separable can be constructed (for some interesting examples see Klein, 1985). The simplest modification allows parallel straight-line criteria that are not orthogonal for the two response types. However, this apparent generalization does not produce an identifiably different model. The angle between the criteria is completely confounded with the parameters of the Gaussian distributions. To see why this is so, recall that the oblique axis rotation that renders the criteria orthogonal to each other and parallel to the axes is accomplished by a linear transformation of the coordinates (see any text on multivariate statistics; for a related result see Ashby & Townsend, 1986, Theorem 2). This linear transformation does not change the quadratic nature of the exponent in the bivariate Gaussian distribution $\phi_2(x,y;\rho)$ (Equation 2). This quadratic form establishes the Gaussian character of the distribution. Thus, the orthogonalized model makes the same predictions as the model with nonorthogonal but parallel criteria, albeit with different variances and correlations.

A more complicated modification of the decisionally separable bivariate Gaussian model allows the criteria to derive from families of lines that are not necessarily parallel and straight. Such models make identifiably different predictions. However, the selection of a family of criterial lines that has a plausible theoretical motivation is difficult. Clearly, the criteria for a rating procedure should not cross each other, which rules out letting each straight-line criterion make its own angle with the axes. One can select instead one of the many more restricted fans and families of curves that do not cross. These sets of criteria have interesting possibilities for representing second-order varieties of interaction, but we do not follow them up here. For the present chapter we leave the bivariate Gaussian model in its relatively pure form as a baseline model.

Maximum likelihood estimates of the parameters of the bivariate Gaussian model can be obtained numerically (for details of the algorithm see Wickens,

1992).[2] For the data in Table 9.1 with cell (1,1) excluded, the estimates of the five high-frequency cutpoints ξ_x are

$$-1.13, \quad -0.21, \quad 0.32, \quad 1.07, \quad \text{and} \quad 1.86\,,$$

and the estimates of the low-frequency cutpoints η_y are

$$-0.97, \quad -0.19, \quad 0.35, \quad 0.96, \quad \text{and} \quad 1.63\,.$$

The standardization of the noise distribution gives these criteria the properties of z-scores with respect to this distribution. They are consistent with what one would expect for a practiced observer using a criterion-based model of this type. They are approximately equally spaced, indicating good utilization of the response categories, and the estimates of ξ_x are roughly similar to those of η_y, indicating consistent numerical use of the rating scale. Estimates of the parameters of the Gaussian distributions are shown in the top portion of Table 9.2.

Before turning to a discussion of the estimates in Table 9.2, consider a visual representation of the parameters. Figure 9.1 pictures the 4 distributions and the 10 cutpoints. The cutpoints are indicated by the horizontal and vertical lines, the distributions by isodensity contours, drawn so as to include 50% of the probability. The means of the distributions are connected by straight lines, creating the quadrilateral in the center of the figure. The variances of the distributions determine the horizontal and vertical axes of the ellipses, and their correlation determines their eccentricity (see Figure 1.2).

An examination of the estimates in Table 9.2 and Figure 9.1 shows four classes of effect. First, the signals affect their proper response; second, in some cases the signals influence the other response; third, the responses are correlated with each other; finally, this correlation interacts with the responses. Each of these effects exemplifies a larger class of influences, so we discuss each briefly.[3]

The direct effect of a signal on its proper response has two parts, one involving the mean, the other the standard deviation. First, for both the low-frequency signal and the high-frequency signal, the mean in the signal condition is higher than the mean in the noise condition. The magnitude of this effect varies slightly over the stimulus types, but is approximately 1.4 times the standard deviations of the pure noise condition. This similarity is presumably due to the calibration of the signal levels at the start of the study. Thus, the distributions are displaced toward higher values when a signal is present. Second, for both signals the standard deviation is larger when a stimulus is present than when it is absent

[2]All analyses reported in this chapter were conducted on an IBM PC- compatible computer using programs written for the purpose in TurboPascal (Borland International, 1989). A copy of these programs can be obtained by supplying the first author with a diskette.

[3]Table 9.7 summarizes the various effects and ties them to the parameters of the several models we discuss in this chapter.

TABLE 9.2
Parameter Estimates for the Bivariate Gaussian Model Fitted to Table 9.1

Stimulus	$\hat{\mu}$	$\hat{\sigma}$	$\hat{\nu}$	$\hat{\tau}$	$\hat{\rho}$
		All Parameters Free			
$(\mathbf{N}_H, \mathbf{N}_L)$	0.00[a]	1.00[a]	0.00[a]	1.00[a]	−0.12
$(\mathbf{N}_H, \mathbf{S}_L)$	−0.05	1.11	1.47	1.39	−0.03
$(\mathbf{S}_H, \mathbf{N}_L)$	1.35	1.44	−0.54	1.08	−0.37
$(\mathbf{S}_H, \mathbf{S}_L)$	1.40	1.51	0.84	1.61	−0.39
		Parameter Estimates For a Simpler Model			
$(\mathbf{N}_H, \mathbf{N}_L)$	0.00[a]	1.00[a]	0.00[a]	1.00[a]	−0.06[b]
$(\mathbf{N}_H, \mathbf{S}_L)$	0.00[a]	1.00[a]	1.47	1.46[b]	−0.06[b]
$(\mathbf{S}_H, \mathbf{N}_L)$	1.32[b]	1.38[b]	−0.49	1.00[a]	−0.37[b]
$(\mathbf{S}_H, \mathbf{S}_L)$	1.32[b]	1.38[b]	0.82	1.46[b]	−0.37[b]

[a]Parameter value fixed by identifiability constraint.
[b]Parameter value fixed by model restriction.

(i.e., $\sigma_{01} < \sigma_{11}$ and $\tau_{h0} < \tau_{h1}$). The combined variation of signal plus noise exceeds that of noise alone, suggesting that the internal response to the signal is variable.

The second type of effect relates a signal to the response that is appropriate to the other signal. In General Recognition Theory, signals that do not show such effects are said to be *perceptually separable* (see chaps. 7 and 8). A positive shift of the means indicates excitation, a negative shift indicates inhibition. In the present data these effects are asymmetrical. There is an inhibitory effect of the high-frequency signal on the low-frequency response, shown by the depression of ν when $\mathbf{S}_H$ is present relative to its value in the corresponding $\mathbf{N}_H$ condition. The shift amounts to about half a standard-deviation unit. The data do not show a corresponding effect of the low-frequency signal on the high-frequency data. Thus, in the mean our observer shows asymmetric perceptual separability, with the parameter μ associated with the high-frequency dimension being unchanged by the low-frequency signal, but with the parameter ν associated with the low-frequency signal being altered by the high-frequency signal.

Failures of perceptual separability other than simple excitation or inhibition are possible but do not appear in these data (testing procedures are given here and in Wickens, 1992). First, the four means may show an interaction in the Analysis of Variance sense. The lack of this interaction is illustrated by the parallelogram form of the means in Table 9.1—had the means interacted, the sides would not be parallel. Second, influences on the variance can appear. There is an inkling of this effect, with both σ and τ being larger in the presence of the opposite signal, but the differences are small and not significant in these data.

Another type of association effect is manifest in the correlation of the responses. In General Recognition Theory the presence of this correlation indicates *perceptual dependence* (see chap. 8). Under the Gaussian model, the only form

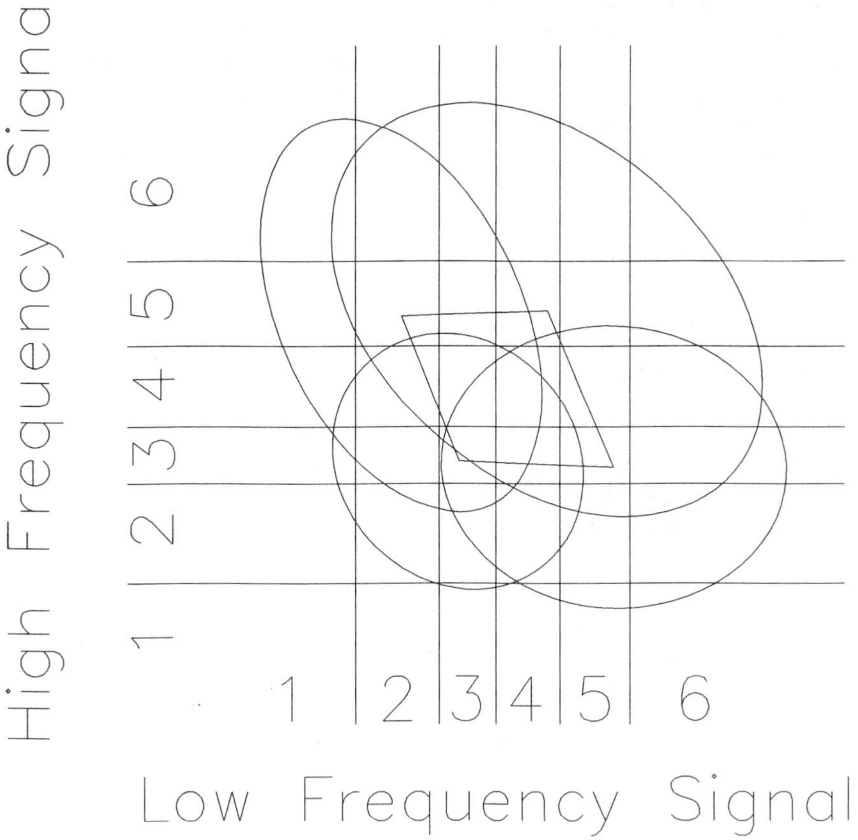

Fig. 9.1. Representation of the bivariate Gaussian model described by the parameters at the top of Table 9.2. The centers of the Gaussian distributions fall at the corners of the quadrilateral, the ellipses enclose half the probability density of each distribution, and the orthogonal lines are the cutpoints.

of association is correlation, so a zero correlation indicates *perceptual independence*. Here, the correlations are all negative, showing that a substantial response to one signal implies a diminished response to the other signal. This effect is different from the inhibition effect just described, for it does not depend on a between-stimulus comparison, but appears in the data from a single-stimulus condition. Two interpretations for this correlation are plausible, one based on the sensory side of the process, the other on the response side. The first possibility is of correlated noise in the sensory system. Such noise has the same role as a generator of variability as the univariate noise postulated in Single-Response Detection Theory. For the present observer, the noise produces a negative correlation between the sensory mechanisms. The response interpretation of the correlation is localized in the generation of the numerical ratings. By this interpretation, extreme ratings on one dimension (either large or small) inhibit similar ratings for the other dimension, producing the negative correlation. Without further assumptions, these data cannot discriminate between these alternatives.

The final effect exhibited in Table 9.2 and Figure 9.1 combines the correlation and the signal-induced effects. The correlation between the responses appears to depend on the stimulus condition. This effect again points to the influence of the high-frequency signal, for the correlation is larger in magnitude when the high-frequency signal is present (about −0.38) than it is when this signal is absent (less than −0.10). In contrast, the low-frequency signal has little or no influence on the correlation.

The parameter differences just described can be submitted to statistical testing. Like any table of discrete data, the observed frequencies f_{hlxy} in Table 9.1 can be compared with a set of theoretical frequencies generated by a model. Let m_{hlxy} denote the estimated expected frequency for cell hlxy under a model. These are the values of $E(f_{\text{hlxy}})$ from Equation 3, with parameter values estimated from the data. A variety of goodness-of-fit statistics are available to compare the m_{hlxy} to the f_{hlxy}, of which the most familiar are the Pearson statistic,

$$X^2 = \sum \frac{(f_{\text{hlxy}} - m_{\text{hlxy}})^2}{m_{\text{hlxy}}},$$

and the likelihood-ratio statistic,[4]

$$G^2 = 2 \sum f_{\text{hlxy}} \, log \, \frac{f_{\text{hlxy}}}{m_{\text{hlxy}}}.$$

If a model fits, these statistics have approximately a chi-square distribution. The degrees of freedom for this comparison equal the number of free observations in the table minus the number of parameters in the model. Each subtable contains 36 frequencies, which are subject to one experimental constraint (summing to 350) and the exclusion of the (1,1) cell, making 34 degrees of freedom available from each subtable. The model has 26 parameters (10 cutpoints, 6 means, 6 variances, and 4 correlations—remember that μ_{00}, σ_{00}, ν_{00}, and τ_{00} are constrained). Accordingly, the reference distribution has $4 \times 34 - 26 = 110$ degrees of freedom. For the bivariate Gaussian model, the test statistics are $X^2 = 201.22$ and $G^2 = 200.42$, respectively. By standard criteria, these values indicate some failure of the model to fully describe the data. Although the comparison to the chi-square sampling distribution is somewhat suspect, for the table contains many small expected frequencies, the failure suggests that some aspect of the behavior goes beyond that captured in the bivariate Gaussian model.

Tests of specific hypotheses about the parameters are often more informative

[4]Throughout this chapter *log x* refers to the natural logarithm.

than tests of global fit, particularly when small cell frequencies lead one to question the accuracy of the chi-square approximation for the goodness-of-fit test. The specific tests compare the fit of a model with that of a hierarchically related model. The difference in statistic value tests the restriction that constrains the general model to the more specific one. For the G^2 statistic, the difference in statistic value constitutes a Likelihood Ratio Test of the restriction hypothesis (see, e.g., Bishop, Fienberg, & Holland, 1975; Wickens, 1989; or Section 1.7). For example, consider the hypothesis that the correlations in all four tables are identical. The model with equal correlation has $G^2 = 225.70$ on 113 degrees of freedom. The difference between this statistic and that of the full model is $\Delta G^2 = 25.28$. It is distributed on $113 - 110 = 3$ degrees of freedom. Comparison of ΔG^2 to a chi-square statistic is unaffected by small cells and clearly rejects the hypothesis of equal correlation.

By appropriately chosen tests, a simple model of the data can be constructed. The parameters of one such model are shown in the bottom panel of Table 9.2. It embodies the following restrictions: (a) the high-frequency means depend only on the high-frequency signal, $\mu_{h0} = \mu_{h1}$; (b) the variances depend only on the presence or absence of the relevant signal, $\sigma_{h0} = \sigma_{h1}$ and $\tau_{01} = \tau_{11}$; and (c) the correlation is the same for both levels of the low-frequency signal, $\rho_{h0} = \rho_{h1}$. Parameters not subject to these constraints differ from each other, leading to the substantive conclusions about the interaction discussed earlier. The goodness-of-fit statistic for the simplified model is $G^2 = 208.59$ on 118 degrees of freedom, so, compared with the fully parameterized model, $\Delta G^2 = 8.17$ on 8 degrees of freedom. The process of data-driven model selection certainly biases this value downward relative to a chi-square distribution, but nonetheless the package of restrictions is clearly satisfactory. The parameter values support the various points discussed in connection with the unrestricted estimates. Concern about the post hoc nature of this model is considerably relieved when one examines the data for five other experimental conditions with the same observer in related tasks and finds that similar restrictions hold for all conditions.

In summary, the bivariate Gaussian model provides a compact description of bivariate rating data, summarizing them in a few readily interpretable parameters. However, its failure to fit accurately suggests that there are aspects of the data that the model does not capture. The bivariate Gaussian model makes strong assertions about the form of the data, some of which may be wrong. Two assertions seem particularly vulnerable. First, the position of the criteria ξ_x and η_y link two aspects of the data that might be considered separately, the marginal frequencies and the pattern of bivariate association. Although this linkage is one of the simplifying strengths of the bivariate Gaussian model, it can influence the quality of the fit. Specifically, any factors that influence the frequencies with which the categories are used but that are not related to the form of the sensory response will bias the measurement of association. Second, the bivariate Gaussian model only allows the response-response association to have a Gaussian form. As shown here, this form has a single-component aspect that cannot describe many other types of association. Deviations from the Gaussian form can influence the estimates of the means and variances of the distributions. Thus, in the remainder of this chapter we examine two models that weaken these assumptions.

THE MULTIPLICATIVE-ASSOCIATION MODEL

We look next at a class of model that allows the scaling of association, in a manner similar to that in a Gaussian distribution, but without dependence on the marginal distributions. In doing so, we turn away from the models based on the latent distributions of General Recognition Theory toward a model that can explicitly represent the association between responses that is embodied in perceptual dependence. The model that we examine here separates the measurement of perceptual dependence from the parameters associated with effects in the marginal distributions, such as the detectability of the signal or the lack of perceptual separability. As an explicit representation of interresponse association, models of this type give the strongest way to investigate perceptual dependence phenomena.

Among the various models that have been proposed to represent association in bivariate contingency tables, two are particularly plausible here.[5] Both are multiplicative models, one for the expected frequencies,

$$E\ (f_{\text{hlxy}}) = \alpha_{\text{hlx}}\beta_{\text{hly}}\ (1 + \phi_{\text{hl}}\xi_{\text{x}}\eta_{\text{y}}) \tag{4}$$

the other for the logarithm of these frequencies,

$$log\ E\ (f_{\text{hlxy}}) = \kappa_{\text{hl}} + \alpha_{\text{hlx}} + \beta_{\text{hly}} + \phi_{\text{hl}}\xi_{\text{x}}\eta_{\text{y}} \tag{5}$$

(Goodman 1985, 1986). The former model is related to the model used in correspondence analysis (e.g., Greenacre, 1984); the latter is a model of multiplicative association (Goodman, 1979), which we refer to as the *multiplicative-association model.*

We do not wish to stray too far from the bivariate Gaussian model, so it is important to realize that although these models are less restrictive than the Gaussian model, both have parameter combinations that are roughly consistent with it. The following argument shows that either model can approximate a Gaussian model (see Wickens & Olzak, 1989, Appendix A-5b). First note that by the mean-value theorem from calculus, the probability in each cell under a latent-density model equals the size of the rectangle of integration times the height of

[5]The statistical arguments in this section and the next are developed in greater detail in the appendix to Wickens & Olzak (1989).

the density function at an interior point. The areas are the products of a row parameter and a column parameter, so the two models roughly mimic the association pattern of a bivariate Gaussian distribution to the extent that they reproduce the form of the Gaussian density function. Consider first the correspondence-analysis model. Let $f(x)$ be a univariate Gaussian density function with variance $1 - \rho^2$. Factoring the bivariate Gaussian density function (Equation 2), one gets

$$\phi_2(x, y) = \sqrt{1 - \rho^2}\, f(x)f(y)\, exp\left(\frac{\rho xy}{1 - \rho_2}\right). \tag{6}$$

Expanding the exponential as a power series gives

$$\phi_2(x, y) = \sqrt{1 - \rho^2}\, f(x)f(y) \left[1 + \frac{\rho xy}{1 - \rho^2} + \frac{(\rho xy)^2}{2(1 - \rho^2)^2} + \cdots \right].$$

When second-order and higher terms are ignored and the constant $\sqrt{1 - \rho^2}$ is combined with either $f(x)$ or $f(y)$, this expression is identical to Equation 4. Now consider the multiplicative-association model. The logarithm of Equation 6 is

$$log\ \phi_2(x, y) = log \sqrt{1 - \rho^2} + \log f(x) + log\, f(y) + \frac{\rho xy}{1 - \rho^2}.$$

This expression is identical in form to Equation 5. The term-for-term matching to Equations 4 and 5 is modified by the identification constraints typically imposed when the parameters are estimated, but the models' form remains the same.

The correspondence between the term in xy in both expansions of Equation 6 and the term in $\xi_x\eta_y$ in both association models indicates that the association parameter ϕ is related to the Gaussian correlation by

$$\phi \approx \frac{\rho}{1 - \rho^2} \quad \text{or} \quad \rho \approx \frac{\sqrt{1 + 4\phi^2} - 1}{2\phi}. \tag{7}$$

This link lets one translate the parameters of the association models to a common ground with those of the bivariate Gaussian model. Goodman (1981) has shown that, for the multiplicative-association model, the quality of this approximation can be quite good.

In our work (Wickens & Olzak, 1989) we have concentrated on the multiplicative-association model of Equation 5 rather than the additive model of Equation 4, in part because of its slightly closer relationship to the Gaussian distribution, and in part because its logarithmic form links it to the models of association that we discuss in the next section.

The quantities ξ_x and η_y in thc multiplicative-association model determine the spacing of the categories in the association portion of the model. Identification of their values requires two restrictions to be imposed on each set. For this problem, the most useful such restrictions fix the mean and variance of the two sets of coefficients with respect to the appropriate marginal distribution

$$\sum_i \xi_i P(X = i) = \sum_j \eta_j P(Y = j) = 0$$

and

$$\sum_i \xi_i^2 P(X = i) = \sum_j \eta_j^2 P(Y = j) = 1 \; .$$

The second of these equations also ensures that ϕ is scaled properly for Equation 7 to apply. All estimates here are chosen to obey these constraints.

Three sets of estimates of ξ_x and η_y are shown in Table 9.3, subject to three levels of constraint on their values. The first set is estimated freely, restricted only by the identification constraints. A test of this model gives $G^2 = 118.65$ on 84 degrees of freedom, which (if the chi-square approximation can be trusted) corresponds to a descriptive level of 0.008. Regardless of the fit of this model, these estimates are unsatisfactory, for they are not monotonically related to the category ordering. Apparently, a consistent placement of the category estimates depends either on support from the marginal distributions (as in the Gaussian model) or on the use of a more constrained model.

The second set of estimates results from imposing an ordinal constraint, so that $\xi_{x-1} \leq \xi_x$ and $\eta_{y-1} \leq \eta_y$ for all x and y. On its face, this model is far more plausible than the free-parameter version. The cost of the restriction is not great. The difference in test statistics between the models is $\Delta G^2 = 10.49$, which is not substantial, although the models do not have the type of hierarchical structure that allow this value to be compared with a chi-square distribution.[6] The association parameters estimated under this model, expressed as correlations using Equation 7, are -0.24, -0.13, -0.36, and -0.42 for the conditions ($\mathbf{N}_H$, $\mathbf{N}_L$), ($\mathbf{N}_H$, $\mathbf{S}_L$), ($\mathbf{S}_H$, $\mathbf{N}_L$), and ($\mathbf{S}_H$, $\mathbf{S}_L$), respectively. Interestingly, although the presence of the high-frequency signal seems to increase the association, the difference is not large. In fact, a model with an identical association of -0.35 for all conditions does not fit significantly worse, having a difference statistic against the free-correlation model of only $\Delta G^2 = 2.75$ on 3 degrees of freedom. This result suggests that the variation in correlation with the high-frequency stimulus that was observed with the bivariate Gaussian model may be interpreted as the flattening of the upper end of the low-frequency association scale, which is the most obvious characteristic of the ordinal estimates in Table 9.3.

The third set of estimates in Table 9.3 is most constrained. Values of ξ_x and η_y are given a uniform spacing, subject to the mean and variance restrictions of the

---

[6]A chi-square comparison is incorrect for at least two reasons. First, the parameter spaces of both models have the same dimension, the ordinal constraints being of range, not of number of parameters. Second, the ordinal constraints can force the selection of a different bilinear association component from that estimated in the free model.

TABLE 9.3
Estimated Association Scale Parameters of the Multiplicative-Association Model (Equation 5) Fitted to the Data from Table 9.1 Under Three Sets of Constraints

	x or y					
Parameter	*1*	*2*	*3*	*4*	*5*	*6*
			Free Estimates			
ξ_x	−0.87	−0.67	−0.29	1.15	0.40	1.52
η_y	−2.11	−0.65	0.60	0.96	0.62	0.36
			Ordinal Constraints			
ξ_x	−1.23	−0.66	−0.64	−0.64	0.43	1.54
η_y	−2.18	−0.61	0.58	0.66	0.66	0.66
			Uniform Spacing			
ξ_x	−1.64	−1.06	−0.48	0.10	0.68	1.26
η_y	−1.51	−0.91	−0.32	0.27	0.86	1.46

identification constraints. Thus, $\xi_x - \xi_{x-1}$ is the same for all x, as is $\eta_y - \eta_{y-1}$ for all y. In the uniformly spaced multiplicative-association model, the association between adjacent categories is identical. The fit of this model is appreciably worse than that of either other model, with $G^2 = 192.97$ on 92 degrees of freedom, and thus $\Delta G^2 = 74.30$ against the ordinal model with 8 degrees of freedom. Apparently, the equal spacing of ξ_x and η_y observed for the bivariate Gaussian model is substantially the result of equal use of the categories, not of the association pattern.

Estimates of the parameters that express the marginal distribution in the ordinal multiplicative-association model are given in Table 9.4. The parameters κ_{hl} express largely the presentation frequencies of the stimulus types and are not particularly interesting here. Both the excitatory effects of the proper signal and the inhibitory effect of the high-frequency signal on the low-frequency response are seen in a shift of the marginal distributions toward larger or smaller values. The parameters are expressed so that positive values indicate a surplus of observations in that condition and negative values indicate a deficiency. Thus, the effect of the low-frequency signal is manifest in the larger values of α_{hlx} for high-numbered responses on $\mathbf{S}_L$ trials and for low-numbered responses on $\mathbf{N}_L$ trials. The elimination of the (1,1) cell from the estimates depresses α_{hl1} and β_{hl1}, particularly for stimulus $(\mathbf{N}_L,\mathbf{N}_H)$, where this response combination is heavily used. These signal effects are manifested in the modulation of these parameters with the response category. The extent of this modulation is measured compactly by the linear tend contrast

$$\alpha_{hl}^{lin} = \frac{1}{\sqrt{70}}(-5\alpha_{hl1} - 3\alpha_{hl2} - \alpha_{hl3} + \alpha_{hl4} + 3\alpha_{hl5} + 5\alpha_{hl6}) .$$

Values of α_{hl}^{lin} are given in the final column of Table 9.4. Another way to obtain a

TABLE 9.4
Estimated Parameters Describing the Marginal Distributions in the Ordinal Multiplicative-Association Model Fitted to the Data from Table 9.1. The Final Column Gives the Linear Trend Component

Stimulus	*x or y* 1	2	3	4	5	6	*Linear Trend*
			High-Frequency Effects (α_{hlx})				
(N_H, N_L)	0.12	0.66	0.44	0.41	−0.32	−1.31	−1.22
(N_H, S_L)	0.13	0.37	0.29	0.17	−0.45	−0.50	−0.69
(S_H, N_L)	−0.81	−0.23	−0.23	0.08	0.42	0.78	1.22
(S_H, S_L)	−1.10	−0.42	−0.38	−0.03	0.52	1.42	1.89
			Low-Frequency Effects (β_{hly})				
(N_H, N_L)	0.15	0.94	0.38	0.33	−0.41	−1.39	−1.41
(N_H, S_L)	−1.30	−0.30	−0.36	0.30	0.57	1.08	1.82
(S_H, N_L)	0.51	1.10	0.49	0.46	−0.82	−1.74	−2.04
(S_H, S_L)	−1.24	−0.46	−0.11	0.48	0.59	0.75	1.64

clearer view of these effects is provided by a detailed parameterization such as that described for the log-linear models in the next section. The effects of the signals on their proper response are obvious in the trend coefficients, but the effects related to perceptual separability are less clear. They are probably obscured by the disruptive effects of the exclusion of cell (1,1). In any event, the multiplicative-association model is not the best model in which to study these effects.

In summary, the multiplicative-association model separates the scale effects determined by the association from those determined by the marginal frequencies. This structured association model expresses the association effects related to perceptual dependence in a simple form. For these data it suggests that the Gaussian model is limited by the even steps imposed on the association by the link to the marginal frequencies. It indicates that the range of the low-frequency association effects are truncated at the upper end and raises the possibility that the inhomogeneous correlation observed with the bivariate Gaussian model may result from its inability to express this truncation (cf. Klein, 1985).

INDEPENDENCE AND CONDITIONAL-INDEPENDENCE MODELS

By relaxing the links between the frequency of category use and the association, the multiplicative-association model lets one separate the ordered structure of perceptual dependence from the marginal distributions. Direct signal effects can be observed in the parameters α_{hlx} and β_{hly}, but their estimates are potentially influenced by the restricted form of the interresponse association. The bilinear form of this association, which was shown to be consistent with the Gaussian distribution, allowed only a single pair of scales in multiplicative combination, as $\phi\xi_x\eta_y$. To examine parameters expressing the marginal distributions, we consider a class of models that allows a broader description of interresponse association. One way to obtain this generality follows the approach of correspondence analysis or canonical correlation by introducing a new pair of scales ξ'_x and η'_y and adding a second multiplicative association term $\phi'_{hl}\xi'_x\eta'_y$ to the model. As many as five such terms can be included. We do not examine these extensions here but turn instead to the models of independence and conditional independence. These models describe the interresponse association very generally and give specific ways to examine the signal effects. They have log-linear form and generalize the type of independence and association measured in an ordinary two-way contingency table.

This approach also returns to the concepts of general recognition theory, but at a different level. The concepts of perceptual separability and independence, discussed in conjunction with the bivariate Gaussian model, refer to properties of the latent distribution that generates the responses. The examination of those properties was conducted in the context of that model. General Recognition Theory also refers to the data-level concepts of sampling independence and marginal response invariance (see chap. 8). The conditional-independence models give explicit tests for hypotheses associated with these concepts.

The fundamental element of this analysis is the independence or the unrelatedness of two classifications—independence in a probabilistic sense when both classifications are subject-generated, as are the two responses here, and unrelatedness when one of the classifications is determined by the experimenter, as are the assignments to the four combinations of signal and noise that create the stimulus types. Unrelatedness of the signal dimension H and the response dimension X in the two-factor HX table formed by collapsing Table 9.1 over L and Y is denoted $H \perp\!\!\!\perp X$. In this table, the hypothesis $H \perp\!\!\!\perp X$ is tested by the conventional test for association in a contingency table with either of the statistics X^2 or G^2. Rejection of this hypothesis implies that the high-frequency signal influences the X response.

A variety of hypotheses of independence are available in three-way or higher tables (see, e.g., Bishop et al., 1975; Wickens, 1989, for discussion of these hypotheses and their associated models). For our purposes, the most important of these hypotheses are conditionally formulated. If H and Y are unrelated at every level of the other signal factor L, then they are said to be conditionally unrelated given this factor, a relationship denoted by $H \perp\!\!\!\perp Y|L$. Conditional unrelatedness of this type does not imply unrelatedness in the marginal distribution (i.e., $H \perp\!\!\!\perp Y$), since H and Y are linked through common dependence on L. The conditional hypothesis excludes this possibility and gives greater power to detect the conditional effects by combining evidence from tests of $H \perp\!\!\!\perp Y$ in the individual HY tables at each level of L. In the present case, one wishes to examine the data for the effects on each response of the opposite signal in the context of the known excitatory effects of the appropriate signal.

In probabilistic terms the hypothesis $H \perp\!\!\!\perp Y|L$ implies that

$$P(Y = y|H = 0, L = l) = P(Y = y|H = 1, L = l) \qquad \text{for } l = 0,1 .$$

This relationship is formally equivalent to *marginal response invariance* in General Recognition Theory, although the definition given in Chapter 8 refers specifically to identification of a particular signal rather than the production of a rating response. A test of the hypothesis $H \perp\!\!\!\perp Y|L$ is a test of marginal response invariance in its most general form.

All the models of unrelatedness or conditional unrelatedness are equivalent to log-linear models for the frequencies in the appropriate frequency table. So the hypothesis $H \perp\!\!\!\perp X$ is equivalent to the model

$$\log \mu_{hx} = \lambda + \lambda_{H(h)} + \lambda_{X(x)} \tag{8}$$

tested in the two-way table of H and X. In the conventional notation here, all the terms of this log-linear model are denoted by λ, with subscripts that indicate the factor(s) over which that term is indexed and, in parentheses, the levels of those factors to which the term applies. The conditional assertion that $H \perp\!\!\!\perp Y|L$ is examined in the three-way HLY table and is equivalent to the model

$$\log \mu_{hly} = \lambda + \lambda_{H(h)} + \lambda_{L(l)} + \lambda_{Y(y)} + \lambda_{HL(hl)} + \lambda_{LY(ly)} . \tag{9}$$

The parameters of this model are not uniquely determined without additional constraint, since any quantity can be added to one estimate and subtracted from another without changing the result. To identify them, they are required to sum to zero over any subscript; for example,

$$\sum_h \lambda_{H(h)} = \sum_l \lambda_{L(l)} = \sum_l \lambda_{LY(ly)} = \sum_y \lambda_{LY(ly)} = 0, \cdots . \tag{10}$$

Expected frequencies necessary to fit these models, and thus to test the corresponding hypotheses of unrelatedness, are readily found. All are calculated by using extensions of the usual formula that gives expected frequencies for the ordinary two-way test for dependence. Thus, if the sums of the frequencies f_{hlxy} over various indices are denoted by dropping the summed subscript, then the expected frequencies for the models $H \perp\!\!\!\perp X$ and $H \perp\!\!\!\perp Y|L$ are[7]

$$m_{hx} = \frac{f_h f_x}{f} \qquad \text{and} \qquad m_{hly} = \frac{f_{hl} f_{ly}}{f_l} .$$

The models are readily fitted by the major statistical computer packages.

For the dual-response detection data, three types of unrelatedness hypotheses are appropriate to test.

[7]The specific formulas for the models described here are given by Wickens & Olzak (1989).

1. Tests of the unrelatedness of each signal to its proper response, $H \perp\!\!\!\perp X$ and $L \perp\!\!\!\perp Y$. Rejection of these hypotheses usually means that the signal is detectable, although it subsumes other effects of the signal such as changes in response variability.

2. Tests of the conditional unrelatedness of each signal and the opposite response, that is, of marginal response invariance. These hypotheses are tested in the context of normal detection, as $H \perp\!\!\!\perp Y|L$ and $L \perp\!\!\!\perp X|H$. Rejection of these hypotheses usually indicates an excitatory or an inhibitory effect, although other forms of association are possible.

3. Tests of the independence of the two responses, conditional on their proper stimulus, $X \perp\!\!\!\perp Y|HL$. In general recognition theory this hypothesis is of *sampling independence,* again as extended to rating responses. Rejection of this hypothesis implies a bivariate response-response association. The association measured by the Gaussian correlation and by the multiplicative-association model are restricted forms of this association. The present model is completely general and subsumes the form of correlation examined in those models along with many other forms.

The relationship of these effects to the latent distributional parameters is a central part of general recognition theory (see chap. 8).

Table 9.5 summarizes these tests using the G^2 statistic. It also reexpresses the hypotheses using the notation for hierarchical log-linear models that specifies the fitted marginal distributions, a description that some readers may find more familiar. The information-transmission statistic T in the last column is discussed later. These tests substantiate the points made in the earlier sections. First, direct association between signal and response is clearly present, as shown by the rejection of the hypotheses $H \perp\!\!\!\perp X$ and $L \perp\!\!\!\perp Y$. This result is hardly surprising. Second, in the conditional tests of the effects on the other signal (the hypotheses $H \perp\!\!\!\perp Y|L$ and $L \perp\!\!\!\perp X|H$), the influence of H on Y is significant, whereas the effect of L on X is not. The high-frequency response shows marginal invariance of the

TABLE 9.5
Tests of Independence and Conditional-Independence Hypotheses for the Data in Table 9.1. The Table Gives both the Hypotheses and Relevant Model as Fitted Marginals. The Last Column Is the Transmitted Information

	Hypothesis	*Model*	G^2	*df*	*T*
$H \perp\!\!\!\perp X$	Undetectable H	[H][X]	381.72	5	0.197
$L \perp\!\!\!\perp Y$	Undetectable L	[L][Y]	413.03	5	0.213
$H \perp\!\!\!\perp Y|L$	Marg. resp. invar. of Y	[HL][LY]	45.26	10	0.023
$L \perp\!\!\!\perp X|H$	Marg. resp. invar. of X	[HL][HX]	4.49	10	0.002
$X \perp\!\!\!\perp Y|HL$	Sampling independence	[HLX][HLY]	306.45	100	0.158
	All effects	[HL][X][Y]	1150.95	130	

low-frequency signal, but the low-frequency response is marginally dependent on the high-frequency signal. Third, the hypothesis X ⫫ Y|HL is rejected, indicating an association between responses within a given signal type. This test is conducted against a very general alternative, allowing any pattern of association effects relating X and Y. Although the generality of this test allows it to detect unusual patterns of association, it has less power to detect correlation-like effects than those based on the more restricted models. Because of this flexibility, it is not necessary to exclude the (1,1) cell from this analysis as was done with the other models.

The final row in Table 9.5 gives the sum of the G^2 statistic for the five effects. As can be shown by an argument that we do not present here (see Wickens, 1989, chap. 6), the five effects form an additive decomposition of the complete set of degrees of freedom associated with any relationship between the stimulus combinations HL and the two responses X and Y. This model tests the hypothesis that the data are random, which is somewhat trivial. However, the additive nature of the decomposition ensures one that all observer-dependent aspects of the data have been captured by the tests in Table 9.5. An analysis such as this provides an attractive Analysis of Variance–like partitioning of the various perceptual interactions.

Assertions such as H ⫫ X or H ⫫ Y|L are null hypotheses, and when they are rejected they imply that an association exists between the corresponding variables. These associations are described by the log-linear parameters estimated from models that introduce the appropriate association to the model of unrelatedness. The HX association in the HX table is measured by the parameter $\lambda_{HX(hx)}$ added to the response-unrelatedness model of Equation 8, and the first component of the HY association conditional on L is obtained by adding $\lambda_{HY(hy)}$ to the marginal-response-invariance model of Equation 9. Log-linear association parameters of this type are shown in Table 9.6 for the effects of the four signals. In the model, there are two series of parameters for each effect, one applying to trials on which the signal is present, the other on trials when the signal is absent. Only the parameters for signal events are shown in Table 9.6, since the identification constraints of Equation 10 make the nonsignal parameters the negative of the signal parameters. The estimates show clearly the form of these associations. The direct signal effects are expressed by λ_{HX} and λ_{LY}. Both these sets of parameters have positive values in the high-numbered cells and negative values in the low-numbered cells, indicating that when a signal is present more high-numbered responses are made. This effect is nicely graded over the confidence levels. As in the multiplicative-association model, these effects are summarized by the linear trend coefficients. The effect of H on Y is described by λ_{HY}, which shows the opposite pattern. The high-frequency signal produces an inhibitory effect on the low-frequency response, comparable to that measured by the differences in μ_{hl} for the bivariate Gaussian model. The effect of L on X, which was not deemed important by the test in Table 9.5, is clearly trivial.

TABLE 9.6
Log-Linear Parameters for Significant Signal Effects for Data from Table 9.1. Only Parameters for the Signal Conditions are Shown; Parameters for the Noise Conditions are the Negative of These

Base Model	*Added Parameter*	*x or y* 1	2	3	4	5	6	*Linear Trend*
$H \perp\!\!\!\perp X$	$\lambda_{HX(hx)}$	−0.59	−0.41	−0.32	−0.12	0.43	1.01	1.28
$L \perp\!\!\!\perp X \mid H$	$\lambda_{LX(lx)}$	−0.07	−0.01	0.04	0.02	−0.04	0.07	0.07
$L \perp\!\!\!\perp Y$	$\lambda_{LY(ly)}$	−0.59	−0.65	−0.38	−0.06	0.51	1.17	1.51
$H \perp\!\!\!\perp Y \mid L$	$\lambda_{HY(hy)}$	0.30	0.18	0.00	−0.03	−0.16	−0.30	−0.48

An index of the size of these effects is useful. As in any testing situation, the value of test statistics such as G^2 are not effect-size measures, for they are roughly proportional to the size of the sample. Many better measures of association exist (see, e.g., Wickens, 1989, chap. 9). For the tests of unrelatedness, a good measure is the *information transmission* between factors, or, for the conditional tests, the *conditional information transmission*. Although it is derived from the axioms of information theory, the quantity T is equal to a rescaling of the G^2 statistic testing the hypotheses of no (conditional) association, the relationship being

$$T = \frac{G^2}{2(\log 2)f} = 0.72135\,\frac{G^2}{f},$$

where f is the total observed frequency (Wickens, 1989, Equation 9.33). The statistic is interpreted as the number of bits of information in one classification that affects another classification. These values are shown in the last column of Table 9.5. From binary signals with equal-frequency events, at most 1 bit of information can be transmitted. In this rather difficult detection task, the signal transmitted only 0.21 bit of information to the response. The inhibitory effect of H on Y is 0.023 bit, and the statistically absent effect of L on X is negligible. The size of the failure of marginal response invariance relative to the detection effect is smaller when measured by the information transmission statistic than when measured by the means in the bivariate Gaussian model (about one ninth here and one third measured by the values of ν_{hl} in Table 9.2). This difference is not an inconsistency, for under the Gaussian model the scaling of the information transmission varies approximately as the square of the shifts in means.[8]

The response-response effect shows a conditional XY transmission of 0.16 bit, or about 80% of the transmission from either stimulus to its proper response.

[8]Briefly, information statistics depend on terms of the form $\Sigma p \log p = E(\log p)$. In a symmetric distribution such as the Gaussian, all odd moments are zero, so T is a function of the even moments, and differences between the Gaussian means enter only in their even powers.

The nature of this effect is harder to interpret than are the signal-response effects. There are 100 degrees of freedom with which to express violations of $X \perp\!\!\!\perp Y|HL$. Even moderate-sized effects distributed over this many degrees of freedom are confusing. Although one can approach the understanding of this association through a table of log-linear parameters, it is generally more productive to treat the association in the context of stronger models. Both the bivariate Gaussian model and the multiplicative-association model provide this specificity. Because of the greater complexity of the pure association parameters, we do not discuss them here.

SUMMARY

We have looked at three models for the description of bivariate rating data. These models differ in the amount and nature of the structure that they imposed on the data. Each provides different information about the data.

1. The bivariate Gaussian model has the strongest form, deriving from an extension of the signal detection rating model to bivariate data. Its parameters are easily interpreted and are the structural parameters of general recognition theory. It is very useful as a way to summarize detection performance. However, its high degree of structure means that it cannot represent some aspects of the data, making it less useful as the basis for an investigation of complex interaction effects.

2. The multiplicative-association model breaks the link between the marginal distributions and the pattern of response-response association that is intrinsic to the Gaussian model. It allows the association of perceptual dependency to be investigated, measuring both how the categories are scaled with respect to the association and the magnitude of that association. The bilinear form of the association, while linking this model to the Gaussian model, limits its value in the examination of the direct excitatory or inhibitory effects of the signal.

3. The general log-linear model is the broadest representation that we consider. This form is well adapted to the examination of direct signal effects, partly because it allows a completely general pattern of association, and partly because it expresses questions about the effects as null hypotheses that are readily tested. It gives direct and maximally powerful tests of the data-descriptive effects of General Recognition Theory. The breadth of its representation limits its value in the examination of response-response effects, which are better measured by the other models.

The three classes of models use different parameterizations, but describe the same type of data. Table 9.7 summarizes these parameters and relates them to the

TABLE 9.7
Summary of the Parameters of the Bivariate Gaussian Model, the Multiplicative-Association Model, and the Log-Linear Models Used in Tests of Conditional Independence

Effect or Influence	*Bivariate Gaussian*	*Multiplicative Assn*	*Log-Linear Models*
Frequency of the stimulus types	f_{hl}	κ_{hl}	$\lambda + \lambda_{H(h)} + \lambda_{L(l)} + \lambda_{HL(hl)}$
Marginal distributions of the high-frequency responses	μ_{hl}, σ_{hl}, and ξ_x	Variation in the distribution of α_{hlx}	$\lambda_{X(x)}$, $\lambda_{HX(hx)}$, $\lambda_{LX(lx)}$, and $\lambda_{HLX(hlx)}$
Marginal distributions of the low-frequency responses	ν_{hl}, τ_{hl}, and η_y	Variation in the distribution of β_{hly}	$\lambda_{Y(y)}$, $\lambda_{HY(hy)}$, $\lambda_{LY(ly)}$, and $\lambda_{HLY(hly)}$
Detection of signals	Variation in μ_{hl} with h and ν_{hl} with l [$\mu_{H(h)}$ and $\nu_{L(l)}$]	Variation in α_{hl}^{lin} with h and β_{hl}^{lin} with l [$\alpha_{H(h)}^{lin}$ and $\beta_{L(l)}^{lin}$]	$\lambda_{HX(h)}^{lin}$ and $\lambda_{LY(l)}^{lin}$ added to independence models
Excitation or inhibition by other signal, perceptual separability	Variation in μ_{hl} with l and ν_{hl} with h [$\mu_{L(l)}$ and $\nu_{H(h)}$]	Variation in α_{hl}^{lin} with l and β_{hj}^{lin} with h [$\alpha_{L(l)}^{lin}$ and $\beta_{H(h)}^{lin}$]	$\lambda_{LX(l)}^{lin}$ and $\lambda_{HY(h)}^{lin}$ added to conditional independence models
Nonadditivity of signal effects	Other variation in μ_{hl} and ν_{hl} [$\mu_{HL(hl)}$ or $\nu_{HL(hl)}$]	Other variation in α_{hl}^{lin} and β_{hl}^{lin} [$\alpha_{HL(hl)}^{lin}$ and $\beta_{HL(hl)}^{lin}$]	$\lambda_{HLX(hl)}^{lin}$ and $\lambda_{HLY(hl)}^{lin}$ in three-way models
Other marginal signal effects	Variation in σ_{hl} and τ_{hl}	Nonlinear variation in α_{hlx} and β_{hly}	Nonlinear variation in parameters of HLX and HLY tables
Association between responses in common to all stimuli	Common value of ρ_{hl} [ρ]	Common value of ϕ_{hl} [ϕ]	Embodied in $\lambda_{XY(xy)}$
First-order scaling of perceptual dependence	ξ_x and η_y	ξ_x and η_y	Embodied in $\lambda_{XY(xy)}$
Variation in first-order perceptual dependence with signal type	Differences in ρ_{hl} [$\rho_{H(h)}$, $\rho_{L(l)}$, and $\rho_{HL(hl)}$]	Differences in ϕ_{hl} [$\phi_{H(h)}$, $\phi_{L(l)}$, and $\phi_{HL(hl)}$]	Embodied in $\lambda_{HXY(hxy)}$, $\lambda_{LXY(lxy)}$, and $\lambda_{HLXY(hlxy)}$
Higher-order perceptual dependence	Not representable	Additional multiplicative terms, $\phi'_{hl}\xi'_x\eta'_y$	$\lambda_{XY(xy)}$, $\lambda_{HXY(hxy)}$, $\lambda_{LXY(lxy)}$, and $\lambda_{HLXY(hlxy)}$

various aspect of the data that they explain. This table lists a series of data effects and for each model indicates which parameters must be examined to measure the effect. Although no single model is optimally suited to represent all characteristics of the data, among them a wide variety of effects can be examined.

For many of the parameters, separate values are estimated for each stimulus condition. The parameters describing the distributions in the bivariate Gaussian model are a good example. For example, the pattern of differences among the four high-frequency means μ_{hl} express the effects of both signals and of their interaction. Any of these sets of parameters can be reparameterized to isolate the influence of each signal and of their interaction. This transformation is essentially the same as that used to express the means in a 2 × 2 Analysis of Variance as main effects and interactions. Using a notation adapted from the log-linear models, μ_{hl} is

$$\mu_{hl} = \mu + \mu_{H(h)} + \mu_{L(l)} + \mu_{HL(hl)} \,. \tag{11}$$

Summation-to-zero constraints in the manner of Equation 10 are required to identify the parameters. With this reparameterization, the four terms on the right describe the overall center of the means, the main-effect shift in mean due to the high-frequency signal, the main-effect shift due to the low-frequency signal, and the interaction of these effects. This form of parameterization is conventional for the log-linear models used in the tests of the conditional-independence hypotheses, but to simplify our notation we have not parameterized the bivariate Gaussian model and the multiplicative-association model in this way, preferring to emphasize the pattern of values, as in Figure 9.1. However, where this type of reparameterization is applicable the revised parameter is noted in brackets in Table 9.7. Only for the parameter μ_{hl} have we listed the main effect and interaction terms separately.

The techniques we have described are essentially data-driven. Except for the broad signal detection model and the context of General Recognition Theory, we do not appeal to any facts from visual theory in our analysis. This atheoretical character increases the applicability to other senses and other forms of perceptual interaction of both the concurrent detection design and its analysis. Of course, we believe that the effects we identify have specific implications for visual theory. An exciting class of models, which we have only begun to explore, links that theory to the statistical models.

ACKNOWLEDGMENT

This work was supported in part by a UCLA Faculty Research Grant to TDW and by US Public Health Service Grant No. EY00360 from the National Institutes of Health to James P. Thomas (renewal, Thomas & LAO). We thank Greg Ashby, Eric Holman, and an anonymous reviewer for comments and suggestions.

III DETECTION, IDENTIFICATION, AND CATEGORIZATION

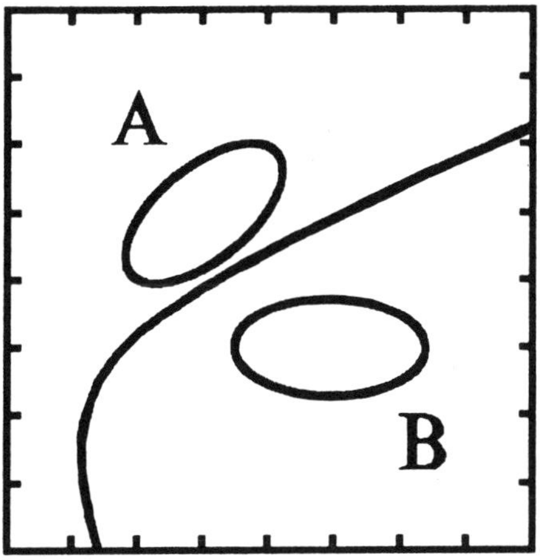

10 Simultaneous Detection and Identification

James P. Thomas
Lynn A. Olzak
University of California at Los Angeles

INTRODUCTION

This chapter concerns the analysis of detection and identification data obtained in psychophysical experiments. The theory and analyses we present were developed in the course of investigating mechanisms underlying visual pattern perception, but are easily generalized to other sensory domains. Specifically, we describe a multidimensional vector model of visual processing and illustrate its application in identifying properties of underlying processing mechanisms. In a general discussion of the model, we consider various questions about the nature of the underlying sensory mechanisms, the internal noise process, and the decision process, including effects of response bias and stimulus uncertainty. Many of these concepts are introduced in the context of the familiar yes-no or rating procedures of Signal Detection Theory. However, the focus of the chapter is on the theoretical analysis of data from the 2 × 2 paradigm, a psychophysical procedure that simultaneously compares the ability to detect the presence of a faint visual stimulus with the ability to identify various properties of that same stimulus. We describe analyses for estimating bandwidths of underlying mechanisms, tests for independence among mechanisms, and provide a brief example in which we test whether the stimulus properties of brightness and darkness are processed via an opponent (bipolar) mechanism or by separate unipolar pathways.

Research Goals

The model and experiments described have the general goal of validating and refining one view, described here, of how local spatial patterns are represented in the visual system. The central concept in both theory and experiment is the psychophysically defined, spatially tuned pathway. This pathway is simultaneously tuned in the space domain (it responds only to a small patch of the visual field) and in the Fourier domain (it responds only to a restricted range of spatial Fourier components, e.g., limited bands of orientations and spatial frequencies). The research has had three specific goals. The first has been to gather additional evidence for the existence of such pathways. The second goal has been to evaluate the role of such pathways in mediating both detection and identification of spatial patterns. The central question here has been whether the representation provided by tuned pathways is the common basis for performance of a wide range of detection, discrimination, and identification tasks. The third goal has been to further define the properties of the pathways themselves. Here the questions have been about the bandwidths of the pathways with respect to spatial frequency and orientation, about the effect of stimulus strength (contrast) on the representation, and about how activity in one pathway affects activity in another.

The Approach

The general approach has been to construct a model of detection and identification in which the representation used in both tasks is the vector of responses by tuned pathways. To the extent that such a model accurately describes both kinds of judgments, the proposition of a common representation is supported. In particular, the model should accurately describe the relationship between the ability to detect the presence of a faint stimulus and to identify its properties and how both abilities are affected by the contrast of the stimuli. Another purpose of the model has been to estimate the bandwidths of the pathways, with respect to orientation and spatial frequency, from the observed relationships between detection and identification performance. Finally, these relationships have been used to test assumptions that the pathways are stochastically independent and do not inhibit one another.

Related Work

Development of the present model has benefited from a rich history of closely related theory and experimentation, on the one hand, and a large group of contemporaries working on the same or similar problems, on the other hand. The basic notion that a stimulus is represented by the pattern of responses in tuned pathways is rooted in Mueller's Doctrine of Specific Nerve Energies and was applied by Helmholtz to the problems of color and pitch perception. The vector model of detection and discrimination described in the third section has its roots in the line-element models of Helmholtz and later workers. At the same time, the model draws heavily from Signal Detection Theory, particularly the work of Tanner (1956). The concepts of bandwidth, and of how such interactions as masking, cross-adaptation, and summation at threshold are related to bandwidth, are closely related to the concept of critical band in psychoacoustics. The formulation presented has gradually evolved, on the one hand, from our own work on detection and identification (Furchner, Thomas, & Campbell, 1977; Olzak, 1981, 1985, 1986; Olzak & Thomas, 1981; Thomas, 1968, 1970; Thomas & Gille, 1979; Thomas, Gille, & Barker, 1982; Thomas, Padilla, & Rourke, 1969; Thomas & Shimamura, 1975). On the other hand, this development has been enormously influenced by those who have worked simultaneously on the same or related problems (Campbell & Robson, 1968; Graham, 1989; Graham & Nachmias, 1971; Nachmias, 1974; Nachmias & Weber, 1975; Pantle & Sekuler, 1968; Sachs, Nachmias, & Robson, 1971; Sekuler, 1965; Watson, 1983; Wilson & Bergen, 1979; Wilson & Gelb, 1984).

MULTIDIMENSIONAL VISUAL REPRESENTATION

At a global level, the basic principle of representation would seem to be one of retinotopic projection or spatial isomorphism. The spatial distribution of light that forms the retinal image is represented at the cortex by a spatial distribution of neural activity, and the two distributions are spatially isomorphic in many ways. At a local level, on the other hand, the process appears to be one of multidimensional analysis and representation in which spatial isomorphism per se plays little role. The model described in this chapter addresses how local properties are represented and how they are used in making detection and identification judgments.

The visual scene can be thought of as composed of many local regions or patches. Each region has its own microstructure, and the question is how the properties of this microstructure are represented. At the primary visual cortex, the patch is represented by a distinct, spatially grouped cluster of neurons, often called a module (Hubel & Wiesel, 1962, 1974). The neurons in the module all have their receptive fields in the same patch of the visual field, but they differ from each other with respect to such things as to which eye they respond best or the size and organization of their receptive fields. Many of the cells within the module are spatially tuned in the sense that each responds only if the patch of the visual scene contains certain properties, such as contours or striations at a particular orientation. The anatomical arrangement of the neurons within the module appears to be determined more by the eye that drives them and their spatial tuning properties than by any principle of local spatial isomorphism (DeValois & DeValois, 1988; Hubel & Wiesel, 1962, 1968, 1974). One hypothesis is that these neurons act as local pattern analyzers, breaking the spatial pattern contained in the patch of visual field into basic components. The local pattern is represented at the cortex by a physiological listing of which components are present and their strengths—that is, by a listing of which spatially tuned neurons respond and the rate of activity in each. There is a close analogy to how the cone systems encode color: Each cone system responds to a somewhat different band of wavelengths, and the wavelength content of the color is represented by the list of activity rates in the three cone systems.

The concept of spatially tuned neural pathways has been supported by a wide range of psychophysical results. Briefly stated, these results demonstrate that even though two spatial patterns are superimposed in space and/or time, they fail to interact in many ways unless they share common pattern elements. For example, the visibility of a pattern composed of vertical stripes is unaffected by superimposing a mask composed of horizontal stripes. Such results have been interpreted to mean that even though the patterns are imaged on the same patch of retina and illuminate the same population of photoreceptors, at some more central level they activate completely separate groups of neurons. Such a separation of effect implies that individual neurons respond only if certain stimulus elements are present and that the character of this tuning differs from one neuron to another. Graham (1985, 1989) has reviewed the many different kinds of spatial and temporal tuning that are indicated by the psychophysical results.

Spatial Fourier analysis has been a useful tool in unifying the physiological and psychophysical results (Robson, 1983). Just as any sound can be represented by a list of pure tone components, varying in amplitude, frequency, and phase, so any spatial pattern can be represented by a list of sinusoidal grating components varying in contrast, spatial frequency, orientation, and spatial phase. The spatial tuning of many cortical cells is well characterized by saying that they respond to only a limited band of spatial Fourier components. That is, if one wants to activate such a cell with a grating stimulus, the grating must not only be imaged within the receptive field of the cell, it must also lie within a restricted band of orientations and within a restricted band of spatial frequencies (DeValois, Albrecht, and Thorell, 1982; DeValois, Yund, & Hepler, 1982; Schiller, Finlay, & Volman, 1976a, 1976b). On the psychophysical side, spatial Fourier analysis also helps to describe the spatial selectivity of many interaction phenomena. Two stimuli interact with one another only if they contain similar Fourier components. For example, adapting to one grating stimulus affects the visibility of a subsequently viewed grating only if the two stimuli are similar in both spatial frequency and orientation. Comparison of the frequency and orientation ranges over which such psychophysical interactions occur with the ranges of frequencies and orientations to which individual cortical neurons respond has supported the hypothesis that the psychophysical interaction occurs only if the stimuli activate common groups of neurons.

THE VECTOR MODEL

Properties of the Individual Pathway

The basic element of the model is the individual tuned pathway. Each patch of the visual field is served by many pathways that differ from each other with respect to their sensitivities to various local properties of the stimulus. The sensitivities could be defined along any set of dimensions, but the usual practice is to define them with respect to local Fourier components, specifically with respect to the orientation, spatial frequency, and phase of the components. Graham (1985, 1989) provides a detailed examination of the stimulus dimensions for which selectivity or tuning has been demonstrated psychophysically.

Each pathway is modeled as a linear filter followed by a (possibly) nonlinear transducer function, with noise added at a third stage. The output of the linear filter is jointly determined by the sensitivity of the pathway to the stimulus and the contrast (or other measure of physical strength) of the stimulus. For simplicity, the pathway is considered to give a single response on each presentation of the stimulus. The response is determined as follows:

$$\boldsymbol{r}_{ij} = \psi[S_{ij}C_j] + \boldsymbol{e}_i \,, \qquad (1)$$

where $\boldsymbol{r}_{ij}$ is the response of pathway i to stimulus j, S_{ij} is the sensitivity of pathway i to stimulus j and is determined by which Fourier components stimulus j contains, C_j is the contrast of the stimulus, ψ is a positive function, and $\boldsymbol{e}_i$ is a random variable representing internal noise. The output of the linear filter stage is given by the product $S_{ij}C_j$. When stimuli are near the detection threshold, the transducer function ψ closely approximates a power function (Thomas, 1983, 1985).

In most models, each pathway is assumed to respond only to local Fourier components that lie within a limited band of spatial frequencies and, at the same time, within a limited band of orientations. One goal of the research described in this chapter has been to estimate the widths of these bands. The term S_{ij} depends on whether the stimulus contains local Fourier components that lie within the joint frequency-orientation sensitivity band of the pathway. Specifically,

$$S_{ij} = \int\int S_i(F, \mathrm{O})L_j(\mathrm{F}, \mathrm{O})\, d\mathrm{F}\, d\mathrm{O} \,, \qquad (2)$$

where $S_i(F, \mathrm{O})$ is the Fourier spectrum of the sensitivity function of the pathway and $L_j(F, \mathrm{O})$ is the Fourier spectrum of the stimulus, given that the stimulus has unit contrast. For additional discussions of pathway sensitivity functions, see Olzak and Thomas, (1986), Thomas (1970), Watson (1983), and Wilson and Gelb (1984).

A critical assumption of this model, and most other models of spatial vision, is that the sensitivity term S_{ij} is independent of the contrast of the stimulus, C_j, and the response of the pathway, $\boldsymbol{r}_{ij}$. Thus, the pathway sensitivity functions are fixed parameters of the visual representation. Relaxing this assumption greatly reduces the power of the models.

Another important set of assumptions concerns the internal noise term $\boldsymbol{e}_i$. It is assumed that $\boldsymbol{e}_i$ is a zero-mean random variable with Gaussian distribution. It has been proposed that the variance of the noise increases as a positive function of the pathway response to the stimulus (Green & Swets, 1974; Nachmias & Kocher, 1970; Thomas, 1983). However, direct tests have failed to support this hypothesis for conditions like those discussed in this chapter (Smith and Thomas,

1989). Therefore, it will be assumed that the noise has unit variance in all pathways and under all conditions. For the present, it will also be assumed that the pathways are stochastically independent of one another—that is, the random variations in e_i are uncorrelated from one pathway to another (i.e., perceptual independence; see Chaps. 8 and 9). However, as noted in the introduction, one purpose in developing the model was to test the assumption of stochastic independence, and tests of the assumption are described later.

Given these assumptions about the internal noise, the expected response, R_{ij}, of pathway i to stimulus j is

$$R_{ij} = \psi[S_{ij}C_j] \ . \qquad (3)$$

The output of the linear filter stage of each pathway may take negative or positive values. An important question is whether R_{ij} also takes positive and negative values. Two extreme cases will be examined. The first possibility is that the pathway responds symmetrically in the positive and negative directions. Specifically,

$$\psi[-(S_{ij}C_j)] = -\psi[S_{ij}C_j] \ . \qquad (4)$$

Following Klein (1985), pathways that respond in this fashion are termed bipolar pathways. The second possibility is that each pathway responds only positively. That is, its expected response is zero if the output of the filter stage is negative. Such a pathway is called unipolar. Full perception of the visual scene requires that unipolar pathways come in pairs, the sensitivity functions of the two members of each pair differing only in sign. That is, if the paired pathways are i and i′,

$$S_{i'j} = -S_{ij} \ .$$

As an illustration, consider two stimuli: one is a bar that is lighter than its background by a given amount; the other is a bar that is darker than the background by the same amount. A bipolar pathway responds to both stimuli, and the expected responses differ only in sign, being positive in one case and negative in the other. A unipolar pathway, on the other hand, responds only to one bar. The set of pathways that respond to the light bar are entirely different from the set of pathways that respond to the dark bar.

By giving oppositely signed responses to stimuli of opposite contrasts, the bipolar pathways embody the antagonism between perceived lightness and darkness that has been recognized since the time of Hering. The unipolar pathways, on the other hand, embody the separate transmission of information about lightness and darkness that is suggested by the existence of distinct on- and off-pathways in the visual system. (See Fiorentini, Baumgartner, Magnussen, Schiller, & Thomas, 1990, for a discussion of both issues.) The question addressed by experiments to be presented later is, which type of pathway provides the best model of simultaneous detection and identification?

Representation of the Visual Scene

It is assumed that the responses of the tuned pathways constitute the entire representation of the visual scene. Thus, each presentation of a stimulus is represented by a vector of n values, each value being the response of one of the n different tuned pathways. Geometrically, the stimulus is represented by a point $\mathbf{r}_j$ in an n-dimensional space, each dimension of the space representing the response of one tuned pathway. The coordinates of the point $\mathbf{r}_j$ are the responses r_{ij} of the individual pathways.

Because of internal noise, the values in the vector fluctuate from one presentation of the stimulus to another. Over many presentations, the geometric representation of the stimulus is an n-dimensional distribution of points. Given the assumptions of Gaussian unit noise in each pathway and stochastic independence between pathways, this distribution is n-dimensional Gaussian with covariance matrix equal to unity. The distribution is centered on the expected response $\mathbf{R}_j$ to the stimulus. The coordinates of $\mathbf{R}_j$ are the expected responses R_{ij} of the individual pathways.

The Perceptual Task

The task of the viewer is to identify which of m different stimulus situations has been presented on a given occasion or trial. If one of the possible situations is a null stimulus, say, a visual field that is uniform or contains only random noise, the task involves a detection component. In many of the situations to be discussed, m = 2. If one of the two situations is a uniform field and the other a structured stimulus, the task is one of simple detection. If both alternatives are structured stimuli, then the task is a simple discrimination.

COMPARING DETECTION AND DISCRIMINATION: YES-NO PROCEDURES

The main topic of this chapter is the analysis of detection and discrimination judgments that are made simultaneously. However, the simplest way to introduce many of the concepts and issues involved is to begin by analyzing the conceptually simpler case in which detection and discrimination judgments are made in separate sets of observations. We start with the situation analyzed by Tanner (1956), and build upon his analysis.

There are three stimulus alternatives: **N**, the null stimulus, which in these experiments is usually a uniform field; **A**, a spatial pattern of low contrast; and **B**, a similar, but not identical, pattern of low contrast. In three separate sets of trials, d''s are measured for the detection of **A** (i.e., discrimination of **A** from **N**), detection of **B** (i.e., discrimination of **B** from **N**), and discrimination of **A** from

B. On each trial, only one of the two alternatives to be distinguished is presented, and the subject judges which. For our analysis the judgment is binary (i.e., yes or no, **A** or **B**). However, the analysis is easily extended to include rating judgments.

Decision Process

Regardless of which d' is measured, the task of the viewer is to distinguish between two alternatives. Figure 10.1 presents the vector representation of the task for the case in which the two alternatives are stimulus **A** and stimulus **B**, and $\mathbf{R_A}$ and $\mathbf{R_B}$ are the expected responses to stimuli **A** and **B**, respectively. The coordinates for $\mathbf{R_A}$ are $R_{i\mathbf{A}}$, the expected responses of the individual pathways; $\mathbf{R_B}$ is analogously located. The distance between the expected responses, $D_{\mathbf{A,B}}$, is the Euclidean sum of the differences between expected responses to the two stimuli in the individual pathways:

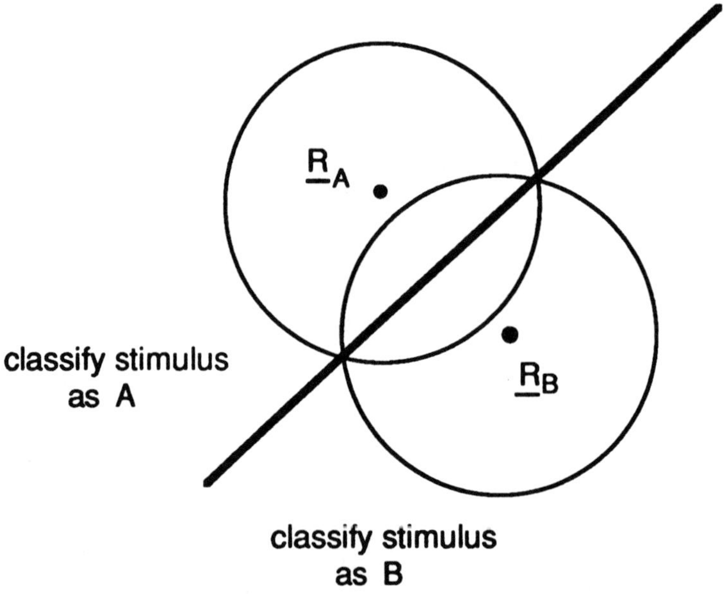

FIG. 10.1. Discrimination between stimulus **A** and stimulus **B**. $\mathbf{R_A}$ and $\mathbf{R_B}$ are the expected responses to stimuli **A** and **B**, respectively. Each circle is a cross section through the n-dimensional distribution of responses to that stimulus and is a contour of equal likelihood. The heavy line is a segment of the intersection of the decision surface with a plane containing the expected responses. The viewer classifies each stimulus presentation as **A** or **B** according to which side of the decision surface the observed response lies.

$$D_{\mathbf{A},\mathbf{B}} = \left[\sum_{i=1}^{n} (R_{i\mathbf{A}} - R_{i\mathbf{B}})^2 \right]^{0.5} . \tag{5}$$

The decision process is represented geometrically by constructing a decision surface that divides the space into two parts, one containing $\mathbf{R_A}$ and the other containing $\mathbf{R_B}$. A particular presentation is classified as stimulus **A** or stimulus **B** according to which part of the space contains the observed response r. If there is no bias and the observer follows a likelihood criterion, the decision surface is a plane perpendicular to, and that bisects, the line segment joining the two expected responses.

Algebraically, the decision process consists of calculating the Euclidean distance between the observed response and the expected response for each stimulus and selecting the stimulus for which this distance is shorter (i.e., minimum distance classification; see chap. 16). Specifically, when there is no response bias, the decision rule is:

$$\text{Select stimulus } \mathbf{A} \text{ if } \left[\sum_{i=1}^{n} (\boldsymbol{r}_i - R_{i\mathbf{A}})^2 \right]^{0.5} < \left[\sum_{i=1}^{n} (\boldsymbol{r}_i - R_{i\mathbf{B}})^2 \right]^{0.5} ,$$

or, equivalently,

$$\text{Select } \mathbf{A} \text{ if } \sum_{i=1}^{n} (\boldsymbol{r}_i - R_{i\mathbf{A}})^2 - \sum_{i=1}^{n} (\boldsymbol{r}_i - R_{i\mathbf{B}})^2 < 0 . \tag{6}$$

The difference in Equation 6 has an expected value of $-D^2_{\mathbf{A},\mathbf{B}}$ when stimulus **A** is presented and $+D^2_{\mathbf{A},\mathbf{B}}$ when stimulus **B** is presented. The standard deviation is $2D_{\mathbf{A},\mathbf{B}}$ in either case. Thus, d' for the discrimination is $D_{\mathbf{A},\mathbf{B}}$.[1] The probability of

---

[1]Proof that $d' = D_{\mathbf{A},\mathbf{B}}$:

Consider the case in which stimulus **A** is presented. In this case $\boldsymbol{r}_i = R_{i\mathbf{A}} + \boldsymbol{e}_i$, where $\boldsymbol{e}_i$ is a zero mean random variable with unit variance and is uncorrelated from pathway to pathway. When this value for $\boldsymbol{r}_i$ is substituted in Equation 6, the decision statistic becomes

$$\sum_{i=1}^{n} (R_{i\mathbf{A}} + \boldsymbol{e}_i - R_{i\mathbf{A}})^2 - \sum_{i=1}^{n} (R_{i\mathbf{A}} + \boldsymbol{e}_i - R_{i\mathbf{B}})^2 ,$$

which simplifies to

$$- \sum_{i=1}^{n} [(R_{i\mathbf{A}} - \mathrm{R}_{i\mathbf{B}})^2 + 2\boldsymbol{e}_i(R_{i\mathbf{A}} - R_{i\mathbf{B}})] .$$

The expected value of this statistic is

$$- \sum_{i=1}^{n} (R_{i\mathbf{A}} - R_{i\mathbf{B}})^2 = -D^2_{\mathbf{A},\mathbf{B}} .$$

a correct response, $p(C)$, that is, selecting **A** when **A** is presented or **B** when **B** is presented, is given by the expression

$$z(C) = \frac{D_{\mathbf{A.B}}}{2}, \tag{7}$$

where $z(C)$ is the standard normal deviate corresponding to $p(C)$.

Figure 10.2 shows the representation of all three stimuli. Under the model, the distance $D_{\mathbf{A.B}}$ is given by the d' for discrimination between stimuli **A** and **B**, $D_{\mathbf{N.A}}$ is given by the d′ for detection of **A,** and $D_{\mathbf{N.B}}$ is given by d' for the detection of **B.** Given these three distances, the angle ϕ formed by the vectors representing the expected responses to stimuli **A** and **B** can be calculated.

The usual question in these experiments is whether stimuli **A** and **B** are processed independently of each other. If the pathways that respond to **A** are entirely different than the pathways that respond to **B**, then the vectors representing **A** and **B** will be orthogonal and angle ϕ will be 90°. Note that in this case the model predicts that the d' for discrimination will be greater than either d' for detection. This counterintuitive prediction has been confirmed a number of times (Kerr, 1974; Olzak & Thomas, 1981; Thomas & Shimamura, 1975). On the other hand, if stimuli **A** and **B** are less than a bandwidth apart, some of the pathways that respond to one stimulus will also respond to the other, and the angle between the vectors will be less than 90°. Finally, if some of the pathways that respond to stimuli **A** and **B** are bipolar and give oppositely signed responses to the two stimuli, the angle between the vectors will be greater than 90°.

Response Bias

Bias is represented by shifting the decision surface closer to one stimulus or the other. The shift is a translation along the line joining the two expected responses: thus, the surface remains a plane perpendicular to the line. Algebraically, the bias is represented by generalizing Equation 6 as follows:

$$\text{Select } \mathbf{A} \text{ if } \sum_{i=1}^{n} (r_i - R_{i\mathbf{A}})^2 - \sum_{i=1}^{n} (r_i - R_{i\mathbf{B}})^2 < \mathrm{K}, \tag{8}$$

where K represents the bias.

The standard deviation of the statistic is

$$2\left[\sum_{i=1}^{n} (R_{i\mathbf{A}} - R_{i\mathbf{B}})^2\right]^{0.5} = 2D_{\mathbf{A.B}}.$$

When stimulus **B** is presented, $\boldsymbol{r}_i = R_{i\mathbf{B}} + \boldsymbol{e}_i$. By analogous substitution and simplification it is found that, when stimulus **B** is presented, the decision statistic has an expected value of $D^2_{\mathbf{A.B}}$ and a standard deviation of $2D_{\mathbf{A.B}}$. Thus, $d' = [D^2_{\mathbf{A.B}} - (-D^2_{\mathbf{A.B}})] / 2D_{\mathbf{A.B}} = D_{\mathbf{A.B}}$.

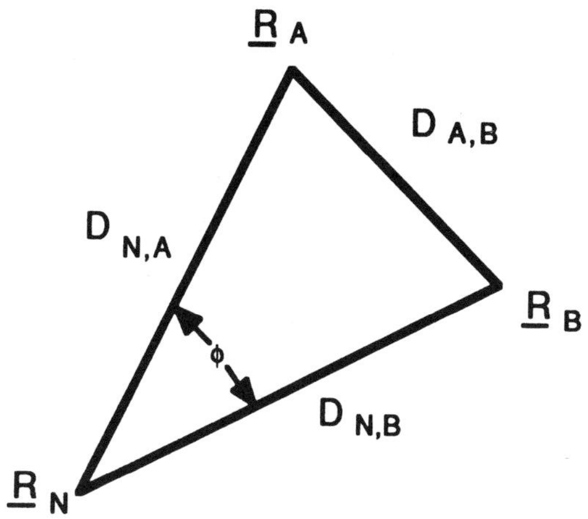

FIG. 10.2. Representation of all three stimulus conditions in vector space. $\mathbf{R}_\mathbf{A}$, $\mathbf{R}_\mathbf{B}$, and $\mathbf{R}_\mathbf{N}$ are the expected responses to stimuli **A**, **B**, and **N**, respectively. The values of d' for detecting **A**, detecting **B**, and discriminating **A** from **B** are measured in separate blocks of trials and used to estimate $D_{\mathbf{N,A}}$, $D_{\mathbf{N,B}}$, $D_{\mathbf{A,B}}$, and ϕ.

Stimulus Uncertainty

Stimulus uncertainty can be introduced by having the observer watch for both stimuli in a detection task. That is, on some trials stimulus **N** is presented, on some trials stimulus **A** is presented, and on the remaining trials stimulus **B** is presented. The task of the observer is to give a binary judgment on each trial: yes, a stimulus was presented; or no, a stimulus was not presented. Following the general decision process described earlier, the observer responds "no stimulus presented" only if the observed response, r, lies closer to the expected response to the null alternative, $\mathbf{R}_\mathbf{N}$, than to either of the expected responses to the stimuli, $\mathbf{R}_\mathbf{A}$ and $\mathbf{R}_\mathbf{B}$. The boundary that represents this decision process is formed by two intersecting planes: one bisects and is perpendicular to the line segment connecting $\mathbf{R}_\mathbf{N}$ and $\mathbf{R}_\mathbf{A}$; the other bisects and is perpendicular to the line segment connecting $\mathbf{R}_\mathbf{N}$ and $\mathbf{R}_\mathbf{B}$. The heavy line in Figure 10.3 represents the intersection of this boundary with the plane containing the expected responses.

The effect of the uncertainty can be seen by comparing the responses the viewer makes in the uncertainty task with those expected when the task is simple discrimination between **N** and **A**. In the latter case, the decision boundary is a single plane, whose intersection with the expected response plane is shown by the broken line in Figure 10.3. For the most part, the judgments of the observer will be the same in the two tasks. However, when the observed response r falls in the wedge of space that projects into the crosshatched area, the viewer responds differently in the two tasks: The response is "no stimulus present" when the task

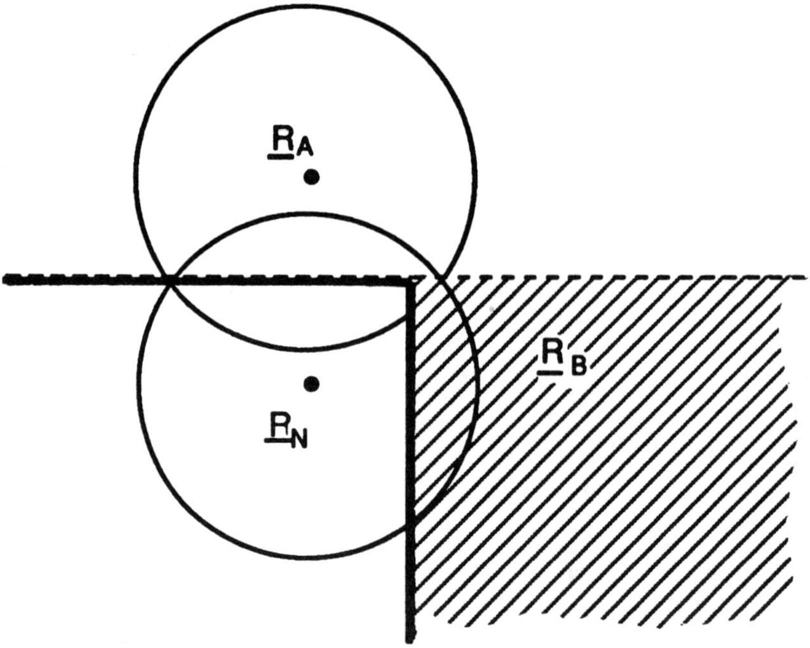

FIG. 10.3. The effect of stimulus uncertainty. In a simple discrimination between stimuli **N** and **A**, the viewer uses the decision surface represented by the broken line. In the uncertainty case, the viewer uses the decision surface represented by the two-segmented heavy line. Responses in the crosshatched area elicit "no" responses in the simple task, but "yes" responses in the uncertainty task. There is an increase in false alarms when stimulus **N** is presented, but not a commensurate increase in hits when stimulus **A** is presented. (The contour of equal likelihood for stimulus **B** is omitted for clarity.)

is simple discrimination between **N** and **A**, and the response is "yes, stimulus present" in the uncertainty task. If responses are classified as hits and false alarms, the change increases the rates of both. However, given the assumption of unit Gaussian noise, the increase in false alarms overbalances the increase in hit rate. If d' is computed from these hit and false alarm rates in the usual fashion, the value obtained underestimates $D_{\mathbf{N,A}}$ by an amount that depends on (a) the lengths of the vectors representing **A** and **B** (i.e., on $D_{\mathbf{N,A}}$ and $D_{\mathbf{N,B}}$), and (b) the similarity of **A** and **B** (i.e., the angle ϕ). (For more detailed treatments of stimulus uncertainty in the context of multiple, tuned-pathway models, see Kramer, Graham, & Yager, 1985, and Pelli, 1985.)

A More General Test of Independent Processing

Given the present model, two stimuli are processed independently when $\phi = 90°$. The computation of this angle from the d''s for detecting **A** and **B** and discriminating **A** from **B** requires the assumption that noise is unit Gaussian and uncorrelated from one pathway to another. Olzak and Thomas (1981) proposed a test of independent processing that uses neither the Gaussian assumption nor the Euclidean distance metric, which flows from the Gaussian assumption. In the Olzak-Thomas paradigm a fourth stimulus alternative is added. The fourth stimulus, **A** + **B**, is a compound formed by superimposing **A** and **B** in time and space. Figure 10.4 shows the representation of the four stimuli for the condition in which **A** and **B** are processed independently of one another. Given the present model, the distances $D_{\mathbf{N},\mathbf{A}+\mathbf{B}}$ and $D_{\mathbf{A},\mathbf{B}}$ are equal and performance in discriminating **A** and **B** must equal performance in detecting the compound, that is, discriminating **A** + **B** from **N**. Olzak and Thomas show that the prediction of equal performance in these two tasks holds even when the Gaussian and Euclidean distance metric assumptions are dropped.

Olzak and Thomas tested the prediction by using grating stimuli that differed in spatial frequencies by factors of 2,3,4, and 6. They found that when the frequencies of the stimuli differed by factors of 4 and 6, performance in discriminating **A** and **B** was better than performance in detecting **A** + **B**. Such results would be obtained (a) if noise is positively correlated from one pathway to another, and/or (b) if some bipolar pathways are involved that give positively signed responses to one stimulus and negatively signed responses to the other.

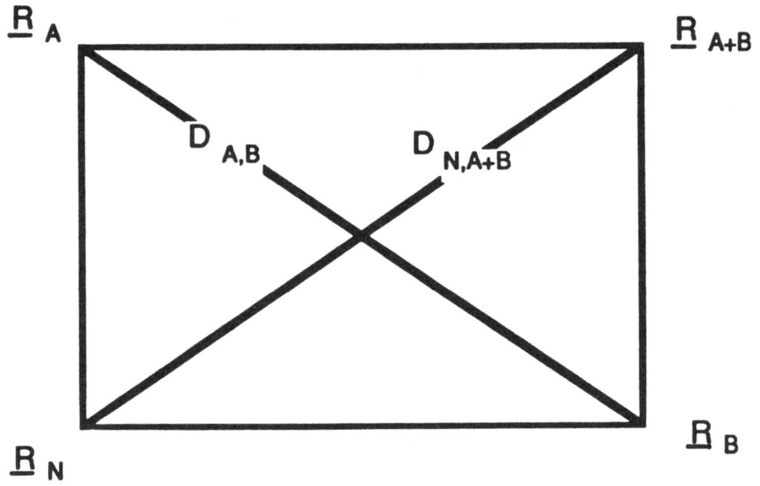

FIG. 10.4. Representation of the four stimulus conditions in the Olzak-Thomas paradigm. $\mathbf{R_N}$, $\mathbf{R_A}$, $\mathbf{R_B}$, and $\mathbf{R_{A+B}}$ are the expected responses to stimuli **N**, **A**, **B**, and the compound **A** + **B**, respectively. The values of d' for detecting the compound stimulus **A** + **B** and for discriminating between stimuli **A** and **B** are measured in separate blocks of trials and used to estimate $D_{\mathbf{N,A+B}}$ and $D_{\mathbf{A,B}}$. When the stimuli **A** and **B** are independently processed, angle ϕ is 90° and performance on these two tasks is predicted to be equal.

The paradigm does not permit distinguishing between these alternatives. However, Chapter 9 describes a paradigm that permits some distinctions to be made.

SIMULTANEOUS DETECTION AND IDENTIFICATION: THE 2 × 2 PROCEDURE

Measuring detection and identification performances in separate blocks of trials, as described in the last section, has two disadvantages: The data on detection and identification are not as comparable as they would be if gathered at the same time, and the process is time consuming. Both disadvantages can be overcome by adopting a procedure in which the subject makes a detection judgment and an identification judgment on each trial. The simultaneous judgment procedure most often used in vision research is a modified two-alternative temporal forced choice, often called the 2 × 2. Besides the benefits just mentioned, this procedure has the additional advantage that the criterion for independent processing does not depend on the assumption that the noise in each pathway has a Gaussian distribution.

We begin by describing the 2 × 2 procedure and then turn to how it has been modeled.

Procedure

The procedure uses three stimuli: **N**, the null stimulus, which is usually a uniform field in vision research; **A**, a faint test stimulus that is imperfectly detectable; and **B**, a similar faint test stimulus. The purpose of the procedure is to compare the ability to distinguish between **A** and **B** with the ability to detect the presence of each. In most cases (and we assume this), stimuli **A** and **B** are equated for detectability to ensure that simple differences in visibility do not aid discrimination.

Each trial contains two temporal observation intervals, sufficiently separated in time to ensure that activity initiated in the visual pathways during one interval is independent of activity initiated in the other. Two of the three stimuli are presented on each trial: The blank stimulus **N** is presented in one observation interval, and one of the two test stimuli, **A** or **B**, is presented in the other interval. Thus, there are four types of trials: **AN** (in which test stimulus **A** is presented in the first interval and **N** in the second interval), **NA**, **BN**, and **NB**.

At the end of each trial, the subject indicates which of the four different stimulus combinations has been presented. The four possible judgments will be called $J_{\mathbf{AN}}$ (meaning the judgment that test stimulus **A** was presented in the first interval and **N** was presented in the second interval), $J_{\mathbf{NA}}$, $J_{\mathbf{BN}}$, and $J_{\mathbf{NB}}$.

The subject's judgment is conceptualized as having two components: The identification component indicates which test stimulus the subject judges to have been presented; the detection component indicates in which interval the test stimulus was presented. These two components are independently scored correct or incorrect. That is, the identification is scored correct if the subject selects the correct test stimulus, regardless of whether the correct interval is selected. Similarly, the detection is scored correct if the correct interval is chosen, regardless of whether the correct test stimulus is selected.

The primary data take the form of two probabilities, of correct detection and of correct identification, for each of the four types of trials. For example, for trials of type **AN**, these probabilities are $p(\mathrm{D}|\mathbf{AN})$ and $p(\mathrm{I}|\mathbf{AN})$, respectively, and are defined as follows:

$$p(\mathrm{D}|\mathbf{AN}) = p(\mathrm{J}_{\mathbf{AN}}|\mathbf{AN}) + p(\mathrm{J}_{\mathbf{BN}}|\mathbf{AN}) , \tag{9}$$

$$p(\mathrm{I}|\mathbf{AN}) = p(\mathrm{J}_{\mathbf{AN}}|\mathbf{AN}) + p(\mathrm{J}_{\mathbf{NA}}|\mathbf{AN}) . \tag{10}$$

The usual practice is to collapse the data over intervals to obtain the four probabilities

$$p(\mathrm{D}|\mathbf{A}) = \tfrac{1}{2}[p(D|\mathbf{AN}) + p(\mathrm{D}|\mathbf{NA})] , \tag{11}$$

$$p(\mathrm{D}|\mathbf{B}) = \tfrac{1}{2}[p(D|\mathbf{BN}) + p(\mathrm{D}|\mathbf{NB})] , \tag{12}$$

$$p(\mathrm{I}|\mathbf{A}) = \tfrac{1}{2}[p(I|\mathbf{AN}) + p(\mathrm{I}|\mathbf{NA})] , \tag{13}$$

$$p(\mathrm{I}|\mathbf{B}) = \tfrac{1}{2}[p(I|\mathbf{BN}) + p(\mathrm{I}|\mathbf{NB})] . \tag{14}$$

The detection measures $p(\mathrm{D}|\mathbf{A})$ and $p(\mathrm{D}|\mathbf{B})$ are examined to determine if the requirement that the two test stimuli be equally detectable has been met. If they are acceptable, the two values are averaged to yield a single measure of detection performance, $p(\mathrm{D})$. Given equal detectability of stimuli **A** and **B**, a difference between $p(\mathrm{I}|\mathbf{A})$ and $p(\mathrm{I}|\mathbf{B})$ indicates a bias in favor of one stimulus or the other. The usual practice is to reduce the effects of any such bias by averaging the two values to obtain a single measure of identification performance, $p(\mathrm{I})$. Thus,

$$p(\mathrm{D}) = \tfrac{1}{2}[p(\mathrm{D}|\mathbf{A}) + p\ (\mathrm{D}|\mathbf{B})] \tag{15}$$

and

$$p(\mathrm{I}) = \tfrac{1}{2}[p(\mathrm{I}|\mathbf{A}) + p(\mathrm{I}|\mathbf{B})] . \tag{16}$$

In many experiments, the observations are repeated with the test stimuli set at different physical strengths (but always equated to each other in detectability at each strength level) in order to obtain psychometric functions for the probability of correct detection and the probability of correct identification. The properties of these psychometric functions help to constrain models of detection and identification. One of the most important properties is that when *log* $z(\mathrm{D})$ and *log* $z(\mathrm{I})$ are plotted as a function of the log of stimulus strength, the two psychometric functions have the same shape and are merely displaced from one another along the performance (vertical) axis (Thomas, 1983). This property has empirical and theoretical importance. The empirical import is that the relationship between detection and identification performances can be described by a single measure: the separation of the two psychometric functions along the performance axis (Thomas, 1983, 1985; Thomas & Gille, 1979). This measure is illustrated in Figure 10.5. The antilog of this separation is called the performance ratio or the I/D ratio, symbolized by θ. The performance ratio approaches 0.0 as the stimuli become so similar as to be indistinguishable, and takes a value of 1.0 when the stimuli are different enough to be processed completely independently. Values greater than 1.0 can be observed when the stimuli are processed by bipolar

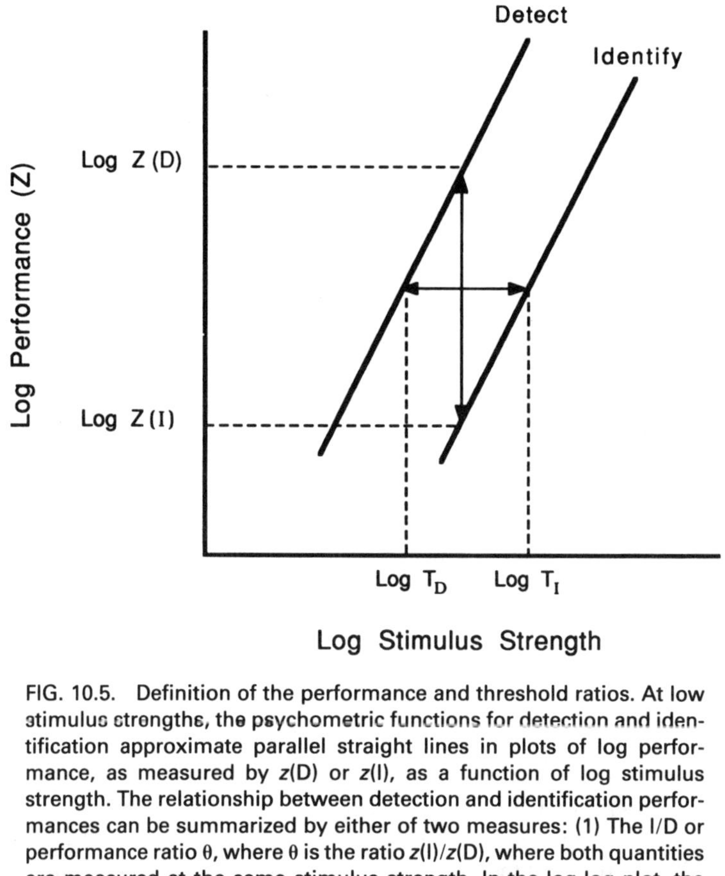

FIG. 10.5. Definition of the performance and threshold ratios. At low stimulus strengths, the psychometric functions for detection and identification approximate parallel straight lines in plots of log performance, as measured by z(D) or z(I), as a function of log stimulus strength. The relationship between detection and identification performances can be summarized by either of two measures: (1) The I/D or performance ratio θ, where θ is the ratio $z(\text{I})/z(\text{D})$, where both quantities are measured at the same stimulus strength. In the log-log plot, the logarithm of this ratio is represented by the vertical separation of the psychometric functions. (2) The threshold ratio. T_D and T_I are the stimulus strengths required to produce $z(\text{D}) = z(\text{I})$ = threshold level of performance. The threshold ratio is the ratio T_I/T_D. In the log-log plot, the logarithm of this ratio is represented by the horizontal separation of the psychometric functions.

pathways, when inhibitory interactions across separate mechanisms are present, or when noise is positively correlated across pathways.

When the range of stimulus strengths is restricted to those for which detection performance can be measured without ceiling effects, the psychometric functions for detection and identification closely approximate straight lines when plotted in log-log coordinates. When only this range is considered, the separation of the functions can also be measured along the stimulus strength axis (Furchner et al., 1977; Watson & Robson, 1981). See Figure 10.5 for an illustration. The antilog of this separation is called the threshold ratio because it is the ratio of the stimulus strengths at which the two types of performance reach a criterion level, or threshold, of accuracy. The threshold ratio is indefinitely large when the stimuli are indistinguishable, and takes a value of 1.0 when the stimuli are processed independently.

The psychometric functions for discrimination between very similar stimuli can be measured over wide ranges of stimulus strength before ceiling effects, if any, are encountered. These functions are negatively accelerated and approach asymptotes at relatively low stimulus strengths. The functions for discriminations of different difficulty are parallel to each other and displaced along the performance axis (Smith & Thomas, 1989; Thomas, 1983). Thus, the I/D ratio can be viewed as a special case of a more general class of performance ratios that describe threshold and suprathreshold discriminations.

Vector Representation of the Procedure

The procedure is modeled by using two orthogonal axes to represent the responses of each tuned pathway. One axis represents the response of the pathway during the first observation interval, and the other axis represents the response during the second interval. The population of pathway responses to each of the four possible stimulus combinations is represented by a 2n-variate Gaussian distribution in a 2n-dimensional space. Each distribution is centered on a point defined by the vector of expected pathway responses to that stimulus combination.

Independent Processing: p(D) = p(I)

Independent processing has three elements: (a) the pathways that respond to stimulus **A** do not respond to stimulus **B**, and vice versa; (b) there are no excitatory or inhibitory interactions between the two sets of pathways; and (c) noise is uncorrelated from one pathway to another. (Element (a) is often called *perceptual separability,* and elements (b) and (c) are associated with *perceptual independence*. Chapters 7–9 provide fuller discussion of perceptual separability and independence.) Given these elements and the assumption of unit-variance Gaussian noise in each pathway, the distributions representing the four different stimulus combinations are identical except for their centroids. Thus, the likelihood of confusing one combination with another depends only on the distance between the respective centroids.

Because the stimuli are equated for detectability, the centroids of the four distributions are equally distant from the origin of the space; that is, the vectors of expected responses defining the centroids are equal in length. If the stimuli are processed independently, each vector is orthogonal to each of the others and the distance between any two centroids equals the distance between any other two. Thus, the likelihood of confusing one stimulus combination with another is the same for all pairs of combinations. Specifically, when the combination **AN** is presented,

$$p(\mathrm{J}_{\mathbf{NA}}|\mathbf{AN}) = p(\mathrm{J}_{\mathbf{BN}}|\mathbf{AN}) = p(\mathrm{J}_{\mathbf{NB}}|\mathbf{AN}) \ , \qquad (17)$$

and so on. When these equalities are substituted in the definitions of detection and identification performance (Equations 9–16), we see that $p(\mathrm{I}) = p(\mathrm{D})$. Thus, equal detection and identification performance is the criterion of independent processing when the 2×2 procedure is used.

In deriving this criterion, we used the assumption of unit-variance Gaussian noise in each pathway. This assumption can be somewhat relaxed without changing the result. For example, the result still holds so long as (a) within each distribution the probability density decreases as a monotonic function of distance from the centroid, and (b) the function is the same for each distribution. As a second example, the criterion can also be derived from classical high-threshold theory by adding to that theory the assumption that, because stimuli **A** and **B** activate completely separate groups of pathways, the viewer will make a correct identification response whenever he or she is in the detect state. This nonparametric or model-free character of the criterion is a major reason for the popularity of the 2×2 procedure.

Estimating Pathway Bandwidths

One application of the 2×2 procedure has been to estimate the bandwidths of the pathways with respect to such stimulus dimensions as orientation (Thomas & Gille, 1979), spatial frequency (Thomas et al., 1982; Watson & Robson, 1981), temporal frequency (Watson & Robson, 1981), and wavelength (Gille, 1984; Mullen & Kulikowski, 1990). In concept, this enterprise is quite simple: One simply varies the separation of the test stimuli, **A** and **B**, along the dimension of interest to define the function relating the performance ratio $z(I)/z(\mathrm{D})$ to stimulus separation. In principle, the ratio is unity only when no pathway responds to both stimuli—that is, when the physical difference between the stimuli equals or exceeds one full bandwidth. Thus, the minimum stimulus separation for which the ratio equals unity is taken as the full bandwidth.

In practice, the method has two difficulties. First, it has been found empirically that the performance ratio increases as a negatively accelerated function of the difference between the stimuli and approaches unity as an asymptote (Gille, 1984; Thomas & Gille, 1979; Thomas et al., 1982). Thus, the minimum stimulus difference for which detection and identification performance are equal cannot be estimated with precision. Second, theoretical simulations have shown that the expected value of the performance ratio closely approximates unity when the stimuli are significantly less than a bandwidth apart (Thomas & Gille, 1979).

The solution to these estimation problems is to make use of the steeply rising portion of the function relating the value of the performance ratio to the physical separation of the stimuli. That is, one needs a model that relates the performance ratio to some measure of independent processing over a wide range of performance ratios and degrees of independence. Such a model has been advanced by Thomas et al. (1982).

The Thomas, Gille, and Barker model takes as its measure of independent processing the angle formed by the two expected vectors of the test stimuli when presented in the same interval (i.e., the angle ϕ as defined earlier). They assumed that the noise in each pathway was unit-variance Gaussian and uncorrelated with noise in other pathways. They derived the following relationship between the performance ratio θ and the angle ϕ formed by the vectors (see p. 1647 of their article)

$$sin \frac{\phi}{2} = \frac{\theta}{(1 + \theta^2)^{0.5}} \ . \tag{18}$$

The relationship defined by Equation 18 is nearly linear from $\phi = 0°$ to $\phi = 90°$, and the following approximation is accurate within error of measurement over this range:

$$\phi = 90\ \theta \ . \tag{19}$$

Bipolar Response to Complementary Stimuli

Many perceptual encoding mechanisms are conceptualized as being bipolar in the sense that they can respond to stimuli by either increasing or decreasing their activity relative to some baseline rate. The opponent color mechanisms are an example. According to opponent color theory, the chroma of a stimulus is encoded by two sets of bipolar pathways. Pathways in one set signal red by increasing their activity, and signal green by decreasing their activity. Pathways in the other set signal yellow and blue in an analogous opponent fashion. The achromatic properties of stimuli are thought to be signaled by a third set of pathways. In Hering's original formulation, these pathways were also bipolar, signaling brightness by an increase in activity and darkness by a decrease. However, recent physiological evidence has suggested that the third group may actually consist of two sets of orthogonal unipolar pathways, one set signaling brightness by an increase in activity and the other set signaling darkness by an increase in activity (Fiorentini et al., 1990). We return to this issue later in the section.

When stimuli are encoded by bipolar pathways, it is possible for identification performance in the 2 × 2 to be more accurate than detection performance; that is, $p(\mathrm{I}) > p(\mathrm{D})$ is possible. Consider the situation in which those pathways that respond to test stimulus **A** either (a) do not respond at all to test stimulus **B** or (b) respond oppositely to **B** than to **A** (i.e., if they respond to **A** by increasing activity, they respond to **B** by decreasing activity, and vice versa). If all pathways that respond to stimulus **A** fall into category 1, then stimuli **A** and **B** are processed independently and $p(\mathrm{I}) = p(\mathrm{D})$. However, if any pathways fall into category 2, then the vectors representing the expected responses to stimuli **A** and **B**, in the same interval, form an angle greater than 90° and $p(\mathrm{I}) > p(\mathrm{D})$. That is, because the angle is greater than 90°, stimulus **A** is less likely to be confused with stimulus **B** presented in the same interval than with either stimulus presented in the other interval. Thus, $p(\mathbf{J_{BN}}|\mathbf{AN})$ is less than either $p(\mathbf{J_{NA}}|\mathbf{AN})$ or $p(\mathbf{J_{NB}}|\mathbf{NA})$ and $p(\mathrm{I}) > p(\mathrm{D})$.

The purest form of bipolar representation occurs in the case of complementary stimuli. For example, red and green are complementary because their chromatic effects are antagonistic to each other, and, when the two colors are combined, their chromatic effects cancel each other. More generally, two stimuli, **A** and **B**, are complementary if, for every pathway i,

$$R_{\mathrm{i}\mathbf{B}} = -R_{\mathrm{i}\mathbf{A}} \,,$$

where $R_{\mathrm{i}\mathbf{A}}$ and $R_{\mathrm{i}\mathbf{B}}$ are the expected responses of the pathway to the two stimuli. In this case, the vectors defining the expected responses to stimuli **A** and **B** within the same interval are collinear. The expected responses to the four stimulus possibilities all lie in a single plane, as illustrated in Figure 10.6.

Klein (1985) and Thomas (1981) independently described a decision model for complementary stimuli that predicts the relative frequencies of the different judgments. In their model, the subject divides the 2n-dimensional response base into four compartments, each containing the expected response to one of the four alternatives. The boundaries between compartments are located according to a likelihood rule; that is, the boundary between any two compartments is the locus of responses that are equally likely given either of the two stimulus alternatives represented. On each trial, the judgment given by the subject is determined by which compartment contains the observed response.

Because the expected responses to the stimulus alternatives lie in a single plane, and given the assumption of uncorrelated unit-variance Gaussian noise in each pathway, the 2n-dimensional response space can be collapsed into the two-dimensional representation in Figure 10.6. The expected responses to stimuli presented in the first interval define one axis of the collapsed space, and the expected responses to stimuli in the second interval define the other axis. The

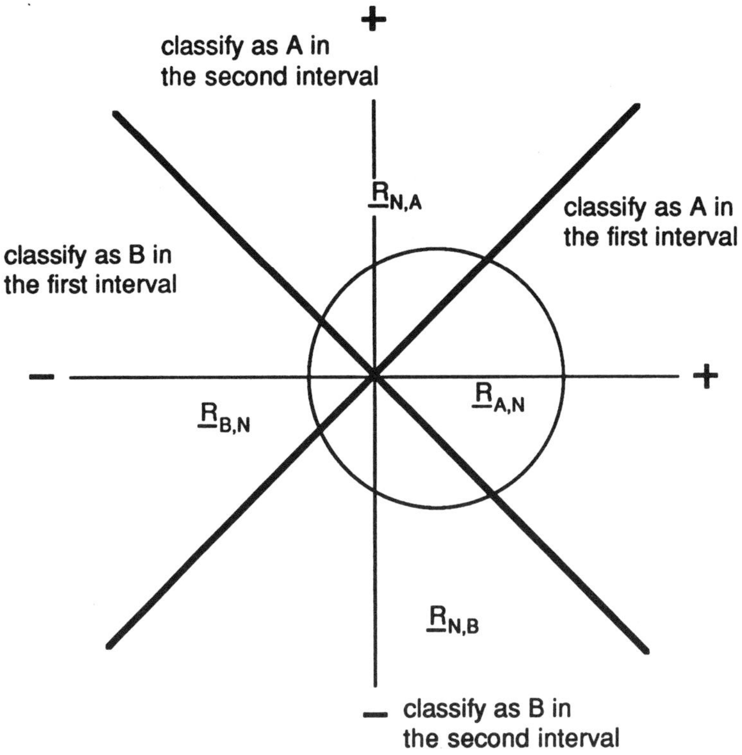

FIG. 10.6. The bipolar 2 × 2 model. $\mathbf{R}_{AN}$, $\mathbf{R}_{BN}$, $\mathbf{R}_{NA}$, and $\mathbf{R}_{NB}$ are the expected responses to stimulus **A** presented in the first interval, **B** presented in the first interval, **A** in the second interval, and **B** in the second interval, respectively. The circle represents a cross section through the 2n-dimensional distribution of responses to **A** in the first interval. The heavy lines represent the decision surface.

vector of pathway responses observed on each trial is represented by its projection onto the plane defined by these axes. The 2n-dimensional distribution of pathway responses that represents each stimulus alternative collapses into a bivariate Gaussian distribution centered on the expected response to that alternative. These bivariate distributions differ from one another only in location and are symmetrically disposed about the origin. The decision boundaries dividing the multidimensional space into four compartments become the diagonal lines that divide the plane into four quadrants. On each trial, the judgment given by the subject is determined by which quadrant contains the projection of the vector of observed pathway responses.

This representation constitutes a model that predicts the relative frequencies of the different possible judgments. The model has one free parameter that, following Klein (1985), we take as the probability of correct identification, $p(\mathrm{I})$.

In terms of the model, $p(\mathrm{I})$ is the probability that the observed response falls on the proximal side of the negative diagonal—that is, on the side nearer the center of the relevant distribution. For example, $p(\mathrm{I}|\mathbf{AN})$ is the probability that the observed response falls above the negative diagonal. Because of the symmetrical disposition of the distributions and decision boundaries, this same value also describes the probability that the response lies on the proximal side of the positive diagonal. To continue the example, $p(\mathrm{I}|\mathbf{AN})$ is also the probability that the response lies below the positive diagonal. Thus, the probabilities of all four possible judgments can be estimated from this one value:

$$p(\mathrm{J}_{\mathbf{AN}}|\mathbf{AN}) = [p(\mathrm{I}|\mathbf{AN})]^2 , \tag{20}$$

$$p(\mathrm{J}_{\mathbf{NA}}|\mathbf{AN}) = p(\mathrm{J}_{\mathbf{NB}}|\mathbf{AN}) = p(\mathrm{I}|\mathbf{AN})\,[1 - p\,(\mathrm{I}|\mathbf{AN})] , \tag{21}$$

$$p(\mathrm{J}_{\mathbf{BN}}|\mathbf{AN}) = [1 - p(\mathrm{I}|\mathbf{AN})]^2 . \tag{22}$$

As Klein (1985) pointed out, the fit of the model can be tested by a χ^2 goodness-of-fit test in order to assess whether the representation is purely bipolar. In practice, one would usually collapse the data over stimuli and intervals and test the following equalities:

$$p(\mathrm{D}, \mathrm{I}) = [p(\mathrm{I})]^2 , \tag{23}$$

$$p(\bar{\mathrm{D}}, \mathrm{I}) = p(\bar{\mathrm{D}}, \bar{\mathrm{I}}) = p(\mathrm{I})[1 - p(\mathrm{I})] , \tag{24}$$

$$p(\mathrm{D}, \bar{\mathrm{I}}) = [1 - p(\mathrm{I})]^2 . \tag{25}$$

Klein applied these tests to two sets of data from the visual psychophysics literature. In one case, in which the task was to detect the motion of a dot and identify the direction of motion, the data were consistent with bipolar representation (Allik, Dzhafarov, & Rauk, 1982); in the other case, in which the task was to detect a low contrast stimulus and identify it as a line or an edge, bipolar representation was rejected (Tolhurst & Dealy, 1975). In the next section, the model is used to ask whether brightness and darkness are represented on a single bipolar dimension or whether they are represented by two orthogonal dimensions.

Brightness and Darkness: One Bipolar Dimension or Two Orthogonal Dimensions?

In the simplest models, each spatially tuned pathway can respond by increasing or decreasing its activity (Thomas, 1968, 1970; Wilson & Bergen, 1979; Wilson & Gelb, 1984). If this is so, then two stimuli that differ only in the sign of their contrast—for example, one is a bright bar on medium background and the other is a dark bar on the same background—will be complementary stimuli. However, there is both physiological and psychophysical evidence that suggests that pathways only increase their activity in response to stimulation and that brightness and darkness are signaled by different sets of pathways (see Fiorentini et al., 1990, for a review of this evidence). For example, one group of pathways would signal the presence of a bright bar by increasing their activity, but would show no change in activity in response to a dark bar. Another set of pathways would signal the dark bar by increasing their activity, but be unresponsive to a bright bar. If this is so, the stimuli are orthogonal rather than complementary.

One way to decide between these alternatives is to conduct a 2×2 experiment using stimuli that differ only in the sign of their contrast and determine which model fits the data: the complementary stimuli model or the orthogonal model.

Thomas (1981) conducted such a test, using two types of stimuli. In both cases, the luminance modulations defining one stimulus were simply opposite in sign to the modulations defining the other. Specifically,

$$\text{stimulus } \mathbf{A} = L_0 + L(x) \; ,$$

$$\text{stimulus } \mathbf{B} = L_0 - L(x) \; ,$$

where L_0 is the luminance of the uniform field constituting the blank stimulus, and $L(x)$ is a function of spatial position x.

One type of stimulus was a low-contrast vertical cosine grating that was spatially windowed along the horizontal axis by multiplying the amplitude of the cosine grating by a Gaussian function with a standard deviation of 0.5°. The spatial frequency of the cosine grating was 0.5 c/deg. For one test stimulus, a bright bar of the grating was centered in the window; for the other test stimulus, a dark bar was centered in the window. The second type of stimulus was a low-contrast vertical bar, 1° wide. For one stimulus, the bar was slightly brighter than the background; for the other stimulus, the bar was slightly darker. Detection and discrimination performance were simultaneously measured at four contrast levels. Stimulus presentations were 1 s in duration with gradual onsets and offsets.

Low-frequency gratings and wide bars were used as the primary stimuli to minimize the effects of involuntary eye movements. Because spatially tuned pathways are sensitive to the position of the image of the stimulus on the retina, eye movements that are large relative to the dimensions of the stimulus cause the assumptions of the complementary stimulus model to be violated. Specifically, the distribution of responses in each pathway to a given stimulus becomes bimodal as the extent of eye movements becomes large relative to the period of the stimulus. However, higher-frequency gratings and thinner bars were also tested.

Results indicated that at low frequencies, for both cosine grating and bar stimuli, identification performance exceeded detection performance, yielding I/D ratios greater than 1.0. The data from three observers, summed over four to eight daily replications each, were statistically tested in two ways. First, expected values for a χ^2 analysis were generated according to three models: the bipolar model with uncorrelated noise, a bipolar model with an additional parameter representing correlated noise, and the independence model with uncorrelated noise. The data unanimously rejected the simple bipolar model for both cosine and bar stimuli. The addition of the extra parameter to this model did not improve the fit: the correlated bipolar also was rejected in all data sets. These results are not consistent with the notion that bright and dark stimuli are complementary stimuli processed by increases and decreases in activity of the same tuned pathways.

The simple independence model was also rejected for low-frequency cosine grating stimuli, but could not be rejected by this analysis for bar stimuli. As a more powerful test of the independence model, the equality of $p(\mathrm{I})$ and $p(\mathrm{D})$ was tested for each observer by a t-test. The data from one observer with the cosine grating stimuli was consistent with the independence model; however, the model was rejected for all other data sets. Although not tested here, an independence model with correlated noise might serve as a better model for these data.

Because of the possible effects of eye movements, caution is necessary in interpreting data gathered with higher-frequency cosine gratings and thinner bars. Nevertheless, the data again consistently reject the simple and correlated-noise forms of the bipolar processing model. The observed relationship between $p(\mathrm{I})$ and $p(\mathrm{D})$ changes as spatial frequency increases (or width decreases), approaching equality near frequencies of 1 to 2 c/deg (or widths of about 0.25°). In this region, the independence model cannot be consistently rejected, although both bipolar models can. For bar stimuli, an I/D ratio of 1.0 represents an asymptote; further decreases in bar width do not affect relative performance on the two tasks. For these thinner bars, the independence model provides a satisfactory fit to all data sets. With cosine gratings, however, detection performance exceeds identification performance at 5 c/deg. Neither the bipolar models nor the independence models account for this result.

SUMMARY

The multidimensional vector model presented here provides a unifying theoretical structure from which observed relationships between detection and identification performance can be interpreted across several psychophysical paradigms. The general formulation of the model stems from traditional line-element models of sensory processing, more recent concepts from psychoacoustics, and the work of many investigators in visual psychophysics over the past two decades. We have illustrated how the current formulation of the model explicitly considers effects of stimulus uncertainty and response bias in the yes-no task, and described a general test of independent processing for this procedure that does not depend on the restrictive Gaussian assumptions of previous analyses.

The specific concepts and analyses presented for the 2×2 paradigm, in which detection and identification performance are simultaneously assessed, extend those formulated for the yes-no tasks of Signal Detection Theory. The 2 × 2 analyses also extend the concepts advanced in Tanner's theory of recognition (1956), in which detection and identification performance are measured in separate blocks of trials.

The vector representation of the 2 × 2 paradigm presented here also leads to tests of independent processing that do not depend on the Gaussian assumption. We demonstrated how a single performance measure, the I/D ratio, describes performance on both detection and identification tasks when they are performed simultaneously. We illustrated (a) how this measure is related to the angle between the vectors in the yes-no task; (b) how it is computed, including procedures to minimize the effects of response bias; and (c) provided examples of its use in tests of independence, in estimates of bandwidth, and in distinguishing unipolar pairs of independent processors from bipolar processing mechanisms.

ACKNOWLEDGMENTS

Development of the vector model, related experiments, and preparation of this chapter were supported by U.S. Department of Health and Human Services research grant EY00360 from the National Eye Institute.

11 Modeling Similarity and Identification When There Are Momentary Fluctuations in Psychological Magnitudes

Daniel M. Ennis
Philip Morris Research Center and Department of Physiology
Medical College of Virginia

To discover the hidden structure in what we observe is a source of great enjoyment and a worthy goal for scientists to achieve. This structure is often revealed by successively employing models of increasing elegance and generality. The physical attributes of any set of objects will never occur at exactly the same value. Similarly, the chemical fluctuations in time and space around each cell, the cacophony in the living world, ensure that mental representations for the same and different objects will not be identical. Explicit models for these fluctuations might be based on known molecular-cellular processes and principles. In the absence of this knowledge, it is often useful to employ models that can be justified on the basis of experience in model fitting. These models may be shown later to have a basis in more fundamental processes, but initially must be viewed as operational. The models to be discussed in this chapter fall into this latter class.

The modest goal of this chapter is to describe models that can be used to explore the consequences of momentary fluctuations in psychological values, irrespective of the processes responsible for these fluctuations. This exploration does indeed lead to the exposition of a hidden structure that cannot be seen from the perspective of models that ignore the existence of momentary fluctuations.

GENERAL PRINCIPLES

An organism's behavior in responding to a stimulus can be modeled as if the organism transduced physical and/or chemical information into mental representations and employed some decision process. Many aspects of this sequence can be expressed in alternative mathematical forms, from which a particular model can be chosen. This selection would be based on fitting the models to experimental findings.

In general, psychological magnitudes can be treated as vectors in which each element of a vector corresponds to a value on a particular psychological continuum. Fluctuations in the vector magnitudes for a particular stimulus may occur because the physical stimulus may not be constant and/or because the information transduced to a mental representation (percept) may change from moment to moment. Fluctuations in the object or in the mental representation of it can be modeled by using particular probability density functions (pdfs). In many probabilistic models, attention is paid only to fluctuations at the psychological level by assuming that stimulus variance is zero, and it has been common to assume that the psychological pdf is normal. Later, I discuss stimulus fluctuation. If f is any psychological pdf, g is a judgment function for a particular task, and $\mathbf{z}$ is a vector that is a function of the momentary psychological magnitudes, then very many tasks in psychology can be modeled based on the simple equation

$$P = \int_D f(\mathbf{z})g(\mathbf{z})\, dz\ , \tag{1}$$

where P is the probability that a particular decision will be made and D is the joint domain of f and g. If f is a multivariate normal density function, then

$$f(\mathbf{z}) = \frac{exp\,\{-0.5(\mathbf{z} - \boldsymbol{\mu})'\boldsymbol{\Sigma}^{-1}(\mathbf{z} - \boldsymbol{\mu})\}}{(2\pi)^{n/2}|\boldsymbol{\Sigma}|^{1/2}}\ . \tag{2}$$

The prime denotes a row vector, and $|\boldsymbol{\Sigma}|$ is the determinant of $\boldsymbol{\Sigma}$, the covariance matrix for the $\mathbf{z}$ values, and $\boldsymbol{\mu}$ is their mean.

SIMILARITY MODELS

Let $\mathbf{x}_i$ and $\mathbf{x}_j$ be vectors (n elements in each vector) of psychological magnitudes corresponding to two objects presented to a subject on a single trial. If the subject were to be presented with exactly the same objects an instant later, these psychological magnitudes might be different. Assume that the momentary psychological values are mutually independently distributed with $\mathbf{x}_i$ having density function f_i and $\mathbf{x}_j$ having density function f_j. The probability densities f_i and f_j are multivariate normal distributions with means $\boldsymbol{\mu}_i$ and $\boldsymbol{\mu}_j$ and covariance matrices $\boldsymbol{\Sigma}_i$ and $\boldsymbol{\Sigma}_j$. Based on the momentary psychological values, $\mathbf{x}_i$ and $\mathbf{x}_j$, the subject decides whether the stimuli are the same or different. Let $\mathbf{z} = \mathbf{x}_i - \mathbf{x}_j$. When n = 2,

$$\boldsymbol{\Sigma} = \begin{bmatrix} \sigma_1^2 + \sigma_3^2 & \rho_1\sigma_1\sigma_2 + \rho_2\sigma_3\sigma_4 \\ \rho_1\sigma_1\sigma_2 + \rho_2\sigma_3\sigma_4 & \sigma_2^2 + \sigma_4^2 \end{bmatrix},$$

where σ_1^2 and σ_2^2 are the variances of the distributions from which x_{i1} and x_{i2} were drawn, respectively; σ_3^2 and σ_4^2 are the variances of the distributions from which x_{j1} and x_{j2} were drawn, respectively; ρ_1 is the correlation coefficient between the dimensions of $\mathbf{x}_i$; and ρ_2 is the correlation coefficient between the dimensions of $\mathbf{x}_j$; and $\boldsymbol{\mu}$ is a vector of differences between the means of the momentary psychological values $\boldsymbol{\mu}_i$ and $\boldsymbol{\mu}_j$.

A general formula for the distance between the vectors $\mathbf{x}_i$ and $\mathbf{x}_j$ is the γ-Minkowski distance d, where

$$d_{ij} = \left[\sum_{k=1}^{n} |z_k|^{\gamma} \right]^{1/\gamma}, \qquad \gamma \geq 1 . \tag{3}$$

If $\gamma = 1$, the distance d is called the *city-block* distance, and if $\gamma = 2$, d is called the *Euclidean* distance.

One can similarly define the distance between population means by

$$\delta_{ij} = \left[\sum_{k=1}^{n} |\mu_{ik} - \mu_{jk}|^{\beta} \right]^{1/\beta}, \qquad \beta \geq 1 . \tag{4}$$

It is extremely important to distinguish d_{ij} and δ_{ij}. The distance d_{ij} is defined only for a particular trial. Once that trial is over, d_{ij} has no further meaning as far as the subject is concerned. On the other hand, δ_{ij} is the distance between the means of the distributions of psychological magnitudes that give rise to d_{ij}. The means and the covariance matrices of these distributions determine the likelihoods of occurrence of values of d_{ij} within a trial. The probability that a subject will ever directly experience psychological magnitudes equal to $\boldsymbol{\mu}_i$ or $\boldsymbol{\mu}_j$ is zero. In many traditional Multidimensional Scaling models that are not probabilistic (deterministic models), it is assumed that a subject will experience psychological magnitudes exactly equal to $\boldsymbol{\mu}_i$ and $\boldsymbol{\mu}_j$ whenever the two stimuli are presented. The difference between d_{ij} and δ_{ij} is central to differentiating between probabilistic models, which allow for fluctuations in psychological magnitudes from trial to trial, and deterministic models that make no probabilistic assumptions.

The Similarity Function

In Equation 1 it can be seen that the probability of making a particular decision depends on f and g. The function g is the judgment function. Suppose that g was concerned with perceived similarity between the momentary values $\mathbf{x}_i$ and $\mathbf{x}_j$. Then g could be called the *similarity function. Similarity* can be defined in terms of d (which is a function of $\mathbf{z}$). Many different forms could be proposed for g. An obvious requirement would be that g decrease as d increases. Shepard (1987) proposed an exponential decay similarity function as a universal principle. A flexible function that includes the exponential decay function is

$$g(d) = exp\ (-d^{\alpha})\ , \qquad \alpha > 0\ . \tag{5}$$

To satisfy the earlier requirement that $g(d)$ decrease as d increases, α must be >0 or $g(d)$ would become larger as d became larger. The value for α may be different for different subjects and experimental conditions, although it is conceivable that α may be a constant.

To use Equation 1, one must specify the probability density function for the momentary psychological magnitudes (for example, Equation 2) and the judgment function to be used in making a decision (for example, Equation 5). Both of these have now been defined, and it follows from Equation 1 that the similarity of two objects over all possible trials is

$$P = \int_{R^n} \frac{exp\ \{-0.5(\mathbf{z} - \boldsymbol{\mu})'\ \boldsymbol{\Sigma}^{-1}(\mathbf{z} - \boldsymbol{\mu})\}}{(2\pi)^{n/2}|\boldsymbol{\Sigma}|^{1/2}}\ exp\ (-d^{\alpha})\ d\mathbf{z}\ . \tag{6}$$

Equation 6 does not include response bias, which can be accounted for by multiplying the right side by a bias parameter. The term P is the *expected value* of g. Since Equation 6 postulates a normal distribution for the psychological magnitudes, originally proposed by Thurstone (1927a), and then uses a general form to define similarity, which was motivated by Shepard's recent (1987) and earlier work, this model of similarity could be called a *Thurstone-Shepard* model.

Equation 6 can be evaluated numerically for a broad range of distance metrics (by varying γ) and similarity functions (by varying α). Computations of this type will be discussed later. There is a case, however, that deserves special mention because it leads to a closed form for Equation 6. If one assumes that the metric of d is Euclidean ($\gamma = 2$) and that in the similarity function $\alpha = 2$, then

$$P = (|\boldsymbol{\Sigma}|\ |\mathbf{J}|)^{-1/2}\ exp\ [\boldsymbol{\mu}'(2\mathbf{J}^{-1} - \mathbf{I})\boldsymbol{\mu}]\ , \tag{7}$$

where $\mathbf{J} = \boldsymbol{\Sigma}^{-1} + 2\mathbf{I}$ and $\mathbf{I}$ is the identity matrix.

The derivation of Equation 7 is given in Ennis, Palen, and Mullen (1988). Naturally, Equation 7 is much faster to compute than Equation 6 for the special case $\alpha = 2$ and $\gamma = 2$. For five-decimal-place accuracy, computational experience suggests a speed improvement of about three to four orders of magnitude. Of course, Equation 7 is only one special case, not necessarily the most important one. A more interesting case may be when $\alpha = 1$ (g is exponential decay) and $\gamma = 1$ (city-block metric).

Ennis and Johnson (in press) recently showed that Thurstone-Shepard similarity models are special cases of moment generating functions of particular random variables. For instance, when $\alpha = 2$ and $\gamma = 2$, Equation 7 is the moment generating function of a quadratic form in normal variables. When $\alpha = 1$ and $\gamma = 1$, then the Thurstone-Shepard similarity model is a special case of the moment generating function of a folded normal random variable. Under the assumption of independent perceptual dimensions,

$$P = \prod_{i=1}^{n} \{exp[(2\mu_i + \sigma_i^2)/2]\Phi[-(\mu_i + \sigma_i^2)/\sigma_i]$$

$$+ exp[-(2\mu_i - \sigma_i^2/2)]\Phi[(\mu_i - \sigma_i^2)/\sigma_i]\} .$$

where μ_i and σ_i^2 are the i-th mean and variance, respectively and Φ is the standard normal distribution function. A more complete generalization with arbitrary covariance matrix for the $\alpha = 1$, $\gamma = 1$ case has not yet been developed.

Equation 5 gives g as a continuous function of d. Suppose that g was, instead, a step function of d. This would mean that g would be 0 or 1, depending on the value of d relative to some threshold or criterion τ. To meet these objectives, let

$$g(d) = 0.5 \{sgn (\tau - d) + 1\} , \quad (8)$$

where sgn is the signum function. The signum function takes the values 1, 1, and -1 whenever $\tau - d$ is greater than, equal to, or less than zero, respectively. For instance, if $\tau - d > 0$, then $d < \tau$, $sgn (\tau - d)$ is 1, and $g(d)$ is 1. Similarly if $\tau = d$, $g(d)$ is 1. However, if $\tau - d < 0$, then $d > \tau$, and $sgn (\tau - d)$ is -1, leading to $g(d) = 0$. Using Equation 1 with this new definition of g results in

$$P = \int_{R^n} \frac{exp \{-0.5(\mathbf{z} - \boldsymbol{\mu})' \Sigma^{-1}(\mathbf{z} - \boldsymbol{\mu})\}}{(2\pi)^{n/2}|\Sigma|^{1/2}} 0.5\{sgn (\tau - d) + 1\}d\mathbf{z} . \quad (9)$$

The value of τ may be fixed or drawn from a probability density function and vary from trial to trial. Ennis and Ashby (1992) showed that Equation 9 can be reduced to a weighted sum of non-central chi-square variables with positive weights,

$$P = Pr(\mathbf{Z} \bullet \mathbf{Z} < \tau^2) = Pr\left(\sum_{k=1}^{n} \lambda_k(\mathbf{W}_k - \omega_k)^2 < \tau^2\right) ,$$

where $\mathbf{W} = \mathbf{P}'\mathbf{A}^{-1}(\mathbf{Z} - \boldsymbol{\mu})$, $\boldsymbol{\omega} = -\mathbf{P}'\mathbf{A}^{-1}\boldsymbol{\mu}$, $\mathbf{P}$ is the normalized orthogonal matrix of eigenvectors of $\mathbf{A}'\mathbf{A}$, $\mathbf{A}$ is a matrix such that $\mathbf{V} = \mathbf{A}\mathbf{A}'$ and $\boldsymbol{\Lambda} = \mathbf{P}'\mathbf{A}'\mathbf{A}\mathbf{P}$, the diagonal matrix of eigenvalues of $\mathbf{A}'\mathbf{A}$. Ennis and Ashby (1992) used the Ruben (1962) series involving central chi-square variables to compute P:

$$Pr(\mathbf{Z} \bullet \mathbf{Z} < \tau^2) = \sum_{j=0}^{\infty} e_j \Pr[\chi^2_{n+2j} < \tau^2/\beta] ,$$

$$\text{where } e_0 = \left[exp\left(-0.5 \sum_{j=1}^{n} \omega_j^2 \right) \right] \prod_{j=1}^{n} (\beta/\lambda_j)^{1/2} ,$$

$$e_r = (1/2r) \sum_{j=0}^{r-1} G_{r-j}e_j \ (r \geq 1) ,$$

$G_r = \Sigma_{j=1}^{n} (1 - \beta/\lambda_j)^r + r\beta \Sigma_{j=1}^{n} (\omega_j^2/\lambda_j)(1 - \beta/\lambda_j)^{r-1}$, and β is a constant. The smallest eigenvalue of $\mathbf{A}'\mathbf{A}$ was chosen for β.

Equations 6 and 9 have been discussed in terms of the expected value of the similarity function, but they also correspond to the probability of giving a *same* response in a same-different task. Data of this kind will be analyzed later by using Equations 6 and 7.

Perceptual Dependence and the Form of the Similarity Function

Ennis and Ashby (1992) recently showed that different probabilistic identification models differ greatly with regard to their sensitivity to perceptual dependence. It was shown that probabilistic identification models based on the idea of response regions (multidimensional Signal Detection Theory) were more sensitive to perceptual dependence than models based on distance comparisons or the Shepard-Luce choice rule. See Ashby (1988), Ashby and Gott (1988), Ashby and Perrin (1988), and Ashby and Townsend (1986) for a discussion of recent developments in multidimensional Signal Detection Theory (see also chaps. 6 and 16). An identification model based on the exponential decay similarity function was particularly insensitive to perceptual dependence. This sensitivity was measured by comparing the difference between identification performance predictions when the variance-covariance matrices and mean difference vectors varied. Cases in which the correlation coefficients of the distributions being considered were either both positive or both negative were of special interest.

Some previous experience in evaluating Equation 9 (the step function) with different covariance matrices, and a comparison of these evaluations with Equation 6, suggested that the sensitivity observed is related to the degree to which the judgment function $g(\mathbf{z})$ approaches a step function. At the opposite extreme to the step function is a linear function of $\mathbf{z}$, the expected value of which (from Equation 1) is a linear function of the mean $\boldsymbol{\mu}$. Multidimensional signal detection identification models can be formulated in terms of Equation 1 by integrating over R^n with $f(\mathbf{z})$ as the probe's probability density function and $g(\mathbf{z})$ as a step function of the likelihoods that $\mathbf{z}$ is a random deviate from the two memory distributions. To test the step function hypothesis, Equation 6 was evaluated for a

FIG. 11.1. The effect of the form of *g*, the judgment function, on the sensitivity of its expected value, *similarity,* to perceptual dependence. (a) Four judgments of the form $g(d) = exp(-d^\alpha)$, where $\alpha = 1, 2, 6$, and 25. (b) The difference between the similarities of two pairs of distributions: In the first pair, correlation correlations between dimensions are both −0.8; in the second pair, correlation coefficients between dimensions are both +0.8. In both cases, $\delta = 1.0$. The curve with the higher asymptote corresponds to distributions with a standard deviation of 0.2, the lower curve corresponds to distributions with a standard deviation of 1.0.

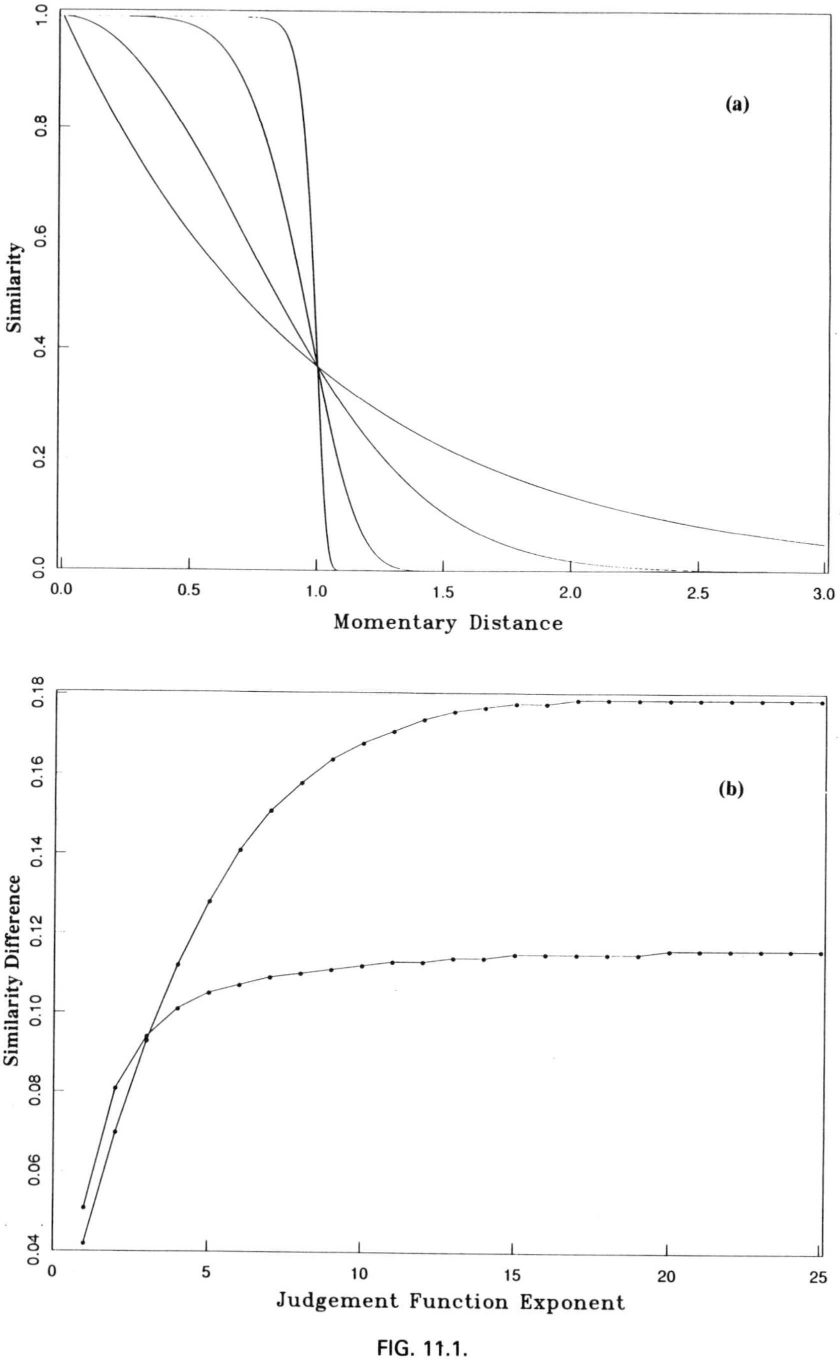

(a)
Similarity
1.0
0.8
0.6
0.4
0.2
0.0
0.0
0.5
1.0
1.5
2.0
2.5
3.0
Momentary Distance
(b)
Similarity Difference
0.18
0.16
0.14
0.12
0.10
0.08
0.06
0.04
0
5
10
15
20
25
Judgement Function Exponent

FIG. 11.1.

series of forms of g and for two cases of perceptual dependence and two levels of distributional overlap. For the basic form $g(\mathbf{z}) = exp\ (-d^{\alpha})$, α was varied from 1 to 25 in unit increments. These functions include exponential decay, Gaussian, and a series that, at $\alpha = 25$, approaches a step function. Figure 11.1a shows the form of g when α is 1, 2, 6, and 25. Figure 11.1b gives the difference between the values of P (from Equation 6) in the two perceptual dependence cases for the two levels of distributional overlap. When $\alpha = 1$, the exponential decay case, the effect of perceptual dependence is very small. As α increases, especially if the level of distributional overlap is not great, the difference between the perceptual dependence cases increases and ultimately saturates. The maximum difference is seen when a step judgment function is operative.

This result has important implications for a variety of models that use Equation 5 to define similarity. One example is the Shepard-Luce choice rule, to be discussed in the next section. If Shepard's suggestion that the exponential decay similarity function formalizes a universal principle, then perceptual dependence will have only a small effect on task performance when objects are perceptually confusable. This theoretical result might be used to test hypotheses concerning the form of g that would then support or refute Shepard's theory concerning the nature of the similarity function.

IDENTIFICATION MODELS

Thurstone-Shepard-Luce Models

One approach to modeling absolute identification is to assume that there are m memory exemplars corresponding to m stimuli $\mathbf{S}_1, \mathbf{S}_2, \ldots, \mathbf{S}_m$. A probe stimulus $\mathbf{S}_k$, which may or may not have been in the original ensemble, is presented. It is assumed that the subject compares this probe to stored exemplars by determining the distances $d_{k1}, d_{k2}, \ldots, d_{km}$ and then uses them in a similarity function such as Equation 5 to determine the similarities. Nosofsky (1986) modeled identification performance on the basis of the *Shepard-Luce* choice rule, which models the probability that a subject will respond by identifying stimulus $\mathbf{S}_k$ as stimulus $\mathbf{S}_i$ (i.e., respond R_i to $\mathbf{S}_k$). As a deterministic model, the choice rule is

$$P(R_i|\mathbf{S}_k) = \frac{b_i h(d_{ki})}{\sum_{j=1}^{m} b_j h(d_{kj})}, \tag{10}$$

where $P(R_i|\mathbf{S}_k)$ is the probability of responding R_i when the stimulus is $\mathbf{S}_k$, b_i is the response bias parameter for R_i, d_{ki} is the distance between $\mathbf{S}_k$ and the memory representation of $\mathbf{S}_i$, and h is a similarity function such as that given in Equation 5:

$$h(d) = exp\ (-d^{\alpha})\ , \qquad \alpha \geq 0\ .$$

In a probabilistic model of identification, one might assume that the Shepard-Luce choice rule was being used within a trial, and interest might then center on the expected value of the right side of Equation 10. Hence, when fluctuations in psychological magnitudes are to be accounted for,

$$P(\mathrm{R_i}|\mathbf{S}_k) = E\left[\frac{\boldsymbol{b}_i h(\boldsymbol{d}_{ki})}{\sum_{j=1}^{m} \boldsymbol{b}_j h(\boldsymbol{d}_{kj})}\right], \tag{11}$$

where E ($\boldsymbol{r}$) is the expected value of $\boldsymbol{r}$.

Consider the special case in which there are only two memory distributions with multivariate normal probability density functions f_i and f_j and a probe with density function f_k. Let $\mathbf{u} = \mathbf{x}_k - \mathbf{x}_i$, $\mathbf{v} = \mathbf{x}_k - \mathbf{x}_j$, and $\mathbf{z} = (\mathbf{u},\mathbf{v})$. Now, $\boldsymbol{\Sigma}$ is the covariance matrix of the joint distribution of $\mathbf{u}$ and $\mathbf{v}$, or $\mathbf{z}$, and $\boldsymbol{\mu}$ is the vector of mean differences previously defined. It can be shown that

$$\boldsymbol{\Sigma} = \begin{bmatrix} \boldsymbol{\Sigma}_1 & \boldsymbol{\Sigma}_2 \\ \boldsymbol{\Sigma}_2 & \boldsymbol{\Sigma}_3 \end{bmatrix}, \qquad \text{with } \boldsymbol{\Sigma}_1 = \boldsymbol{\Sigma}_k + \boldsymbol{\Sigma}_i,\ \boldsymbol{\Sigma}_2 = \boldsymbol{\Sigma}_k, \text{ and } \boldsymbol{\Sigma}_3 = \boldsymbol{\Sigma}_k + \boldsymbol{\Sigma}_j\,.$$

The judgment function introduced in Equation 1 can now be defined as a function of $\mathbf{z}$ by using the Shepard-Luce choice rule and rewriting Equation 10 as

$$g(\mathbf{z}) = \frac{\mathrm{b}_i h(d_{ki})}{\sum_{j=1}^{m} \mathrm{b}_j h(d_{kj})}\,. \tag{12}$$

Applying Equation 1 to obtain the choice probability, we need only integrate over the vector space composed of all 2n-tuples represented by $\mathbf{z}$, weighting each element of the space by its probability of occurrence (given by the multivariate normal density function), or

$$P(\mathrm{R_i}|\mathbf{S}_k)$$

$$= \int_{R^n}\int_{R^n} \frac{exp\,\{-0.5(\mathbf{z}-\boldsymbol{\mu})'\boldsymbol{\Sigma}^{-1}(\mathbf{z}-\boldsymbol{\mu})\}}{(2\pi)^n|\boldsymbol{\Sigma}|^{1/2}}\ \frac{\boldsymbol{b}_i h(d_{ki})}{\boldsymbol{b}_i h(d_{ki}) + \boldsymbol{b}_j h(d_{kj})}\, d\mathbf{z}\,. \tag{13}$$

Since Equation 13 includes models that are probabilistic extensions of the Shepard-Luce choice rule, these models can be referred to as *Thurstone-Shepard-Luce* models.

If $\alpha = 1$ and $\gamma = 1$, h is an exponential decay function and the metric of d_{ki} is city block. If $\alpha = 2$ and $\gamma = 2$, h is a Gaussian function and the metric of d_{ki} is Euclidean.

Identification Models Based on Ordinal Decision Rules

An alternative decision making process to the Shepard-Luce choice rule is to select a response based on the relative size of the momentary distances d_{ki} and

d_{kj}. If $d_{ki} < d_{kj}$, then the subject would give R_i as the response, for instance. The probabilistic model for this type of decision rule is identical (with two memory representations) to a Thurstonian variant of Torgerson's Method of Triads (Torgerson, 1958) and to a probabilistic generalization of Coombs' preference unfolding model (Coombs, 1964). Special cases of this model have been discussed by Ennis and Mullen (1986a), Mullen and Ennis (1987), Mullen, Ennis, De Doncker, and Kapenga (1988), and Ennis, Mullen, and Frijters (1988). A major problem with this model had been the computing time needed to handle numerical integration of a 2n-fold integral. Reduction of this integral to a single integral, for all values of n, is given in Mullen and Ennis (1991) and discussed in Chapter 5. This form of the model contributes importantly to solving the computational problem posed by the 2n-fold integral. Reference to the use of the model for absolute identification is given in Chapter 5.

Identification Models Based on Category Distributions

Nosofsky (1986, 1990; see also chap. 14) discussed a model of categorization that was based on the context theory of classification proposed by Medin and Schaffer (1978). In this model, one assumes that a subject stores category exemplars in memory and that the probability of giving a category I response to stimulus $\mathbf{S}_k$ is

$$P(R_I|\mathbf{S}_k) = b_I \sum_{i \in C_I} L_i(I)s_{ki} \Big/ \sum_J b_J \sum_{j \in C_J} L_j(J)s_{kj} , \tag{14}$$

where b_J is the response bias parameter for category C_J, $L_j(J)$ is the likelihood that exemplar$_j$ is presented during training as a member of category C_J, and s_{ki} is the similarity of exemplar$_k$ and exemplar$_i$.

In the previous section on Thurstone-Shepard-Luce models, it was assumed that each stimulus representation (either a probe or a memory representation) can be treated as a random value from a particular probability distribution. In this way, it was possible to capture the effect of momentary fluctuations in psychological magnitudes. It was also assumed that subjects make within-trial decisions based on single instances of stimulus and memory representations that were assumed to have been drawn from these distributions. The categorization model in Equation 14 is a deterministic model with a finite set of training exemplars making up each category and a finite set of likelihoods that each exemplar has been presented during training. Imagine, instead, that a category contains an infinite number of category exemplars with likelihoods of occurrence determined by a probability density function. The categories may now be viewed as the distributions corresponding to memory representations of individual stimuli, and Equation 14 can be extended to yield identification probabilities for *particular* stimulus values. Hence,

$$P(\mathrm{R_i}|\mathbf{S}_\mathrm{k}) = \mathrm{b_i} \int_{R^n} f_\mathrm{i}(\mathbf{x})h(d_\mathrm{ki})\, d\mathbf{x} \Big/ \sum_{\mathrm{j}=1}^{\mathrm{m}} \mathrm{b_j} \int_{R^n} f_\mathrm{j}(\mathbf{x})h(d_\mathrm{kj})\, d\mathbf{x}\ . \tag{15}$$

All terms in Equation 15 have been defined in the previous sections. Note that Equation 1 has been used in the numerator and denominator to obtain the expected values of the similarity of stimulus $\mathbf{S}_\mathrm{k}$ to each of the m memory representations.

Equation 14 was a deterministic model for the categorization of a particular stimulus and, hence, made no allowance for the possibility that the probe's mental representation may be a random variable. A more general model than Equation 15 is one in which presentation of the probe stimulus evokes a momentary value from a probability distribution itself. Thus, it is also necessary to integrate over the probe or stimulus pdf. Thinking again in terms of Equation 1, where

$$g_\mathrm{k}(\mathbf{x}_\mathrm{k}) = \mathrm{b_i} \int_{R^n} f_\mathrm{i}(\mathbf{x})h(d_\mathrm{ki})\, d\mathbf{x} \Big/ \sum_{\mathrm{j}=1}^{\mathrm{m}} \mathrm{b_j} \int_{R^n} f_\mathrm{j}(\mathbf{x})h(d_\mathrm{kj})\, d\mathbf{x}\ ,$$

this means that

$$P(\mathrm{R_i}|\mathbf{S}_\mathrm{k}) = \int_{R^n} f_\mathrm{k}(\mathbf{x})g_\mathrm{k}(\mathbf{x})\, d\mathbf{x}\ . \tag{16}$$

Equation 16 gives the probability of identifying stimulus $\mathbf{S}_\mathrm{k}$ as stimulus $\mathbf{S}_\mathrm{i}$, based on the assumption that probes and memory representations of stimuli can be modeled as if they were drawn from particular probability distributions. A deterministic categorical model, such as that in Equation 14 can be viewed as a special case of this model in which there are a finite number of elements in each category with a corresponding finite set of likelihoods of occurrence of each element.

RESOLUTION OF SHEPARD-NOSOFSKY PARADOX

Shepard (1987) proposed the exponential decay similarity function as a general form or universal principle of considerable importance when organisms make decisions about how to react to novel stimuli. Shepard has also given arguments in support of the city-block metric, when psychological dimensions are separable (they can be attended to separately), and of the Euclidean metric, when psychological dimensions are integral (they cannot be attended to separately). Working with separable stimuli, Nosofsky (1986) provided very strong support for the Euclidean metric and a Gaussian form for the similarity function, which appeared to be incompatible with Shepard's theory. Both Nosofsky and Shepard used deterministic models and, therefore, did not take momentary fluctuations in the psychological magnitudes into account. Nosofsky's stimuli were highly similar, suggesting that perceptual variance should be included formally in models of his data. Equation 6 presents a form that should lead to a modified Gaussian relationship between P and δ. The extent of modification depends on the similarity function exponent α and the metric defining the within-trial distance d. As can be seen from Figures 11.2, 11.3a, and 11.3b, when the similarity function within a trial is exponential decay, the relationship between P and δ appears to be much more Gaussian in form than exponential decay. These results are discussed in Ennis et al. (1988) and Ennis (1988a, 1988b). Based on these theoretical findings, it would be reasonable to infer a Gaussian similarity function if a deterministic model is used to uncover the underlying form in the presence of perceptual noise. Thus, although subjects may actually use an exponential decay similarity function in making decisions, this function may not be uncovered by using a deterministic modeling approach to the data.

It has also been shown (Ennis, 1988a) that if subjects actually use an exponential decay similarity function and the city-block metric *within a trial* to determine d, then the Euclidean metric distance δ between *stimulus means* is at least as satisfactory in relating similarity to distance as is the city-block metric. Thus, the two hidden components—the form of the similarity function and the choice of

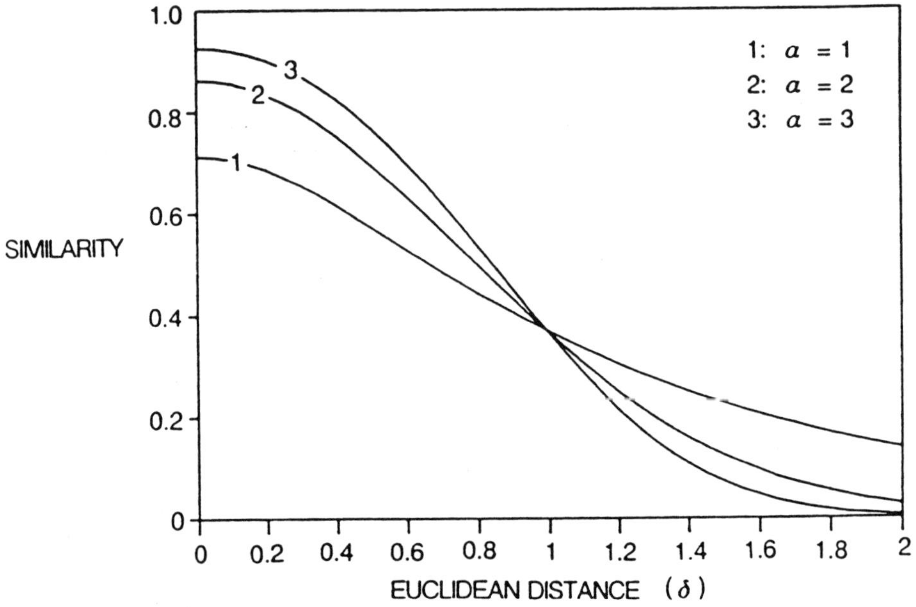

FIG. 11.2. Expected value of similarity as a function of the Euclidean distance between the means of the distributions of psychological magnitudes for values of α of 1, 2, and 3 in the similarity function $g(d) = exp\ (-d^{\alpha})$.

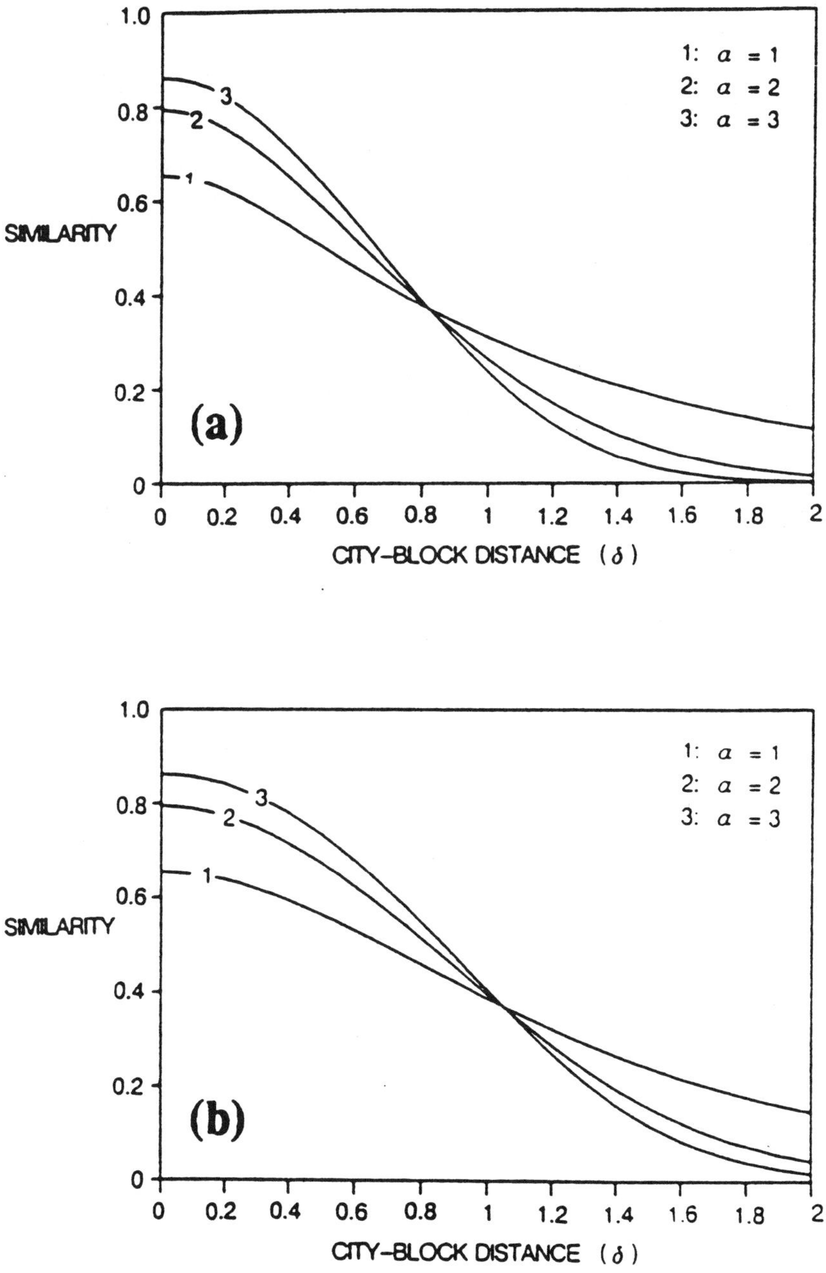

FIG. 11.3. Expected value of similarity as a function of the city-block distance between the means of the distributions of psychological magnitudes for values of α of 1, 2, and 3 in the similarity function $g(d) = exp\ (-d^{\alpha})$. (a) Means differ on one axis only; (b) means differ equally on both axes.

metric—may not be revealed by ploying a deterministic model in the presence of momentary fluctuations or noise. Further comments on this issue are in Nosofsky (1988b) and Shepard (1988).

Nosofsky (1985a) used the Shepard-Luce choice rule, Equation 10, to fit the absolute identification performance data of Kornbrot (1978) on tones. Both the exponential decay and the Gaussian similarity functions were used to model the data. The latter yielded a significantly better fit than the former for a neutral condition and a payoff-biased condition. Equation 16, a probabilistic identification model, was used with a constant variance for stimuli and memory distributions of 1.0 to fit the same data. The exponential decay function fit the data at least as well the deterministic or probabilistic Gaussian models in the neutral condition (based on minimum chi-square and nonlinear least-squares fits). In the payoff-biased condition, the exponential decay probabilistic model fit significantly better than its deterministic counterpart but not as well as the Gaussian probabilistic or deterministic models. However, all of the models were comparable when distance or squared distance in the similar function was multiplied by a rate-decreasing parameter [i.e., c in $g(d) = exp\ (-cd^{\alpha})$]. This model provides further support for the idea that when the exponential decay similarity function is operative, it may require an appropriate probabilistic model to reveal it.

MULTIVARIATE PARAMETER ESTIMATION

To use any of the models given earlier in fitting a data set, one must have an efficient, reliable procedure for parameter estimation. The parameters of interest in the probabilistic models are γ, the metric-defining parameter; α, the exponent in the similarity function; $\boldsymbol{\mu}_i$ and $\boldsymbol{\Sigma}_i$, the vector of means and the covariance matrix, respectively, of the stimulus or memory distributions. Hypotheses concerning γ and α can be tested by specifying values of these parameters (e.g., 1 or 2) rather than allowing them to vary freely. This approach reduces the problem to one of estimating means and covariance matrices under assumptions concerning the metric and form of the similarity function. There are several approaches to solving the estimation problem, one of which is to use the Levenberg-Marquardt Algorithm for Nonlinear Least-Squares estimation (Dennis and Schnabel, 1983). Let **a** be a vector containing the parameters to be estimated.

Define

$$q_{ij}(\mathbf{a}) = p_{ij} - P_{ij} \ ,$$

where p_{ij} is the observed proportion of judgments involving a comparison of $\mathbf{S}_i$ and $\mathbf{S}_j$ (this could be a same-different judgment or an identification error in which the response to presenting $\mathbf{S}_i$ is $\mathbf{S}_j$), and P_{ij} is the theoretical value obtained by solving the equation corresponding to the model being tested at the parameter values **a**. Let $\mathbf{q}(\mathbf{a})$ be a vector with typical element $q_{ij}(\mathbf{a})$. The value to be minimized is the residual sum of squares $\mathbf{q}(\mathbf{a})'\mathbf{q}(\mathbf{a})$. If $\mathbf{a}^0$ is an initial estimate of $\mathbf{a}$, a series of approximations are computed as

$$\mathbf{a}^{n+1} = \mathbf{a}^n - [\alpha_n \mathbf{D}_n + \mathbf{J}_n' \mathbf{J}_n]^{-1} \mathbf{J}_n' \mathbf{q}(\mathbf{a}^n) ,$$

where $\mathbf{J}_n$ is the Jacobian matrix (matrix of partial derivatives) evaluated at $\mathbf{a}^n$, $\mathbf{D}_n$ is a diagonal matrix with entries equal to the diagonal of $\mathbf{J}_n'\mathbf{J}_n$, and α_n is the Marquardt parameter, a positive constant. One usually approximates $\mathbf{J}_n$ by using finite differences in double precision. The Marquardt parameter, initially 0.01, is quadrupled if the residual sum of squares increases from one iteration to the next, and is halved if it decreases.

Parameter Estimation Using "Same-Different" Judgments

Thirty-six means and standard deviations were selected so that pairwise similarity values, P_{ij}, would be in the range 0.5 to 1.0. This selection ensured a high degree of distributional overlap. Figure 11.4 shows the 36 distributions with two standard-deviation equal-probability contours. One of the stimuli was assigned

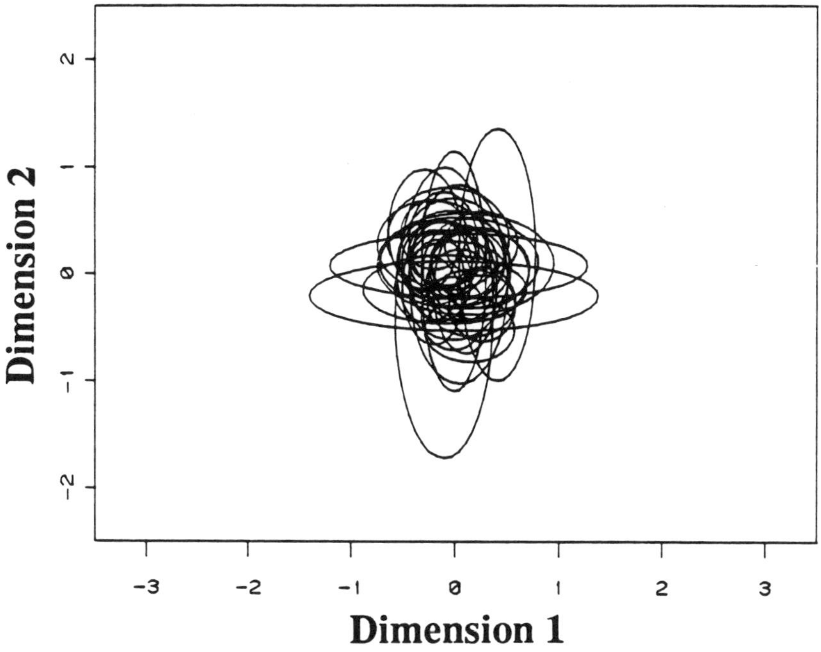

FIG. 11.4. Thirty-six highly overlapping distributions with different covariance matrices. Each distribution is represented by its two standard-deviation equal-probability contour.

the mean vector **O**. All correlation coefficients were assigned the value 0.0. For $\alpha = 2$ and $\gamma = 2$, the matrix of 666 similarity values (all stimulus pairs including self-comparisons) was obtained by solving Equation 7 for the selected means and standard errors. An iterative nonlinear least-squares algorithm, as described before, was used to estimate the means and covariance matrices from the matrix of paired simulated similarity values. A key to solving this problem and avoiding local minima is the generation of good initial estimates of the parameters.

An attempt to accurately recover all of the parameters for the 36 stimuli (all means and standard deviations) in one stage failed. Various strategies for estimating the parameters led to a successful analysis that was conducted in three stages. In the first stage, randomly generated values of the means were obtained, and it was assumed that all standard deviations were 0.2 and that correlation coefficients were 0.0. The value of 0.2 for the standard deviations was chosen because it yields a self-similarity value of about 0.85, which roughly corresponded to the average diagonal value of the same-different matrix. Parameter estimates were obtained that minimized the residual sum of the squares, $\mathbf{q}(\mathbf{a})'\mathbf{q}(\mathbf{a})$. The parameter values at this minimum were then used as the starting configuration for a second stage in which all standard deviations were assumed to be equal across dimensions for a stimulus, but were allowed to vary across stimuli. The parameter estimates at the minimum from this stage were used as the starting configuration for the final stage in which the standard deviations were allowed to vary across stimuli and dimensions. The residual sum of squares at this minimum was <0.001.

The results of this analysis are given in Ennis et al. (1988), who show that estimates of the parameters differed from the original values only in the third decimal place. A plot of the recovered configuration was indistinguishable from a mirror image of Figure 11.4. Unlike traditional Multidimensional Scaling Analysis based on deterministic models, the solution configuration from the type of probabilistic model used may not be invariant to rotation. This orientational uniqueness is a consequence of variance inequality.

An analysis of the Rothkopf (1957) Morse code data that used Equation 7 to model the same-different judgments is given in Ennis et al. (1988). They pointed out that differences between pairs of identical stimuli obtained from same-different judgments can be viewed as a consequence of differences in variances on one or more of the dimensions involved in the decision process. Ashby and Perrin (1988) have also provided this kind of interpretation of self-similarity. This means that P_{ii} will be closer to 1.0 when the variance is small than when it is large. In the Rothkopf Morse code data, many of the same-different judgment proportions for pairs of identical stimuli differ from each other, and many are less than 1.0. In a deterministic model in which the proportions depend on δ, the probability for self-similarity must always be 1.0 when $\delta = 0$ and a judgment function of the form $g(\delta) = exp\,(-\delta^{\alpha})$ is used. This is not true for a probabilistic model, such as that in Equations 6 and 7. In these models, the within-trial distance d will almost always be different from zero when δ is zero because psychological magnitudes for a stimulus vary from moment to moment.

With the closed form, Equation 7, where $\alpha = 2$ and $\gamma = 2$, the Rothkopf Morse code data was modeled for the cases of equal and unequal variance within a stimulus distribution. The unequal-variance model gave a slightly lower residual sum of squares than did the equal-variance model, but the configurations of means for the stimuli were almost identical and the fit improvement was not significant at $p < 0.05$. Ennis et al. (1988) plotted the relationship between the size of the standard error for a stimulus distribution and the degree to which that stimulus is isolated from the other stimuli in the set under study (measured by the average Euclidean distance between a stimulus and all the other stimuli). The size of the standard error was shown to decrease with increasing degree of isolation of a stimulus from the others in the ensemble. Stimuli located near many other stimuli therefore had distributions with the largest variance. Shepard's (1963) nonmetric Multidimensional Scaling Analysis of the same data yielded a configuration of points that were quite similar to the location of the means of the distributions from probabilistic modeling. Certainly, the same interpretation of the dimensions (number of signal components and the dots-dashes ratio) would have resulted from both analyses. This result is consistent with the fact that many of the same-different judgment probabilities were less than 0.5, suggesting, in the absence of response bias, that many pairs of signals were not highly confusable.

An analysis of the Rothkopf data when $\alpha = 1$ and $\gamma = 1$ (the exponential decay, city-block metric model) using Equation 6, solved numerically, resulted in a configuration with a lower residual sum of squares than that obtained when $\alpha = 2$ and $\gamma = 2$ ($p < 0.01$). Some problems still remain to be solved with respect to local minima and computing efficiency for this case, and these will be taken up in a future paper. Based on the previous discussion concerning the judgment function and metric, the $\alpha = 1$ and $\gamma = 1$ case should fit the data best if the perceptual dimensions are separable. If the dimensions are integral, one would expect γ to be 2.

PROBABILISTIC PSYCHOPHYSICS

In all of the models discussed so far, momentary fluctuations have been assumed to occur in the psychological magnitudes. Where specific probability density functions have been considered, attention has been restricted to multivariate normal functions, although Equation 1 is not necessarily restricted to this model. It is valuable to attempt to model performance in psychological tasks in terms of psychological *and* stimulus parameters because such models are likely to shed light on the material basis for perceptions. From the standpoint of modeling efficiency, it can be shown also that in many cases this type of model requires fewer parameters than models that ignore stimulus parameters. Ennis and Mullen (1992) recently developed a general structure for connecting psychophysical models with Thurstonian models. The purpose of this section is to introduce some of these ideas and to point the discussion beyond probabilistic models that have all been based on Thurstonian concepts.

Assume there are several objects with a common attribute that can be measured on a single physicochemical continuum. (A generalization to many continua will be mentioned later.) A stimulus magnitude $\boldsymbol{\phi}_i$ is the value on this continuum for a stimulus object. Let f_1 (ϕ_i) be some probability density function of $\boldsymbol{\phi}_i$. Following a psychophysical transformation, the stimulus magnitude is represented mentally by a psychological magnitude $\boldsymbol{\psi}_i$. Let g (ϕ_i) be any *one-to-one* function of ϕ_i that can operate on the entire domain of f_1. Since g is one-to-one, it is invertible, because for $g(\phi_1) = g(\phi_2)$ the only solution is $\phi_1 = \phi_2$. The pdf of $\boldsymbol{\psi}_i$, $h_1(\psi_i)$, is

$$f_1 \circ g^{-1} (\psi_i) \left| \frac{dg^{-1} (\psi_i)}{d\psi_i} \right| ,$$

where $(f_1 \circ g^{-1})(\psi_i)$ is a composition function. If variation inherent in the biological system of the organism was zero, then each time an object with a stimulus value was presented, it would be represented mentally by exactly the same psychological magnitude after the action of the transduction mechanism. However, it is more realistic to imagine that this value is a parameter, such as the mean, of a distribution of psychological magnitudes. The psychological magnitude $\boldsymbol{\psi}_i$ is then a parameter in a probability density function of momentary psychological magnitudes, $x_i|\psi_i$, which may occur if central or peripheral noise is present, for instance. Let $f_2(x_i|\psi_i)$ be any pdf of $x_i|\psi_i$. Since the pdfs of $\boldsymbol{\psi}_i$ and $x_i|\psi_i$ are h_1 and f_2, the pdf of x_i is

$$\int_D f_2(x_i|\psi_i)h_1(\psi_i)\, d\psi_i \, , \tag{17}$$

where D is the domain of h_1.

The function f_1 may be a multivariate pdf of a vector of physicochemical measures instead of the single variable ϕ_i. The function g, a one-to-one function, would map vectors from the domain space of f_1 to either single values (if g is a real-valued function) or vectors (if g is a vector-valued function) in the range space of g. Similar steps to those taken in deriving Equation 17 can be taken to derive the pdf of $\mathbf{x}_i$ (the vector equivalent of x_i, the momentary psychological magnitude). If $\mathbf{z}$ is some function of the momentary values in a trial, in terms of Equation 1, its pdf would be f. Returning to Equation 1, models for a great many psychological measures and tasks can be derived, such as similarity and identification performance. However, unlike many of the *specific* models discussed in this chapter, special requirements for f_1, f_2, and g would be needed to ensure a multivariate normal pdf for the momentary psychological magnitudes $\mathbf{x}_i$. Ennis and Mullen (1992) discuss one such case leading to a unidimensional normal pdf.

In other models discussed in this chapter, no attention was given to stimulus parameters or to processes that might have led to the percepts. In this sense, the probabilistic models already discussed are much more restrictive than the models in this section. These models, however, require a great deal of work before they can be put to use in modeling experimental results.

SOME COMPUTING NOTES

Integral expressions such as Equations 6, 9, 13, and 16 were evaluated numerically on Gould 32/97 and Trace Multiflow computers. An adaptive routine by Genz and Malik (1980) was found to be useful for multiple integration. A check for gross errors in the numerical computations was achieved by conducting large-scale (100,000 trials per estimate) Monte Carlo evaluations.

In some cases, such as the evaluation of Equation 13, significant saving in computer time can be achieved by using Cholesky Factorization to avoid the need to compute $f(\mathbf{z})$. Taking the standard multivariate normal pdf, one can select values on each dimension (for example, the median of equal-probability intervals) and convert them to values in probabilistically equivalent intervals from the multivariate normal pdf of interest. This is achieved by computing $\mathbf{Z} = \mathbf{AY} + \boldsymbol{\mu}$, where $\mathbf{A}$ is a lower triangular matrix such that $\mathbf{LL}' = \boldsymbol{\Sigma}, \mathbf{Y}$ is a vector with a standard multivariate normal pdf, and $\boldsymbol{\mu}$ is the mean of the desired pdf. Since the interval bounding each $\mathbf{Z}$ is probabilistically equivalent to each corresponding interval bounding $\mathbf{Y}$, it is only necessary to compute the probability contents of these intervals once. Numerical integration of $f(\mathbf{Z})g(\mathbf{Z})$ then becomes a dot product operation with a constant vector of probability weights [a vector computed from $f(\mathbf{Z})$ at particular values of $\mathbf{Z}$] for all values of $\boldsymbol{\Sigma}$ and $\boldsymbol{\mu}$. These values can be computed once, stored, and reused as needed. It is still necessary, of course, to compute $g(\mathbf{Z})$ for all values of $\mathbf{Z}$. In some cases, this approach to numerical integration can lead to significant improvements in computing speed compared with adaptive numerical integration of the entire function. See Chapter 1 for a more thorough discussion of this technique.

CONCLUDING REMARKS

Changes occur continuously in the physical and chemical properties of stimuli in the world. Neither do our biological transduction and information processing systems remain static from moment to moment. Although universal principles governing acquisition of information, judgment, and behavior may exist, they may not be revealed by using deterministic or static models of these processes.

One approach to modeling fluctuations or changes in psychological magnitudes from moment to moment is to treat the information-containing vectors probabilistically. A general approach to thinking about and formulating probabilistic models for many psychological tasks was presented in this chapter with specific applications to similarity and identification performance. It was shown that probabilistic models may be useful in revealing the nature of the judgment function and the distance metric when stimuli are perceptually similar, and this led to a resolution of a paradox created when a deterministic model had been used to model identification performance. As a self-criticism, it must be pointed out that the probabilistic models chosen are somewhat arbitrary. A framework for building models with more concrete connections to physicochemical measures, however, has been sketched in the section on probabilistic psychophysics.

12 Developing and Characterizing Multidimensional Thurstone and Luce Models for Identification and Preference

A. A. J. Marley
McGill University

INTRODUCTION

A class of situations that has received considerable theoretical and empirical study in psychology, statistics, and economics involves the selection of the single "best" option from some available set of multidimensional options. Two of the major examples of relevance to this book are *preference* and (*absolute*) *identification.* In a typical preference situation a person has simultaneously available some finite set of options from which he or she is to select the most preferred according to some (usually specified) criterion; typical preference situations involve the selection of the preferred mode of transportation among, say, automobile, bus, and subway; the preferred investment portfolio from some set of available options; the preferred house from several currently on the market. In an (absolute) identification situation a person is usually presented with one option from some fixed set of options, which he or she is required to identify, usually in terms of a response from some simple set of responses that have previously been associated with the possible options; a typical identification situation involves identifying which pure tone has been presented from some set of pure tones that vary in, say, frequency and loudness. Note that it is possible to design an identification situation that has the structure of a preference situation—that is, with all the options simultaneously available; a typical situation would be the identification of the brightest of some simultaneously presented set of monochromatic lights.

For simplicity in the following introduction, I refer to *choice*(*s*) (*among the available options*) without distinguishing between preference and identification situations, and I call the relevant models *choice models.* Particularly in psychology and economics it is often the case that such choices (decisions) are *stochastic*—that is, repeated decisions in the "same" situation will not necessarily lead to identical choices; such stochastic choice is conceptualized as being due either to variability in the decisions of a given individual or to variability in the decisions across individuals or both. This chapter summarizes recent theoretical work on certain *probabilistic* (or *stochastic*) *choice models* that have been developed for dealing with such probabilistic (or stochastic) choice data.

There have traditionally been two major classes of such stochastic choice models (Colonius, 1984; Falmagne, 1985; Hilton, 1985, Luce, 1977a, 1977b, 1986; Luce & Suppes, 1965; this book): *random function models* assume that choices are based on some, usually deterministic, function of the values of an appropriate random vector over the available options; *constant function models* assume that choices are based on some deterministic function of appropriate, possibly vector-valued, functions over the available options.[1] Many common probabilistic choice models are both constant and random function (utility) models, the most familiar being random utility models based on multivariate dependent *probit* (or normal) distributions and those based on multivariate dependent *logit* (or extreme value) distributions. Luce (1977a, 1977b) gives excellent summaries of theoretical and empirical results on these two classes of models at that date, with the chapters in this book presenting much recent work.

As is clear from those chapters, significant additional work has been done on probit and logit models since Luce wrote his reviews, and one purpose of this chapter is to selectively summarize that work. To constrain the chapter to a reasonable length and to avoid extensive overlap with other chapters, I emphasize the development of a general random function model that includes the probit and logit models as special cases. The results obtained are important, for although the logit model has been extensively developed as a random function model in the preference case (Marley, 1989a, 1989b), no satisfactory development has been given for the logit identification model as a random function model. (Townsend & Landon, 1983, and van Santen & Bamber, 1981, present one such representation, and I later discuss in detail why I do not consider their solutions to be entirely satisfactory.) Also, in line with the theme of the book, I concentrate on models for options that have an explicit multidimensional structure.

The relevant multidimensional choice models are usually developed and motivated in one of three distinct fashions. The first assumes that the probability distributions representing the stimuli belong to some multivariate family, such as the multivariate probit (normal) or multivariate logit (extreme value), and then

[1]The definition of constant function models given here is inadequate. Marley (1989a, 1991b) discusses the difficulty of giving a brief, adequate definition of this concept. Also, I use the word *function* for the random and constant models, rather than the traditional word *utility*, to emphasize the (possibly) multidimensional nature of the representations.

adds a superstructure of memory structures, decision rules, and so on, to obtain predictions of the choice probabilities. This is my approach in the first two sections of the chapter, where I first present a general framework for describing a large class of multidimensional choice models and then give Poisson process interpretations of various of those models, including the multivariate probit and logit models.

The second approach to developing models based on probability distributions, which is not represented in this chapter, begins by stating a set of desirable properties for the distributions and then derives distributions with such properties; that is, one develops or uses a *characterization theorem* for the underlying distribution (Galambos, 1981, 1982, 1987; Galambos & Kotz, 1978). Recent examples of the latter approach are Iverson (1979, 1987) and Iverson and Sheu (1992) for the univariate normal distribution and Marley (1989a, 1989b) for the multivariate extreme value distribution.

The third modeling approach begins with the relevant choice probabilities, states some plausible constraints on them (perhaps including that they are compatible with some underlying distributional model of the form just discussed), and then attempts to infer what structures (e.g., distributions) would lead to choice probabilities satisfying the stated constraints. An outstanding example of this approach is Yellott's (1977) characterization of Luce's choice model for preference as the unique random utility model that has independent distributions differing only in their means for different options and that satisfies his *k-copies condition;* Marley and Colonius (1992) give an alternative characterization of Luce's choice model and of the transition probabilities of Tversky's (1972a, 1972b) elimination-by-aspects model, which assumes choice reaction times are available as well as choice probabilities.

Inferring underlying structures (e.g., distributions) from a set of choice probabilities is much harder than "simply" assuming some distributional representation and deriving the choice probabilities; as a consequence there are not many relevant results, especially in the multivariate case. A variant of this approach is to attempt to characterize plausible *aggregation rules* for combining the choice probabilities on unidimensional options to yield the choice probabilities on the associated multidimensional options, and then to study which choice models satisfy the obtained aggregation rules. As a motivating example, consider that aggregating preference probabilities satisfying Luce's choice model via an arithmetic mean will usually *not* give probabilities satisfying that model (Luce, 1959, p. 8), whereas Luce's choice model *is* "closed" under weighted geometric mean aggregation (Marley, 1991b, and this chapter). In the second half of the chapter, I develop results that show that under reasonable conditions arithmetic or weighted geometric means are the only possible aggregation functions. These results are somewhat disappointing because they suggest that only a small class of random function models with *independent* distributions will satisfy such relations. Nonetheless, the techniques do give interesting interpretations of several important models, particularly of the *biased-choice model* when the similarity functions satisfy either the *exponential* or *Gaussian Multidimensional Scaling* (*MDS*) *choice model* (e.g., see chap. 13). For these latter models, the results give an interesting representation of the overall choice probabilities over multidimensional options as a weighted geometric mean of the component choice probabilities over the unidimensional components of the options; this is a surprising result for the exponential Multidimensional Scaling Model, which is usually applied to stimuli with "integral" dimensions and which at first sight does not seem decomposable in the manner just mentioned. A short section then discusses possible empirical tests of this result.

The discussion section considers the reasonableness of the various models, especially of their representations by Poisson processes, given the potentially large spatial and temporal storage requirements of such representations (in the brain); these issues lead to a consideration of the relations between the present proposals and recent connectionist and "neural" models of similar tasks.

MULTIDIMENSIONAL RANDOM FUNCTION MODELS

In this and the next several sections I assume that there is a finite set T (respectively, W) of potential stimuli (respectively, responses) available, and that in any given situation some subset $S \subseteq T$ with $|S| \geq 2$ (respectively, $R \subseteq W$ with $|R| \geq 2$) is relevant; I also assume that each element of T (respectively, W) is different, an important assumption for developing the later models. Finally, I assume that choices are *stochastic*—that is, the same choice is not necessarily made on repeated presentations of the same stimulus or stimulus set. Also, for the present, I do not explicitly include in the notation the multidimensional nature of the stimuli and, possibly, of the responses; however, such is required later when I consider decompositions of choice probabilities over multidimensional stimuli in terms of choice probabilities over component unidimensional stimuli.

Let $S = \{\mathbf{s}_1, \ldots, \mathbf{s}_n\}$ be the currently relevant subset of options (stimuli). In the preference case, there are choice probabilities $P(\mathbf{s}_i{:}S)$, $i = 1, \ldots, n$, corresponding to the probability of selecting option $\mathbf{s}_i$ as "best" in S. In the identification case, with $R = \{\mathbf{r}_1, \ldots, \mathbf{r}_n\}$ denoting the available responses, there are conditional choice probabilities $P(\mathbf{r}_i|\mathbf{s}_k{:}S)$, $i, k = 1, \ldots n$, of making response $\mathbf{r}_i$ to stimulus $\mathbf{s}_k$, where response $\mathbf{r}_i$ is "correct" for stimulus $\mathbf{s}_i$, $i = 1, \ldots, n$. Clearly, without specifying any structure on the stimulus and/or response spaces, the mapping of stimuli to responses is arbitrary; later, when I explicitly consider the multidimensional nature of the stimuli and responses, the mapping is no longer arbitrary—experiments usually use a natural *compatible mapping* (Luce, 1986) between the stimulus and response spaces.

Note that, for notational simplicity, in the remainder of the chapter $P(i{:}S)$ stands for $P(\mathbf{s}_i{:}S)$ and $P(i|k{:}S)$ stands for $P(\mathbf{r}_i|\mathbf{s}_k{:}S)$.

I now present the basic notation for the proposed (multidimensional) general random function models for preference and absolute identification, give simple examples, and then present equivalent multidimensional Poisson process representations of subclasses of those models. I first state the models very generally, without explicit detail regarding what form "memory" takes, then expand on these points in the examples. The models extend van Santen and Bamber's (1981) *finite and infinite state confusion models* to explicitly include memory, so I call them *state confusion models with memory.*

The general process mapping from stimulus to response in these models is:

1. A sample value is generated of the "sensory state" associated with the currently presented stimulus.
2. Sample values are generated for the "memory" values.
3. These sample sensory and memory values determine the response, possibly probabilistically.

Thus, with $\boldsymbol{I}_k$ an indicator random variable with values in $\{1, \ldots, n\}$ that stands for the response made to stimulus $\mathbf{s}_k$, we have

$$\boldsymbol{I}_k = D(\mathbf{s}_k, \mathbf{m}) ,$$

where

$\mathbf{s}_k$ is the (real-valued) random vector associated with stimulus k
$\mathbf{m}$ is the (real-valued) memory[2] random vector
D is the possibly random function that maps combined sensory and memory random vectors onto a response

Although the notation does not show it, each of these random variables can, and normally will, depend on the context S; this dependence is made explicit when I present the equivalent distributional version of this class of models. Note that given the possibility of such dependence on the set S, *any* set of absolute identification data on *any* finite set S can be fit by a finite sensory state version of this model. Take $\mathbf{s}_k = s_k$ with probability 1, $\mathbf{m}$ arbitrary (or, rather, unnecessary), and $D(\mathbf{s}_k, \mathbf{m}) = i$ with probability $P(i|k{:}S)$. However, such generality gives no "implementation" of the decision function D; also, in actual applications, we either already have in mind some form for the random variable $\mathbf{s}_k$, for example, distributed as a multivariate normal, or we are given a representation of

[2]I later let m stand for the number of dimensions in the stimulus (and memory) state space. This use of **m** and m with distinct meanings is somewhat undesirable, but **m** is a good mnemonic for memory, and the use of m for dimension agrees with the notation of various other authors.

the response probabilities $P(\mathrm{i}|\mathrm{k}{:}\mathrm{S})$ in terms of stimulus, memory, and decision parameters and we want to know if the preceding model can generate such probabilities with a "sensible" mapping between the stimulus, memory, and decision parameters in the assumed representation and in the model (see van Santen & Bamber, 1981, and this chapter). Note that allowing the internal state representation of individual stimuli to depend on the available set S gives a form of *context dependence*. Although many contemporary models do not assume such context dependence, significant amounts of data appear to require it for their explanation; these data and relevant models are presented briefly in the discussion section.

Returning to the interpretation of the model, stage 2 "memory" would normally be used for, say, storing *referent* or *prototype* values or distributions for each possible stimulus in the experiment; stage 3 "memory" would be used to store the *decision rule* (deterministic or probabilistic) that maps the combined sensory and stage 2 memory values onto a response. This is a rather arbitrary separation of the overall memory requirements of the task, and a different, possibly more detailed, notation might eliminate this distinction; however, the current notation agrees with the way most models are presented. Note that no matter how one allocates the memory requirements, a worst-case decision rule is possible that requires explicit storage of the desired response for each possible sensory state. This is clearly not possible, with finite memory resources, for infinite state spaces. Thus, we must either consider any infinite state space model to be an approximation to an actual finite space model or study simpler decision rules that approximate the "correct" rule; see Example 1 later. Finally, note that there is much debate regarding whether the decision function D is always deterministic (see, for instance, Ashby & Gott, 1988; Ashby & Maddox, 1990; Nosofsky, this volume); it is clear from the foregoing formulation that the answer to this question depends on where one places various "memories" in the model.

When the foregoing class of state confusion models with memory is represented in the usual distribution form, we obtain

$$P(\mathrm{i}|\mathrm{k}{:}\mathrm{S}) = \int_{\mathbf{S}\times\mathbf{M}} f_{\mathrm{S}}(\mathbf{s}|\mathrm{k})h_{\mathrm{S}}(\mathbf{m})g_{\mathrm{R}}(\mathrm{i}|\mathbf{s}, \mathbf{m})\, d\mathbf{s}\, d\mathbf{m}\ ,$$

where

$f_{\mathrm{S}}(\cdot|\mathrm{k})$ is the sensory state distribution associated with stimulus k when S is the set of possible stimuli;
$h_{\mathrm{S}}(\cdot)$ is the memory state distribution when S is the set of possible stimuli;
$g_{\mathrm{R}}(\mathrm{i}|\cdot,\cdot)$ is the probability of response i when R is the set of possible responses, given particular internal state and memory values;
$\mathbf{S}$ (respectively, $\mathbf{M}$) is the sensory (respectively, memory) state space.

The model can be specialized to preference in various ways. For instance, in standard preference experiments where the options in S are simultaneously perceptually available, we might have

$$P(\mathrm{i}{:}\mathrm{S}) = \int_{\mathbf{S}} f_{\mathrm{S}}(\mathbf{s}) g_{\mathrm{R}}(\mathrm{i}|\mathbf{s})\, d\mathbf{s}\ ,$$

where $\mathbf{s}$ is an n·m component vector of sensory-based sample values with the components (j − 1)m + k, k = 1, . . . , m, corresponding to the current vector-valued utility of option j. Similarly, when the options in S are not perceptually present, we might have

$$P(\mathrm{i}{:}\mathrm{S}) = \int_{\mathbf{M}} h_{\mathrm{S}}(\mathbf{m}) g_{\mathrm{R}}(\mathrm{i}|\mathbf{m})\, d\mathbf{m}\ ,$$

where $\mathbf{m}$ is an n·m component vector of memory-based utility values exactly paralleling the previous vector $\mathbf{s}$ of sensory-based utility values. I do not discuss preference further; see Chapter 6 for related representations in the context of *General Recognition Theory* (Ashby & Gott, 1988; Ashby & Townsend, 1986).

This *General Recognition Theory* corresponds to the subclass of state confusion models with memory where $h_{\mathrm{S}}(\cdot)$ is arbitrary (or, rather, unnecessary) and there are exclusive and exhaustive subsets $\mathrm{D}_{\mathbf{S}}(\mathrm{j})$, j = 1, . . . , n, of the state space $\mathbf{S}$ with

$$g_{\mathrm{R}}(\mathrm{i}|\mathbf{s}, \mathbf{m}) = \begin{cases} 1 & \text{if } \mathbf{s} \in \mathrm{D}_{\mathbf{S}}(\mathrm{i})\ , \\ 0 & \text{if otherwise}\ . \end{cases}$$

Thus, in General Recognition Theory,

$$P(\mathrm{i}|\mathrm{k}{:}\mathrm{S}) = \int_{\mathrm{D}_{\mathbf{S}}(\mathrm{i})} f_{\mathrm{S}}(\mathbf{s}|\mathrm{k})\, d\mathbf{s}\ .$$

In particular, (a) the sensory state distributions may depend on the context S; (b) no "memory" is used other than for retaining the decision rule; (c) the region of integration is independent of the specific sensory state on a trial. Examples 2 and 3 later are state confusion models with memory that do not satisfy the second or third condition in their given representation. However, further work is needed to show that the relevant identification probabilities *cannot* be represented by a general recognition model; such results might follow if Marley's (1971, especially Theorem 5) techniques could be extended to identification probabilities generated by multidimensional distributions.

I now give examples of the class of state confusion models with memory that assume normal (respectively, exponential) sensory distributions and that produce Thurstone (respectively, Luce) models for absolute identification.

Example 1. Multidimensional Signal Detection Model for an Ideal Observer

The sensory distribution $f_S(\cdot|k)$ for stimulus $\mathbf{s}_k$ is multivariate normal with mean μ_k and variance-covariance matrix $\boldsymbol{\Sigma}_k$. The (ideal observer) person responds $\mathbf{r}_i$ whenever the current sample value $\mathbf{s}$ is such that $f_S(\mathbf{s}|i) > f_S(\mathbf{s}|j)$ for all $j \neq i$. Thus,

$$P(i|k{:}S) = \int_{D_{\mathbf{s}}(i)} \frac{exp\,\{-0.5(\mathbf{s} - \boldsymbol{\mu}_k)^t\boldsymbol{\Sigma}_k^{-1}(\mathbf{s} - \boldsymbol{\mu}_k)\}}{(2\pi)^{n/2}|\boldsymbol{\Sigma}_k|^{1/2}}\, d\mathbf{s}\ ,$$

where $D_{\mathbf{s}}(i) = \{\mathbf{s}|f_S(\mathbf{s}|i) > f_S(\mathbf{s}|j)\ \forall j \neq i\}$.
This is clearly a special case of the general model (and of general recognition theory) with $h_S(\cdot)$ arbitrary (or, rather, unnecessary), and with

$$g_R(i|\mathbf{s}, \mathbf{m}) = \begin{cases} 1 & \text{if } \mathbf{s} \in D_{\mathbf{s}}(i), \\ 0 & \text{if otherwise .} \end{cases}$$

This representation makes it clear that the "simple" *ideal observer decision function,* determined by the regions $D_{\mathbf{s}}(j)$, $j = 1, \ldots, n$, will in general require extensive memory for its storage. As already mentioned, this is one reason why it is important to study the ability of rules such as the *general linear* (*hyperplane*) *classifier* (Ashby & Gott, 1988; Ennis & Ashby, 1991) to (approximately) solve such decision problems; the presumption being that such "simpler" rules can be implemented in the brain with less memory. However, detailed implementations of such rules are seldom formulated in the psychophysical literature, in contrast to related work in the "neural network" literature (e.g., Lacouture, 1990; Lacouture and Marley, 1992).

Example 2. Probabilistic Multidimensional Scaling Models

In these models the sample memory vector $\mathbf{m}$ has the form $(\mathbf{m}_1, \ldots, \mathbf{m}_n)$ with $\mathbf{m}_i$, $i = 1, \ldots, n$, a sample "referent" vector for stimulus s_i; thus, each $\mathbf{m}_i$ takes values in the sensory state space $\mathbf{S}$. There is also a metric d over $\mathbf{S} \times \mathbf{S}$, and the decision rule has the form

$$g_R(i|\mathbf{s}, \mathbf{m}) = \begin{cases} 1 & \text{if } d(\mathbf{s}, \mathbf{m}_i) < d(\mathbf{s}, \mathbf{m}_j) \quad \forall\, j \neq i, \\ 0 & \text{if otherwise .} \end{cases}$$

Example 3. Biased-Choice Model

This model assumes that

$$P(i|k{:}S) = \frac{\beta_i \eta_{ik}}{\sum_{j=1}^{n} \beta_j \eta_{ij}}\ ,$$

where $\eta_{ik} = \eta_{ki} \geq 0$, $\eta_{ii} = 1$, $\beta_j \geq 0$, and $\sum_{j=1}^{n} \beta_j = 1$.

Various authors, including van Santen and Bamber (1981) (respectively, Townsend & Landon, 1983) derived a representation of this model as an infinite state confusion model, using double exponential (respectively, exponential) distributions. I now present the simpler exponential representation, which can be motivated by Poisson processes, discuss why I feel this representation is not entirely satisfactory, and then reinterpret various finite and infinite state confusion models, including this one, in terms of multidimensional Poisson processes.

Given an identification experiment with $|S| = n$, consider the following sensory state and decision function distributions, where $\mathbf{s} = (s_1, \ldots, s_n)$ with each s_i a nonnegative real, and with the η, β parameters as just presented:

$$f_S(\mathbf{s}|k) = \prod_{j=1}^{n} \eta_{jk} e^{-\eta_{jk} s_j} ,$$

and

$$g_R(i|\mathbf{s}, \mathbf{m}) = g_R(i|\mathbf{s}) = \begin{cases} 1 & \text{if } \frac{s_i}{\beta_i} < \frac{s_j}{\beta_j} \quad \forall\, j \neq i, \\ 0 & \text{otherwise} . \end{cases}$$

In words, the internal state vectors are of dimension $|S|$, and response i is made to stimulus k if component i of the state vector, weighted by β_i^{-1}, is *less than* the corresponding quantity for all other components $j \neq i$. Thus, if $\mathbf{a}_k(j)$ denotes the time of occurrence of some "event" associated with response j when stimulus k occurs—with "events" occurring earlier on average for plausible responses—the foregoing representation corresponds to having

$$\Pr[\mathbf{a}_k(j) > t_j] = exp\ -\eta_{jk} t_j, \qquad t_j \geq 0 ,$$

and

$$P(i|k{:}S) = \Pr\left[\frac{\mathbf{a}_k(i)}{\beta_i} < \frac{\mathbf{a}_k(j)}{\beta_j} \quad \forall\, j \neq i\right]$$

$$= \frac{\beta_i \eta_{ik}}{\sum_{j=1}^{n} \beta_j \eta_{jk}} ,$$

the final equality being a standard result (e.g., Marley & Colonius, 1992) regarding the representation of the (biased) choice model.[3] Thus, we have a mathematically correct representation of the biased-choice model as an infinite state confusion model; van Santen and Bamber (1981) show that there is no exact finite state confusion model with this representation. I now give arguments why I

[3]We can identify "time" in this representation with real time, and the time to the first "event" with the decision time. If the similarity and bias parameters do not depend on the context S, then the representation makes the erroneous prediction that decision time *decreases* with increasing set size. See Marley (1989a, 1989b) and Marley and Colonius (1992) for further discussion of related reaction time models.

feel this representation is unsatisfactory, and proceed to what I consider a more satisfactory representation.

Suppose that the mean of each stimulus s can be represented at the sensory state level by a nonnegative m-component vector $(u_1(s), \ldots, u_m(s))$; note that the dimension m currently has *no* relation to the dimension n of the internal state representation just proposed. A very common, and well-supported assumption (Shepard, 1957; see also chap. 13), is that absolute identification data satisfy the biased-choice model with

$$\eta_{ik} = exp - d^{\alpha}(i, k), \qquad \alpha > 0 ,$$

where

$$d(i, k) = \left[\sum_{g=1}^{m} |u_g(s_i) - u_g(s_k)|^p \right]^{1/p}, \qquad p \geq 1 .$$

As Takane and Shibayama state (in chap. 13), the case $\alpha = 1$, $p = 2$ (respectively, $\alpha = 2$, $p = 2$) is usually appropriate for stimuli with *integral* (respectively, *separable*) dimensions. The first case ($\alpha = 1$, $p = 2$)—$\eta_{ik} = exp - d(i, k)$ and $d(i, k)$ Euclidean distance—is sometimes called the *exponential Multidimensional Scaling* (MDS) *choice model;* the second case ($\alpha = 2$, $p = 2$)—$\eta_{ik} = exp - d^2(i, k)$ and $d(i, k)$ Euclidean distance—is sometimes called the *Gaussian Multidimensional Scaling* (MDS) *choice model.*

Now, my major objection to the random function representation of the biased-choice model given earlier is that, with the preceding representation of the similarity measures η, the random variable $\mathbf{a}_k(j)$ depends on the distance $d(j, k)$, yet no *process* model is given to motivate such a dependence; a secondary objection is that in the given random function representation, the typical bias term β_j is "simply" a scaling factor applied to the time of occurrence of the "event" associated with $\mathbf{a}_k(j)$, again with no *process* interpretation or motivation being given for such an assumption.

What might a process interpretation of these stages look like? Focusing on $\mathbf{a}_k(j)$, it might be related to that presented earlier for probabilistic Multidimensional Scaling models: For instance, one might wish to assume that

$$\mathbf{a}_k(j) = g[d(\mathbf{s}_k, \mathbf{m}_j)] ,$$

where g is a strictly increasing function, d is the Euclidean metric, $\mathbf{s}_k$ is a sample vector from a sensory state distribution associated with stimulus k, of mean $[u_1(s_k), \ldots, u_m(s_k)]$, and $\mathbf{m}_j$ is a sample vector from a memory (referent) distribution for stimulus j, of mean $[u_1(s_j), \ldots, u_m(s_j)]$. However, to my knowledge, no one has produced such a probabilistic Multidimensional Scaling model that generates random variables $\mathbf{a}_k(j)$ that are exponentially distributed as required by the preceding representation. It might even be possible to prove that no such (independent) random variables exist.

Of course, this might not be the "correct" approach. Some other process model involving, say, random trees or random directed graphs, might yield a sensible "reason" for the forms of the random variables $\mathbf{a}_k(j)$; again, I am not aware of such representations being available at this time. I therefore now develop alternative representations of various state confusion models, including Thurstone (respectively, Luce biased-choice) models, by using Poisson processes over continuous (respectively, discrete) spaces.

MULTIDIMENSIONAL POISSON PROCESS MODELS

I develop most of the following results for *finite* state confusion models with the understanding that they can be extended to *infinite* state models by limiting arguments and/or by using measure-theoretic ideas. Relevant techniques can be found in Karlin and Taylor (1981) for continuous multidimensional Poisson processes and in Ben-Akiva and Watanatada (1981), Cohen (1980), Cosslett (1987), Dagsvik (1988), and Resnick and Roy (1990, 1991, 1992) for continuous-choice models.

Consider again General Recognition Theory with a finite state space $\mathbf{S}$; that is, there are distributions $f(\mathbf{s}|k)$ for $k = 1, \ldots, n$ (note that for simplicity f is for now assumed to be independent of the stimulus set S) and an exclusive and exhaustive partitioning $D_{\mathbf{S}}(j)$, $j = 1, \ldots, n$, of $\mathbf{S}$, such that

$$P(i|k:S) = \sum_{\mathbf{s} \in D_{\mathbf{S}}(i)} f(\mathbf{s}|k) \ .$$

I now reinterpret this model in terms of independent Poisson processes. Assume that $\mathbf{S}$ is represented in some way in the brain and that when stimulus k is presented there is associated with each state $\mathbf{s} \in \mathbf{S}$ an independent Poisson process with mean pulse rate $f(\mathbf{s}|k)$, equivalently mean interpulse time $[f(\mathbf{s}|k)]^{-1}$. Now assume that the finite set of Poisson processes associated with the set of states $\mathbf{S}$ is simultaneously monitored and that response i is made if the first Poisson process to generate a pulse belongs to the set $D_{\mathbf{S}}(i)$ as defined before. Letting $\mathbf{t}_k(\mathbf{s})$ denote the time of occurrence of the first "event" associated with state $\mathbf{s}$ when stimulus k is presented, we have

$$\Pr[\mathbf{t}_k(\mathbf{s}) > t] = exp - f(\mathbf{s}|k)t, \qquad t > 0 \ ;$$

therefore,

$$\begin{aligned} P(i|k:S) &= \Pr[s \in D_{\mathbf{S}}(i) \text{ and } t_k(\mathbf{s}) < t_k(\mathbf{w}) \quad \forall\, \mathbf{w} \neq \mathbf{s}] \\ &= \sum_{\mathbf{s} \in D_{\mathbf{S}}(i)} \Pr[t_k(\mathbf{s}) < t_k(\mathbf{w}) \quad \forall\, \mathbf{w} \neq \mathbf{s}] \end{aligned}$$

$$= \sum_{\mathbf{s}\in \mathbf{D_S}(i)} \frac{f(\mathbf{s}|k)}{\Sigma_{\mathbf{w}\in S} f(\mathbf{w}|k)}$$

$$= \sum_{\mathbf{s}\in \mathbf{D_S}(i)} f(\mathbf{s}|k)$$

$$= \Pr[\mathbf{s} \in \mathbf{D_S}(i)] \ .$$

Clearly, when the state space is infinite, one can either approximate it more and more accurately by appropriate finite state spaces (Ben-Akiva & Watanatada, 1981) or represent it directly in terms of continuous (multidimensional) Poisson processes (Karlin & Taylor, 1981). In either case the relevant Poisson argument in the infinite case will again clearly yield

$$P(i|k{:}S) = \int_{D_{\mathbf{S}}(i)} f(\mathbf{s}|k)\, d\mathbf{s} \ ,$$

the general recognition model.

If this were the extent of the application of the Poisson approach, then it might be of limited interest; therefore, I now develop it further. In the previous example the state space **S** was divided into a set of exclusive *and* exhaustive decision regions $\mathbf{D_S}(j)$, $j = 1, \ldots, n$. However, overall accuracy might be improved at the expense of increased reaction time but with reduced memory load by reducing the size of the regions $\mathbf{D_S}(j)$ so that they no longer form an exhaustive set (but for now I retain exclusivity). For example, assume that there exist constants $c_j > 0$, $j = 1, \ldots, n$, with

$$D_{\mathbf{S}}(j) = \{s | f(\mathbf{s}|j) > c_j\} \ ,$$

such that $\mathbf{D_S}(j) \neq \emptyset$, and let

$$\mathbf{D_S} = \bigcup_{j=1}^{n} \mathbf{D_S}(j) \ .$$

Then paralleling the previous development, we have

$$\begin{aligned} P(i|k{:}S) &= \Pr[\mathbf{s} \in D_{\mathbf{S}}(i) \text{ and } t_k(\mathbf{s}) < t_k(\mathbf{w}) \quad \forall\, w \in D_{\mathbf{S}} - D_{\mathbf{S}}(i)] \\ &= \sum_{\mathbf{s}\in D_{\mathbf{S}}(i)} \Pr[t_k(\mathbf{s}) < t_k(\mathbf{w}_j) \quad \forall\, \mathbf{w}_j \in D_{\mathbf{S}}(j),\ j \neq i] \\ &= \sum_{\mathbf{s}\in D_{\mathbf{S}}(i)} \frac{f(\mathbf{s}|k)}{\Sigma_{\mathbf{w}\in \mathbf{D_S}} f(\mathbf{w}|k)} \\ &= \frac{\Sigma_{\mathbf{s}\in D_{\mathbf{S}}(i)} f(\mathbf{s}|k)}{\Sigma_{j=1}^{n} \Sigma_{\mathbf{w}_j\in \mathbf{D_S}(j)} f(\mathbf{w}_j|k)} \end{aligned}$$

Again, the continuous version becomes

$$P(\mathrm{i}|\mathrm{k}:\mathrm{S}) = \int_{\mathbf{D_s}(\mathrm{i})} f(\mathbf{s}|\mathrm{k})\, d\mathbf{s} \Big/ \sum_{\mathrm{j}=1}^{\mathrm{n}} \int_{\mathbf{D_s}(\mathrm{j})} f(\mathbf{w}|\mathrm{k})\, d\mathbf{w}.$$

In both the discrete and continuous cases, the representation is beginning to look like a choice model for identification. I now show that with plausible forms for the distributions $f(.|\mathrm{k})$ and the regions $\mathbf{D_s}(\mathrm{j})$ we *do* obtain the (unbiased) choice model for absolute identification, which I then extend to the biased form.

Assume that the distribution $f(.|\mathrm{k})$ is determined by its mean $\mathbf{u}(\mathbf{s}_\mathrm{k})$, where $\mathbf{u}(\mathrm{s}_\mathrm{k})$ is an m-component (real-valued) vector, and that for any state $\mathbf{s}$,

$$f(\mathbf{s}|\mathrm{k}) = h[d(\mathbf{s}, \mathbf{u}(\mathrm{s}_\mathrm{k}))] ,$$

where d is a metric and h is strictly decreasing. For convenience assume that $\mathbf{u}(\mathrm{s}_\mathrm{k})$ is actually one of the (finite) states $\mathbf{s}$, and assume that the decision region $\mathbf{D_s}(\mathrm{j})$ for response j is given by

$$\mathbf{D_s}(\mathrm{j}) = \left\{ \mathbf{s} | f(\mathbf{s}|\mathrm{j}) = \max_{\mathbf{w}} f(\mathbf{w}|\mathrm{j}) \right\} .$$

Clearly, given such a structure for $f(.|\mathrm{k})$, the actual $\max_{\mathbf{w}} f(\mathbf{w}|\mathrm{j})$ occurs when $\mathbf{w} = \mathbf{u}(\mathrm{s}_\mathrm{j})$. Thus, the previous formula gives

$$P(\mathrm{i}|\mathrm{k}:\mathrm{S}) = \frac{h[\mathrm{d}(\mathbf{u}(\mathrm{s}_\mathrm{i}), \mathbf{u}(\mathrm{s}_\mathrm{k}))]}{\Sigma_{\mathrm{j}=1}^{\mathrm{n}}\ h(d(\mathbf{u}(\mathrm{s}_\mathrm{j}), \mathbf{u}(\mathrm{s}_\mathrm{k}))]}$$

$$= \frac{\eta_{\mathrm{ik}}}{\Sigma_{\mathrm{j}=1}^{\mathrm{n}}\ \eta_{\mathrm{jk}}} ,$$

where $\eta_{\mathrm{ik}} = h[d(\mathbf{u}(\mathrm{s}_\mathrm{i}), \mathbf{u}(\mathrm{s}_\mathrm{k}))]$, that is, the choice model for absolute identification in the special case where the response biases are equal, and $\eta_{\mathrm{ik}} = \eta_{\mathrm{ki}}$, $\eta_{\mathrm{ii}} = \eta_{\mathrm{kk}}$ for all i, k. I now extend the development to the case of general bias terms.

Thus far we have a Poisson process with mean rate $f(\mathbf{s}|\mathrm{k})$ associated with each state $\mathbf{s}$ when stimulus k is presented, and response j is made if an "event" associated with state $\mathbf{u}(\mathrm{s}_\mathrm{j})$ is the first to occur in sampling from these processes. Now replace this decision rule by the assumption that events associated with state $\mathbf{u}(\mathrm{s}_\mathrm{j})$ are "filtered" by a probability β_j; that is, the event is only recorded, or passed on to the decision center, with probability β_j. As a consequence, the process associated with response j when stimulus k is presented becomes a Poisson process with rate $\beta_\mathrm{j}\eta_{\mathrm{jk}}$, and clearly we then obtain

$$P(\mathrm{i}|\mathrm{k}:\mathrm{S}) = \frac{\beta_\mathrm{i}\eta_{\mathrm{ik}}}{\Sigma_{\mathrm{j}=1}^{\mathrm{n}}\ \beta_\mathrm{j}\eta_{\mathrm{jk}}} ,$$

that is, the biased-choice model.

Why do I consider this motivation of the biased-choice model better than that given earlier, based on van Santen and Bamber's (1981) or Townsend and Landon's (1983) result? The major reason is that in the present development the *sensory* distributions $f(.|k)$ are context-independent; in fact, $f(.|k)$ depends only on stimulus k. In the earlier development we required sensory distributions $f_S(.|k)$ that were highly dependent on all the elements in the stimulus set S. This dependence "falls out" of the present model by the selection of the *referent* sensory state for identifying each stimulus, and hence the associated response. The bias terms also have a natural interpretation in terms of filtering the basic Poisson processes. A further advantage of the current approach is that with a *fixed* set of sensory state distributions $f(.|k)$, k = 1, . . . , n, by varying the size of the decision regions $D_S(j)$ for responses j = 1, . . . , n we can move from a case of the biased-choice model (when each decision region is a particular point as before) to a case of the General Recognition Theory (when we have a particular set of exclusive and exhaustive decision regions; see the initial argument of this section). In particular, if the distributions $f(.|k)$, k = 1, . . . , n, are multivariate normal (as in Example 1), then by appropriately defining the decision regions we can either obtain a biased-choice model (with particular similarity measures determined by the form of the multivariate normal distribution) or a multivariate Thurstone model. This is an important result since all previous state confusion representations of these two models have required different distributions $f(.|k)$ for each model—normals for Thurstone models (the most common signal detection models) and context-dependent double exponentials or exponentials for Luce models (biased-choice models).

Before turning to other applications of the Poisson approach, note that the foregoing representations were for state confusion models with memory where the only "memory" was, in fact, that involved in the decision rule. Although models involving "referent" or "prototype" memory can also be represented by Poisson processes, the required spatial storage requirements (in the brain) become much larger, perhaps unreasonably so (see the discussion section). It is also possible that models that place "referents" in the sensory state space, as in the preceding representation of the biased-choice model, rather than in some separate "memory" can capture the essential properties of the more general models.

The present approach is easily extended to *categorization*. In a typical categorization experiment, each stimulus $\mathbf{s}_k$ is associated by the experimenter with some response category **J** with a probability $L(\mathbf{J}|k)$. The subject's task, upon presentation of stimulus $\mathbf{s}_k$, is to assign it to a (correct?) response category from the set $\mathscr{C}$ of available categories, and our task is to model the probabilities $P(\mathbf{J}|k)$, $\mathbf{J} \in \mathscr{C}$, of the subject responding "category **J**" given stimulus k; for simplicity, I have omitted in the notation, but not in the results, the dependence of these probabilities on the stimulus set S. An obvious extension of the Poisson model to such experiments assumes that the person observes a set of Poisson processes, one for each stimulus that has been presented in the experiment, and bases decisions on the process yielding the first "event" for the currently presented stimulus. Clearly, if the categories are disjoint, the person can respond with response category **J** whenever a Poisson "event" associated with that category occurs. However, the categories are *not* always disjoint, so the subject should perhaps allow an "event" (identification of a stimulus) to contribute to a specific response category to the extent that the (possibly incorrectly) identified stimulus has been associated by the experimenter with that category. Thus, assume that events associated with the identification of stimulus j are "filtered" in their contribution to response category **J** by a quantity $Q(\mathbf{J}|\mathrm{j})$, which may or may not equal the corresponding objective probability $L(\mathbf{J}|\mathrm{j})$. Combining these processes, we write the overall Poisson rate associated with response category **J** when stimulus $\mathbf{s}_k$ is presented as

$$\sum_{j=1}^{n} Q(\mathbf{J}|\mathrm{j})\eta_{jk} \, .$$

Note that when the categories overlap—certain stimuli have been identified by the experimenter as examples of more than one category—the Poisson processes for the various response categories are *not* independent: For instance, if the state $\mathbf{u}(\mathbf{s}_k)$ is the referent state for stimulus k, and stimulus k belongs to more than one category, then a pulse from the Poisson process associated with state $\mathbf{u}(\mathbf{s}_k)$ is considered to be evidence for each of those categories. For now we can ignore such dependencies (making the following result an approximation), or we can assume that an independent copy of the sensory states, and the corresponding Poisson processes, is associated with each response category. (Generalizations of Marley's, 1989a, 1989b, and McFadden's, 1978, work is required to develop exact results that incorporate dependencies among the Poisson processes.) So, assuming independence, we obtain

$$P(\mathbf{J}|\mathrm{k}) = \sum_{j=1}^{n} Q(\mathbf{J}|\mathrm{j})\eta_{jk} \Big/ \sum_{\mathbf{H}\in\mathscr{C}} \sum_{h=1}^{n} Q(\mathbf{H}|\mathrm{h})\eta_{hk} \, .$$

This is a slight generalization of the *context-* or *exemplar-based* (*likelihood*) *model* (Nosofsky, 1990), one of the most general and most successful recent models of categorization performance. Nosofsky's definition has $Q(\mathbf{J}|\mathrm{j}) = b_{\mathbf{J}}L(\mathbf{J}, \mathrm{j})$, where $b_{\mathbf{J}}$ is a response bias probability and $L(\mathbf{J}, \mathrm{j})$ is the likelihood of stimulus j being presented and being specified by the experimenter as being in category **J**. Nosofsky is one of the major proponents of the latter model, having related several of its special cases to other models (Nosofsky, 1990), particularly by considering various forms for the similarly measures η in terms of continuous and/or discrete "feature" representations. He has also considered the special case where the model reduces to a prototype model (Nosofsky, this volume), and applied it to recognition data (Nosofsky, 1988a, this volume; Nosofsky, Clark, & Shin, 1989).

To illustrate these points, consider a *prototype* version of the model from the current Poisson perspective. A prototype of a category is a single point in the sensory space that measures the central tendency of the relevant category examples; let $r(\mathbf{J})$ denote the prototype or referent for response category $\mathbf{J}$. Then an obvious development of the Poisson modeling approach yields

$$P(\mathbf{J}|\mathrm{k}) = \frac{b_{\mathbf{J}}\eta_{r(\mathbf{J})\mathrm{k}}}{\sum_{\mathbf{H}\in\mathscr{C}} b_{\mathbf{H}}\eta_{r(\mathbf{H})\mathrm{K}}},$$

a form of the biased-choice model with the similarities being between the presented stimulus (rather, its mean state value) and the prototypes (defined in the state space). Clearly, one can develop intermediate models between the single prototype model and the complete exemplar model by allowing each category to have *several* prototypes associated with it in such a way that the state space is efficiently covered without storing all the exemplars; Kanerva's (1988) *sparse distributed memory model* and Kruschke's (1992) *ALCOVE model* are motivated by similar efficiency concerns.

In Chapter 14, Nosofsky (see also Nosofsky et al., 1989) assumes that in a "new" versus "old" item recognition task the *total* weight in the previous model is calculated for the presented stimulus; the stimulus is then categorized as "old" if and only if this total weight is greater than a criterion value. There are numerous ways to implement a similar rule in the Poisson model, related to neural counting and timing models (Luce & Green, 1972). For instance, the person could use a *counting rule:* Take a fixed time, count the total number of filtered pulses over the whole stimulus array in that time, and respond "old" versus "new" based on that total. Or the person could use a *timing rule:* Take a fixed count, measure the time to achieve this count from the filtered processes over the whole array, and respond "old" versus "new" based on that time.

In fact, Poisson-based counting and timing models can be applied to all of the experimental paradigms described in this chapter, leading to models for reaction times as well as for choice probabilities (Luce, 1986; Marley, 1981; Ratcliff, 1978). Thus, given a stimulus, each response has an associated random count (respectively, time), and the response is selected that has the largest count (respectively, smallest time); that is, the responses are determined by a *random utility model* (Luce & Suppes, 1965; Marley, 1989a); allowing the count and/or time to depend on set size is one way to avoid the previously mentioned erroneous prediction of the Poisson representation of the biased-choice model that reaction time decreases with set size. Finally, for large counts and/or times, the relevant distributions are approximately normal with means and variances that depend on the bias and similarity parameters (Edgell & Geisler, 1980; Marley, 1981; Stern, 1987). Thus, we obtain a class of Thurstone models with a structure similar to van Santen and Bamber's (1981) double exponential and Townsend and Landon's (1983) exponential representation of the biased-choice model; this class of Thurstone models is not identical to the multidimensional signal detection models presented earlier, since the present models explicitly involve similarity parameters, whereas the earlier models are stated in terms of means and variance-covariance matrices.

Clearly, there is no difficulty in extending any of the foregoing models for categorization, recognition, and so forth, to the case of infinite state Poisson processes. However, without some thought, one cannot get back to an analogous general recognition model for, say, categorization. The reason is that in General Recognition Theory, the state "function" $f(.|\mathrm{k})$ for a given stimulus k is interpreted as a distribution function; thus *every* state $\mathbf{s}$ is possible, with probability density $f(\mathbf{s}|\mathrm{k})$, and hence a distribution of category responses $Q(\mathbf{J}|\mathbf{s})$ must be given for every state. This latter constraint is not required in the "referent"-based Poisson interpretation. Given these preambles, it is clear that a version of the general recognition model appropriate for categorization is that

$$P(\mathrm{J}|\mathrm{k}) = \int_{\mathbf{S}} f(\mathbf{s}|\mathrm{k}) Q(\mathrm{J}|\mathbf{s})\, d\mathbf{s} ,$$

with the omitted normalizing factor equal to unity; at this point, the Poisson representation of this model should be clear. Ashby and Gott (1988) and Ashby and Perrin (1988) fit this model to their data with deterministic decision rules, that is, $Q(\mathbf{J}|\mathbf{s})$ equal to 0 or 1 for all $\mathbf{J}$, $\mathbf{s}$.

As mentioned, a significant portion of Nosofsky's work on the context model concerns specific representations of the similarity functions η_{ij}, $i, j \in S$. Most of these representations are of the form

$$\eta_{ij} = exp - d^{\alpha}(\mathrm{i}, \mathrm{j}), \qquad \alpha > 0 ,$$

where

$$d(\mathrm{i}, \mathrm{j}) = \left(\sum_{g=1}^{m} w_S(g) |u_g(\mathrm{i}) - u_g(\mathrm{j})|^p \right)^{1/p} , \qquad p \geq 1 ,$$

with $\mathbf{u}(\mathrm{k}) = (u_1(\mathrm{k}), \ldots, u_m(\mathrm{k}))$ the vector of scale values for stimulus k, and $w_S(g) \geq 0$, $g = 1, \ldots, m$, a set of "attention" weights for dimension g in context S. Two commonly proposed cases are the exponential MDS choice model ($\alpha = 1$, $p = 2$) and the Gaussian MDS choice model ($\alpha = 2$, $p = 2$). Although such forms for the similarity functions η are compatible with the Poisson process model, there is nothing in its structure as given that requires such similarity functions. Some such motivations have been presented for the exponential case by Shepard (1986, 1987) and by Staddon and Reid (1990) for the exponential and Gaussian cases. In the next section, using an axiomatic approach, I produce further (weak) arguments for various such representations of the similarity parameters.

CHARACTERIZING RELATIONS BETWEEN CHOICE PROBABILITIES ON UNIDIMENSIONAL AND MULTIDIMENSIONAL OPTIONS

In the previous sections I studied various models for absolute identification of multidimensional stimuli, with the models being easily specialized to preference. These models were motivated on the basis of plausible distributions and/or Poisson processes, rather in some more basic axiomatic fashion; also, the probabilities were assumed to be for the overall identification or preference of multidimensional options with no models given for choice on the unidimensional components of those options. Consequently, no relations were suggested between overall choice probabilities on multidimensional options and component choice probabilities on the associated unidimensional options; such relations are studied in this section. I focus on absolute identification, because the results there are somewhat more complex than for preference, yet it is clear from those results what the parallel preference results would be; the preference results actually appear in Marley (1991b).

First, I need to extend the notation $P(\mathrm{j}|\mathrm{k}:\mathrm{S})$ for the overall choice probabilities to explicitly mention the component dimensions and the choice probabilities on those dimensions. Thus, let the current set of stimuli be $\mathrm{S} = \{\mathbf{s}_1, \ldots, \mathbf{s}_n\}$, where for $\mathrm{i} = 1, \ldots, \mathrm{n}$, $\mathbf{s}_i = (\mathrm{s}_{i(1)} \ldots, \mathrm{s}_{i(m)})$ is an m-component vector representing stimulus i; I use the subscript and parenthetical notation so that I can later, without confusion, let i denote (i(1), . . . , i(m)), where the latter vector is meant to identify the components of stimulus i. Similarly, the current set of responses is $\mathrm{R} = \{\mathbf{r}_1, \ldots, \mathbf{r}_n\}$, where for $\mathrm{i} = 1, \ldots, \mathrm{n}$, $\mathbf{r}_i = (\mathbf{r}_{i(1)}, \ldots, \mathbf{r}_{i(m)})$ is an m-component vector representing response i. Also, I assume that the experiment has a complete or orthogonal design in that

$$\mathrm{S} = \prod_{j=1}^{m} \mathrm{S}_j, \qquad \mathrm{R} = \prod_{j=1}^{m} \mathrm{R}_j ,$$

where for $\mathrm{j} = 1, \ldots, \mathrm{m}$,

$$\mathrm{S}_j = \{\mathbf{s}_{i(j)}, \mathrm{i} = 1, \ldots, \mathrm{n}\}, \qquad \mathrm{R}_j = \{\mathbf{r}_{i(j)}, \mathrm{i} = 1, \ldots, \mathrm{n}\}$$

are the set of possible stimulus (respectively, response) values across the stimulus (respectively, response) set on dimension j. Finally, I assume that response $\mathbf{r}_i$ is "correct" for stimulus $\mathbf{s}_i$. Nosofsky (1985b) presents data from a typical such experiment in which subjects were presented with 1 of 16 stimuli. The stimuli were lines that varied independently in length (four levels) and angle of orientation (four levels). The progression from one level to the next on each dimension was linear in the physical scale. The four values on each dimension were combined orthogonally to yield the 16 stimuli, and the possible responses were 16 buttons arranged in a 4 × 4 panel, with the mapping from stimuli to correct responses being "compatible" in the obvious sense. Clearly, many other designs are possible, varying aspects of the experiment such as the dimension of the responses, the mapping from stimuli to responses, and so forth. However, to deal fully with all such variants requires extensive additional notation, with little (at this point) additional theoretical gain; therefore, I restrict the notation and the discussion to the general complete/orthogonal design.

Throughout this section I assume that $S = \{\mathbf{s}_1, \ldots, \mathbf{s}_n\}$, $R = \{\mathbf{r}_1, \ldots, \mathbf{r}_n\}$ are specific n-element sets with $S \subseteq T$, $R \subseteq W$, where T, W are the master sets; in fact, the results hold for arbitrary $S \subseteq T$, $R \subseteq W$, with $|S| = |R| = n > 2$. Also, since in identification experiments the stimulus and response sets are of the same size n, no confusion arises by letting $N = \{1, \ldots, n\}$ denote both the stimulus set and the response set, and letting i, k, . . . , $1 \leq i, k \leq n$, denote arbitrary stimuli and/or responses.

Now let $P_g(j|k{:}S)$ denote the probability of making, in context S, component g of response j [i.e., $\mathbf{r}_{j(g)}$ or more briefly j(g)] to component g of stimulus k [i.e., $\mathbf{s}_{k(g)}$ or more briefly k(g)], where the response is to be made "with respect to dimension g." The phrase in quotation marks is intentionally vague because the component choice leading to $P_g(j|k{:}S)$ can be determined in various ways, some of which I discuss later. For now, think of the whole stimulus as being presented with the person being instructed to only "attend to" the currently relevant dimension of the stimulus and to only make the relevant component of the overall response. Given that people have limited attentional capacity, it will normally be in the person's interests to obey the instructions in order to optimize performance within the attentional constraints.

In the remainder of the chapter, a *structure of identification probabilities* is a pair (S, *P*) where $P(i|k{:}S)$ [respectively, $P_g(i|k{:}S)$, $g = 1, \ldots, m$] is the overall (respectively, component) probability of making response i (respectively, the g-th component of response i) to stimulus k in the set S. Note that a complete notation would extend the notation (S, *P*) to include the P_g, $g = 1, \ldots, m$. Also, I refer to (S, *P*), (S, *Q*), and so on, on a fixed set S as a *class of identification probabilities on S.*

Before proceeding, I make various technical comments concerning the notation $P_g(j|k{:}S)$ for the probability of making component g of response j "with respect to dimension g." First, the notation $P(j(g)|k{:}S)$ might appear clearer and more accurate; however, the axioms and models that I present later for combining identification probabilities across dimensions are more clearly stated when the dimensions g, $g = 1, \ldots, m$, are separately identified in the notation. Second, it is important to remember that $P_g(j|k{:}S)$ is the probability of responding with component g of response j, and thus this quantity does *not* depend on any other component h, $h \neq g$, of response j. In particular, if we have two responses i,j that agree on component g, that is, $i(g) = j(g)$, then *by definition* $P_g(i|k{:}S) = P_g(j|k{:}S)$. Also, the component probabilities $P_g(j|k{:}S)$, $g = 1, \ldots,$ m, have no necessary relation to the overall probabilities $P(j|k{:}s)$. It is the purpose of this section to study and motivate such relations. However, one possible such relation is

$$P(j|k{:}S) = \prod_{g=1}^{m} P_g(j|k{:}S) \ ,$$

which arises if the overall response is selected by a series of independent judgments for each component g, g = 1, . . . m; in this case, we would also have (from independence) that $P_g(j|k{:}S) = \Sigma_{\{r:r(g)=j(g)\}} P(r|k{:}S)$.

I now use the biased-choice model to illustrate the later general results. To simplify the notation, I write

$$P(j|k{:}S) \sim v_S(j|k)$$

when the identification probabilities have the form

$$P(j|k{:}S) = \frac{v_S(j|k)}{\Sigma_{h=1}^{n} v_S(h|k)}$$

for some nonnegative scale v_S. Of course, any set of identification probabilities on a fixed set S can be represented by such a scale v_S by simply letting $v_S(j|k) = P(j|k{:}S)$. However, we are usually interested in specific forms of v_S defined for all $S \subseteq T$. For example, the biased-choice model (for choice between multidimensional options) has

$$P(i|k{:}S) \sim \beta(i)\eta(i, k) \ ,$$

where I have changed the notation for the bias and similarity measures in an obvious way to make it suited to my next points.

Continuing with the biased-choice model, assume that the unidimensional absolute identification probabilities[4] also satisfy that model; that is, for g = 1, . . . , m,

$$P_g(i|k{:}S) \sim \beta_g(i)\eta_g(i, k) \ .$$

Now if there are nonnegative weights w(g), g = 1, . . . , m, such that

$$\eta(i, k) = \prod_{g=1}^{m} \eta_g(i, k)^{w(g)}$$

[4]Phrases such as "unidimensional . . . probabilities" (respectively, "multidimensional . . . probabilities") should be interpreted as meaning " . . . probabilities over unidimensional options" (respectively, " . . . probabilities over multidimensional options")—that is, it is the options, not the probabilities, that are uni- or multidimensional. The phrasing used is clearly more compact and should not lead to confusion.

and

$$\beta(i) = \prod_{g=1}^{m} \beta_g(i)^{w(g)} ,$$

then

$$P(i|k:S) \sim \prod_{g=1}^{m} P_g(i|k:S)^{w(g)} .$$

This final formula is an example of *weighted geometric mean aggregation.*

In particular, this development shows that the biased-choice model is "closed" under weighted geometric mean aggregation; that is, if the component identification probabilities satisfy the biased-choice model, then so does a weighted geometric mean of those identification probabilities. Note, however, that one can propose such a geometric mean aggregation rule *without* knowing the "form" of the component and overall identification probabilities. One of the main results of this section is a characterization of when a set of component and overall identification probabilities are so related; the second main result is a similar characterization of *arithmetic mean aggregation,* that is, where the overall identification probabilities are an arithmetic average of the component identification probabilities.

When w(g) = 1 for all g = 1, . . . , m, the preceding representation reduces to

$$P(i|k:S) = \prod_{g=1}^{m} P_g(i|k:S) ,$$

which has the interpretation that the overall response is the result of independently selecting each component of the response. Nosofsky (1985b) showed that the biased-choice model is "closed" under weighted geometric mean aggregation in this case; in other words, he obtained a special case of the foregoing general result. Note that given *any* component identification probabilities P_g, g = 1, . . . , m, one can combine them in the previous manner (based on independence) to obtain a set of predicted overall identification probabilities *P*. For instance, one might assume that the identification probabilities on each dimension are generated by independent *unidimensional* Thurstonian models, in which case the special case combination rule yields overall identification probabilities that satisfy a *multidimensional* Thurstonian model. However, it is probably not the case that the overall identification probabilities then satisfy a *unidimensional* Thurstonian model. I have not proved this result, but based on Marley (1971) I expect it to hold. In this sense, the Thurstonian representation is not closed under weighted geometric mean aggregation, whereas the biased-choice model is closed under this operation (shown earlier). Later, I discuss what models other than the biased-choice model satisfy this closure property.

One might wonder if the biased-choice model is closed under a large class of aggregation functions in addition to the weighted geometric mean. I do not have complete results on this question, although intuitively its answer is no. In particular, the biased-choice model is not closed under arithmetic mean aggregation, which, as mentioned, is the second rule that I characterize in this section. To show this result, consider the arithmetic mean form

$$P(\mathrm{i}|\mathrm{k}:\mathrm{S}) = \sum_{\mathrm{g}=1}^{\mathrm{m}} \mathrm{w}(\mathrm{g}) P_{\mathrm{g}}(\mathrm{i}|\mathrm{k}:\mathrm{S})$$

with nonnegative weights w(g) that sum to 1 (which conserves probability). It is routine to check that almost any "arbitrarily" selected set of component identification probabilities satisfying the biased-choice model will not, when combined arithmetically, give overall identification probabilities satisfying that model. The easiest way to see this fact is to note that for any three elements j, k, l $\in$ S, for the biased-choice model to hold we must have

$$P(\mathrm{j}|\mathrm{l}:\mathrm{S})P(\mathrm{l}|\mathrm{k}:\mathrm{S})P(\mathrm{k}|\mathrm{j}:\mathrm{S}) = P(\mathrm{j}|\mathrm{k}:\mathrm{S})P(\mathrm{k}|\mathrm{l}:\mathrm{S})P(\mathrm{l}|\mathrm{j}:\mathrm{S})$$

(simply substitute the expressions for the identification probabilities in this equation and remember that η, η_g are symmetric functions). Now assume that the biased-choice model holds on a three-element set {1, 2, 3} over two dimensions {1, 2} with all the bias terms equal and with the following similarity values, where omitted values are supplied by symmetry and by $\eta_g(i, i) = 1$, i = 1,2,3, g = 1,2:

Dimension 1. $\eta_1(1, 2) = 2, \quad \eta_1(1, 3) = 3, \quad \eta_1(2, 3) = 4$,
Dimension 2. $\eta_2(1, 2) = 5, \quad \eta_2(1, 3) = 6, \quad \eta_2(2, 3) = 7$.

Now combine the resulting identification probabilities arithmetrically with equal weights of 1/2. A check of the final values shows that the previously stated necessary condition for the biased choice model is not satisfied, yielding the desired result that an arithmetic combination of biased-choice models is not necessarily a biased-choice model. This result parallels that of Luce (1959, p. 8), discussed in Marley (1991b), showing that arithmetic averages of preference probabilities satisfying the choice axiom need not themselves satisfy that axiom.

Having illustrated two aggregation rules, I now give some answers to the general question, what are plausible aggregation rules for combining component identification probabilities for unidimensional options to yield overall identification probabilities for the corresponding multidimensional options? I show that under certain reasonable conditions the aggregation function must be either an arithmetic or weighted geometric mean. After presenting the main results, I discuss the biased-choice model, especially MDS versions, in more detail in the light of those results.

I first develop the arithmetic mean result, then the geometric mean result. The notation and results in each case extend those of Marley (1991b) for preference probabilities, and although I discuss the motivation of the various conditions here I do not give references to their use in other contexts; those references are given in Marley (1991b). I also assume that each experiment has at least three stimuli and three responses; for smaller set sizes additional solutions are possible besides arithmetic and weighted geometric means (Marley, 1991b). Remember that I am assuming that $S \subseteq T$, $R \subseteq W$, with $|S| = |R| = n$, and I am letting $N = \{1, \ldots, n\}$, with i, j, . . . , $i, j \in N$, denote arbitrary stimuli and/or responses.

Assumption M1 (simple marginalization property). For a structure of identification probabilities (S, P), $S \subseteq T$, and for each $k \in S$,

$$P(i|k{:}S) = F_S[i, P_1(i|k{:}S), \cdots, P_m(i|k{:}S)] ,$$

where F_S is a function that may depend on the elements of the set S.

Note that F_S does *not* depend on (stimulus) k. For completeness, I should allow the possibility that F also depends on the response set R; however, it is easy to reinterpret the results with this additional condition, and carrying the additional notation is not warranted.

I call Assumption M1 simple marginalization because it is a special case of the marginalization property considered in the context of opinion aggregation (Genest, 1984; McConway, 1981). Clearly, aggregation by simple marginalization is similar to the way univariate or marginal distributions are aggregated to form multivariate distributions; nonetheless, here the P_i are not necessarily the marginals of P.

The main result of this section is that provided $|S| > 2$, the marginalization property, plus some regularity and existence conditions (given later), imply that F_S has the form of an arithmetic mean, with weights that can depend on S. However, when $|S| = 2$, the class of solutions is much larger. Marley (1991b) gives the solutions in the preference case when $|S| = 2$; these are easily adapted to the absolute identification situation.

I now state the required additional existence and regularity conditions.

Assumption M2. For any m-dimensional real vectors $(r_1, \ldots, r_m)$, $(s_1, \ldots, s_m)$ with $r_g, s_g, r_g + s_g \in [0, 1]$, $g = 1, \ldots, m$, and for $S \subseteq T$ with $|S| = 3$, for each $k \in S$ it is possible to select identification probabilities $P_g(.|k{:}S)$ and $h, i, j \in S$ such that for $g = 1, \ldots, m$,

$$P_g(h|k{:}S) = r_g, \quad P_g(i|k{:}S) = s_g, \quad P_g(j|k{:}S) = 1 - (r_g + s_g) .$$

Note that this condition holds vacuously unless $|S| \geq 3$.

This is a technical assumption that allows the application of functional equation results to our problem. This assumption is somewhat strange in that we are dealing with finite sets T, yet we want the total set of available probabilities to be quite dense. Nonetheless, the assumption is plausible for the usual choice models for absolute identification, for example, Luce's biased-choice model. Although it is probably worthwhile in the future to study weaker versions of this condition, it is nonetheless Assumption M1 (and not Assumption M2) that is the major constraint. (Falmagne, 1981, discusses the use of conditions similar to Assumption M2 in other situations and presents weaker versions of those conditions. Also, Aczel & Dhombres, 1989, chap. 6, discuss the related general problem of *conditional* functional equations.)

Assumption M3 (dominance principle). For structures of identification probabilities (S, P), (S, Q), $S \subseteq T$, if $P_g(i|k{:}S) < Q_g(i|k{:}S)$ for all g = 1, . . . , m, then $P(i|k{:}S) < Q(i|k{:}S)$.

This is clearly a form of monotonicity for the function F_S in Assumption M1.

Assumption M4 (zero preservation property). For a structure of identification probabilities (S, P), $S \subseteq T$, if $P_g(i|k{:}S) = 0$ for all g = 1, . . . , m, then $P(i|k{:}S) = 0$.

This condition obviously says that if every component of response i has zero probability of being made to stimulus k in the component experiments, then this response is never made to stimulus k in the overall experiment; that is, if the response i is not in the "confusion set" of stimulus k on any of the dimensional judgments, then it is not in the corresponding overall confusion set.

THEOREM 12.1. If a class of identification probabilities on a finite set S satisfies Assumption M1 and M2, then, provided $|S| > 2$, there exist weights $w_S(g)$, g = 1, . . . , m, and a fixed probability measure $\Psi(\cdot{:}S)$ over S such that $\Sigma_{g=1}^{m} wS(g) \leq 1$ and for each structure of identification probabilities (S, P),

$$P(i|k{:}S) = \sum_{g=1}^{m} w_S(g) P_g(i|k{:}S) + \left[1 - \sum_{g=1}^{m} w_S(g)\right] \Psi(i{:}S) .$$

If Assumptions M2 and M3 hold, then this representation has $w_S(g) \in [0, 1]$, and if Assumptions M1, M2, and M4 hold, then $\Sigma_{g=1}^{m} w_S(g) = 1$.

Proof: The statement of Marley's (1991b) Theorem 1 exactly parallels that of Theorem 12.1, except that where we have a class of identification probabilities on a set S he has a class of choice probabilities on a set S; that is, for each $x \in S$ there is a set of choice probabilities $P_g(x{:}S)$, g = 1, . . . , m, [respectively, $P(x{:}S)$], that are the probabilities of choosing the option x from the set S on dimension g (respectively, overall). However, no properties of x, S are used in the proof of Marley's (1991b) Theorem 1 beyond those stated in his Assumptions M1–M4, which parallel the corresponding conditions just given. Thus, if in Marley's (1991b) Theorem 1 we reinterpret $P(x{:}S)$, $P_g(x{:}S)$, $g = 1, \ldots, m$, as a set of identification probabilities conditioned on a stimulus k, then we immediately obtain the result.

I call the representation of Theorem 1 *arithmetic mean aggregation.* As in Marley (1991b), it is unclear how to interpret negative weights in this context, although examples with such weights can be constructed that satisfy the probability constraints (Genest, 1984). Thus it is reasonable to add Assumptions M3 and/or M4. Also note that the theorem gives no constraint on the form of the (nonnegative) weights $w_S(g)$ and the probability distribution Ψ, only that they exist. The obvious interpretation is that $w_S(g)$ is the probability of "attending" to dimension g and basing the choice on that dimension alone, and that $1 - \Sigma_{g=1}^{m} w_S(g)$ is the probability of choosing "randomly" according to the distribution Ψ. Note that since the weights depend on the context S, such a strategy can lead to quite complex patterns of choices, which will not superficially appear to be determined at any given choice opportunity by a single dimension.

I demonstrated earlier that the biased-choice model is not closed under arithmetic mean aggregation, and I am not aware of any common choice model that is so closed. What I would consider as an example would be some model that has the same "form" for the component and overall identification probabilities, with these probabilities related by an arithmetic mean formula, thereby paralleling my earlier demonstration that the biased-choice model is closed (has the same form) under weighted geometric mean aggregation.

I now present the second set of assumptions that lead to weighted geometric mean aggregation rules. As in the previous section, I present various assumptions, motivating them as I proceed. For simplicity, I assume *nonzero* identification probabilities. First, for a structure of identification probabilities (S, P), $S \subseteq T$, and $i,j \in N$, let

$$L_S^P(i,j|k) = \frac{P(i|k{:}S)}{P(j|k{:}S)} ;$$

that is, $L_S^P(i, j|k)$ is the likelihood or odds ratio for choosing response i versus response j in context S according to the measure P. Similar notation is used for the corresponding unidimensional odds ratios.

Assumption L1 (likelihood independence property). For any structure of nonzero identification probabilities (S, P), $S \subseteq T$, and $i, j, k \in N$,

$$L_S^P(i,j|k) = F_S[L_S^{P_1}(i,j|k), \ldots, L_S^{P_m}(i,j|k)] ,$$

where F_S is a function that may depend on S.

Clearly, this condition states that it does not matter in calculating likelihood ratios whether one first calculates them on the individual dimensions and then combines these ratios over dimensions, or simply calculates likelihood ratios of the choice probabilities on the multidimensional set. Again, note that F_S is assumed not to depend on the current stimulus k.

I now show that, under certain "technical" conditions, when $|S| \geq 3$ the only solutions to Assumption L1 are weighted geometric means.

Assumption L2 (solvability). For $S \subseteq T$ with $|S| > 2$ and for every $\mathbf{a} = (a_1, \ldots, a_m)$, $\mathbf{b} = (b_1, \ldots, b_m)$, a_i, b_i positive reals, for each $k \in S$ it is possible to select a structure of nonzero identification probabilities (S,P) and $h, i, j \in S$ such that for $g = 1, \ldots, m$,

$$L_S^{P_g}(h, i|k) = a_g, \qquad L_S^{P_g}(i, j|k) = b_g .$$

Note that this condition requires $|S| \geq 3$. Similar comments can be made about it as were made previously about Assumption M2.

Assumption L3 (dominance principle). For structures of nonzero identification probabilities (S, P), (S, Q), $S \subseteq T$, and $i,j,k \in N$, if

$$L_S^P(i, j|k) \leq L_S^Q(i, j|k), \qquad g = 1, \ldots, m ,$$

then

$$L_S^P(i, j|k) \leq L_S^Q(i, j|k) .$$

This is again a monotonicity condition for F_S in Assumption L1.

THEOREM 12.2. If a class of nonzero identification probabilities on a finite set S satisfies Assumptions L1–L3, then provided $|S| \geq 3$ there exist nonnegative constants $w_S(g)$, $g = 1, \ldots, m$, such that

$$P(i|k:S) = \prod_{g=1}^{m} P_g(i|k:S)^{w_S(g)} \Big/ \sum_{h \in S} \prod_{g=1}^{m} P_g(h|k:S)^{w_S(g)} .$$

Again, the proof exactly parallels that of Marley's (1991b) Theorem 2. I call the representation of Theorem 12.2 *weighted geometric mean aggregation*.

As mentioned at the beginning of this section, when $w_S(g) = 1$ for all $g = 1, \ldots, m$, the representation becomes

$$P(i|k:S) = \prod_{g=1}^{m} P_g(i|k:S) ,$$

which has the obvious interpretation that the overall response is selected by independently selecting each component of the response. Regrettably, there is no obviously parallel "process" interpretation for the case of general weights $w_S(g)$, $g = 1, \ldots, m$.

Note that the results of Theorems 12.1 and 12.2 do not explicitly restrict the "form" of the component and overall identification probabilities; they only give relations between these probabilities. It is therefore of interest to know when the component and overall identification probabilities are of the same "form." Marley (1991a, 1992) has studied the parallel question for choice and ranking probabilities without providing a complete solution. Here I present an extension of one of his examples that satisfies weighted geometric mean aggregation and includes the biased-choice model as a special case. Remember, I previously showed that the biased-choice model is not closed under arithmetic aggregation but that it is closed under weighted geometric mean aggregation. In that demonstration I used weights that did not depend on the set S, but the result continues to hold in the general case provided we allow the overall similarity measures η and the biases b to depend on the set S through the weights. This is considered a reasonable thing to do.

For my general example, suppose there are nonnegative quantities $\eta_g(i, j|k)$ that measure the *plausibility* of response i versus response j on dimension g given that stimulus k has been presented. Now assume that

$$P_g(i|k{:}S) \sim b_g(i) \prod_{j \neq i} \eta_g(i,j|k)^{1/\theta(S)},$$

with $\theta(S) > 0$. Thus, if the representation of Theorem 12.2 also holds, then

$$P(i|k{:}S) \sim b_S(i) \prod_{j \neq i} \eta_S(i,j|k)^{1/\theta(S)},$$

where

$$\eta_S(i,j|k) = \prod_{g=1}^{m} \eta_g(i,j|k)^{w_S(g)}$$

and

$$b_S(i) = \prod_{g=1}^{m} b_g(i)^{w_S(g)}.$$

This is the *generalized Rotondo model* (Marley, 1991a) extended to absolute identification. Note that the component and overall identification probabilities are all of the same form, and that the model reduces to the biased-choice model when $\theta(S) = |S|$ and

$$\eta_g(i,j|k) = \frac{\eta_g(i, k)}{\eta_g(j, k)}.$$

In the preference case the generalized Rotondo model can handle various (context-dependent) phenomena that are beyond the scope of Luce's choice model (Marley, 1991a; Rotondo, 1986), so one might expect similar generality in absolute identification.

This is the end of my general aggregation results. In the next section I discuss how one might attempt to test them, and in the discussion section I consider whether there are plausible aggregation functions besides arithmetic and geometric means.

ISSUES ASSOCIATED WITH EXPERIMENTAL TESTS OF AGGREGATION THEOREMS

I now discuss the difficulties of designing experiments that adequately test a model that satisfies weighted geometric mean aggregation. I focus on the biased-choice model, discussing the MDS case in detail, especially the exponential and Gaussian versions. I show that a generalized version of the MDS model formally satisfies weighted geometric aggregation, but that it is not obviously true that the relevant data will be thus aggregable.

First, however, I need to briefly discuss possible experimental designs for the collection of the component identification data. There are two relevant aspects to such designs: the Data Collection Method and the Stimulus Presentation Method. I discuss three methods under each heading.

Data Collection Methods

1. The component probabilities are obtained as the marginals of the relevant overall probabilities; that is,

$$P_g(\mathrm{i}|\mathrm{k:S}) = \sum_{\{\mathrm{r:r(g)=i(g)}\}} P(\mathrm{r}|\mathrm{k:S}) .$$

This does not seem to make much sense as a way to "estimate" the component probabilities, which we would normally expect to be estimated separately from the overall probabilities, for instance, as in methods 2 and 3. Nonetheless, as previously discussed, the component and overall probabilities will satisfy this relation in the independent case where

$$P(\mathrm{r}|\mathrm{k:S}) = \prod_{\mathrm{g=1}}^{\mathrm{m}} P_g(\mathrm{r}|\mathrm{k:S}) .$$

2. The component probabilities are obtained in specific blocks in which the

subject is instructed to "only attend to" the relevant dimension of the presented stimulus.

If such blocks are separate, say on different days, then it is reasonable to expect the subject to comply with the instruction, to the extent possible with the given (integral or separable) stimuli; see the sequel.

3. The component probabilities are obtained on specific trials on which the subject is instructed to "only attend to" the relevant dimension of the presented stimulus; however, trials for different dimensions and for the overall judgments are (randomly) intermixed.

In this case, it is not clear how well the subject will be able to obey the instructions to only attend to the relevant dimension, especially if changing attention (weights) takes time and/or learning.

Stimulus Presentation Methods

1. Only component g of the stimulus is presented.
2. All components of the stimulus are presented but the values on each "irrelevant" dimension are equal across the stimulus set; each equal value may or may not be one of those used in other parts of the experiment.
3. All components of the stimulus are presented with their values being those used in other parts of the experiment.

Clearly, Method 1 is only possible when the stimulus can be broken up into their individual components (dimensions); this is seldom the case even with so-called separable stimuli. Using Method 2 implicitly assumes that the "irrelevant" component values are truly irrelevant; otherwise there is no reason to expect to be able to combine the obtained component identification probabilities to obtain or predict the overall identification probabilities. Method 3 is clearly the easiest to defend, but it can still be combined with Data Collection Methods 2 and 3 to yield (probably) different results.

I now discuss the MDS choice model in the context of these Data Collection and Stimulus Presentation Methods. I first develop the model in very general form with various "attention" weights being dependent on the stimulus set S, whereas later I remove such dependence for many of the weights. However, in this way I show that the most general form satisfies geometric mean aggregation, and I can then easily develop the special cases as needed.

Using the notation for stimulus means introduced previously, consider the metric

$$d(\mathrm{i}, \mathrm{k}) = \left(\sum_{\mathrm{g}=1}^{\mathrm{m}} w_{\mathrm{S}}(\mathrm{g}) |u_{\mathrm{g}}(\mathrm{i}) - u_{\mathrm{g}}(\mathrm{k})|^{\mathrm{p}} \right)^{1/\mathrm{p}}, \qquad \mathrm{p} \geq 1 ,$$

where

$$w_S(g) \geq 0 \, ,$$

and let

$$d_g(i, k) = v_S(g)|u_g(i) - u_g(k)| \, ,$$

where $v_S(g) > 0$ for every g. Then clearly

$$d^p(i, k) = \sum_{g=1}^{m} x_S(g) d_g^p(i, k)$$

with

$$x_S(g) = \frac{w_S(g)}{v_S^p(g)} \, .$$

Now consider the following (generalized) MDS choice model representation of the overall and component choice probabilities: $\alpha > 0$ and

$$P(i|k{:}S) \sim \beta_S(i) \; exp - \frac{d^p(i, k)}{d^\alpha(i, k)} \, ,$$

and

$$P_g(i|k{:}S) \sim \beta_g(i) \; exp - \frac{d_g^p(i, k)}{d^\alpha(i, k)} \, , \qquad g = 1, \ldots, m \, ,$$

with

$$\beta_S(i) = \prod_{g=1}^{m} \beta_g(i)^{u_S(g)} \, .$$

Then it is easily checked that

$$P(i|k{:}S) \sim \prod_{g-1}^{m} \{P_g(i|k{:}S)\}^{x_S(g)} \, ;$$

that is, the overall identification probabilities are a weighted geometric mean of the component identification probabilities.

Note that, in general, in these representations both the component and the overall similarity measures, that is,

$$\eta_g(i, k) = exp - \frac{d_g^p(i, k)}{d^\alpha(i, k)}$$

and

$$\eta(i, k) = exp - \frac{d^p(i, k)}{d^\alpha(i, k)}$$

depend on the set S (as do the overall bias parameters) through the weights $v_S(g)$ and $w_S(g)$. Now it is accepted that the overall similarity measure η should depend on S through the "attention" weights w_S (e.g., Nosofsky, 1986), and I now discuss whether it is reasonable to have the component similarity measures η_g depend on S through the attention weights. Since the usual idea is that total attentional capacity is limited, it is customary to assume that $\Sigma_{g=1}^{m} w_S(g) = 1$. I implicitly assume this constraint, although it has minor impact on the conclusions. Also, I refer to *integral* and *separable* stimulus dimensions: Integral dimensions are those that combine into relatively unanalyzable unitary wholes, whereas separable dimensions are highly analyzable, remaining psychological distinct when in combination (Garner, 1974; Nosofsky, 1987; Shepard, 1964; see also chap. 7).

I now consider some special cases of the (generalized) MDS model in the context of Data Collection Methods and Stimulus Presentation Methods.

Special Case 1. $\alpha = 0$

The model reduces to

$$P(i|k{:}S) \sim \beta_S(i) exp\ -d^p(i, k)$$

and

$$P_g(i|k{:}S) \sim \beta_g(i) exp\ -d_g^p(i, k)\ .$$

Thus, each component identification probability only depends on the distance and the weight on that component. Also, when $p = 2$ we obtain the Gaussian MDS choice model, which is usually assumed to hold for separable dimensions. In the obvious sense the identification probabilities are themselves separable (independently decomposable) across dimensions. Such results (as data) seem most likely to be obtained with Data Collection Method 2 and any of the Stimulus Presentation Methods, assuming that the dimensions are truly separable. Given all these provisos, we would also expect the attention weight on each component to equal 1; that is, $v_S(g) = 1$ for $g = 1, \ldots, m$.

Special Case 2. $\alpha = p - 1$

The model reduces to

$$P(i|k{:}S) \sim \beta_S(i)\ exp\ -d(i, k)$$

and

$$P_g(i|k{:}S) \sim \beta_g(i)\ exp\ -\frac{d_g^p(i, k)}{d^{p-1}(i, k)}\ .$$

In this case, when $p = 2$ we obtain the exponential MDS choice model on the *overall* choice probabilities, but the component choice probabilities are not independent of the overall distances. However, the exponential MDS choice model is usually considered appropriate for integral dimensions, which might fit in with the previous result. In particular, if the experiment is run with Data Collection Method 3 and Stimulus Presentation Method 3, then it is conceivable (although obviously not necessary) that the component identification probabilities (data) will have the preceding form. Note that in this case we would not necessarily expect all the weights $v_S(g)$ on the individual dimensions to equal 1, the idea being that since the stimuli are integral and the one-dimensional judgments are (randomly) intermixed with the overall judgments, the person does not necessarily have the time or ability to move the full attentional resources to the given dimension on each trial.

Finally, note that all of the results are driven by the desire to fit the general MDS choice model into the weighted geometric mean aggregation framework. A more common interpretation of the exponential MDS choice model would assume that

$$P(i|k{:}S) \sim \beta_S(i)\ exp\ -d(i,\ k)$$

and

$$P_g(i|k{:}S) \sim \beta_g(i)\ exp\ -d_g(i,\ k)\ ,$$

with

$$d^2(i,\ k) = \sum_{g=1}^{m} x_S(g) d_g^2(i,\ k)$$

and

$$\beta_S(i) = \prod_{g=1}^{m} \beta_g(i)^{u_S(g)}\ .$$

This version does *not* satisfy weighted geometric mean aggregation.

This discussion is clearly not complete. I only introduced the MDS choice models as motivating examples, but it is nonetheless interesting to see the issues that are raised by these models when one looks at possible combinations of component identification probabilities to yield overall identification probabilities.

DISCUSSION

I have presented basic results for three approaches to developing probabilistic models of absolute identification, with some comments on probabilistic models of categorization and recognition. The first approach "simply" assumes some distributional structure for the sensory, memory, and response processes; the second approach reformulates various distributional models in terms of Poisson processes; the third approach relates the identification probabilities for multidimensional options to the identification probabilities on their unidimensional projections. The biased-choice model can be motivated via each of the approaches and is currently the only model that I am aware of with this property. For instance, Thurstone models do not appear to be closed under either of the aggregation rules presented in the fourth section. Thus, an interesting open question is, what class of state confusion models (with memory?) or Poisson process models (although this class has not been explicitly defined) satisfies either arithmetic or geometric mean aggregation as defined in the fourth section? If we restrict attention to sensory distributions and Poisson processes that are context independent (i.e., depend only on the current stimulus), perhaps the class of such models is not much larger than the biased-choice model (Marley, 1991a, 1991b and the fourth section of this chapter). An alternate approach would be to study (models satisfying) relations other than arithmetic and geometric mean combination. For instance, there is much recent interesting work on developing and characterizing multidimensional probability distributions in terms of functions of their univariate marginals (Alsina, 1989; Marshall & Olkin, 1988; Schweizer & Sklar, 1983). It is a standard result that any multivariate distribution $\boldsymbol{F}[x_1, \ldots, x_m]$ can be expressed as a function $\boldsymbol{H}$ of its univariate marginals $\boldsymbol{F}_i(x_i)$, $i = 1, \ldots, m$; that is, $\boldsymbol{F}[x_1, \ldots, x_m] = \boldsymbol{H}[\boldsymbol{F}_1(x_1), \ldots, \boldsymbol{F}_m(x_m)]$. The contribution of recent work is to study specific combination functions $\boldsymbol{H}$ with interesting properties. Clearly, these results could fruitfully be used to develop multivariate distributions for the (sensory) components of state confusion models. The question regarding aggregation at the level of the identification probabilities essentially then concerns what combination functions $\boldsymbol{H}$ at the level of the state distributions also yield an aggregation function at the level of the identification probabilities. Alsina's (1989) work suggests that the class of solutions will be quite limited, and Latta (1979) and Marley (1982, 1991a) discuss related issues, such as how one might represent choices over a multielement set in terms of choices over its binary subsets.

For absolute identification (and preference), I have shown a formal equivalence between a class of Poisson process models and certain state confusion models. However, I have not seriously studied the spacial storage requirements for the Poisson process representation. Clearly, for large-dimensional stimuli and/or large state or memory spaces, placing the whole (sensory) state space "in the brain" (the Poisson models) as opposed to "in the world" (the confusion models) requires considerable capacity and, with more than three dimensions, considerable ingenuity in solving the embedding, or "packing," problem. Only when the stimulus dimensions are "independent" are these storage and packing problems easily solved, by representing each stimulus dimension separately by its own unidimensional spatial Poisson process (Nosofsky, 1985b). On the other hand, confusion models, particularly with infinite state spaces, implicitly assume that the relevant internal states and decision variables are continuous-valued vectors, which themselves require extensive spatial and/or temporal storage and comparison capacities. Thus, although at first the storage requirements of the Poisson representation might appear unrealistic, further study and comparison with other approaches might change this opinion, or perhaps lead to the conclusion that all current approaches are unrealistic in terms of storage and computational requirements!

I have not placed much emphasis on the possibility that the state representations and Poisson processes might be context-dependent—that is, that they might depend on the full stimulus (and response) context, not just on the current stimulus. However, there is much data that seem to require such context dependence; for instance, it is known that absolute identification performance has a very low upper limit corresponding to perfect identification of no more than four to eight stimuli. The "standard" explanations of this phenomenon use sensory state representations that are highly context dependent on the number and range of stimuli in the experiment (see, for instance, Durlach & Braida, 1969; Marley & Cook, 1984, 1986; Vickers, 1979). Related data and theory concern the amount of a limited total capacity "attention" paid to the component dimensions in multidimensional absolute identification (e.g., Nosofsky, 1986; fifth section of this chapter). Finally, suggestions are frequently made in the neurophysiological and "neural" modeling literature that only six to eight levels of a given sensory dimension are available and/or required for many sensory tasks (see, for instance, Arbib, 1989; Ballard, 1986; Rosenfeld & Touretzky, 1988). Together these results not only show the importance of context in determining the sensory representation and the allocation of attention, but also the plausibility of models based on a small number of internal states, with the allocation of states to external stimuli being adjusted dynamically, depending on the context. Such approaches, based on assuming small numbers of internal states, overcome the concerns regarding the complexity of context-independent Poisson representations.

The models presented in this chapter describe the choice probabilities in simple stimulus-response mapping tasks, and they implicitly assume asymptotic performance. The models must be extended to reaction time, to more complex tasks, and, especially, to learning. In fact, only learning methods can currently solve complex tasks such as saying a printed word (e.g., Hinton, 1989; Sejnowski & Rosenberg, 1987). Clearly, recent connectionist approaches (McClelland & Rumelhart, 1986; Rumelhart & McClelland, 1986) are important in this context, with the work on stochastic *Boltzmann machines* (Aarts & Korst, 1989) being very similar in motivation to the Poisson models presented here. However, until recently, little connectionist work within psychology has been devoted to the study of "simple" tasks such as identification, categorization, and recognition. There are currently signs of a major upswing in interest in these topics. For instance, see Lacouture (1990) and Lacouture and Marley (1992) on identification, Pavel, Gluck, and Henkle (1988) on categorization, Ratcliff (1990) on recognition, and Aha and McNulty (1989), Aha and Goldstone (1990), and Kruschke (1992) for concept and category learning. The latter works are especially relevant and interesting in the present context since they were partially motivated by the desire to implement a learning algorithm compatible with Nosofsky's (1986, 1987) *generalized context model,* especially the attention-focusing weights (see earlier in this chapter). Finally, Shepard's (1987, 1990; Shepard & Kannappans, 1991) and Staddon and Reid's (1990) recent work is similar in spirit to the Poisson models of this chapter.

In conclusion, the "classical" and superficially "trivial" absolute identification task continues to be a testing ground for theoretical developments in mathematical psychology, and it can perhaps also become a benchmark task for the serious application of the newer connectionist learning models to psychological data.

ACKNOWLEDGMENTS

This work was supported by the Natural Science and Engineering Research Council of Canada. Parts of the chapter are based on an invited address at the Twenty First Annual Meeting of the Society for Mathematical Psychology, Northwestern University, July 1988, and a Colloquium at the Irvine Research Unit in Mathematical Behavioral Sciences, January 1990. I thank R. Duncan Luce, director of that unit, for inviting me to spend a month there. I have also benefited from the comments of Greg Ashby and Rob Nosofsky.

13 Structures in Stimulus Identification Data

Yoshio Takane
Tadashi Shibayama
McGill University

INTRODUCTION

Stimulus identification data have attracted considerable attention from many researchers (e.g., Ashby & Perrin, 1988; Keren & Baggen, 1981; Nosofsky, 1985b; J. E. K. Smith, 1980, 1982; Takane & Shibayama, 1986; Townsend & Ashby, 1982; Townsend & Landon, 1982). In a stimulus identification experiment one of n stimuli is randomly selected and presented on each trial, and the subject's task is to identify the stimulus. The basic data thus consists of a set $f_{j/i}$ (i = 1, . . . , n; j = 1, . . . , n) of frequencies of response j when stimulus i is presented, with $f_i = \Sigma_j f_{j/i}$ the total number of presentations of stimulus i.

Various models have been proposed for stimulus identification data (e.g., Ashby & Perrin, 1988; Keren & Baggen, 1981; Luce, 1963a; Nakatani, 1972; Shepard, 1957; Townsend, 1971). Typically, these models attempt to predict $p_{j/i}$, the probability of response j when stimulus i is presented. The models are distinguished by different submodels assumed for $p_{j/i}$. Two major classes of models have been proposed. (We exclude, from our account, the more recently proposed general recognition model by Ashby and Perrin, 1988, since it is treated in Chaps. 6–8, and 16. Also, see Ashby and Lee, 1991.) One class is similarity-choice models, and the other is sophisticated guessing models (J. E. K. Smith, 1980; Townsend & Landon, 1982).

In the similarity-choice models, a model of stimulus similarity is postulated, and the strength of a response when a stimulus is presented is defined as a function of the stimulus similarity and the bias for that response. A response is assumed chosen with probability proportional to its response strength relative to other alternative responses. This class of models includes the unrestricted similarity-choice model (sometimes called the biased-choice model; Luce, 1963a). The Euclidean distance-choice model [sometimes called the MDS (Multidimensional Scaling) choice model; Shepard, 1957; Nosofsky, 1985b], and the unique feature-choice model (Keren& Baggen, 1981; Tversky, 1977). These models have been systematically compared by Takane and Shibayama (1986).

In the sophisticated guessing models, a presentation of a stimulus is assumed to generate an internal state, called a confusion set, characterized by a set of admissible responses. Its probability is defined as a function of stimulus similarities/dissimilarities. A response is chosen from the admissible responses in the confusion set with probability proportional to the response bias. The confusion probability is the sum, over all possible confusion sets, of probabilities leading to a certain response when a certain stimulus is presented. This class of models includes various versions of Nakatani's (1972) confusion-choice model, the all-or-none (AON) model (Broadbent, 1967; Townsend, 1971), the overlap (OVLP) activation model (Townsend, 1971), and the informed guessing model (Pachella, Smith, & Stanovich, 1978). The latter three models are also considered special cases of the similarity-choice models (see fourth section).

There has been considerable effort to establish relationships among various models of stimulus identification data. See Marley (chap. 12), Nosofsky (in press), Takane and Shibayama (1986), Townsend and Ashby (1982), Townsend and Landon (1982, 1983), and van Santen and Bamber (1981), each presenting a somewhat different viewpoint for relating the models.

This chapter compares goodness of fit (GOF) of the models in the two classes. A general strategy for model comparison is presented first (second section). It is illustrated by three examples for assessing the stability of confusion probabilities across contexts (across trials, across subjects, and across other stimulus conditions). In the third section, the similarity-choice models are briefly reviewed. Then, two related issues will be addressed, namely, fitting ADDTREE and EXTREE to stimulus identification data, and the problem of d (exponential) versus d^2 (Gaussian) in the exponent of the Euclidean distance-choice model. In the fourth section, the sophisticated guessing models are discussed along with their relationships. Empirical results are presented in the fifth section.

A STRATEGY FOR MODEL COMPARISON

Different models of stimulus identification data postulate different submodels for $p_{j/i}$. Whichever submodels are assumed, however, the likelihood of the total set of observations may be written as

$$L = \prod_{i} \prod_{j} (p_{j/i})^{f_{j/i}} , \qquad (1)$$

where $p_{j/i}$ may be further constrained in various ways. Model parameters are determined in such a way as to maximize the log of L. Note that the definition of L does not include terms that are not related to model parameters. These terms do not affect the maximum likelihood estimates.

Once the maximum likelihood is obtained, Akaike's (1974) Information Criterion (AIC) can readily be calculated and used for model comparison. This statistic is defined as

$$AIC\ (\mathrm{q}) = -2\ ln\ L^*(\mathrm{q}) + 2\mathrm{n}(\mathrm{q})\ , \tag{2}$$

where $L^*(\mathrm{q})$ is the maximum likelihood and n(q) is the effective number of parameters in model q. The first term on the right side of Equation 2, $-2\ ln\ L^*(\mathrm{q})$, indicates a badness of fit of model q to the current data set. A reasonably good fit to the current data set is crucial; otherwise there is no way that the model can fit to future observations well. However, a goodness of fit to the current data set can be improved, as desired, by simply increasing the number of model parameters. An improved fit obtained this way, however, may not work favorably for predicting future observations, since additional parameters to be estimated tend to produce less reliable parameter estimates. To avoid overparametrization, the AIC penalizes additional use of parameters by adding 2n(q) to $-2\ ln\ L^*(\mathrm{q})$. The AIC is an estimate of $-2\ E\ [ln\ L(\mathrm{q})]$, minus twice the expected log-likelihood. However, on average, $-2\ ln\ L^*(\mathrm{q})$ underestimates $E[-2\ ln\ L(\mathrm{q})]$ as much as 2n(q). Adding 2n(q) to $-2\ Ln\ L^*(\mathrm{q})$ thus corrects this bias.

A smaller value of AIC indicates a better-fitting model. In an actual model comparison process, maximum likelihoods of competing models are obtained by fitting them to the data. The AICs are then calculated according to Equation 2, and the model associated with the smallest value of AIC is chosen as the best-fitting model. This procedure is called the minimum AIC procedure. Note that only relative values of AIC (which is larger or smaller) are relevant in the comparison process. Consequently, a constant may be added to AIC values without loss of generality. In Table 13.5, for example, AIC values are adjusted, so that the AIC of the saturated model is equal to zero. This is also why the maximum likelihood used to calculate AIC need not include the terms common to all models compared.

The minimum AIC optimizes predictability. Consequently, the best model identified by the minimum AIC procedure does not imply that the model is correct. It only means the model is best among competing models in the sense that it gives predictions closest to those produced by the correct model (i.e., future observations). The minimum AIC procedure eliminates certain restrictions associated with the asymptotic chi-square goodness-of-fit test. A significance level need not be chosen arbitrarily, and more than two models can be compared simultaneously. Also, the models compared need not be hierarchically ordered in their complexity.

The philosophy underlying the minimum AIC procedure is radically different from that underlying conventional statistical significance testing procedures. However, the following example, drawn from the situation in which the chi-square GOF test is also feasible, may illuminate what the minimum AIC procedure really does in much broader contexts. Let the model q = 1 be a special case of the model q = 2. The minimum AIC procedure selects a model according to whether $AIC\ (1) - AIC\ (2) \gtrless 0$. Since $AIC\ (1) = -2\ ln\ L^*(1) + 2n(1)$ and $AIC\ (2) = -2\ ln\ L^*(2) + 2n(2)$, $AIC\ (1) - AIC\ (2) \gtrless 0$ is equivalent to $-2[ln\ L^*(1) - ln\ L^*(2)] \gtrless 2[n(2) - n(1)]$. The left side of this inequality is equal to the asymptotic chi-square statistic. The minimum AIC procedure in this instance is thus equivalent to the chi-square GOF test with $2[n(2) - n(1)]$ used as the critical value. The significance level of this chi-square test can be found, if desired, by working backward from $2[n(2) - n(1)]$. The minimum AIC procedure thus incorporates a built-in significance level. To ask if an observed difference in two AIC values is statistically significant is like asking if the observed difference in GOF is close to the built-in significance level or significantly far from it. No such significance tests are available in the statistical literature. See Sakamoto, Ishiguro, and Kitagawa (1986) for more detailed accounts of the AIC statistic.

The following three examples demonstrate elementary uses of the minimum AIC procedure. More examples will be given in the following sections.

Example 1 (Constancy of $p_{j/i}$ Over Trials)

The product multinomial form of the likelihood function, Equation 1, presupposes independently replicated trials. This implies that $p_{j/i}$ is constant throughout the trials. Whether this is so can be verified by the following procedure. Trials are first grouped into several blocks. Let $p_{j/i(k)}$ and $f_{j/i(k)}$ denote, respectively, $p_{j/i}$ and $f_{j/i}$ for block k. The likelihood of $\{f_{j/i(k)}\}$, $k = 1, \ldots, K$ (where K is the number of blocks) is then stated as

$$L = \prod_{k} \prod_{i} \prod_{j} (p_{j/i(k)})^{f_{j/i(k)}} . \tag{3}$$

Under the hypothesis that $p_{j/i(k)} = p_{j/i}$ for all k, Equation 3 reduces to Equation 1. The problem thus becomes one of comparing the goodness-of-fit of Model 1 and Model 3. The maximum likelihood estimate (MLE) of $p_{j/i}$ in Equation 1 is given by $f_{j/i}/f_j$. This model uses $n(n - 1)$ independent parameters. The MLE of $p_{j/i(k)}$ in Equation 3, on the other hand, is given by $f_{j/i(k)}/f_{j(k)}$, where $f_{j(k)} = \Sigma f_{j/i(k)}$. Model 3 uses $Kn(n - 1)$ independent parameters.

Nosofsky (1987) collected "learning" identification data on 12 Munsell colors. The stimuli had constant hue (5R), but varied in brightness and saturation. The data were collected while subjects were still improving their performance. An experimental session was organized into three blocks of 108 trials each, and 34 subjects participated in the experiment. Model 1 and Model 3 were fitted to

Nosofsky's data. The AIC value was found to be 28,394.7 [(n(q) = 396] for Model 3 and 29,678.0 [(n(q) = 132] for Model 1, indicating that Model 3 was the better fitting model. As expected, confusion probabilities are not constant across the blocks. To justify Model 1, we must collect identification data after $p_{j/i}$'s have reached their "asymptotes" by a sufficient number of practice trials. Note that the result by no means implies that Model 3 is correct. It is possible that $p_{j/i(k)}$ may still vary within the blocks.

Example 2 (Constancy of $p_{j/i}$ Across Subjects)

Confusion data are often aggregated across subjects. This, however, assumes that $p_{j/i}$'s are constant across the subjects. Whether the $p_{j/i}$'s are constant can be tested similar to Example 1, provided that individual data are also available. "Blocks" in Example 1 are simply replaced by "subjects," and the problem reduces to a comparison between Model 3 and Model 1.

Townsend and Landon (1982) suspected significant individual differences in performing the stimulus identification task, and consequently analyzed each of four subjects' data separately. One of their original purposes was to test the Constant-Ratio Rule (see Example 3), and four different subsets of five letters (**A**, **E**, **F**, **H**, **X**) were employed. Set 1 included all letters, set 2 only (**A**, **E**, **F**, **H**), set 3 (**A**, **E**, **X**), and set 4 (**F**, **H**, **X**). Each stimulus was presented 240 times for each set and for each subject. For the purpose of testing the individual differences, only set 1 and set 2 were used here. Set 1 yielded the AIC value of 12,141.7 [n(q) = 80] for Model 3 and 12,230.4 [n(q) = 20] for Model 1. Set 2 yielded the AIC value of 8,953.9 [n(q) = 48] for Model 3 and 8,975.0 [n(q) = 12] for Model 1. For both sets, Model 3 was found to be the better-fitting model, indicating that the individual differences were indeed substantial. Townsend and Landon (1982) made the right decision in analyzing individual data.

Examples 1 and 2 concerned the constancy of $p_{j/i}$. When the constancy assumption is grossly violated, the use of Model 1 can be problematic. The problem is known as "overdispersion" (e.g., McCullagh & Nelder, 1983), in which the variance of $f_{j/i}$ becomes much larger than what is expected from the multinomial distributional assumption due to the variability in $p_{j/i}$ (Kraemer, 1988). The quasi-likelihood proposed by McCullagh and Nelder (1983) can incorporate an additional dispersion term to deal with the overdispersion problem often encounted in contingency table analyses.

Example 3 (Constant-Ratio Rule)

Let M and S denote sets of stimuli such that $S \subseteq M$ (i.e., S is a subset of M). Let $p_{j/i}(M)$ and $p_{j/i}(S)$ denote $p_{j/i}$ when the stimulus sets in identification tasks are restricted to M and S, respectively. The Constant-Ratio Rule (CRR; Clarke, 1957) stipulates that $p_{j/i}(S)$ is proportional to $p_{j/i}(M)$ for $i, j \in S$. That is,

$$p_{j/i}(S) = c p_{j/i}(M) , \tag{4}$$

for some $c \neq 0$. However, $\Sigma_{j \in S} p_{j/i}(S) = 1$, so that $c\ \Sigma_{j \in S} p_{j/i}(M) = 1$, or $c = 1/\Sigma_{j \in S} p_j/_i(M)$. Using this expression for c, we can write Equation 4 more explicitly as

$$p_{j/i}(S) = p_{j/i}(M) \Big/ \sum_{k \in S} p_{k/i}(M) . \tag{5}$$

The right side of Equation 5 is equal to the conditional probability of $p_{j/i}(M)$ given S, which is denoted by $p_{j/i}(M/S)$. The CRR states that $p_{j/i}$ is essentially context-free, and the only effect of reducing the stimulus set M to S is that the probability of inadmissible responses under S is redistributed over admissible responses under S in proportion to $p_{j/i}(M)$ for $i, j \in S$. An alternative way of stating the same property is that $p_{k/i}/p_{j/i}$ does not depend on the stimulus set. That is,

$$\frac{p_{k/i}(M)}{p_{j/i}(M)} = \frac{p_{k/i}(S)}{p_{j/i}(S)} \qquad \text{for } i, j, k \in S . \tag{6}$$

Many researchers have investigated the CRR (Clarke, 1957; Hodge & Pollack, 1962; Morgan, 1974; Townsend & Landon, 1982). The latter two used the Likelihood Ratio Test. The CRR can also be tested by using the minimum AIC procedure. Let $f_{j/i}(M)$ and $f_{j/i}(S)$ be observed confusion frequencies, when the stimulus sets are M and S, respectively. Under the CRR, the ML estimate of $p_{j/i} = p_{j/i}(S) = p_{j/i}(M/S)$ is given by $\hat{p}_{j/i} = [f_{j/i}(S) + f_{j/i}(M)]/[f_j(S) + f_j(M/S)]$, where $f_i(S) = \Sigma_{j \in S} f_{j/i}(S)$ and $f_i(M/S) = \Sigma_{j \in S} f_{j/i}(M)$. This value of $\hat{p}_{j/i}$ is used in Model 1 to obtain the maximum likelihood under the CRR hypothesis. The CRR uses $s(s - 1)$ parameters, where s is the number of stimuli in S. Under the non-CRR hypothesis the ML estimates of $p_{j/i(1)} \equiv p_{j/i}(S)$ and $p_{j/i(2)} \equiv p_{j/i}(M/S)$ are given by

$$\hat{p}_{j/i(1)} = \frac{f_{j/i}}{f_i(S)} \qquad \text{and} \qquad \hat{p}_{j/i(2)} = \frac{f_{j/i}(M)}{f_i(M/S)} ,$$

which are substituted for $p_{j/i(k)}$, $k = 1,2$, in Model 3 to obtain the maximum likelihood under this hypothesis. Model 3 in this case uses twice as many parameters as Model 1. The AICs are calculated in the same way as before, and the model comparison proceeds just as in the previous examples.

The foregoing procedure will be demonstrated with Townsend and Landon's (1982) data. This data set was briefly described in Example 2. There were four subjects (D.X., M.X., G.X., and A.X.), and each subject's data were analyzed separately. This is in accordance with the results of Example 2. Four stimulus sets were employed with set 1, with stimuli (**A**, **E**, **F**, **H**, **X**) serving as the master set for all the other three sets, set 2 with (**A**, **E**, **F**, **H**), set 3 with (**A**, **E**, **X**), and set 4 with (**F**, **H**, **X**). Results are reported in Table 13.1. For each pair of stimulus sets, the minimum AIC solution is indicated by an "a."

TABLE 13.1
Tests of Constant-Ratio Rule with Townsend and Landon's (1982) Data

Subject	Data Sets M	Data Sets S	Stimuli in M and Those in S (underlined)	CRR	Non-CRR	Difference in n(q)
D.X.	(1),	(2)	**A E F H X**	4,202.2[a]	4,207.4	12
	(1),	(3)	**A E F H X**	1,696.9[a]	1,698.5	6
	(1),	(4)	**A E F H X**	1,679.3	1,674.6[a]	6
M.X.	(1),	(2)	**A E F H X**	4,439.5[a]	4,454.8	12
	(1),	(3)	**A E F H X**	2,125.8[a]	2,131.7	6
	(1),	(4)	**A E F H X**	1,960.1	1,954.0[a]	6
G.X.	(1),	(2)	**A E F H X**	4,056.2[a]	4,070.4	12
	(1),	(3)	**A E F H X**	1,812.4[a]	1,817.4	6
	(1),	(4)	**A E F H X**	1,975.1[a]	1,975.5	6
A.X.	(1),	(2)	**A E F H X**	4,175.7[a]	4,192.0	12
	(1),	(3)	**A E F H X**	1,839.4	1,837.0[a]	6
	(1),	(4)	**A E F H X**	1,921.8	1,918.0[a]	6

[a]Minimum AIC.

Neither the CRR nor the non-CRR hypothesis is uniformly better than the other. However, there are twice as many cases supporting the CRR as cases against the CRR. This is probably because M and S are fairly similar in Townsend and Landon's data. Intuitively, the more similar M and S are, the higher is the chance that the CRR holds. The similarity between M and S may be measured by s/m, where s and m are the numbers of stimuli in S and M, respectively.

The pattern of cases in favor of the CRR across subjects and different pairs of stimulus sets agrees perfectly with the results obtained by Townsend and Landon (1982), using the Likelihood Ratio Chi-Square Test. For set 1 versus set 2, all the four subjects favored the CRR. This case had the highest similarity between M and S. For set 1 versus set 3, three favored the CRR, but for set 1 versus set 4 only one subject favored the CRR. These two cases shared three stimuli each, and consequently the similarity between M and S is considered approximately equal.

An error analysis was conducted to identify $p_{j/i}$'s for which the discrepancy between $\hat{p}_{j/i}$ under the CRR and $\hat{p}_{j/i}(S)$ and $\hat{p}_{j/i}(M/S)$ under the non-CRR was large. The discrepancy is measured by

$$z_{ij} = \pm \left\{ 2f_{j/i}(S)[ln\, \hat{p}_{j/i}(S) - ln\, \hat{p}_{j/i}] + 2f_{j/i}(M)\left[ln\, \hat{p}_{j/i}\left(\frac{M}{S}\right) - ln\, \hat{p}_{j/i} \right] \right\}^{1/2}$$

(Pierce and Schafer, 1986), which approximately follows the standard normal distribution. Note, however, that the z_{ij}'s are not independent across j. Stimulus-response pairs for which z_{ij} exceeds ± 2.58 [$\Pr(z \geq |2.58|) = 0.01$] are listed in Table 13.2. Stimuli **F** and **X** seem to be causing most of the problem.

TABLE 13.2
Stimulus Pairs That Violate CRR in Townsend and Landon's (1982) Data

	Data Sets		*Pair*		*p in the Master Set*	*p in the Reduced Set*
Subject	*M*	*S*	*Stimulus*	*Response*	*(M)*	*(S)*
D.X.	(1),	(4)	F	X	.27	.13
M.X.	(1),	(4)	X	F	.06	.14
A.X.	(1),	(3)	X	A	.06	.13
A.X.	(1),	(4)	H	F	.07	.14

Hodge and Pollack's (1962) data (see fifth section) were also analyzed in a similar manner. Results were similar. The CRR does not seem to hold universally, and how likely it holds depends on the similarity between the stimulus sets.

SIMILARITY-CHOICE MODELS

All the models considered in the previous section impose some form of equality restrictions on $p_{j/i}$. This section deals with a group of models, called similarity-choice models, that specify explicit submodels under $p_{j/i}$. In this section, the similarity-choice models are briefly reviewed, and then two related issues are addressed, namely, fitting ADDTREE and EXTREE and comparing d and d^2 in the Euclidean distance-choice model.

Brief Review

In the similarity-choice models, $p_{j/i}$ is assumed proportional to the strength of response j when stimulus i is presented. Denote the response strength by t_{ij}. Then $p_{j/i} = v_i t_{ij}$ for some v_i. But since $\Sigma_j p_{j/i} = v_i \Sigma_j t_{ij} = 1$, $v_i = 1/\Sigma_j t_{ij}$, and thus

$$p_{j/i} = \frac{t_{ij}}{\Sigma_k \, t_{ik}} \,. \tag{7}$$

A variety of similarity-choice models are obtained by specializing t_{ij} in various ways.

In Luce's (1963a) unrestricted similarity-choice model, it is assumed that

$$t_{ij} = w_j s_{ij} \,, \tag{8}$$

where w_j (≥ 0, $\Sigma_j w_j = 1$) is the bias for response j, and s_{ij} is the similarity between stimuli i and j ($0 \leq s_{ij} = s_{ji} \leq s_{ii} = s_{jj} = 1$). By substituting Equation 8 in Equation 7, we can write the model more explicitly as

$$p_{j/i} = \frac{w_j s_{ij}}{\Sigma_k \, w_k s_{ik}} \,. \tag{9}$$

The model is called the unrestricted similarity-choice model, since there is no further restriction imposed on s_{ij}. The model is sometimes called the biased-choice model.

The unrestricted similarity-choice model is known to be a special case of the quasi-symmetry model for square contingency tables, which states

$$p_{ij} = ca_i b_j g_{ij} \ ,$$

where p_{ij} is the joint probability of row i and column j, c is some constant, a_i ($\Pi_i a_i = 1$) is the effect of row i, b_j ($\Pi_j b_j = 1$) is the effect of column j, and g_{ij} ($g_{ij} = g_{ji}$; $\Pi_i g_{ij} = \Pi_j g_{ij} = 1$) is the interaction effect between row i and column j. Since $p_{j/i} = p_{ij}/p_i$, where $p_i = \Sigma_j p_{ij}$, $p_{j/i}$ is given by

$$p_{j/i} = \frac{b_j g_{ij}}{\Sigma_k \ b_k g_{ik}} \ . \tag{10}$$

Model 9 is derived from Equation 10 by setting $s_{ij} = g_{ij}/(g_{ii}g_{jj})^{1/2}$ and $w_j = b_j g_{jj}{}^{1/2}/\Sigma_k b_k g_{kk}{}^{1/2}$. One important property of the quasi-symmetry model is the cycle condition (Caussinus, 1965)

$$p_{ij} p_{jk} p_{ki} = p_{ik} p_{kj} p_{ji} \ ,$$

which implies

$$p_{j/i} p_{k/j} p_{i/k} = p_{k/i} p_{j/k} p_{i/j} \ ,$$

for the unrestricted similarity-choice model (J. E. K. Smith, 1982). In the unrestricted similarity-choice model, $0 \leq s_{ij} = s_{ji} \leq s_{ii} = s_{jj} = 1$ also implies the column constraint

$$p_{i/i} \geq p_{i/j}$$

for all j. It has been shown (Townsend & Landon, 1982) that these two conditions are necessary and sufficient for the unrestricted similarity-choice model.

It follows from Equation 9 that

$$ln\left(\frac{p_{j/i}}{p_{i/i}}\right) = (ln\ w_j - ln\ w_i) + ln\ s_{ij} \ . \tag{11}$$

This implies that Model 9 decomposes $ln(p_{j/i}/p_{i/i})$ into two parts, a skew-symmetric part and a symmetric part, and represents the former by $ln\ w_j - ln\ w_i$ and the latter by $ln\ s_{ij}$.

In the Euclidean distance-choice model, stimuli are represented as points in multidimensional space. The distance between stimuli i and j, d_{ij}, is assumed related to s_{ij} by $s_{ij} = exp\ (-d_{ij})$ or $s_{ij} = exp(-d_{ij}^2)$. This leads to

$$p_{j/i} = \frac{w_j\ exp\ (-d_{ij})}{\Sigma_k\ w_k\ exp\ (-d_{ik})} \ , \tag{12}$$

or

$$p_{j/i} = \frac{w_j \, exp\,(-d_{ij}^2)}{\Sigma_k \, w_k \, exp\,(-d_{ij}^2)} \,. \tag{13}$$

Model 12 is sometimes called exponential MDS-choice model, Model 13 the Gaussian MDS-choice model (see also chap. 14; MDS stands for multidimensional scaling). There has been controversy over which of the two MDS-choice models, 12 or 13, better accounts for stimulus identification data (Nosofsky, 1985a, 1985b, 1986; Shepard, 1986, 1988). The issue will be addressed in the third section (see also chap. 11).

The MDS-choice model can also be derived from Krumhansl's (1978) distance-density model. Let $r_{ij} = d_{ij} + a_i^* + b_j^*$ or $r_{ij} = d_{ij}^2 + a_i^* + b_j^*$ be the distance-density model, where a_i^* and b_j^* are, respectively, the stimulus and response density parameters. Let $t_{ij} = exp\,(-r_{ij})$ in Equation 7. Model 12 or 13 is obtained, depending on which r_{ij} is used to define t_{ij}. In either case, $w_j = exp\,(-b_j^*)$.

In the unique feature-choice model (Keren & Baggen, 1981; Tversky, 1977) t_{ij} is specialized in yet another way. Let

$$y_{ia} = \begin{cases} 1, & \text{if stimulus i has feature } a, \\ 0, & \text{otherwise}, \end{cases}$$

and define $x_{ija} = y_{ia}(1 - y_{ja})$, and $x_{jia} = y_{ja}(1 - y_{ia})$. The x_{ija} takes the value 1 if stimulus i, but not stimulus j, has feature a, and is zero otherwise. The x_{jia}, on the other hand, takes the value 1 if feature a is unique to stimulus j. Let h_{ij} be the (asymmetric) dissimilarity between stimuli i and j, defined by

$$h_{ij} = \sum_a (x_{ija} \mathrm{b}_a + x_{jia} \mathrm{c}_a) \,, \tag{14}$$

where b_a and c_a are the dissimilarity contributions of feature a, when the feature is unique to stimulus i ($x_{ija} = 1$) and stimulus j ($x_{jia} = 1$), respectively. Let $t_{ij} = exp\,(-h_{ij})$ in Equation 7. Then

$$p_{j/i} = \frac{w_j^* \, exp\,(-e_{ij})}{\Sigma_k \, w_k^* \, exp\,(-e_{ik})} \,, \tag{15}$$

where

$$w_j^* = exp\left(\sum_a u_a^* y_{ja}\right) ,$$

and

$$e_{ij} = \Sigma v_a^* |y_{ia} - y_{ja}|^q \,, \tag{16}$$

with $q \geq 1$, $u_a^* = (b_a - \mathrm{c}_a)/2$ and $v_a^* = (\mathrm{b}_a + \mathrm{c}_a)/2$. This indicates that the unique feature model is a special case of Model 9, in which both w_j and s_{ij} are constrained in special ways (J. E. K. Smith, 1982); that is, $w_j = w_j^*$ and $s_{ij} = exp$

$(-e_{ij})$. The e_{ij} in Equation 16 can be considered the q-th power of the Minkowski power metric. In the special case q = 2, e_{ij} is equal to the square of the Euclidean distance. Thus, the unique feature-choice model can also be viewed as a special case of Equation 13, where $w_j = w_j^*$ and $d_{ij}^2 = e_{ij}$ defined by a set of prescribed features.

It may be assumed that c_a is proportional to b_a; that is, $c_a = cb_a$ for some c but for all a. Then Equation 14 reduces to

$$h_{ij} = \sum_a (x_{ija} + x_{jia}c)b_a \ . \tag{17}$$

This model is called the restricted unique feature model, as opposed to Equation 14, which is called the general unique feature model.

When we further assume that $b_a = c_a$, Equation 14 reduces to the symmetric-difference model

$$q_{ij} = \sum_a (x_{ija} + x_{jia})b_a \ , \tag{18}$$

which may be substituted for d_{ij}^2 in Equation 13 to obtain

$$p_{j/i} = \frac{w_j \, exp\, (-q_{ij})}{\Sigma_k \, w_k \, exp\, (-q_{ik})} \ . \tag{19}$$

This model plays an important role in fitting ADDTREE and EXTREE to stimulus identification data.

Fitting ADDTREE and EXTREE

In the additive similarity tree (ADDTREE; Sattath & Tversky, 1977; see also chap. 3), dissimilarity between two stimuli is represented by the length of a path connecting them. The extended similarity tree (EXTREE; Corter & Tversky, 1986) is similar, except that some segments of paths have markers. Whenever a path connecting two stimuli includes segments with common markers, those segments are excluded from the total path length. That is, they are not counted toward the overall dissimilarity between the stimuli. There is one-to-one correspondence between ADDTREE and EXTREE representations and the symmetric difference model, Equation 18, defined on a set of features determined by the tree structure. Given the tree structure, then, ADDTREE and EXTREE can be fitted to the stimulus identification data by using Equation 18.

Let us illustrate, using Keren and Baggen's (1981) data. This data set pertains to 10 rectangular digits used in digital clocks and calculators. There were eight subjects, but stimulus exposure duration was adjusted for each subject to minimize individual differences in performance, and the data were pooled across the subjects. Keren and Baggen's data have been analyzed and reanalyzed previously by several authors (Keren & Baggen, 1981; J. E. K. Smith, 1982; Takane &

Shibayama, 1986). Takane and Shibayama, in particular, used their data to systematically compare various similarity-choice models.

Figure 13.1 displays an EXTREE structure derived from Keren and Baggen's data by Corter and Tversky (1986). A feature set can be extracted from the tree that defines the symmetric-difference metric. In the tree a feature corresponds with a branch. In the figure it corresponds with a segment of a path between a terminal node (representing a stimulus) and the root that connects all the stimuli in the stimulus set. There are 19 such segments numbered from 1 to 19. Four of them are marked by special symbols (**C**, **D**, **E**, & **H**). Segments having direct contact with terminal nodes represent features unique to the stimuli corresponding to the nodes. Digit 2, for example, has only one feature (feature 1) unique to the stimulus. Digit 1 has features 2, 4, 5, and 19. Feature sets that characterize other stimuli can be obtained in a similar manner. Table 13.3 displays the feature indicator matrix for the 10 digits corresponding to the EXTREE structure presented in Figure 1.

Dissimilarity between digits 1 and 2 is obtained by summing the contributions

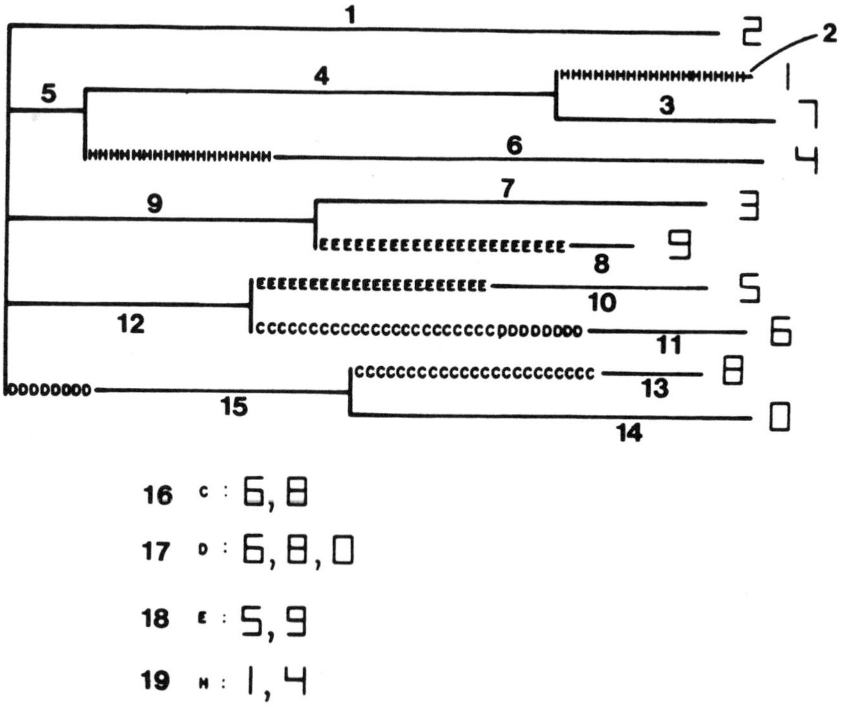

FIG. 13.1. Optimal EXTREE structure for Keren & Baggen's (1981) data. *Note.* From "Extended Similarity Trees" by J. E. Corter and A. Tversky, 1986, *Psychometrika, 51,* p. 443. Copyright 1986 by the Psychometric Society. Reprinted by permission.

TABLE 13.3
Feature Matrix Corresponding to the EXTREE Structure Given in Figure 13.1 for Keren & Baggen's (1981) Data

	Features																		
Stimuli	*1*	*2*	*3*	*4*	*5*	*6*	*7*	*8*	*9*	*10*	*11*	*12*	*13*	*14*	*15*	*16*	*17*	*18*	*19*
1	0	1	0	1	1	0	0	0	0	0	0	0	0	0	0	0	0	0	1
2	1	0	0	0	0	0	0	0	0	0	0	0	0	0	0	0	0	0	0
3	0	0	0	0	0	0	1	0	1	0	0	0	0	0	0	0	0	0	0
4	0	0	0	0	1	1	0	0	0	0	0	0	0	0	0	0	0	0	1
5	0	0	0	0	0	0	0	0	0	1	0	1	0	0	0	0	0	1	0
6	0	0	0	0	0	0	0	0	0	0	1	1	0	0	0	1	1	0	0
7	0	0	1	1	1	0	0	0	0	0	0	0	0	0	0	0	0	0	0
8	0	0	0	0	0	0	0	0	0	0	0	0	1	0	1	1	1	0	0
9	0	0	0	0	0	0	0	1	1	0	0	0	0	0	0	0	0	1	0
10	0	0	0	0	0	0	0	0	0	0	0	0	0	1	1	0	1	0	0

of features 1, 2, 4, 5, and 19. Marked feature 19 is included because it is unique to digit 1. Dissimilarity between digits 1 and 4 is defined by features 2, 4, and 6. Feature 19 is not included because it is commonly shared by the two digits. Our analysis obtains optimal weights for the features, which, when added, give overall dissimilarities between the stimuli.

The ADDTREE structure (not displayed) obtained by Corter and Tversky (1986) is similar to the EXTREE structure. It is identical to the EXTREE structure without marked features except that digit groups (8, 0), (5, 6), (3, 9), (1, 7, 4), and (2) are not joined simultaneously. In ADDTREE, (8, 0) and (5, 6) are joined first, then (8, 0, 5, 6) with (3, 9), and then (8, 0, 5, 6, 3, 9), (1, 7, 4) and (2) simultaneously. The ADDTREE structure contains 17 features. The feature indicator matrix can be constructed in the same way as in Table 13.3.

Both the ADDTREE and the EXTREE structures were fitted to Keren and Baggen's data. ADDTREE yielded the AIC value of 164.1 with 26 parameters. (There are nine independent bias parameters.) EXTREE provided the AIC value of 56.1 with 28 parameters. With just two more parameters this improvement in fit is rather impressive. EXTREE also does considerably better than the Euclidean distance-choice models with comparable numbers of parameters. (See Table 13.8.) However, EXTREE does not fit as well as the best fitting model found by Takane and Shibayama (1986), that is, the unrestricted similarity-choice model.

Apart from the fact that it did not provide the best-fitting model, there is an obvious limitation to this analysis. It presupposes that the optimal tree structure is known beforehand. The "optimal" tree structures used were obtained by Corter and Tversky (1986), but there is no guarantee that they are optimal with respect to the model and the fitting criterion used here. Indeed, the weight for feature 8 in EXTREE was estimated to be negative, and in order to avoid the improper solution the feature had to be eliminated. This indicates that the true optimal structure could be different from the one fitted.

Table 13.4 shows the stimulus-response pairs for which the discrepancy between observed and predicted probabilities is large. For thc pairs of stimuli for which the predicted probability is underestimated, new markers could be added to part of the features unique to the stimuli, increasing the similarity between them. Overestimation of confusion probabilities is more difficult to deal with. There is one such pair in the table, stimulus 2 and response 9. One way to handle this case is obviously to increase the weight for feature 2 while attaching a common marker to this feature as well as features unique to all other digits except digit 9. This is admittedly ad hoc, however; the meaning of the marked feature is not entirely clear.

Comparison Between d and d^2

As noted, two versions of the Euclidean distance-choice model have been proposed, d and d^2 in the exponent. There has been some controversy as to which of the two works better. This section examines existing empirical evidence and reports results on a numerical experiment designed to shed some light on the issue.

Kornbrot (1978) compared the GOF of d and a logistic version of Thurstone's successive categories model (SCM) for unidimensional stimuli (pure tones varying in intensity) and found that the latter fitted the data considerably better. Nosofsky (1985a) reanalyzed Kornbrot's data by d^2 and found that it provided comparable fits to SCM. Nosofsky (1985b, 1986) also presented data sets involving multidimensional stimuli (semicircles of varying size with a spoke in each semicircle oriented in a different angle from a horizontal baseline) to which d^2 fitted appreciably better than d. Ashby and Perrin (1988) report analyses of Townsend, Hu, and Ashby's (1981) data, for which they found d^2 worked consistently better.

Table 13.5 summarizes these results. In the table the AIC values have been

TABLE 13.4
Stimulus Pairs with Large Discrepancies Between Observed and Predicted Probabilities from EXTREE

Stimulus	*Response*	*Observed p*	*Predicted p*
2	6	.047	.013
1	6	.015	.002
0	7	.025	.007
2	9	.007	.046
3	7	.040	.019
9	8	.082	.046

TABLE 13.5
Comparison Between d and d^2 for Various Data Sets

Source		Data	d	d^2
Kornbrot (1978)	1	D.P. (natural cond.)	33.4	−44.5[a]
	2	D.J. (natural cond.)	60.3	−19.1[a]
dim = 2	3	D.P. (biased cond.)	350.9	−23.4[a]
	4	D.J. (biased cond.)	296.3	−47.0[a]
Nosofsky (1985b)	1	Subject 1	216.7	−233.4[a]
dim = 2	2	Subject 2	212.1	−162.4[a]
(1986)	1	Subject 1	1,262.2	−71.2[a]
dim = 2	2	Subject 2	1,015.0	7.9[a]
(1987)	1	Block 1	21.7[a]	792.1
dim = 2	2	Block 2	−54.0[a]	472.2
	3	Block 3	−48.1[a]	379.2
Townsend & Landon (1982)	1	D.X. (5 stimuli)	−14.9[a]	48.0
		(4 stimuli)	5.4[a]	21.8
dim = 2	2	M.X. (5 stimuli)	−11.3[a]	17.8
		(4 stimuli)	−4.1[a]	11.8
	3	G.X. (5 stimuli)	15.5[a]	141.7
		(4 stimuli)	−1.6[a]	40.4
	4	A.X. (5 stimuli)	−9.4[a]	44.8
		(4 stimuli)	1.6[a]	29.6
Townsend, Hu, & Ashby,	1	Observer 1 (gap)	21.5	5.9[a]
(1981)[b]	2	Observer 2 (gap)	19.6	4.3[a]
	3	Observer 3 (gap)	10.5	−2.0[a]
dim = 2	4	Observer 4 (gap)	−0.1	−3.2[a]
	5	Observer 1 (no gap)	11.5	−0.9[a]
	6	Observer 2 (no gap)	1.5	−5.0[a]
	7	Observer 3 (no gap)	4.3	−5.2[a]
	8	Observer 4 (no gap)	13.1	5.9[a]

[a]A better solution.
[b]Results obtained by Ashby & Perrin (1988).

adjusted so that the AIC of the saturated model takes the value of zero in each case. Table 13.5 is supplemented by the results from two more studies that, unlike those mentioned, favor d. Nosofsky (1987) used colors of constant hue (5R in Munsell notation), but varying in brightness and saturation, and Townsend and Landon (1982) used five letters of the alphabet and their subsets (see Examples 2 and 3). The results reported in Table 13.5 are very orderly in the sense that one model is consistently better than the other within each study. Data sets collected within a study use the same stimuli and the same experimental procedure.

Shepard (1986, 1988) attributed Nosofsky's (1985b, 1986) results to peculiarities in his data collection procedures and argued that d must be favored on empirical and theoretical grounds. Indeed, almost all the data sets analyzed prior to Nosofsky favored d. Data sets to be discussed in the fifth section present four such examples. They are Keren and Baggen's (1981) data on rectangular digits (used previously), Wickelgren's (1965) data on different forms of verbs, Hodge and Pollack's (1962) data on tones varying in intensity, frequency, and duration (briefly mentioned in Example 3), and Clark and Stafford's (1969) data on consonant-vowel combinations. All of these data favor d in the exponent of the Euclidean distance-choice model. Tables 13.8 and 13.9, in particular, present systematic comparisons of various models fitted to Keren and Baggen's data and Hodge and Pollack's data, respectively.

Table 13.6 presents a summary of existing empirical results concerning the choice between d and d^2. The table indicates for each study mentioned whether d or d^2 is favored, whether the data are individual or aggregated, whether the stimuli have separable or integral dimensions, and whether practice trials were extensive, moderate, or minimal.

The last three variables are thought to be important in distinguishing the two cases. Individual data tend to favor d^2, although there is one exception. Townsend and Landon's (1982) data are individual data, yet favor d. Stimuli with separable dimensions tend to favor d^2, although in some cases deciding whether relevant stimulus dimensions are separable or integral is not so straightforward. For some stimulus sets, it is difficult even to see any obvious dimensional structures. The letters used by Townsend and Landon, the rectangular digits used by Keren and Baggen, the different verb forms used by Wickelgren, and the consonant-vowel combinations used by Clark and Stafford are such examples. They are tentatively classified as having "integral" dimensions, meaning that there are no obvious separable dimensions or that the task involved may require something more cognitive than perceptual (e.g., integration of unidentifiable dimensions).

A larger number of practice trials seem to favor d^2. Nosofsky's (1987) data, unlike his two previous studies, favor d. The data were obtained with minimal practice trials. The reason, however, could be that the data are aggregated or that the stimuli have integral dimensions. Because of the generally high correlations among the variables considered, it is impossible to tear apart their confounding effects and draw any sensible conclusion as to which variable is causing a particular effect. To isolate the effects of the variables, one must conduct a factorial experiment in which all possible combinations of levels of the variables are equally represented.

One thing seems clear, however. Whether s_{ij} is a strictly convex (downward) function of d or whether there is an inflection point near $d = 0$ is not likely to be an important factor in deciding which of the two models works better in particular situations. What counts most is what happens where d is large. Whereas *exp* $(-d^2)$ approaches 0 very quickly as d increases, *exp* $(-d_{ij})$ does not. Although part of the difference is mitigated by adjusting the overall size of the stimulus configuration, it still remains that *exp* $(-d_{ij})$ has a heavier tail. The unsquared distance d is thus favored in situations where the heavy tail is required. Aggre-

TABLE 13.6
A Summary of Empirical Results Concerning the Choice Between *d* and d^2

Data Set	d/d^2	*Data (Individual/ Aggregated)*	*Stimuli (Separable/ Integral)*	*Practice (Extensive/ Moderate/ Minimal)*	*Description of Stimuli*
Kornbrot (1978)	d^2	Ind	Sep (unidimensional)	Ext	1-s bursts of 500-Hz pure tones varying in intensity
Nosofsky (1985b)	d^2	Ind	Sep	Ext	Circles of varying size with a
(1986)	d^2	Ind	Sep	Ext	spoke in each circle oriented in a different angle
(1987)	d	Agg	Int	Min	Colors of constant hue, but varying in brightness and saturation
Townsend & Landon (1982)	d	Ind	Int(?)	Mod	Five letters of alphabet (A, E, F, H, X) their subset
Townsend, Hu, & Ashby (1981)	d^2	Ind	Sep	Mod	A vertical and a horizontal line segment presented together, alone or not presented
Keren & Baggen (1981)	d	Agg	Int(?)	Mod	Rectangular digits
Wickelgren (1965)	d	Agg	Int	?	Forms of verbs
Hodge & Pollack (1962)	d	Agg	Int(?)	Ext	Tones varying in intensity, frequency, & duration
Clark & Stafford (1965)	d	Agg	Int	?	Vowel-consonant and consonant-vowel combinations

gated data tend to require heavier tails because of the individual differences in identification performance. Minimal practice trials also tend to require heavier tails, because at initial stages subjects can confuse rather distinct stimuli (i.e., they make the sort of errors that they should not make, if only well-practiced).

The following numerical experiment on Nosofsky's (1987) data clarifies our argument. The data were collected while subjects were still in learning phases. Significant improvements in identification performance can be observed over blocks of trials, as verified in Example 2. The min(f_{ij}, c) (where c is some integer) was subtracted from each of the off-diagonal elements of the confusion frequency tables and added back to the corresponding diagonal elements. This is supposed to simulate what happens when subjects make fewer and fewer careless mistakes as they become more proficient in the task. Both d and d^2 were fitted to the "corrected" tables with the value of c incremented systematically.

The results are shown in Table 13.7. In all three blocks, d fitted better for smaller values of c, but the difference between d and d^2 diminished as the value of c increased until d^2 took over.

TABLE 13.7
Numerical Experiments on Nosofsky's (1987) Data

	Error Frequency Corrected $-c$	d	d^2
Block 1	0	13,781.7[a]	14,452.1
	−12	6,072.5[a]	6,236.3
	−15	4,925.7[a]	4,940.6
	−18	3,990.6	3,939.1[a]
	−19	3,722.9	3,672.9[a]
	−20	3,466.3	3,426.2[a]
	−21	3,208.2	3,176.1[a]
Block 2	0	8,409.4[a]	8,935.6
	−3	6,544.4[a]	6,582.0
	−4	6,141.2[a]	6,141.8
	−5	5,789.6	5,774.9[a]
	−6	5,619.5	5,429.6[a]
	−7	5,317.4	5,139.1[a]
	−8	5,049.8	4,831.3[a]
	−9	4,756.9	4,525.4[a]
Block 3	0	6,123.2[a]	6,550.5
	−3	4,752.8[a]	5,094.8
	−4	4,379.0[a]	4,652.3
	−5	4,020.4[a]	4,216.6
	−6	3,555.6	3,517.8[a]
	−7	3,276.3	3,234.7[a]
	−8	3,098.1	2,984.8[a]
	−9	2,899.3	2,804.1[a]

[a]Minimum AIC solution.

A larger value of c was needed to get this reversal in block 1, which included the most initial trials. The results are as expected. If, however, the variabilities in p over subjects and over trials are indeed what make the data more in line with d, then there is not much substance in this model, because those are the situations that should be avoided in collecting stimulus identification data according to the results of the second Section.

Our finding is consistent with Ennis (1988a; see also Ennis, Palen, & Mullen, 1988; chap. 11), who attempted to reconcile the two models by postulating multivariate distributions for the stimulus representations. For confusable stimuli for which "perceived similarity may vary from moment to mement because of variation in the mental representations of the stimulus objects" (Ennis, 1988a, p. 408), d^2 provides the better model. However, for discriminable stimuli that "cannot be confused because of this variation" (Ennis, 1988a, p. 408), d could be the better model. Shepard (1988), on the other hand, argues that for discriminable stimuli that "are nevertheless close enough in psychological space to be judged . . . likely to have the same important consequence" (Shepard, 1988, p. 416), d should be favored. Clearly, what Shepard has in mind is the stimulus generalization context. However, how relevant is his argument to the stimulus identification context? Stimulus identification data are usually collected under a pressure to minimize the error probability and consequently, rather distinct, from stimulus generalization data. None of the data sets for which we found d fitted better are, strictly speaking, stimulus generalization data.

SOPHISTICATED GUESSING MODELS

In this section, sophisticated guessing models (SGM) are discussed in some detail. The general form of the SGM is presented first, followed by its specialization, Nakatani's (1972) confusion-choice model. The symmetric SGM, another specialization of the general SGM, is then discussed along with its relation to the similarity-choice models, the AON and OVLP models. Some introductory remarks about the models were given in the introduction.

In the SGM, a presentation of a stimulus is assumed to generate a confusion set c, which is a set of admissible responses. A response is chosen among the admissible responses according to the bias of the response. Let C_j denote the set of all confusion sets that include j as an admissible response plus the null set, which includes no admissible responses. Let $p_{c/i}$ be the probability of confusion set c when stimulus i is presented. Then the general SGM can be written as

$$p_{j/i} = \sum_{c \in C_j} p_{c/i} \left(\frac{b_j}{\sum_{k \in c} b_k} \right), \tag{20}$$

where b_j is the bias parameter for response j (J. E. K. Smith, 1980). This b_j is analogous to w_j in the similarity-choice models. One exception should be allowed in Equation 20. When c is null, $\Sigma_{k \in c} b_k$ should be interpreted as the sum of b_k over all possible (not necessarily admissible) responses. Most SGM do not allow the null confusion set, but some, such as Nakatani's confusion-choice model, do.

Nakatani's Confusion-Choice Model

Various specializations of Equation 20 are possible. In Nakatani's (1972) confusion-choice model, it is assumed that

$$p_{c/i} = \prod_{k} (p_{ik})^{r_{k/c}} (1 - p_{ik})^{1-r_{k/c}} , \tag{21}$$

where p_{ik} is the marginal probability of response k being admissible for stimulus i, and $r_{k/c}$ is defined as

$$r_{k/c} = \begin{cases} 1 & \text{if } k \in c, \\ 0 & \text{otherwise} . \end{cases}$$

In Nakatani's original model, stimuli are represented in multidimensional Euclidean space. Each p_{ik} is assumed to be a decreasing function of the distance d_{ik} between stimulus i and response k (which is supposed to coincide with stimulus k). More specifically, d_{ik} is assumed to follow the standard normal distribution, and p_{ik} is set equal to the probability that d_{ik} falls within a threshold denoted by t_k. For ease of computation, however, this was replaced by

$$p_{ik} = \{1 + exp\ (-(t_k - d_{ik})]\}^{-1} \tag{22}$$

here.

The preceding model is analogous to the Euclidean distance-choice model since it assumes a representation of stimuli in multidimensional Euclidean space, and confusion probabilities are related to distances between the stimulus points. The d_{ik} in Equation 22 may be replaced by the unrestricted dissimilarity parameter δ_{ik} ($\delta_{ii} = 0$), analogous to s_{ik} in the unrestricted similarity-choice model. This, however, turns out to be equivalent to what Townsend and Landon (1982) called the modified Nakatani model, which does not restrict p_{ik} in any way. This follows from

$$logit\ (p_{ik}) = ln \left(\frac{p_{ik}}{1 - p_{ik}} \right) = t_k - \delta_{ik} ,$$

and

$$logit\ (p_{kk}) = t_k ,$$

which establish the one-to-one correspondence between $\{p_{ik}\}$ and $\{\delta_{ik}, t_k\}$. Alternatively, d_{ik} in Equation 22 may be replaced by h_{ij} in Equations 14 or 17 or by q_{ij}

in Equation 18. This leads to the unique feature versions of Nakatani's confusion-choice model.

There is one important departure in our implementation of Nakatani's confusion-choice model. The bias parameters are defined as

$$b_j = \frac{f_j}{f} \tag{23}$$

(Hojo, 1982), where $f_j = \Sigma_i f_{j/i}$ and $f = \Sigma_j f_j$. In Nakatani's original procedure, b_j was estimated according to the Least-Squares Criterion, whereas t_k was calculated in an ad hoc manner. Ideally, both b_j and t_k should be estimated according to a well-defined statistical criterion. This was attempted. Too often, however, it led to numerical difficulties. It was decided that t_k was estimated by the maximum likelihood method, and b_j by Equation 23. This decision was dictated because there was no ready-made formula available for t_j, whereas Equation 23 for b_j was obvious (Hojo, 1982).

Symmetric SGM, AON, and OVLP Models

In the symmetric SGM, it is assumed that $p_{c/i} = p_{c/j}$ whenever i and j are in c, and that $p_{c/i} = 0$ whenever i is not in c (Noreen, 1978). The first assumption states that the probability of a confusion set evoked by a stimulus in the set is equal across all stimuli in the confusion set (i.e., $P_{c/i} \equiv p_c$ for all $i \in c$). The second assumption states that the confusion sets evoked by stimulus i always include response i as an admissible response. (Nakatani's confusion-choice model does not satisfy these conditions.) Under these assumptions, Equation 20 becomes

$$p_{j/i} = \sum_{c \in C_{ij}} p_c \left(\frac{b_j}{\Sigma_{k \in c}\, b_k} \right), \tag{24}$$

where C_{ij} is the set of all the confusion sets that include i and j.

The model can be rewritten as

$$p_{j/i} = b_j z_{ij}\,, \tag{25}$$

where

$$z_{ij} = \sum_{c \in C_{ij}} \left(\frac{p_c}{\Sigma_{k \in c}\, b_k} \right)$$

and $\Sigma_j b_j = 1$. Note that $z_{ij} = z_{ji}$ (z_{ij} is symmetric). This is the reason for the name symmetric SGM. Also, $z_{ii} \geq z_{ij}$ for all j. This inequality holds, since $C_{ii} = C_i \supseteq C_{ij}$. Model 25 can be further rewritten in the form of Equation 9 by setting

$$s_{ij} = \frac{z_{ij}}{(z_{ii} z_{jj})^{1/2}} \qquad \text{and} \qquad w_j = \frac{b_j (z_{jj})^{1/2}}{\Sigma_k\, b_k (z_{kk})^{1/2}}$$

(J. E. K. Smith, 1980). This implies that the symmetric SGM is a special case of the similarity-choice model. (Note that Equation 25 satisfies the cycle condition and the column constraint, which are necessary and sufficient for the unrestricted similarity-choice model.) However, the reverse is not necessarily true. Although Equation 9 can be put in the form of Equation 25 by letting

$$z_{ij} = \frac{s_{ij}}{v_i v_j} \sum_k v_k w_k \qquad \text{and} \qquad b_j = \frac{v_j w_j}{\Sigma_k v_k w_k} ,$$

where $v_i = \Sigma_j w_j s_{ij}$, it could lead to inadmissible values of p_c in the symmetric SGM.

Equation 25 along with the conditions on z_{ij} ($z_{ii} \geq z_{ij} = z_{ji} \leq z_{jj}$) is important, since any models that can be expressed in the form of Equation 25 are special cases of the symmetric SGM and, consequently, special cases of the similarity-choice model. In the all-or-none model (Townsend, 1971), it is assumed that stimulus i is identified perfectly with probability p_i, but with the remaining probability, $1 - p_i$, a confusion state is evoked that elicits response j with probability b_j^*. The model can be formally written as

$$p_{j/i} = \begin{cases} (1 - p_i)b_j^* & \text{for } j \neq i , \\ p_i + (1 - p_i)b_i^* & \text{for } j = i , \end{cases} \tag{26}$$

where $\Sigma_j b_j^* = 1$. This model can be rewritten in the form of Equation 25 by setting

$$z_{ij} = a_i a_j \left(\frac{\Sigma_k b_k^*}{a_k} \right) \qquad \text{for } j \neq i$$

and

$$b_j = \frac{b_j^*}{a_j} \bigg/ \left(\sum_k \frac{b_k^*}{a_k} \right) ,$$

where $a_i = 1 - p_i$ and

$$z_{ii} = \left[a_i^2 + \frac{a_i(1 - a_i)}{b_i^*} \right] \sum_k a_k b_k^* .$$

It can be easily verified that

$$z_{ii} \geq z_{ij} = z_{ji} \leq z_{jj} .$$

By implication, the AON model is also a special case of the similarity-choice models.

In the overlap model (Townsend, 1971), it is assumed that with probability p_{ii} stimulus i is identified perfectly. With probability p_{ij}, a confusion state is generated in which the only admissible responses are i and j. The response j is chosen with probability $b_j/(b_i + b_j)$. The model is written as

$$p_{j/i} = \begin{cases} p_{ij}\left(\dfrac{b_j}{b_i + b_j}\right) & \text{for } j \neq i\ , \\ p_{ii} + \sum\limits_{k \neq i} p_{ik}\left(\dfrac{b_i}{b_i + b_k}\right) & \text{for } j = i\ , \end{cases} \tag{27}$$

where $\Sigma\, b_j = 1$ and $\Sigma\, p_{ij} = 1$ for all i. This model is also a special case of the symmetric SGM. Let

$$z_{ij} = \frac{p_{ij}}{b_i + b_j} \qquad \text{for } j \neq i\ ,$$

and

$$z_{ii} = \sum_{k \neq i} z_{ik} + \frac{p_{ii}}{b_i}\ .$$

Then Equation 27 can be rewritten in the form of Equation 25, indicating that the OVLP model is a special case of the symmetric SGM, which in turn is a special case of the similarity-choice models. Again, it can be easily verified that $z_{ii} \geq z_{ij} = z_{ji} \leq z_{jj}$. There is one-to-one correspondence between parameters in the OVLP model and those in the unrestricted similarity-choice model. However, a proper solution in the latter may correspond with an improper (inadmissible) solution in the former. A proper solution in the former, on the other hand, always leads to a proper solution in the latter.

The informed guessing model (Pachella et al., 1978) is similar to the OVLP model, except that it has one additional parameter. This additional parameter represents the probability of an uninformative confusion state assumed possible in the informed guessing model. In this confusion state, any response is admissible, and a response is chosen with probability equal to its response bias. When the probability of this confusion state is assumed to be zero, the informed guessing model reduces to the OVLP model. It can be easily verified, however, that even with the additional parameter the informed guessing model is a special case of the symmetric SGM.

A hierarchy of the SGM is presented in Figure 13.2. It would be interesting to compare the GOF of the models discussed in this section as well as those discussed in the third section on an empirical basis.

SOME EMPIRICAL RESULTS

The models discussed in the previous section were applied to four data sets, and the results are reported in this section. The four data sets are from Keren and Baggen (1981), Wickelgren (1965), Hodge and Pollack (1962), and Clark and Stafford (1969). All are empirically interesting. However, they are all aggregated data, and the results may be confounded with individual differences.

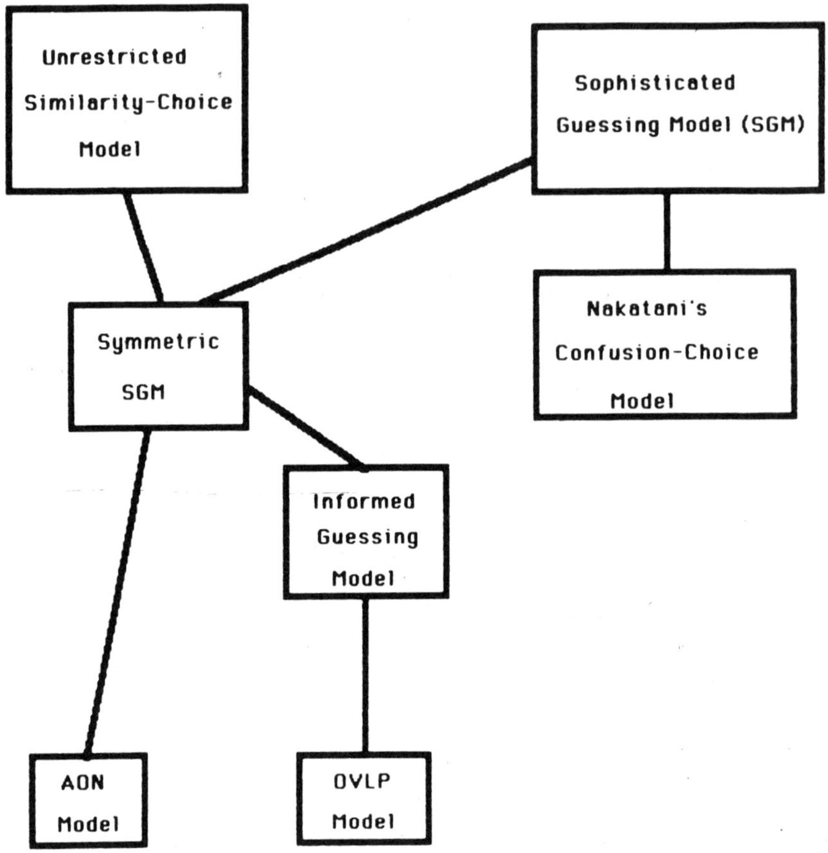

FIG. 13.2. A hierarchy of sophisticated guessing models.

Keren and Baggen's Data

The Keren and Baggen data set was used by Takane and Shibayama (1986) to compare similarity-choice models discussed in the third section. It was found that the unrestricted similarity-choice model fit the data best. ADDTREE and EXTREE were fit as special cases of the unique feature-choice model. However, neither ADDTREE nor EXTREE fit as well as the unrestricted similarity-choice model.

Sophisticated guessing models, including the AON and the OVLP models and Nakatani's confusion-choice model with various (dis)similarity models, were fit in this study, and results are reported in Table 13.8. The main entries in the table are the AIC values and the effective numbers of parameters in the fitted models given in parentheses. It is immediately clear that the AON model does not provide a good fit. This model seems too naive, not only for this data set but also for all other data sets discussed in this section. The OVLP model, on the other

TABLE 13.8
Summary of GOF Statistics for Keren and Baggen's (1981) Data

	Response Model		
Similarity Model	*Similarity-Choice Model*		*Confusion-Choice Model*
0. Saturated Model	17.4 (90)		
1. Unrestricted similarity model	5.6 (54)		8.6 (54)
2. Euclidean distance model	*d*	d^2	
dim = 2	220.3 (26)	1,148.8 (26)	42.6 (27)
dim = 3	79.2 (33)	438.2 (33)	11.5 (34)
dim = 4	35.6 (39)	90.9 (39)	9.5 (40)
dim = 5	40.9 (44)	20.5 (44)	7.9 (45)
3. Unique feature model			
General asymmetric			
7 features	199.3 (14)		11.6 (24)
9 features	95.3 (16)		−3.8[a] (26)
Restricted asymmetric			
7 features	273.7 (8)		18.0 (18)
9 features	122.5 (10)		5.3 (20)
Symmetric-difference			
7 features	197.5 (16)		16.1 (17)
9 features	91.5 (18)		9.4 (19)
4. ADDTREE	164.1 (26)		131.4 (25)
EXTREE	56.1 (28)		26.5 (28)
5. All-or-none model	680.3 (19)		
6. Overlap model			
Proper	5.6 (54)		

AIC-6170.
Effective number of model parameters in parentheses.
[a]Minimum AIC solution.

hand, yielded a proper solution with the GOF equivalent to that of the unrestricted similarity-choice model.

Nakatani's confusion-choice model with various (dis)similarity submodels compares favorably with its similarity-choice model counterparts. In particular, one version of the unique feature model combined with the confusion-choice model was found to work remarkably well. The stimuli used in Keren and Baggen's experiment were 10 rectangular digits defined by subsets of seven segmented features (the seven-feature case). Two additional features, open left and open right, were included in the nine-feature case. The general asymmetric unique feature model (Model 14), with the nine features, combined with the confusion-choice model, proved to be the best fitting model among all the models fitted. This model uses far fewer parameters [n(q) = 26] than the unrestricted similarity-choice model [n(q) = 54]. This result was somewhat surprising, after having obtained disappointing results with the unique feature-choice models (Takane & Shibayama, 1986) using the same set of features. It seems, however, that whenever the OVLP model yields a proper solution without explicit constraints on its parameters, Nakatani's confusion-choice model generally works very well, and a unique feature model may be found that provides an excellent fit to the data.

Wickelgren's Data

The results for Wickelgren's (1965) data are remarkably similar to those of Keren and Baggen's data. Again, the OVLP model yielded a proper solution without explicit constraints on model parameters, Nakatani's confusion-choice model generally worked very well, and a version of the unique feature confusion-choice model turned out to be the best-fitting model. The stimuli used in Wickelgren's experiment were eight consonant-vowel combinations (fa, af, fo, of, na, an, no, on). Subsets of the stimuli were presented to the subjects, who were asked to recall them shortly after. Three features of the stimuli, the order of the two types of elements (CV or VC), the type of vowel (a or o), and the type of consonant (f or n), were taken as an initial feature set. All possible interactions among the three features (1 and 2, 1 and 3, 2 and 3, and 1, 2, and 3) were then added to form a seven-feature set. The symmetric-difference unique feature model (Model 18) with the seven features combined with the confusion-choice model was found to be the best-fitting model. From the result of the four-dimensional Euclidean distance confusion-choice model, it was conjectured that a subset of the seven features (original three features, 1, 2, and 3, plus the interaction between 1 and 3) might work even better. This was tried, but was found to be not as good as the full seven-feature set.

Hodge and Pollack's Data

The results are somewhat different for Hodge and Pollack's (1962) data, which are summarized in Table 13.9. Hodge and Pollack's data were briefly mentioned in Example 3. The data pertain to eight tones constructed by factorial combinations of two levels each of three physical attributes: frequency (1,000 Hz, 1,006 Hz); intensity (80 dB, 81 dB), and duration (320 ms, 367 ms).

The OVLP model yielded an improper solution; some probabilities were estimated to be negative, and nonnegativity constraints had to be imposed to obtain a proper solution. The GOF of the proper solution (AIC = 57.4) was, however, appreciably worse than that of the improper solution (AIC = 13.8). Still, Nakatani's confusion-choice model fared reasonably well in comparison with its similarity-choice model counterparts. However, the saturated model, in which no special submodels were assumed under $p_{j/i}$, turned out to be the best-fitting model (AIC = 6.5).

The best nonsaturated model was the four-dimensional unsquared Euclidean distance-choice model (AIC = 9.0). The first three of the four dimensions in this model roughly corresponded with the three physical attributes (frequency, inten-

TABLE 13.9
Summary of GOF Statistics for Hodge and Pollack's (1962) Data

	Response Model		
Similarity Model	*Similarity-Choice Model*		*Confusion-Choice Model*
0. Saturated Model		6.5[a] (56)	
1. Unrestricted similarity model	13.8 (35)		13.5 (35)
2. Euclidean distance model	d	d^2	
dim = 2	171.7 (20)	958.9 (20)	57.9 (21)
dim = 3	14.4 (25)	284.9 (25)	26.7 (26)
dim = 4	9.0[a] (29)	80.1 (29)	10.1 (30)
dim = 5	14.9 (32)	45.0 (32)	11.5 (33)
3. Unique feature model			
General asymmetric			
4 features	245.3 (8)		25.8 (16)
7 features	28.1 (14)		20.7 (22)
Symmetric-difference			
4 features	116.5 (11)		22.4 (12)
7 features	28.1 (14)		14.7 (14)
4. All-or-none model		539.5 (15)	
5. Overlap model			
Improper		13.8 (35)	
Proper		57.4 (35)	

AIC-14450.
Effective number of model parameters in parentheses.
[a]Minimum AIC solution.

sity, and duration) of the stimuli. The fourth dimension represented the three-way interaction among the three attributes. Since all the attributes had only two levels, they were coded into binary features. The unique feature models were fit using these features. However, no unique feature models were found to fit as well as the saturated model. Subsequently, the feature set was incremented by including all two-way interactions, which improved the fit, but not as much as desired. Note that with the seven features (three main effects plus interactions among them) the general asymmetric unique feature-choice model and the symmetric-difference unique feature-choice model provide an identical GOF, which seems to be the case in general.

Clark and Stafford's Data

The fourth data set was reported by Clark and Stafford (1969). The results were similar to those of Hodge and Pollack's data. The stimuli were eight different forms of verbs embedded in sentences. Subjects were shown the sentences and asked to remember the verb. Verbs differed in tense (present or past), in perfective form, and in progressive form. An example would be: (a) watch, (b) watched, (c) is watching, (d) was watching, (e) has watched, (f) had watched, (8) has been watching, and (i) had been watching.

As in Hodge and Pollack's data, an improper solution was obtained from the OVLP model. This was due to large proportions of errors in the two data sets. The OVLP model requires $p_{i/i} \geq \Sigma_j p_{i/j}$ (J. E. K. Smith, 1980). The difference between the improper solution and the constrained proper solution is much larger, however, in Clark and Stafford's data than in Hodge and Pollack's data. The informed guessing model may be a better choice under this circumstance. However, the informed guessing model suffers from a different kind of problem; model parameters in the informed guessing model are not uniquely determined.

Nakatani's confusion-choice model worked reasonably well. However, the minimum AIC solution was found to be the two-dimensional unsquared Euclidean distance-choice model (AIC = 5.8). The two dimensions in this model roughly corresponded with two of the three defining features of the verb forms: perfective or not perfective and progressive or not progressive. Attempts were made to fit the unique feature models using the defining features of the stimuli and the interactions among them. However, no unique feature models were found to fit better than the best Euclidean distance-choice model.

CONCLUDING REMARKS

This chapter compared a number of existing models of stimulus identification data. One important model was omitted, the general recognition model by Ashby and Perrin (1988). This model is very general and can explain a variety of phenomena that could not be explained by other models. It was not considered here, despite its promise, primarily because it is still under development and because it is too general. In most cases, only specialized models can be fit, and it is not clear what specializations are necessary in particular situations. This situation can improve rapidly (see chaps. 6–8 and 16), however, and the full comparison between this model and the kinds of models discussed in this chapter would undoubtedly be interesting. Such attempts are already underway (Ashby & Lee, 1991).

ACKNOWLEDGMENTS

This work has been supported by Grant A6394 from the Natural Sciences and Engineering Research Council of Canada to the first author. Thanks are due to Greg Ashby, Tony Marley, and an anonymous reviewer for their helpful comments on an earlier version of this paper, to Milton Hodge for providing Hodge and Pollack's data, to Jim Corter for providing the ADDTREE and EXTREE structures, to Marion McGlynn for running the analyses in the third section, and to Marina Takane for preparing Figure 13.2.

14 Exemplar-Based Approach to Relating Categorization, Identification, and Recognition

Robert M. Nosofsky
Indiana University

This chapter provides an overview of an exemplar-based approach to relating performance in tasks of multidimensional perceptual categorization, identification, and recognition. By *categorization,* I mean a choice experiment in which people classify distinct items into groups, whereas in *identification* each item is assigned a unique response. *Recognition* refers to a memory paradigm in which people judge whether items are "old" (previously experienced) or "new."

At the heart of the present approach is the assumption that people represent categories by storing individual exemplars in memory, and make classification decisions on the basis of similarity comparisons with the stored exemplars. This exemplar view of category representation strongly motivates the study of relations among categorization, identification, and recognition. Presumably, when people learn to identify stimuli, a unique representation of each item is stored in memory. Furthermore, the extent to which individual items are confused is determined by similarity relations among the items (e.g., Lockhead, 1970; Luce, 1963a; Shepard, 1958b). If categorization decisions are also based on similarity relations among individually stored items, then one might be able to *predict* categorization performance given knowledge of performance in an identification paradigm involving the same set of stimuli. Likewise, if individual exemplars are stored in memory during category learning, then this fact should be corroborated by postacquisition recognition memory tests.

A conceptual difficulty associated with using an exemplar-similarity model to relate categorization, identification, and recognition, however, is that similarities among exemplars may not be invariant across the paradigms. The present theory adopts a Multidimensional Scaling (MDS) approach to representing context-dependent changes in similarity. Exemplars are represented as points in a multidimensional psychological space, with similarity assumed to be a decreasing function of distance in the space. Similarities change systematically because of the influence of selective attention processes that stretch and shrink the space along its component dimensions.

The idea is illustrated in Figure 14.1, which shows a set of eight stimuli varying along three binary-valued dimensions (color—black or white, shape—triangle or circles, and size—large or small). The stimuli are represented by the vertices of a cube, with each face of the cube corresponding to a value along one of the dimensions. Figure 14.1 illustrates the situation in which subjects begin to attend selectively to the color dimension. The space is stretched along the color dimension and shrunk along the unattended size and shape dimensions. Note that by selective attention to the color dimension, the black stimuli are rendered more

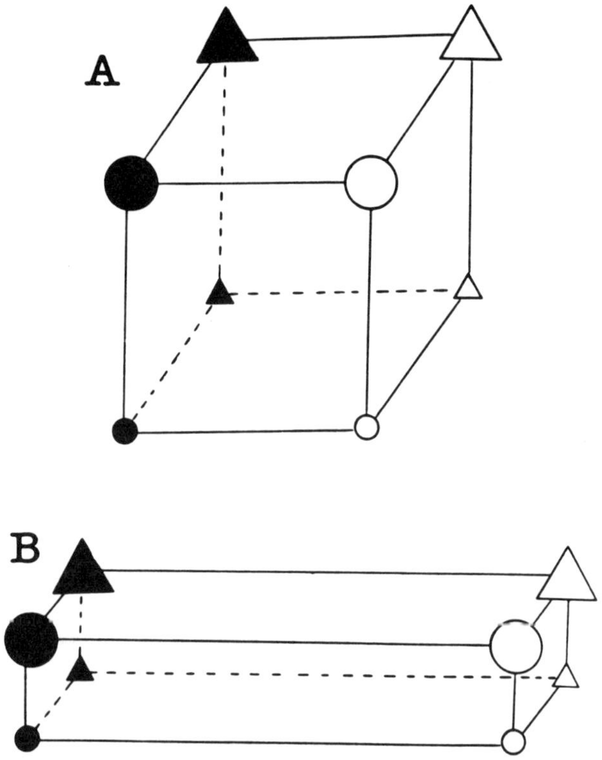

FIG. 14.1. Schematic illustration of the role of selective attention in modifying similarities among exemplars. *Note.* From "Attention, similarity, and the Identification-Categorization Relationship" by R. M. Nosofsky, 1986, *Journal of Experimental Psychology: General, 115,* p. 39–57. Copyright 1986 by American Psychological Association. Reprinted by permission.

similar to one another and less similar to the white stimuli. Now, suppose subjects were required to classify all black stimuli into one category and all white stimuli into a second category. Then the selective attention process illustrated in Figure 14.1 would greatly benefit performance, because it would serve to maximize within-category similarities and to minimize between-category similarities. In effect, subjects would be optimizing similarity relations for the categorization problem at hand. To summarize the key idea, Figure 14.1 is intended to illustrate that identification and categorization decisions may be based on similarities among individual exemplars, but similarities among those exemplars may change systematically because of the influence of selective attention.

The chapter is organized as follows. The first section provides an overview of the theoretical framework and the general approach to relating identification and categorization. The second section focuses on how the MDS-based exemplar model has been used to analyze identification confusion data, whereas the third section illustrates the exemplar-based approach to predicting categorization from identification. The last section considers the categorization-recognition relation.

As developed thus far, the present model departs from most others in this volume in that it uses a deterministic MDS approach: Each exemplar is represented as a single point rather than as a probabilistic distribution of points in the space. In principle, however, the model could be extended by incorporating a probabilistic MDS approach. Potential benefits of such an extension are discussed at various points in the chapter.

MDS-BASED EXEMPLAR MODEL: THE GENERALIZED CONTEXT MODEL

The exemplar model is referred to as the *generalized context model* (GCM) (Nosofsky, 1986), because it is a generalization of the context model of classification proposed by Medin and Schaffer (1978). The GCM also builds closely on classic models and approaches proposed by Shepard and his colleagues for predicting and relating identification and categorization performance (Shepard, 1957, 1958b; Shepard & Chang, 1963; Shepard, Hovland, & Jenkins, 1961).

According to the GCM, the strength with which stimulus i is associated with category J is found by summing the (weighted) similarity of stimulus i to all exemplars of category J and then multiplying by the response bias for category J. This strength is then divided by the sum of strengths for all categories to determine the conditional probability with which stimulus i is classified in category J:

$$P(\mathrm{R_J}|\mathrm{S_i}) = b_\mathrm{J} \sum_{\mathrm{j}\in \mathrm{C_J}} N_\mathrm{j}\, \eta_\mathrm{ij} \Big/ \sum_{\mathrm{K}} b_\mathrm{K} \sum_{\mathrm{k}\in \mathrm{C_K}} \mathrm{N_k}\, \eta_\mathrm{ik}\ , \tag{1}$$

where b_J is the category J response bias, N_j is an exemplar-strength term, and η_ij is the similarity between exemplars i and j. (Throughout this chapter, uppercase letters are used as subscripts to index categories, category responses, and category-level parameters, whereas lowercase letters are used as subscripts to index individual stimuli, identification responses, and stimulus-level parameters.) Nosofsky (1990, 1991a) discusses numerous factors that may affect exemplar strength; however, except where noted otherwise, it is assumed throughout that all exemplars have equal strength and the N_j terms are set equal to unity.

In the special case in which each stimulus defines its own category (i.e., an identification experiment), the decision rule in the GCM reduces to that of the classic *similarity-choice model* (SCM) for predicting identification confusion data (e.g., Luce, 1963a; Shepard, 1957; J. E. K. Smith, 1980; Townsend & Landon, 1983). The probability that stimulus i is identified as stimulus j is given by

$$P(\mathrm{R_j}|\mathbf{S_i}) = \frac{b_{\mathrm{j}}\,\eta_{\mathrm{ij}}}{\Sigma_{\mathrm{k}}\, b_{\mathrm{k}}\,\eta_{\mathrm{ik}}}. \tag{2}$$

As noted by J. E. K. Smith (1980) and Townsend and Landon (1983), the SCM provides accurate quantitative descriptions of identification confusion data in a wide variety of experimental situations and continues to serve as a standard against which alternative models of identification confusion are compared (e.g., Ashby & Perrin, 1988; Townsend & Ashby, 1982).

The relation between Equations 1 and 2 suggests a straightforward means by which to predict categorization from identification. First, one could conduct an identification experiment and fit the SCM to the confusion data, thereby deriving estimates of all of the η_{ij} interexemplar similarity parameters. Then, for any given categorization paradigm involving the same set of stimuli, one could substitute the derived η_{ij} values into Equation 1, thereby obtaining (bias-free) predictions of categorization performance. Unfortunately, an approach essentially like the one suggested here was attempted in a classic study of the identification-categorization relation conducted by Shepard et al. (1961) and was shown to fail dramatically. More recently, Nosofsky (1986, 1987, 1989) has demonstrated failings of this straightforward approach. According to the present view, the main problem with the approach is that the η_{ij} similarity values are (generally) not invariant across identification and categorization. A theory is needed that allows for systematic changes in similarity relations.

In the GCM, each exemplar is represented as a point in an M-dimensional space. The distance between exemplars i and j (d_{ij}) is computed by using the (weighted) Minkowski power model formula (e.g., Carroll & Wish, 1974):

$$d_{\mathrm{ij}} = c\left[\sum_{\mathrm{m=1}}^{\mathrm{M}} w_{\mathrm{m}}|x_{\mathrm{im}} - x_{\mathrm{jm}}|^{\mathrm{r}}\right]^{1/\mathrm{r}}, \tag{3}$$

where x_{im} is the psychological value of exemplar i on dimension m, w_m ($0 \leq w_m \leq 1$, $\Sigma w_m = 1$) is the weight given to dimension m in calculating psychological distance, and c is a sensitivity parameter reflecting overall discriminability in the psychological space. The w_m parameters are interpreted as "attention weights." The constraint that the weights sum to unity reflects the assumption of a limited-capacity system: If more attention is devoted to one dimension, then less attention remains to be devoted to remaining dimensions. The geometric interpretation of the attention weights is that of stretching and shrinking of the psychological space along its coordinate axes, as illustrated in Figure 14.1. A cornerstone of the theory is the assumption that the selective attention weights describe the systematic changes in interexemplar similarities that occur across identification and categorization.

The similarity between exemplars i and j is computed from the transformation

$$\eta_{ij} = exp\ (-d_{ij}^{p})\ . \tag{4}$$

The values of r and p in Equations 3 and 4 that provide the best fits to data appear to depend on experimental conditions, as discussed in the next section. The value $r = 2$ in Equation 3 yields the Euclidean metric, whereas $r = 1$ yields the city-block metric. The value $p = 1$ in Equation 4 yields an exponential decay similarity function, whereas $p = 2$ yields a Gaussian similarity function.

The general approach to predicting and relating identification and categorization can now be outlined. First, one models a set of identification confusion data, using the SCM. However, rather than allowing all of the η_{ij} values to be free parameters, one computes the η_{ij} values from a derived MDS solution for the exemplars. That is, one represents each stimulus as a point in a multidimensional space and computes similarities between exemplars, using Equations 3 and 4. The MDS "solution" is defined as the one that yields a maximum likelihood fit to the identification confusion data when used in conjunction with Equations 2, 3, and 4. For appropriately structured stimulus sets, this *MDS-choice model* (Equations 2, 3, and 4) often yields quantitative fits to data that are essentially as good as that of the full version of the SCM (without the MDS assumptions). Once the MDS solution is derived, one has a great deal of predictive power, because now for any given categorization paradigm involving the same set of stimuli, one can use the MDS solution in conjunction with the GCM (Equations 1, 3, and 4) to predict classification performance. Because the MDS solution will have been derived from the identification data, few parameters remain to be estimated for predicting categorization. The critical parameters are generally the attention weights in Equation 3, which describe how the structure of the multidimensional space is modified as a result of selective attention processes.

MDS-CHOICE MODEL ANALYSES OF IDENTIFICATION CONFUSION DATA

This section illustrates the first step in the method for relating identification and categorization, namely using the MDS-choice model to analyze identification confusion data. Various versions of the model are compared on their ability to account for the detailed structure of a set of identification confusions. For convenience in making comparisons, the summary fits for the various models that are involved are all presented in Table 14.1. The main output of the analyses is an MDS solution for the stimulus set, together with information regarding the metric structure of the underlying psychological space.

The standard statistical technique of Likelihood Ratio Testing (e.g., see Wickens, 1982) is used for evaluating and comparing the identification models, as well as the categorization and recognition models discussed in the third and fourth sections. In general, the categorization data are summarized in n × m confusion matrices, where n is the number of stimuli and m is the number of categorization responses (for identification, n = m). The entry in cell (i, j) of the matrix gives the frequency with which stimulus i was classified in category j (f_{ij}). It is assumed that the data for each stimulus are multinomially distributed, and the distributions for each stimulus are independent. Then the (natural) log-likelihood of a data set, given the parameters in the model, is given by

$$ln\ L = \sum_i ln\ N_i! - \sum_i \sum_j ln\ f_{ij}! + \sum_i \sum_j f_{ij}\ ln\ P(R_j|S_i)\ , \tag{5}$$

where N_i is the frequency with which stimulus i was presented, f_{ij} is the observed frequency with which stimulus i was classified in category j, and $P(R_j|S_i)$ is the predicted probability with which stimulus i is classified in category j. Let $ln\ L(F)$ denote the log-likelihood for a full model under consideration, and let $ln\ L(R)$ denote the log-likelihood for a restricted version of that model that arises by constraining some of the parameters a priori. Assuming the restricted model is correct, the quantity $G^2 = -2[ln\ L(R) - ln\ L(F)]$ is distributed asymptotically as

TABLE 14.1
Summary of Fits for Identification Confusion Models

Model	*ln L*	*SSE*	*%Var*	
	Subject 1			
Perfect-fitting	−215.6	0	100.0	(240)
Full SCM	−263.12	948	99.4	(135)
Unconstrained MDS-choice	−293.82	1,510	99.0	(45)
Constrained MDS-choice	−311.12	2,344	98.5	(21)
Bias-independent MDS-choice	−319.07	3,779	97.5	(36)
	Subject 2			
Perfect-fitting	−290.66	0	100.0	(240)
Full SCM	−359.30	1,736	98.2	(135)
Unconstrained MDS-choice	−405.85	2,643	97.3	(45)
Constrained MDS-choice	−464.31	4,928	94.9	(21)
Bias-independent MDS-choice	−456.86	6,159	93.6	(36)

Note: Values in parentheses give number of free parameters used by each model.

a χ^2 random variable, with degrees of freedom equal to the number of parameters constrained in moving from the full to the restricted model. If the observed value of G^2 exceeds the critical value, then the restricted model can be rejected relative to the full model, and one would conclude that some of the parameters were constrained inappropriately. Finally, note that an overall test of goodness of fit for a model is a special case of Likelihood Ratio Testing. One compares the fit of the model to that of a fully saturated model that fits the data perfectly. See Chapter 1 for a more thorough review of goodness-of-fit testing.

In the following example, the data are from an identification experiment reported by Nosofsky (1985b). The stimuli were semicircles with a radial line embedded in them. The semicircles had four levels of size and four levels of angle combined orthogonally to yield the set of 16 stimuli illustrated in Figure 14.2. On any given trial a stimulus was selected randomly from the set and presented with a brief duration. Subjects identified the stimuli by pressing 1 of 16 buttons arranged in a 4 × 4 grid. For example, if the subject believed that the stimulus had size level i and angle level j, then he or she pressed the button in row i and column j of the response grid. The identification confusion matrices obtained for two subjects tested over an extended period of time (6,400 observations each, not including practice) are reported in Nosofsky (1985b, Table 1).

As an initial step in the analysis, the full version of the SCM (Equation 2) was fitted to the two sets of confusion data by using a maximum likelihood criterion. A scatterplot of observed against predicted confusion frequencies is shown in Figure 14.3 (top panels). Although the discrepancies between predicted and observed confusion frequencies are statistically significant, by usual criteria the

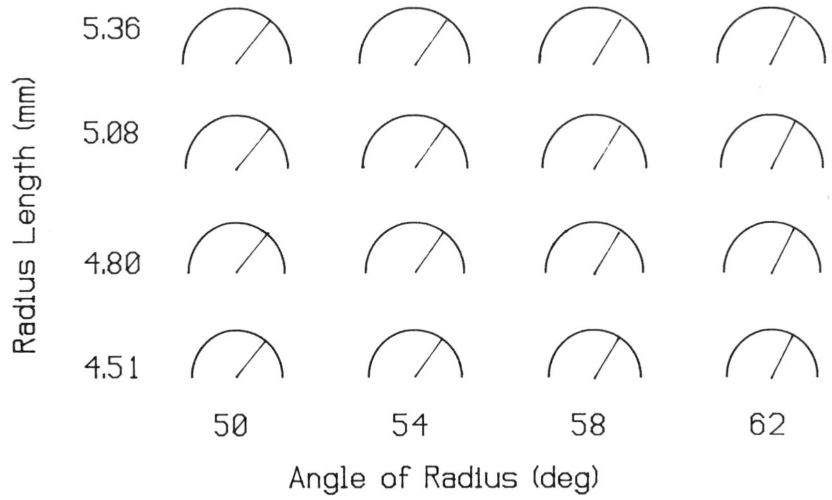

FIG. 14.2. Illustration of stimulus set used in Nosofsky's (1985b) experiment.

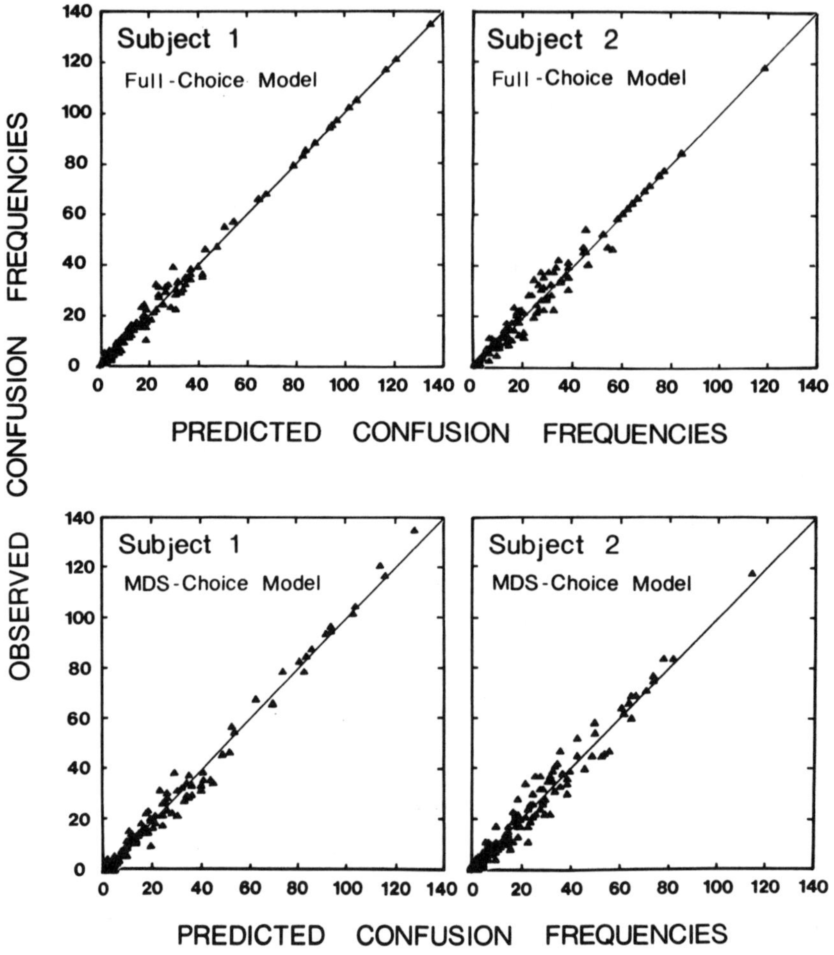

FIG. 14.3. Observed confusion frequencies plotted against predicted confusion frequencies. Top panel: full SCM; bottom panel: MDS-choice model. *Note.* From "Overall Similarity and the Identification of Separable-Dimension Stimuli" by R. M. Nosofsky, 1985, *Perception and Psychophysics, 38,* p. 415–432. Copyright 1985 by Psychonomic Society. Reprinted by permission.

fits would be regarded as excellent. The model accounts for 99.4% and 98.2% of the variance in subject 1's and subject 2's data, respectively. At the very least, the SCM would be competitive with alternative models and provides a convenient framework within which to further analyze the data.

The next step in the analysis was to fit the MDS-choice model to the confusion data. Each stimulus was represented as a point in a two-dimensional space, the distance between stimuli i and j was calculated from Equation 3 and transformed to a similarity measure by using Equation 4, and the derived similarities were then substituted into Equation 2. The free parameters in the model are the MDS coordinates (the values of x_{im}) that appear in Equation 3 and the set of response bias parameters (b_k) in Equation 2. (In fitting the identification data, the sensitivity and weight parameters in Equation 3 are not identifiable with respect to the MDS coordinates, so they are set at default values; $c = 1.00$, $w_1 = w_2 = 1.00$.) A general computer search routine is used to search for the maximum likelihood parameters, and numerous starting configurations are used to guard against local minima. Finally, to apply the model, one needs to know the value of r in Equation 3 (the form of the distance metric) and the value of p in Equation 4 (the form of the similarity function). For the present data set, extensive preliminary analyses pointed clearly to a Euclidean distance metric and a Gaussian similarity function. Some of these preliminary analyses are discussed in depth later in this section.

The fit of the Gaussian-Euclidean MDS-choice model is illustrated in the bottom panels of Figure 14.3. The model accounted for 99.0% and 97.3% of the variance in subject 1's and subject 2's data, respectively. More impressive, Likelihood Ratio Tests indicated that the fit of the MDS-choice model was not significantly worse than that of the full SCM for either subject 1 [$\chi^2(90) = 61.4$, $p > 0.40$] or subject 2 [$\chi^2(90) = 93.8$, $p > 0.30$]. Thus, the MDS approach yielded a precise quantitative account of the similarity structure inherent in each subject's data. The MDS solutions that yielded maximum likelihood fits to the data for each subject are illustrated in Figure 14.4 (the exact values of the coordinates are given in Nosofsky, 1985b, Table 3). Not surprisingly, the MDS solutions closely reflect the physical space that defines the stimuli.

The MDS-choice model can be used to ask additional questions about identification processes. In the previous analyses, each stimulus was represented by two freely varying coordinate parameters (although there are 16 stimuli, only 30 of the coordinate parameters are truly free parameters, because the MDS solution is translation-invariant). However, it is plausible that the perceived level of size for a stimulus is independent of the stimulus's angle, and likewise that the perceived level of angle is independent of the stimulus's size. This condition is represented in the MDS-choice model by assuming that all stimuli with the same physical value of angle have the same first coordinate (x_{i1}) and all stimuli with the same physical value of size have the same second coordinate (x_{i2}). Because in the present stimulus set there are four levels of angle and four levels of size, and the coordinates corresponding to the lowest level on each dimension can be arbitrarily set equal to zero (translation invariance), there are only 6 free coordinate parameters rather than 30. For subject 1, the fit of this constrained MDS-choice model was found *not* to be significantly worse than that of either the unconstrained MDS-choice model [$\chi^2(24) = 34.6$, $p > 0.05$] or the full SCM [$\chi^2(114) = 96.0$, $p > 0.80$], and the model accounted for 98.5% of the data. For

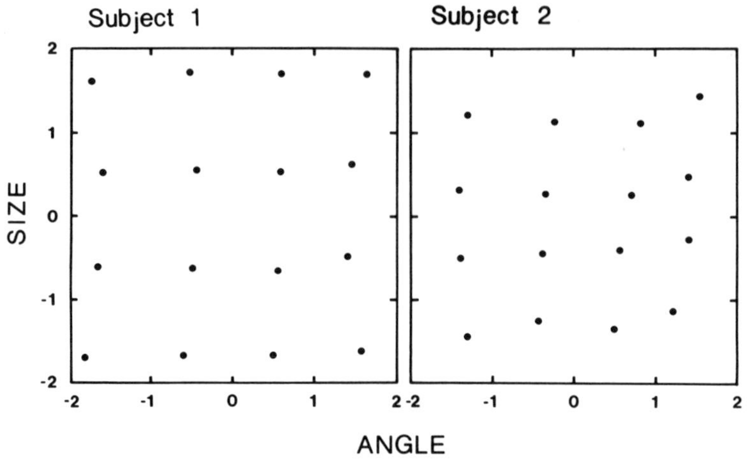

FIG. 14.4. MDS solutions derived by fitting the MDS-choice model to Nosofsky's (1985b) identification confusion data. *Note.* From "Overall Similarity and the Identification of Separable-Dimension Stimuli," by R. M. Nosofsky, 1985, *Perception and Psychophysics, 38,* p. 415–432. Copyright 1985 by Psychonomic Society. Reprinted by permission.

subject 2, however, the fit of the constrained MDS-choice model was significantly worse than that of the unconstrained models. Apparently, although the dimensions were perceived in a separable manner for subject 1, they were not for subject 2.

The preceding analyses tested for perceptual separability of the dimensions within the framework of the MDS-choice model. Likewise, one can also test for a form of bias independence. Instead of defining a separate bias parameter for each stimulus (as in Equation 2), one could define bias parameters corresponding to each dimension level. Let $b_a(i)$ and $b_s(j)$ denote the bias for responding with angle i and size j, respectively. If these biases operate independently, then the overall bias for responding angle i–size j would be given by $b_{a,s}(i,j) = b_a(i)b_s(j)$. Thus, in the present situation, instead of estimating 16 bias parameters (15 of which are free to vary) as in the full version of the MDS-choice model, one needs to estimate only 8 bias parameters (only 6 of which are free to vary, 3 per dimension) in the bias-independent version of the model. However, the bias-independent model fit the data significantly worse than the full model for both subject 1 [$\chi^2(9) = 50.5$ $p < 0.05$] and subject 2 [$\chi^2(9) = 102.0$, $p < 0.05$]. Additional analyses revealed that a major source of the bias nonindependence was a tendency for the subjects to avoid giving identical component responses (e.g., angle 1, size 1).

As stated earlier, the MDS-choice model analysis also provides information regarding the appropriate distance metric and similarity function for describing the structure of the confusion data. For example, a graphical comparison contrasting the Euclidean and city-block metrics and the exponential and Gaussian similarity functions is provided in Figure 14.5 for subject 1. In each graph, the maximum likelihood η_{ij} similarity parameters for the full SCM are plotted against a set of corresponding distance values (d_{ij}). These distance values were computed from the (constrained) MDS solutions that yielded maximum likelihood fits to the confusion data. Four such sets of distance values were computed:

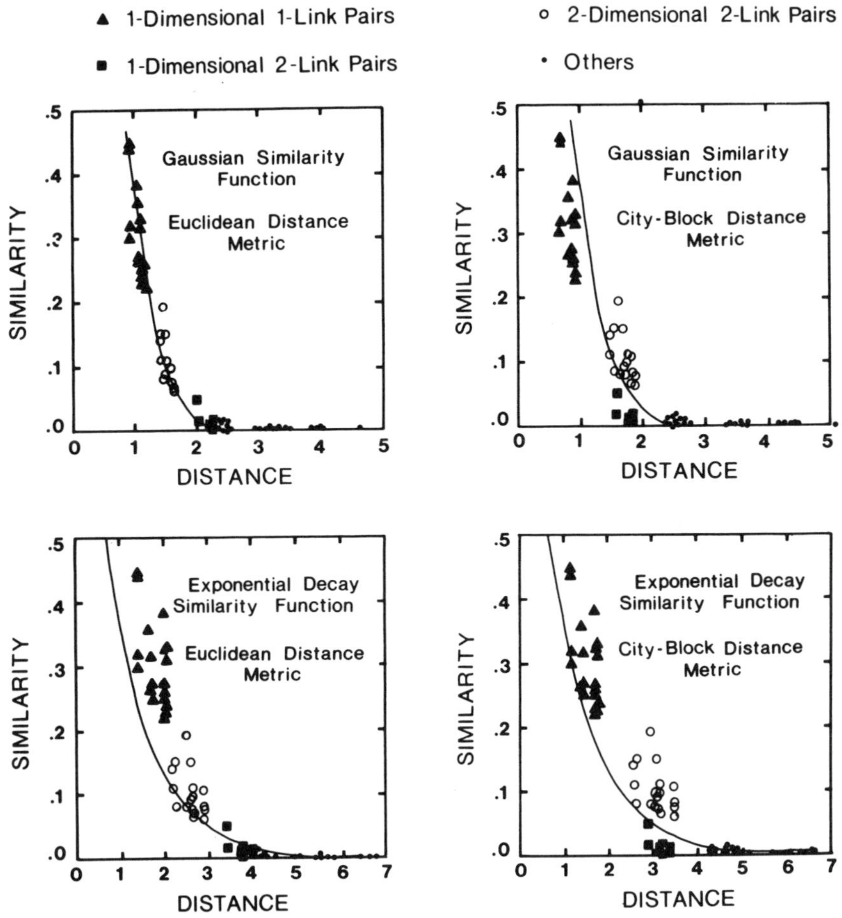

FIG. 14.5. Graphical comparison of the alternative similarity functions and distance metrics on their ability to account for the similarity structure inherent in subject 1's identification confusion data. (The Gaussian function in the upper two panels has a point of inflection at distance = $\sqrt{0.5}$. This point of inflection is not shown because the plot of the function starts at distance = 1.0.) *Note.* From "Overall Similarity and the Identification of Separable-Dimension Stimuli" by R. M. Nosofsky, 1985, *Perception and Psychophysics, 38,* p. 415–432. Copyright 1985 by Psychonomic Society. Reprinted by permission.

one from the MDS solution in which a Euclidean metric and Gaussian similarity function were assumed, a second from the MDS solution that assumed a Euclidean metric and exponential similarity function, and so forth. The solid curve in each graph shows the theoretical function relating similarity to distance. It is evident from inspection that the Gaussian-Euclidean version of the MDS-choice model accurately captures the similarity structures, whereas the remaining alternatives all fail dramatically and in highly systematic ways (see Nosofsky, 1985b, pp. 422–423, for additional discussion).

The support for a Euclidean distance metric and Gaussian similarity function contrasts with many previous findings and conclusions. In particular, for "separable-dimension" stimuli, such as the present semicircles (e.g., Garner, 1974; Shepard, 1964), much evidence suggests that the distance metric is city block (see chap. 7). Also, extensive research points to an exponential decay function as providing an excellent description of the relation between similarity and psychological distance (e.g., see Shepard, 1958a, 1987). Indeed, the support for these alternative functions is so pervasive that Shepard (1987) proposed them as candidates for universal laws of psychological generalization and developed a cognitive process model to account for these laws.

One of the main differences between the present experiment and previous ones that explored the nature of the similarity function and the distance metric is that the present stimuli were highly confusable. By contrast, in most previous experiments that examined these issues, the stimuli were readily discriminable. In discussing Nosofsky's (1985b, 1986) data, Shepard (1986, 1988) drew a distinction between failures of perceptual discrimination and the process of generalization. The latter is a cognitive act on the part of an organism in which a new stimulus—clearly discriminable from a previously experienced one—is nevertheless judged to have the same consequences or belong to the same class as the original. Shepard (1986) conjectured that in Nosofsky's (1985b) experiment, the Gaussian gradient may have been reflecting "perceptual noise" in the stimulus representations, and not the cognitive form of similarity intrinsic to generalization.

In subsequent work, Ennis (1988a; Ennis, Palen, & Mullen, 1988; see also chaps. 5 and 11) formalized these ideas in terms of a stochastic multivariate theory of similarity. Instead of representing each exemplar as a single point in the multidimensional space, as in Nosofsky's (1985b, 1986) approach, exemplars were represented as Gaussian-distributed multivariate random vectors. These Gaussian distributions model the perceptual noise in the stimulus representations. Ennis then showed in simulation work that even if the similarity between any two individual points in these distributions was an exponential decay function of their distance, after integrating over all possible pairs of such points the function relating similarity to distance between the means of the exemplar distributions could look Gaussian in form. Thus, this stochastic theory of similarity provides an attractive avenue to reconciling Nosofsky's (1985b) results with

Shepard's (1987) theory, although the detailed quantitative accuracy of Ennis's model remains to be tested on Nosofsky's (1985b) data.

PREDICTING CATEGORIZATION FROM IDENTIFICATION

Whereas the previous section focused on MDS-choice model analyses of identification confusion data, the present section illustrates applications of the GCM (Equations 1, 3, and 4) to categorization confusion data. The main theme involves the prediction of categorization performance given knowledge of performance in an identification paradigm involving the same set of stimuli.

The first set of data that is considered is from a series of experiments conducted by Nosofsky (1989). The stimuli were essentially the same as those used in Nosofsky's (1985b) experiment described in the second section. However, whereas Nosofsky (1985b) analyzed matrices obtained for individual subjects, the present analyses are for data matrices collapsed over many subjects. The reason for focusing on multiple-subject data is that the categorization experiments include "transfer" stimuli. These stimuli are not assigned by the experimenter to any category. We are interested instead in how subjects will generalize from the original training items to these new items. The process of generalization, of course, is a major facet of categorization. To obtain reliable sample sizes for testing models, we must collect multiple observations for the transfer stimuli. The problem with collecting multiple observations from individual subjects is that once a decision is made with regard to the category membership of a transfer stimulus, this decision may influence subsequent ones. For example, once an observer classifies a transfer stimulus into a category a certain number of times, the observer may treat the transfer stimulus as an actual category exemplar and augment his or her category representation with that exemplar (cf. Nosofsky, 1986, pp. 50–51). To avoid the potential complications involved in presenting individual transfer stimuli numerous times, we adopt the alternative approach of testing multiple subjects, each of whom sees each transfer stimulus just a couple of times. Of course, this latter methodology also has its pitfalls, among them that the model parameters across different subjects may vary.

The category structures tested in Nosofsky's (1989) experiment are illustrated in Figure 14.6. As in the identification experiment discussed in the previous section, there were four levels of both size and angle combined orthogonally to yield a 16-member stimulus set. Cells in the 4×4 grids that are labeled with a 1 and 2 represent training exemplars assigned by the experimenter to categories 1 and 2, respectively. Empty cells represent unassigned transfer stimuli. Each category structure can be described in terms of a simple rule. In the *size* categorization, small stimuli are assigned to category 1 and large stimuli to category 2. In the *angle* categorization, stimuli with low angles are assigned to category 1

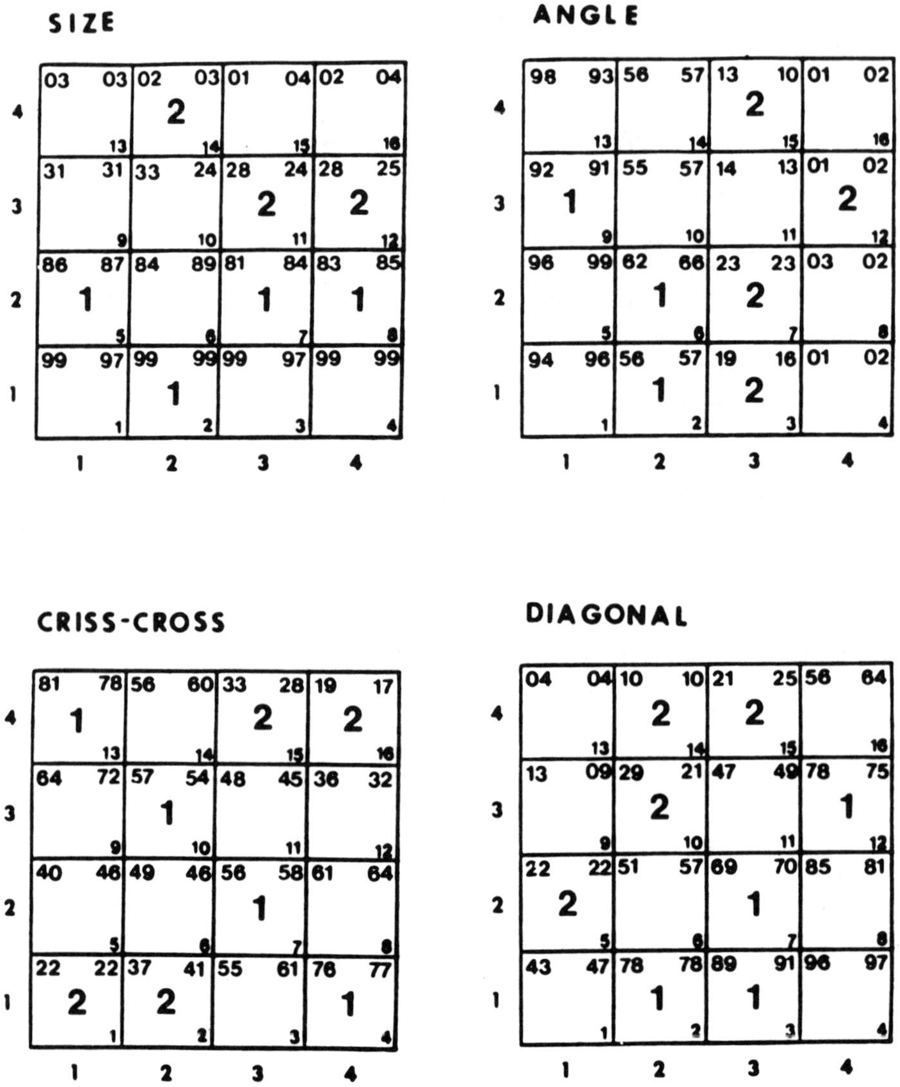

FIG. 14.6. Category structures tested by Nosofsky (1989). Columns represent different levels of angle, and rows represent different levels of size. Boldface numbers in the center of each cell indicate category assignments for each exemplar. Values in upper right of each cell are observed category 1 response probabilities; values in upper left of each cell are GCM-predicted category 1 response probabilities. *Note.* From "Further Tests of an Exemplar-Similarity Approach to Relating Identification and Categorization" by R. M. Nosofsky, 1989, *Perception and Psychophysics, 45,* p. 279–290. Copyright 1989 by Psychonomic Society. Reprinted by permission.

and stimuli with high angles to category 2. The *crisscross* categorization can be described as a continuous biconditional rule: Large stimuli with low angles and small stimuli with high angles are assigned to category 1, and the reverse for category 2. Finally, the *diagonal* categorization is so named because the category exemplars can be partitioned by drawing a diagonal line through the two-dimensional space.

The asymmetric structures associated with the size and angle categorizations (see Figure 14.6) were used to provide clear evidence for the operation of a selective attention process. Consider, for example, the angle categorization. Transfer stimulus 14 is highly similar to a category 2 training exemplar, namely stimulus 15. Indeed, without selective attention operating, the exemplar model predicts that stimulus 14 will be classified in category 2. However, if subjects attended selectively to the relevant angle dimension, the psychological space would be "stretched" along the angle dimension and "shrunk" along the size dimension. In this case, transfer stimulus 14 becomes more similar to the exemplars of category 1, and the exemplar model predicts that it would be classified in category 1. An analogous situation arises for transfer stimulus 9 in the size categorization.

In the experiment, separate groups of approximately 40 subjects participated in each categorization condition. Each condition started with a training phase immediately followed by a transfer phase. During the training phase, only assigned category exemplars were presented, and corrective feedback was provided on every trial. During the transfer phase, assigned exemplars as well as transfer stimuli were presented. The goal is to predict quantitatively the probability with which each individual stimulus was classified into either category 1 or 2 during the transfer phase.

To apply the GCM, we need an MDS solution for the exemplars. As was the case in Nosofsky's (1985b) experiment, an identification condition was conducted. However, instead of testing two individual subjects for an extensive period of time, approximately 40 subjects were tested, each for a single session of 150 trials (plus 200 trials of practice). The identification confusion data cumulated over all subjects were analyzed by using the MDS-choice model. The model provided a fairly good fit to the data, and the two-dimensional solution that was derived had the same grid-like structure as already illustrated in Figure 14.4 (see Figures 3 and 4 of Nosofsky, 1989). The precise coordinates for the maximum likelihood MDS solution are provided in Table 3 of Nosofsky (1989). The MDS-choice model analyses also provided evidence for a Gaussian similarity function and a Euclidean distance metric, as was found in Nosofsky's (1985b) study that used individual subject data. These functions are assumed in applying the GCM to the categorization data.

The probability with which each stimulus was classified by the subjects into category 1 is given by the values in the upper right of each cell in Figure 14.6. The GCM (Equations 1, 3, and 4) can be used to predict each data set by estimating three parameters: a category response-bias parameter b_1 that appears in Equation 1 (with $b_2 = 1 - b_1$), the overall sensitivity parameter c that appears in Equation 3, and an attention-weight parameter w_1 that appears in Equation 3 (with $w_2 = 1 - w_1$). Recall that all of the MDS coordinates (the values of x_{im} in Equation 3) as well as the values of r and p in Equations 3 and 4 were estimated previously by fitting the MDS-choice model to the identification confusion data.

The GCM was fitted to each set of categorization data using a maximum likelihood criterion (Equation 5). The maximum likelihood parameters and summary fits for the model are provided in Table 14.2. (The table also shows the parameters and fits for various restricted versions of the model described subsequently.) The predicted probabilities with which each stimulus was classified in category 1 are shown along with the observed probabilities in Figure 14.6 (upper left of each cell). A scatterplot of the observed against predicted probabilities is provided in Figure 14.7. It is evident from inspection that the GCM provides an impressive quantitative fit to the categorization data. It accounts for 99.4%, 99.6%, 95.2%, and 98.4% of the variance in the size, angle, crisscross, and diagonal categorizations, respectively. The scatterplot in Figure 14.7 indicates that the quantitative predictions are accurate across the entire range of the probability space. Indeed, the model was not rejected in Likelihood Ratio Tests of overall goodness of fit in any of the four conditions [average $\chi^2(13) = 18.0$, $p > 0.05$], despite fairly large sample sizes (approximately 100 observations for each of the 16 stimuli in each condition).

TABLE 14.2
Maximum Likelihood Parameters and Summary Fits for Full and Restricted Versions of the Exemplar-Similarity Categorization Model

		Parameters			*Fits*		
Condition	*Model*	*c*	w_1	b_1	*SSE*	*% Var*	*− lnL*
Size	Unconstrained	1.60	.10	.50	.015	99.4	40.8
	Equal attention	2.38	(.50)	.49	.077	97.0	72.0
	Equal bias	1.60	.10	(.50)	.015	99.4	40.8
Angle	Unconstrained	3.20	.98	.43	.010	99.6	44.3
	Equal attention	3.57	(.50)	.45	.305	86.4	164.3
	Equal bias	3.09	1.00	(.50)	.029	98.7	56.8
Crisscross	Unconstrained	1.62	.80	.45	.025	95.2	47.7
	Equal attention	1.23	(.50)	.45	.087	83.1	64.6
	Equal bias	3.00	.93	(.50)	.046	91.1	56.7
Diagonal	Unconstrained	2.42	.81	.49	.023	98.4	48.3
	Equal attention	1.81	(.50)	.48	.217	85.0	109.4
	Equal bias	2.42	.81	(.50)	.021	98.6	49.1

Note: Values in parentheses were constrained a priori. The parameter w_1 gives the attention weight for angle, and $1 - w_1$ the attention weight for size. *SSE* = sum of squared deviations between predicted and observed category 1 probabilities; *% Var* = percentage of variance accounted for; *ln L* = log-likelihood.

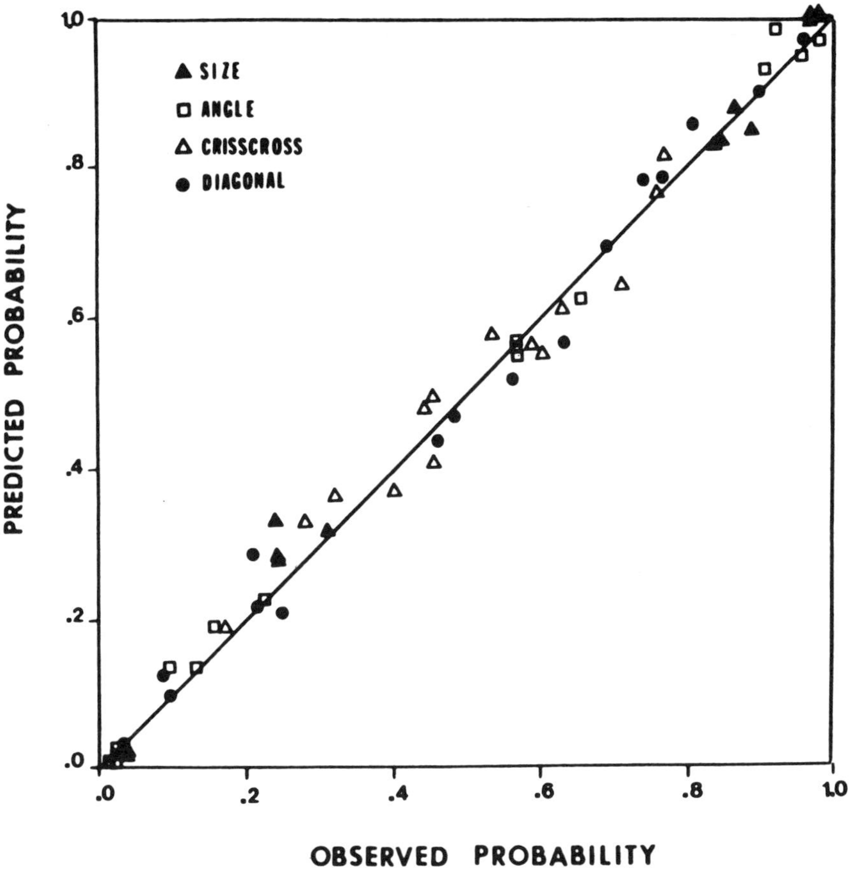

FIG. 14.7. Scatterplot of observed against GCM-predicted category 1 response probabilities. (This is Figure 6 of Nosofsky, 1989.) *Note.* From "Further Tests of an Exemplar-Similarity Approach to Relating Identification and Categorization" by R. M. Nosofsky, 1989, *Perception and Psychophysics, 45,* p. 279–290. Copyright 1989 by Psychonomic Society. Reprinted by permission.

For demonstrating the critical role of the attention weight parameters in achieving these fits, a restricted version of the GCM was fitted to the data in which the weights were held fixed at 0.5. This restricted model assumes that the distribution of attention over the two dimensions in each categorization condition was the same as in the identification condition. As shown in Table 14.2, this restricted GCM fit the data far worse than the full model. Likelihood Ratio Tests indicated that the attention weights were significantly different from 0.5 in all conditions [$\chi^2(1) = 62.4, 240.0, 33.8$, and 122.2, in the size, angle, crisscross, and diagonal categorizations, respectively].

As discussed earlier, transfer stimulus 14 in the angle categorization provides a good example to illustrate the role of the attention parameters (see Figure 14.6).

Without selective attention operating, the GCM predicts that stimulus 14 will be classified into category 1 with probability 0.18; but with selective attention operating, the predicted value is 0.56, which is close to the observed value of 0.57. With nondifferential weighting of the dimensions, stimulus 14 is more similar overall to the exemplars of category 2 than of category 1. But after selective attention to the relevant angle dimension, the space is stretched along the horizontal axis and shrunk along the vertical axis, making stimulus 14 more similar to the exemplars of category 1. Note that this selective attention strategy is optimal in the context of the angle categorization. By attending selectively to angle, subjects maximize their ability to discriminate between the exemplars of the contrasting categories.

A restricted version of the GCM was also fitted to the data in which the bias parameter was held fixed at $b_1 = 0.50$ (nondifferential response bias). As indicated in Table 14.2, this bias-free model fit the categorization data essentially as well as the full version of the model. Indeed, Likelihood Ratio Tests indicated that the bias parameter did not differ significantly from 0.5 in either the size or diagonal categorizations [average $\chi^2(1) = 0.80$, $p > 0.05$], although it did in the crisscross and angle categorizations [average $\chi^2(1) = 21.5$, $p < 0.01$]. Presumably, the bias parameter would play a more important role in situations in which differential payoffs for alternative category responses were provided, a priori probabilities of categories were manipulated, and so forth.

Rules and Exemplars

In additional studies of the identification-categorization relation, attempts have been made to provide severe tests of the exemplar model by designing category structures for which alternative classification strategies might be expected to operate. An example from an experiment conducted by Nosofsky, Clark, and Shin (1989) is illustrated in Figure 14.8. For reasons to be explained shortly, we used stimulus components that were highly separable in nature, namely a line that varied in length and a tone that varied in pitch. There were four levels of length and four levels of pitch combined orthogonally to yield a 16-member stimulus set. In Figure 14.8, stimuli enclosed by circles represent category 1 training exemplars, stimuli enclosed by triangles represent category 2 training exemplars, and unenclosed stimuli are transfer items. The general procedure was the same as discussed previously for Nosofsky's (1989) experiment, with a classification training phase followed by transfer tests.

The motivation behind testing the category structure in Figure 14.8 was the idea that subjects might learn and represent the category by forming a conjunctive rule: If an item has a length greater than or equal to 3 *and* a pitch less than or equal to 2 then it belongs to category 1; otherwise it belongs to category 2. (Alternatively, the structure could be described by a disjunctive rule: If an item has a length less than or equal to 2 *or* a pitch greater than or equal to 3 then it

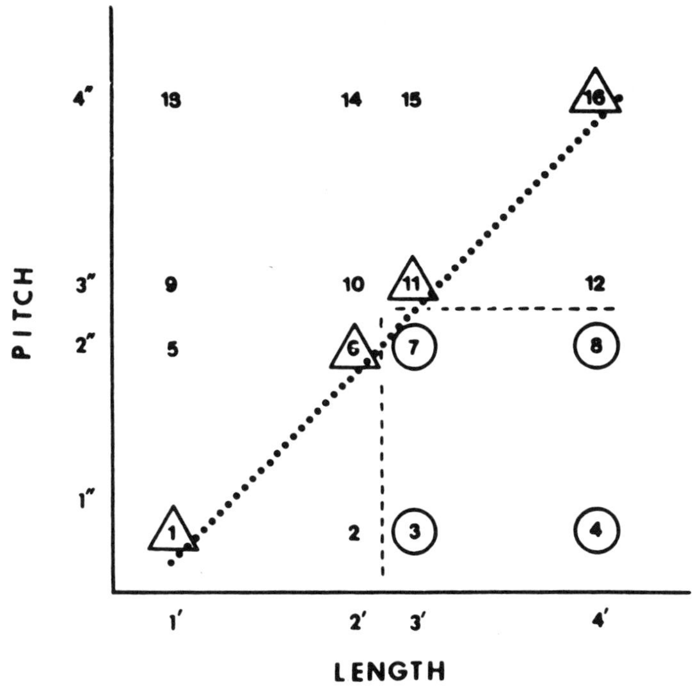

FIG. 14.8. Conjunctive-rule category structure tested by Nosofsky et al. (1989). Physical values of line length were 28, 90, 110, and 180 mm; physical values of pitch were 100, 1,000, 1,050, and 2,400 Hz. Unequal spacings were used to more clearly contrast the predictions of the conjunctive-rule and exemplar-similarity models. *Note.* From "Rules and Exemplars in Categorization, Identification, and Recognition" by R. M. Nosofsky, S. E. Clark, and H. J. Shin, 1989, *Journal of Experimental Psychology: Learning, Memory, and Cognition, 15,* p. 282–304. Copyright 1989 by American Psychological Association. Reprinted by permission.

belongs to category 2; otherwise it belongs to category 1.) The decision boundary defined by such a logical rule is illustrated by the dashed lines in Figure 14.8. Note that application of this classification strategy entails separate processing of each dimension and combining individual decisions about the values on each dimension in making a categorization response. In designing the experiment, it was thought that using the highly separable dimensions of line length and tone pitch would promote the use of such an "independent-decisions" strategy (cf. Ashby & Gott, 1988; Shaw, 1982).

The critical items of interest in the design are transfer stimuli 2 and 12 (see Figure 14.8). If subjects represented the categories by forming the simple conjunctive rule, then these critical transfer stimuli should be classified in category

2. By contrast, suppose that subjects represented the categories by storing individual exemplars in memory. Then transfer stimuli 2 and 12 should be classified in category 1, because they are each highly similar to a category 1 training exemplar. For this category structure, global selective attention to dimensions could not account for a pattern in which both critical transfer stimuli were classified into category 2, because attending primarily to one dimension would move classification tendencies for stimuli 2 and 12 in opposite directions.

Contrary to the predictions of the conjunctive-rule model, and in agreement with the predictions of the exemplar-based GCM, the overwhelming tendency in the experiment was for subjects to classify both critical transfer stimuli into category 1. Furthermore, the GCM yielded a good quantitative fit to the overall pattern of classification data, accounting for over 90% of the response variance. Of course, alternative logical rules could be proposed that would also account for the observed pattern of results. One such rule is illustrated by the dotted linear boundary in Figure 14.8. It corresponds to the rule that if the level on dimension 2 is greater than or equal to the level on dimension 1, then the item belongs in category 2; otherwise it belongs in category 1. (One can question the psychological plausibility of such a rule in the present situation, however, because it entails comparing a magnitude of pitch to a magnitude of length.) In principle, because a "rule" can be essentially anything, it is impossible to contrast the exemplar model with the entire class of logical rule-based models. The main point of experiments such as the one just described has been to challenge the exemplar model by contrasting its predictions with those of explicitly formalized rule-based models that seem plausible in particular settings. In most such tests to date, the exemplar model has remained stubborn and appears to provide accurate quantitative predictions of classification performance even in situations in which categories are describable in terms of simple logical rules (Nosofsky, 1984, 1987, 1991c; Nosofsky et al., 1989).

Similarity and Frequency

The main focus thus far in this section has been on the roles of similarity and selective attention processes in determining categorization. Another fundamental variable known to affect learning, memory, and decision making is frequency or repetition. The GCM represents the role of frequency in terms of changes in the values of the exemplar-strength parameters (N_j) in Equation 1. Presumably, as the frequency with which an exemplar is presented during categorization training increases, the strength with which that exemplar is represented in memory also increases.

Nosofsky (1988c) conducted an experiment designed to test the frequency-sensitive exemplar model. The stimuli were 12 Munsell color chips of a constant red hue but varying along the dimensions of brightness and saturation. A two-

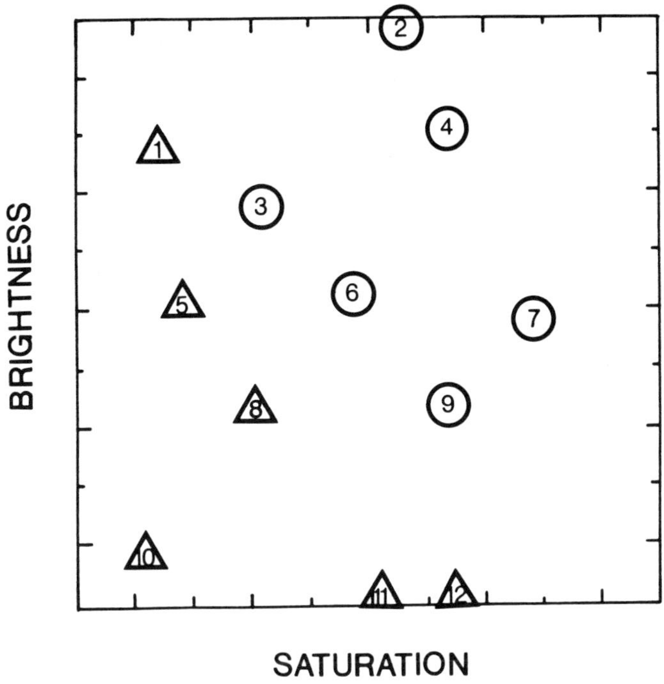

FIG. 14.9. Category structure tested by Nosofsky (1988c). Stimuli enclosed by circles are members of target category, stimuli enclosed by triangles are members of contrast category. *Note.* From "Similarity, Frequency, and Category Representations" by R. M. Nosofsky, 1988, *Journal of Experimental Psychology: Learning, Memory, and Cognition, 14,* p. 54–65. Copyright 1988 by American Psychological Association. Reprinted by permission.

dimensional scaling solution for the colors is shown in Figure 14.9. (The solution was derived on the basis of confusions observed during an identification learning condition, as described previously.) In the main experiment, subjects learned to classify the colors into the two categories illustrated in Figure 14.9. I will refer to the set of stimuli enclosed by circles as the *target* category, and to the set of stimuli enclosed by triangles as the *contrast* category. Following the categorization learning phase, a transfer phase was conducted in which subjects made goodness-of-example (or "typicality") judgments for each of the 12 colors, as well as classification confidence judgments.

The main experimental manipulation was that during training, individual colors were presented with high frequency. In one condition, color 2 was presented five times as often as any of the other colors, whereas in two other conditions colors 7 and 6 were presented with high frequency. This frequency manipulation had a dramatic impact on subjects' postacquisition classification confidence judgments and typicality ratings. First, relative to a baseline condition in which all colors were presented with equal frequency, classification confidence and typicality ratings for the high-frequency colors increased substantially. Indeed, a crossover effect was observed, in which color 2 was rated as the best example of the target category when it was presented with high frequency, whereas color 7 was rated as the best example of the target category when it was presented with high frequency. More interesting, classification confidence and typicality ratings also changed for stimuli that were similar to the high-frequency exemplars. In the condition in which color 2 was presented with high frequency, typicality ratings increased substantially for its neighbor color 4, whereas in the condition in which color 7 was presented with high frequency, typicality ratings increased substantially for color 9 (see Figure 14.9). Finally, typicality ratings *decreased* for members of the contrast category that were similar to the high-frequency exemplars. For example, color 8 was judged as a worse example of the contrast category when color 6 of the target category was presented with high frequency.

A fair metaphorical summary of the results is that the high-frequency stimulus acted as a "magnet" in the psychological space, drawing nearby stimuli toward it. Indeed, good quantitative fits to the classification and typicality data were achieved by using the frequency-sensitive version of the GCM (Equation 1), with the assumption that the exemplar-strength terms were proportional to the relative frequencies of the stimuli.[1] This frequency-sensitive model accurately captured the joint, interactive roles of similarity and frequency on subjects' classification judgments.

Prototype and Exemplars

Tests of the MDS-based exemplar model have also involved systematic quantitative comparisons with MDS-based prototype models, where the prototype is defined as the centroid over all category exemplars in the multidimensional space (e.g., Reed, 1972). In the prototype model, instead of summing the similarity of a probe to all category exemplars, one computes the similarity of the probe to the category centroid. In all comparisons to date, the evidence has been overwhelmingly in favor of the exemplar model (e.g., Medin & Schaffer, 1978; Medin & Smith, 1981; Nosofsky, 1987, 1988c, 1991b; Shin, 1990) in experiments involving a wide variety of category structures and stimulus materials. A review of these comparisons and a theoretical treatment of relations between prototype and exemplar models is provided by Nosofsky (in press).

[1]More recent research suggests, however, that exemplar strength is a negatively accelerated, increasing function of presentation frequency (Nosofsky, 1991a, 1991c).

CATEGORIZATION AND RECOGNITION

The focus thus far has been to illustrate the exemplar-based approach to relating identification and categorization. The exemplar-based GCM has been extended to also account for relations between categorization and old-new recognition memory (Nosofsky, 1988a, 1991b; Nosofsky et al., 1989). The central assumption in the model is that, whereas categorization decisions are based on the similarity of a probe to the exemplars of a target category *relative* to the exemplars of contrast categories (as in Equation 1), recognition decisions are based on the *absolute* summed similarity of a probe to all exemplars stored in memory. This absolute summed similarity gives a measure of overall "familiarity," with higher familiarity values leading to higher recognition probabilities. The idea that recognition decisions are based on a global match to information stored in memory forms a core assumption of various recent quantitative models (e.g., Gillund & Shiffrin, 1984; Hintzman, 1986, 1988; Murdock, 1982). A unique contribution of the present work has been to show that fined-grained differences in recognition probabilities can be predicted on the basis of fine-grained differences in summed similarities among items. Also, because categorization and recognition judgments are assumed to be based on different decision rules, the GCM has been able to account for certain "dissociations" between the two paradigms that previous investigators have cited as evidence against exemplar-only memory models (Nosofsky, 1988a, 1991b).

The Formal Model

The following section describes the formal approach used by Nosofsky (1991b) for relating categorization and recognition. It entails a modification of the general approach described earlier. In Equation 1, the degree to which a probe "activates" a category is deterministically related to the summed similarity of the probe to the category exemplars. Responding is probabilistic because a probabilistic decision rule is used. A problem with this approach is that Ashby and Gott (1988) and Ashby and Maddox (1990) have presented convincing evidence of the use of deterministic decision rules in certain classification paradigms. In the modified model that is now discussed, the category activation functions are assumed to be random variables, while a deterministic decision rule is used. This modified model can describe classification decision-making behavior ranging from what appears to be probabilistic to completely deterministic.

The underlying spirit of the model is the same as before. Exemplars are represented as points in a multidimensional space, the distance between exemplars i and j is computed from Equation 3, and this distance is transformed to a similarity measure (η_{ij}) by using Equation 4. The degree to which probe i "activates" exemplar j in memory is given by

$$a_{ij} = N_j \cdot \eta_{ij} + e_j \,, \tag{6}$$

where N_j and η_{ij} are defined as before and the e_j's are independent and identically distributed normal random variables with mean zero and variance σ^2. Thus, the activation of exemplar j is determined jointly by its strength in memory, its similarity to the presented probe i, and random noise. The "evidence" for category J given presentation of probe i is found by summing the activations of probe i to all exemplars of category J,

$$E_{J,i} = \sum_{j \in C_J} a_{ij} \,. \tag{7}$$

In a two-category experiment, the decision rule is to respond category 1 if the evidence for category 1 exceeds the evidence for category 2 by a critical amount,

$$E_{1,i} - E_{2,i} > b \,, \tag{8}$$

where b is a response bias parameter. Note that categorization decisions are based on the *relative* activations for the two categories, that is, the magnitude of $E_{1,i}$ relative to $E_{2,i}$.

For recognition, the decision rule is to respond "old" if the summed activation for both categories exceeds a criterion x_c:

$$E_{1,i} + E_{2,i} > x_c \,. \tag{9}$$

Thus, for recognition, what is important is the absolute summed activation for both categories, not their activations relative to one another.

As explained by Nosofsky (1991b), the predicted categorization and recognition probabilities are derived from the decision rules in Inequalities 8 and 9 by using a numerical approximation to the integrals of appropriate normal density functions. The parameters in the model are the sensitivity and attention weight parameters in the distance function (Equation 3), the category bias parameter b, the recognition criterion x_c, and the error variance (σ^2) associated with the random variables e_j. If the error variance is large, then responding appears to be probabilistic, whereas, as the error variance goes to *zero*, responding becomes entirely deterministic.

There are numerous possible process interpretations of the locus of the error variance or "noise" in subjects' categorization and recognition judgments. For example, instead of representing an exemplar as a single point in the psychological space, exemplars could be represented as distributions of points, as in probabilistic MDS models (e.g., Ennis et al., 1988; see also chaps. 2–6). Then, upon presentation of a probe, momentary psychological values from each of these distributions would be sampled and the similarity between the probe and each momentary value computed. Other likely sources of noise are noise in the actual similarity computations, noise in subjects' memory for the category assignments of the exemplars, as well as noise in the criterion settings (the values of b and x_c

in Inequalities 8 and 9, respectively). The system of Equations 6–9 should be viewed as an approximation to a complete process-model account of the noise in categorization judgments.

Although the version of the exemplar model with the deterministic decision rule (Equations 3, 4, and 6–9) was introduced in this section on the categorization-recognition relation, the same model could be applied in an attempt to account for the categorization-identification relation. The fundamental assumption in the modeling is that people represent categories by storing individual exemplars in memory, and make classification decisions on the basis of similarity to the stored exemplars. Whether a probabilistic or a deterministic decision rule is used is an important question, but one that is orthogonal to the issue of the nature of the category representation.

Experimental Tests

In an experiment designed to test the categorization-recognition model (Nosofsky, 1991b), subjects learned to classify the schematic faces illustrated in Figure 14.10. The faces varied along four (trinary-valued) continuous dimensions: eye height, eye separation, nose length, and mouth height. The five faces in the top row of Figure 14.10 were the category 1 training exemplars, whereas the bottom five faces were the category 2 training exemplars. Following a training phase, subjects were tested in a transfer phase in which they were presented with the 10 old training exemplars plus 24 new faces formed by new combinations of the dimension values. For each face presented during transfer, subjects first judged whether it was old or new, and then classified it into category 1 or 2.[2]

To apply the exemplar-similarity model, we need an MDS solution for the faces. Figure 14.11 shows an MDS solution for the 34 faces that was derived on the basis of direct similarity judgments. (A traditional Euclidean MDS model was used.) A four-dimensional solution accounted well for the similarity ratings data, and the psychological dimensions could be readily interpreted in terms of the physically manipulated dimensions of eye height, eye separation, nose length, and mouth height. Figure 14.11 also illustrates the category structures embedded in the MDS solution. The stimuli enclosed by circles are the category 1 training exemplars, whereas the stimuli enclosed by triangles are the category 2 training exemplars. Note that four exemplars in each category form a prototypical cluster in the plot of dimension 1 versus dimension 2, whereas the fifth exemplar is relatively atypical and falls close to the (hypothetical) category boundary. (These atypical exemplars correspond to the second faces in the top and bottom rows of Figure 14.10.) The MDS solution shown in Figure 14.11 was used in conjunction with the extended GCM to quantitatively predict subjects' categorization and recognition judgments for each of the 34 faces.

[2]The stimuli and category structures used in this experiment were the same as those used in an earlier study by Reed (1972).

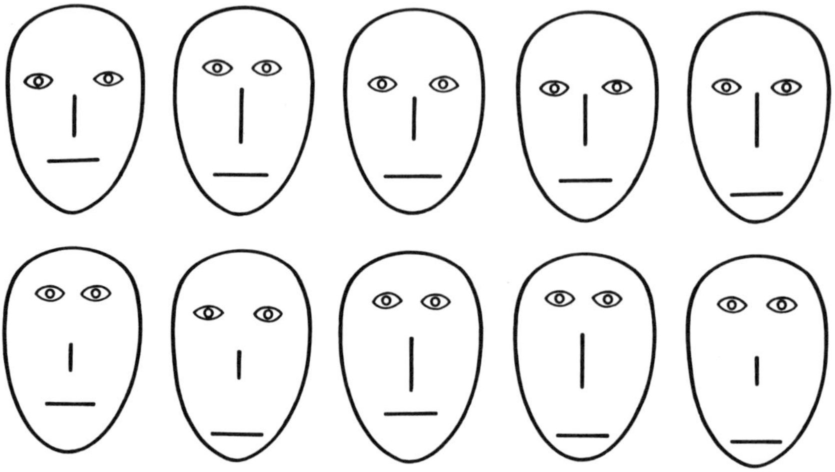

FIG. 14.10. Illustration of the schematic faces used as training items in Nosofsky's (1991b) experiment. Faces in top row are members of category 1, faces in bottom row are members of category 2. *Note.* From "Tests of an exemplar model for relating perceptual classification and recognition memory" by R. M. Nosofsky, 1991, *Journal of Experimental Psychology: Human Perception and Performance, 17,* p. 3–27. Copyright 1991 by American Psychological Association. Reprinted by permission.

Before proceeding to the results of the theoretical analyses, it is useful to gain some preliminary insight into the nature of the categorization-recognition relation that was observed in the experiment. Figure 14.12 provides a scatterplot of observed recognition probabilities against a "classification confidence" measure. The classification confidence for face i [cc (i)] was defined as $cc\ (i) = 2*|P(R_1|\mathbf{S}_i) - 0.5|$, where $P(R_1|\mathbf{S}_i)$ denotes the probability with which face i was classified in category 1. Thus, for faces that are classified with probability near unity into either category 1 or 2, the confidence measure will be near unity, whereas for faces that are classified with probability close to 0.5, the confidence measure will be near zero. The motivation behind plotting the recognition probabilities against the classification confidences is the following intuition expressed by various researchers regarding exemplar-only memory models: If classification

FIG. 14.11. Illustration of category structures and transfer stimuli embedded in MDS solution for the faces. Stimuli enclosed by circles are members of category 1; stimuli enclosed by triangles are members of category 2. *Note.* From "Tests of an exemplar model for relating perceptual classification and recognition memory" by R. M. Nosofsky, 1991, *Journal of Experimental Psychology: Human Perception and Performance, 17,* p. 3–27. Copyright 1991 by American Psychological Association. Reprinted by permission.

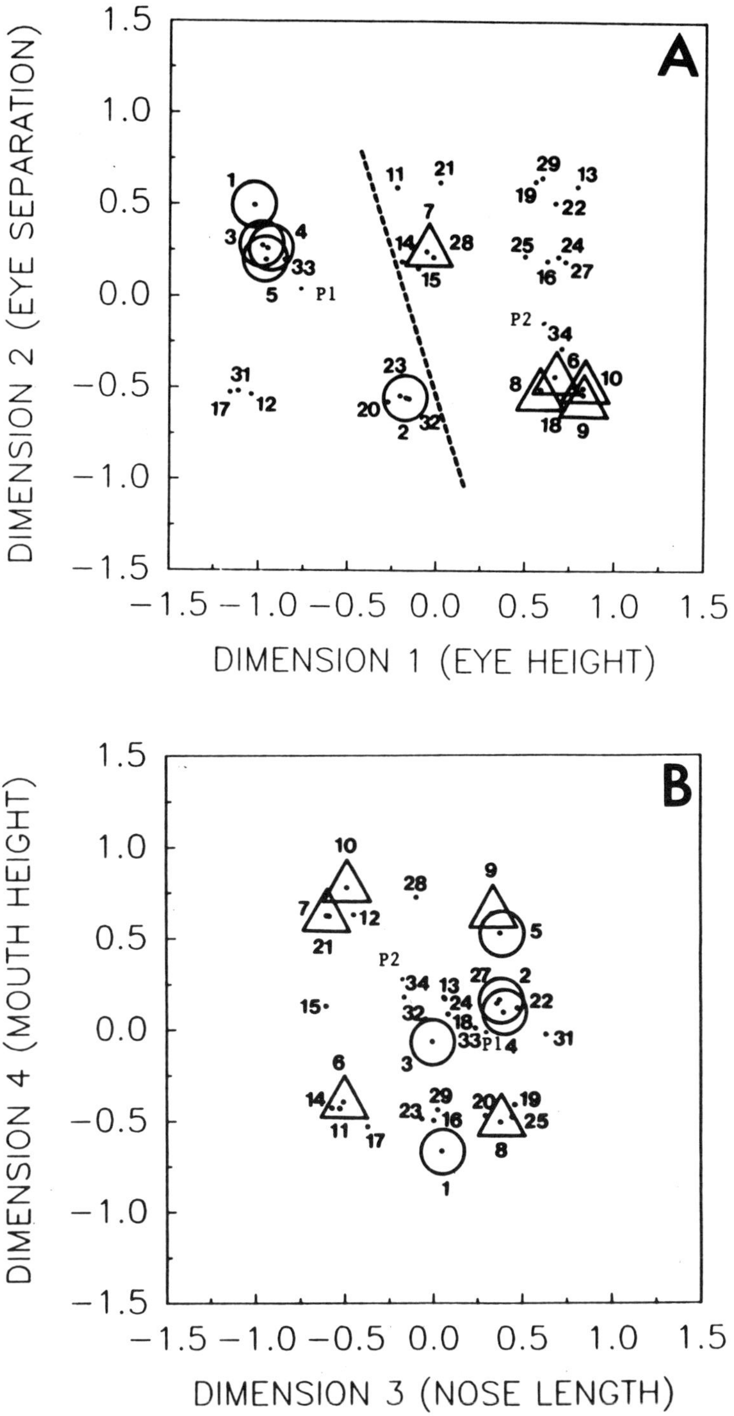
A
DIMENSION 2 (EYE SEPARATION)
DIMENSION 1 (EYE HEIGHT)
1.5
1.0
0.5
0.0
−0.5
−1.0
−1.5
−1.5 −1.0 −0.5 0.0 0.5 1.0 1.5
P1
P2
B
DIMENSION 4 (MOUTH HEIGHT)
DIMENSION 3 (NOSE LENGTH)
1.5
1.0
0.5
0.0
−0.5
−1.0
−1.5
−1.5 −1.0 −0.5 0.0 0.5 1.0 1.5
P1
P2

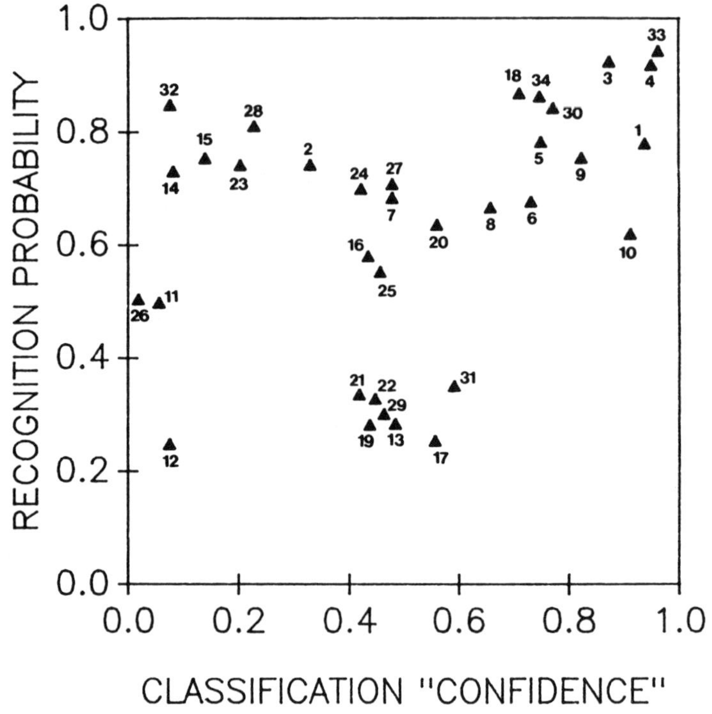

FIG. 14.12. Scatterplot of observed recognition probabilities against observed classification confidences. *Note.* From "Tests of an exemplar model for relating perceptual classification and recognition memory" by R. M. Nosofsky, 1991, *Journal of Experimental Psychology: Human Perception and Performance, 17,* p. 3–27. Copyright 1991 by American Psychological Association. Reprinted by permission.

and recognition judgments are based on the same information, then there should be a strong correlation between recognition and classification. That is, subjects should be more confident about classifying items that they believe are "old" than items that they believe are "new" (Anderson, Kline, & Beasley, 1979; Metcalfe & Fisher, 1986). As is clear from inspection of the scatterplot, however, there is little correlation between the recognition probabilities and the classification confidences ($r = 0.36$). Indeed, various examples exist in which classification confidence is low, yet recognition probability is high (faces 14, 15, 23, 28, and 32), and in which confidence classification is at least moderate, yet recognition probability very low (faces 13, 17, 19, 22, 29, and 31).

Despite the apparent dissociation displayed in Figure 14.12, the extended GCM (Equations 3, 4, and 6–9) accounted well for both types of judgments within a unified framework (see Nosofsky, 1991b, for details of the theoretical analyses). Scatterplots of observed against predicted categorization and recognition probabilities are shown in Figure 14.13. The model accounted for 95.9%

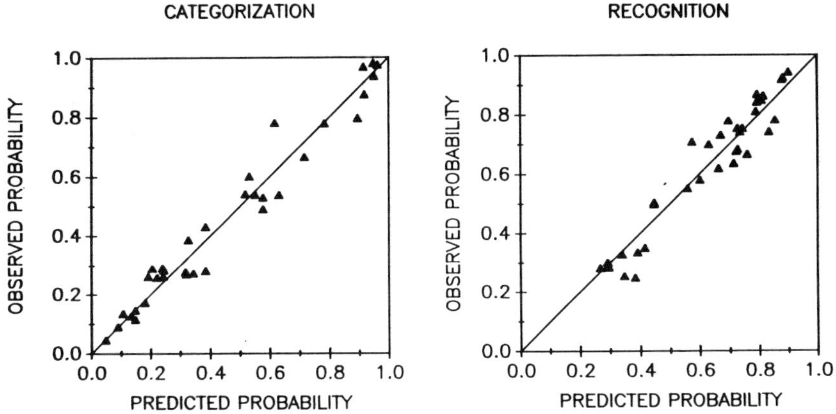

FIG. 14.13. Scatterplot of observed against predicted classification and recognition probabilities. *Note.* From "Tests of an exemplar model for relating perceptual classification and recognition memory" by R. M. Nosofsky, 1991, *Journal of Experimental Psychology: Human Perception and Performance, 17,* p. 3–27. Copyright 1991 by American Psychological Association. Reprinted by permission.

and 91.9% of the variance in the categorization and recognition probabilities, respectively.

To gain insight into the workings of the model, consider again the MDS solution for the exemplars in Figure 14.11 and the categorization-recognition scatterplot in Figure 14.12. Faces 14, 15, 23, 28, and 32 are examples of faces that received high recognition probabilities but for which three was low classification confidence. Inspection of the plot of dimension 1 versus dimension 2 reveals that these faces are located in a central portion of the multidimensional space, so are moderately similar to numerous training exemplars. Furthermore, these faces are highly similar to at least one training exemplar. Thus, absolute summed similarity for these faces is high, explaining their high recognition probabilities. However, both categories of exemplars exert competing influence for these faces, so there is low classification confidence associated with them. By contrast, faces 13, 19, 22, and 29 are examples of faces that had low recognition probabilities but for which there was moderate classification confidence. Inspection of Figure 14.11 reveals that these faces are located in an isolated region of the multidimensional space, explaining their low recognition probabilities. However, in a *relative* sense, these faces are clearly more similar to the exemplars of category 2 than to the exemplars of category 1, so they are classified in category 2 with moderately high probability. Finally, faces 3, 4, and 33 are examples of faces that are highly similar to several training exemplars from only the *same* category, explaining jointly their high recognition probabilities and classification confidences.

Another important result of the model-based analyses was that the maximum likelihood distributions of attention weights differed significantly for categorization and recognition. Although this finding might seem an embarrassment to the model, a moment's reflection suggests that it is a plausible occurrence. In particular, dimensions that are highly diagnostic for discriminating between the two categories may be useless for distinguishing between old and new items, and vice versa. To take an extreme example, suppose that all the faces presented during the training phase were red, and the new faces presented during the transfer phase were blue. The color of a face would be useless for deciding its category membership, and subjects would presumably give it zero weight in making classification decisions. However, virtually all weight would be focused on the color dimension for purposes of making old-new recognition judgments. Indeed, in the analyses reported by Nosofsky (1991b), it was found that the top performers came close to optimizing their distribution of attention weights for purposes of categorization. Furthermore, the best-fitting distribution of recognition weights, although not theoretically optimal, led to levels of recognition performance that far exceeded what could have been achieved had the subjects used the same weights that they had used for categorization. Thus, just as selective attention processes play a key role in shaping the identification-categorization relation, so they appear to do in shaping the categorization-recognition relation.

In summary, this section illustrated an exemplar-based approach to modeling the categorization-recognition relation. According to the model, both categorization and recognition decisions involve similarity computations performed on a common representational substrate, namely collections of individual category exemplars. However, whereas categorization decisions are based on the relative degree of within-category to between-category similarity, recognition decisions are based on the absolute summed similarity of a probe to all exemplars stored in memory. Because different decision rules are involved, the model is able to predict low correlations between categorization and recognition, a phenomenon that previous investigators have cited as evidence against exemplar-only memory models. Furthermore, detailed quantitative analyses suggest that subjects may adopt different selective attention strategies when making categorization and recognition decisions. This finding seems reasonable, because, in general, different distributions of attention over the psychological dimensions will serve to optimize categorization and recognition performance.

SUMMARY

This chapter provided an overview of an MDS-based exemplar model of categorization performance. The model has proved capable of providing detailed quantitative fits to sets of classification data involving multidimensional perceptual stimuli, often with a minimum of parameter estimation. More important than the ability of the model to simply fit categorization data, however, has been its ability to characterize relations between categorization and other fundamental cognitive processes, namely identification and recognition. These achievements are important, because the development of formal models that provide unified quantitative accounts of performance across domains is a central goal of cognitive and mathematical psychology.

ACKNOWLEDGMENT

This work was supported by Grants BNS 87-19938 from the National Science Foundation and PHS R01 MH48494-01 from the National Institute of Mental Health to Indiana University.

15 On the Similarity of Categorization Models

Michael M. Cohen
Dominic W. Massaro
Program in Experimental Psychology
University of California
Santa Cruz, CA

INTRODUCTION

Most chapters in this book describe probabilistic multidimensional models of perceptual and cognitive tasks. This fact acknowledges several important properties of human information processing. First, performance is not deterministic, but is variable or probabilistic. A subject responds in one way to a stimulus on one trial and responds in another way on another trial. Thus, performance is often characterized by some probability value representing overall response probability to a repeated presentation of a stimulus. Probabilistic performance might result from probabilistic differences in processing, probabilistic differences in the physical stimulus information from trial to trial, or probabilistic representations of prototype items in memory. Second, the term *multidimensional* refers to the multiple sources of information that influence perception and cognition (Massaro & Cohen, 1991; Massaro & Friedman, 1990).

In a previous paper, Massaro & Friedman (1990) presented and compared various existing models of how multiple sources of information influence perception and decision. The question they addressed was how individuals process two or more sources of information that may reinforce or conflict to various degrees. The models were analyzed in terms of a prototypical pattern recognition task and the application of extant models to this task. The central concerns were the processes assumed by the models, the similarities and differences in predictions of the models, their optimality properties, and empirical validity.

Our goal in this chapter is to extend the analyses carried out by Massaro and Friedman (1990) by comparing several additional classes of models. The models analyzed and tested by Massaro and Friedman were the fuzzy logical model of perception (FLMP), a two-layer connectionist model (CMP), a model derived from the Theory of Signal Detection (TSD), a linear integration model (LIM) derived from results of Functional Measurement, and a model based on Multidimensional Scaling (MDS). The goal of these analytical and descriptive exercises was to lay the groundwork for valid experimental tests of the models. Simulations of the models and predictions of the results by the same models were carried out to provide a measure of identifiability or the extent to which the models can be distinguished from one another. The models were also contrasted against empirical results from tasks with two and four response alternatives and with graded responses. The results indicated FLMP was optimal (mathematically equivalent to Bayes' theorem) and was the only psychological model to provide an adequate account of performance in these tasks.

This chapter attempts to formulate the models previously shown to be inadequate, in such a manner to bring them in line with the predictions of the FLMP and with empirical results. In contrast to our general research strategy of strong inference (Platt, 1964) and competition between models, we attempt a reconciliation of current models. We will see that, in some cases, there are straightforward formulations that give equivalence among some models and the FLMP. In other cases, an additional free parameter or some other modification is necessary to bring a model in line with the devised predictions. The model classes that we will consider are FLMP, Gaussian MDS model (GMM), exponential MDS model (EMM), TSD, Feedforward connectionist model (FCM), and interactive activation and competition (IAC). Some of these models are based on spatial representations, others are grounded in probability or truth value, and others are described in activation of neural-like units. Each of these different representational foundations is referred to as a model's currency (Massaro & Friedman, 1990). As in Massaro and Friedman (1990), we first present each of these models theoretically in the context of a prototypical pattern recognition task combining two sources of stimulus information and allowing two possible responses. We then consider how the models compare in a four-response task. For both the two- and four-response situations, we derive predictions of the models, compare these predictions to those of other models, and test the models against one another with hypothetical FLMP data and experimental data, using model-fitting techniques. We do not completely describe the psychological theory underlying each model because adequate summaries are available elsewhere (Massaro & Friedman, 1990, Shepard, 1987).

PROTOTYPICAL TWO-RESPONSE CATEGORIZATION TASK

We use a letter-processing task carried out by Massaro and Hary (1986), with categories G and Q as the response alternatives. Two sources of information were manipulated with a number of levels of each source of information. A range of letters between G and Q was created by independently varying the obliqueness of the straight line and the closedness of the gap in the letter (Figure 15.1). Seven levels of closedness were made by removing 0, 2, 3, 4, 7, 9 and 10 points from the right side of the oval of a capital letter Q. Similarly, the obliqueness of the line varied between the horizontal and 11, 21, 29, 38, 51, and 61 degrees of obliqueness measured from the horizontal. The resultant 49 test letters make up the factorial design.

Nine subjects saw each of the test letters (shown in Figure 15.1) for 400 ms 12 times in random order (Massaro & Hary, 1986). On each trial they labeled the test letter as a Q or a G. Figure 15.2 gives the observed performance for two typical subjects. The probability of a Q response given each test letter is the dependent variable. Because the Q and G identifications sum to 1, the probability of a Q response to each test letter, *P*(Q), completely represents the identification judgments. Thus, we have 49 independent observations to describe performance given the 49 test letters.

FUZZY LOGICAL MODEL OF PERCEPTION

We initiate our derivation of specific models with the FLMP. We begin with this model because it has proven successful in accounting for a wide range of categorization results (Massaro, 1987b; Massaro & Friedman, 1990; McClelland, 1991). Thus, the model's predictions serve as a standard for the predictions of other models.

Underlying the FLMP is the assumption that well-learned patterns are recognized in accordance with a general algorithm, regardless of the modality or

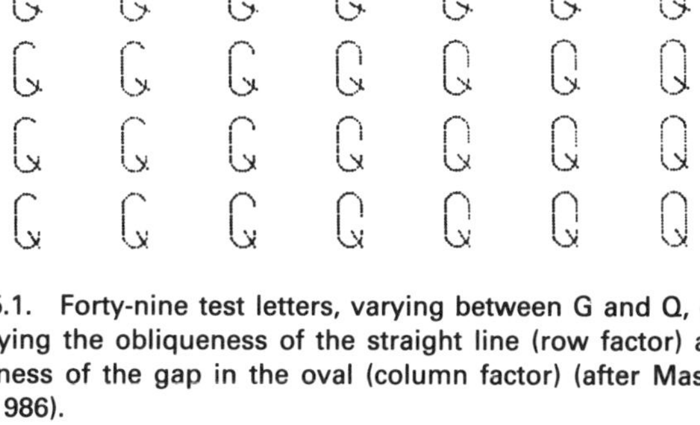

FIG. 15.1. Forty-nine test letters, varying between G and Q, created by varying the obliqueness of the straight line (row factor) and the closedness of the gap in the oval (column factor) (after Massaro & Hary, 1986).

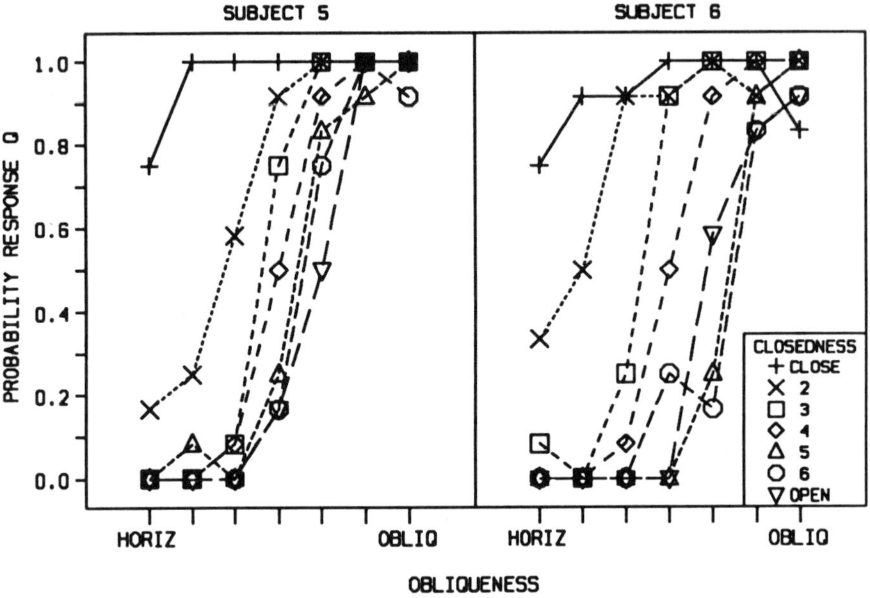

FIG. 15.2. Observed probability of Q responses for the 49 test letters presented in Figure 15.1 (created by varying the obliqueness of the straight line and the closedness of the gap in the oval) The results are for two typical subjects (from Massaro & Hary, 1986).

nature of the patterns (Massaro, 1984, 1987a; Oden, 1981, 1984). The model consists of three operations in perceptual recognition: feature evaluation, feature integration, and pattern classification. Continuously valued features are evaluated, integrated, and matched against prototype descriptions in memory, and an identification decision is made on the basis of the relative goodness of match of the stimulus information with the relevant prototype descriptions.

Given multiple features, it is useful to have a common metric representing the degree of match of each feature. Two features that define a prototype can be related to one another more easily if they share a common currency. To serve this purpose, fuzzy truth values (Goguen, 1969; Zadeh, 1965) are used because they provide a natural representation of the degree of match. Fuzzy truth values lie between 0 and 1, corresponding to a proposition being completely false and completely true. The value 0.5 corresponds to a completely ambiguous situation, whereas 0.7 would be more true than false, and so on. Fuzzy truth values, therefore, not only can represent continuous rather than categorical information, but they also can represent different kinds of information.

The three operations between presentation of a pattern and its categorization, as illustrated in Figure 15.3, can be formalized mathematically. Feature evaluation gives the degree to which a given dimension supports each test alternative. Given a test letter in the QG task, the featural evaluation stage determines the

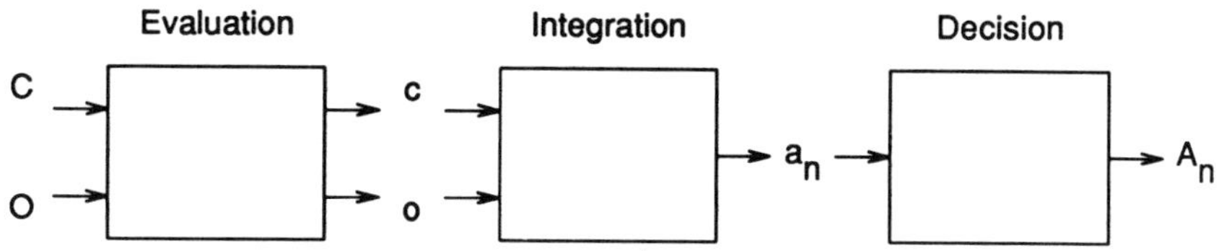

FIG. 15.3. Schematic representation of the three stages of processing in the FLMP. The three stages are illustrated for the sources of information closedness *C* and obliqueness *O* in the G_7Q task. The evaluation of the degree to which the oval is closed and the straight line is oblique produce values *c* and *o* that are made available to the integration process. Integration of the values gives an overall value a_n indicating the degree of support for alternative n. The decision process maps the information made available to it into a response A_n.

degree to which each of the alternatives A_n (in this case Q and G) are supported by each feature of the visual information. The physical input (represented in uppercase) is transformed to a psychological value (represented in lowercase); for example, closedness *C* would be transformed to c, and analogously for dimension obliqueness *O*. The notation is listed at the end of the chapter. Each dimension provides a feature value at feature evaluation. Using fuzzy truth values, we assign a value between 0 and 1 to the closedness and obliqueness dimensions, indicating the degree to which these features support the Q and G alternatives. To develop hypothetical predictions of the FLMP model, we used the following feature values: for closedness, going from open to closed, 0.01, 0.10, 0.30, 0.50, 0.70, 0.90, 0.99; and for obliqueness, going from horizontal to oblique, 0.03, 0.20, 0.40, 0.60, 0.80, 0.92, 0.95.

These features values are then integrated within the Q and G prototypes. The prototypes are defined by:

Q: closed oval and oblique line
G: open oval and horizontal line

Given a prototype's *independent* specifications for the oval and straight-line features, the value of one of these features cannot change the value of the other feature at feature integration. Given a two-alternative forced-choice task and the opposing features being manipulated, it is reasonable to assume that closed and open are opposites (or negations) of one another, as are oblique and horizontal. Using the definition of fuzzy negation as 1 minus the feature value (Zadeh, 1965), we can represent the prototypes in terms of the degree to which the oval is closed and the line is oblique:

Q: closed and oblique
G: (1 - closed) and (1 - oblique)

The integration of the features defining each prototype can be represented by the product of the feature values. Feature integration consists of a multiplicative combination of feature values supporting a given alternative. These products are represented in Figure 15.3 by the lowercase a_n. If c_j and o_k are the hypothetical feature values from stimulus level j of closedness and k of obliqueness supporting alternative Q, then the total support is given by the product c_j and o_k. Similarly, the support for G, the other alternative, is given by the product of $(1 - c_j)$ and $(1 - o_k)$. Figure 15.4 shows the total support for alternatives G and Q given the hypothetical feature values. The linear results reflect the multiplicative integration of the feature values.

The third operation is decision, which uses a Relative Goodness Rule (RGR) based on the support for each of the test alternatives to give the probability that a given alternative is selected. In this case, the probability of response Q given a specific stimulus C_jO_k is

$$P(Q|C_j \text{ and } O_k) = \frac{c_j o_k}{c_j o_k + (1 - c_j)(1 - o_k)}, \tag{1}$$

where the denominator is equal to the sum of the merit of all relevant alternatives. Figure 15.5 shows the probability of selecting alternative Q given the support for each alternative shown in Figure 15.4.

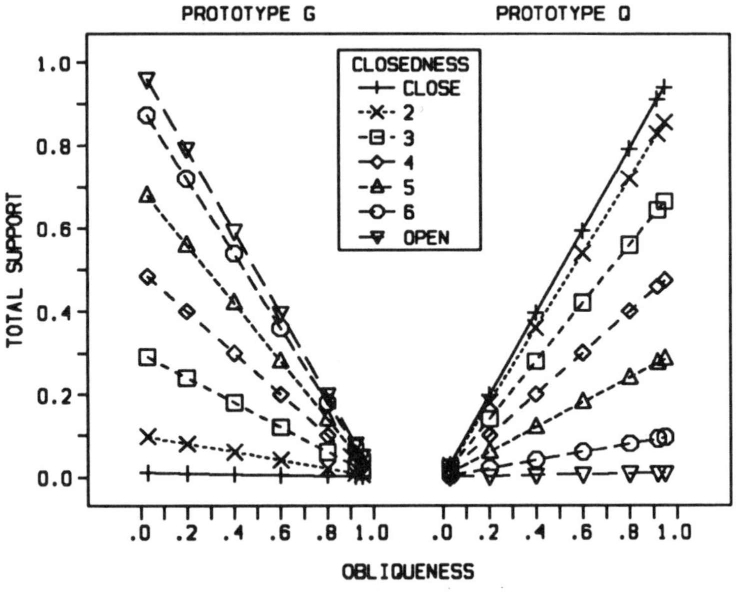

FIG. 15.4. Total support for alternative Q and G prototypes based on hypothetical closedness and obliqueness features given in the text. The locations on the abscissa are scaled according to the value of the obliqueness feature.

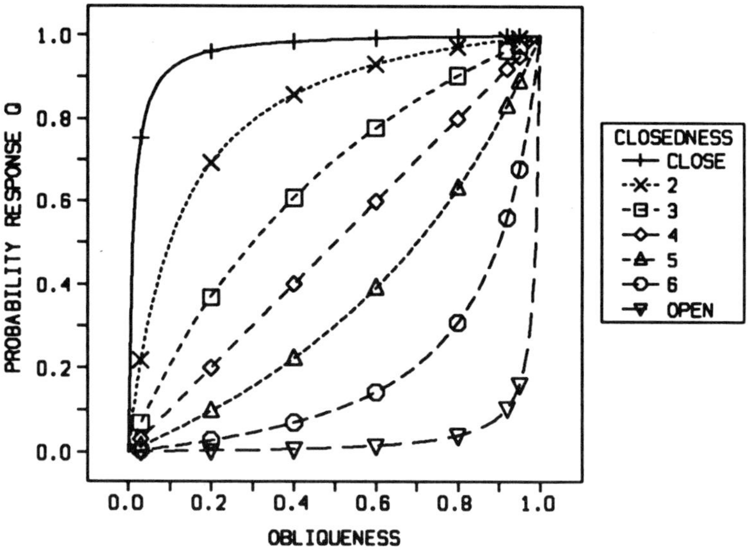

FIG. 15.5. Probability for alternative Q based on the total support for the Q and G prototypes shown in Figure 15.4. The locations on the abscissa are scaled according to the value of the obliqueness feature.

To summarize, evaluation in the FLMP involves the representation of each source of information in terms of a truth value, between 0 and 1, indicating the merit of an alternative. Integration consists of a multiplicative combination of truth values. The decision utilizes an RGR.

BAYESIAN PROBABILITY MODEL

The Bayesian approach to combining multiple sources of information has at its core a theorem derived independently by Reverend Thomas Bayes (about 1701–1761) and Pierre Laplace (1749–1827) (Stigler, 1986). This theorem states that

$$P(h_1|e) = \frac{P(e|h_1)P(h_1)}{\Sigma_i\, P(e|h_i)P(h_i)}\,, \tag{2}$$

where $P(h_i|e)$ is the probability that some hypothesis h_i is true given that some evidence e is observed; $P(e|h_i)$ is the probability of the evidence e, given that the hypothesis h_i is true, and $P(h_i)$ is the a priori probability of the hypothesis h_i. The probability of hypothesis h_1 given some evidence e is equal to the probability of the evidence given the hypothesis times the a priori probability of the hypothesis, divided by the sum of analogous products for all possible hypotheses. If the a priori probabilities of all possible hypotheses are equal, Bayes' theorem reduces to

$$P(h_1|e) = \frac{P(e|h_1)}{\Sigma_i P(e|h_i)} . \tag{3}$$

Bayes' theorem specifies how different sources of evidence are combined. Given two independent pieces of evidence e_1 and e_2 and equal a priori probabilities, the probability of a hypothesis h_1 is equal to

$$P(h_1|e_1 \text{ and } e_2) = \frac{P(e_1 \text{ and } e_2|h_1)}{\Sigma_i P(e_1 \text{ and } e_2|h_i)} \tag{4}$$

$$= \frac{P(e_1|h_1)P(e_2|h_1)}{\Sigma_i P(e_1|h_i)P(e_2|h_i)} . \tag{5}$$

Equation 5 has a direct correspondence to our evaluation and integration processes. It describes optimal information integration in the currency of probability under two assumptions. First, the prior probabilities of all relevant response alternatives are equal. Second, it is assumed that the sources of evidence are evaluated independently of one another, as assumed for the FLMP. Following our QG paradigm example, and analogous to Equations 5 and 6,

$$P(\mathrm{Q}|C_j \text{ and } O_k) = \frac{P(C_j|\mathrm{Q})P(O_k|\mathrm{Q})}{P(C_j|\mathrm{Q})P(O_k|\mathrm{Q}) + P(C_j|\mathrm{G})P(O_k|\mathrm{G})} \tag{6}$$

gives the probability of selecting Q based on the two sources of information C and O, with $P(C|\mathrm{Q})$ representing evaluation of the closedness source (in terms of the subjective probability "currency") and $P(O|\mathrm{Q})$ representing separate evaluation of the obliqueness source. Comparing Equations 1 and 6, we see a direct correspondence between the fuzzy feature values in the FLMP and the probabilities of evidence given hypotheses in the Bayesian probability model (BPM), as well as the common use of an RGR.

One difference between the FLMP and the Bayesian predictions is that the two alternatives are defined as negations of their sources of information in the FLMP. Thus, closed and open are assumed to be negations, as are oblique and horizontal. The probabilities $P(e|h_1)$ and $P(e|h_2)$ in Bayes' theorem need not sum to 1 as do the corresponding fuzzy features. When applied to a factorial design with two response alternatives, however, we should note that the predictions of the BPM, given in Equation 6, can be rearranged [by dividing top and bottom by $P(C_j|\mathrm{Q})P(O_k|\mathrm{Q})$] to give the form

$$P(\mathrm{Q}|C_j \text{ and } O_k) = \frac{1}{1 + \left[\frac{P(C_j|\mathrm{G})}{P(C_j|\mathrm{Q})}\right]\left[\frac{P(O_k|\mathrm{G})}{P(O_k|\mathrm{Q})}\right]} \tag{7}$$

or the equivalent

$$P(\mathrm{Q}|C_j \text{ and } O_k) = \frac{1}{1 + l_{\mathrm{GQ}}(C_j)l_{\mathrm{GQ}}(O_k)} , \tag{8}$$

where

$$l_{GQ}(C_j) = \frac{P(C_j|G)}{P(C_j|Q)} \tag{9}$$

is the likelihood ratio of category G to Q given evidence C_j, and

$$l_{GQ}(O_k) = \frac{P(O_k|G)}{P(O_k|Q)} \tag{10}$$

is the likelihood ratio of category G to Q given evidence O_k. Given that each fraction on the right side of the denominator of Equation 8, is indexed by a single subscript, a single value of likelihood ratio is sufficient for each source of evidence. We call equations like Equation 8 the canonical *likelihood product form* and note that it is an instance of the more general form given in Green and Swets (1974, Appendix 1-A, Equation 1.A.7):

$$P(h_j|e_1, e_2, \cdots, e_i, \cdots, e_n) = \left[1 + \frac{P(h_k)}{P(h_j)} \prod_{i=1}^{n} l_{kj}(e_i)\right]^{-1}, \tag{11}$$

where $e_1, e_2, \ldots, e_n$ are n events (sources of evidence) concerning hypotheses h_j and h_k and $l_{kj}(e_i)$ is the likelihood ratio of hypothesis h_k to h_j for evidence e_i. The likelihood product form for the FLMP can be obtained from Equation 1 by dividing top and bottom by $c_j o_k$:

$$P(Q|C_j \text{ and } O_k) = \left[1 + \left(\frac{1 - c_j}{c_j}\right)\left(\frac{1 - o_k}{o_k}\right)\right]^{-1}, \tag{12}$$

from which we obtain

$$l_{GQ}(C_j) = \frac{1 - c_j}{c_j}, \tag{13}$$

$$l_{GQ}(O_k) = \frac{1 - o_k}{o_k} \tag{14}$$

for the likelihood ratios in the FLMP. Comparing Equations 8 and 12, we see that the BPM and FLMP (and any other that can be put in this form) are mathematically equivalent. We call any model that can be put in likelihood product form a member of the class of likelihood product models (LPM).

GAUSSIAN MDS MODEL

The GMM considers perceptual features as dimensions in a multidimensional psychological space. Figure 15.6 illustrates the model using our QG categorization example. In the figure, the center of each prototype distribution is denoted by a symbol (e.g., Q in the upper right quadrant), surrounded by concentric circles indicating 1, 2, and 3 standard deviations from the center. Feature analy-

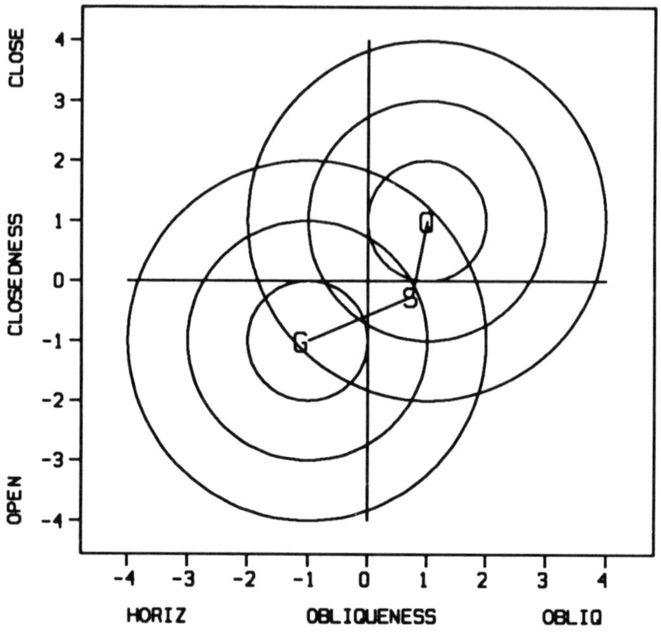

FIG. 15.6. Gaussian multidimensional model of QG paradigm. The letters G and Q represent the center of the probabilistic prototype distributions corresponding to G and Q, respectively. The concentric circles indicate 1, 2, and 3 standard deviations from the center, as described by the Gaussian. The letter **S** represents a stimulus input with coordinates [*o, c*].

sis locates a stimulus event at a point in the space. In our notation, [*obliqueness, closedness*] indicates a specific location as a coordinate pair in the multidimensional space. For expositional simplicity rather than theoretical necessity, we assume that the prototypes are symmetrically centered at $[P, P]$ and $[-P, -P]$. In the example in Figure 15.6, $P = 1$. Given a pair of perceptual features associated with a stimulus (denoted by **S** in Figure 15.6), the perceiver evaluates the similarity of **S** to each of the prototypes by transforming the distance between **S** and each prototype according to the Gaussian $exp\ (-d^2)$(Nosofsky, 1986; Ennis, 1988a). We examine two forms of the GMM, using different metrics: a Euclidean GMM (GMM-E) and a city-block GMM (GMM-CB). For the GMM-E, the Euclidean distances $d(\mathbf{S}, \mathrm{Q})$ and $d(\mathbf{S}, \mathrm{G})$ from stimulus **S** at $[o_k, c_j]$ to the center of the Q and G prototype distributions are given by

$$d(\mathbf{S}, \mathrm{Q}) = \sqrt{(P - o_k)^2 + (P - c_j)^2} \tag{15}$$

and

$$d(\mathbf{S}, \mathrm{G}) = \sqrt{(-P - o_k)^2 + (-P - c_j)^2}\ . \tag{16}$$

Transforming these Euclidean distances by the Gaussian function, we arrive at the similarities

$$s(\mathbf{S}, \mathrm{Q}) = exp\ \{-[(P - o_k)^2 + (P - c_j)^2]\} \tag{17}$$

and

$$s(\mathbf{S}, \mathrm{G}) = exp\ \{-[(P - o_k)^2 + (-P - c_j)^2)\}\ . \tag{18}$$

Given these similarities, the perceiver uses an RGR (Shepard, 1957, Nosofsky, 1986) to decide among alternatives. Putting the similarities in an RGR, we have

$$P(\mathrm{Q}|c_j, o_k) = \frac{exp\ \{-[(P - o_k)^2 + (P - c_j)_2]\}}{exp\ \{-[(P - o_k)^2 + (P - c_j)^2]\} + exp\ \{-[(-P - o_k)^2 + (-P - c_j)^2]\}}\ . \tag{19}$$

Because *exp* (a + b) = *exp* (a) *exp* (b), we can factor Equation 19 as follows:

$$P(\mathrm{Q}|c_j, o_k) = \frac{exp\ [-(P - o_k)^2]\ exp\ [-(P - c_j)^2]}{exp\ [-(P - o_k)^2]\ exp\ [-(P - c_j)^2] + exp\ [-(-P - o_k)^2]\ exp\ [-(-P - c_j)^2]}\ . \tag{20}$$

With the factoring of the exponential terms into products, we see clearly the multiplicative combination of the two sources of information in the model. Given this factoring, we can draw the equivalences:

$$P(c|\mathrm{Q}) = exp\ [-(P - c_j)^2]\ , \tag{21}$$

$$P(c|\mathrm{G}) = exp\ [-(-P - c_j)^2]\ , \tag{22}$$

$$P(o|\mathrm{Q}) = exp\ [-(P - o_k)^2]\ , \tag{23}$$

$$P(o|\mathrm{G}) = exp\ [-(-P - o_k)^2]\ . \tag{24}$$

For the likelihood product form of the model (viz. Equation 8) we have

$$l_{\mathrm{GQ}}(C_j) = exp\ [(P - c_j)^2 - (-P - c_j)^2] = exp\ [-4Pc_j]\ , \tag{25}$$

$$l_{\mathrm{GQ}}(O_k) = exp\ [(P - o_k)^2 - (-P - o_k)^2] = exp\ [-4Po_k]\ . \tag{26}$$

Figure 15.7 shows how the hypothetical QG stimuli, whose response probabilities are shown in Figure 15.5, are arranged in the two-dimensional space.

To summarize, the GMM-E conceptualizes the representation of stimuli and prototypes as occurring in a multidimensional space, with the perceiver using the Gaussian-transformed Euclidean distances as similarities that are then translated to response probabilities with an RGR. Theoretical analysis shows that the model is a member of the LPM class.

An interesting note regarding the use of a Euclidean distance measure here is that it is what makes the GMM-E consistent with the FLMP, which is based on the assumption of *independent* fuzzy feature values. This runs contrary to the common belief that the Euclidean distance is more appropriate for integral dimensions, whereas the alternative city-block distance measure,

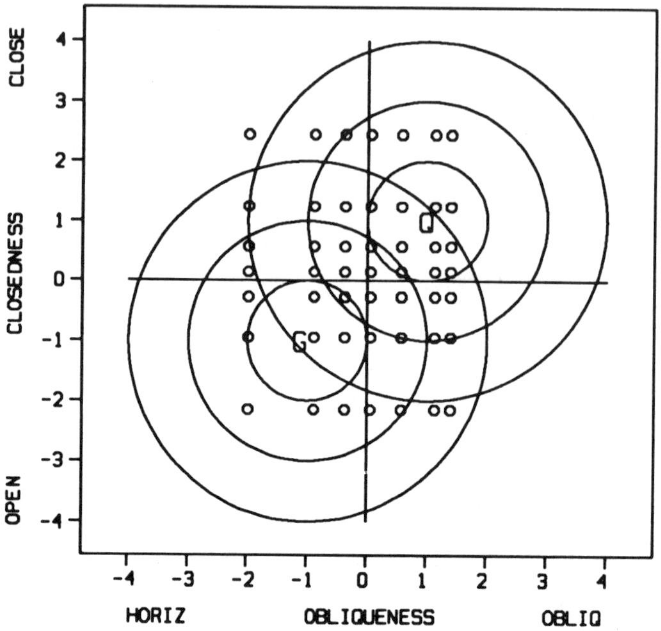

FIG. 15.7. Gaussian multidimensional model of QG paradigm showing location of hypothetical stimuli, assuming Euclidean distance metric.

$$d(\mathbf{S}, \mathrm{Q}) = |P - o_k| + |P - c_j| \,, \tag{27}$$

is more appropriate for separable dimensions (Shepard, 1964). For the GMM-CB in which the latter measure is used, the similarity (e.g., to Q) using a Gaussian function is

$$s(\mathbf{S}, \mathrm{Q}) = exp. \{-[(P - o_k)^2 + 2|P - c_j||P - o_k| + (P - c_j)^2]\} \,, \tag{28}$$

which is not factorable into two parts containing c and o independently and, thus, is not a member of the LPM class. Another way to look at this situation would be to say that the critical factor here for independence is that the exponent α in the similarity function $exp\ (-d\alpha)$ equals the exponent r in the Minkowski distance equation.

Although the original derivation of MDS stressed similarities of stimuli to response alternatives (and functions relating distances to similarities) in the MDS space, the model is mathematically equivalent to one based on probabilities of stimuli belonging to response categories. In this view, each alternative would be represented by a bivariate normal probability distribution (reflecting the variability of category instances in the world) centered at a particular location in the space, rather than by a single point. The MDS models discussed here can be considered relatively simple models, subsumed by the more general formalization called *General Recognition Theory* (Ashby & Gott, 1988; Ashby & Perrin 1988; Ashby & Townsend, 1986). Ashby and Perrin (1988) offer a general Gaussian recognition model as an alternative to traditional MDS models. In that model, similarity is a function of the overlap of perceptual distributions. They argue that similarity judgments between two stimuli result from a judgment of the degree to which a pair of perceptual distributions overlaps. The decision process divides the similarity space into response regions, one associated with each response. Identification judgments are not constrained by any distance axioms. Ashby and Gott (1988) found evidence for integration and for an optimal noise-free decision process in that subjects did not make independent decisions on each component or use the distance to each prototype. See Chapters 6 and 16 for a more thorough discussion of General Recognition Theory.

EXPONENTIAL MDS MODEL

The exponential MDS model (Shepard, 1957) is essentially equivalent to the Gaussian MDS model discussed in the fifth section, except that distance is translated into similarity by the negative exponential $exp\ (-d)$ rather than the Gaussian $exp\ (-d^2)$. As with the GMM, we examine two different metrics: a Euclidean EMM (EMM-E) and a city-block EMM (EMM-CB). For the EMM-E, distances are computed in the same way as for the GMM-E, given in Equations 15 and 16:

$$s(\mathbf{S}, \mathrm{Q}) = exp\ [-\sqrt{(P - o_k)^2 + (P - c_j)^2}] \tag{29}$$

and

$$s(\mathbf{S}, \mathrm{G}) = exp\ [-\sqrt{(-P - o_k)^2 + (-P - c_j)^2}]\ . \tag{30}$$

Putting these similarities in an RGR, we have

$$\mathrm{p}(\mathrm{Q}|\mathrm{c_j}, \mathrm{o_k}) = \frac{exp\ [-\sqrt{(P - o_k)^2 + (P - c_j)^2}]}{exp\ [-\sqrt{(P - o_k)^2 + (P - c_j)^2}] + exp\ [-\sqrt{(-P - o_k)^2 + (-P - c_j)^2}]}\ . \tag{31}$$

Because of the square root term in the exponentials, the support (similarities) for the two alternatives cannot be factored into two parts containing c and o independently. Thus, this model makes different mathematical predictions from those of the LPM class.

If a city-block rather than Euclidean distance is used, however, then the EMM model falls within the LPM. For the EMM-CB, the distances to each prototype are

$$d(\mathbf{S}, \mathrm{Q}) = |P - o_k| + |P - c_j| \tag{32}$$

and

$$d(\mathbf{S}, \mathrm{G}) = |-P - o_k| + |-P - c_j|\ , \tag{33}$$

and corresponding similarities, instead of Equations 29 and 30, will be

$$s(\mathbf{S}, \mathrm{Q}) = exp\ [-(|P - o_k| + |P - c_j|)] \tag{34}$$

and

$$s(\mathbf{S}, \mathrm{G}) = exp\ [-(|-P - o_k| + |-P - c_j|)]\ . \tag{35}$$

Putting these similarities in an RGR, we have

$$p(\mathrm{Q}|c_j, o_k) = \frac{exp\ [-(|P - o_k| + |P - c_j|)]}{exp\ [-(|P - o_k| + |P - c_j|)] + exp\ [-(|-P - o_k| + |-P - c_j|)]} \tag{36}$$

which can be factored into

$$p(\mathrm{Q}|c_j, o_k) = \frac{exp\ (-|P - o_k|)\ exp\ (-|P - c_j|)}{exp\ (-|P - o_k|)\ exp\ (-|P - c_j|) + exp\ (-|-P - o_k|)\ exp\ (-|-P - c_j|)}\ . \tag{37}$$

We can then draw the equivalences

$$P(c|\mathrm{Q}) = exp\ (-|P - c_{\mathrm{EMM}}|)\ , \tag{38}$$

$$P(c|\mathrm{G}) = exp\ (-|-P - c_{\mathrm{EMM}}|)\ , \tag{39}$$

$$P(o|\mathrm{Q}) = exp\ (-|P - o_{\mathrm{EMM}}|)\ , \tag{40}$$

$$P(o|\mathrm{G}) = exp\ (-|-P - o_{\mathrm{EMM}}|) \tag{41}$$

and construct the likelihood ratios

$$l_{\mathrm{GQ}}(C_j) = exp\ (|P - c_j| - |-P - c_j|)\ , \tag{42}$$

$$l_{\mathrm{GQ}}(O_k) = exp\ (|P - o_k| - |-P - o_k|) \tag{43}$$

for the likelihood product form. Figure 15.8 shows how the QG stimuli, whose response probabilities are shown in Figure 15.5, are arranged in the two-dimensional space given the city-block metric. For this solution P was set to 6. Thus, this EMM-CB is an LPM class member, and, at least for identification performance with two prototypes, the EMM-CB is equivalent to the GMM-E, both of which are LPM class members. This equivalence exists even though the two distance metrics make different predictions regarding ordering of distances between pairs of stimuli. When there are more than two prototype locations on a given dimension, however, the constraints imposed by the different similarity and distance functions between prototypes cause the EMM-CB and the GMM-E to make different predictions. Nosofsky (1985b, 1987) proved this result for two-dimensional data sets in which there are 16 prototypes, with 4 prototype locations equally spaced on each dimension. Given only two prototypes locations on each dimension, however, the locations of stimuli on each dimension are not constrained in this fashion.

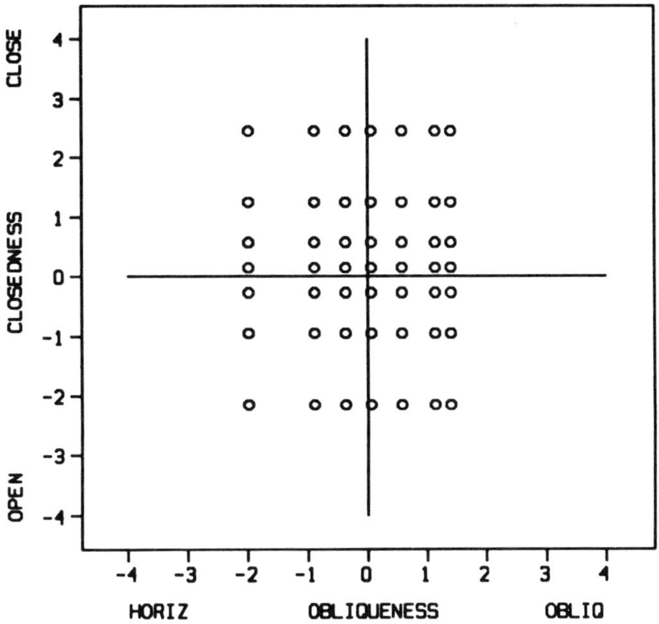

FIG. 15.8. EMM multidimensional space for QG task showing location of hypothetical stimuli, assuming a city block metric.

THEORY OF SIGNAL DETECTION

The original TSD model (Green & Swets, 1974; Peterson, Birdsall, & Fox, 1954) offers a framework for a categorization model. This model also serves as a foundation for the multivariate TSD model General Recognition Theory (Ashby & Townsend, 1986). The multivariate TSD model is illustrated in Figure 15.9, as applied to our QG two-response categorization task. As in the GMM model, we have Q and G prototypes defined as distributions located symmetrically at $[P, P]$ and $[-P, -P]$ (with $P = 1$) in a multidimensional feature space. We assume equal uncorrelated variance for each prototype (and stimulus) distribution. In terms of the notation of this volume, we would say that the covariance matrix of the model is the identity matrix (ones on the main diagonal and zeros elsewhere). We assume that the perceiver establishes a decision rule based on the use of a criterion at the line of equal likelihood between alternatives Q and G. This decision rule is equivalent to the minimum distance bound described by Ashby and Gott (1988). Given the symmetric locations of the alternative distributions, the criterion lies on the main antidiagonal ($c + o = 0$).

In this model it is assumed that stimuli are noisy, varying in location from trial to trial, with bivariate normal distributions. The distributions for three stimuli are

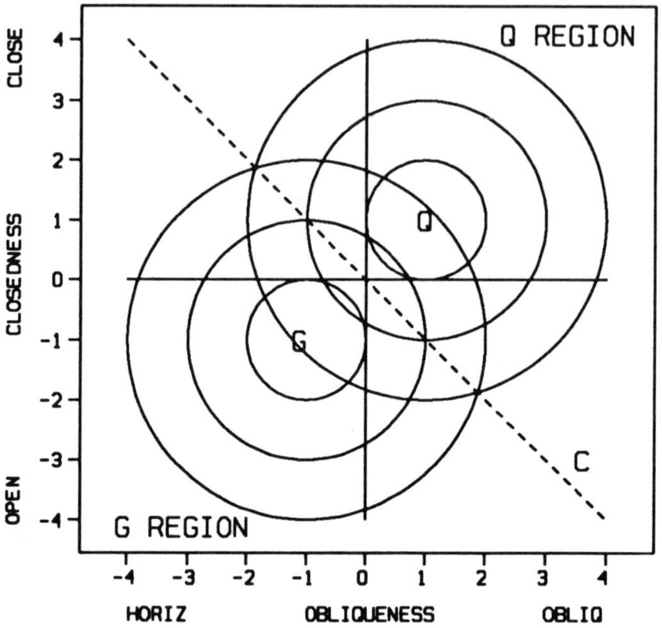

FIG. 15.9. Multidimensional TSD model of QG task. The Q and G prototypes are defined as distributions located symmetrically in a multidimensional feature space, indicated by G and Q corresponding to the centers. In addition, a criterion (C) at the line of equal likelihood between the two prototype distributions is shown.

shown in the center of the two-dimensional space in Figure 15.10. On a given trial, if the stimulus falls in the Q region, above and to the right of the criterion line, then a Q response is made. Similarly, for the G region below and to the left of the criterion line, a G response is made. Given that the stimuli are noisy, however, the two-dimensional location of a stimulus will sometimes fall in one region and sometimes in the other. To predict response probabilities, we must determine what volume of each stimulus distribution (what proportion) falls into each region. These proportions are related to the distance of the center of the distribution from the criterion line. Taking a hypothetical stimulus on the main diagonal centered at $[c, o]$ (e.g., the stimulus in Figure 15.10 at [0.33, 0.33]), we can see that the Euclidean distance d back along the main diagonal to the criterion line is given by

$$d = \sqrt{x^2 + x^2} = \sqrt{2x^2} = \sqrt{2}x \,, \tag{44}$$

where $x = c = o$. Given that $x = (c + \mathrm{o})/2$, we arrive at

$$d = \sqrt{2}\,\frac{c + o}{2} = \frac{1}{\sqrt{2}}\,(c + o) \tag{45}$$

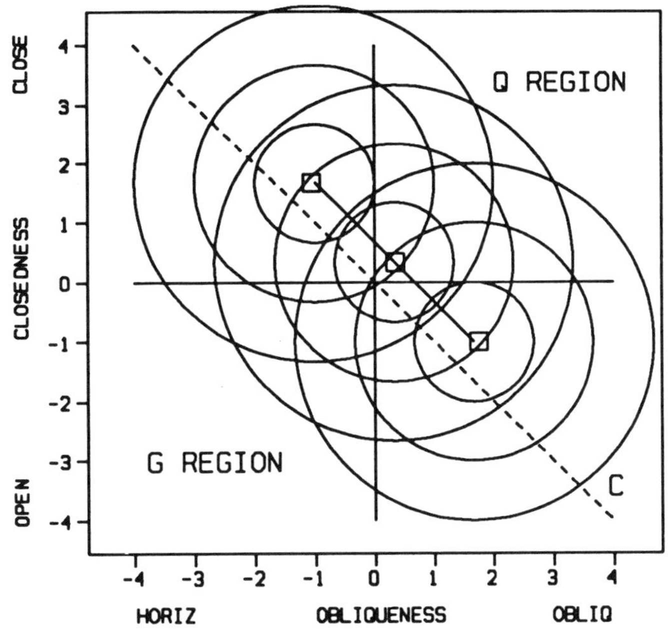

FIG. 15.10. Multidimensional TSD model of QG task. Three stimulus distributions, equidistant from the criterion line, are shown in the multidimensional space.

when the stimulus falls on the main diagonal. We can also see that the other two hypothetical stimuli that lie on the same antidiagonal have the same distance to the criterion line, since an antidiagonal line has an equation of the form $c + o = k$, with the result that the distance must always be $k/\sqrt{2}$. If we assume equal variance, uncorrelated normal distributions, then the probability of a Q response is given by

$$P(\mathrm{Q}|C_{\mathrm{j}} \text{ and } O_{\mathrm{k}}) = \Phi\left(\frac{1}{\sqrt{2}}(c_{\mathrm{j}} + o_{\mathrm{k}})\right). \tag{46}$$

where $\Phi(x)$ is the cumulative standard normal distribution (see chap. 1). We call this model the normal TSD (TSD-N). The predictions of this model are mathematically different from the LPM (to what degree, we will evaluate later).

Rather than the cumulative normal area Φ, suppose we substitute the similar corrected logistic cumulative function

$$L(x) = \frac{1}{1 + exp\,(-kx)} \tag{47}$$

(with correction factor $k = \pi/\sqrt{3}$ to equate for the variance $\pi^2/3$ of the logistic) in Equation 46. We then obtain

$$P(\mathrm{Q}|C_j \text{ and } O_k) = \frac{1}{1 + exp\left[\frac{-k}{\sqrt{2}}(c_j + o_k)\right]} = \frac{1}{1 + exp\left[\frac{-\pi}{\sqrt{6}}(c_j + o_k)\right]} \tag{48}$$

$$= \frac{1}{1 + exp\left(\frac{-\pi}{\sqrt{6}} c_j\right) exp\left(\frac{-\pi}{\sqrt{6}} o_k\right)} . \tag{49}$$

We call this model the logistic TSD (TSD-L). This model is equivalent to the likelihood product form with the assignments

$$l_{GQ}(C_j) = exp\left(\frac{-\pi}{\sqrt{6}} c_j\right) \tag{50}$$

and

$$l_{GQ}(O_k) = exp\left(\frac{-\pi}{\sqrt{6}} o_k\right) . \tag{51}$$

We can also draw the equivalences

$$exp\left(-\frac{\pi}{\sqrt{6}} c_{GMM}\right) = \frac{1 - c_{FLMP}}{c_{FLMP}} , \tag{52}$$

$$exp\left(-\frac{\pi}{\sqrt{6}} o_{GMM}\right) = \frac{1 - o_{FLMP}}{o_{FLMP}} , \tag{53}$$

or, going in the other direction,

$$c_{GMM} = \frac{-\sqrt{6}}{\pi} ln\left(\frac{1 - c_{FLMP}}{c_{FLMP}}\right) , \tag{54}$$

$$o_{GMM} = \frac{-\sqrt{6}}{\pi} ln\left(\frac{1 - o_{FLMP}}{o_{FLMP}}\right) . \tag{55}$$

Given these relationships, Figure 15.11 shows how the QG stimuli whose hypothetical response probabilities are shown in Figure 15.5 are arranged in the two-dimensional space given the logistic TSD model. To summarize, we find a mathematical equivalence between the TSD-L and the LPM class of models, and a strong similarity (due to the similarity of the cumulative normal and the corrected logistic) to those theories for the TSD-N.

Massaro and Friedman (1990) derived a somewhat different formulation of TSD. Their starting point was the derivation of Green and Swets (1974, Appendix 9-A) for the optimal combination of two observations in a detection task. With both observations in the detection task taken into account, the d' value for the two-observation task was proven to be

$$d' = \sqrt{(d'_1)^2 + (d'_2)^2} , \tag{56}$$

where d'_1 and d'_2 are the d's of the single observations. This solution was extended by Massaro and Friedman to take into account the directions of the component

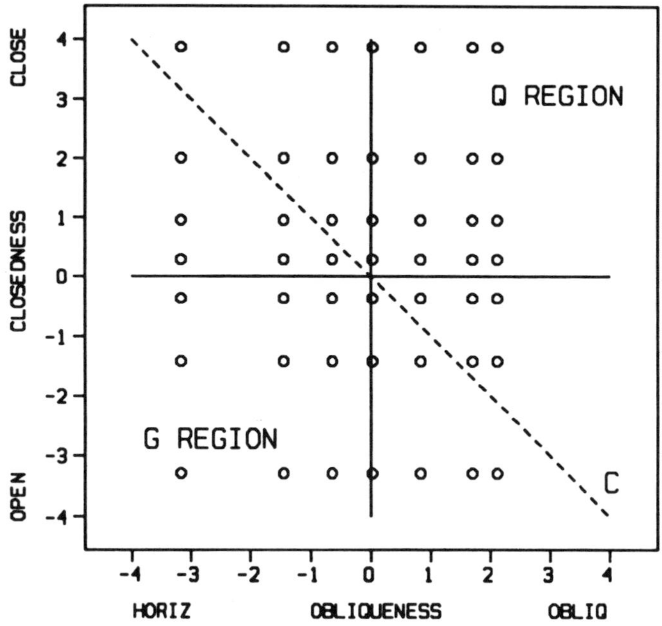

FIG. 15.11. Multidimensional TSD-L model of QG task showing location of hypothetical stimuli assuming a logistic cumulative function.

distances by adjusting the signs in Equation 56 to preserve direction. The current implementation of the TSD, however, places the observations in a multidimensional space and derives the predictions on the basis of their location with respect to a criterion line. Thus, the model departs from the TSD framework as described by Green and Swets (1974) and has many of the same properties of the MDS models.

FEEDFORWARD CONNECTIONIST MODEL

Network models are to some extent grounded in the metaphor of neural information processing. These models are usually referred to as connectionist, because information is represented in terms of the connections among the neural-like units (Minsky & Papert, 1968, 1988; Rosenblatt, 1958; Rumelhart & McClelland, 1986). These units are assumed to exist at different layers; for example, NETtalk (Sejnowski & Rosenberg, 1987) consists of units at the input, hidden, and output layers. The units interact with one another via connections with positive or negative weights that are either specified in advance or learned through feedback. Because of the extreme power of models with hidden units, we consider only a specific two-layer connectionist model that is most comparable to the alternative models that we have considered.

The FCM is assumed to have input and output layers of neural units, with all input units connected to all output units. It is assumed that each source of information and each response alternative is represented by a single unit at the input layer. Figure 15.12 gives a schematic representation of two input units connected to two output units for our QG task.

The output units accumulate the sums of input activations. Each of these is given by the multiplicative combination of an input activation and a weight *w*, which we assume is either 1 or -1. With two inputs c_j and o_k, the activation entering output unit Q is $c_j + o_k$, Analogous to the use of negation in the FLMP, it can be assumed that the weight on the activation entering output unit G is the negative of the weight entering Q (Massaro & Cohen, 1987). In this case, the activation entering output unit G is $(-c_j + -o_k)$. Although an additional "threshold" unit connected to each output unit is sometimes assumed in connectionist models, its use with just two response alternatives is not necessary to bring the model into line with the FLMP. The total activation leaving an output unit is given by the sum of the input activations, passed through a sigmoid squashing function (Rumelhart, Hinton, & Williams, 1986) (which is, incidently, equivalent to the logistic function):

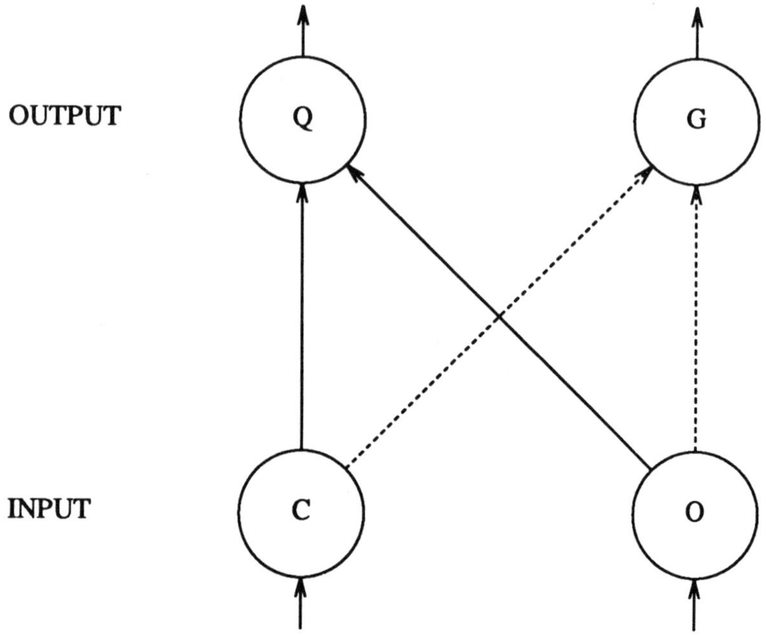

FIG. 15.12. An FCM model for the QG task. The two layers of units contain input units corresponding to the features Closedness (C) and Obliqueness (O), and output units for the alternatives Q and G. Solid arrows indicate connections with weight 1, and dashed arrows indicate connections with weight -1.

$$act_Q = \frac{1}{1 + exp\,[-(c_j + o_k)]}\,, \tag{57}$$

$$act_G = \frac{1}{1 + exp\,[-(-c_j + -o_k)]}\,. \tag{58}$$

The "neural processing" of a connectionist model does not specify completely the stimulus-response function. The activations at the output layer have to be mapped into a response, and a RGR has been assumed to describe this mapping (Rumelhart et al., 1986):

$$P(Q|C_j \text{ and } O_k) = \frac{\dfrac{1}{1 + exp\,[-(c_j + o_k)]}}{\dfrac{1}{1 + exp\,[-(c_j + o_k)]} + \dfrac{1}{1 + exp\,[-(-c_j + -o_k)]}}\,. \tag{59}$$

Since

$$\frac{1}{1 + exp\,(-x)} + \frac{1}{1 + exp\,(x)} = 1\,, \tag{60}$$

the denominator of Equation 59 is equal to 1, and we can simplify Equation 59 to

$$P(Q|C_j \text{ and } O_k) = \frac{1}{1 + exp\,[-(c_j + o_k)]} = \frac{1}{1 + exp\,(-c_j)\,exp\,(-o_k)}\,. \tag{61}$$

This is equivalent to the likelihood product form with the assignments

$$l_{GQ}(C_j) = exp\,(-c_j) \tag{62}$$

and

$$l_{GQ}(O_k) = exp\,(-o_k)\,, \tag{63}$$

and we can also draw the equivalences

$$exp\,(-c_{FCM}) = \frac{1 - c_{FLMP}}{c_{FLMP}}\,, \tag{64}$$

$$exp\,(-o_{FCM}) = \frac{1 - o_{FLMP}}{o_{FLMP}}\,, \tag{65}$$

or, going in the other direction,

$$c_{FCM} = -ln\left(\frac{1 - c_{FLMP}}{c_{FLMP}}\right)\,, \tag{66}$$

$$o_{FCM} = -ln\left(\frac{1 - o_{FLMP}}{o_{FLMP}}\right)\,. \tag{67}$$

To summarize, evaluation in the FCM consists of the activation and inhibition of neural-like units. Integration involves the summation of the separate activations, which are then passed through the sigmoid squashing function. Decision follows the RGR. Mathematical analysis of this FCM reveals that it is also an LPM (for two-response alternatives).

IAC MODELS

Interactive activation models are similar in spirit and design to feedforward models. However, IAC models assume that processing occurs over many processing cycles rather than just one. Furthermore, there are inhibitory lateral connections among units within a layer and two-way connections between units in different layers as illustrated in Figure 15.13. According to interactive activation, the information from one source can modify the processing (and representation) of other information sources (McClelland & Elman, 1986; McClelland & Rumelhart, 1981). Presentation of stimulus information from one source activates (and laterally inhibits) input units associated with that source, as illustrated in Figure 15.13. In this IAC model network, the two units for a given input layer receive complementary inputs. For example, if the CL unit receives 0.8, then the OP unit receives 0.2. These input units in turn activate the memory units of the top layer, which in turn feed backward and activate the input units associated with the other input source, and so on, during several cycles of processing. Contrary to most uses of the IAC, we are taking the activations of the highest level units as determinate of the response.

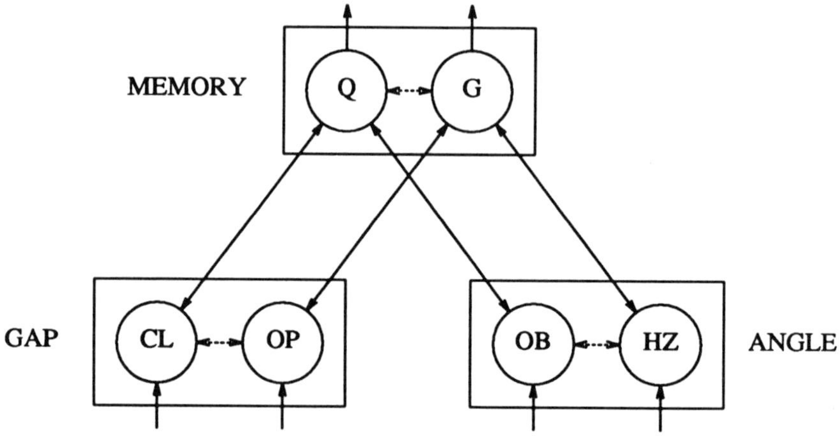

FIG. 15.13. An IAC model for the QG task. The three layers of units contain input units corresponding to the gap and angle features, respectively, and to the "prototypes" or memory of G and Q. Units between layers have bidirectional excitatory connections indicated by solid arrows. Units within a layer have bidirectional inhibitory connections indicated by dashed arrows.

The formal algorithm of the IAC model is as follows (McClelland & Rumelhart, 1988). Initially, for each unit i, the activation act_i is set to the resting level *rest*. Then, on each computation cycle of the model for each unit i, the excitatory input exc_i and inhibitory input inh_i are computed from the product of the activation of the sending units act_i and path weights w_{ij} as follows:

$$exc_i = \sum_j \max(0, w_{ij})\max(0, act_j) , \quad (68)$$

$$inh_i = \sum_j \min(0, w_{ij})\max(0, act_j) . \quad (69)$$

All weights w_{ij} are either $+1$ or -1, so Equation 68 adds up all the activations on positive pathways and Equation 69 adds up all the activations on negative pathways. Activations less than 0 are ignored in these summations. Next, for each unit i, the summed net input net_i is computed from the weighted sum of the exc_i, inh_i, and external inputs ext_i:

$$net_i = \alpha\ exc_i + \gamma\ inh_i + estr\ ext_i , \quad (70)$$

where α is the weight on excitatory connections, γ is the weight on inhibitory connections, and *estr* is the weight on external inputs. Next, the change of activation for each unit for the upcoming cycle Δact_i is computed as follows:

$$\text{if } net_i > 0, \quad \Delta act_i = net_i\ (M - act_i) - decay(act_i - rest) , \quad (71)$$

$$\text{if } net_i < 0, \quad \Delta act_i = net_i(act_i - m) - decay(act_i - rest) , \quad (72)$$

where M is the maximum allowed activation, m is the minimum allowed activation, and *decay* is the rate of activation decay. Then each act_i is adjusted by adding the Δact_i:

$$act_i = act_i + \Delta act_i . \quad (73)$$

Finally, each act_i is adjusted, if necessary, to remain in the interval m to M:

$$\text{if } act_i > M, \quad act_i = M , \quad (74)$$

$$\text{if } act_i < m, \quad act_i = m . \quad (75)$$

In most simulations, the IAC model has been used with the following standard set of control parameters: $estr = 0.1$, $\alpha = 0.1$, $\gamma = 0.1$, $decay = 0.1$, $M = 1.$, $m = -0.2$, and $rest = -0.1$ (McClelland, 1991). In some simulations of the IAC model, running averages across cycles have been used rather than those directly computed at the cycle of interest (McClelland, 1991). We utilize the latter. Typically, 60 cycles of processing are carried out.

In McClelland and Rumelhart's (1981) original formulation of the model, which we call the IAC-RGR, the activations were translated into strengths by the exponential function

$$S_i = exp\ (k\ act_i) \tag{76}$$

(with k commonly equal to 5), and these strengths were evaluated by an RGR to obtain the probability of a response. For the QG task, the form is

$$P(\mathrm{Q}) = \frac{S_\mathrm{Q}}{S_\mathrm{Q} + S_\mathrm{G}}\ . \tag{77}$$

Due to certain incorrect predictions of the IAC model pointed out by Massaro (1989) (further discussed in the next section), the IAC model was revised to use a best-one-wins (BOW) decision rule applied directly to the activations, with normal noise being added to the input feature values. We call this model the IAC-BOW. We examine both the original and revised IAC model.

The IAC model is basically additive with nonlinearities introduced by the change in additivity as activation boundaries are approached (Equations 71 and 72), by nonlinear decay (Equations 71 and 72), and by the activation and competition processes over time. Given the nonlinear characteristics of the model, it is, unfortunately, impossible to examine exactly the mathematical behavior of this model by a general closed-form analysis, and we have to be content with our simulations and empirical analysis given in the next two sections.

We note, however, an important demonstration by McClelland (1991) that a model closely related to the IAC-BOW—the *Boltzmann machine* (Hinton and Sejnowski, 1983, 1986)—at its equilibrium state can be reduced to multiplicative terms, each representing a single source of information, and is thus equivalent to the FLMP.

MODEL TESTS WITH HYPOTHETICAL TWO-RESPONSE DATA

The predictions of each model were fit to the predictions of the FLMP (the hypothetical 49 data points shown in Figure 15.5) using the analysis program STEPIT (Chandler, 1969). A model is represented to STEPIT as an algorithm for computing the sum of squared deviations between the observed and predicted data as a function of a set of parameters. By iteratively adjusting the parameters of the model, STEPIT minimizes the deviations between the observed and predicted points. Thus, STEPIT finds a set of parameter values that, when put in the model, come closest to predicting the observed data. The metric of goodness of fit used is the root-mean-squared deviation (RMSD) between the observed and predicted data. Although many of these models are expected to fit the hypothetical data perfectly, it is of interest to examine the parameter values from the fits. For some of these models we could directly compute the parameters from those found for the FLMP, but not all models have exact transforms, and it is worthwhile to carry out the fitting procedures for all models. It also may be, for example, that some of the parameter estimates are illogical or not meaningful. Therefore, even though mathematically equivalent, models could be distinguished on the basis of the reasonableness of the parameter estimates. For the most part, the estimated parameters are presented in figure form.

For the fit of the FLMP, 14 parameters were used, 7 for the *c* feature values and 7 for the *o* features. There was a perfect fit to the data. The fit of the FLMP model to the data is shown in Figure 15.5.

For the fit of the BPM, 28 parameters were used, 7 each for the $P(c|Q)$, $P(c|G)$, $P(o|Q)$, and $P(o|G)$ probabilities. As expected, there was a perfect fit to the FLMP predictions.

For the fit of the GMM models, 14 parameters were used, 7 for the spatial *c* coordinates and 7 for the *o* coordinates. Figure 15.7 gives the locations of the best-fitting stimulus locations for the GMM-E (a perfect fit). Although theoretically different, the GMM-CB provided an extremely close fit (RMSD = 0.0060) with a slightly different arrangement of the stimuli.

The EMM models also used 14 parameters for spatial coordinates. Figure 15.8 gives the locations of the best-fitting stimulus locations for the EMM-CB (a perfect fit). Interestingly, the EMM-E gave an almost perfect fit of (RMSD = 0.0002). This similarity of models has been previously noted by Indow (1974) and Ennis (1988a), who reported a number of cases in which city-block data are well fit by Euclidean distance.

The TSD models also used 14 parameters for spatial coordinates. Figure 15.11 gives the locations of the best-fitting stimulus locations for the TSD-L (a perfect fit). Although theoretically different from the FLMP, the TSD-N did a respectable (RMSD = 0.0064) job of mimicking the FLMP predictions.

The fit of the IAC models is somewhat more complex. We begin with a fit of the IAC-RGR with the typical *k* value of 5. This model used 14 parameters representing the 7 *c* and 7 *o* input feature values. To fit this model, the IAC algorithm (McClelland & Rumelhart, 198) (recoded in FORTRAN [f77] for use with STEPIT) was run to compute the target activations after 60 time cycles. The fit of this model was relatively poor (RMSD = 0.0457). To understand the nature of the problem the IAC-RGR has in mimicking the FLMP predictions, we plot in the left panel of Figure 15.14 the fit transformed by the inverse logistic. In the figure, we can see that while the inverse logistic of the FLMP hypothetical data is additive, five of the seven IAC-RGR predicted lines tend to converge at both ends. This nonadditivity of the effects of the two variables was originally pointed out by Massaro (1989) in an analysis of the combination of phonological context and stimulus information in the TRACE model (McClelland & Elman, 1986), which is closely related to the IAC. This nonadditivity disagrees with the classically observed additivity.

To improve the fit of the IAC-RGR, we set the *k* value to 15. The right panel of Figure 15.14 gives the inverse logistic of the predicted probability of a Q response for the FLMP and the IAC-RGR with $k = 15$. As can be seen in this

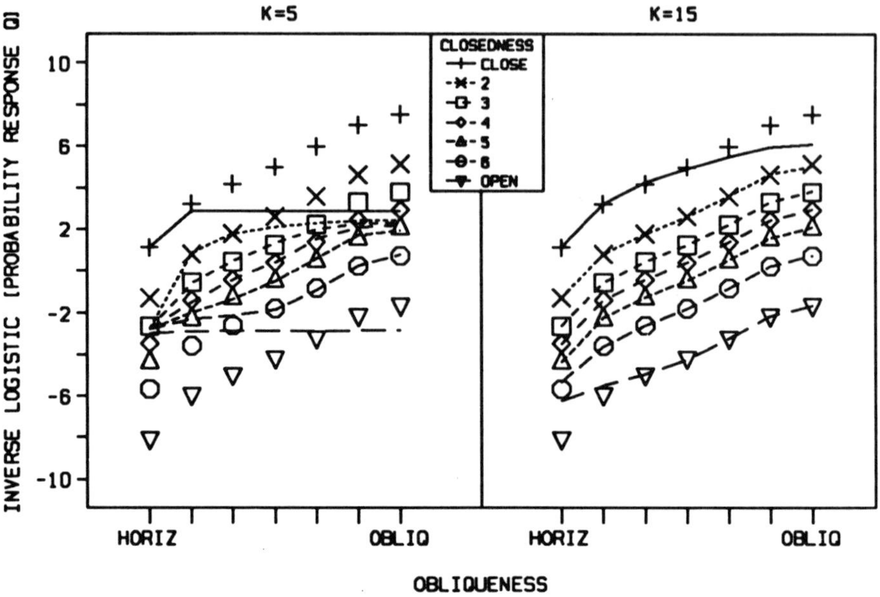

FIG. 15.14. Inverse logistic transform of the predicted probability of a Q response according to the FLMP (points) and IAC-RGR model (lines) for k = 5 (left panel) and k = 15 (right panel).

figure, the IAC-RGR with k = 15 gave a good much better fit (RMSD = 0.0007), although there was still a slight nonadditivity. Table 15.1 gives the best-fitting feature values found by STEPIT for the k = 5 and k = 15 cases. Although using larger k values allows better mimicking of the FLMP, this is an unattractive solution because the input feature values take on unrealistic values.

For the IAC-RGR to mimic the FLMP predictions, the input features must be very close to neutral values, with a very small range of feature values. In fact, a small range of feature values also occurred for the interior five levels of the k = 5 case. Thus, the IAC-RGR model can only mimic the FLMP predictions by

TABLE 15.1
Estimated Input Feature Values for Two IAC-RGR Models (with k = 5 and k = 15) for Best Fit of Hypothetical Data

		Level							
Feature	*k*	*1*	*2*	*3*	*4*	*5*	*6*	*7*	*Range*
Closedness	5	.0001	.4869	.4946	.4993	.5038	.5112	.9999	.9998
	15	.4966	.5007	.5030	.5044	.5059	.5082	.5123	.0157
Obliqueness	5	.2636	.4932	.4986	.5029	.5085	.5145	.5173	.2537
	15	.4896	.4932	.4949	.4963	.4980	.4998	.5006	.0110

having the activations of the response units fall in a relatively neutral, non-asymptotic range. The left and right panels of Figure 15.15 give the response activations for the Q and G units for the $k = 5$ and $k = 15$ cases, respectively. Within the relatively neutral range, the activation values are less susceptible to the nonlinearities of the IAC and therefore can better approximate the hypothetical data. Thus, the model involves something closer to an addition of individual effects, transformed at the end by an exponential—that is, more like the multiplication of the two effects (which is what happens in the FLMP and related models). Figure 15.16 illustrates how the activations from the two cases are shaped by transforming them into strength values. The difference in the strength scales on the two graphs should be noted; the strengths resulting from $k = 15$ are about 15 times larger. Comparing the right panel of Figure 15.16 with Figure 15.4, we see that the IAC-RGR with k = 15 is able to replicate to some extent the multiplicative fan predicted by the FLMP. In summary, the IAC-RGR can apparently mimic the noninteractive nature of the LPM, but only by staying in a restricted linear parameter range. The small range of feature values is particularly damaging to a neural network interpretation because neurons are unlikely to represent activations to this fine level of resolution.

We now evaluate the IAC-BOW model with its alternative decision process of

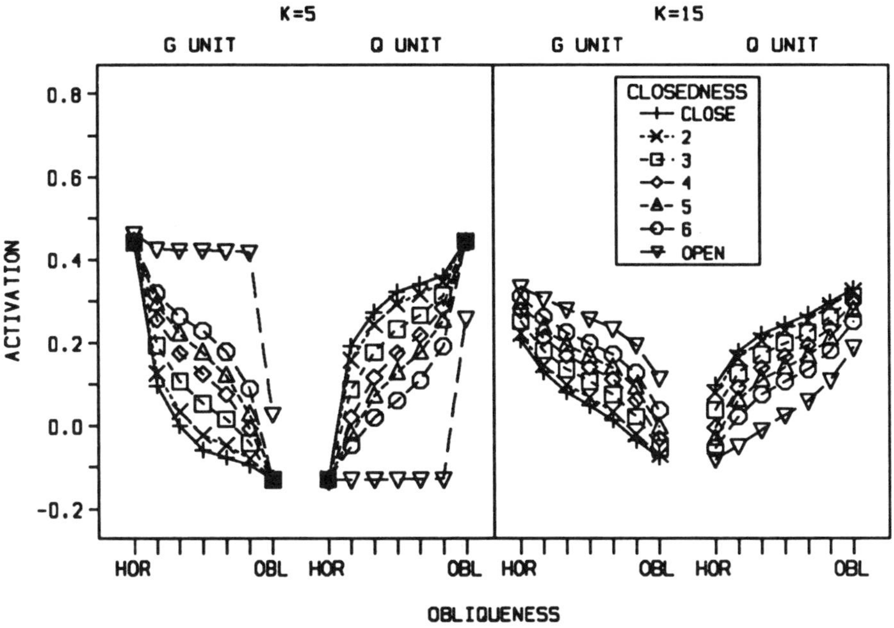

FIG. 15.15. Activation of the G and Q units for the IAC-RGR model with $k = 5$ (left panel) and $k = 15$ (right panel) given the hypothetical parameter values in Table 15.1.

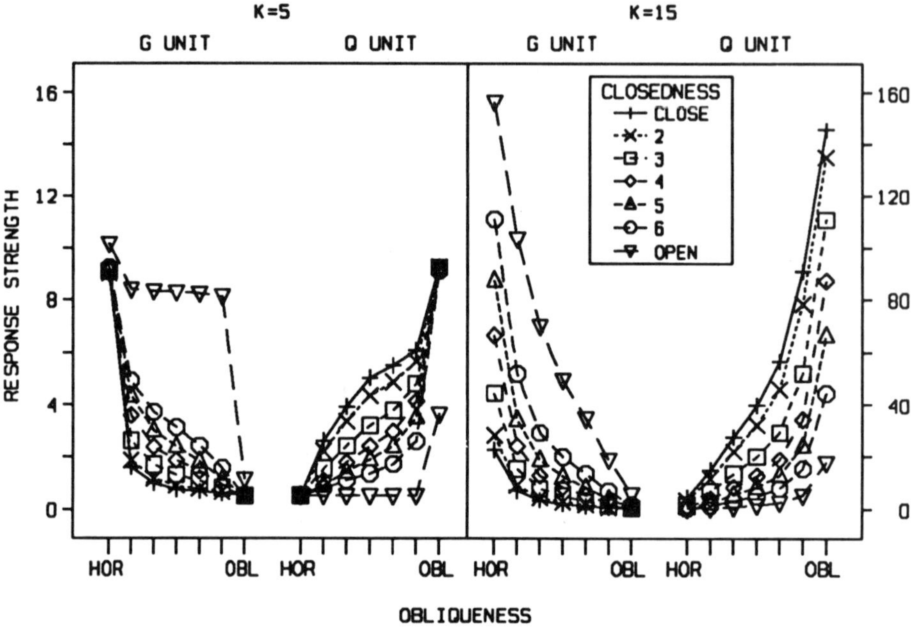

FIG. 15.16. The strengths of the G and Q response alternatives for the IAC-RGR model with $k = 5$ (left panel) and $k = 15$ (right panel) given the activations in Figure 15.15. Note difference in response strength scales for the two panels.

choosing the response with the highest activation. To compute the model's predictions, we first set the 49 probabilities of a Q response given the 7 closedness times 7 obliqueness conditions to 0, and reset the random number generator. Then for each of the 49 conditions 1,000 simulated trials occurred. On each simulated trial random deviates, from a normal (Gaussian) distribution computed by the Box-Muller Method (Press, Flannery, Teukolsky, & Vetterling, 1988; see also chap. 1) with a standard deviation (which was allowed to vary) initially set at 0.14142, were added to each of the current pair of parameters (for closedness and obliqueness). Then the IAC algorithm (McClelland & Rumelhart, 1988) was run to compute the target activations after 60 time cycles. If the final activation of the Q unit was greater than or equal to the final activation of the G target, then $\frac{1}{1000}$ was added to the probability of a Q response. For the parameter estimation routine to operate properly, we had to employ the same sequence of random numbers on each overall computation run. This allowed STEPIT to make reliable adjustments in the parameter values, even though noise was being added to the input.

The IAC with the BOW decision rule gave a good fit to the FLMP predictions (RMSD = 0.0090) with the noise standard deviation at 0.1251. Figure 15.17 shows the fit of the model in terms of the inverse logistic of the proportion of Q

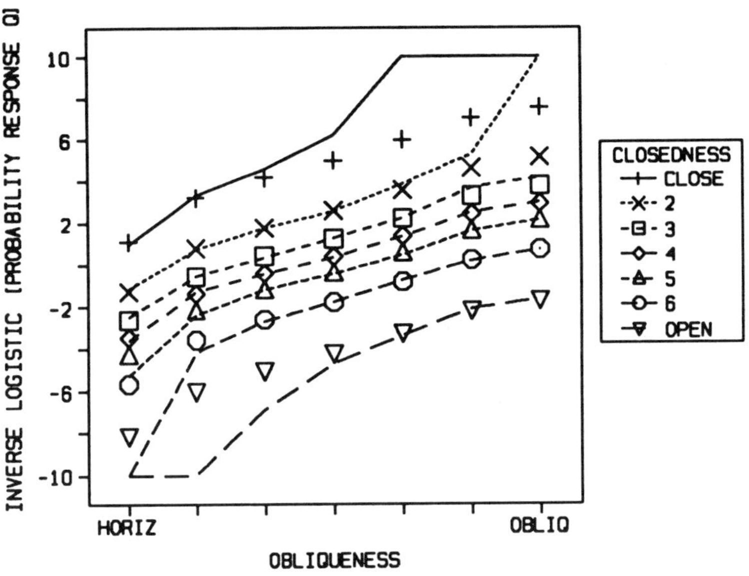

FIG. 15.17. Inverse logistic transform of the predicted probability of a Q response according to the FLMP (points) and IAC-BOW model (lines).

responses. We note some deviations from additivity, but those are mostly due to the problem of computing the inverse logistic for 0 and 1. In those cases, the value was set at ± 10.

Table 15.2 summarizes the fits of the various models, giving the RMSDs between the FLMP predictions and the predicted data for each model. As can be seen in the table, the FLMP, BPM, GMM-E, EMM-CB, TSD-L, and FCM models all had perfect fits to the FLMP hypothetical data, as predicted by the theoretical analysis. Of all the models not exactly equivalent to the FLMP, the GMM-CB, EMM-E, TSD-N, IAC-RGR15 did a good job at mimicking the FLMP, the latter model doing so with unrealistic parameter values. Only the IAC-RGR5 made different predictions.

MODEL TESTS WITH EXPERIMENTAL QG DATA

Given the subtle differences between the LPM class and most of the others (and the large difference for the IAC-RGR5) observed for the pure hypothetical data, it is of interest to see whether we can discriminate among these models with real experimental data. Of course, we expect all the LPM class to give the same goodness of fit and predictions, but it is worthwhile to present the fits so that the parameters of the models can be examined. Table 15.3 gives the RMSD for each model for each of the nine subjects in the QG task, a fit of a mean subject, and

TABLE 15.2
Model Fits of Hypothetical FLMP Data

Model	*RMSD*
FLMP	.0000
BPM	.0000
GMM-E	.0000
GMM-CB	.0060
EMM-E	.0002
EMM-CB	.0000
TSD-L	.0000
TSD-N	.0064
FCM	.0000
IAC-RGR5	.0457
IAC-RGR15	.0007
IAC-BOW	.0090

the mean of the subject fits. We will graph the observed and predicted data for the two typical subjects shown in Figure 15.2.

For the fit of the FLMP, 14 parameters were used, 7 for the *c* feature values and 7 for the *o* features. The average RMSD for the model was 0.0507. Figure 15.18 shows the observed and predicted data for the typical subjects with the abscissa scaled according to the obtained obliqueness parameters. Table 15.3 shows that all models of the LPM class achieved the same goodness of fit. The related GMM-CB, EMM-E, TSD-N, IAC-RGR15 did not give a significantly different fit. Of particular interest is the goodness of fit of the IAC-RGR5—the only model different from the FLMP and related models in fitting the hypothetical data in the previous section. The RMSDs of the IAC-RGR5 were compared with those of the FLMP by using an ANOVA for the nine subject fits, and were found to be significantly worse for the IAC-RGR5, ($F(1, 8) = 30.64$, $p = 0.001$). Therefore, at least one of the models can be distinguished on the basis of actual results, and the IAC-RGR5 is falsified by the fit of the data from the QG experiment of Massaro and Hary (1986).

PROTOTYPICAL FOUR-RESPONSE CATEGORIZATION TASK

Given the successful reconciliation of a number of models for the two-response task, it is worthwhile to extend our analysis to a prototypical four response alternative task, carried out by Massaro, Tseng, and Cohen (1983). The four

TABLE 15.3
RMSDs for Model Fits of QG Experimental Data for Nine Individual Subjects, Fit of the Mean Subject, and Average of the Nine Subject Fits

Model	*S1*	*S2*	*S3*	*S4*	*S5*	*S6*	*S7*	*S8*	*S9*	*SM*	*AVE*
FLMP	.0346	.0637	.0973	.0444	.0312	.0543	.0487	.0284	.0539	.0369	.0507
BPM	.0346	.0637	.0973	.0444	.0312	.0543	.0487	.0284	.0539	.0369	.0507
GMM-E	.0346	.0637	.0973	.0444	.0312	.0543	.0487	.0284	.0539	.0369	.0507
GMM-CB	.0432	.0637	.0974	.0449	.0290	.0629	.0485	.0302	.0542	.0371	.0527
EMM-E	.0346	.0636	.0973	.0444	.0312	.0543	.0487	.0284	.0539	.0369	.0507
EMM-CB	.0346	.0637	.0973	.0444	.0312	.0543	.0487	.0284	.0539	.0369	.0507
TSD-L	.0346	.0637	.0973	.0444	.0312	.0543	.0487	.0284	.0539	.0369	.0507
TSD-N	.0354	.0624	.0961	.0446	.0322	.0561	.0483	.0292	.0542	.0384	.0509
FCM	.0346	.0637	.0973	.0444	.0312	.0543	.0487	.0284	.0539	.0369	.0507
IAC-RGR5	.0518	.0719	.1014	.0610	.0482	.0569	.0645	.0487	.0611	.0445	.0628
IAC-RGRK	.0327	.0634	.0991	.0445	.0297	.0493	.0476	.0286	.0536	.0350	.0498
IAC-BOW	.0358	.0604	.0968	.0487	.0329	.0571	.0480	.0296	.0525	.0378	.0513

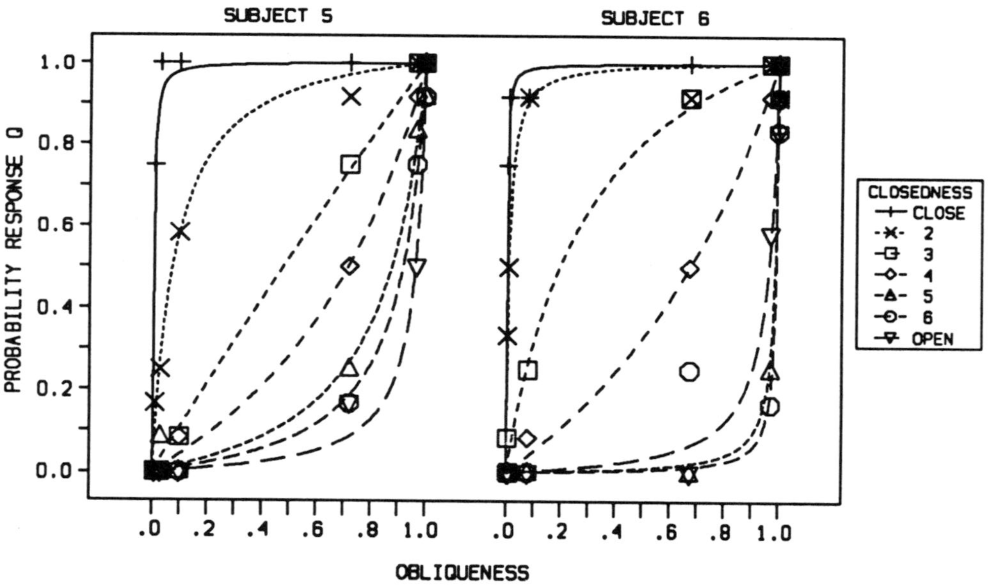

FIG. 15.18. Observed (points) and predicted (lines) probability of Q responses for the forty-nine test letters presented in Figure 15.1 for two typical subjects. The predictions are for the FLMP model and the locations on the abscissa are scaled according to the estimated value of the obliqueness feature.

responses in the experiment were four words in Mandarin Chinese. The experiment used a factorial design with seven levels of each of two factors. These factors were the format structure of the vowel in the monosyllabic words and the fundamental frequency (F_0) contour (tone) during the vowel. Mandarin Chinese is a tone language, and both of these sources of information are functional to distinguish different words. The formant structure was varied to make a continuum of vowel sounds between /i/ and /y/. (The vowel /y/ is articulated in the same manner as /i/, except with the lips rounded.) The F_0 contour varied between falling-rising to falling during the vowel. Six native Chinese speakers participated for four days, with each subject giving a total of 48 responses to each of the 49 test stimuli. The subjects identified each of the 49 test stimuli as one of the four words. Figure 15.19 shows the data for a single typical subject as a function of vowel and tone level for the four responses.

FOUR-RESPONSE FLMP

In the four-response version of the FLMP the prototypes are defined by:

i-FR: vowel /i/ and falling-rising tone
i-F: vowel /i/ and falling tone

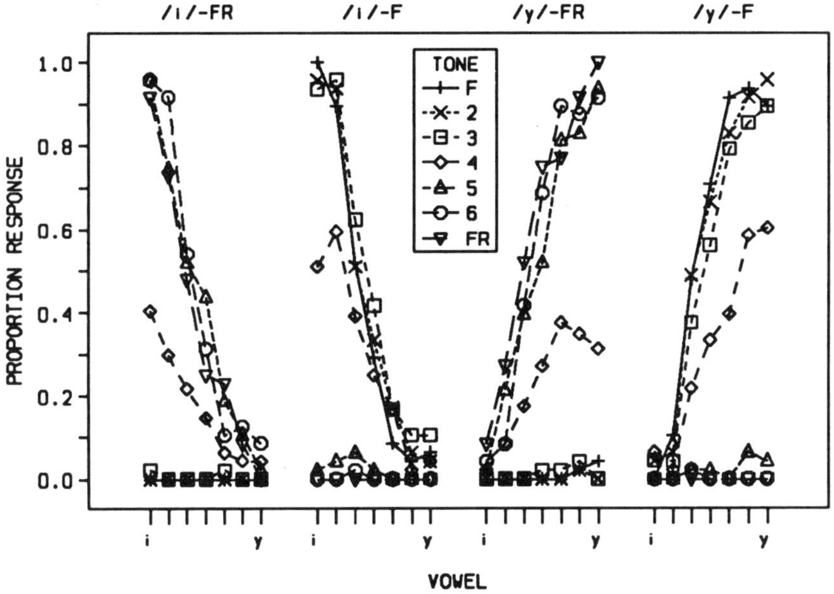

FIG. 15.19. Mean observed proportion of responses for a typical subject as a function of vowel and tone level for the four responses. (After Massaro, Tseng & Cohen, 1983).

y-FR: vowel /y/ and falling-rising tone
y-F: vowel /y/ and falling tone

In thc implementation of the model, it is assumed that the vowel /i/ and vowel /y/ features are opposites (or negations) of one another, as are falling-rising and falling tones. Thus, we can represent the prototypes' goodnesses in terms of the degree to which the vowel is /y/ (y) and the tone is falling (F), and with the multiplicative definition of conjunction:

i-FR: $(1 - y) \times (1 - F)$
i-F: $(1 - y) \times F$
y-FR: $y \times (1 - F)$
y-F: $y \times F$

These prototypes are then evaluated by a RGR. The probability of a y-F response, for example, is given by

$$P(\text{y-F}|Y_j \text{ and } F_k) = \frac{(y_j)(f_k)}{(1 - y_j)(1 - f_k) + (1 - y_j)(f_k) + (y_j)(1 - f_k) + (y_j)(f_k)} . \quad (78)$$

Noting that the denominator of Equation 78 is always the quantity 1, we can simplify the response predictions to

$$P(\text{i-FR}|Y_j \text{ and } F_k) = (1 - y_j)(1 - f_k) \quad (79)$$

$$P(\text{i-F}|Y_j \text{ and } F_k) = (1 - y_j)(f_k) \quad (80)$$

$$P(\text{y-FR}|Y_j \text{ and } F_k) = (y_j)(1 - f_k) \quad (81)$$

$$P(\text{y-F}|Y_j \text{ and } F_k) = (y_j(f_k) \quad (82)$$

To generate the FLMP predictions, the following hypothetical feature values were used for vowel /y/, going from /i/ to /y/: 0.01, 0.10, 0.30, 0.50, 0.70, 0.90, 0.99, and for tone falling, going from falling-rising to falling: 0.03, 0.20, 0.40, 0.60, 0.80, 0.92, 0.95. Figure 15.20 shows the support for the four alternatives given these hypothetical feature values (and also the probability of responding with those alternatives since the denominator of the RGR is 1).

FOUR-RESPONSE BPM

For the four-response BPM, the probabilities of the four responses are computed from the probabilities of evidence $P(Y_j|\text{y})$, $P(Y_j|\text{i})$, $P(F_k|\text{FR})$, $P(F_k|\text{F})$. The probability of a y-F response, for example would be given by

$$P(\text{y-F}|Y_j \text{ and } F_k) = \frac{P(Y_j|\text{Y})P(\text{F}_k|\text{F})}{P(Y_j|\text{I})P(F_k|\text{FR}) + P(Y_j|\text{I})P(F_k|\text{F}) + P(Y_j|\text{Y})P(F_k|\text{FR}) + P(Y_j|\text{Y})P(F_k|\text{F})} . \quad (83)$$

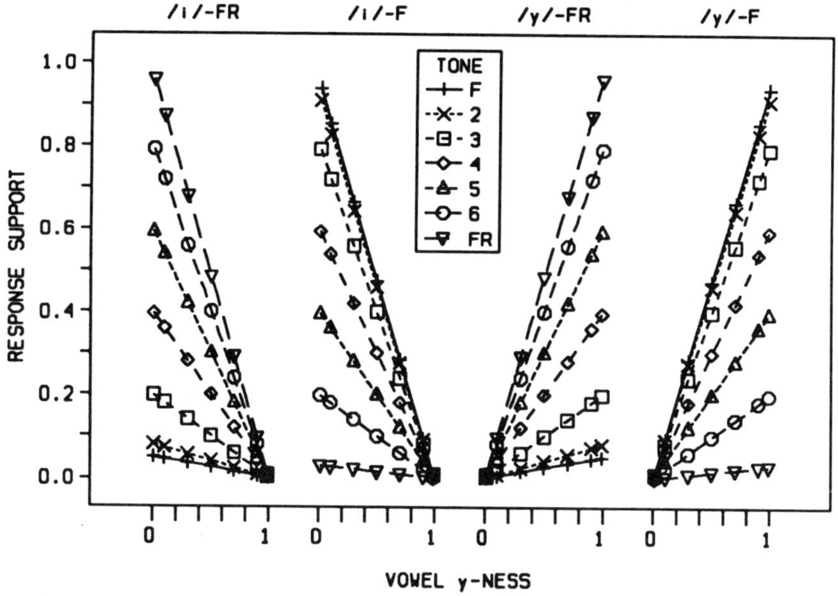

FIG. 15.20. Support for alternative i-FR, i-F, y-FR, and y-F prototypes based on hypothetical vowel and tone features given in the text. The locations on the abscissa are scaled according to the y-ness of the vowel feature.

As with the two-response case, the FLMP and the BPM differ in that for the FLMP the alternatives are defined as using *complementary* features. Thus, in the FLMP, i and FR are assumed to be complements of y and F, respectively. For the BPM, however, the probabilities $P(e|h_1)$ and $P(e|h_2)$ need not sum to 1. Let us consider again Equation 83, which, by dividing top and bottom by $P(Y_j|\text{y})P(F_k|\text{F})$ can be rewritten as

$$P(\text{y-F}|Y_j \text{ and } F_k) = \frac{1}{\dfrac{P(Y_j|\text{i})P(F_k|\text{FR})}{P(Y_j|\text{y})P(F_k|\text{F})} + \dfrac{P(Y_j|\text{i})P(F_k|\text{F})}{P(Y_j|\text{y})P(F_k|\text{F})} + \dfrac{P(Y_j|\text{y})P(F_k|\text{FR})}{P(Y_j|\text{y})P(F_k|\text{F})} + 1} \quad (84)$$

$$= \frac{1}{\dfrac{P(Y_j|\text{i})}{P(Y_j|\text{y})}\dfrac{P(F_k|\text{FR})}{P(F_k|\text{F})} + \dfrac{P(Y_j|\text{i})}{P(Y_j|\text{y})}\dfrac{P(F_k|\text{F})}{P(F_k|\text{F})} + \dfrac{P(Y_j|\text{y})}{P(Y_j|\text{y})}\dfrac{P(F_k|\text{FR})}{P(F_k|\text{F})} + 1}$$

$$= \frac{1}{\dfrac{P(Y_j|\text{i})}{P(Y_j|\text{y})}\dfrac{P(F_k|\text{FR})}{P(F_k|\text{F})} + \dfrac{P(Y_j|\text{i})}{P(Y_j|\text{y})} + \dfrac{P(F_k|\text{FR})}{P(F_k|\text{F})} + 1}$$

or the equivalent

$$= \frac{1}{l_{\text{iy}}(Y_j)l_{\text{FR F}}(F_k) + l_{\text{iy}}(Y_j) + l_{\text{FR F}}(F_k) + 1}. \quad (85)$$

where l_{iy} (Y_j) is the likelihood ratio of vowel i to vowel y given evidence Y_j, and $l_{FR\ F}(F_k)$ is the likelihood ratio of tone FR to tone F given evidence F_k. The likelihood product form (i.e., Equation 85) for other responses also requires $l_{yi}(Y_j)$, which is the reciprocal of $l_{IY}(Y_j)$, and $l_{F\ FR}(F_k)$, which is the reciprocal of $l_{FR\ F}(F_k)$. Thus, for each combination of closedness and obliqueness conditions, only two likelihood ratios (one for each source of evidence) are needed. For the BPM, the likelihood ratios are given by

$$l_{IY}(Y_j) = \frac{P(Y_j|i)}{P(Y_j|y)} \tag{86}$$

and

$$l_{FR\ F}(F_k) = \frac{P(F_k|FR)}{P(F_k|F)} \ . \tag{87}$$

Similarly, for the FLMP, the likelihood ratios are given by

$$l_{IY}(Y_j) = \frac{1 - y_j}{y_j} \tag{88}$$

and

$$l_{FR\ F}(F_k) = \frac{1 - f_k}{f_k} \tag{89}$$

As in the two-alternative case, both the FLMP and BPM are members of the LPM class.

FOUR-RESPONSE GMM

The GMM for the four-response task is similar to that for two responses except that there are four prototype locations. We assume that the prototypes are symmetrically centered in a multidimensional space with dimensions vowel and tone, at $[P, P]$ for y-F, at $[P, -P]$ for y-FR, at $[-P, P]$ for i-F, and at $[-P, -P]$ for i-FR. Figure 15.21 shows the arrangement of the prototype distributions in the multidimensional space. The Euclidean distances from stimulus **S** at $[y_j, f_k]$ to the four prototype locations are given by

$$d(\mathbf{S}, \text{y-F}) = \sqrt{(P - y_j)^2 + (P - f_k)^2} \ , \tag{90}$$

$$d(\mathbf{S}, \text{y-FR}) = \sqrt{(P - y_j)^2 + (-P - f_k)^2} \ , \tag{91}$$

$$d(\mathbf{S}, \text{i-F}) = \sqrt{(-P - y_j)^2 + (P - f_k)^2} \ , \tag{92}$$

and

$$d(\mathbf{S}, \text{i-FR}) = \sqrt{(-P - y_j)^2 + (-P - f_k)^2} \ . \tag{93}$$

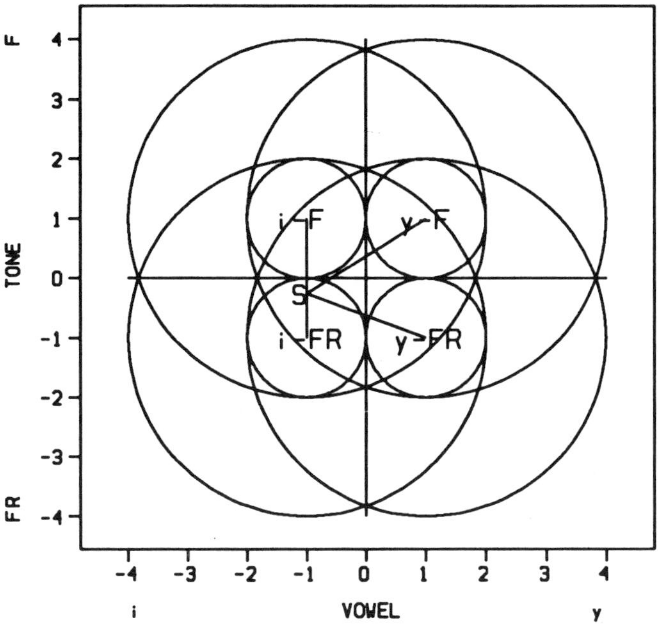

FIG. 15.21. Gaussian multidimensional model of four response paradigm. The labels y-F, y-FR, i-F and i-FR represent the center of the probabilistic prototype distributions corresponding to the four response categories. The concentric circles indicate 1, and 3 standard deviations from the center, as described by the bivariate normal.

Given the Gaussian similarity function, we can compute the similarities

$$s(\mathbf{S}, \text{y-F}) = exp\,\{-[(P - y_j)^2 + (P - f_k)^2]\}\,, \tag{94}$$

$$s(\mathbf{S}, \text{y-FR}) = exp\,\{-[(P - y_j)^2 + (-P - f_k)^2]\}\,, \tag{95}$$

$$s(\mathbf{S}, \text{i-F}) = exp\,\{-[(-P - y_j)^2 + (P - f_k)^2]\}\,, \tag{96}$$

$$s(\mathbf{S}, \text{i-FR}) = exp\,\{-[(-P - y_j)^2 + (-P - f_k)^2]\}\,. \tag{97}$$

These similarities can then be factored into

$$s(\mathbf{S}, \text{y-F}) = exp\,[-(P - y_j)^2]\; exp\,[-(P - f_k)^2]\,, \tag{98}$$

$$s(\mathbf{S}, \text{y-FR}) = exp\,[-(P - y_j)^2]\; exp\,[-(-P - f_k)^2]\,, \tag{99}$$

$$s(\mathbf{S}, \text{i-F}) = exp\,[-(-P - y_j)^2]\; exp\,[-(P - f_k)^2]\,, \tag{100}$$

$$s(\mathbf{S}, \text{i-FR}) = exp\,[-(-P - y_j)^2]\; exp\,[-(-P - f_k)^2]\,, \tag{101}$$

from which we can draw, using the terminology of the FLMP and BPM:

$$p(Y_j|\text{y}) = exp\,[-(P - y_j)^2]\,, \tag{102}$$

$$p(Y_j|\text{i}) = exp\ [-(-P - y_j)^2]\ , \tag{103}$$

$$p(F_k|\text{F}) = exp\ [-(P - f_k)^2]\ , \tag{104}$$

$$p(F_k|\text{FR}) = exp\ [-(-P - f_k)^2]\ . \tag{105}$$

With these probabilities obtained, we can use Equation 83 for the rest of the derivation. For the likelihood product form we derive the likelihood ratios:

$$l_{\text{IY}}(Y_j) = exp\ [(P - y_j)^2 - (-P - y_j)^2] = exp\ (-4Py_j)\ , \tag{106}$$

$$l_{\text{FR F}}(F_k) = exp\ [(P - f_k)^2 - (-P - f_k)^2] = exp\ (-4Pf_k)\ . \tag{107}$$

Figure 15.22 shows how our 49 hypothetical stimuli are arranged in the multidimensional space.

For the alternative GMM-CB model with the city-block distance measure, the distance between the stimulus **S** and, for example, y-F would be

$$d(\mathbf{S}, \text{y-F}) = |P - y_j| + |P - f_k|\ , \tag{108}$$

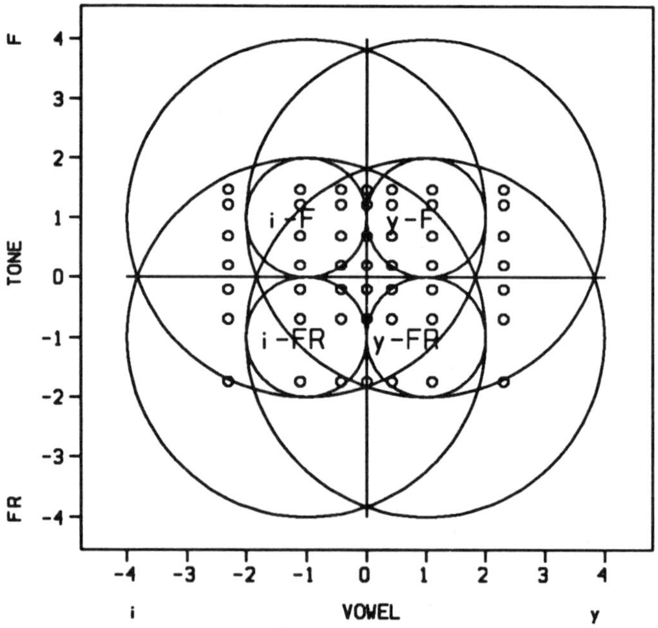

FIG. 15.22. Gaussian multidimensional model of four response paradigm. The labels y-F, y-FR, i-F and i-FR represent the center of the probabilistic prototype distributions corresponding to the four response categories. The concentric circles indicate 1, and 3 standard deviations from the center, as described by the bivariate normal. The small circles give the locations of the hypothetical stimuli.

for which the similarity function would be

$$s(\mathbf{S}, \text{y-F}) = exp\,\{-[(P - f_k)^2 + 2|P - y_j||P - f_k| + (P - y_j)^2]\}\,. \quad (109)$$

As with the two-response case, these similarities are not factorable, and thus the GMM-CB is not a member of the LPM class.

FOUR-RESPONSE EMM

The derivation of the EMM for four responses is very similar to that for the four-response GMM, except that the exponential similarity function is used. For the EMM-CB, the city-block distances from stimulus **S** at $[y_j, f_k]$ to the four prototype locations are given by

$$d(\mathbf{S}, \text{y-F}) = |P - y_j| + |P - f_k|\,, \quad (110)$$

$$d(\mathbf{S}, \text{y-FR}) = |P - y_j| + |-P - f_k|\,, \quad (111)$$

$$d(\mathbf{S}, \text{i-F}) = |-P - y_j| + |P - f_k|\,, \quad (112)$$

$$d(\mathbf{S}, \text{i-FR}) = |-P - y_j| + |-P - f_k|\,. \quad (113)$$

Given the exponential similarity function, we can compute the similarities

$$s(\mathbf{S}, \text{y-F}) = exp\,[-(|P - y_j| + |P - f_k|)]\,, \quad (114)$$

$$s(\mathbf{S}, \text{y-FR}) = exp\,[-(|P - y_j| + |-P - f_k|)]\,, \quad (115)$$

$$s(\mathbf{S}, \text{i-F}) = exp\,[-(|-P - y_j| + |P - f_k|)]\,, \quad (116)$$

$$s(\mathbf{S}, \text{i-FR}) = exp\,[-(|-P - y_j| + |-P - f_k|)]\,. \quad (117)$$

These similarities can then be factored into

$$s(\mathbf{S}, \text{y-F}) = exp\,[-|P - y_j|]\;exp\,[-|P - f_k|]\,, \quad (118)$$

$$s(\mathbf{S}, \text{y-FR}) = exp\,[-|P - y_j|]\;exp\,[-|-P - f_k|]\,, \quad (119)$$

$$s(\mathbf{S}, \text{i-F}) = exp\,[-|-P - y_j|]\;exp\,[-|P - f_k|]\,, \quad (120)$$

$$s(\mathbf{S}, \text{i-FR}) = exp\,[-|-P - y_j|]\;exp\,[-|-P - f_k|]\,. \quad (121)$$

from which we can draw

$$p(Y_j|\text{y}) = exp\,(-|P - y_j|)\,, \quad (122)$$

$$p(Y_j|\text{i}) = exp\,(-|-P - y_j|)\,, \quad (123)$$

$$p(F_k|\text{F}) = exp\,(-|P - f_k|)\,, \quad (124)$$

$$p(F_k|\text{FR}) = exp\,(-|-P - f_k|)\,. \quad (125)$$

Given these probabilities, we can return to Equation 83 in the BPM section for the rest of the derivation. For the likelihood product form we can derive the likelihood ratios:

$$l_{\mathrm{IY}}(Y_{\mathrm{j}}) = exp\ (|P - y_{\mathrm{j}}| - |-P - y_{\mathrm{j}}|)\ , \tag{126}$$

$$l_{\mathrm{FR\ F}}(F_{\mathrm{k}}) = exp\ (|P - f_{\mathrm{k}}| - |-P - f_{\mathrm{k}}|)\ . \tag{127}$$

For the alternative EMM-E model with the Euclidean distance measure, the distance between the stimulus **S** and, for example, y-F is

$$d(\mathbf{S}, \text{y-F}) = \sqrt{(P - y_{\mathrm{j}})^2 + (P - f_{\mathrm{k}})^2} \tag{128}$$

for which the similarity function is

$$s(\mathbf{S}, \text{y-F}) = exp\ [-\sqrt{(\mathrm{P} - \mathrm{y_j})^2 + (\mathrm{P} - \mathrm{f_k})^2}]\ . \tag{129}$$

As with the two-response case, these similarities are not factorable, and thus the EMM-E is not a member of the LPM class.

FOUR-RESPONSE TSD

The TSD model is illustrated for the four-response task in Figure 15.23. As in the four-response GMM model, the prototypes are defined as distributions located symmetrically at $[P, P]$, $[P, -P]$, $[-P, P]$, and $[-P, -P]$ (with $P = 1$) in a multidimensional feature space. We assume the covariance matrix associated with each prototype (and stimulus) distribution is the same scalar multiple of the identity matrix. We also assume that the perceiver establishes a decision rule based on the use of criterion lines of equal likelihood that separate the space into four regions, one for each response. Given the symmetric locations of the alternative distributions, the criterion lines lie on the main axes of the space, as shown in Figure 15.23.

On each trial, the subject simply determines what region the stimulus has occurred in and responds accordingly. As in the previous TSD model, we assume that stimuli are noisy. Figure 15.24 shows a typical bivariate normal stimulus distribution centered at [0.7,0.7]. Given a stimulus distribution **S** centered at $[y_{\mathrm{j}}, f_{\mathrm{k}}]$, we can simply determine what volume (proportion) falls in each response region. Looking at the figure, we can see that the area to the right of the vertical axis is $\Phi(y_{\mathrm{j}})$. Similarly, the area above the horizontal axis is $\Phi(f_{\mathrm{k}})$. Since the area in the upper right quadrant is that fraction of the distribution to the right times the fraction above (and similarly for the other quadrants), we arrive at the following formulas:

$$P(\text{i-FR}|\mathbf{S}) = [1 - \Phi(y_{\mathrm{j}})]\ [1 - \Phi(f_{\mathrm{k}})]\ , \tag{130}$$

$$P(\text{i-F}|\mathbf{S}) = [1 - \Phi(y_{\mathrm{j}})]\ \Phi(f_{\mathrm{k}})\ , \tag{131}$$

$$P(\text{y-FR}|\mathbf{S}) = \Phi(y_{\mathrm{j}})\ [1 - \Phi(f_{\mathrm{k}})]\ , \tag{132}$$

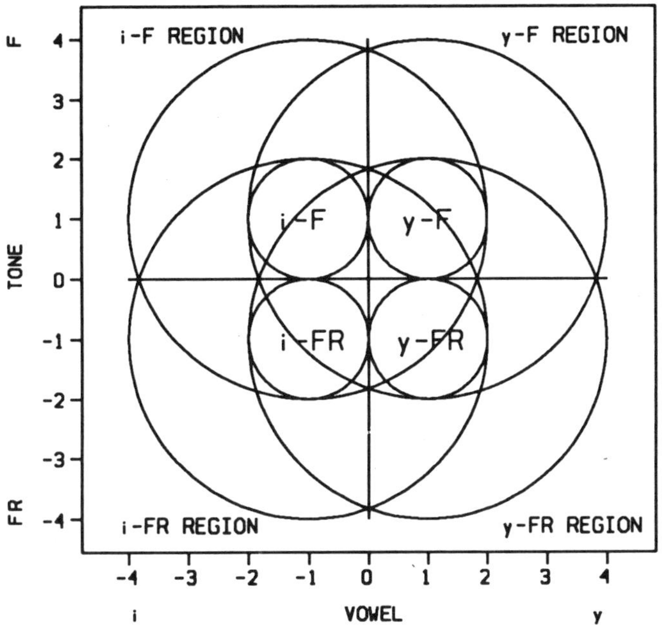

FIG. 15.23. Multidimensional TSD model of four response task. The four prototypes are defined as distributions located symmetrically in a multidimensional feature space, indicated by y-F, y-FR, i-F, and i-FR corresponding to the centers. The main axes divide the space into four response regions.

$$P(\text{y-F}|\mathbf{S}) = \Phi(y_j)\,\Phi(f_k)\,. \tag{133}$$

Comparing Equations 130–133 with Equations 79–81 of the FLMP, we can draw the simple equivalences:

$$y_{\text{FLMP}} = \Phi(y_{\text{TSD}}) \tag{134}$$

and

$$f_{\text{FLMP}} = \Phi(f_{\text{TSD}})\,. \tag{135}$$

Similarly, for the likelihood product form, we have the likelihood ratios:

$$\mathrm{l}_{\mathrm{IY}}(\mathrm{Y}_j) = \frac{1 - \Phi(y_j)}{\Phi(y_j)} \tag{136}$$

and

$$l_{\text{FR F}}(F_k) = \frac{1 - \Phi(f_k)}{\Phi(f_k)} \tag{137}$$

The hypothetical four-response stimuli are arranged in the multidimensional

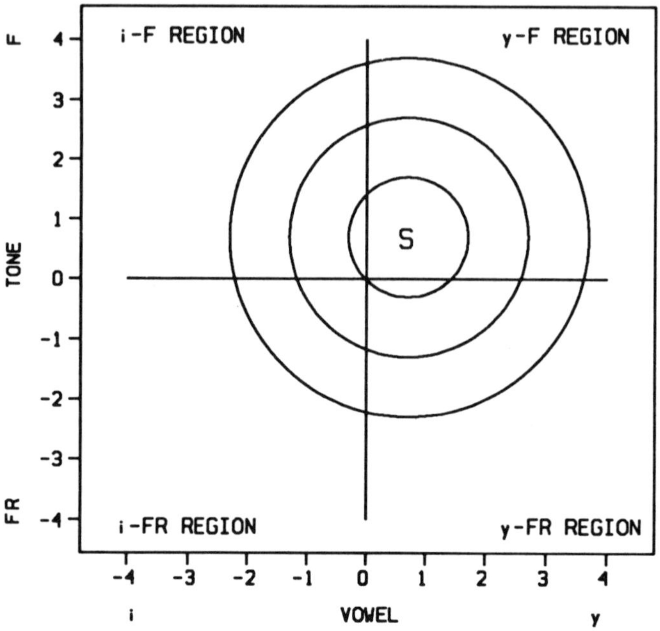

FIG. 15.24. Multidimensional TSD model of four response task with space divided into four response regions. A stimulus distribution indicated by S is centered at [.7, .7].

space in Figure 15.25. To summarize, we find an exact mathematical equivalence between the TSD and the FLMP when using an equal variance, uncorrelated bivariate normal stimulus distribution. To put things another way, we can interpret the fuzzy feature values to be the cumulative normal areas of the multidimensional scale values.

FOUR-RESPONSE FCM

At first glance, the FCM for four responses appears quite similar to that for two. In a recent report, however, Massaro and Friedman (1990) demonstrated that an FCM becomes nonequivalent to the FLMP when three or more response alternatives exist. This FCM has a strong constraint on its predicted response probabilities when more than two response alternatives exist. In the four-response task, for example, the maximum predicted probability for any response is limited to 0.5.

To overcome this constraint, we can add a threshold unit to the network, as illustrated in Figure 15.26. This unit is connected to each of the output units with a positive weight of 1, as with other excitatory connections. The revised FCM

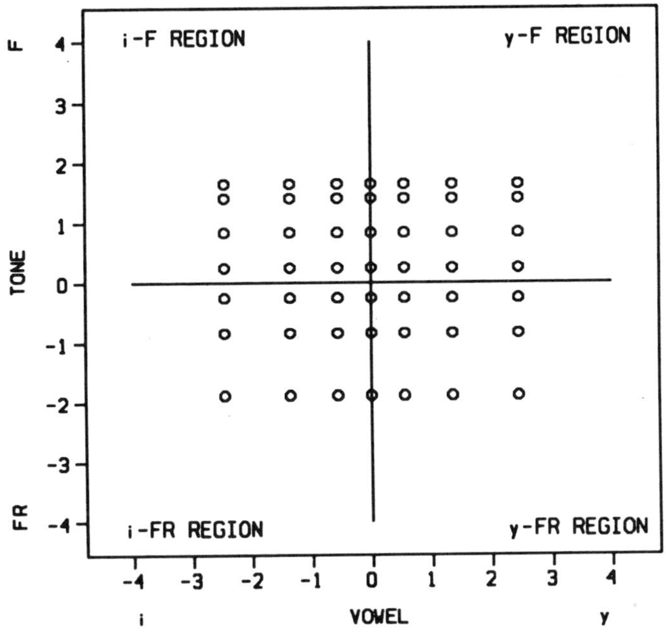

FIG. 15.25. Multidimensional TSD model of four response task with space divided into four response regions. Small circles show locations of hypothetical stimuli.

with a threshold is called the FCM-T. In this model, the additional free threshold parameter is sufficient to bring the model into close correspondence with the LPM class of models. The parameter functions in somewhat the same way as the k value in the IAC model in that it alters the effect of the function producing the response strengths in the RGR. Figure 15.27 provides a demonstration of how the threshold works for the FCM. To see more clearly the problem that the threshold corrects, let us first consider the overall pattern of predicted responses for a hypothetical pair of input features. Suppose the *y* and *f* features for the FLMP are both 0.9. The resulting goodnesses for y-F, y-FR, i-F, and i-FR prototypes in the FLMP would then be 0.810, 0.090, 0.090, and 0.010, respectively. For the FCM with no threshold and with the *y* and *f* input features both at 3.7, the resulting activations for y-F, y-FR, i-F, and i-FR would then be 0.976, 0.500, 0.500, and 0.024, respectively, as illustrated by the first four symbols in Figure 15.27. Two differences between the FLMP and FCM are apparent. First, the FLMP prototype goodnesses sum to 1, but the activations of the FCM sum to 2. This follows from the additive combination of the separate activations for the FCM. Since these sums are in the denominator of the RGR, and the numerator for the FCM can be at most 1, the highest proportion of response that the FCM can predict is 0.5, which is clearly incorrect. The second difference between the

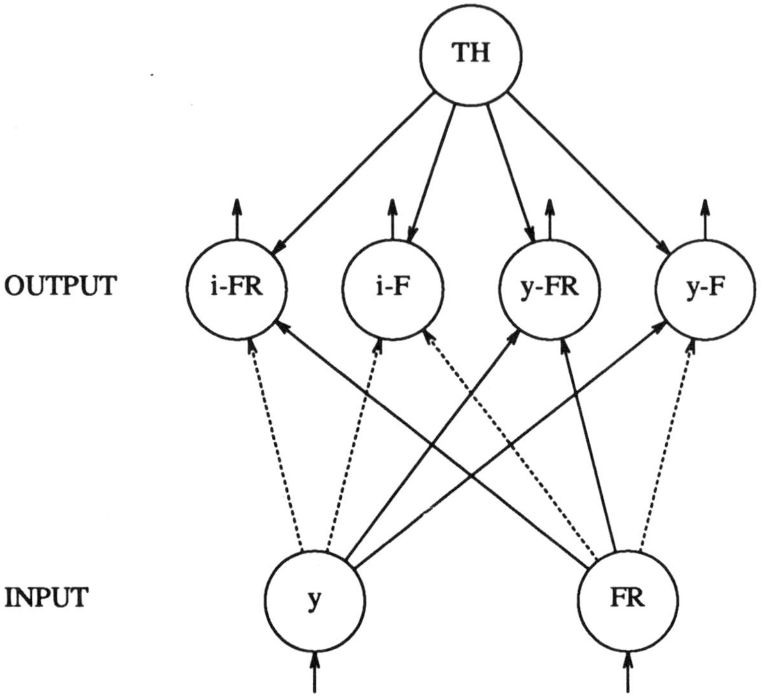

FIG. 15.26. FCM-T for the four-response task. Input and output layers are shown and also an additional threshold unit (TH). Solid arrows indicate connections with weight 1, and dashed arrows indicate connections with weight −1.

models concerns the goodness of the two responses with conflicting information. For the FCM, the goodness of the two responses are centered on the scale at 0.5 (because the opposing features sum to zero). For the FLMP, however, the goodnesses of the responses are both at 0.09.

Now consider what happens when we add a threshold value of −2.3 to each response unit in the FCM. The arrows in the figure indicate this leftward shift of 2.3, which results in the second set of four points in Figure 15.27. In this case, the resulting activations for y-F, y-FR, i-F, and i-FR would then be 0.802, 0.091, 0.091, and 0.002, respectively. These sum to 0.986 and have the center activation asymmetry (not at 0.5 activation for conflicting input values) of the FLMP. This biasing effect of the threshold thus allows the FCM to mimic the overall characteristics of the FLMP.

The mathematics of the four-response FCM-T are not as tractable as for the two-response case. For the network in Figure 15.26 we have the activations:

$$a_{\text{y-F}} = \frac{1}{1 + exp\,[-(y_j + f_k + th)]}\,, \tag{138}$$

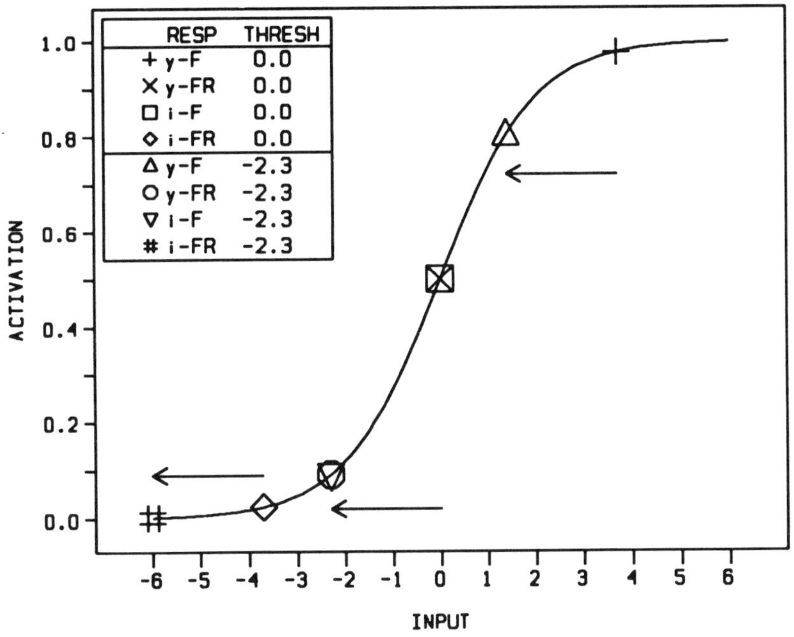

FIG. 15.27. Sigmoid activation curve showing unbiased (threshold = 0.0) and negatively biased (threshold = −2.3) activations. See text for details.

$$a_{\text{y-FR}} = \frac{1}{1 + exp\,[-(y_j - f_k + th)]}\,, \tag{139}$$

$$a_{\text{i-F}} = \frac{1}{1 + exp\,[-(-y_j + f_k + th)]}\,, \tag{140}$$

$$a_{\text{i-FR}} = \frac{1}{1 + exp\,[-(-y_j - f_k + th)]}\,. \tag{141}$$

Given a RGR decision rule, we have (e.g., for y-F):

$$P(\text{y-F}|Y_j \text{ and } F_k) = \tag{142}$$

$$\frac{\dfrac{1}{1 + exp\,[-(y_j + f_k + th)]}}{\dfrac{1}{1 + exp\,[-(y_j + f_k + th)]} + \dfrac{1}{1 + exp\,[-(y_j - f_k + th)]} + \dfrac{1}{1 + exp\,[-(-y_j + f_k + th)]} + \dfrac{1}{1 + exp\,[-(-y_j - f_k + th)]}}.$$

If $th = 0$, we get an ordinary FCM, in which the denominator always sums to 2, producing predictions no greater than 0.5, clearly an incorrect result. If $th \neq 0$, we get the FCM-T, which cannot be factored and is thus mathematically different from the LPM.

FOUR-RESPONSE IAC MODELS

The application of the IAC to the four-response task is straightforward. Figure 15.28 shows the network we used, which contains layers for vowel and tone feature inputs and a layer of memory units for the four-response alternatives. Within each layer, although not shown in the figure, there is mutual inhibition. Each of the memory units receives support from (and sends support back to) one unit in each input layer. The y-F memory unit, for example, is connected to the y vowel unit and the F tone unit.

For the IAC-RGR, each activation after 60 cycles was transformed by Equation 76 to a strength value. For the IAC-RGR5, k was fixed at 5. For the IAC-RGRK, k was an additional free parameter allowed to vary. For both of these models, the resulting strengths were evaluated for a decision using a RGR. For a y-F response, for example, the probability of a response was

$$P(\text{y-F}) = \frac{S_{\text{y-F}}}{S_{\text{y-F}} + S_{\text{y-FR}} + S_{\text{i-F}} + S_{\text{y-FR}}} . \tag{143}$$

For the IAC-BOW model, 1000 simulated trials with Gaussian noise added to the inputs were run with 60 cycles, and the response on each trial was made on the basis of which memory unit had the highest activation on each trial.

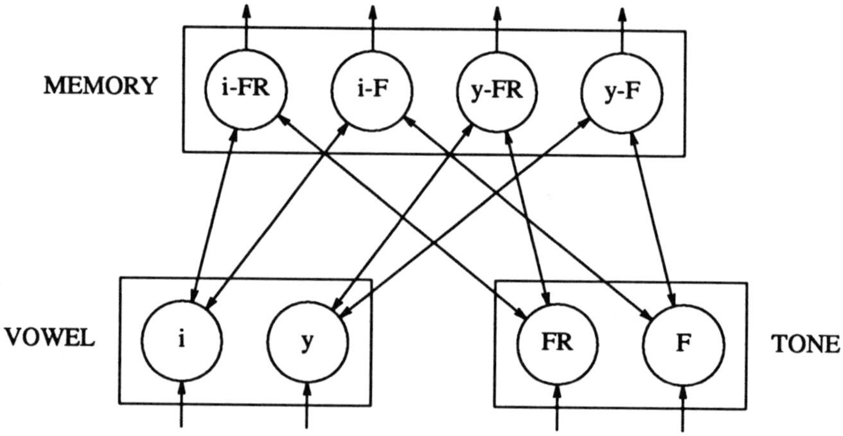

FIG. 15.28. An IAC model for the four-response task. The three layers of units contain input units corresponding to the vowel and tone features, respectively, and to the "prototypes" or memory of i-FR, i-F, y-FR, and y-F. Units between layers have bidirectional excitatory connections indicated by arrows. Bidirectional inhibitory connections exist between all unit pairs within each layer, but have been omitted from the figure for clarity.

MODEL TESTS WITH HYPOTHETICAL FOUR-RESPONSE DATA

The predictions of each model were fit to the predictions of the FLMP (the hypothetical 196 data points shown in Figure 15.20) by using STEPIT. For the fit of the FLMP, 14 parameters were used, 7 for the *y* feature values and 7 for the *f* features. The predictions of this model are shown in Figure 15.20. Table 15.4 summarizes the fits of the various models, giving the RMSDs between the observed and predicted data for each model. As can be seen in the table, the FLMP, BPM, GMM-E, EMM-CB, and TSD-N models all had perfect fits, as predicted by the theoretical analysis. Relative to the two-response task, the alternative metric MDS model versions GMM-CB (RMSD = 0.0205 versus 0.0060 for two-response) and EMM-E (RMSD = 0.0093 versus 0.0002 for two-response) models provided slightly different predictions. As expected, the non-threshold FCM did very poorly (RMSD = 0.2721), whereas the FCM-T gave a good fit (RMSD = 0.0002), mimicking the FLMP with *th* = −8. For the IAC models, the IAC-RGR5 once again gave different predictions (RMSD = 0.0457), and the IAC-RGRK had a good fit to the FLMP predictions (RMSD = 0.0030) with k = 80 and an extremely small range for the feature values. The IAC-BOW provided a good fit (RMSD = 0.0091) with the noise standard deviation at 0.1466.

TABLE 15.4
Model Fits of Hypothetical FLMP Data

Model	*RMSD*
FLMP	.0000
BPM	.0000
GMM-E	.0000
GMM-CB	.0205
EMM-E	.0093
EMM-CB	.0000
TSD-N	.0000
FCM	.2712
FCM-T	.0002
IAC-RGR5	.0521
IAC-RGRK	.0030
IAC-BOW	.0091

MODEL TESTS WITH EXPERIMENTAL FOUR-RESPONSE DATA

As with the two-response experimental data, it is of interest to see whether we can discriminate among these models with real experimental data. Table 15.5 gives the RMSD for each model for each of the six subjects in the QG task, a fit of a mean subject, and the mean of the subject fits. The FLMP and theoretically equivalent (BPM, GMM-E, EMM-CB, TSD) models all had fits of about RMSD = 0.0426. Figure 15.29 shows the fit of the FLMP for the typical subject shown in Figure 15.19. Of the remaining models, none differed significantly from the FLMP in goodness of fit, except the nonthreshold FCM (RMSD = 0.2364), $F(1, 5) = 371.1$, $p < 0.001$, and the IAC-RGR5 (RMSD = 0.0804), $F(1, 5) = 111.5$, $p < 0.001$. For the IAC-RGRK model, the additional k parameter averaged 9.2 and for the IAC-BOW model the standard deviation of the input noise averaged 0.133.

SUMMARY

Several models of categorization were developed and analyzed within the context of prototypical pattern recognition tasks. These tasks involve the independent manipulation of two sources of information. The subject categorizes the stimulus event by choosing among two- or four-response alternatives. This task has been

TABLE 15.5
RMSDs for Model Fits of Four-Response Experimental Data for Six Individual Subjects, Fit of Mean Subject, and Average of Six Subject Fits

Model	*S1*	*S2*	*S3*	*S4*	*S5*	*S6*	*SM*	*AVE*
FLMP	.0331	.0397	.0300	.0450	.0360	.0715	.0265	.0426
BPM	.0326	.0393	.0295	.0449	.0359	.0714	.0262	.0423
GMM-E	.0331	.0397	.0300	.0450	.0360	.0715	.0265	.0426
GMM-CB	.0322	.0387	.0319	.0433	.0348	.0693	.0273	.0417
EMM-E	.0333	.0373	.0293	.0435	.0353	.0705	.0254	.0415
EMM-CB	.0331	.0397	.0300	.0450	.0360	.0715	.0265	.0426
TSD	.0331	.0397	.0300	.0450	.0360	.0715	.0265	.0426
FCM	.2392	.1994	.2203	.2609	.2561	.2423	.2210	.2364
FCM-T	.0309	.0388	.0300	.0425	.0362	.0664	.0264	.0408
IAC-RGR5	.0770	.0686	.0605	.0927	.0816	.1018	.0714	.0804
IAC-RGRK	.0394	.0379	.0300	.0521	.0375	.0776	.0455	.0458
IAC-BOW	.0329	.0395	.0283	.0455	.0358	.0723	.0291	.0424

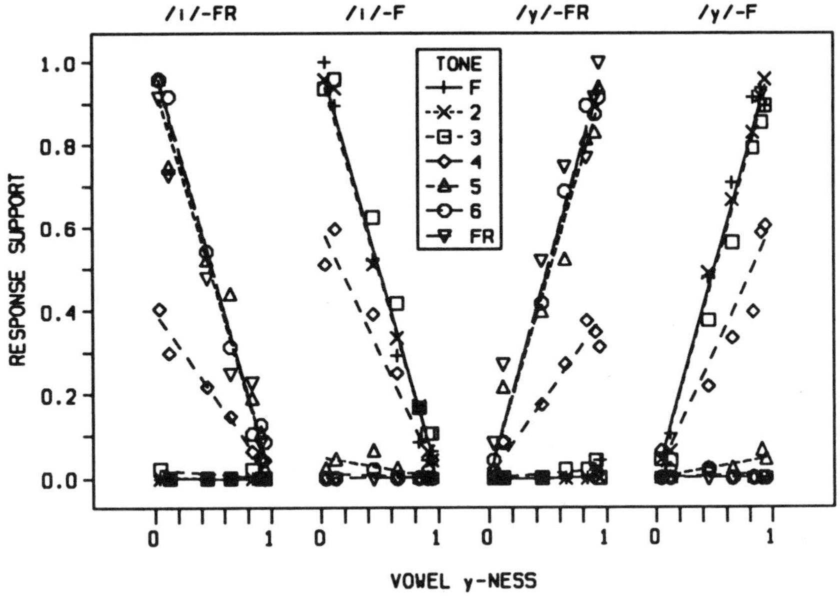

FIG. 15.29. Observed (points) and predicted (lines) proportion of i-FR, i-F, y-FR, and y-F responses for a typical subject. Predictions are for the FLMP and locations on the abscissa are scaled according to the y-ness of the vowel feature parameters.

used in a variety of empirical settings, and a set of prototypical results has been observed. Given that a fuzzy logical model of perception has consistently provided a good description of results in this paradigm, the model's predictions were used as the target predictions for the other models. Evaluation, integration, and decision processes are considered for each model. Important features are whether evaluation is noisy, whether integration follows Bayes' theorem, and whether decision consists of a criterion rule or a relative goodness rule.

The models developed and compared with the FLMP include a model based on Bayes' theorem, models based on multidimensional scaling, the Theory of Signal Detection, a feedforward two-layer connectionist model, and an interactive activation connectionist model. Theoretical analysis of the models reveals that most can be reduced to a canonical likelihood product form. We call this class of models likelihood product models. The required likelihood ratios for this form are given in Tables 15.6 and 15.7 for the two- and four-response tasks, respectively. Additionally, model fits were carried out to determine to what extent the nonequivalent models can make similar predictions.

With two-response alternatives, the results show that all of the models, except the IAC-RGR model, can be brought into line with the predictions of the FLMP and the observed results. Even the IAC model can be saved if activations are

TABLE 15.6
Table of Likelihood Ratios for Likelihood Product Form of Two-Response Models

Model	$l_{GO}(C_j)$	$l_{GO}(O_k)$
FLMP	$\frac{1 - c_j}{c_j}$	$\frac{1 - o_k}{o_k}$
BPM	$\frac{P(C_j \mid G)}{P(C_j \mid Q)}$	$\frac{P(O_k \mid G)}{P(O_k \mid Q)}$
GMM-E	$exp\ (-4Pc_j)$	$exp\ (-4Po_k)$
GMM-CB	—	—
EMM-E	—	—
EMM-CB	$exp\ (\lvert P - c_j \rvert - \lvert -P - c_j \rvert)$	$exp\ (\lvert P - o_k \rvert - \lvert -P - o_k \rvert)$
TSD-N	—	—
TSD-L	$exp\left(-\frac{\pi}{\sqrt{6}} c_j\right)$	$exp\left(-\frac{\pi}{\sqrt{6}} o_k\right)$
FCM	$exp\ (-c_j)$	$exp\ (-o_k)$
IAC-RGR	—	—
IAC-BOW	—	—

TABLE 15.7
Table of Likelihood Ratios for Likelihood Product Form of Four-Response Models

Model	$l_{IY}(Y_j)$	$l_{FRF}(F_k)$
FLMP	$\frac{1 - y_j}{y_j}$	$\frac{1 - f_k}{f_k}$
BPM	$\frac{P(Y_j \mid Y)}{P(Y_j \mid I)}$	$\frac{P(F_k \mid FR)}{P(F_k \mid F)}$
GMM-E	$exp\ (-4Py_j)$	$exp\ (-4Pf_k)$
GMM-CB	—	—
EMM-E	—	—
EMM-CB	$exp\ (\lvert P - y_j \rvert - \lvert -P - y_j \rvert)$	$exp\ (\lvert P - f_k \rvert - \lvert -P - f_k \rvert)$
TSD-N	$\frac{1 - \Phi(y_j)}{\Phi(y_j)}$	$\frac{1 - \Phi(f_k)}{\Phi(f_k)}$
FCM	—	—
FCM-T	—	—
IAC-RGR	—	—
IAC-BOW	—	—

multiplied by a very large constant that has the effect of making activations additive when transformed to logistic values or if a BOW decision rule is used instead of a RGR. With four-response alternatives, similar outcomes are observed except for the FCM. The FCM cannot match the target results unless an additional threshold unit is assumed. The additional free parameter given by the threshold unit makes it possible for a FCM-T to predict the target results.

Given the equivalences found among the models, simple predictions of response probabilities in these categorization tasks are not sufficient to distinguish among the models. Some of these models (e.g., the EMM-CB and GMM-E) can be discriminated when more complex prototype structures are considered (Nosofsky, 1985b, 1987). Other dependent measures, such as ratings, similarity judgments, and reaction times, might also permit tests among the models. For example, it has been shown that the FLMP can account for the dynamics or time-course of processing when a categorization task is embedded in a backward-masking task (Massaro & Cohen, 1991). The IAC model had difficulty predicting these same results. To date, the other models have not been systematically developed to make predictions about the time course of processing. Future work should address this issue because psychologists should be concerned with differentiating among models of human performance (Townsend, 1990). Many of the models presented here assumed equal, uncorrelated distributions. We acknowledge that this is not always the case (e.g., with the correlated stimulus dimensions used by Ashby and Gott, 1988), and the theoretical comparison of models should be extended to more general distribution models (see chap. 16).

List Symbols

act_i	activation of unit i
a_n	support for prototype n in FLMP
α	excitatory strength parameter in IAC
A_n	degree of support for response n in FLMP
BPM	Bayesian probability model
c_{EMM}	closedness coordinate in EMM
c_{FCM}	closedness activation in FCM
c_{FLMP}	closedness feature value in FLMP
c_{GMM}	closedness coordinate in GMM
c_{TSD}	closedness coordinate in TSD
C_j	closedness stimulus level j
c_j	closedness feature value of C_j
d(a,b)	distance from a to b in space
decay	rate of activation decay parameter in IAC
d'	*d* prime metric

e	event or source of evidence
$estr$	external strength parameter in IAC
EMM-CB	exponential multidimensional model—city-block metric
EMM-E	exponential multidimensional model—euclidean metric
exc_i	excitatory inputs to unit i in IAC
$exp\ (x)$	2.71828^x
ext_i	external inputs to unit i in IAC
F_0	fundamental frequency or pitch
FCM	feedforward connectionist model
FCM-T	feedforward connectionist model with threshold
F	Chinese falling tone
FR	Chinese falling-rising tone
F_k	falling-tone stimulus level k
f_k	falling-tone feature value from F_k
FLMP	fuzzy logical model of perception
f_{FLMP}	falling-tone feature value of FLMP
f_{TSD}	falling-tone coordinate of TSD
γ	inhibitory strength parameter in IAC
GMM-CB	Gaussian multidimensional model—city-block metric
GMM-E	Gaussian multidimensional model—euclidean metric
h_i	hypothesis i
i	vowel /i/ as in "she"
IAC-BOW	interactive activation and competition model—best-one-wins rule
IAC-RGR	interactive activation and competition model—relative goodness rule
inh_i	inhibitory inputs to unit i in IAC
$L(x)$	cumulative logistic function of x
l_{kj}	likelihood ratio of hypothesis k to hypothesis j
LPM	likelihood product model
M	maximum activation level parameter in IAC
m	minimum activation level parameter in IAC
net_i	summed input activation to unit i in IAC
o_{EMM}	obliqueness coordinate of EMM
o_{FCM}	obliqueness activation of FCM
o_{FLMP}	obliqueness feature value of FLMP
o_{GMM}	obliqueness coordinate of GMM

o_{TSD}	obliqueness coordinate of TSD
O_k	obliqueness stimulus level k
o_k	obliqueness feature value from O_k
$\Phi(x)$	cumulative normal function of x
rest	resting activation level parameter in IAC
s(a,b)	similarity of a and b
S_i	strength of response i in IAC
TSD-L	Theory of Signal Detection model—cumulative logistic distribution
TSD-N	Theory of Signal Detection model—cumulative normal distribution
w_{ij}	weight to unit i from unit j in IAC
y	Chinese vowel /y/, rounded version of /i/
y_{FLMP}	y-ness feature value of FLMP
Y_j	y-ness stimulus level j
y_j	y-ness feature value from Y_j
y_{TSD}	y-ness coordinate of TSD

ACKNOWLEDGMENTS

We thank Greg Ashby, an anonymous reviewer, and Antoinette Gesi for their helpful comments. The authors of this collaborative effort are listed in alphabetical order. The research reported in this paper and the writing of the paper were supported, in part, by grants to Dominic W. Massaro from the Public Health Service (PHS R01 NS 20314), the National Science Foundation (BNS 8812728), a James McKeen Cattell Fellowship, and the graduate division of the University of California, Santa Cruz.

16 Multidimensional Models of Categorization

F. Gregory Ashby
Department of Psychology
University of California at Santa Barbara

Categorization is fundamentally important in perception and cognition. Everyday we make hundreds of categorization judgments. In the words of George Lakoff (1987), "every time we see something as a *kind* of thing, for example, a tree, we are categorizing" (p. 5).

The long history of categorization as a topic of intellectual curiosity and scientific investigation is in keeping with the important role that it plays in our everyday lives. The oldest theory of human categorization, known as the Classical Theory, dates back to Aristotle. The Classical Theory assumes that a category can be represented as a set of necessary and sufficient conditions (e.g., Bruner, Goodnow, & Austin, 1956; Smith & Medin, 1981). Therefore, the categorization process is a matter of testing whether the object in question possesses each of these conditions. If it does, it is judged to be a member of the category. If any of the conditions are missing, it cannot be a member of the category. For example, an equilateral triangle: (a) is a closed figure, (b) has three sides, (c) has all sides of equal length, and (d) is constructed only of line segments. Any figure that has these four properties is an equilateral triangle, and every equilateral triangle has these four properties.

Classical Theory remained dominant through the first half of this century, but in the 1950s it began to suffer heavy criticism. First, Wittgenstein (1953) pointed out that the exemplars of some categories did not all share the same properties. In fact, exemplars of some categories, like "games," might not have any properties in common. For example, most games involve competition, but some do not (e.g., ring-around-the-rosy). Second, Wittgenstein argued that one exemplar that satisfies all of the necessary and sufficient conditions of a category should be as good an example of that category as any other exemplar that satisfies the same set of necessary and sufficient conditions. He argued that chess is better than dice at representing the category "game." It appears that the Classical Theory of categorization cannot account for these facts.

Experimental support for Wittgenstein's conjecture about differences in goodness of example came from studies by Rips, Shoben, and Smith (1973) and by Rosch (1973b; see also, McCloskey & Glucksberg, 1979; Mervis & Rosch, 1981; Rosch, 1975). In both studies, subjects were presented with the name of a category exemplar and were then asked to indicate its typicality or representativeness with respect to that category. For example, subjects reliably rated a robin as a more typical bird than a goose, and a deer as a more typical mammal than a pig. Furthermore, the most typical category member, called the prototype, shows advantages over other exemplars in a variety of categorization tasks. For example, the prototypes are the first exemplars learned by children (Mervis, 1980; Rosch, 1973b), and they are likely to be named first when subjects are asked to recall all members of a category (Mervis, Catlin, & Rosch, 1976). In addition, if subjects are asked to verify whether a probe item is a member of a category, the fastest yes responses are to the category prototypes (Rips, Shoben, & Smith, 1973; Rosch, 1973b).

Rosch persuasively argued that a viable theory of categorization must account for these prototypicality effects (1973a, 1973b, 1977; see also Homa, Sterling, & Trepel, 1981; Rosch, Simpson, & Miller, 1976). As a consequence, Prototype Theory was proposed as an alternative to Classical Theory. The idea is that a category is distributed around its most typical member, called the prototype (Posner & Keele, 1968, 1970). Reed (1972) formalized these ideas with what he called the prototype model, which assumes that, when asked to assign a stimulus to one of several categories, the subject responds with the category possessing the most similar prototype. Prototype Theory is able to account for many of the results that were troublesome to Classical Theory. For example, because a category is no longer a set of necessary and sufficient conditions, there is no reason to expect category exemplars to all share some property in common. Also, as the similarity of an exemplar to the prototype increases, the typicality of that exemplar with respect to the category increases, so Prototype Theory nicely accounts for the main typicality effects.

Although Prototype Theory was seen as an improvement over the Classical Theory of categorization, it soon began to suffer its own criticisms. These came from two directions (see Smith & Medin, 1981, for a more thorough discussion of these). First, in most instantiations of Prototype Theory, similarity was assumed to be inversely related to psychological distance. Several chapters in Part II of this volume have questioned the empirical validity of this assumption (see also, Ashby & Perrin, 1988; Krumhansl, 1978; Tversky, 1977; Tversky & Gati, 1982). The second line of attack was more damaging. Essentially, simple Prototype Theory assumes that the mental representation of a category consists of a single example, namely the prototype. A number of studies have shown convincingly that other category exemplars, besides the prototype, can have pronounced effects on categorization performance (e.g., Brooks, 1978; Hayes-Roth & Hayes-Roth, 1977; Medin & Schaffer, 1978; Medin & Schwanenflugel, 1981; Neumann, 1974; Reber, 1976; Reber & Allen, 1978; Walker, 1975). For example, it has been demonstrated that categorization performance may be affected if the exemplars possess correlated attributes (e.g., Ashby & Gott, 1988; Ashby & Maddox, 1990, 1992; Medin, Altom, Edelson, & Freko, 1982).

Rosch (1975, 1978) acknowledged the difficulties with the simple prototype model and proposed that, instead of representing a category as a single prototype, subjects often choose multiple prototypes. For example, both robin and sparrow seem to be prototypes for the category "bird." In a categorization task, a subject might recall all prototypes of each relevant category, compute similarity of the test stimulus to each of these prototypes, and then somehow select a response.

As the number of prototypes that describe a category increases it begins to make less sense to call them prototypes. Eventually the model becomes an *exemplar* model. In its extreme form, Exemplar Theory postulates no special role for the prototype. Instead, on each trial, subjects are assumed to perform some sort of global match between the representation of the presented stimulus and the memory representation of *every* exemplar of each category and to choose a response on the basis of these similarity computations. This idea was elaborated and formalized by several investigators (Brooks, 1978; Estes, 1986; Hintzman, 1986; Medin & Schaffer, 1978; Nosofsky, 1986). Exemplar theories have successfully accounted for a wide variety of categorization results (see, e.g., Smith & Medin, 1981; see also chap. 14). Even so, it seems unlikely that the global matching operation includes *all* members of each category, especially in tasks involving the *natural* categories with which we are most familiar. For example, when deciding that a chicken is a bird, it seems unlikely that we compute the similarity of the chicken in question to every bird we have ever seen.

Closely related to exemplar theory is *General Recognition Theory* (GRT; Ashby, 1988, 1989; Ashby & Gott, 1988; Ashby & Lee, 1991; Ashby & Maddox, 1990, 1991a, in press; Ashby & Perrin, 1988; Ashby & Townsend, 1986). Like Exemplar Theory, GRT assumes that categorization performance depends on all category exemplars. Rather than assuming that subjects match the stimulus representation to the memory representation of every exemplar of each category, GRT assumes that the subject learns to assign responses to regions of the perceptual space. On each trial, the subject determines in which region the stimulus representation falls and then emits the associated response. Several versions of the theory can be formulated, depending on how the subject divides the perceptual space into response regions. Like Exemplar Theory, GRT has been found to provide a better description of categorization data in a variety of situations than either the Classical Theory or Prototype Theory (Ashby & Gott, 1988; Ashby & Maddox, 1990, 1992).

In spite of the apparently large differences between each of these categorization theories, all categorization models make three kinds of assumptions: (a) *representation* assumptions, (b) *retrieval* assumptions, and (c) *response selection* assumptions. The representation assumptions describe the internal representation of the stimulus and the contrasting categories. Most of the theories described explicitly assume that the perceptual effect of a stimulus presentation can be represented as a point in a multidimensional space, but the theories differ on the issue of whether there is variability in the percepts associated with a single stimulus and in how categories should be represented.

The retrieval assumptions form the soul of the categorization theories. They describe the exact information that must be collected before a response can be made. For example, exemplar theories state that the subject must compute the similarity of the stimulus representation to the memory representation of every exemplar of each category. GRT assumes that the subject needs only to determine the location of the stimulus representation within the perceptual space.

Finally, the response selection assumptions describe how the subject selects a response after all the relevant information has been collected. The major point of contention between the current models is whether response selection is *deterministic* or *probabilistic*. A deterministic response selection process always chooses the same response given the same information, whereas a probabilistic process does not.

The remainder of this chapter examines each assumption class in turn. This provides a common language from which to describe and formally compare the various theories. The discussion begins with the representation assumptions, proceeds with the response selection assumptions, and finishes with the retrieval assumptions.

REPRESENTATION ASSUMPTIONS

Prototype, Exemplar, and General Recognition Theories all assume that the percept associated with any single exposure to a stimulus can be represented as a point in a multidimensional space. This assumption is not without controversy. Tversky, among others, has argued persuasively for nonnumeric representation (Sattath & Tversky, 1977; Tversky, 1972b, 1977). When a stimulus is represented as a point in a multidimensional space, there must be some other point that is its nearest neighbor. Geometric models impose an upper bound on the number of stimuli that can share the same nearest neighbor. For example, when points are distributed on a line, any single point can be the nearest neighbor of at most two other points. In two dimensions, a point can be the nearest neighbor to at most five other points. This bound is even sharper if it is assumed that the points are samples from a continuous probability distribution. In an examination of 100 data sets, Tversky and Hutchinson (1986) found this upper bound to be satisfied with most perceptual data sets but to be violated with many conceptual data sets. Violations were most severe in conceptual data sets containing a superordinate category label. For example, Mervis, Rips, Rosch, Shoben, and Smith (1975) found that 18 of 20 fruit names were judged to be most related to the word "fruit." In summary, the assumption that a percept can be represented as a point in a multidimensional space seems valid with perceptual stimuli. With some conceptual stimulus sets, especially those containing a superordinate category label, the assumption may be inappropriate. A later section considers this point in more detail.

To formalize the notion that any single exposure to a stimulus can be represented as a point in a multidimensional space, consider a stimulus ensemble in which each member can be defined by a set of coordinates in some physical space of dimension s. Suppose the subject's percept of each stimulus can be defined by a set of coordinates in some perceptual space of dimension r. Denote the coordinates of stimulus $\mathbf{S}_i$ in the physical space by the vector $\mathbf{y}_i$ and in the perceptual space by $\mathbf{x}_i$. Let the psychophysical function ψ map the physical space into the perceptual. Thus

$$\psi(\mathbf{y}_i) = \mathbf{x}_i \, . \tag{1}$$

Essentially, this is the perceptual representation assumed by the prototype and exemplar models considered here.

GRT extends this representation by assuming

$$\psi(\mathbf{y}_i) = \mathbf{x}_{pi} = \mathbf{x}_i + \mathbf{e}_{pi} \, , \tag{2}$$

where $\mathbf{e}_{pi}$ is a random vector with mean $\mathbf{0}$. All applications to date have assumed that $\mathbf{e}_{pi}$ is multivariate normal with covariance matrix $\mathbf{\Sigma}_{pi}$. Therefore, in GRT, the perceptual effects of *each* exemplar of a category are represented by a multivariate probability distribution. A category is represented perceptually as a probability mixture of the individual exemplar distributions. When a category contains a finite number of exemplars, the probability density function of the perceptual effects associated with category A is

$$f_A(\mathbf{x}) = \sum_{i \in C_A} p_A(i) f_i(\mathbf{x}) \, , \tag{3}$$

where $p_A(i)$ is the probability that exemplar $\mathbf{S}_i$ is presented as a member of category A, and $f_i(\mathbf{x})$ is the probability density function of $\mathbf{x}_{pi}$.

Several special cases of the Equation 2 GRT representation are of particular interest. Stimulus-invariant GRT models assume that all covariance matrices are equal; that is, $\mathbf{\Sigma}_{pi} = \mathbf{\Sigma}_p$ for all values of i. If, in addition, the covariance matrix $\mathbf{\Sigma}_p$ is assumed to be diagonal, the result is a stimulus-invariant uncorrelated GRT model. Finally, a simple GRT model assumes that $\mathbf{\Sigma}_p$ is some scalar multiple of the identity matrix (i.e., $\mathbf{\Sigma}_p = \sigma_p^2\mathbf{I}$).

Whereas many of the models make the same assumptions about the perceptual representation of the single presentation of a stimulus, there is less agreement about how a category should be represented in the stimulus (i.e., physical) space. The Classical Theory is mute with respect to representation. Exemplar Theories assume no specific category structure. Prototype Theories often assume that a category is distributed around its prototype and thus that the prototype plays the role of a centroid (e.g., Homa, Sterling, & Trepel, 1981). GRT has gone further and assumed that the structure of many natural categories can be effectively modeled by the multivariate normal distribution (Ashby & Maddox 1990, 1991a, 1992). The argument proceeds as follows.

What properties characterize the categories with which we are most familiar? First, most natural categories have a very large, if not unlimited, number of exemplars. Second, the dimensions of natural categories are continuous-valued. Third, many natural categories overlap. Fourth, the distribution of exemplars within a category tends to be unimodal and symmetric, or at least this is the null hypothesis of most subjects when they are confronted with an unfamiliar category (Flannagan, Fried, & Holyoak, 1986; Fried & Holyoak, 1984).

Although it is common in psychological research to construct categories with only a few exemplars, this practice has only limited ecological validity (Homa, Sterling, & Trepel, 1981). Think of all the handwritten characters that we categorize as the letter "a," all of the trees that we call "pine," all of the objects that we call "chair," or all of the people that we call "Caucasian." In fact, it is difficult to think of any natural categories that have only a few exemplars.

Another common experimental practice is to use binary-valued dimensions when constructing exemplars of an artificial category. This practice also has limited ecological validity. For example, trees vary continuously in height, in girth, in hue, and in the texture of their bark. One popular experimental setting that consistently uses binary-valued dimensions is disease diagnosis. In these tasks, subjects are told that a battery of tests has been given to a patient, that each test can be either positive or negative, and that a certain pattern of test results is characteristic of a particular disease. The subjects are then given the outcome of a set of tests and asked to make a diagnosis. Is this realistic? How many medical tests actually give binary-valued results? For example, high blood pressure could indicate heart disease, but blood pressure does not have either a single high value or a single low value. Instead, it is continuous-valued. A physician might decide on the basis of some continuous-valued blood pressure level that a patient has high blood pressure, but then it is the decision that is binary-valued, not the percept. Even a simple home pregnancy test is not binary-valued. For a variety of reasons, the testing material will display a continuum of hues, even if the woman is pregnant.

Still another characteristic of experimenter-defined categories is that they do not overlap, and so perfect categorization is possible. Although many natural categories also share this property, many do not. The same handwritten character may one time signify the letter "a" and another time the letter "c." A person might look like the prototype of one race but be a member of another. In these cases, perfect categorization is impossible, and, precisely for this reason, overlapping categories are the most theoretically interesting. Virtually all theories of categorization predict that subjects will never confuse vegetables and automobiles, but only a few (if any) can predict the categorization errors that occur when wine tasters separate Zinfandels and Pinot Noirs.

Finally, there is preliminary empirical evidence that subjects enter categorization tasks with the expectation that the exemplars of each category are symmetrically and unimodally distributed around some prototype (Flannagan et al., 1986; Fried & Holyoak, 1984). It is difficult to say whether natural categories objectively possess this property. For example, are more birds similar to the prototypical robin than to the atypical chicken? Perhaps so, but if we are interested in human categorization performance, then all that really matters is the subject's expectation about the category. Therefore, our category model should have the exemplars symmetrically distributed around a single prototypical value.

A model that possesses each of these four properties is the multivariate normal distribution. It assumes an unlimited number of exemplars, its dimensions are continuous-valued, it postulates a few extremely atypical members, and thus will overlap with nearby categories, and it is unimodal and symmetric. Therefore, in what follows, the exemplars in a category are assumed to be normally distributed on each perceptual dimension. For example, consider the stimuli in Figure 16.1. In one case, we might be dealing with categories of rectangles. Within each category, the length and width of the rectangles are normally distributed. In another case, the category exemplars might be the circular stimuli in Figure 16.1b. Within each of these categories, the size of the circle and the orientation of the radial line are normally distributed.

Let the mean of category A be denoted by $\boldsymbol{\mu}_A$ and the covariance matrix by $\boldsymbol{\Sigma}_A$. In a normal distribution, the mean, median, and mode are all equal, so $\boldsymbol{\mu}_A$ is a good candidate for the category prototype. For example, in Figure 16.1, the two rectangles might correspond to the means of two different categories. The exact length and width of the two rectangles would then specify the coordinates of each category mean.

For stimuli like those in Figure 16.1, we expect the psychophysical function ψ to be approximately linear. In this case, if the $\mathbf{y}_i$ (i.e., the stimulus coordinates) are normally distributed, then so are the $\mathbf{x}_i$ (i.e., their mean percepts). In fact, for convenience, assume that $\mathbf{x}_i = \mathbf{y}_i$. If the distribution of perceptual noise depends on the stimulus (i.e., if $\boldsymbol{\Sigma}_{pi} \neq \boldsymbol{\Sigma}_{pj}$ when $i \neq j$), then this model has an infinite number of free parameters. Therefore, when GRT is applied to experiments with normally distributed categories, some simplifying assumptions are needed, such as perceptual noise is stimulus-invariant. In this case, Equation 2 implies that the perceived category A distribution, $f_A(\mathbf{x})$, is multivariate normal with mean vector

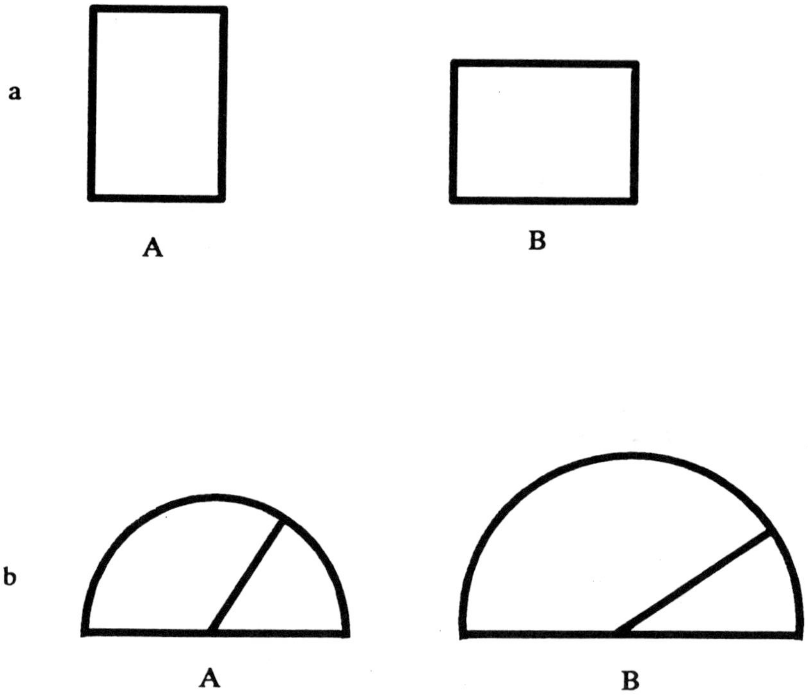

FIG. 16.1. Examples of experimental stimuli.

$\boldsymbol{\mu}_{Ap} = \boldsymbol{\mu}_A$ and covariance matrix $\boldsymbol{\Sigma}_{Ap} = \boldsymbol{\Sigma}_A + \boldsymbol{\Sigma}_p$. In other words, a probability mixture of multivariate normal distributions itself has a multivariate normal distribution if the mixture distribution is multivariate normal.

Another interpretation of this model is that although category J has covariance matrix $\boldsymbol{\Sigma}_J$, because of perceptual error, the subject perceives it to have covariance matrix $\boldsymbol{\Sigma}_{Jp} = \boldsymbol{\Sigma}_J + \boldsymbol{\Sigma}_p$. Thus, on each trial, the subject's task is to determine whether the percept $\mathbf{x}_p$ is a member of perceived category A, with mean vector $\boldsymbol{\mu}_{Ap} = \boldsymbol{\mu}_A$ and covariance matrix $\boldsymbol{\Sigma}_{Ap} = \boldsymbol{\Sigma}_A + \boldsymbol{\Sigma}_p$, or a member of perceived category B, with mean vector $\boldsymbol{\mu}_{Bp} = \boldsymbol{\mu}_B$ and covariance matrix $\boldsymbol{\Sigma}_{Bp} = \boldsymbol{\Sigma}_B + \boldsymbol{\Sigma}_p$.

GRT therefore specifies two different sources of variation: within-exemplar and between-exemplar. Within-exemplar variation is described by the covariance matrix $\boldsymbol{\Sigma}_p$. Ashby and Maddox (1991a) assumed that the perceptual variability was equal on each stimulus dimension and that no perceptual correlation existed. Under these conditions $\boldsymbol{\Sigma}_p = \sigma_p^2\mathbf{I}$. Within-exemplar variation is therefore completely determined by the perceptual noise variance σ_p^2. The amount of perceptual noise to be expected is determined by the integrity of the stimulus presentation. Tachistoscopic presentation, low contrast, or masking would all be expected to increase perceptual noise. Between-exemplar variation, described by $\boldsymbol{\Sigma}_A$, is determined by the nature of the category. In general, between-exemplar variation will increase with the pairwise dissimilarity of the category exemplars. With highly discriminable stimuli presented for long durations at high contrast, within-exemplar variation may often be negligible when contrasted with between-exemplar variation; that is, the variances on the main diagonal of $\mathbf{\Sigma}_A$ may be orders of magnitude larger than the perceptual noise variance σ_p^2. In this case, the perceptual representation of each exemplar may be approximated as a point in a multidimensional space and the category as a distribution of exemplar points.

RESPONSE SELECTION ASSUMPTIONS

Two kinds of response selection assumptions are popular. The first assumption is that given a stimulus with perceptual coordinates $\mathbf{x}$, the probability of responding $\mathbf{R}_A$ is computed from the similarity-choice model (Luce, 1963a; Shepard, 1957). Specifically, in a categorization task with categories A and B,

$$P(\mathbf{R}_A|\mathbf{x}) = \frac{\beta_A \eta_{\mathbf{x}A}}{\beta_A \eta_{\mathbf{x}A} + \beta_B \eta_{\mathbf{x}B}}, \quad (4)$$

where β_J is the response bias toward category J and $\eta_{\mathbf{x}J}$ is the similarity of the stimulus to category J. Without loss of generality, one can assume that $\beta_B = 1 - \beta_A$.

This response model has been incorporated into the most widely known exemplar models, namely, the context model (Medin & Schaffer, 1978) and the generalized context model (Nosofsky, 1986). In this case $\eta_{\mathbf{x}J}$ is equal to the sum of the similarities of stimulus $\mathbf{x}$ to all exemplars in category J. The similarity-choice response selection model has also been incorporated into a probabilistic prototype model (Ashby & Maddox, in press; Nosofsky, 1987). In this case $\eta_{\mathbf{x}J}$ equals the similarity of $\mathbf{x}$ to the category J prototype.

The major competing hypothesis is that response selection is a deterministic process. Let $h(\mathbf{x})$ be some function of the perceptual coordinates with the property that $\mathbf{x}$ is more likely to be a member of category A when $h(\mathbf{x})$ is negative and a member of category B when $h(\mathbf{x})$ is positive. For example, in exemplar or prototype models $h(\mathbf{x})$ might equal $\eta_{\mathbf{x}B} - \eta_{\mathbf{x}A}$. Then the deterministic decision rule is to

$$\text{Respond } \mathbf{R}_A \text{ if } h(\mathbf{x}) < \delta\text{; otherwise respond } \mathbf{R}_B\ .$$

Note that δ is a bias parameter. When $\delta > 0$, response $\mathbf{R}_A$ is favored, and when $\delta < 0$, response $\mathbf{R}_B$ is favored.

It is rarely the case, however, that categorization data appear deterministic, especially if between-category similarity is high. It is important to realize that this fact does not falsify the notion of a deterministic decision process. The presence of perceptual and criterial noise obscure deterministic responding. For example, consider some exemplar, say $\mathbf{S}_i$ of category A. Variability in the response to the presentation of $\mathbf{S}_i$ might come from any of several sources. First, the subject's percept of $\mathbf{S}_i$ may vary over trials. This variability is called perceptual noise. Second, even in the absence of perceptual noise, the subject's memory of δ may vary over trials. This variability is called criterial noise.

With perceptual noise, the perceived value of the stimulus is $\mathbf{x}_p = \mathbf{x} + \mathbf{e}_p$, and with criterial noise the subject determines the referent to be $\delta + e_c$, where e_c is a random variable with mean 0. Under these conditions, the rule becomes

$$\text{Respond } \mathbf{R}_A \text{ if } h(\mathbf{x}_p) < \delta + e_c; \text{ otherwise respond } \mathbf{R}_B . \tag{5}$$

Note that this rule is no longer deterministic in the sense that the same response is always given to the same stimulus $\mathbf{x}$. However, it is deterministic in the sense that response $\mathbf{R}_A$ is given with probability 1.0 if $h(\mathbf{x}_p) < \delta + e_c$.

A number of studies have attempted to test whether subjects use deterministic or probabilistic decision rules, by using an experimental paradigm known as the numerical decision task (Hammerton, 1970; Healy & Kubovy, 1977; Kubovy & Healy, 1977; Kubovy, Rapoport, & Tversky, 1971; Lee & Janke, 1964, 1965; Ward, 1973; Weissmann, Hollingsworth, & Baird, 1975). In this task, two categories are created by specifying two univariate normal distributions of numbers. On each trial, a number is sampled from one of the distributions and presented to the subject. The subject's task is to assign the stimulus to one of the two categories. In general, these studies have favored deterministic rules over probabilistic rules. For example, Kubovy and his colleagues (Kubovy & Healy, 1977; Kubovy et al., 1971) found that a fixed cutoff accounted for the data significantly better than a probabilistic decision rule (Lee's, 1963, micromatching model), but that it still mispredicted a small percentage of the responses (5.87% in Kubovy et al., 1971).

Ashby and Gott (1988) reported the results of a number of categorization experiments with stimuli like the rectangles in Figure 16.1 (except the right vertical and bottom horizontal segments were deleted). Each task involved two categories (A and B), and the exemplars in each category had bivariate normal distributions. In some conditions, responding was highly deterministic. This was especially true in conditions in which the optimal decision rule was to give response A if the vertical length was less than the horizontal length, and response B if the vertical length was greater than the horizontal length. Note that in this case, no internal referent is required, and thus there should be no criterial noise. With response-terminated displays of high contrast, perceptual noise should be small, so under these conditions a deterministic decision process with perceptual and criterial noise predicts near-deterministic responding. These data are extremely difficult for models with probabilistic decision processes to predict.

In most experiments, however, perceptual and criterial noise are expected. Although probabilistic and deterministic decision rules appear very different, in these cases they often make similar predictions. In fact, the following result, due to Ashby and Maddox (in press), shows that it is always possible to construct a deterministic decision rule that is mathematically equivalent to the similarity-choice model.

Proposition 16.1: Assume there is no perceptual noise (so that Equation 1 holds). Suppose that a subject uses the decision rule:

$$\text{Respond } \mathbf{R}_A \text{ if } ln\,(\eta_{\mathbf{x}A}) - ln\,(\eta_{\mathbf{x}B}) > \delta + e_c\,;$$
$$\text{otherwise respond } \mathbf{R}_B\,.$$

where the criterial noise e_c is assumed to have a logistic distribution with mean 0 and variance σ_c^2 (i.e., see Equation 20 of chap. 1). Then the probability of responding $\mathbf{R}_A$, given $\mathbf{x}$, is

$$P(\mathbf{R}_A|\mathbf{x}) = \frac{\beta\eta_{\mathbf{x}A}^{\gamma}}{\beta\eta_{\mathbf{x}A}^{\gamma} + (1 - \beta)\eta_{\mathbf{x}B}^{\gamma}}, \tag{6}$$

where

$$\gamma = \frac{\pi}{\sqrt{3}\,\sigma_c} \quad \text{and} \quad \beta = \frac{e^{\delta\gamma}}{1 + e^{\delta\gamma}}.$$

Thus, the Proposition 16.1 deterministic decision rule predicts exactly the same response probabilities as the similarity-choice model when $\gamma = 1$ or, equivalently, when the criterial noise variance $\sigma_c^2 = \pi^2/3$.

Suppose the Equation 6 model is fit to a set of categorization data, and accurate estimates of the γ parameter are obtained. These parameter estimates can be used to determine whether responding is more or less variable than predicted by the similarity-choice model. If $\gamma < 1$, the transition from a small value of $P(\mathbf{R}_A|\mathbf{x})$ to a large value is more gradual than predicted by the similarity-choice model; responding is too variable. If $\gamma > 1$, the transition is more abrupt than the similarity-choice model predicts; that is, the subject is responding with too little variability.

Ashby and Maddox (1991a) fit the Equation 6 model to the data from four experiments, each involving the two stimulus sets illustrated in Figure 16.1. Each experiment involved (bivariate) normally distributed categories. For 24 of the 28 subjects, the estimated value of γ was greater than 1.0 in the best-fitting version of the Equation 6 model. Thus, in these experiments, responding was less variable than the similarity-choice model predicts.

RETRIEVAL ASSUMPTIONS

Decision Bound Models

General Recognition Theory

General Recognition Theory (GRT) assumes that on each trial a practiced subject divides the perceptual space into regions and associates a category label with each region (Ashby, 1989; Ashby & Gott, 1988; Ashby & Maddox, 1990,

1991a, 1992). On each trial the subject determines in which region the stimulus representation falls and then emits the associated response. The line or curve separating two response regions is called the *decision bound*. Several versions of the theory can be formulated, depending on how the subject divides the perceptual space into response regions. The five versions considered in this chapter are: (a) the general quadratic classifier, (b) the optimal classifier, (c) the general linear classifier, (d) the minimum distance classifier, and (e) the independent decisions classifier.

In each of these models it is possible to define a function h, with the property that points on the decision bound satisfy $h(\mathbf{x}) = 0$, points in the region assigned to response $\mathbf{R}_A$ satisfy $h(\mathbf{x}) < 0$, and points in the region assigned to response $\mathbf{R}_B$ satisfy $h(\mathbf{x}) > 0$. Thus, with perceptual and criterial noise and with a response bias, GRT models assume the subject uses the Equation 5 decision rule. The probability of responding $\mathbf{R}_A$ is therefore

$$\begin{aligned} P(\mathbf{R}_A|\mathbf{x}) &= P[h(\mathbf{x}_p) < \delta + e_c|\mathbf{x}] \\ &= P[h(\mathbf{x}_p) - e_c < \delta|\mathbf{x}] \\ &= P[h(\mathbf{x}_p) + e_c < \delta|\mathbf{x}]\ . \end{aligned} \tag{7}$$

The latter equality holds because the distribution of e_c is symmetric (i.e., normal) with mean zero.

Suppose $h(\mathbf{x}_p)$ is normally distributed with mean $\mu_{h(\mathbf{x})}$ and variance $\sigma^2_{h(\mathbf{x})}$. Then Equation 7 reduces to

$$P(\mathbf{R}_A|\mathbf{x}) = \Phi\left(\frac{\delta - \mu_{h(\mathbf{x})}}{\sqrt{\sigma^2_{h(\mathbf{x})} + \sigma^2_c}}\right), \tag{8}$$

where $\Phi(\mathbf{z})$ is the cumulative Z distribution function evaluated at $\mathbf{z}$.

The General Quadratic Classifier. When $\Sigma_A \neq \Sigma_B$ the optimal classifier uses a quadratic decision bound. Suppose a subject attempts to respond optimally but underestimates one of the within-category correlation coefficients or overestimates the amount of variability along a stimulus dimension in one of the categories. In this case, the subject will use a quadratic rule, but not the one that is optimal for this problem. The general quadratic classifier assumes only that the subject uses *some* quadratic decision bound.

With two perceptual dimensions x_1 and x_2, every quadratic bound satisfies

$$h(x_1,x_2) = a_1x_1^2 + a_2x_2^2 + a_3x_1x_2 + b_1x_1 + b_2x_2 + c_0 = 0 \tag{9}$$

for some constants a_1, a_2, a_3, b_1, b_2, and c_0. An example is shown in Figure 16.2a. Suppose, for illustrative purposes, that the categories depicted in Figure 16.2 contain exemplars like the circular stimuli in Figure 16.1b. Let dimension x_1 correspond to perceived size, and dimension x_2 correspond to perceived orientation. Note that the exemplars in category B have more variability on the size

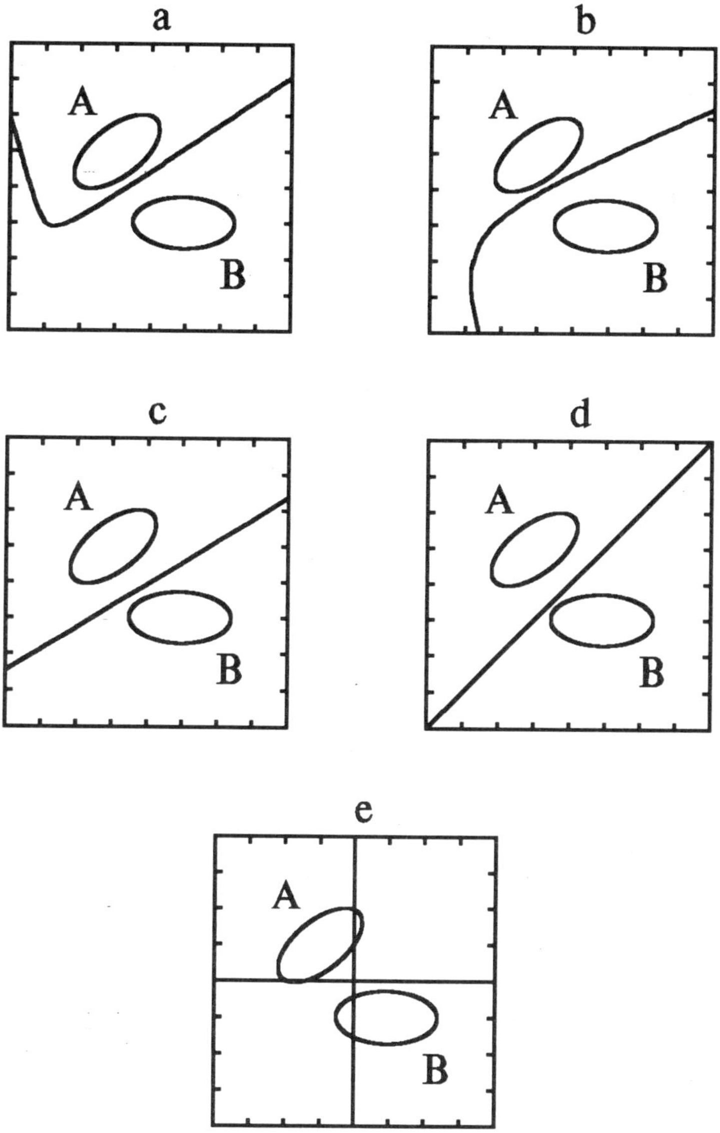

FIG. 16.2. Decision bounds predicted by five versions of General Recognition Theory: (a) the general quadratic classifier; (b) the optimal classifier; (c) the general linear classifier; (d) the minimum distance classifier; and (e) the independent decisions classifier.

dimension than on the orientation dimension. In category A the amount of variability on each dimension is the same, but size and orientation are positively correlated.

Note that Equation 9 can be rewritten as

$$h(x_1, x_2) = [x_1, x_2] \begin{bmatrix} a_1 & \frac{1}{2} a_3 \\ \frac{1}{2} a_3 & a_2 \end{bmatrix} \begin{bmatrix} x_1 \\ x_2 \end{bmatrix} + [b_1, b_2] \begin{bmatrix} x_1 \\ x_2 \end{bmatrix} + c_0 = 0 ,$$

or, equivalently, as

$$h(\mathbf{x}) = \mathbf{x}' \mathbf{A} \mathbf{x} + \mathbf{b}' \mathbf{x} + c_0 = 0 . \quad (10)$$

Now $\mathbf{x}_p$ is normally distributed (with mean $\mathbf{x}$ and covariance matrix $\mathbf{\Sigma}_p$), but since $h(\mathbf{x}_p)$ is quadratic in $\mathbf{x}_p$, $h(\mathbf{x}_p)$ is not normally distributed. In fact, $h(\mathbf{x}_p) + e_c$ has the distribution of the sum of four independent random variables: two with noncentral chi-square distributions and two with normal distributions (Khatri, 1980). In many cases, the distribution of this sum is approximately normal. The mean and variance of $h(\mathbf{x}_p)$ are equal to (e.g., Ashby & Maddox, 1991a; Khatri, 1980)

$$\mu_{h(\mathbf{x})} = trace\ (\mathbf{A\Sigma}_p) + \mathbf{x}'\mathbf{A}\mathbf{x} + \mathbf{b}'\mathbf{x} + c_0 \quad (11)$$

and

$$\sigma^2_{h(\mathbf{x})} = 2\ trace\ (\mathbf{A\Sigma}_p)^2 + (\mathbf{b} + 2\mathbf{A}\mathbf{x})'\ \mathbf{\Sigma}_p(\mathbf{b} + 2\mathbf{A}\mathbf{x}) , \quad (12)$$

so the probability of responding $\mathbf{R}_A$ on trials when a stimulus with mean percept $\mathbf{x}$ is presented can be approximated by Equation 8, with $\mu_{h(\mathbf{x})}$ and $\sigma^2_{h(\mathbf{x})}$ given in Equations 11 and 12.

Note that, in this model, $\mu_{h(\mathbf{x})}$ depends on $\mathbf{\Sigma}_p$ and on the perceptual coordinates $\mathbf{x}$, but not on σ^2_c. In addition, $\sigma^2_{h(\mathbf{x})}$ depends on $\mathbf{x}$ as well as σ^2_p. Thus, σ^2_p and σ^2_c are identifiable; that is, it is possible to uniquely estimate each source of variability. Separate estimates of perceptual and criterial noise have been obtained in the past (e.g., Nosofsky, 1983), but these required a comparison of performance across several different conditions. The general quadratic classifier is one of the first models to permit independent estimation of perceptual and criterial noise from the same data set.

The Optimal Classifier. The optimal classifier places the decision bound so that overall categorization accuracy is maximized. If the two relevant categories are A and B and both categories occur with equal probability, then accuracy is maximized if the subject computes the likelihood ratio $l(\mathbf{x}) = f_A(\mathbf{x})/f_B(\mathbf{x})$ and responds A when $l(\mathbf{x}) > 1$ and B when $l(\mathbf{x}) < 1$. The decision bound is the set of all $\mathbf{x}$ such that

$$h(\mathbf{x}) = -ln\ [l(\mathbf{x})] = 0\ .$$

In all but a few special cases, this bound is nonlinear.

When the category exemplars are normally distributed, the optimal decision bound has an especially simple form. Under these conditions, the decision bound satisfies (e.g., Ashby & Gott, 1988; see, also, Equation 26 of chap. 1)

$$\begin{aligned} h(\mathbf{x}) &= \tfrac{1}{2}(\mathbf{x} - \boldsymbol{\mu}_A)'\boldsymbol{\Sigma}_A^{-1}(\mathbf{x} - \boldsymbol{\mu}_A) - \tfrac{1}{2}(\mathbf{x} - \boldsymbol{\mu}_B)'\boldsymbol{\Sigma}_B^{-1}(\mathbf{x} - \boldsymbol{\mu}_B) \\ &\quad + \tfrac{1}{2}\ ln \left(\frac{|\boldsymbol{\Sigma}_A|}{|\boldsymbol{\Sigma}_B|}\right) \\ &= 0\ . \end{aligned} \tag{13}$$

Note that this bound is quadratic in **x**, and, thus, like the general quadratic classifier, the optimal classifier always uses a quadratic decision bound when the categories are normally distributed. An example of the optimal decision bound is given in Figure 16.2b.

Note that Equation 13 can be rewritten as

$$\begin{aligned} h(\mathbf{x}) &= \mathbf{x}'[\tfrac{1}{2}(\boldsymbol{\Sigma}_A^{-1} - \boldsymbol{\Sigma}_B^{-1})]\mathbf{x} + (\boldsymbol{\mu}_B'\boldsymbol{\Sigma}_B^{-1} - \boldsymbol{\mu}_A\boldsymbol{\Sigma}_A^{-1})\mathbf{x} \\ &\quad + \left[\boldsymbol{\mu}_A'\boldsymbol{\Sigma}_A^{-1}\boldsymbol{\mu}_A - \boldsymbol{\mu}_B'\boldsymbol{\Sigma}_B^{-1}\boldsymbol{\mu}_B' + ln\left(\frac{|\boldsymbol{\Sigma}_A|}{|\boldsymbol{\Sigma}_B|}\right)\right] \\ &= 0\ , \end{aligned}$$

and thus the optimal classifier is a special case of the general quadratic classifier with

$$\mathbf{A} = \tfrac{1}{2}\ (\boldsymbol{\Sigma}_A^{-1} - \boldsymbol{\Sigma}_B^{-1})\ ,$$

$$\mathbf{b} = \boldsymbol{\mu}_B'\boldsymbol{\Sigma}_B^{-1} - \boldsymbol{\mu}_A'\boldsymbol{\Sigma}_A^{-1}\ ,$$

and

$$c_0 = \boldsymbol{\mu}_A'\boldsymbol{\Sigma}_A^{-1}\boldsymbol{\mu}_A - \boldsymbol{\mu}_B'\boldsymbol{\Sigma}_B^{-1}\boldsymbol{\mu}_B + ln\left(\frac{|\boldsymbol{\Sigma}_A|}{|\boldsymbol{\Sigma}_B|}\right)\ .$$

The General Linear Classifier. In the general linear classifier, the decision bound is constrained to be linear, but no restrictions are placed on its slope and intercept. The general linear classifier can be viewed as a special case of the general quadratic classifier in which all elements of the **A** matrix of Equation 10 are zero. Thus, the decision bound satisfies

$$h(\mathbf{x}) = \mathbf{b}'\mathbf{x} + c_0 = 0\ ,$$

and the mean and variance of $h(\mathbf{x}_p)$ equal

$$\mu_{h(\mathbf{x})} = \mathbf{b}'\mathbf{x} + c_0 \tag{14}$$

and

$$\sigma^2_{h(\mathbf{x})} = \mathbf{b}' \, \Sigma_p \mathbf{b} \, . \tag{15}$$

In this case, however, because $h(\mathbf{x}_p)$ is a linear function of $\mathbf{x}_p$, it is normally distributed, so Equation 8 holds exactly with $\mu_{h(\mathbf{x})}$ and $\sigma^2_{h(\mathbf{x})}$ given by Equations 14 and 15.

Note that $\sigma^2_{h(\mathbf{x})}$ no longer depends on the stimulus coordinates $\mathbf{x}$. Also, $\mu_{h(\mathbf{x})}$ no longer depends on Σ_p. Therefore, all we can hope to estimate in Equation 8 is the sum $\sigma^2_{h(\mathbf{x})} + \sigma^2_c$. Hence, so long as the decision bound is linear in $\mathbf{x}$, it is impossible to separately estimate perceptual and criterial noise variance from the same data set. Only their sum can be estimated uniquely.

An example of general linear classification is shown in Figure 16.2c. The bound illustrated there is the *most accurate general linear classifier.* A subject using this bound will have higher overall categorization accuracy than a subject using any other linear bound. To find the most accurate general linear classifier, we need to find the vector $\mathbf{b}$ and scalar c_0 that maximizes accuracy. Unfortunately, no analytic solution to this problem is known. However, it can be shown that for the most accurate linear classifier, there exists a constant α in the interval $0 \leq \alpha \leq 1$ such that the following constraint is satisfied (Anderson, 1962; Fukunaga, 1972; Peterson & Mattson, 1966):

$$\mathbf{b} = [\alpha\Sigma_A + (1 - \alpha)\Sigma_B]^{-1}(\boldsymbol{\mu}_B - \boldsymbol{\mu}_A) \, .$$

Once $\mathbf{b}$ is known, c_0 can be shown to equal

$$c_0 = - \frac{\alpha(\mathbf{b}'\Sigma_A\mathbf{b})\mathbf{b}'\boldsymbol{\mu}_B + (1 - \alpha)(\mathbf{b}'\Sigma_B\mathbf{b})\mathbf{b}'\boldsymbol{\mu}_A}{\alpha(\mathbf{b}'\Sigma_A\mathbf{b}) + (1 - \alpha)(\mathbf{b}'\Sigma_B\mathbf{b})} \, .$$

Therefore, for a given value of α, both $\mathbf{b}$ and c_0 can be determined, and then Equations 14, 15, and 8 can be used to find overall accuracy (see also chap. 1). The most accurate linear bound can be identified by using a numerical minimization routine to find that value of α that maximizes accuracy.

The Minimum Distance Classifier. The minimum distance classifier assumes the subject responds with the category that has the nearest (i.e., most similar) mean. This strategy is equivalent to using the bound of equidistance (Ashby & Gott, 1988; see also chap. 10), which in the two category case is the line that bisects and is orthogonal to the chord connecting the two means. Specifically, the minimum distance bound is given by

$$h(\mathbf{x}) = (\boldsymbol{\mu}_B - \boldsymbol{\mu}_A)\,'\mathbf{x} + \tfrac{1}{2}(\boldsymbol{\mu}_A'\boldsymbol{\mu}_A - \boldsymbol{\mu}_B'\boldsymbol{\mu}_B) = 0 \, .$$

An example of minimum distance classification is shown in Figure 16.2d. Note that every point on the bound is equidistant from the two category means. Thus, all points above the Figure 16.2d bound are closer to the A mean and all points below the bound are closer to the B mean. Minimum distance classifiers are associated with distributed memory models that assume pattern recognition is based on cross-correlation (e.g., Hinton & Anderson, 1981; see, Ashby & Gott, 1988, for a proof).

The minimum distance classifier is a special case of the general linear classifier in which

$$\mathbf{b} = \boldsymbol{\mu}_B - \boldsymbol{\mu}_A$$

and

$$c_0 = \tfrac{1}{2}(\boldsymbol{\mu}_A{}'\boldsymbol{\mu}_A - \boldsymbol{\mu}_B{}'\boldsymbol{\mu}_B) \,.$$

Thus, $h(\mathbf{x}_p)$ is normally distributed with mean

$$\mu_{h(\mathbf{x})} = (\boldsymbol{\mu}_B - \boldsymbol{\mu}_A)\,'\mathbf{x} + \tfrac{1}{2}(\boldsymbol{\mu}_A'\boldsymbol{\mu}_A - \boldsymbol{\mu}_B'\boldsymbol{\mu}_B) \qquad (16)$$

and variance

$$\sigma^2_{h(\mathbf{x})} = (\boldsymbol{\mu}_B - \boldsymbol{\mu}_A)\,'\boldsymbol{\Sigma}_p\,(\boldsymbol{\mu}_B - \boldsymbol{\mu}_A)\,, \qquad (17)$$

so $P(\mathbf{R}_A|\mathbf{x})$ can be computed exactly from Equation 8, with $\mu_{h(\mathbf{x})}$ and $\sigma^2_{h(\mathbf{x})}$ given in Equations 16 and 17.

If the variability in any category around the mean is not uniform in every direction, then the minimum distance classifier will perform more poorly than the most accurate general linear classifier. In Figure 16.2, for example, the general linear classifier predicts higher categorization accuracy than the minimum distance classifier. In separate experiments reported by Ashby and Gott (1988) and Ashby and Maddox (1990), subjects did use the most accurate linear rule rather than minimum distance classification.

The nested relation between these four versions of GRT is illustrated by the Figure 16.3 Venn diagram. With two normally distributed categories, the optimal decision bound is always quadratic, so the optimal classifier is always a special case of the general quadratic classifier. The general linear and minimum distance classifiers are also special cases of the general quadratic classifier, regardless of the category distributions. Also note that the optimal classifier overlaps with the general linear classifier. With normal distributions the region of overlap includes exactly those cases for which $\boldsymbol{\Sigma}_A = \boldsymbol{\Sigma}_B$. Finally, note that the optimal classifier and the minimum distance classifier overlap. The intersection of these two models includes all cases in which the two category covariance matrices equal $\boldsymbol{\Sigma}_A = \boldsymbol{\Sigma}_B = \sigma^2\mathbf{I}$.

The Independent Decisions Classifier. The independent decisions classifier assumes a two-stage decision process (e.g., Ashby & Gott, 1988; Ashby & Maddox, 1990; Shaw, 1982; Townsend & Ashby, 1982). In the first stage, a separate decision is made about each component (e.g., whether it is large or small, present or absent), and then in the second stage the results of these decisions are used to select a response. For example, with stimuli like those in

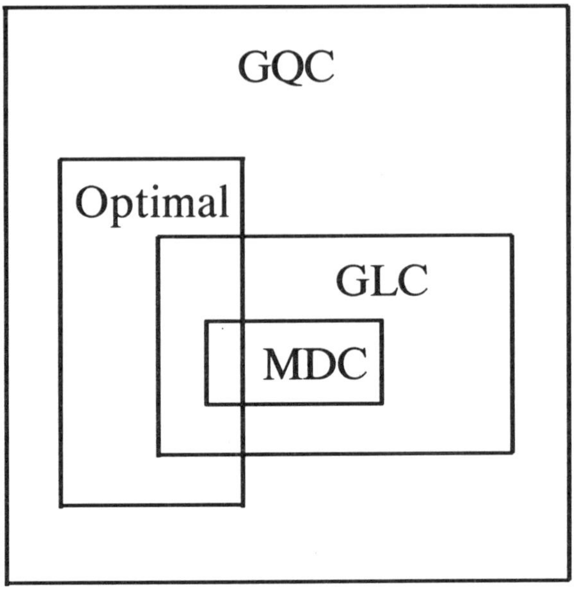

FIG. 16.3. Venn diagram showing the relations between different versions of General Recognition Theory. (GQC = general quadratic classifier, Optimal = optimal classifier, GLC = general linear classifier, and MDC = minimum distance classifier).

Figure 16.1b, the subject might decide whether the size is small or large and then whether the orientation is small or large. If a stimulus is presented that is judged to have a small size and a large orientation, the subject responds A.

Independent decisions models have enjoyed great popularity. For example, the idea of independent decisions forms the basis of high-threshold models (e.g., Blackwell, 1963) as well as feature-analytic models of letter identification (e.g., Townsend & Ashby, 1982). In feature-analytic models, separate decisions are first made about the presence or absence of each stimulus feature. Next, the list of perceived features is compared with a stored listed of the features known to be contained in each letter. Finally, a response is selected on the basis of this matching process.

Independent decisions is also equivalent to *decisional separability.* In both cases, the subject's decision about the level of one component does not depend on the perceived value of the other. When stimulus components are *perceptually separable,* it is easy to attend to one and ignore the other, so decisional separability and, consequently, independent decisions are most likely to occur when the stimulus components are perceptually separable (see chaps. 7 and 8).

In terms of GRT, independent decisions and, therefore, decisional separability is always identified with decision bounds that are parallel to the coordinate axes. An example is shown in Figure 16.2e. A subject making independent decisions might begin by setting a criterion x_{1o} on the perceived size dimension. Note that a circle with a perceived size greater than x_{1o} will fall to the right of the vertical bound in Figure 16.2e. The subject next sets a criterion x_{2o} on the perceived orientation dimension. Any circle with a radial arm that has perceived orientation greater than x_{2o} will fall above the horizontal bound. Using these bounds, the subject responds A to any stimulus falling in the upper left quadrant and B to any stimulus falling in the lower right quadrant. Stimuli falling in either other quadrant contain ambiguous or contradictory information, and, in these cases, independent decisions models often assume that subjects will respond by guessing.

In the Figure 16.2 example, the independent decisions classifier postulates two decision bounds, which are defined by the following linear discriminant functions:

$$h_1(x_1, x_2) = x_1 - x_{1o} = 0 \qquad \text{and} \qquad h_2(x_1, x_2) = x_{2o} - x_2 = 0\ .$$

Let δ_1 and e_{c1} (δ_2 and e_{c2}) be the response bias and criterial error on the first (second) discriminant function, and let $\mathbf{e}_p' = (e_{px}, e_{py})$. In addition, assume that $\Sigma_p = \sigma_p^2\mathbf{I}\cdot$ Then the probability of an $\mathbf{R}_A$ response is given by

$$\begin{aligned} P(\mathbf{R}_A|\mathbf{x}) &= P[h_1(\mathbf{x} + \mathbf{e}_p) < \delta + e_{c1},\, h_2(\mathbf{x} + \mathbf{e}_p) < \delta + e_{c2}|\mathbf{x}] \\ &= P[x_1 - x_{1o} + e_{px} < \delta + e_{c1},\, x_{2o} - x_2 + e_{py} < \delta + e_{c2}|\mathbf{x}] \\ &= P[e_{px} - e_{c1} < \delta_1 + x_{1o} - x_1,\, e_{py} - e_{c2} < \delta_2 + x_2 - x_{2o}|\mathbf{x}] \\ &= \Phi\left(\frac{\delta_1 + x_{1o} - x_1}{\sqrt{\sigma_p^2 + \sigma_c^2}}\right)\Phi\left(\frac{\delta_2 + x_2 - x_{2o}}{\sqrt{\sigma_p^2 + \sigma_c^2}}\right), \end{aligned}$$

where e_{c1} and e_{c2} are assumed to be independent and identically distributed.

Nosofsky, Clark, and Shin (1989) recently investigated a probabilistic version of the independent decisions model.

Classical Theory of Categorization

According to the Classical Theory, a category is defined by a set of necessary and sufficient conditions. For example, suppose category A is defined by the conditions $C_1, C_2, \ldots, C_n$. Then any stimulus satisfying conditions C_1 to C_n must be an exemplar of category A. The Classical Theory therefore suggests that a subject decides whether a stimulus is a member of category A by separately examining these n conditions and by making a binary decision about whether each one is satisfied.

If the subject is focusing on these n conditions, then it seems plausible that each condition would correspond to a unique perceptual dimension (or to a unique set of perceptual dimensions). For example, suppose category A is the set of all tall blue objects. Condition C_1 holds if the object is tall, and condition C_2 holds if it is blue. Then with respect to this category there are two relevant sets of perceptual dimensions: those associated with height and those associated with hue. Suppose as in Figure 16.4, that dimension x_1 corresponds to perceived height and dimension x_2 corresponds to hue. The presentation of a test stimulus can be represented by the ordered pair (x_1, x_2). The subject must now examine this pair and decide whether conditions C_1 and C_2 are met. This is accomplished by setting a criterion on each dimension. For example, the object may be considered tall if its height exceeds 2 m, and it may be considered blue if the wavelength it most efficiently reflects is less than 485 nm.

This process can be formalized in the following way. Let x_{1o} be the criterion on dimension x_1 and x_{2o} the criterion on dimension x_2. Then the Classical Theory predicts that the subject will adopt a decision rule of the following sort:

Assign the object to category A if $x_1 > x_{1o}$ *and* if $x_2 < x_{2o}$.

Note that the decision bounds $x_1 = x_{1o}$ and $x_2 = x_{2o}$ divide the perceptual space into rectangular response regions. In the Figure 16.4 example, the lower right quadrant is assigned to category A. The percept of any object that falls in this region will be considered tall and blue and will therefore be assigned to category A.

Note that we have established the following fact: The Classical Theory of categorization always predicts decision bounds that are parallel to the coordinate axes. As we saw in the preceding section, decision bounds of this type are also

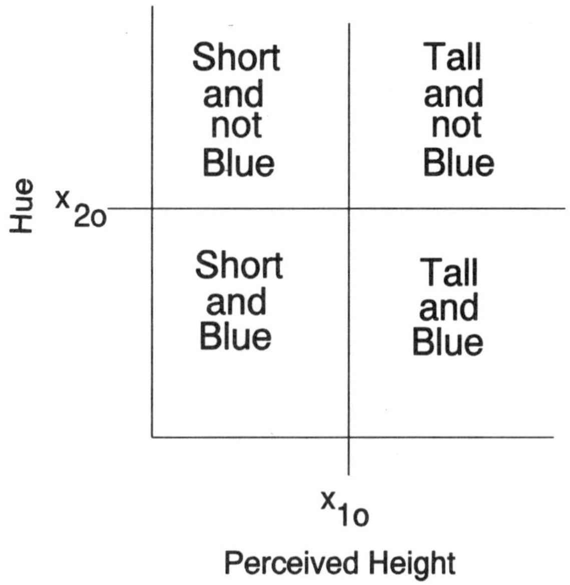

FIG. 16.4. Decision bounds predicted by the Classical Theory of categorization.

associated with independent decisions models and with decisional separability. Thus, for example, the Classical Theory of categorization postulates the same decision process as feature-analytic models of letter identification. In addition, the association between the Classical Theory and decisional separability suggests that the Classical Theory of categorization is most likely to hold when the stimulus dimensions are perceptually separable.

Given this more formal description, we might now reexamine the criticisms that were thought earlier to falsify the Classical Theory. First, the classical approach was criticized because in some categories, not all exemplars share the same properties. Clearly, all exemplars within the same rectangular region of Figure 16.4 share the same properties. The criticism, then, is that the response region for some categories might sprawl out of a single quadrant. To handle this case, the Classical Theory might be generalized to allow a category to be defined as the union of subcategories, each of which has a rectangular response region. For example, the category "games" can be viewed as the union of "competitive games" and "noncompetitive games of pleasure." Each of these subcategories might satisfy the classical definition of a category. In Figure 16.4, this generalization means that the response region assigned to a category might include more than one quadrant. Suppose a new category is created by taking the union of the lower right quadrant with one other response region. There are three possibilities. Note that in two of these, all exemplars in the resulting category share at least one property; that is, they are all either tall or blue. However, if we define the response region of the new category as the union of the upper left and lower right regions then there is no property that all exemplars share. This is the case that bothered Wittgenstein (1953), but note that even in this case the decision rule can be written as:

$$\text{Assign the object to category A if } x_1 > x_{1o} \text{ and } x_2 < x_{2o}$$
$$\textit{or} \text{ if } x_1 < x_{1o} \text{ and } x_2 > x_{2o} \,,$$

which still preserves the principles of the Classical Theory.

The other criticisms to the Classical Theory that were discussed involve typicality effects. In the simplest possible typicality or goodness-of-example experiment, a single category is indicated, and then exemplars from that category are presented to the subject. The subject's task is to indicate how typical or how good an example each exemplar is of the indicated category. The well-replicated results are that prototypical exemplars receive higher typicality ratings (e.g., Rosch, 1973b, 1975). In fact, even categories whose members are defined by a set of necessary and sufficient conditions show prototypicality effects. For example, Armstrong, Gleitman, and Gleitman (1983) showed that most people rate 8 as a better example of an even number than 18, and they are also faster to verify that 8 is indeed an even number.

The decision bounds predicted by the classical theory (and illustrated in Figure 16.2e and in Figure 16.4) are meant to be used in a task where the subject is asked to decide whether a particular exemplar is a member of one category or another. That is, the bounds separate the relevant categories. In the simple typicality experiment, there is only one category, so it makes no sense for the subject to construct such bounds. In fact, even if a subject wanted to construct such bounds, he or she would not know how to do so. For example, suppose the category in question was "sports cars." Does the subject construct bounds to separate "sports cars" from "sedans," from "station wagons," or from "pickup trucks"?

Any typicality effects observed in this experiment, therefore, provide little (if any) information about the decision rules that subjects use in categorization tasks. Instead, they provide information about category structure. Specifically they indicate that categories usually have some central member that is most typical of the category and that as we move away from this "prototype" (i.e., as similarity to the prototype decreases) typicality decreases. If typicality is interpreted as likelihood, then data in which the most central member of a category is judged the most typical supports the assumption that the exemplars of categories are normally distributed. They do not constitute evidence against the Classical Theory (e.g., Armstrong et al., 1983).

On the other hand, in some typicality experiments, contrasting categories are present. In such cases, subjects are frequently asked to make categorization responses *and* typicality judgments about the same set of stimuli, and it is often found that the nature of the contrasting category influences the subject's typicality judgments (Nosofsky, 1988a). Thus, typicality judgments are context-sensitive. Because these more complex experiments involve categorization responses, they have the potential to provide much information about the decision bound a subject is using. To fully account for the data from such an experiment, we must construct some model of how context influences typicality judgments. Once such a model is constructed, however, it may be possible to incorporate it directly into the Classical Theory of categorization.

Superordinate Categories

Another advantage of decision bounds is that they suggest a natural way to deal with the problem of superordinate category labels. For example, in the study of Mervis et al. (1975), relatedness judgments were collected on 20 fruit names along with the superordinate label "fruit." As discussed earlier, the problem for geometric models was that for 18 of the 20 fruit names, "fruit" was judged the most highly related concept in the group. If each word is represented as a point in a multidimensional space, then "fruit" must be the nearest neighbor to 18 other points. However, suppose that instead of representing each fruit name as a point, it is represented by a response region. For example, one region is associated with the category label "apple" and contains the representations of all objects called "apples." Similarly, one region is associated with the superordinate category label "fruit" and contains the representations of all objects called "fruit." But since "apples" and "oranges" are both called "fruit," the "fruit" response region must contain the response regions assigned to "apples" and to "oranges." The response regions of a superordinate category label, therefore, are defined by the union of the response regions of its subordinate category names. The "fruit" region is the union of the regions associated with each species of fruit. Similarly, the "apple" region is the union of the regions associated with each subspecies of apple (e.g., Mackintosh, Red Delicious).

A natural way to define the similarity of category A to category B is as the proportion of the category A distribution that falls in the category B response region (Ashby & Perrin, 1988). Since the probability that a subject will confuse an apple and orange or an apple and pear is low, this model predicts that the proportion of the "fruit" distribution that falls in the "apple" region should exceed the proportion of either the "orange" or the "pear" distribution that falls in the "apple" region. Thus, subjects should judge "fruit" and "apple" to be more similar or related than "orange" and "apple" or "pear" and "apple." The superordinate category name should be judged most related to *almost all* subordinate category members. The major exception occurs when a pair of subordinate category members is extremely similar. For example, the proportion of the "orange" distribution falling in the "lemon" response region might be greater than the proportion of the "fruit" distribution falling in the "lemon" region, and thus we might expect "orange" and "lemon" to be more related than "fruit" and "lemon." This is exactly what Mervis et al. found.

Exemplar Models

Single-Exemplar Models

A Single Fixed Exemplar—Prototype Theory. Deterministic prototype models assume the subject responds with the category containing the most similar prototype (e.g., Reed, 1972). When the exemplars of a category are normally distributed, the mean, median, and mode are all equal, and so, by most definitions, the prototype can be interpreted as the category mean. The "most similar prototype" is usually interpreted as the prototype whose representation is least distant from the representation of the stimulus in the perceptual space.

Consider a categorization task with two categories A and B. In this case, responding with the label associated with the nearest category mean is equivalent to dividing the space into two regions. In one region, all points are closer to the A mean, and in the other region all points are closer to the B mean. The points on the boundary separating the two regions are all equidistant from the two means. It is straightforward to show that the line of equidistance bisects and is orthogonal to the chord connecting the two means. We have thus established the following: The prototype model postulates the same decision bounds as the minimum distance classifier of General Recognition Theory.

Like the classical model, the prototype model (called the comparative distance model by Smith & Medin, 1981) always predicts linear decision bounds. However, whereas the bounds predicted by the classical model are constrained to be vertical and/or horizontal, prototype bounds may have any slope. On the other hand, in the absence of response bias, the prototype bound is completely determined by the position of the category means, whereas a subject obeying the classical theory has the freedom to choose the criteria x_{1o} and x_{2o}. However, for the sake of comparison, suppose that x_{1o} and x_{2o} are placed so that categorization accuracy is maximized.

First, consider the case in which the covariance matrices describing categories A and B are both equal to $\mathbf{\Sigma} = \mathbf{\Sigma}_A = \mathbf{\Sigma}_B = \sigma^2\mathbf{I}$, where $\mathbf{I}$ is the identity matrix. These constraints cause the optimal bound, given in Equation 13, to reduce to the minimum distance bound. No model, therefore, can predict more accurate categorization performance under these conditions than the prototype model. Because subjects seem to be very good at maximizing categorization accuracy, it is no wonder, then, that Prototype Theory is usually thought to be more valid than the Classical Theory.

If the two prototypes have the same coordinate on one dimension, the classical model is equivalent to the prototype model. In this situation, the two models both predict that the subject will ignore the dimension on which the prototypes are identical and set a criterion on the other dimension.

If the two prototypes differ on both dimensions, the classical model predicts that the subject will divide the space into four quadrants, as in Figures 16.2e and 16.4. Two of these quadrants will be assigned a response, but the other two signal ambiguous information, so presumably a subject would guess to any exemplar falling in either of these regions. With normally distributed categories, some exemplars must necessarily fall into these two ambiguous quadrants, so the classical model predicts that during categorization, subjects will eventually encounter objects that they do not know how to categorize and will respond by guessing. The prototype model, however, predicts that subjects never guess. They may encounter objects that are atypical of both categories, but the object in question will be more similar to one prototype than the other, and so response selection is unambiguous.

There are instances, however, in which the classical model predicts higher categorization accuracy than the prototype model. An example is given in Figure 16.5. Note that the two categories have identical prototypes, so the prototype model predicts that subjects will guess on every trial and thus, that categorization accuracy will be at chance levels. The classical model predicts the solid line decision bounds. Response A is given to any exemplar falling in the upper right or lower left quadrants, and response B is given to any exemplar falling in the upper left or lower right quadrants. Because of the negative correlation between

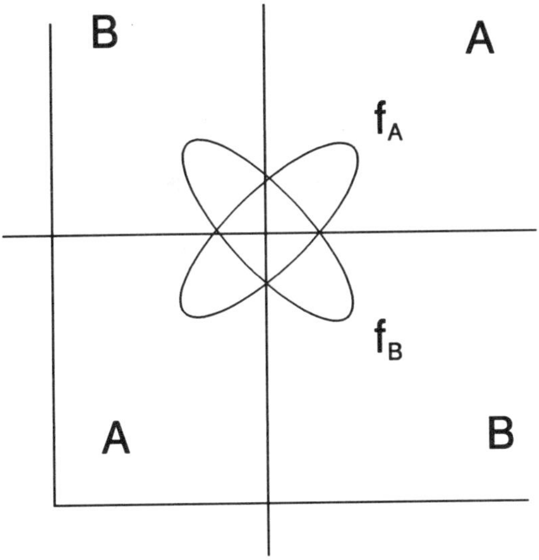

FIG. 16.5. Contours of equal likelihood for which the Classical Theory of categorization predicts better performance than Prototype Theory.

the component values in category B and the positive correlation in A, the bounds predicted by the classical model turn out to be optimal in this case (the optimal bound is hyperbolic). Therefore, the classical model predicts that categorization accuracy will be significantly better than chance. Pilot work with the Figure 16.5 categories (using the line stimuli of Ashby & Gott, 1988) indicated that subjects can learn this categorization task. Also, Nosofsky (1986) reported the results of a task that used the Figure 16.1b stimuli and in which the two relevant categories had a structure very similar to Figure 16.5. The major difference was that, instead of normal distributions, each category contained four exemplars (and perfect performance was possible). After extensive practice, the two subjects averaged 75% correct.

Taken together with the data that shows that subjects will reject minimum distance classification in favor of more complex but accurate decision strategies, these data indicate that minimum distance classification has no privileged role in human categorization behavior. A better first approximation of experienced categorization performance is provided by the optimal classifier. The classical model and/or the prototype model might accurately account for the results of some experiment, but only because the category structures are such that they happen to make identical predictions to the optimal model. In fact, this hypothesis also explains why the prototype model is usually superior to the classical model. If two arbitrary multivariate distributions are chosen, minimum distance classification will generally predict higher categorization accuracy than an independent decisions strategy.

Even so, minimum distance classification is guaranteed to be optimal only if the category covariance matrices are all scalar multiples of the identity.[1] Although this condition may be approximately satisfied with some categories, most natural categories are probably not similarly constrained. If the amount of variability along any dimension or if the amount of covariation between any pair of dimensions differs for the two categories, then the optimal bound will be nonlinear. For example, suppose the relevant dimensions when classifying two species of birds are feather length and beak color. Then, in general, minimum distance classification will be optimal only if the variability in feather length and beak color is equal both within and across species and if these two variables are uncorrelated within both species. These constraints seem overly restrictive and unlikely to hold in general.

Probabilistic versions of prototype theory have been constructed from the similarity-choice model (i.e., Equation 4) by assuming that the similarity of a stimulus with perceptual coordinates $\mathbf{x}$ to category A, $\eta_{\mathbf{x}A}$, is equal to the similarity of $\mathbf{x}$ to the prototype of category A (Ashby & Maddox, in press; Nosofsky, 1987). In these models, similarity is assumed to be a monotonically decreasing function of the psychological distance between point representations of the stimulus and the prototype. Suppose the perceptual space is n-dimensional. Let $(x_{i1}, x_{i2}, \ldots, x_{in})$ be the coordinates of the perceptual representation of stimulus S_i, and denote the proportion of attention allocated to dimension k by w_k. Then one possibility is to assume that the psychological distance between stimuli S_i and S_j is given by

$$d_{ij} = \left[\sum_{k=1}^{n} w_k |x_{ik} - x_{jk}|^r \right]^{1/r} . \tag{18}$$

This weighted distance metric forms the basis of Carroll's INDSCAL Multidimensional Scaling (MDS) model (e.g., Carroll & Chang, 1970; Carroll & Wish, 1974).

The exponent r, which is constrained to be greater than or equal to 1.0, defines the nature of the distance metric. The most popular cases occur when r = 1 (city-block distance) and when r = 2 (Euclidean distance). In MDS, the city-block metric usually provides the best account of the data when the stimulus dimensions are separable (Attneave, 1950; Garner, 1974; Shepard, 1964; Torgerson, 1958; however, see Dunn, 1983; Nosofsky, 1986), and the Euclidean metric usually provides the best account when the dimensions are integral (e.g., Att-

[1]This statement is not exactly true. Minimum distance classification is optimal in one other special case. This is when the two covariance matrices are equal and one of the eigenvectors is parallel to the minimum distance bound.

neave, 1950; Nosofsky, 1987; Shepard, 1964, 1986, 1987; Torgerson, 1958; see also chap. 7).

Two specific functions relating psychological distance to similarity have become popular. The *exponential decay function* assumes that the similarity between stimuli $\mathbf{S}_i$ and $\mathbf{S}_j$ is given by (e.g., Ennis, 1988a; Nosofsky, 1986, 1988b; Shepard, 1957, 1964, 1986, 1987)

$$\eta_{ij} = exp\ (-d_{ij})\ . \tag{19}$$

In contrast, the *Gaussian function* assumes (e.g., Ennis, 1988a; Ennis, Mullen, & Frijters, 1988; Nosofsky, 1986, 1988b; Shepard, 1986, 1987, 1988)

$$\eta_{ij} = exp\ (-d_{ij}^2)\ . \tag{20}$$

Previous applications of models that combine an MDS representation with the similarity-choice model have paired the exponential similarity function with either the city-block distance metric (Nosofsky, 1985a; Shepard, 1957, 1987) or the Euclidean metric (Nosofsky, 1987), or else they have paired the Gaussian similarity function with the Euclidean metric (Nosofsky, 1985b, 1986). See Chapters 11, 13, and 14 for more details on this controversy.

In probabilistic models, the analogue of a decision bound is the contour for which $P(\mathbf{R}_A|\mathbf{x}) = 0.5$. In probabilistic prototype models, $P(\mathbf{R}_A|\mathbf{x}) > 0.5$ on one side of this contour and $P(\mathbf{R}_A|\mathbf{x}) < 0.5$ on the other. It is straightforward to show that the $P(\mathbf{R}_A|\mathbf{x}) = 0.5$ contour is coincident with the minimum distance bound only if the attention allocated to dimension x_1 equals the attention allocated to dimension x_2; that is, if and only if $w_1 = w_2$. Any other distribution of attention will result in a linear bound (at least with the Euclidean distance metric) with a slope that is different from the minimum distance bound. In this way, the weighted probabilistic prototype model has much the same flexibility as the general linear classifier. In fact, Ashby and Maddox (in press) showed that if the noise has a logistic distribution (i.e., so that Φ in Equation 8 is the standard logistic cumulative distribution function; see Equation 20 of chap. 1), then the weighted probabilistic prototype model with a Gaussian similarity function and Euclidean distance metric can exactly mimic any general linear classifier in which the slope of the decision bound has the same sign as the slope of the minimum distance bound (i.e., either both bounds have positive slopes or they both have negative slopes). The attention weights give the prototype model the flexibility to change the slope of the decision bound, and the response bias provides a mechanism for changing the intercept.

A Single Random Exemplar. Ennis and his colleagues have investigated deterministic and probabilistic versions of a model that assumes the subject matches the stimulus representation to the memory representation of one exemplar drawn randomly from each category (Ennis & Ashby, 1991; Ennis & Mullen, 1986a; Ennis, Palen, & Mullen, 1988; Mullen & Ennis, 1987, 1991;

Mullen, Ennis, de Doncker, & Kapenga, 1988; see also De Soete, Carroll, & DeSarbo, 1986; Zinnes & MacKay, 1983, 1987; see also chaps. 2, 5, and 11). In the deterministic version, called the *probabilistic multidimensional scaling* (PMDS) model, the subject is assumed to respond with the name of the category with the most similar (i.e., the nearest) exemplar. In the probabilistic version, called the *stochastic choice* model, the subject is assumed to compute the similarity of the stimulus to the exemplar chosen from each category and then to use these similarity values in conjunction with the similarity-choice model (Equation 4) to determine the probability of each response alternative. As of yet, neither of these models has been applied to categorization, but they have been used successfully to model data from similarity and preference experiments (De Soete et al., 1986; Ennis & Mullen, 1986a; Mullen & Ennis, 1987, 1991; Mullen et al., 1988; Zinnes & MacKay, 1983, 1987).

Ennis and Ashby (1991) compared the single-exemplar models to several of the decision bound models with respect to their sensitivity to within category correlation. Humans display a great deal of sensitivity to correlation in these kinds of categorization tasks (Ashby & Gott, 1988; Ashby & Maddox, 1990, 1992), so the correct categorization model should also display such sensitivity. Ennis and Ashby examined predicted categorization accuracy in a task with categories A and B. The exemplars in the two categories varied on two dimensions, and within each category the correlation coefficient between dimensions was 0, 0.4, or 0.8. These three values were factorially combined across categories to yield nine separate conditions. Another nine conditions were created by factorially combining the correlations 0, −0.4, and −0.8. The category means and variances were held constant across conditions.

The predictions of the following models were investigated: (a) the optimal classifier, (b) the general linear classifier, (c) the minimum distance classifier, and (d) the PMDS model. Each of these assumed a deterministic decision process, and no perceptual or criterial noise was assumed. In addition, two versions of the stochastic choice model were investigated: (e) the city-block distance–exponential similarity function model, and (f) the Euclidean distance–Gaussian similarity function model.

For each model and condition, Ennis and Ashby (1991) computed the probability of a correct response on trials when a probe from category A was presented. Rather than compare the models with respect to the magnitude of the accuracy values that they predicted, the models were compared with respect to the variability in their predicted accuracy values across conditions. The more variable a model's predictions, the more sensitive it is to category covariance structure.

The most sensitive model, of course, was the optimal classifier. Next came the general linear classifier, followed by the minimum distance model. Then came the PMDS model and the Euclidean–Gaussian stochastic choice model, which were about equally sensitive. The least sensitive model was the city-block–exponential stochastic choice model. In fact, this latter model displayed almost no variability across experimental conditions. Thus, empirical evidence that subjects are sensitive to category covariance structure disconfirms the city-block–exponential stochastic choice model.

Perhaps the biggest surprise was that the minimum distance model displayed more sensitivity to category covariance structure than either version of the stochastic choice model. Because the category means were the same in all conditions, the minimum distance model predicted the same decision bound in all conditions. Therefore, the probability of a correct categorization on A trials was unaffected by the correlation within category B. However, it was affected by the correlation within category A. As the correlation within category A varied, the proportion of category A exemplars falling in the A response region varied and, consequently, so did the predicted accuracy on A trials.

Multiple-Exemplar Models

The (Generalized) Context Model. Recently, it has become popular to assume that categorization is based on a match of the stimulus representation to the representation of all exemplars of every category (Brooks, 1978; Estes, 1986; Hintzman, 1986; Medin & Schaffer, 1978; Nosofsky, 1986; Restle, 1961). Perhaps the most widely known of these exemplar models is the *context model,* developed by Medin and Schaffer (1978) as an application and extension of the similarity-choice model (Equation 4). As originally proposed, the context model assumed stimuli had binary values on each dimension. Nosofsky (1986; see chap. 14) generalized the context model to continuous-valued stimulus dimensions, and he explicitly considered the role that selective attention plays in the categorization process. According to both versions, the similarity of a stimulus with perceptual coordinates $\mathbf{x}$ to the elements of category A is equal to

$$\eta_{\mathbf{x}A} = \sum_{j \in \mathbf{C}_A} \eta_{\mathbf{x}j} , \tag{21}$$

where $j \in \mathbf{C}_A$ represents all $\mathbf{S}_j$ that are members of category A.

In Nosofsky's (1986) *generalized context model* (GCM) the similarity between a pair of stimuli is assumed to be a monotonically decreasing function of the psychological distance between point representations of the two stimuli. The psychological distance between stimuli $\mathbf{S}_i$ and $\mathbf{S}_j$ is given by

$$d_{ij} = c \left[\sum_{k=1}^{n} w_k |x_{ik} - x_{jk}|^r \right]^{1/r} , \tag{22}$$

which is the weighted distance metric from the INDSCAL MDS model (Equation 18) multiplied by a nonnegative parameter c that is assumed to scale the psychological space. The parameter c can be interpreted as a measure of overall stimulus discriminability and so would be expected to increase with increased exposure duration and/or as subjects gain experience with the stimuli (Nosofsky, 1986). Similarity is related to psychological distance through either the exponential or Gaussian similarity functions (Equation 19 or 20). The context model and the GCM have successfully accounted for categorization performance with stimuli constructed from separable and integral dimensions under a variety of different conditions (Busemeyer, Dewey, & Medin, 1984; Medin, Altom, Edelson, & Freko, 1982; Medin & Schaffer, 1978; Medin & Schwanenflugel, 1981; Smith & Medin, 1981; see also chap. 14).

Deterministic Exemplar Models. The GCM assumes a probabilistic decision process. Given the same percept, the model assumes that sometimes the subject will give one response and sometimes another. In contrast, one could assume that the subject always gives the response associated with the greatest summed similarity. Ashby and Maddox (1991a, in press) investigated a deterministic exemplar model that contains the GCM as a special case.

In the Ashby and Maddox model, the subject is assumed to use the Proposition 16.1 decision rule:

$$\text{Respond } \mathbf{R}_A \text{ if } ln\,(\Sigma\eta_{\mathbf{x}A}) - ln\,(\Sigma\eta_{\mathbf{x}B}) > \delta + e_c\,; \quad \text{otherwise respond } \mathbf{R}_B\,; \tag{23}$$

where the criterial noise, represented by e_c, is assumed to have a logistic distribution with mean 0 and variance σ_c^2 and, as before, the subject is biased toward $\mathbf{R}_A$ if $\delta > 0$. As Proposition 16.1 indicates, this model is equivalent to the GCM when $\gamma = 1$. In other words, the GCM can be interpreted as a deterministic exemplar model in which the criterial noise variance $\sigma_c^2 = \pi^2/3$.

The form of the Equation 23 decision rule suggests an alternative deterministic exemplar model in which the similarity of probe $\mathbf{x}$ to category J is determined by $\Sigma\, \eta_{\mathbf{x}J}$ rather than by $ln\,(\Sigma\eta_{\mathbf{x}J})$. Although the resulting model does not contain the GCM as a special case, Nosofsky (chap. 14) discusses a deterministic exemplar model that is mathematically equivalent to this alternative.

The predictions of deterministic exemplar models can be described in the language of decision bounds in the same way as the other categorization models discussed in this chapter. In the exemplar model, the decision bound is that set of points for which summed similarity to the two categories is equal. On one side of this bound, summed similarity is greater to category A, and on the other side it is greater to category B. This decision bound also has meaning in the probabilistic GCM because, as can be seen in Equation 4, when summed similarities are equal the response probabilities are equal, at least in the absence of response bias. In probabilistic models, the decision bound corresponds to the contour for which $P(\mathbf{R}_A|\mathbf{x}) = 0.5$, and, therefore, the GCM and both of the deterministic exemplar models described earlier predict identical decision bounds. One way to compare exemplar theories with other categorization theories is to examine the nature of the decision bounds that they predict.

To begin, it is important to distinguish between decision bounds in the stimulus space and decision bounds in the perceptual space. For example, the Equation 13 bound predicted by the GRT optimal classifier is optimal only in the stimulus space. To compute the optimal bound in the perceptual space, we must replace $\boldsymbol{\mu}_A$, $\boldsymbol{\mu}_B$, $\boldsymbol{\Sigma}_A$, and $\boldsymbol{\Sigma}_B$ in Equation 13 with the mean vectors and covariance matrices of the *perceived* category distributions—that is, with $\boldsymbol{\mu}_{Ap}$, $\boldsymbol{\mu}_{Bp}$, $\boldsymbol{\Sigma}_{Ap}$, and $\boldsymbol{\Sigma}_{Bp}$. In the perceptual error model developed here, $\boldsymbol{\mu}_{Jp} = \boldsymbol{\mu}_J$ and $\boldsymbol{\Sigma}_{Jp} = \boldsymbol{\Sigma}_J + \boldsymbol{\Sigma}_p$, for J = A and B. In some situations, for example, when minimum distance classification is optimal, the addition of perceptual noise will not change the optimal bound. However, in many cases, the two bounds will differ. If $\boldsymbol{\Sigma}_A \neq \boldsymbol{\Sigma}_B$, so that the optimal stimulus bound is nonlinear, then the optimal bound in the perceptual space will be less curved than the optimal stimulus bound. This is because adding $\boldsymbol{\Sigma}_p$ to both $\boldsymbol{\Sigma}_A$ and $\boldsymbol{\Sigma}_B$ reduces their differences and makes the optimal bound more nearly linear.

Nosofsky (1990) and Ashby and Maddox (in press) showed that when the distance metric is Euclidean and the similarity function is Gaussian, then there exist certain parameter settings for which the decision bounds predicted by the exemplar models and by the GRT optimal classifier are identical *in the perceptual space*. If $\boldsymbol{\Sigma}_p = \sigma_p^2\mathbf{I}$, the equivalence relation requires no response bias and equal attention allocated to each stimulus dimension.[2] The discriminability parameter **c** of Equation 22 is related to the GRT perceptual noise variance via $\mathbf{c} = 1/\sigma_p$.

The GRT and exemplar models are thus equally sensitive to category covariance structure. However, the two models treat suboptimality differently. The exemplar models stress the importance of selective attention, which indirectly affects the decision bound. The GRT models assume that the subject operates on the decision bound directly. When the optimal bound is linear, then manipulating attention is essentially equivalent to changing the decision bound slope and intercept. However, if the optimal bound is nonlinear, then the effects of manipulating attention will be limited. In this case, the general quadratic classifier is more powerful than the exemplar models. Of course, if the direct action of the subject is one of selective attention, then the extra power of the general quadratic classifier (in the form of extra free parameters) is wasted.

Empirical Comparisons

Ashby and Maddox (1990, 1992; see also Ashby & Gott, 1988) reported the results of a number of categorization experiments with stimuli like those in Figure 16.1. Each task involved two categories (A and B), and the exemplars in each category had bivariate normal distributions. Given data from such an experiment, two questions are of immediate interest. First, what is the shape of the

[2]In general, the equivalence relation requires that the perceptual covariance matrix $\boldsymbol{\Sigma}_p$ be diagonal and identical for every exemplar in both categories. If either of these assumptions fails, then the exemplar bounds are suboptimal.

decision bound that best separates the subject's A and B responses? Second, which model best predicts the data?

Across a variety of experiments, Ashby and Maddox (1990, 1992) tested whether each subject's A and B responses were best separated by the optimal bound, the most accurate linear bound, the minimum distance bound, or the independent decisions bounds. Although subjects responded suboptimally in some experiments, the best predictor of the categorization performance of experienced subjects, across all the experiments, was the optimal bound. This was true regardless of whether the optimal rule involved minimum distance, general linear, or nonlinear classification. Similar results were found with the rectangular and circular stimuli, and thus it made little difference whether the components of the stimuli were integral or separable.

Ashby and Maddox (1991a) examined the ability of a number of categorization models to account for the data collected in these experiments. When the optimal bound was linear, the best fits were obtained with the general linear classifier or, equivalently, with the probabilistic weighted prototype model. The deterministic exemplar model performed almost as well, but the GCM fit worse than the other models. The poor performance of the GCM appeared to result because responding was less variable than predicted by the GCM.

When the optimal bound was quadratic, the general quadratic classifier provided fits that were substantially better than any other model. The GCM and the deterministic exemplar model each fit the data from one experiment about equally well, but in a second experiment the deterministic exemplar model performed better than the GCM. The prototype model and the general linear classifier provided the poorest fits. The poor fits of the exemplar models in the quadratic conditions apparently occurred because subjects responded suboptimally in these experiments, but in a fashion that required the full flexibility of the general quadratic classifier to mimic. Specifically, a manipulation of attention weights or response biases proved inadequate.

SUMMARY AND CONCLUSIONS

When models of the categorization process are constructed, it is vital to carefully distinguish between the construct of a category and the act of categorization. The Classical Theory does not explicitly separate these two components. Prototype and Exemplar Theories have traditionally represented a category as a set of points in a multidimensional perceptual space. Exemplar Theory has made no explicit assumptions about the distribution of these points but Prototype Theory assumes that the category representation is dominated by the prototype. Both theories have been more explicit about the act of categorization, specifying it as a process in which the presented stimulus is globally matched to the memory representation of one or more category exemplars, and then a response is selected on the basis of these matching operations. General Recognition Theory also represents the perceptual effect of an exemplar as a point in a multidimensional space, but, unlike the other theories, it postulates that variability in the perceptual process over trials causes variability in the exemplar representation. In addition, GRT explicitly considers the effects of category structure on the categorization process.

The multivariate normal distribution provides a powerful model of a natural category. It nicely accounts for the major (context free) typicality effects without any reference to the act of categorization. As a model of category structure, the multivariate normal assumption is easily incorporated into each of the major categorization theories that were discussed in this chapter (e.g., Nosofsky, 1988b). Once this is done, the various models can be compared by examining the decision bounds that they predict in the multidimensional perceptual space.

The act of categorization can also be subdivided into two components. The first involves accessing the categorical information that is assumed relevant to the decision-making process, and the second involves using this information to select a response. Table 16.1 illustrates the relations between various categoriza-

TABLE 16.1
Relations Between Various Categorization Models

			Response Selection	
			Probabilistic	*Deterministic*
Exemplar	Single Exemplar	Fixed	Probabilistic Prototype Model (Ashby & Maddox, in press; Nosofsky, 1987)	Prototype Model (Reed, 1972)
		Random	Stochastic Choice Model (Ennis et al., 1988; Ennis & Ashby, 1991)	PMDS Model (De Soete et al., 1986; Ennis & Mullen, 1986; Zinnes & MacKay, 1983, 1987)
	Multiple exemplar		Context Model (Medin & Schaffer, 1978) Generalized Context Model (Nosofsky, 1986)	Deterministic Exemplar Model (Ashby & Maddox, 1991a; Nosofsky, Chapter 14)
Decision Bounds	General quadratic		?	General Recognition Theory (Ashby & Maddox, 1991a)

(continued)

TABLE 16.1 (*Continued*)

		Response Selection	
		Probabilistic	*Deterministic*
Decision Bounds	Optimal	?	General Recognition Theory (Ashby & Gott, 1988; Ashby & Maddox, 1991a)
	General linear	?	General Recognition Theory (Ashby & Gott, 1988; Ennis & Ashby, 1991)
	Minimum distance	(equivalent to Probabilistic Prototype Model)	General Recognition Theory (Ashby & Gott, 1988; Ennis & Ashby, 1991) (equivalent to Prototype Model)
	Independent decisions	Probabilistic Rule Model (Nosofsky et al., 1989)	General Recognition Theory (Ashby & Gott, 1988) Classical Theory (Bruner et al., 1956; Smith & Medin, 1981)

tion models with respect to these components. Rows indicate different retrieval assumptions, columns different response selection assumptions. Thus, all models in the same row or column differ only on one assumption.

Although models in different cells in Table 16.1 make different processing assumptions, a number of equivalence relations can be stated. Because classifying by the most similar prototype is the same as classifying by the nearest centroid, the probabilistic minimum distance classifier is equivalent to the probabilistic prototype model. Similarly, the deterministic minimum distance model is equivalent to the deterministic prototype model. In addition, we have already seen that the weighted probabilistic prototype model is a special case of the general linear classifier and that the GCM is a special case of the deterministic exemplar model proposed by Ashby and Maddox (in press).

Of the two components detailed in Table 16.1, the retrieval component is the one with which the various theories are most concerned. The Classical Theory assumes the subject generates the criteria x_{1o} and x_{2o} that determine whether the stimulus satisfies the necessary conditions. This generation process might involve retrieval of the criterion values from memory, or the subject might compute the values on each trial in some way. Prototype Theory assumes the subject matches the perceptual representation of the stimulus to the memory representation of the category prototypes, and Exemplar Theory assumes the subject matches the perceptual representation to the memory representation of all exemplars of each category. General Recognition Theory assumes the subject generates the response label associated with the region in which the perceptual representation falls. Ideally, we desire a method for testing between these alternatives. Unfortunately, however, predictions of the models depend also on the second response selection component.

The most widely known versions of the Classical Theory, Prototype Theory, and General Recognition Theory all assume a deterministic decision process. Thus, these models all differ only in the first component. An empirical advantage for one model, therefore, supports its retrieval assumptions. The GCM assumes a probabilistic decision process, so it differs from the other models in both components. Differences in goodness of fit between the GCM and GRT could, therefore, be due to either component. The development of the deterministic exemplar model described in Proposition 16.1 will make it easier to compare decision bound and exemplar models of categorization.

References

Aarts, E., & Korst, J. (1989). *Simulated annealing and Boltzmann machines: A stochastic approach to combinatorial optimization and neural computing*. New York: Wiley.

Abdel-Aty, S. H. (1954). Approximate formulae for the percentage points and the probability integral of the non-central chi-square distribution. *Biometrika, 41*, 538–540.

Abramowitz, M., & Stegun, A. (Eds.). (1965). *Handbook of mathematical functions*. New York: Dover.

Aczel, J., & Dhombres, J. (1989). *Functional equations in several variables*. New York: Cambridge University Press.

Aha, D. W., & McNulty, D. M. (1989). Learning relative attribute weights for independent, instance-based concept descriptions. *Proceedings of the Eleventh Annual Conference of the Cognitive Society* (pp. 530–537). Hillsdale, NJ: Lawrence Erlbaum Associates.

Aha, D. W., & Goldstone, R. L. (1990). Learning attribute relevance in context in instance-based learning algorithms. In *Proceedings of the Twelfth Annual Conference of the Cognitive Science Society* (pp. 141–148). Hillsdale, NJ: Lawrence Erlbaum Associates.

Akaike, H. (1974). A new look at the statistical model identification. *IEEE Transactions on Automatic Control, 19*, 716–723.

Akaike, H. (1977). On entropy maximization. In P. R. Krishnaiah (Ed.), *Applications of statistics* (pp. 27–41). Amsterdam: North-Holland.

Allik, J., Dzhafarov, E., & Rauk, M. (1982). Position discrimination may be better than detection. *Vision Research, 22*, 1079–1081.

Alsina, C. (1989). *Synthesizing judgments given by probability distribution functions*. Unpublished manuscript, Departemento de Matematicas y Estadistica, Universidad Politecnica de Catalunya.

Anderson, J. R., Kline, P. J., & Beasley, C. M. (1979). A general learning theory and its application to schema abstraction. In G. H. Bower (Ed.), *The psychology of learning and motivation*. New York: Academic Press.

Anderson, T. W. (1962). *An introduction to multivariate statistical analysis*. New York: Wiley.

Arbib, M. A. (1989). *The metaphorical brain 2: Neural networks and beyond*. New York: Wiley.

Armstrong, S. L., Gleitman, L. R., & Gleitman, H. (1983). What some concepts might not be. *Cognition, 13*, 263–308.

Ashby, F. G. (1988). Estimating the parameters of multidimensional signal detection theory from simultaneous ratings on separate stimulus components. *Perception & Psychophysics, 44,* 195–204.

Ashby, F. G. (1989). Stochastic general recognition theory. In D. Vickers & P. L. Smith (Eds.), *Human information processing: Measures, mechanisms, and models* (pp. 435–457). Amsterdam: Elsevier.

Ashby, F. G., & Gott, R. E. (1988). Decision rules in the perception and categorization of multidimensional stimuli. *Journal of Experimental Psychology: Learning, Memory, and Cognition, 14,* 33–53.

Ashby, F. G., & Lee, W. W. (1991). Predicting similarity and categorization from identification. *Journal of Experimental Psychology: General, 120,* 150–172.

Ashby, F. G., & Maddox, W. T. (1990). Integrating information from separable psychological dimensions. *Journal of Experimental Psychology: Human Perception and Performance, 16,* 598–612.

Ashby, F. G., & Maddox, W. T. (1991a). *A decision bound theory of categorization.* Manuscript submitted for publication.

Ashby, F. G., & Maddox, W. T. (1991b). A response time theory of perceptual independence. In J. P. Doigon & J. C. Falmagne (Eds.), *Mathematical psychology: Current developments.* New York: Springer-Verlag.

Ashby, F. G., & Maddox, W. T. (1991c). *A response time theory of separability and integrality in speeded classification.* Manuscript submitted for publication.

Ashby, F. G., & Maddox, W. T. (1992). Complex decision rules in categorization: Contrasting novice and experienced performance. *Journal of Experimental Psychology: Human Perception and Performance, 18,* 50–71.

Ashby, F. G., & Maddox, W. T. (in press). Relations between prototype, exemplar, and decision bound models of categorization. *Journal of Mathematical Psychology.*

Ashby, F. G., & Perrin, N. A. (1988). Toward a unified theory of similarity and recognition. *Psychological Review, 95,* 124–150.

Ashby, F. G., & Townsend, J. T. (1986). Varieties of perceptual independence. *Psychological Review, 93,* 154–179.

Attneave, F. (1950). Dimensions of similarity. *American Journal of Psychology, 63,* 516–556.

Attneave, F. (1959). *Applications of information theory to psychology.* New York: Holt, Rinehart, & Winston.

Bahadur, R. R. (1961). A representation of the joint distribution of responses to n dichotomous items. In H. Solomon (Ed.), *Studies in item analysis and prediction* (pp. 158–168). Stanford: Stanford University Press.

Ballard, D. H. (1986). Cortical connections and parallel processing: Structure and function. *Behavioral and Brain Sciences, 9,* 67–120.

Beals, R., Krantz, D. H., & Tversky, A. (1968). The foundations of multidimensional scaling. *Psychological Review, 75,* 127–142.

Beaver, R. J. (1983). Log-linear models for multivariate paired comparison experiments with ties. *Journal of Statistical Planning and Inference, 7,* 209–218.

Beck, J. (1966). Effect of orientation and of shape similarity on perceptual grouping. *Perception & Psychophysics, 1,* 300–302.

Becker, G. M., DeGroot, M. H., & Marschak, J. (1963). Probabilities of choice among very similar objects. *Behavioral Science, 8,* 306–311.

Becker, M. P., & Clogg, C. C. (1988). A note on approximating correlations from odds ratios. *Sociological Methods and Research, 16,* 407–424.

Ben-Akiva, M., & Watanatada, T. (1981). Application of a continuous spatial choice logit model. In C. F. Manski & D. McFadden (Eds.), *Structural analysis of discrete data with econometric applications.* Cambridge, MA: MIT Press.

Bennett, J. F., & Hays, W. L. (1960). Multidimensional unfolding determining the dissimilarity of ranked preference data. *Psychometrika, 25,* 27–43.

Bezembinder, T., & Bossuyt, P. (1989). Strong stochastic transitivity in a multidimensional probabilistic unfolding model. *Journal of Mathematical Psychology, 33,* 496–499.

Bickel, P. J., & Doksum, K. A. (1977). *Mathematical statistics.* San Francisco: Holden-Day.

Biederman, I., & Checkosky, S. F. (1970). Processing redundant information. *Journal of Experimental Psychology, 83,* 486–490.

Bindra, D., Donderi, D. C., & Nishisato, S. (1968). Decision latency of "same"-"different" judgments. *Perception & Psychophysics, 3,* 121–130.

Bindra, D., Williams, J. A., & Wise, J. S. (1965). Judgments of sameness and difference: Experiments on decision time. *Science, 150,* 1625–1627.

Bishop, Y. M. M., Fienberg, S. E., & Holland, P. W. (1975). *Discrete multivariate analysis: Theory and practice.* Cambridge, MA: MIT Press.

Blackwell, H. R. (1963). Neural theories of simple visual discriminations. *Journal of the Optical Society of America, 53,* 129–160.

Bock, R. D. (1975). *Multivariate statistical methods in behavioral research.* New York: McGraw Hill.

Bock, R. D., & Böckenholt, U. (1987). *Multiqual III: Log-linear analysis of nominal or ordinal qualitative data by the method of maximum likelihood.* Chicago: National Educational Resources.

Böckenholt, I., & Gaul, W. (1986). Analysis of choice behavior via probabilistic ideal point and vector models. *Applied Stochastic Models and Data Analysis, 2,* 209–226.

Böckenholt, U. (1988). A logistic representation of multivariate paired comparison models. *Journal of Mathematical Psychology, 32,* 44–63.

Böckenholt, U. (1990). Multivariate Thurstonian models. *Psychometrika, 55,* 391–404.

Böckenholt, U. (1992). Loglinear representation for multivariate choice data. *Mathematical Social Sciences, 23.*

Böckenholt, U., & Böckenholt, I. (1990). Modeling individual differences in unfolding preference data: A restricted latent class approach. *Applied Psychological Measurement, 14,* 257–269.

Borland International (1989). *Turbo Pascal 5.5.* Scotts Valley, CA: Author.

Bornstein, M. H., & Monroe, M. D. (1980). Chromatic information processing: Rate depends on stimulus location in the category and psychological complexity. *Psychological Research, 42,* 213–225.

Box, G. E. P., & Muller, M. A. (1958). A note on the generation of random normal deviates. *Annals of Mathematical Statistics, 29,* 610–613.

Bradley, R. A. (1984). Paired comparisons: Some basic procedures and examples. In P. R. Krishnaiah & P. K. Sen (Eds.), *Handbook of statistics* (Vol. 4, pp. 299–326). New York: North-Holland.

Bradley, R. A, & Terry, M. E. (1952). Rank analysis of incomplete block designs. I: The method of paired comparisons. *Biometrika, 39,* 324–345.

Broadbent, D. E. (1967). Word frequency effect and response bias. *Psychological Review, 74,* 1–15.

Brooks, L. (1978). Nonanalytic concept formation and memory for instances. In E. Rosch & B. B. Lloyd (Eds.), *Cognition and categorization.* Hillsdale, NJ: Erlbaum.

Bruner, J. S., Goodnow, J., & Austin, G. (1956). *A study of thinking.* New York: Wiley.

Bulgren, W. G. (1971). On representations of the doubly non-central F distribution. *Journal of the American Statistical Association, 66,* 184–186.

Burns, B., & Shepp, B. E. (1988). Dimensional interactions and the structure of psychological space: The representation of hue, saturation, and brightness. *Perception & Psychophysics, 43,* 494–507.

Burns, B., Shepp, B. E., McDonough, D., & Weiner-Ehrlich, W. K. (1978). The relation between stimulus analyzability and perceived dimensional structure. In G. H. Bower (Ed.), *The psychology of learning and motivation* (Vol. 12, pp. 77–115). New York: Academic Press.

Busemeyer, J. R., Dewey, G. I., & Medin, D. L. (1984). Evaluation of exemplar-based generalization and the abstraction of categorical information. *Journal of Experimental Psychology: Learning, Memory, and Cognition, 10,* 638–648.

Callaghan, T. C. (1984). Dimensional interaction of hue and brightness in preattentive field segregation. *Perception & Psychophysics, 36,* 25–34.

Callaghan, T. C. (1989). Interference and dominance in texture segregation: Hue, geometric form, and line orientation. *Perception & Psychophysics, 45,* 299–311.

Callaghan, T. C., Lasaga, M. I., & Garner, W. R. (1986). Visual texture segregation based on orientation and hue. *Perception & Psychophysics, 39,* 32–38.

Campbell, F. W., & Robson, J. G. (1968). Application of Fourier analysis to the visibility of gratings. *Journal of Physiology, 197,* 551–556.

Carroll, J. D. (1972). Individual differences and multidimensional scaling. In R. N. Shepard, A. K. Romney, & S. B. Nerlove (Eds.), *Multidimensional scaling: Theory and applications in the behavioral science* (Vol. 1). New York: Seminar Press.

Carroll, J. D. (1976). Spatial, non-spatial and hybrid models for scaling. *Psychometrika, 41,* 439–463.

Carroll, J. D. (1980). Models and methods for multidimensional analysis of preferential choice (or other dominance) data. In E. D. Lantermann & H. Feger (Eds.), *Similarity and choice* (pp. 234–289). Bern: Huber.

Carroll, J. D., & Chang, J. J. (1970). Analysis of individual differences in multidimensional scaling via an N-way generalization of Eckart-Young decomposition. *Psychometrika, 35,* 283–319.

Carroll, J. D., & Chang, J. J. (1972). *IDIOSCAL (individual differences in orientation scaling): A generalization of INDSCAL allowing idiosyncratic reference systems.* Paper presented at the meeting of the Psychometric Society, Princeton, NJ.

Carroll, J. D., DeSarbo, W. S., & De Soete, G. (1988). Stochastic tree unfolding (STUN) models: Theory and application. In H. H. Bock (Ed.), *Classification and related methods of data analysis* (pp. 421–430). Amsterdam: North-Holland.

Carroll, J. D., DeSarbo, W. S., & De Soete, G. (1989). Two classes of stochastic tree unfolding models. In G. De Soete, H. Feger, & K. C. Klauer (Eds)., *New developments in psychological choice modeling* (pp. 161–176). Amsterdam: North-Holland.

Carroll, J. D., & De Soete, G. (1990). Fitting a quasi-Poisson case of the GSTUN (General Stochastic Tree UNfolding) model and some extensions. In M. Schader & W. Gaul (Eds.), *Knowledge, data and computer-assisted decisions* (pp. 93–102). Berlin: Springer-Verlag.

Carroll, J. D., De Soete, G., & DeSarbo, W. S. (1990). Two stochastic multidimensional choice models for marketing research. *Decision Sciences, 21,* 337–356.

Carroll, J. D., & Wish, M. (1974). Models and methods for three-way multidimensional scaling. In D. H. Krantz, R. C. Atkinson, R. D. Luce, & P. Suppes (Eds.), *Contemporary developments in mathematical psychology* (Vol. 2). San Francisco: Freeman.

Cartwright, D. (1941). Relation of decision-time to the categories of response. *American Journal of Psychology, 54,* 174–196.

Caussinus, H. (1965). Contribution a l'analyse statistique tableau de correlation. *Ann. Fac. Sci.,* Univ. Toulouse, *29,* 77–182.

Chandler, J. P. (1965). STEPIT—Finds local minima of a smooth function of several parameters. *Behavioral Science, 14,* 81–82.

Cheng, P. W., & Pachella, R. G. (1984). A psychophysical approach to dimensional separability. *Cognitive Psychology, 16,* 279–304.

Chou, Y., & Arthur, K. H. (1985). New representations for the doubly noncentral F distribution and derived distributions. *Communications in Statistics. Volume A. Theory and Methods, 14,* 527–534.

Chow, G. C. (1981). A comparison of information and posterior probability criteria for model selection. *Journal of Econometrics, 16,* 21–33.

Clark, H. H., & Stafford, R. A. (1969). Memory for semantic features in the verb. *Journal of Experimental Psychology, 80*, 326–334.

Clarke, F. R. (1957). Constant-ratio rule for confusion matrices in speech communication. *Journal of the Acoustical Society of America, 29*, 715–720.

Cohen, M. A. (1980). Random utility systems: The infinite case. *Journal of Mathematical Psychology, 22*, 1–23.

Colonius, H. (1984). *Stochastische Theorien individuallen Wahlverhaltens*. Berlin: Springer-Verlag.

Coombs, C. H. (1950). Psychological scaling without a unit of measurement. *Psychological Review, 57*, 148–158.

Coombs, C. H. (1964). *A theory of data*. New York: Wiley.

Corcoran, D. W. J. (1967). Perceptual independence and recognition of two-dimensional auditory stimuli. *The Journal of the Acoustical Society of America, 42*, 139–142.

Corter, J. E., & Tversky, A. (1986). Extended similarity trees. *Psychometrika, 51*, 429–451.

Cosslett, S. R. (1988). *Extreme-value stochastic processes: A model of random utility maximization for a continuous choice set*. Unpublished manuscript, Department of Economics, Ohio State University.

Cunningham, J. P. (1978). Free trees and bidirectional trees as representations of psychological distance. *Journal of Mathematical Psychology, 17*, 165–188.

Dagsvik, J. K. (1988). *The continuous generalized extreme value model with special reference to static models of labor supply* (Discussion Paper No. 31). Oslo, Norway: Central Bureau of Statistics.

David, H. A. (1988). *The method of paired comparisons* (2nd ed.). London: Griffin.

David, H. A., & Trivedi, M. C. (1962). *Pair, triangle and duo-trio tests*. Technical Report 55. Blacksburg, VA: Virginia Polytechnic Institute, Department of Statistics.

Davidson, R. R., & Bradley, R. A. (1969). Multivariate paired comparisons: The extensions of a univariate model and associated estimation and test procedures. *Biometrika, 56*, 81–95.

Davidson, R. R., & Bradley, R. A. (1970). Multivariate paired comparisons: Some large sample results on estimation and tests of equality of preference. In M. L. Puri (Ed.), *Nonparametric techniques in statistical inference* (pp. 111–125). Cambridge: Cambridge University Press.

Davidson, R. R., & Bradley, R. A. (1971). A regression relationship for multivariate paired comparisons. *Biometrika, 58*, 555–560.

Davidson, R. R., & Farquhar, P. H. (1976). A bibliography on the method of paired comparisons. *Biometrics, 32*, 241–252.

Davoodzadeh, J., & Beaver, R. J. (1983). Models for multivariate paired comparison with ties. *Journal of Mathematical Psychology, 25*, 269–281.

Debreu, G. (1960). [Review of *Individual choice behavior: A theoretical analysis*]. *American Economic Review, 50*, 186–188.

Dempster, A. P., Laird, N. M., & Rubin, D. B. (1977). Maximum likelihood estimation from incomplete data via the EM algorithm. *Journal of the Royal Statistical Society, Series B, 39*, 1–38.

Dennis, J. E. Jr., & Schnabel, R. B. (1983). *Numerical methods for unconstrained optimization and nonlinear equations* (pp. 221–228). Englewood Cliffs, NJ: Prentice-Hall.

DeSarbo, W. S., De Soete, G., Carroll, J. D., & Ramaswamy, V. (1988). A new stochastic ultrametric unfolding methodology for assessing competitive market structure and deriving market segments. *Applied Stochastic Models and Data Analysis, 4*, 185–204.

DeSarbo, W. S., De Soete, G., & Jedidi, K. (1987). Probabilistic multidimensional scaling models for analyzing consumer choice behavior. *Communication and Cognition, 20*, 93–116.

DeSarbo, W. S., Oliver, R. L., & De Soete, G. (1986). A probabilistic multidimensional scaling vector model. *Applied Psychological Measurement, 10*, 79–98.

De Soete, G. (1983a). A least squares algorithm for fitting additive trees to proximity data. *Psychometrika, 48*, 621–626.

De Soete, G. (1983b). On the relation between two generalized cases of Thurstone's law of comparative judgment. *Mathétiques et Sciences Humaines, 21,* 45–57.

De Soete, G. (1990). A latent class approach to modeling pairwise preferential choice data. In M. Schader & W. Gaul (Eds.), *Knowledge, data and computer-assisted decisions* (pp. 103–113). Berlin: Springer-Verlag.

De Soete, G., & Carroll, J. D. (1983). A maximum likelihood method for fitting the wandering vector model. *Psychometrika, 48,* 553–566.

De Soete, G., & Carroll, J. D. (1986). Probabilistic multidimensional choice models for representing paired comparisons data. In E. Diday, Y. Escoufier, L. Lebart, J. Pagès, Y. Schektman, & R. Tommasone (Eds.), *Data analysis and informatics* (Vol. 4, pp. 485–497). Amsterdam: North-Holland.

De Soete, G., & Carroll, J. D. (1990). Probabilistic multidimensional choice models for marketing research. In A. de Fonténay, M. H. Shugard, & D. S. Sibley (Eds.), *Telecommunications demand modelling: An integrated view* (pp. 167–184). Amsterdam: North Holland.

De Soete, G., Carroll, J. D., & DeSarbo, W. S. (1986). The wandering ideal point model: A probabilistic multidimensional unfolding model for paired comparisons data. *Journal of Mathematical Psychology, 30,* 28–41.

De Soete, G., Carroll, J. D., & DeSarbo, W. S. (1989). The wandering ideal point model for analyzing paired comparisons data. In G. De Soete, H. Feger, & K. C. Klauer (Eds.), *New developments in psychological choice modeling* (pp. 123–137). Amsterdam: North-Holland.

De Soete, G., & DeSarbo, W. S. (1991). A latent class probit model for analyzing pick any/N data. *Journal of Classification, 8,* 45–63.

De Soete, G., DeSarbo, W. S., Furnas, G. W., & Carroll, J. D. (1984). The estimation of ultrametric and path length trees from rectangular proximity data. *Psychometrika, 49,* 289–310.

De Valois, K. K., & Tootell, R. B. H. (1983). Spatial-frequency-specific inhibition in cat striate cortex cells. *Journal of Physiology, 336,* 359–376.

De Valois, R. L., Albrecht, D. G., & Thorell, L. G. (1982). Spatial frequency selectivity of cells in Macaque visual cortex. *Vision Research, 22,* 545–559.

De Valois, R. L., & De Valois, K. K. (1988). *Spatial vision.* New York: Oxford University Press.

De Valois, R. L., Yund, E. W., & Hepler, N. (1982). The orientation and direction selectivity of cells in Macaque visual cortex. *Vision Research, 22,* 531–544.

Devroye, L. (1986). *Non-uniform random variate generation.* New York: Springer-Verlag.

Digby, P. G. N. (1983). Approximating the tetrachoric correlation coefficient. *Biometrics, 40,* 753–757.

Dixon, P., & Just, M. A. (1978). Normalization of irrelevant dimensions in stimulus comparisons. *Journal of Experimental Psychology: Human Perception and Performance, 4,* 36–46.

Dobson, A. G. (1974). Unrooted trees for numerical taxonomy. *Journal of Applied Probability, 11,* 32–42.

Dunn, J. C. (1983). Spatial metrics of integral and separable dimensions. *Journal of Experimental Psychology: Human Perception and Performance, 9,* 242–257.

Durlach, N. I., & Braida, L. D. (1969). Intensity perception. I: Preliminary theory of intensity resolution. *Journal of the Acoustical Society of America, 46,* 372–383.

Edgell, S. E., & Geisler, W. S. (1980). A set-theoretic random utility model of choice behavior. *Journal of Mathematical Psychology, 21,* 265–278.

Eijkman, E., & Vendrik, J. K. (1965). Can a sensory system be specified by its internal noise? *The Journal of the Acoustical Society of America, 37,* 1102–1109.

Emmerich, D. S., Gray, C. S., Watson, C. S., & Tanis, D. C. (1972). Response latency, confidence and ROCs in auditory signal detection. *Perception & Psychophysics, 11,* 65–72.

Ennis, D. M. (1988a). Confusable and discriminable stimuli: Comment on Nosofsky (1986) and Shepard (1986). *Journal of Experimental Psychology: General, 117,* 408–411.

Ennis, D. M. (1988b). Technical comment: Toward a universal law of generalization. *Science, 242,* 944.

Ennis, D. M., & Ashby, F. G. (1991). *The relative sensitivities of same-different and identification judgment models to perceptual dependence*. Manuscript submitted for publication.

Ennis, D. M., & Johnson, N. L. (in press). Thurstone-Shepard similarity models as special cases of moment generating functions. *Journal of Mathematical Psychology.*

Ennis, D. M., & Mullen, K. (1986a). A multivariate model for discrimination methods. *Journal of Mathematical Psychology, 30,* 206–219.

Ennis, D. M., & Mullen, K. (1986b). Theoretical aspects of sensory discrimination. *Chemical Senses, 11,* 513–522.

Ennis, D. M., & Mullen, K. (1992). Probabilistic psychophysics with noisy stimuli. *Mathematical Social Sciences, 23.*

Ennis, D. M., Mullen, K., & Frijters, J. E. R. (1988). Variants of the method of triads: Unidimensional Thurstonian models. *British Journal of Mathematical and Statistical Psychology, 41,* 25–36.

Ennis, D. M., Mullen, K., Frijters, J. E. R., & Tindall, J. (1989). Decision conflicts: Within trial resampling in Richardson's method of triads. *British Journal of Mathematical and Statistical Psychology, 42,* 265–269.

Ennis, D. M., Palen, J. J., & Mullen, K. (1988). A multidimensional stochastic theory of similarity. *Journal of Mathematical Psychology, 32,* 449–465.

Estes, W. K. (1986). Array models for category learning. *Cognitive Psychology, 18,* 500–549.

Falmagne, J-C. (1981). On a recurrent misuse of a classical functional equation result. *Journal of Mathematical Psychology, 23,* 190–193.

Falmagne, J-C. (1985). *Elements of psychophysical theory.* New York: Oxford University Press.

Farley, J. U., Katz, J., & Lehmann, D. R. (1978). Impact of different comparison sets on evaluation of a new subcompact car. *Journal of Consumer Research, 5,* 138–142.

Fechner, G. (1860, 1966). *Elements of Psychophysics, Vol. 1.* Translation by H. E. Adler. New York: Holt, Rinehart, & Winston, Inc.

Felfoldy, A. (1974). Repetition effects in choice reaction time to multidimensional stimuli. *Perception & Psychophysics, 15,* 453–459.

Felfoldy, G., & Garner, W. R. (1971). The effects on speeded classification of implicit and explicit instructions regarding redundant dimensions. *Perception & Psychophysics, 9,* 289–292.

Fidell, S. (1970). Sensory function in multimodal signal detection. *The Journal of the Acoustical Society of America, 47,* 1009–1015.

Fienberg, S. E. (1979). Log-linear representation for paired comparison models with ties and within-pair order effects. *Biometrics, 35,* 479–481.

Fienberg, S. E., & Larntz, K. (1976). Log-linear representation for paired and multiple comparison models. *Biometrika, 63,* 245–262.

Fiorentini, A., Baumgartner, G., Magnussen, S., Schiller, P., & Thomas, J. P. (1990). The perception of brightness and darkness: Relations to neuronal receptive fields. In L. Spillman and J. S. Werner (Eds.), *The neurophysiological foundations of visual perception.* New York: Academic Press.

Flannagan, M. J., Fried, L. S., & Holyoak, K. J. (1986). Distributional expectations and the induction of category structure. *Journal of Experimental Psychology: Learning, Memory, and Cognition, 12,* 241–256.

Foard, C. F., & Kemler-Nelson, D. G. (1984). Holistic and analytic modes of processing: The multiple determinants of perceptual analysis. *Journal of Experimental Psychology: General, 113,* 94–111.

Fried, L. S., & Holyoak, K. J. (1984). Induction of category distributions: A framework for classification learning. *Journal of Experimental Psychology: Learning, Memory, and Cognition, 10,* 234–257.

Fukunaga, K. (1972). *Introduction to statistical pattern recognition.* New York: Academic Press.

Furchner, C. S., Thomas, J. P., & Campbell, F. (1977). Detection and discrimination of simple and complex patterns at low spatial frequencies. *Vision Research, 17,* 827–836.

Furnas, G. W. (1980). *Objects and their features: The metric representation of two class data.* Unpublished doctoral dissertation, Stanford University, Stanford.

Galambos, J. (1981). Extreme value theory in applied probability. *Mathematical Scientist, 6*, 13–26.

Galambos, J. (1982). The role of functional equations in stochastic model building. *Aequationes Mathematicae, 25*, 21–41.

Galambos, J. (1987). *The asymptotic theory of extreme order statistics* (2nd ed.). Malabar, FL: Krieger.

Galambos, J., & Kotz, S. (1978). Characterizations of probability distributions. In *Lecture notes in mathematics* (Vol. 675). Heidelberg: Springer-Verlag.

Garner, W. R. (1962). *Uncertainty and structure as psychological concepts*. New York: Wiley.

Garner, W. R. (1970). The stimulus in information processing. *American Psychologist, 25*, 350–358.

Garner, W. R. (1974). *The processing of information and structure*. New York: Wiley.

Garner, W. R. (1977). The effect of absolute size on the separability of the dimensions of size and brightness. *Bulletin of the Psychonomics Society, 9*, 380–382.

Garner, W. R. (1983). Asymmetric interactions of stimulus dimensions in perceptual information processing. In T. Tighe, & B. E. Shepp (Eds.), *Perception, cognition and development: Interactional analyses* (pp. 77–102). Hillsdale, NJ: Lawrence Erlbaum Associates.

Garner, W. R. (1988). Facilitation and interference with a separable redundant dimension in stimulus comparison. *Perception & Psychophysics, 44*, 321–330.

Garner, W. R., & Felfoldy, G. L. (1970). Integrality of stimulus dimensions in various types of information processing. *Cognitive Psychology, 1*, 225–241.

Garner, W. R., Hake, H. W., & Eriksen, C. W. (1956). Operationism and the concept of perception. *Psychological Review, 63*, 149–159.

Garner, W. R., & Haun, F. (1978). Letter identification as a function of perceptual limitation and type of attribute. *Journal of Experimental Psychology: Human Perception and Performance, 4*, 199–209.

Gati, I., & Tversky, A. (1982). Representations of qualitative and quantitative dimensions. *Journal of Experimental Psychology: Human Perception and Performance, 8*, 325–340.

Genest, C. (1984). Pooling operators with the marginalization property. *The Canadian Journal of Statistics, 12*, 153–163.

Genz, A. C., & Malik, A. A. (1980). Remarks on algorithm 006: An adaptive algorithm for numerical integration over an N-dimensional rectangular region. *Journal of Computing and Applied Mathematics, 6*, 295–302.

Gille, J. G. (1984). Detection and identification of color increments to a white background. *Journal of the Optical Society of America A, 1*, 1241 (Abstract).

Gillund, G., & Shiffrin, R. M. (1984). A retrieval model for both recognition and recall. *Psychological Review, 91*, 1–67.

Goguen, J. A. (1969). The logic of inexact concepts. *Synthese, 19*, 325–373.

Goodman, L. A. (1979). Simple models for the analysis of association in cross-classification having ordered categories. *Journal of American Statistical Association, 74*, 537–552.

Goodman, L. A. (1981). Association models and the bivariate normal for contingency tables with ordered categories. *Biometrika, 68*, 347–355.

Goodman, L. A. (1985). The analysis of cross classified data having ordered and/or unordered categories: association models, correlation models, and asymmetry models for contingency tables with or without missing entries (1983 Henry L. Reitz Memorial). *Annals of Statistics, 13*, 10–69.

Goodman, L. A. (1986). Some useful extensions of the usual correspondence analysis approach and the usual log-linear models approach in the analysis of contingency tables. *International Statistical Review, 54*, 243–309.

Goodman, L. A. (1987). The analysis of a set of multidimensional contingency tables using log linear models, latent class models, and correlation models: The Solomon data revisited. In A. E. Gelfand (Ed.), *Contributions to the theory and application of statistics*. New York: Academic Press.

Gottwald, R. L., & Garner, W. R. (1975). Filtering and condensation tasks with integral and separable dimensions. *Perception & Psychophysics, 18,* 26–28.

Graham, N. (1981). The visual system does crude Fourier analyses of patterns. In S. Grossberg (Ed.), *Mathematical psychology and psychophysiology.* Providence, RI: American Mathematical Society.

Graham, N. (1985). Detection and identification of near-threshold visual patterns. *Journal of the Optical Society of America A, 2,* 1468–1482.

Graham, N. (1989). *Visual pattern analyzers.* New York: Oxford University Press.

Graham, N., Kramer, P., & Haber, N. (1985). Attending to the spatial frequency and spatial position of near-threshold visual patterns. In M. I. Posner & O. S. M. Marin (Eds.), *Attention and performance* (Vol. 6). Hillsdale, NJ: Lawrence Erlbaum Associates.

Graham, N., Kramer, P., & Yager, D. (1987). Signal detection models for multidimensional stimuli: Probability distributions and combination rules. *Journal of Mathematical Psychology, 31,* 192–206.

Graham, N., & Nachmias, J. (1971). Detection of grating patterns containing two spatial frequencies: A comparison of single-channel and multiple-channel models. *Vision Research, 11,* 251–259.

Grau, J. W., & Kemler-Nelson, G. K. (1988). The distinction between integral and separable dimensions: Evidence for the integrality of pitch and loudness. *Journal of Experimental Psychology: General, 117,* 347–370.

Graybill, F. A. (1976). *Theory and application of the linear model.* North Scituate, MA: Duxbury Press.

Green, D. M. (1958). Detection of multiple component signals in noise. *The Journal of Acoustical Society of America, 30,* 904–911.

Green, D. M., & Birdsall, T. G. (1978). Detection and recognition. *Psychological Review, 85,* 192–206.

Green, D. M., & Swets, J. A. (1974). *Signal detection theory and psychophysics.* New York: Krieger.

Greenacre, M. J. (1984). *Theory and application of correspondence analysis.* London: Academic Press.

Grier, J. B. (1971). Nonparametric indexes for sensitivity and bias: Computing formulas. *Psychological Bulletin, 75,* 424–429.

Gulliksen, H. (1958). Comparatal dispersion: A measure of accuracy of judgment. *Psychometrika, 23,* 137–150.

Halff, H. M. (1976). Choice theories for differentially comparable alternatives. *Journal of Mathematical Psychology, 14,* 244–246.

Hammerton, M. (1970). An investigation into changes in decision criteria and other details of a decision-making task. *Psychonomic Science, 21,* 203–204.

Handel, S., & Imai, S. (1972). The free classification of analyzable and unanalyzable stimuli. *Perception & Psychophysics, 12,* 108–116.

Hayes-Roth, B., & Hayes-Roth, F. (1977). Concept learning and the recognition and classification of exemplars. *Journal of Verbal Learning and Verbal Behavior, 16,* 119–136.

Healy, A. F., & Kubovy, M. A. (1977). A comparison of recognition memory to numerical decision: How prior probabilities affect cutoff location. *Memory & Cognition, 5,* 3–9.

Hefner, R. A. (1958). *Extensions of the law of comparative judgment to discriminable and multidimensional stimuli.* Unpublished doctoral dissertation, University of Michigan.

Heiser, W., & De Leeuw, J. (1981). Multidimensional mapping of preference data. *Mathématiques et Sciences Humaines, 73,* 39–96.

Hilton, R. W. (1985). *Probabilistic choice models and information.* Sarasota, FL: American Accounting Association.

Hinton, G. E. (1989). Connectionist learning procedures. *Artificial Intelligence, 40,* 185–234.

Hinton, G. E., & Anderson, J. A. (Eds.). (1981). *Parallel models of associative memory.* Hillsdale, NJ: Lawrence Erlbaum Associates.

Hinton, G. E., & Sejnowski, T. J. (1983). Analyzing cooperative computation. *Proceedings of the Fifth Annual Conference of the Cognitive Science Society.*

Hinton, G. E., & Sejnowski, T. J. (1986). Learning and relearning in boltzmann machines. In D. Rumelhart, J. L. McClelland, & the PDP research group (Eds.), *Parallel distributed processing: Explorations in the microstructure of cognition* (Vol. 1). Cambridge, MA: Bradford Books.

Hintzman, D. L. (1986). "Schema abstraction" in a multiple-trace memory model. *Psychological Review, 93,* 411–428.

Hintzman, D. L. (1988). Judgments of frequency and recognition memory in a multiple-trace memory model. *Psychological Review, 95,* 528–551.

Hirsch, J., Hylton, R., & Graham, N. (1982). Simultaneous recognition of two spatial frequency components. *Vision Research, 22,* 365–375.

Hodge, M. H., & Pollack, I. (1962). Confusion matrix analysis of single and multidimensional auditory displays. *Journal of Experimental Psychology, 63,* 129–142.

Hogg, R. V., & Craig, A. T. (1978). *Introduction to mathematical statistics* (4th ed.). New York: Macmillan.

Hojo, H. (1982). Confusion-choice model for multidimensional scaling: Modification of Nakatani's model. *Japanese Psychological Research, 24,* 211–215.

Holland, P. W. (1987). *The Dutch identity: A new tool for the study of item response theory models* (Report No. 87–78). Princeton, NJ: Educational Testing Service.

Homa, D., Sterling, S., & Trepel, L. (1981). Limitations of exemplar-based generalization and the abstraction of categorical information. *Journal of Experimental Psychology: Human Learning and Memory, 7,* 418–439.

Hope, A. C. (1968). A simplified Monte Carlo significance test procedure. *Journal of the Royal Statistical Society, Series B, 30,* 582–598.

Horan, C. B. (1969). Multidimensional scaling: Combining observations when individuals have different perceptual structures. *Psychometrika, 34,* 139–165.

Hubel, D. H. (1982). Exploration of the primary visual cortex, 1955–78. *Nature, 299,* 515–524.

Hubel, D. H., & Livingstone, M. S. (1985). Complex-unoriented cells in a subregion of primate area 18. *Nature, 315,* 325–327.

Hubel, D. H., & Weisel, T. N. (1959). Receptive fields of receptive single neurones in the cat's striate cortex. *Journal of Physiology (London), 148,* 574–591.

Hubel, D. H., & Weisel, T. N. (1962). Receptive fields, binocular interaction, and functional architecture in the cat's visual cortex. *Journal of Physiology, 160,* 106–123.

Hubel, D. H., & Weisel, T. N. (1968). Receptive fields and functional architecture of monkey striate cortex. *Journal of Physiology, 195,* 215–243.

Hubel, D. H., & Weisel, T. N. (1974). Uniformity of monkey striate cortex: A parallel relationship between field size, scatter, and magnification factor. *Journal of Comparative Neurology, 158,* 295–305.

Hyman, R., & Well, A. (1967). Judgments of similarity and spatial models. *Perception & Psychophysics, 2,* 233–248.

Hyman, R., & Well, A. (1968). Perceptual separability and spatial models. *Perception & Psychophysics, 3,* 161–165.

Imhof, J. P. (1961). Computing the distribution of quadratic forms in normal variables. *Biometrika, 48,* 419–426.

IMSL Library Reference Manual (1979). New York: International Mathematical and Statistical Libraries.

Indow, T. (1974). Applications of multidimensional scaling in perception. In E. C. Carterette, &

M. P. Friedman (Eds.), *Handbook of perception: Vol. 2. Psychophysical judgment and measurement*. New York: Academic Press.

Iverson, G. J. (1979). Conditions under which Thurstone Case III representations for binary choice probabilities are also Fechnerian. *Journal of Mathematical Psychology, 20,* 263–271.

Iverson, G. J. (1987). Thurstonian psychophysics: Case III. *Journal of Mathematical Psychology, 31,* 219–247.

Iverson, G. J., & Sheu, C. F. (1992). Characterizing random variables in the context of signal detection theory. *Mathematical Social Sciences, 23.*

James, W. (1890). *Principles of psychology.* New York: Holt.

Johnson, N. L., & Kotz, S. (1970). *Continuous univariate distributions* (Vol. 2). New York: Wiley.

Johnson, N. L., & Kotz, S. (1975). On some generalized Farlie-Gumbel-Morgenstern distributions. *Communications in Statistics, 4,* 415–427.

Johnson, N. L., & Kotz, S. (1977). On some generalized Farlie-Gumbel-Morgenstern distributions. II: Regression, correlation and further generalizations. *Communications in Statistics, 6,* 485–496.

Julesz, B. (1981). Textons, the element of texture perception, and their interactions. *Nature, 290,* 91–97.

Julesz, B. (1985). Preconscious and conscious processes in vision. In C. Chagas, R. Gattass, & C. Gross (Eds.), *Pattern recognition mechanisms.* Berlin: Springer-Verlag.

Kadlec, H., & Townsend, J. T. (1992). Implications of marginal and conditional detection parameters for the separabilities and independence of perceptual dimensions. *Journal of Mathematical Psychology, 36.*

Kanerva, P. (1988). *Sparse distributed memory.* Cambridge, MA: Bradford/MIT Press.

Kapenga, J. A., de Doncker, E., Mullen, K., & Ennis, D. M. (1987). The integration of the multivariate normal density function for the triangular method. In P. Keast & G. Fairweather (Eds.), *Numerical integration* (pp. 321–328). Norwell, MA: Reidel.

Karlin, S., & Taylor, H. K. (1981). *A second course in stochastic processes.* New York: Academic Press.

Keren, G., & Baggen, S. (1981). Recognition models of alphanumeric characters. *Perception & Psychophysics, 29,* 234–246.

Kerr, L. G. (1974). Detection and identification of monochromatic stimuli under chromatic contrast. *Vision Research, 14,* 1095–1105.

Khatri, C. G. (1980). Quadratic forms in normal variables. In P. R. Krishnaiah (Ed.), *Handbook of statistics* (Vol. 1, pp. 443–469). Amsterdam: North-Holland.

Klatzky, R. L., Lederman, S., & Reed, C. (1987). There's more to touch than meets the eye: The salience of object attributes for haptics with and without vision. *Journal of Experimental Psychology: General, 116,* 356–369.

Klatzky, R. L., Lederman, S., & Reed, C. (1989). Haptic integration of object properties: Texture, hardness, and planar contour. *Journal of Experimental Psychology: Human Perception and Performance, 15,* 45–57.

Klein, S. A. (1985). Double judgment psychophysics: Problems and solutions. *Journal of the Optical Society of America A, 2,* 1560–1585.

Klingberg, F. L. (1941). Studies in measurement of the relations between sovereign states. *Psychometrika, 6,* 335–352.

Knuth, D. E. (1981). *The art of computer programming* (2nd ed.). Reading, MA: Addison-Wesley.

Koehler, K. J., & Ridpath, H. (1982). An application of a biased version of the Bradley-Terry-Luce model to professional basketball results. *Journal of Mathematical Psychology, 25,* 187–205.

Kornbrot, D. E. (1978). Theoretical and empirical comparison of Luce's choice model and logistic Thurstone model of categorical judgment. *Perception & Psychophysics, 24,* 193–208.

Kraemer, H. C. (1988). Assessment of 2 × 2 associations: Generalization of signal detection methodology. *The American Statistician, 42,* 37–49.

Kramer, P., Graham, N., & Yager, D. (1985). Simultaneous measurement of spatial-frequency summation and uncertainty effects. *Journal of the Optical Society of America A, 2,* 1533–1542.

Krantz, D. H. (1967). Rational distance function for multidimensional scaling. *Journal of Mathematical Psychology, 4,* 226–245.

Krantz, D. H. (1974). Measurement theory and qualitative laws in psychophysics. In D. H. Krantz et al. (Eds.), *Contemporary developments in mathematical psychology* (Vol. 2). San Francisco: Freeman.

Krantz, D. H., & Tversky, A. (1971). Conjoint-measurement analysis of composition rules in psychology. *Psychological Review, 78,* 151–169.

Krantz, D. H., & Tversky, A. (1975). Similarity of rectangles: An analysis of subjective dimensions. *Journal of Mathematical Psychology, 12,* 4–34.

Krumhansl, C. L. (1978). Concerning the applicability of geometric models to similarity data: The interrelationship between similarity and spatial density. *Psychological Review, 85,* 445–463.

Kruschke, J. K. (1992). ALCOVE: An exemplar-based connectionist model of category learning. *Psychological Review, 99,* 22–44.

Kruskal, J. B. (1978). Factor analysis and principal components. I: Bilinear models. In W. H. Kruskal & J. M. Tanur (Eds.), *International encyclopedia of statistics* (Vol. 1, pp. 307–330). New York: Free Press.

Kruskal, J. B., Young, F. W., & Seery, J. B. (1973). *How to use KYST, a very flexible program to do multidimensional scaling unfolding.* Murray Hill, NJ: Bell Laboratories.

Kubovy, M., & Healy, A. F. (1977). The decision rule in probabilistic categorization: What it is and how it is learned. *Journal of Experimental Psychology: General, 106,* 427–446.

Kubovy, M., Rapoport, A., & Tversky, A. (1971). Deterministic vs. probabilistic strategies in detection. *Perception & Psychophysics, 9,* 427–429.

Lacouture, Y. (1990). *Connectionist models of choice and reaction time in psychophysics and word recognition.* Unpublished doctoral dissertation, McGill University, Department of Psychology.

Lacouture, Y., & Marley, A. A. J. (1991). *A connectionist model of choice and reaction time in absolute identification.* Manuscript submitted for publication.

Lakoff, G. (1987). *Women, fire, and dangerous things.* Chicago: University of Chicago press.

Latta, R. B. (1979). Composition rules for probabilities from paired comparisons. *Annals of Statistics, 7,* 349–371.

Lazarsfeld, P. F., & Henry, R. W. (1968). *Latent structure analysis.* Boston: Houghton Mifflin.

Lazarte, A. A., & Schönemann, P. H. (1991). Saliency metric for subadditive dissimilarity judgments of rectangles. *Perception & Psychophysics, 49,* 142–158.

Lee, W. (1963). Choosing among confusably distributed stimuli with specific likelihood ratios. *Perceptual and Motor Skills, 16,* 445–467.

Lee, W., & Janke, M. (1964). Categorizing externally distributed stimulus samples for three continua. *Journal of Experimental Psychology, 68,* 376–382.

Lee, W., & Janke, M. (1965). Categorizing externally distributed stimulus samples for unequal molar probabilities. *Psychological Reports, 17,* 79–90.

Levy, R. M., & Haggbloom, S. J. (1971). Tests of a multidimensional discrimination model of stimulus identification. *Psychonomic Science, 25,* 203–204.

Livingstone, M. S., & Hubel, D. H. (1988). Segregation of form, color, movement, and depth: Anatomy, physiology, and perception. *Science, 240,* 740–749.

Lockhead, G. R. (1966). Effects of dimensional redundancy on visual discrimination. *Journal of Experimental Psychology, 72,* 94–104.

Lockhead, G. R. (1970). Identification and the form of multidimensional discrimination space. *Journal of Experimental Psychology, 85,* 1–10.

Lockhead, G. R., & King, M. C. (1977). Classifying integral stimuli. *Journal of Experimental Psychology: Human Perception and Performance, 3,* 436–443.

Lockhead, G. R. (1979). Holistic versus analytic process models: A reply. *Journal of Experimental Psychology: Human Perception and Performance, 5,* 746–755.

Lord, F. (1962). [Review of *Studies in item analysis and prediction*]. *Psychometrika, 27,* 207–213.

Lord, F., & Novick, M. R. (1968). *Statistical theories of mental test scores.* Reading, MA: Addison-Wesley.

Luce, R. D. (1959). *Individual choice behavior.* New York: Wiley.

Luce, R. D. (1963a). Detection and recognition. In R. D. Luce, R. R. Bush, & E. Galanter (Eds.), *Handbook of mathematical psychology* (Vol. 1, pp. 103–189). New York: Wiley.

Luce, R. D. (1963b). A threshold theory for simple detection experiments. *Psychological Review, 70,* 61–79.

Luce, R. D. (1977a). The choice axiom after twenty years. *Journal of Mathematical Psychology, 15,* 215–233.

Luce, R. D. (1977b). Thurstone's discriminal processes fifty years later. *Psychometrika, 42,* 461–490.

Luce, R. D. (1986). *Response times. Their role in inferring elementary mental organization.* New York: Oxford University Press.

Luce, R. D., & Green, D. M. (1972). A neural timing theory for response times and the psychophysics of intensity. *Psychological Review, 79,* 14–57.

Luce, R. D., & Suppes, P. (1965). Preference, utility, and subjective probability. In R. D. Luce, R. R. Bush, & E. Galanter (Eds.), *Handbook of mathematical psychology* (Vol. 3, pp. 249–410). New York: Wiley.

MacAdam, D. L. (1942). Visual sensitivities to color difference in daylight. *Journal of Optical Society of America, 32,* 247–274.

MacKay, D. B. (1989). Probabilistic multidimensional scaling: An anisotropic model for distance judgments. *Journal of Mathematical Psychology, 33,* 187–205.

MacKay, D. B., & Dröge, C. (1990). Extensions of probabilistic perceptual maps with implications for competitive positioning and choice. *International Journal of Research and Marketing, 7,* 265–282.

MacKay, D. B., & Zinnes, J. L. (1981). Probabilistic scaling of spatial distance judgments. *Geographical Analysis, 13,* 21–37.

MacKay, D. B., & Zinnes, J. L. (1986). A probabilistic model for the multidimensional scaling of proximity and preference data. *Marketing Science, 5,* 325–344.

Marley, A. A. J. (1971). Conditions for the representation of absolute judgment and pair comparison isosensitivity curves by cumulative distributions. *Journal of Mathematical Psychology, 8,* 554–590.

Marley, A. A. J. (1981). Multivariate stochastic processes compatible with "aspect" models of similarity and choice. *Psychometrika, 46,* 421–428.

Marley, A. A. J. (1982). Random utility models with all choice probabilities expressible as 'functions' of the binary choice probabilities. *Mathematical Social Sciences, 3,* 39–56.

Marley, A. A. J. (1989a). Random utility family that includes many of the 'classical' models and has closed form choice probabilities and choice reaction times. *British Journal of Mathematical and Statistical Psychology, 42,* 13–36.

Marley, A. A. J. (1989b). Addendum to "A random utility family that includes many of the 'classical' models and has closed form choice probabilities and choice reaction times." *British Journal of Mathematical and Statistical Psychology, 42,* 280.

Marley, A. A. J. (1991a). Aggregation theorems and multidimensional stochastic choice models. *Theory and Decision, 34,* 81–87.

Marley, A. A. J. (1991b). Context-dependent probabilistic choice models based on measures of binary advantage. *Mathematical Social Sciences, 21.*

Marley, A. A. J. (1992). Aggregation theorems and the combination of probabilistic rank orders. In D. E. Critchlaw, M. A. Fligner, & J. S. Verducci (Eds.), *Probability models and data analysis for ranking data: Lecture notes in statistics*. New York: Springer-Verlag.

Marley, A. A. J., & Colonius, H. (1992). The "horse race" random utility model and its competing risks interpretation. *Journal of Mathematical Psychology, 35*.

Marley, A. A. J., & Cook, V. T. (1984). A fixed rehearsal capacity interpretation of limits on absolute identification performance. *British Journal of Mathematical and Statistical Psychology, 37*, 136–151.

Marley, A. A. J., & Cook, V. T. (1986). A limited capacity rehearsal model for psychophysical judgments applied to magnitude estimation. *Journal of Mathematical Psychology, 30*, 339–390.

Marr, D. (1982). *Vision*. San Francisco: Freeman.

Marshall, A. W., & Olkin, I. (1988). Families of multivariate distributions. *Journal of the American Statistical Association, 83*, 834–841.

Massaro, D. W. (1984). Building and testing models of reading processes. In P. D. Pearson (Ed.), *Handbook of reading research* (pp. 111–146). New York: Longman.

Massaro, D. W. (1987a). Integrating multiple sources of information in listening and reading. In D. A. Allport, D. G. MacKay, W. Prinz, & E. Scheerer (Eds.), *Language perception and production: Shared mechanisms in listening, speaking, reading, and writing* (pp. 111–129). London: Academic Press.

Massaro, D. W. (1987b). *Speech perception by ear and eye: A paradigm for psychological inquiry*. Hillsdale, NJ: Lawrence Erlbaum Associates.

Massaro, D. W. (1989). Testing between the TRACE model and the fuzzy logical model of speech perception. *Cognitive Psychology, 21*, 398–421.

Massaro, D. W., & Cohen, M. M. (1987). Process and connectionist models of pattern recognition. *Proceedings of the Ninth Annual Conference of the Cognitive Science Society* (pp. 258–264). Hillsdale, NJ: Lawrence Erlbaum Associates.

Massaro, D. W., & Cohen, M. M. (1991). Interactive activation and the interaction of sensory information and context in perception. *Cognitive Psychology, 23*, 558–614.

Massaro, D. W., & Friedman, D. (1990). Models of integration given multiple sources of information. *Psychological Review, 97*, 225–252.

Massaro, D. W., & Hary, J. M. (1986). Addressing issues in letter recognition. *Psychological Research, 48*, 123–132.

Massaro, D. W., Tseng, C., & Cohen, M. M. (1983). Vowel and lexical tone perception in Mandarin Chinese: Psycholinguistic and psychoacoustic contributions. *Quantitative Linguistics, 19*, 76–102.

McClelland, J. L. (1991). Stochastic interactive processes and the effect of context on perception. *Cognitive Psychology, 23*, 1–44.

McClelland, J. L., & Elman, J. L. (1986). The TRACE model of speech perception. *Cognitive Psychology, 18*, 1–86.

McClelland, J. L., & Rumelhart, D. E. (1981). An interactive activation model of context effects in letter perception. I: An account of basic findings. *Psychological Review, 88*, 375–407.

McClelland, J. L., & Rumelhart, D. E. (Eds.). (1986). *Parallel distributed processing: Explorations in the microstructure of cognition. Vol. 2: Psychological and biological models*. Cambridge, MA: Bradford/MIT Press.

McClelland, J. L., & Rumelhart, D. E. (1988). *Explorations in parallel distributed processing: A handbook of models, programs, and exercises*. Cambridge, MA: MIT Press.

McCloskey, M., & Glucksberg, S. (1979). Decision processes in verifying category membership statements: Implications for models of semantic memory. *Cognitive Psychology, 11*, 1–37.

McConway, K. J. (1981). Marginalization and linear opinion pools. *Journal of the American Statistical Association, 76*, 410–414.

McCullagh, P., & Nelder, J. A. (1983). *Generalized linear models*. London: Chapman and Hall.

McFadden, D. (1978). Modelling the choice of residential location. In A. Karlquist et al. (Eds.), *Spatial interaction theory and planning models*. Amsterdam: North-Holland.

McGee, V. C. (1968). Multidimensional scaling of n sets of similarity measures: A nonmetric individual differences approach. *Multivariate Behavioral Research, 3*, 233–248.

McLachlan, G. J., & Basford, K. E. (1988). *Mixture models*. New York: Dekker.

Medin, D. L., Altom, M. W., Edelson, S. M., & Freko, D. (1982). Correlated symptoms and simulated medical classification. *Journal of Experimental Psychology: Learning, Memory, and Cognition, 8*, 37–50.

Medin, D. L., & Schaffer, M. M. (1978). Context theory of classification learning. *Psychological Review, 85*, 207–238.

Medin, D. L., & Schwanenflugel, P. J. (1981). Linear separability in classification learning. *Journal of Experimental Psychology: Human Learning and Memory, 1*, 335–368.

Melara, R. D. (1989a). Dimensional interaction between color and pitch. *Journal of Experimental Psychology: Human Perception and Performance, 15*, 69–79.

Melara, R. D. (1989b). Similarity relations among synthetic stimuli and their attributes. *Journal of Experimental Psychology: Human Perception and Performance, 15*, 212–231.

Melara, R. D., & Marks, L. E. (1990a). Hard and soft interacting dimensions: Differential effects of dual context on classification. *Perception & Psychophysics, 47*, 307–325.

Melara, R. D., & Marks, L. E. (1990b). Perceptual primacy of dimensions: Support for a model of dimensional interactions. *Journal of Experimental Psychology: Human Perception and Performance, 16*, 398–414.

Melara, R. D., & O'Brien, T. P. (1987). Interaction between synthetically corresponding dimensions. *Journal of Experimental Psychology: General, 116*, 323–336.

Mervis, C. B. (1980). Category structure and the development of categorization. In R. Spiro, B. C. Bruce, & W. F. Brewer (Eds.), *Theoretical issues in reading comprehension*. Hillsdale, NJ: Lawrence Erlbaum Associates.

Mervis, C. B., Catlin, J., & Rosch, E. (1976). Relationships among goodness-of-example, category norms, and word frequency. *Bulletin of the Psychonomic Society, 7*, 283–284.

Mervis, C. B., Rips, L., Rosch, E., Shoben, E. J., & Smith, E. E. (1975). [Relatedness of concepts]. Unpublished data.

Mervis, C. B., & Rosch, E. (1981). Categorization of natural objects. *Annual Review of Psychology, 32*, 89–115.

Metcalfe, J., & Fisher, R. P. (1986). The relation between recognition memory and classification learning. *Memory & Cognition, 14*, 164–173.

Minsky, M., & Papert, S. (1968, 1988). *Perceptrons*. Cambridge, MA: MIT Press.

Monahan, J. S., & Lockhead, G. R. (1977). Identification of integral stimuli. *Journal of Experimental Psychology: General, 106*, 94–110.

Morgan, B. J. T. (1974). On Luce's choice axiom. *Journal of Mathematical Psychology, 11*, 107–123.

Morrison, D. F. (1967). *Multivariate statistical methods*. New York: McGraw-Hill.

Mullen, K., & Ennis, D. M. (1987). Mathematical formulation of multivariate Euclidean models for discrimination methods. *Psychometrika, 52*, 235–249.

Mullen, K., & Ennis, D. M. (1991). A simple multivariate probabilistic model for preferential and triadic choices. *Psychometrika, 56*, 69–75.

Mullen, K., Ennis, D. M., de Doncker, E., & Kapenga, J. A. (1988). Multivariate models for the triangular and duo-trio methods. *Biometrics, 44*, 1169–1175.

Mullen, K. T., & Kulikowski, J. J. (1990). Wavelength discrimination at detection threshold. *Journal of the Optical Society of America A, 7*, 733–742.

Murdock, B. B. (1985). An analysis of the strength-latency relationship. *Memory & Cognition, 13*, 511–521.

Murdock, B. B. Jr. (1982). A theory for the storage and retrieval of item and associative information. *Psychological Review, 89*, 609–626.

Murdock, B. B., & Anderson, R. E. (1975). Encoding, storage, and retrieval of item information. In R. L. Solso (Ed.), *Information processing and cognition: The Loyola Symposium*. Hillsdale, NJ: Lawrence Erlbaum Associates.

Nachmias, J. (1974). *A new approach to bandwidth estimation of spatial frequency channels*. Paper presented at the meeting of the Association for Research in Vision and Ophthalmology, Sarasota, FL.

Nachmias, J., & Kocher, E. C. (1970). Visual detection and discrimination of luminance increments. *Journal of the Optical Society of America, 60*, 382–389.

Nachmias, J., & Weber, A. (1975). Discrimination of simple and complex gratings. *Vision Research, 15*, 217–224.

Nakagami, S. (1961). An example of consumer's preference test: On the application of method of paired comparison. *Reports on Statistical Applications in Research, 8*, 165–171.

Nakatani, L. H. (1972). Confusion-choice model for multidimensional psychophysics. *Journal of Mathematical Psychology, 9*, 104–129.

Nakayama, K., & Silverman, G. H. (1986). Serial and parallel processing of visual feature conjunctions. *Nature, 320*, 264–265.

Neumann, P. G. (1974). An attribute frequency model for the abstraction of prototypes. *Memory & Cognition, 2*, 241–248.

Noble, B., & Daniel, J. W. (1977). *Applied linear algebra*. Englewood Cliffs, NJ: Prentice-Hall.

Nolte, L. W., & Jaarsma, D. (1967). More on the detection of one of M orthogonal signals. *The Journal of the Acoustical Society of America, 41*, 497–505.

Noreen, D. (1978). *Testable properties of some models of confusion*. Handout for a talk at the joint meeting of the Psychometric Society and the Society for Mathematical Psychology, Hamilton, Ontario, Canada.

Nosofsky, R. M. (1983). Information integration and the identification of stimulus noise and criterial noise in absolute judgment. *Journal of Experimental Psychology: Human Perception and Performance, 9*, 299–309.

Nosofsky, R. M. (1984). Choice, similarity, and the context theory of classification. *Journal of Experimental Psychology: Learning, Memory, and Cognition, 10*, 104–114.

Nosofsky, R. M. (1985a). Luce's choice model and Thurstone's categorical judgment model compared: Kornbrot's data revisited. *Perception & Psychophysics, 37*, 89–91.

Nosofsky, R. M. (1985b). Overall similarity and the identification of separable-dimension stimuli: A choice model analysis. *Perception & Psychophysics, 38*, 415–432.

Nosofsky, R. M. (1986). Attention, similarity, and the identification-categorization relationship. *Journal of Experimental Psychology: General, 115*, 39–57.

Nosofsky, R. M. (1987). Attention and learning processes in the identification and categorization of integral stimuli. *Journal of Experimental Psychology: Learning, Memory, and Cognition, 13*, 87–108.

Nosofsky, R. M. (1988a). Exemplar-based accounts of relations between classification, recognition, and typicality. *Journal of Experimental Psychology: Learning, Memory, and Cognition, 14*, 700–708.

Nosofsky, R. M. (1988b). On exemplar-based representations: Reply to Ennis (1988). *Journal of Experimental Psychology: General, 117*, 412–414.

Nosofsky, R. M. (1988c). Similarity, frequency, and category representations. *Journal of Experimental Psychology: Learning, Memory, and Cognition, 14*, 54–65.

Nosofsky, R. M. (1989). Further tests of an exemplar-similarity approach to relating identification and categorization. *Perception & Psychophysics, 45*, 279–290.

Nosofsky, R. M. (1990). Relations between exemplar-similarity and likelihood models of classification. *Journal of Mathematical Psychology, 34*, 393–418.

Nosofsky, R. M. (1991a). Stimulus bias, asymmetric similarity, and classification. *Cognitive Psychology, 23*, 91–140.

Nosofsky, R. M. (1991b). Tests of an exemplar model for relating perceptual classification and recognition memory. *Journal of Experimental Psychology: Human Perception and Performance, 17,* 3–27.

Nosofsky, R. M. (1991c). Typicality in logically-defined categories: Exemplar-similarity versus rule instantiation. *Memory & Cognition, 19,* 131–150.

Nosofsky, R. M. (in press). Exemplars, prototypes, and similarity rules. In A. Healy, S. Kosslyn, & R. Shiffrin (Eds.), *Festschrift for W. K. Estes.* Hillsdale, NJ: Lawrence Erlbaum Associates.

Nosofsky, R. M., Clark, S. E., & Shin, H. J. (1989). Rules and exemplars in categorization, identification, and recognition. *Journal of Experimental Psychology: Learning, Memory, and Cognition, 15,* 282–304.

Oden, G. C. (1981). A fuzzy propositional model of concept structure and use: A case study in object identification. In G. W. Lasker (Ed.), *Applied systems and cybernetics* (Vol. 6, pp. 2890–2897). Elmsford, NY: Permagon Press.

Oden, G. C. (1984). Dependence, independence, and emergence of word features. *Journal of Experimental Psychology: Human Perception and Performance, 10,* 394–405.

Olzak, L. A. (1981). Inhibition and stochastic interactions in spatial pattern perception. *Dissertation Abstracts International, 42,* 1651B (University Microfilms No. 8121021).

Olzak, L. A. (1985). Interactions between spatially tuned mechanisms: Converging evidence. *Journal of the Optical Society of America A, 2,* 1551–1559.

Olzak, L. A. (1986). Widely separated spatial frequencies: Mechanism interactions. *Vision Research, 26,* 1143–1153.

Olzak, L. A., & Kramer, P. (1984). Inhibition between spatially tuned mechanisms: Temporal influences. *Journal of the Optical Society of America A, 1,* 1290 (Abstract).

Olzak, L. A., & Thomas, J. P. (1981). Gratings: Why frequency discrimination is sometimes better than detection. *Journal of the Optical Society of America, 71,* 64–70.

Olzak, L. A., & Thomas, J. P. (1986). Seeing spatial patterns. In K. R. Boff, L. Kaufman, & J. P. Thomas (Eds.), *Handbook of perception and human performance* (Vol. 1). New York: Wiley-Interscience.

Olzak, L. A., & Wickens, T. D. (1983). The interpretation of detection data through direct multivariate frequency analysis. *Psychological Bulletin, 93,* 574–585.

Owens, D. B. (1956). Tables for computing bivariate normal probabilities. *Annals of Mathematical Statistics, 27,* 1075–1090.

Pachella, R. G., Smith, J. E. K., & Stanovich, K. E. (1978). Qualitative error analysis and speeded classification. In N. J. Castellan & F. Restle (Eds.), *Cognitive theory* (Vol. 3). Hillsdale, NJ: Lawrence Erlbaum Associates.

Palen, J. J., & Ennis, D. M. (1991). *A single integral form for the bivariate normal distribution function.* Unpublished manuscript, Philip Morris Research Center, Richmond, VA.

Pantle, A., & Sekuler, R. (1968). Size detecting mechanisms in human vision. *Science, 162,* 1146–1148.

Pantle, A., & Sekuler, R. (1969). Contrast response of human visual mechanisms sensitive to orientation and direction of motion. *Vision Research, 9,* 397–406.

Papoulis, A. (1965). *Probability, random variables, and stochastic processes.* New York: McGraw-Hill.

Parzen, E. (1960). *Modern probability theory and its applications.* New York: Wiley.

Patnaik, P. B. (1949). The non-central chi-square and F-distribution and their applications. *Biometrika, 36,* 202–232.

Pavel, M., Gluck, M. A., & Henkle, V. (1988). Generalizations by humans and multi-layer adaptive networks. *Proceedings of the Tenth Annual Conference of the Cognitive Science Society* (pp. 680–687). Hillsdale, NJ: Lawrence Erlbaum Associates.

Pearson, K. (1901). Mathematical contributions to the theory of evolution. VII: On the correlation of characters not quantitatively measurable. *Philosophical Transactions of the Royal Society (London), Series A, 195A,* 1–47.

Pelli, D. G. (1985). Uncertainty explains many aspects of visual contrast detection and discrimination. *Journal of the Optical Society of America A, 2,* 1508–1531.

Perrin, N. A. (1986). The GRT of preference: A new theory of choice. Unpublished doctoral dissertation, Ohio State University.

Perrin, N. A., & Ashby, F. G. (1991). A test of perceptual independence with dissimilarity data. *Applied Psychological Measurement, 15,* 79–93.

Peterson, D. W., & Mattson, R. L. (1966). A method of finding linear discriminant functions for a class of performance criteria. *IEEE Transactions on Information Theory, IT-12,* 380–387.

Peterson, W. W., & Birdsall, T. G. (1953). *The theory of signal detectability* (Tech. Rep. No. 13) University of Michigan, Electronic Defense Group.

Peterson, W. W., Birdsall, T. G., & Fox, W. C. (1954). The theory of signal detectability. *Transactions of the IRE Professional Group on Information Theory, PGIT-4* (pp. 171–212).

Pierce, D. A., & Schafer, D. W. (1986). Residuals in generalized linear models. *Journal of the American Statistical Association, 81,* 977–986.

Platt, J. R. (1964). Strong inference. *Science, 146,* 347–353.

Posner, M. I. (1964). Information reduction in the analysis of sequential tasks. *Psychological Review, 71,* 491–504.

Posner, M. I., & Keele, S. W. (1968). On the genesis of abstract ideas. *Journal of Experimental Psychology, 77,* 353–363.

Posner, M. I., & Keele, S. W. (1970). Retention of abstract ideas. *Journal of Experimental Psychology, 83,* 304–308.

Press, W. H., Flannery, B. P., Teukolsky, S. A., & Vetterling, W. T. (1988). *Numerical recipes: The art of scientific computing.* Cambridge: Cambridge University Press.

Price, R. (1964). Some non-central F-distributions expressed in closed form. *Biometrika, 51,* 107–122.

Pruzansky, S., Tversky, A., & Carroll, J. D. (1982). Spatial versus tree representations of proximity data. *Psychometrika, 47,* 3–24.

Ramsay, J. O. (1978). Confidence regions for multidimensional scaling analysis. *Psychometrika, 43,* 145–160.

Ramsay, J. O. (1980). The joint analysis of direct ratings, pairwise preferences, and dissimilarities. *Psychometrika, 45,* 149–165.

Ratcliff, R. (1978). A theory of memory retrieval. *Psychological Review, 85,* 59–108.

Ratcliff, R. (1990). Connectionist models of recognition and memory-constraints imposed by learning and forgetting functions. *Psychological Review, 97,* 285–308.

Reber, A. S. (1976). Implicit learning of synthetic languages: The role of instructional set. *Journal of Experimental Psychology: Human Memory and Learning, 2,* 88–94.

Reber, A. S., & Allen, R. (1978). Analogical and abstraction strategies in synthetic grammar learning: A functionalist interpretation. *Cognition, 6,* 189–221.

Reed, C. L., Lederman, S. J., & Klatzky, R. L. (1990). Haptic integration of planar size with hardness, texture, and planar contour. *Canadian Journal of Psychology, 44,* 522–545.

Reed, S. K. (1972). Pattern recognition and categorization. *Cognitive Psychology, 3,* 382–407.

Resnick, S. I., & Roy, R. (1990). Multivariate extremal processes, leader processes and dynamic choice models. *Advances in Applied Probability, 22,* 309–331.

Resnick, S. I., & Roy, R. (1991). Random USC functions, max-stable processes and continuous choice. *Annals of Applied Probability, 1,* 267–292.

Resnick, S. I., & Roy, R. (1992). On min-stable horse races with infinitely many horses. *Mathematical Social Sciences, 23.*

Restle, F. A. (1961). *Psychology of judgment and choice.* New York: Wiley.

Richardson, M. W. (1938). Multidimensional psychophysics. *Psychological Bulletin, 35,* 659–660.

Rips, L. J., Shoben, E. J., & Smith, E. E. (1973). Semantic distance and the verification of semantic relations. *Journal of Verbal Learning and Verbal Behavior, 12,* 1–20.

Robson, J. G. (1983). Frequency domain in visual processing. In O. J. Braddick & A. C. Sleigh (Eds.), *Physical and biological processing of images.* Berlin: Springer-Verlag.

Ronacher, B., & Bautz, W. (1985). Human pattern recognition: Individually different strategies in analyzing complex stimuli. *Biological Cybernetics, 51,* 249–261.

Rosch, E. (1973a). Natural categories. *Cognitive Psychology, 4,* 328–350.

Rosch, E. (1973b). On the internal structure of perceptual and semantic categories. In T. E. Moore (Ed.), *Cognitive development and the acquisition of language.* New York: Academic Press.

Rosch, E. (1975). Cognitive reference points. *Cognitive Psychology, 7,* 532–547.

Rosch, E. (1977). Human categorization. In N. Warren (Ed.), *Studies in cross-cultural psychology.* London: Academic Press.

Rosch, E. (1978). Principles of categorization. In E. Rosch & B. B. Lloyd (Eds.), *Cognition and categorization.* Hillsdale, NJ: Lawrence Erlbaum Associates.

Rosch, E., Simpson, C., & Miller, R. S. (1976). Structural bases of typicality effects. *Journal of Experimental Psychology: Human Perception and Performance, 2,* 491–502.

Rosenblatt, F. (1958). The perceptron: A probabilistic model for information storage and organization in the brain. *Psychological Review, 65,* 386–407.

Rosenfeld, R., & Touretzky, D. S. (1988). Coarse-coded symbolic memories and their properties. *Complex Systems, 2,* 463–484.

Rothkopf, E. Z. (1957). A measure of stimulus similarity and errors in some paired-associate learning tasks. *Journal of Experimental Psychology, 53,* 93–101.

Rotondo, J. (1986). *A generalization of Luce's choice axiom and a new class of choice models.* Paper presented at the 51st Annual Meeting of the Psychometric Society, Toronto, Canada.

Ruben, H. (1962). Probability content of regions under spherical normal distributions. IV: The distribution of homogeneous and non-homogeneous quadratic functions of normal variables. *Annals of Mathematical Statistics, 34,* 542–570.

Rumelhart, D. E. (1971). *A multicomponent theory of confusion among briefly exposed characters* (CHIP 22). San Diego: University of California, Center for Human Information Processing.

Rumelhart, D. E., Hinton, G. E., & Williams, R. J. (1986). Learning internal representations by error propagation. In D. E. Rumelhart & J. L. McClelland (Eds.), *Parallel distributed processing: Explorations in the microstructure of cognition: Vol. 1. Foundations.* Cambridge, MA: Bradford/MIT Press.

Rumelhart, D. E., & McClelland, J. L. (Eds.) (1986). *Parallel distributed processing: Explorations in the microstructure of cognition: Vol. 1. Foundations.* Cambridge, MA: Bradford/MIT Press.

Rumelhart, D. E., & Greeno, J. G. (1971). Similarity between stimuli: An experimental test of the Luce and Restle choice models. *Journal of Mathematical Psychology, 8,* 370–381.

Sachs, M. B., Nachmias, J., & Robson, J. G. (1971). Spatial frequency channels in human vision. *Journal of the Optical Society of America, 61,* 1176–1186.

Sakamoto, Y., Ishiguro, M., & Kitagawa, G. (1986). *Akaike information criterion statistics.* Dordrecht: Reidel.

Sankaran, M. (1959). On the non-central chi-square distribution. *Biometrika, 46,* 235–237.

Sattath, S., & Tversky, A. (1977). Additive similarity trees. *Psychometrika, 42,* 319–345.

Schiller, P. H., Finlay, B. L., & Volman, S. F. (1976a). Quantitative studies of single-cell properties in monkey striate cortex. II: Orientation specificity and ocular dominance. *Journal of Neurophysiology, 39,* 1320–1333.

Schiller, P. H., Finlay, B. L., & Volman, S. F. (1976b). Quantitative studies of single-cell properties in monkey striate cortex. III: Spatial frequency. *Journal of Neurophysiology, 39,* 1334–1351.

Schönemann, P. H. (1977). Similarity of rectangles. *Journal of Mathematical Psychology, 16,* 161–165.

Schönemann, P. H., & Wang, M. M. (1972). An individual difference model for the multidimensional analysis of preference data. *Psychometrika, 37,* 275–309.

Schwarz, G. (1978). Estimating the dimensions of a model. *Annals of Statistics, 6,* 461–464.

Schweizer, B., & Sklar, A. (1983). *Probabilistic metric spaces.* New York: North-Holland.

Sejnowski, T. J., & Rosenberg, C. R. (1987). Parallel networks that learn to pronounce English text. *Complex Systems, 1,* 145–168.

Sekuler, R. (1965). Spatial and temporal determinants of visual backward masking. *Journal of Experimental Psychology, 70,* 401–406.

Shaw, M. L. (1982). Attending to multiple sources of information. I: The integration of information in decision making. *Cognitive Psychology, 14,* 353–409.

Shepard, R. N. (1957). Stimulus and response generalization: A stochastic model relating generalization to distance in psychological space. *Psychometrika, 22,* 325–345.

Shepard, R. N. (1958a). Stimulus and response generalization: Tests of a model relating generalization to distance in psychological space. *Journal of Experimental Psychology, 55,* 509–523.

Shepard, R. N. (1958b). Stimulus and response generalization: Deduction of the generalization gradient from a trace model. *Psychological Review, 65,* 242–256.

Shepard, R. N. (1963). Analysis of proximities as a technique for the study of information processing in man. *Human Factors, 5,* 33–48.

Shepard, R. N. (1964). Attention and the metric structure of the stimulus space. *Journal of Mathematical Psychology, 1,* 54–87.

Shepard, R. N. (1986). Discrimination and generalization in identification and classification: Comment on Nosofsky. *Journal of Experimental Psychology: General, 115,* 58–61.

Shepard, R. N. (1987). Toward a universal law of generalization for psychological science. *Science, 237,* 1317–1323.

Shepard, R. N. (1988). Time and distance in generalization and discrimination: Comment on Ennis (1988). *Journal of Experimental Psychology: General, 117,* 415–416.

Shepard, R. N. (1990). Neural nets for generalization and classification: Comment on Staddon and Reid (1990). *Psychological Review, 97,* 579–580.

Shepard, R. N., & Chang, J. J. (1963). Stimulus generalization in learning of classifications. *Journal of Experimental Psychology, 65,* 94–102.

Shepard, R. N., Hovland, C. I., & Jenkins, H. M. (1961). Learning and memorization of classifications. *Psychological Monographs, 75* (13, Whole No. 517).

Shepard, R. N., & Kannappans, S. (1991). Connectionist implementation of a theory of generalization. In R. P. Lippman, J. Moody, & D. S. Touretsky (Eds.), *Advances in neural information processing systems 3.* San Mateo, CA: Morgan Kaufmann.

Sheppard, W. F. (1899). On the application of the theory of error to cases of normal distribution and normal correlation. *Philosophical Transactions of the Royal Society of London, Series A, 192,* 101–167.

Shin, H. J. (1990). *Similarity-scaling studies of "dot patterns" classification and recognition.* Unpublished doctoral dissertation, Indiana University.

Sjöberg, L. (1975). Uncertainty of comparative judgment and multidimensional structure. *Multivariate Behavioral Research, 10,* 207–218.

Sjöberg, L. (1977). Choice frequency and similarity. *Scandinavian Journal of Psychology, 18,* 103–115.

Sjöberg, L. (1980). Similarity and correlation. In E. D. Lantermann & H. Feger (Eds.), *Similarity and choice* (pp. 70–87). Bern: Huber.

Sjöberg, L., & Capozza, D. (1975). Preference and cognitive structure of Italian political parties. *Italian Journal of Psychology, 2,* 391–402.

Slater, P. (1960). The analysis of personal preferences. *British Journal of Statistical Psychology, 13,* 119–135.

Smith, B. G., & Thomas, J. P. (1989). Why are some spatial discriminations independent of contrast? *Journal of the Optical Society of America A, 6,* 713–724.

Smith, E. E. (1968). Choice reaction time: An analysis of the major theoretical positions. *Psychological Bulletin, 69,* 77–110.

Smith, E. E., & Medin, D. L. (1981). *Categories and concepts.* Cambridge, MA: Harvard University Press.

Smith, J. D., & Kemler-Nelson, D. G. (1984). Overall similarity in adults' classification: The child in all of us. *Journal of Experimental Psychology: General, 113,* 137–159.

Smith, J. E. K. (1980). Models of identification. In R. S. Nickerson (Ed.), *Attention and performance* (Vol. 8). Hillsdale, NJ: Lawrence Erlbaum Associates.

Smith, J. E. K. (1982). Recognition models evaluated: A commentary on Keren and Baggen. *Perception & Psychophysics, 31,* 183–189.

Smith, J. E. K. (1992). Alternative biased choice models. *Mathematical Social Sciences,* in press (due, Feb. 1992).

Smith, L. B. (1989). A model of perceptual classification in children and adults. *Psychological Review, 96,* 125–144.

Smith, L. B., & Kemler, D. G. (1977). Developmental trends in free classification: Evidence for a new conceptualization of perceptual development. *Journal of Experimental Child Psychology, 24,* 279–298.

Smith, L. B., & Kemler, D. G. (1978). Levels of experienced dimensionality in children and adults. *Cognitive Psychology, 10,* 502–523.

Snedecor, G. W., & Cochran, W. (1967). *Statistical methods* (6th ed.). Ames, IA: Iowa State University Press.

Sorkin, R. D., Pohlmann, L. D., & Gilliom, J. D. (1973). Simultaneous two-channel signal detection. III: 630- and 1400-Hz signals. *The Journal of the Acoustical Society of America, 53,* 1045–1050.

Staddon, J. E. R., & Reid, A. K. (1990). On the dynamics of generalization. *Psychological Review, 97,* 576–578.

Stern, H. S. (1987). *Gamma processes, paired comparisons, and ranking.* Unpublished doctoral dissertation, Stanford University, Department of Statistics.

Stigler, S. M. (1986). *The history of statistics: The measurement of uncertainty before 1900.* Cambridge, MA: Belknap Press.

Strauss, D. (1981). Choice by features: An extension of Luce's choice model to account for similarities. *British Journal of Mathematical and Statistical Psychology, 22,* 188–196.

Suppes, P., Krantz, D. H., Luce, R. D., & Tversky, A. (1989). *Foundations of measurement* (Vol. 2). New York: Academic Press.

Swets, J. A. (1984). Mathematical models of attention. In R. Parasuraman & D. R. Davies (Eds.), *Varieties of attention.* Orlando, FL: Academic Press.

Swets, J. A., & Pickett, R. M. (1982). *Evaluation of diagnostic systems: Methods from signal-detection theory.* New York: Academic Press.

Takane, Y. (1980). Maximum likelihood estimation in the generalized case of Thurstone's law of comparative judgment. *Japanese Psychological Research, 22,* 188–196.

Takane, Y. (1987). Analysis of covariance structures and probabilistic binary choice data. *Cognition and Communication, 20,* 45–62.

Takane, Y., & Shibayama, T. (1985). Comparison of models for stimulus recognition data. *Proceedings of the Multidimensional Data Analysis Workshop.* Leiden, Netherlands: DSWO Press.

Takane, Y., & Shibayama, T. (1986). Comparison of models for stimulus recognition data. In J. de Leeuw, W. Heiser, J. Meulman, & F. Critchley (Eds.), *Multidimensional data analysis.* Leiden: Netherlands, DSWO Press.

Tang, P. C. (1938). Power of the F-test in terms of the non-central F distribution. *Statistics Research Memoirs, 2,* 126–149.

Tanner, W. P. (1956). Theory of recognition. *The Journal of the Acoustical Society of America, 28,* 882–888.

Tanner, W. P., & Swets, J. A. (1954). A decision-making theory of visual detection. *Psychological Review, 61*, 401–409.

Taylor, M. M., Lindsay, P. H., & Forbes, S. M. (1967). Quantification of shared capacity processing in auditory and visual discrimination. *Acta Psychologica, 27*, 223–229

Thomas, J. P. (1968). Receptive field model for visual perception. *Proceedings of the 76th Annual Convention of the American Psychological Association*, 107–108.

Thomas, J. P. (1970). Model of the function of receptive fields in human vision. *Psychological Review, 77*, 121–134.

Thomas, J. P. (1981). Do channels give symmetrical positive and negative responses? *Supplement to Investigative Ophthalmology and Visual Science, 20*, 124.

Thomas, J. P. (1983). Underlying psychometric function for detecting gratings and identifying spatial frequency. *Journal of the Optical Society of America, 73*, 751–758.

Thomas, J. P. (1985). Detection and identification: How are they related? *Journal of the Optical Society of America, 2*, 1457–1467.

Thomas, J. P., & Gille, J. (1979). Bandwidths of orientation channels in human vision. *Journal of the Optical Society of America, 69*, 652–660.

Thomas, J. P., Gille, J., & Barker, R. A. (1982). Simultaneous visual detection and identification: Theory and data. *Journal of the Optical Society of America, 72*, 1642–1651.

Thomas, J. P., Padilla, G. J., & Rourke, D. L. (1969). Spatial interactions in identification and detection of compound visual stimuli. *Vision Research, 9*, 283–292.

Thomas, J. P., & Shimamura, K. K. (1975). Inhibitory interaction between visual pathways tuned to different orientations. *Vision Research, 15*, 1373–1380.

Thurstone, L. L. (1927a). A law of comparative judgment. *Psychological Review, 34*, 273–286.

Thurstone, L. L. (1927b). Psychophysical analysis. *American Journal of Psychology, 38*, 368–389.

Thurstone, L. L. (1927c). Three psychophysical laws. *Psychological Review, 34*, 424–432.

Tiku, M. L. (1965). Series expansions for the doubly non-central F distribution. *Australian Journal of Statistics, 7*, 78–89.

Tolhurst, D. J., & Dealy, R. S. (1975). The detection and identification of lines and edges. *Vision Research, 15*, 1367–1372.

Torgerson, W. S. (1951). *A theoretical and empirical investigation of multidimensional scaling*. Unpublished doctoral dissertation, Princeton University.

Torgerson, W. S. (1958). *Theory and methods of scaling*. New York: Wiley.

Townsend, J. T. (1971). Theoretical analysis of an alphabetic confusion matrix. *Perception & Psychophysics, 9*, 40–50.

Townsend, J. T. (1990). Serial vs. parallel processing: Sometimes they look like Tweedledum and Tweedledee but they can (and should) be distinguished. *Psychological Science, 1*, 46–54.

Townsend, J. T., & Ashby, F. G. (1982). Experimental test of contemporary mathematical models of visual letter recognition. *Journal of Experimental Psychology: Human Perception and Performance, 8*, 834–864.

Townsend, J. T., Hu, G. G., & Ashby, F. G. (1980). A test of visual feature sampling independence with orthogonal straight lines. *Bulletin of the Psychonomic Society, 15*, 163–166.

Townsend, J. T., Hu, G. G., & Ashby, F. G. (1981). Perceptual sampling of orthogonal straight line features. *Psychological Research, 43*, 259–275.

Townsend, J. T., Hu, G. G., & Evans, R. J. (1984). Modeling feature perception in brief displays with evidence for positive interdependencies. *Perception & Psychophysics, 36*, 35–49.

Townsend, J. T., Hu, G. G., & Kadlec, H. (1988). Feature sensitivity, bias, and interdependencies as a function of intensity payoffs. *Perception & Psychophysics, 43*, 575–591.

Townsend, J. T., & Landon, D. E. (1982). An experimental and theoretical investigation of the constant-ratio rule and other models of visual letter confusion. *Journal of Mathematical Psychology, 25*, 119–162.

Townsend, J. T., & Landon, D. E. (1983). Mathematical models of recognition and confusion in psychology. *Mathematical Social Sciences, 4*, 25–71.

Treisman, A. M., & Gelade, G. (1980). A feature-integration theory of attention. *Cognitive Psychology, 12,* 97–136.

Treisman, A. M., & Gormican, S. (1988). Feature analysis in early vision: Evidence from search asymmetries. *Psychological Review, 95,* 15–48.

Tucker, L. R. (1960). Intra-individual and inter-individual multidimensionality. In H. Gulliksen & S. Messick (Eds.), *Psychological scaling: Theory and applications.* New York: Wiley.

Tucker, L. R. (1972). Relations between multidimensional scaling and three-mode factor analysis. *Psychometrika, 37,* 3–28.

Tversky, A. (1972a). Choice by elimination. *Journal of Mathematical Psychology, 9,* 341–367.

Tversky, A. (1972b). Elimination by aspects: A theory of choice. *Psychological Review, 79,* 281–299.

Tversky, A. (1977). Features of similarity. *Psychological Review, 84,* 327–352.

Tversky, A., & Gati, I. (1982). Similarity, separability and the triangle inequality. *Psychological Review, 89,* 123–154.

Tversky, A., & Hutchinson, J. W. (1986). Nearest neighbor analysis of psychological spaces. *Psychological Review, 93,* 3–22.

Tversky, A., & Krantz, D. H. (1969). Similarity of schematic faces: A test of interdimensional additivity. *Perception & Psychophysics, 5,* 124–128.

Tversky, A., & Krantz, D. H. (1970). The dimensional representation and the metric structure of similarity data. *Journal of Mathematical Psychology, 7,* 572–597.

Tversky, A., & Russo, J. E. (1969). Substitutability and similarity in binary choices. *Journal of Mathematical Psychology, 6,* 1–12.

Tversky, A., & Sattath, S. (1979). Preference trees. *Psychological Review, 86,* 542–573.

Ura, S. (1960). Pair, triangle and duo-trio tests. *Japanese Union of Scientists and Engineers, 7,* 107–119.

Van Putten, W. L. J. (1982). Maximum likelihood estimates for Luce's choice model. *Journal of Mathematical Psychology, 25,* 163–174.

Van Santen, J. P. H., & Bamber, D. (1981). Finite and infinite state confusion models. *Journal of Mathematical Psychology, 24,* 101–111.

Vickers, D. (1979). *Decision processes in visual perception.* New York: Academic Press.

Walker, J. H. (1975). Real-world variability, reasonableness judgments, and memory representations for concepts. *Journal of Verbal Learning and Verbal Behavior, 14,* 241–252.

Wandell, B. A. (1982). Measurement of small color differences. *Psychological Review, 89,* 281–302.

Wang, M. M., Schönemann, P. H., & Rusk, J. G. (1975). A conjugate gradient algorithm for the multidimensional analysis of preference data. *Multivariate Behavioral Research, 10,* 45–99.

Ward, L. M. (1973). Use of Markov-encoded sequential information in numerical signal detection. *Perception & Psychophysics, 14,* 337–342.

Ward, T. B. (1983). Response tempo and separable-integral responding: Evidence for an integral-to-separable processing sequence in visual perception. *Journal of Experimental Psychology: Human Perception and Performance, 9,* 103–112.

Ward, T. B. (1985). Individual differences in processing stimulus dimensions: Relation to selective processing abilities. *Perception & Psychophysics, 37,* 471–482.

Ward, T. B., Foley, C. M., & Cole, J. (1986). Classifying multidimensional stimuli: Stimulus, task and observer factors. *Journal of Experimental Psychology: Human Perception and Performance, 12,* 211–225.

Watson, A. B. (1983). Detection and recognition of simple spatial forms. In O. J. Braddick & A. C. Sleigh (Eds.), *Physical and biological processing of images.* New York: Springer-Verlag.

Watson, A. B., & Robson, J. G. (1981). Discrimination at threshold: Labeled detectors in human vision. *Vision Research, 21,* 1115–1122.

Webster, M. A., & De Valois, R. L. (1985). Relationship between spatial-frequency and orientation tuning of striate-cortex cells. *Journal of the Optical Society of America A, 2,* 1124–1132.

Weiner-Ehrlich, W. K. (1978). Dimensional and metric structures in multidimensional stimuli. *Perception & Psychophysics, 24,* 399–414.

Weintraub, D. J. (1971). Rectangle discriminability: Perceptual relativity and the law of Pragnanz. *Journal of Experimental Psychology, 88,* 1–11.

Weissmann, S. M., Hollingsworth, S. R., & Baird, J. C. (1975). Psychophysical study of numbers. III: Methodological applications. *Psychological Research, 38,* 97–115.

Wickelgren, W. A. (1965). Similarity and intrusion in short-term memory for consonant-vowel diagrams. *The Quarterly Journal of Experimental Psychology, 17,* 241–247.

Wickelgren, W. A. (1967). Strength theories of disjunctive visual disection. *Perception & Psychophysics, 2,* 331–337.

Wickens, T. D. (1982). *Models for behavior.* San Francisco: Freeman.

Wickens, T. D. (1989). *Multiway contingency table analysis for the social sciences.* Hillsdale, NJ: Erlbaum.

Wickens, T. D. (1992). Maximum-likelihood estimation of a bivariate Gaussian rating model with excluded data. *Journal of Mathematical Psychology, 36.*

Wickens, T. D., & Olzak, L. A. (1989). The statistical analysis of concurrent detection ratings. *Perception & Psychophysics, 45,* 514–528.

Wilson, H., & Bergen, J. (1979). A four-mechanism model for threshold spatial vision. *Vision Research, 19,* 19–32.

Wilson, H. R., & Gelb, D. J. (1984). Modified line-element theory for spatial frequency and width discrimination. *Journal of the Optical Society of America A, 1,* 124–131.

Wittgenstein, L. (1953). *Philosophical investigations.* New York: Macmillan.

Wood, C. C. (1974). Parallel processing of auditory and phonetic information in speech discrimination. *Perception & Psychophysics, 15,* 501–508.

Yellott, J. I. Jr. (1977). The relationship between Luce's choice axiom, Thurstone's theory of comparative judgment, and the double exponential distribution. *Journal of Mathematical Psychology, 15,* 109–144.

Young, G., & Householder, A. S. (1938). Discussion of a set of points in terms of their mutual distances. *Psychometrika, 3,* 19–21.

Yule, G. U. (1900). On the association of attributes in statistics. *Philosophical Transactions Series A, 194,* 257–319.

Zadeh, L. A. (1965). Fuzzy sets. *Information and Control, 8,* 338–353.

Zagorski, M. (1975). Perceptual independence of pitch and loudness in a signal detection experiment: A processing model for 2ATFC (21FC) experiments. *Perception & Psychophysics, 17,* 525–531.

Zinnes, J. L., & Griggs, R. A. (1974). Probabilistic multidimensional unfolding analysis. *Psychometrika, 39,* 327–350.

Zinnes, J. L., & Mackay, D. B. (1983). Probabilistic multidimensional scaling: Complete and incomplete data. *Psychometrika, 48,* 27–48.

Zinnes, J. L., & Mackay, D. B. (1987). Probabilistic, multidimensional analysis of preference ratio judgments. *Communication and Cognition, 20,* 17–44.

Zinnes, J. L., & MacKay, D. B. (1989). Probabilistic multidimensional analysis of preference ratio judgments. In G. De Soete, H. Feger, & K. C. Klauer (Eds.), *New developments in psychological choice modeling* (pp. 177–205). Amsterdam: North-Holland.

Zinnes, J. L., & Wolff, R. P. (1977). Single and multidimensional same-different judgments. *Journal of Mathematical Psychology, 16,* 30–50.

Author Index

Numbers in italics *denote pages with complete bibliographic information.*

A

B

F

G

H

P

R

S

Y

Z

Subject Index

D

E

F

G